# Essentials of Sociology

Sixth Edition

Basirico | Cashion | Eshleman

Publisher and Marketing Manager: Richard Schofield

Managing Editor: Joyce Bianchini

Permissions Coordinator, Project Research and Development: Jenefier Winchell

Production and Fulfillment Manager: Janai Bryand

Cover and Interior Design: Esther Scannell

Typesetting Manager: Suzanne Schmidt

Proofreader: Annie Schofield

Pre-Production Coordinator and Photo Researcher: Tommi Morgenthal



For information, address BVT Publishing, LLC, P.O. Box 492831, Redding, CA 96049-2831

Some ancillaries, including electronic and printed components, may not be available to customers outside of the United States.

Photo Credits: Cover photo from Getty

Vital Source eBook ISBN: 978-1-62751-347-0

Loose Leaf ISBN: 978-1-62751-348-7

Softcover ISBN: 978-1-62751-349-4

Textbook+ ISBN: 978-1-62751-350-0

Textbook+ Loose Leaf Bundle ISBN: 978-1-62751-352-4

eBook+ ISBN: 978-1-62751-351-7

# About the Authors

**Laurence ("Larry") Basirico** earned his BA in sociology from Hofstra University (1972) and his MA (1974) and PhD (1983) at Stony Brook University. He is professor of sociology at Elon University where he has been since 1983. He was chair of the Department of Sociology and Anthropology from 1994 to 2004 and resumed his role as department chair in 2009. Dr. Basirico's research primarily has been in the areas of social interaction, identity, socialization, the family and culture—as applied specifically to rock groups, arts and crafts communities, family reunions, and marital relationships. His major teaching areas are introduction to sociology, self and society, and the family. Dr. Basirico was also dean of international programs at Elon for 5 years (2004 to 2009), spearheading one of the most successful study abroad programs in the United States and overseeing efforts to internationalize the campus. While he was dean, Elon won the prestigious Paul Simon Internationalization of the Campus Award, the highest award given by NAFSA: Association of International Educators.

In 1988, he joined forces with J. Ross Eshleman and Barbara G. Cashion to write *Sociology: An Introduction* (Scott Foresman, Little Brown, and then with HarperCollins Publisher)—the precursor for this textbook. That book was one of the first sociology textbooks that focused on how students could apply sociology in their lives. He assumed primary responsibility for *Introduction to Sociology* with BVT Publishing beginning with the 4th edition.

Dr. Basirico is married with three children and lives in Burlington, North Carolina. He is a lifelong music lover and learner dedicated primarily to guitar these days, but with a background in piano. He regularly walks around golf courses chasing a little white ball into never-before-seen natural habitats.

**J. Ross Eshleman,** PhD, received his doctorate from Ohio State University and is currently professor emeritus at Wayne State University. His past teaching experience includes serving as department chair of sociology at Wayne State University and Appalachian State University, two Fulbright grants to the Philippines at the University of Santo Tomas and De La Salle College, a year with the National Science Foundation, and two university teaching awards.

Dr. Eshleman has directed five institutes for teachers of high school sociology with grants through the National Science Foundation. His publications include numerous editions (10 of his own and 2 co-authored) of a sociology of the family text.

**Barbara G. Cashion** received her PhD from the University of Maryland and taught at a variety of universities, including Georgetown University in Washington, D.C., and Shippensburg University of Pennsylvania. She has special interest in the sociology of medicine and has worked in group health insurance settings at the National Institute of Mental Health (NIMH) and in the pharmaceutical field.

Dr. Cashion has published on related topics in a variety of journals. She is currently retired from teaching and is living in Hagerstown, Maryland. There she continues to develop her interests in music and fine arts, especially in the sociology of American art. Dr. Cashion has two daughters and four grandchildren.

# Contents in Brief

# Contents

GOLD IS REAL MONEY
WANT JOBS? LOWER TAX
END THE FED
NO MO
FOR CO
BANKERS
END THE F
SPEED LIMIT

facebook

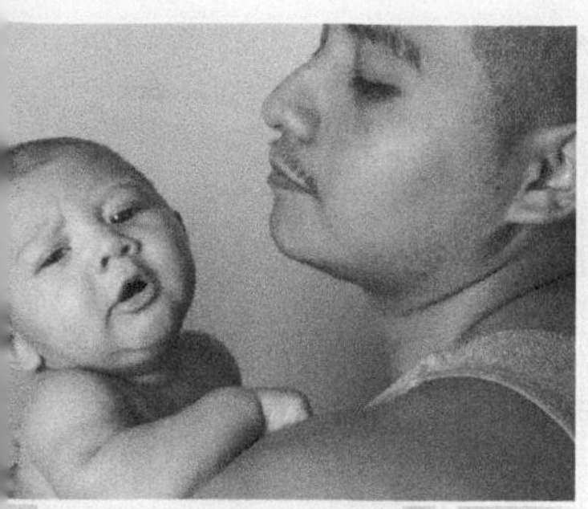

For Thiev
JUSTICE F
202-544-
HONK IF
YOU
OPPOSE
AIG
cutives
Bonuses
r Thieves!
USTICE FIRST

## 8 Racial and Ethnic Differentiation 185

## 9 Gender Differentiation 217

We Can Do It!

## 12 Educational Groups and Systems 303

## 13 Political and Economic Groups and Systems 329

POLLING PLACE
VOTE HERE
6:00 A.M. - 7:00 P.M.

CUT CARBON POLLUTION,
UNLOCK
CLEAN
ENERGY

# Preface

**Our purpose in writing** this text is to convey both the excitement of sociology and its relevance to our lives. The excitement of sociology comes from what it studies: social life and social organization. Sociology encompasses all aspects of society: family life, community change, individual development, group differences, and gender inequality, to name a few. It involves a unique way of looking at the world in which we live, forcing us to question the obvious and understand how society and behavior are patterned and organized. People are discovering that sociology provides them with unique skills and abilities in research methods, in applying social theory in the working world, and in using their understanding of social processes, organization, and change.

## New to This Edition

**As with each new edition,** we have retained the characteristics of our *Essentials of Sociology* text that make it stand out and have incorporated updates and revisions to ensure accuracy and currency. This edition continues to include an emphasis on the relevance of sociology with sections in each chapter on how students can apply specific sociological theories and/or concepts to their professional and personal lives.

The major changes to this edition revolve around ensuring currency, accuracy, and formatting updates. We did not change the topics for the opening vignettes because they have been so favorably reviewed and because they retain their relevance to the central ideas of each chapter. However, each vignette has been updated to include references to current events so that students can relate to them more effectively. All of the citations have been checked (and revised if necessary) to ensure that they are as current and accurate as possible. Almost every table and figure has been updated with the most current data available. Of course, the text has been revised where needed to broaden discussions that the authors deemed especially important. For example, there is a new section on beliefs in Chapter 3 in the section dealing with the elements of culture. Chapter 4 contains a new section on role relationships with a focus on Talcott Parsons' pattern variables, an often-overlooked discussion in many contemporary introductory texts yet vitally important to understanding the impact that roles have on social interaction.

Changes to the format include moving the opening vignette from the very beginning of each chapter to embedding it in a box a little after the chapter begins, thus providing a better perspective from which the vignette can be understood. Key terms were included at the end of each chapter in previous editions, but this new edition places them in the margins in each chapter close to where they are discussed in the text. Most of the photographs have been changed to try to ensure relevance to the students' lives. We believe that our book offers a traditional, solid introduction to sociology that encourages students to see its relevance in their lives and the world around them.

# SUPPLEMENTS & RESOURCES

## Instructor Supplements

A complete teaching package is available for instructors who adopt this book. This package includes an **online lab**, **instructor's manual**, **test bank**, **course management software**, and **PowerPoint™ slides**.

| | |
|---|---|
| BVT*Lab* | An online lab is available for this textbook at www.BVTLab.com, as described in the BVT*Lab* section below. |
| Test Bank | An extensive test bank is available to instructors in both hard copy and electronic form. Each chapter has 120 to 150 multiple choice questions ranked by difficulty and style, as well as 20 written-answer questions. Each question is referenced to the appropriate section of the text to make test creation quick and easy. |
| Course Management Software | BVT's course management software, Respondus, allows for the creation of tests and quizzes that can be downloaded directly into a wide variety of course management environments such as Blackboard, WebCT, Desire2Learn, ANGEL, E-Learning, eCollege, Canvas, Moodle, and others. |
| PowerPoint Slides | A set of PowerPoint slides includes about 30 slides per chapter, comprising a chapter overview, learning objectives, slides covering all key topics, key figures and charts, as well as summary and conclusion slides. |

## Student Resources

Student resources are available for this textbook at www.BVTLab.com. These resources are geared toward students needing additional assistance as well as those seeking complete mastery of the content. The following resources are available:

| | |
|---|---|
| Practice Questions | Students can work through hundreds of practice questions online. Questions are multiple choice or true/false in format and are graded instantly for immediate feedback. |
| Flashcards | BVT*Lab* includes sets of flashcards for each chapter that reinforce the key terms and concepts from the textbook. |
| Chapter Summaries | A convenient and concise chapter summary is available as a study aid for each chapter. |
| PowerPoint Slides | All instructor PowerPoints are available for convenient lecture preparation and for students to view online for a study recap. |

## BVT*Lab*

BVT*Lab* is an affordable online lab for instructors and their students. It includes an online classroom with grade book and chat room, a homework grading system, extensive test banks for quizzes and exams, and a host of student study resources.

| | |
|---|---|
| Course Setup | BVT*Lab* has an easy-to-use, intuitive interface that allows instructors to quickly set up their courses and grade books, and to replicate them from section to section and semester to semester. |
| Grade Book | Using an assigned passcode, students register themselves in the grade book; all homework, quizzes, and tests are then automatically graded and recorded. |
| Chat Room | Instructors can post discussion threads to a class forum and then monitor and moderate student replies. |
| Student Resources | All student resources for this textbook are available in BVT*Lab* in digital form. |
| eBook | A web-based eBook is available within the lab for easy reference during online classes, homework, and study sessions. |

Even if a class is not taught in the lab, students can still utilize the many student resources described above

## Customization

BVT's Custom Publishing Division can help you modify this book's content to satisfy your specific instructional needs. The following are examples of customization:

- Rearrangement of chapters to follow the order of your syllabus
- Deletion of chapters not covered in your course
- Addition of paragraphs, sections, or chapters you or your colleagues have written for this course
- Editing of the existing content, down to the word level
- Customization of the accompanying student resources and online lab
- Addition of handouts, lecture notes, syllabus, etc.
- Incorporation of student worksheets into the textbook

All of these customizations will be professionally typeset to produce a seamless textbook of the highest quality, with an updated table of contents and index to reflect the customized content.

# Acknowledgments

**We wish to acknowledge** the input and contributions of many people. How do we express an intellectual debt to the scholars, researchers, teachers, and students who provided the ideas, data, and findings used here? For the three of us, this includes many people. Special thanks to our spouses and children who have taught us as much as we have taught them. We also thank our teachers, those people who have sparked our interest in sociology and helped us develop our ability to think through the issues of the discipline. We extend our thanks to our professional colleagues at Elon University, Shippensburg University, and Wayne State University who have supported us in our daily activities.

We want to thank the many instructors who used previous editions of our text and provided us with valuable feedback. We are especially grateful for the comments and suggestions offered during preparation of this edition. We also thank the editors and contributors to this edition of the work for their dedication to maintaining currency and relevance. Special thanks to Savannah Bradley who served as Laurence Basirico's research assistant in helping with the revisions for the 6th edition.

Finally, we would like to acknowledge the following scholars who, from the outset, have provided review of our manuscript, from which successive editions (including this one) have come:

| | |
|---|---|
| David A. Gay | University of Central Florida |
| Lee F. Hamilton | Montana State University |
| Gary D. Hartley | Simpson College |
| Harlowe Hatle | University of South Dakota |
| A. C. Higgins | SUNY, Albany |
| Tim Johnson | Central College |
| Tye Craig Johnson | University of South Carolina |
| Cheryl A. Joseph | College of Notre Dame |
| Barbara Karcher | Kennesaw State College |
| James H. Leiding | East Stroudsburg University |
| Martin L. Levin | Emory University |
| Jerry Lewis | Kent State University |
| Margarite Martin | Gonzago University |
| Barbara McCoy | Northeast Mississippi Community College |
| Richard B. Miller | Missouri Southern State College |
| Man J. Molseed | University of Michigan, Flint |
| Kay Mueller | Baylor University |
| Donna Phillips | San Bernardino Valley College |
| William G. Roy | University of California, Los Angeles |
| William A. Schwab | University of Arkansas |
| Dwayne M. Smith | Tulane University |
| Thomas Sparhawk | Georgia Southern College |
| James Sutton | Chattanooga State Technical Community College |
| Nancy Terjesen | Kent State University |
| Kathleen A. Tiemann | University of North Dakota |
| Steven Vassar | Mankato State University |
| Richard Veach | Whatian Community College |
| Robert Wooley | Mansfield University |

# An Open Invitation to Our Readers:

**We feel it is imperative** to make sure that our textbook is as current, relevant, and engaging as possible, and that it provides the greatest utility benefit to instructors and students alike. If you have any comments and/or suggestions from which future editions of this book may benefit, please let us know. We welcome your emails and will give due consideration to each and every one. Please send your communications to: contactus@bvtpublishing.com.

*People who like to avoid shocking discoveries, who prefer to believe that society is just what they were taught in Sunday school, who like the safety of the rules ... should stay away from sociology.*

PETER BERGER

# PART ONE

# SOCIOLOGICAL PERSPECTIVES AND METHODS

Sociology, like other social sciences, has a unique perspective that is supported by over 200 years of theories and research. Part I of this book discusses the core ingredients of the sociological perspective, it's basic theories and the research tools that sociologists use to do their work. As you will read, one of the main goals of the sociological approach is to "debunk" or to critically analyze our everyday ways of explaining the world—which are often the result of our individual, selective experiences. As Peter Berger notes in his above quote, some of the explanations you discover for the conditions of your personal lives, interpersonal relationships, and the larger facets of society—such as family, government, religion, economics, healthcare, education and other social phenomenon that are central to how we live—may challenge your way of thinking and may, at times, make you uncomfortable. However, our goal is not to make you uncomfortable, but rather to help you develop the skills that are necessary to understand society in such a way that you are an engaged, productive, compassionate citizen within your personal life—locally, nationally, and globally.

CHAPTER 1

# The Sociological Perspective

## SYNOPSIS

**What Is Sociology?**

- The Sociological Imagination
- Sociology and Popular Wisdom
- Sociology and the Other Social Sciences

**The Development of Sociology**

- Auguste Comte
- Herbert Spencer
- Karl Marx
- Emile Durkheim
- Max Weber
- Harriet Martineau

**The Development of Sociology in America**

**The Major Theoretical Perspectives in Sociology**

- Structural Functional Theory
- Conflict Theory
- Symbolic Interaction Theory
- Exchange Theory
- Evolutionary Theory
- Additional Theoretical Perspectives and the Future of Sociological Theory

## 1.1 WHAT IS SOCIOLOGY?

What is **sociology**? Sociology is the scientific study of human behavior, social groups, and society. Sociology is concerned with every aspect of the self in relationships with others and every aspect of the social world that affects a person's thoughts or actions. As stated by the American Sociological Association in a booklet titled *21st Century Careers with an Undergraduate Degree in Sociology* (2009), sociology is the study of *social life* and the social causes and consequences of human behavior. The term *social life* encompasses all interpersonal relationships, all groups or collections of persons, and all types of social organizations. The "causes and consequences of human behavior" encompass how these relationships, groups, and organizations are interrelated; how they influence personal and interpersonal behavior; how they affect and are affected by the larger society;

**Sociology**
The study of human society and social life and the social causes and consequences of human behavior

## Focal Point

# THE SOCIOLOGY OF RAMPAGE SHOOTING

Mass killings seem to be occurring more often now than in the past, not only in the United States, but in other countries as well. Rampage shootings—such as those that occurred at the Sandy Hook Elementary School in Connecticut, Virginia Polytechnic University, a movie theatre in Colorado, a youth camp in Norway, and a political gathering at a supermarket in Arizona—have captured the attention of people around the world.

During the weeks and months following these events, newspaper articles abounded with speculations about the possible motives for the shootings and especially about how, in retrospect, the killers had manifested problematic psychological characteristics well before the deadly incidents had taken place.

Much like yourself, the shooting victims probably thought that school, the movies, camp, or an informal meeting with a politician in a shopping center were very safe activities held in places where crime is limited to petty theft and other nonviolent offenses. However, in recent years the media have bombarded us with images of school violence. We hear commentary from multiple news agencies and television personalities suggesting that schools, once thought to be safe havens for children, have become killing fields. Heated political arguments for and against gun control, as means of curtailing violence, result. How much of this is truth and how much is myth? Are young people becoming increasingly violent? Does a proliferation of weapons make societies safer or more dangerous? Should we arm our students with bulletproof vests before sending them

*Philadelphia Mayor Michael Nutter speaks during a demonstration in Philadelphia in August 2013. The event was held in support of legislation HR 1565 to expand background checks for gun sales.* (AP Wide World Photo)

how they change or why they remain static; and what the consequences are of these factors. This definition reflects the belief that people can be understood only in the context of their contacts, associations, and communications with other people. The very heart of sociology then—its concern with the complexities and subtleties of human social life—makes it a discipline that is highly relevant, not only to professional sociologists, but also to people in virtually every line of work and at every level.

Thus sociology may consider a wide range of general questions, such as the following:

1. How do groups influence individual human behavior?
2. What are the causes and consequences of a particular system of social order?
3. What social factors contribute to a particular social change?
4. What purpose is served by a particular social organization?
5. What are the causes and consequences of a particular social system?

Other areas investigated by sociologists include racial and ethnic relationships, prejudice and discrimination, power and politics, jobs and income, families and family life, school systems and the educational process, social control, organizations, bureaucracies, groups and group dynamics, leisure, healthcare systems, military systems, women's movements, and labor movements. The stratification of people by wealth, education, power, and such differences as gender or age may also be examined. As off to school? Are students safer if they attend schools in rural areas rather than in inner cities? After such horrific incidents, and others like them, it is easy to focus exclusively on the characteristics of the killers and/or to blame society for a decline in morality. Some have even suggested that such rampages are the result of severely differing values (political or otherwise) or the availability of guns. These explanations tend to be quick reactions to tragedies that may or may not be accurate or worthwhile explanations.

As sociologists, we feel that to answer questions about why incidents such as these take place, we should first consider what Peter Berger suggests in *Invitation to Sociology*: **"The first wisdom of sociology is this—things are not what they seem"** (1963). As a sociology student, you will be asked to examine issues based on a critical analysis, rather than simply relying on the media or your own personal experiences to answer questions related to social phenomena. It is best to examine issues from various points of view, particularly those directly affected by the phenomenon.

> *... the first wisdom of sociology is this—things are not what they seem.*
>
> Peter Berger

For example, Cybelle Fox and David J. Harding (2005) investigated school shootings from the point of view of **organizational deviance** rather than focusing so much on the characteristics of the killers. "From a sociological perspective, what is perhaps most surprising is that, with few exceptions, school officials were unaware that the shooters in these incidents were experiencing severe emotional, social, and/or behavioral problems or that they had such rage against the institution" (Fox & Harding, 2005, p. 69). Their approach looks not so much at individual killers but at what organizations do or do not do to perpetuate the situation.

Our point here is not that we are shifting the blame from the individual to society. Rather, our point is to reaffirm Berger's contention that "things are not what they seem" and that sociology offers us perspectives, theories, and methods to analyze events in such a way that we go well beyond our immediate reactions and what might seem to be common sense. Then, we can gain a more accurate and helpful understanding of the causes and consequences of events. This does not mean that sociology always finds answers that are different from our initial assumptions (although sometimes the two are very different). Sociology employs, instead, a critical analysis that enables us to feel more confident in explanations and to have explanations, hopefully, that are more useful in helping stem disasters such as rampage shootings.

**Organizational deviance**
Occurs when events are created by or exist within organizations that do not conform to the organization's goals or expectations and that produce unanticipated and harmful outcomes

you can see, sociology is an extremely broad field. It provides knowledge that directly applies to occupations that involve evaluation, planning, research, analysis, counseling, and problem solving. In its most comprehensive sense, sociology can be regarded as including every aspect of social life—its causes, its forms and structures, its effects, and its changes and transformations.

## 1.1a The Sociological Imagination

Throughout this course you will likely be asked to "step outside your box" and to view social issues as an outsider. The purpose of this request is to help you develop a **sociological imagination**—a quality of mind that allows us to understand the influence of history and biography on our interactive processes (Mills, 1956). Although published in 1959, Mills' description of what sociological thinking entails is just as accurate today. In other words, our experiences guide our perceptions. A school building may be seen as a place of work by a teacher, as a place of study by a student, as a tax liability by a homeowner, as a fire hazard by a firefighter, and as a particular structural design by a builder. In the same way, sociologists consider the social world from their own unique perspective.

As a student, you will develop not only a sociological imagination but also a sociological perspective. What is the **sociological perspective**? It is a conscious effort

**Sociological imagination**
The ability to see how history and biography—together—influence our lives

**Sociological perspective**
A way of looking at society and social behavior that involves questioning the obvious, seeking patterns, and looking beyond the individual in an attempt to discern social processes

to question the obvious and to remove us from familiar experiences, allowing for our critical and objective examination. This sort of *empirical* (based on observation or experiment) investigation enables us to determine whether our generalizations about society are accurate. These investigations could involve asking questions about poverty in a wealthy nation, about the social forces leading to unionization, or about the effects of divorce on family life and on children. Ultimately, it requires us to consider issues such as employment, income, education, gender, age, and race—and how these and other externalities influence people's experiences.

This perspective also entails efforts to see beyond individual experiences. The sociologist tries to interpret patterns—the regular, recurrent aspects of social life. An awareness of interaction patterns and group processes can help us to understand the relationship between our personal experiences and the society in which we live.

Social rules and conventions influence our lives and our actions, including how parents may plan for the arrival of a child whose gender is known beforehand. (Shutterstock)

Human behavior is, to a large extent, shaped by the groups to which people belong, by social interactions, and by the surrounding social and cultural context. Apart from the social and cultural context, for example, it may be extremely difficult to understand the spontaneous, simultaneous, and collective shout that occurs when a person with a wooden stick hits a round object over the head of a person standing on a field and wearing a thick leather glove on one hand but not on the other. It may be difficult to understand the anger of people in a neighborhood when children are bused to a school in a different neighborhood. It may be difficult to understand why people often become overtly vehement in their disagreements about policies concerning taxes, healthcare, gun control, abortion, public prayer, same sex marriages, and other persistent controversial issues. Behaviors such as these are reflections of the group, the institution, and the society in which they occur. Because individual behavior can be understood only in its social and cultural context, the sociological perspective considers the individual as part of the larger society. It notes how the society is reflected in individuals and attempts to discover patterns in behaviors and regularity in events.

The sociological perspective operates at two levels, termed **macrosociology** and **microsociology**. The difference relates to the size of the unit of analysis. Macro-level analysis deals with large-scale structures and processes: broad social categories, institutions, and social systems, such as war, unemployment, and divorce. Solutions to these problems are sought at the structural or organizational level.

**Macrosociology**

A level of sociological analysis concerned with large-scale structures and processes, such as war and unemployment

**Microsociology**

The level of sociological analysis concerned with small-scale units such as individuals in small group or social interactions

One example of macrosociological analysis is the study of how societies transition from an agricultural economic system to an industrial one. Micro-level analysis, on the other hand, is concerned with how individuals behave in social situations. The social problems of a veteran, an unemployed worker, or a divorcée would be subjects for microsociological research. Solutions would be sought at the personal or interpersonal level. One example of microsociological analysis is the study of university classroom conformity, where the researcher observes the day-to-day patterns of behavior and socialization occurring among those enrolled in the class. The sociological perspective involves investigations of problems on both scales.

**thinking** SOCIOLOGICALLY

1. It was suggested that human behavior is, to a large extent, shaped through our social interactions and cultural contexts. Discuss ways in which members of our communities influence our everyday choices. More personally, to what extent are you solely responsible for your own condition or destiny? To what extent do you think that people have free will? Think of free will not only in terms of freedom to do what one desires to do but also in terms of how we do what we desire. Do we determine what we desire?
2. In regard to school shootings, how does the sociological imagination help us to understand the events at the recent rampage shootings, such as in the movie theatre in Colorado or the elementary school in Newton, Connecticut?

## 1.1b Sociology and Popular Wisdom

It is widely assumed, sometimes accurately so, that research findings tend to support what we already know. We all have some idea as to why people act the way they do and how society works. As social beings, most of us were raised in families and communities. Everyone has learned to obey traffic signals and danger signs. We have all heard the debate and rhetoric of presidential and local political campaigns. We have all read newspapers and heard television reports that remind us continually of crime, racial conflicts, poverty, inflation, pollution, AIDS, and teenage pregnancies. We all understand social life—our own experiences make us experts in human behavior and in the nature of society. Let us examine a few examples to prove our point. Aren't the following statements obviously true?

1. People who commit rampage shootings are obviously mentally ill and suddenly snapped before the incident.
2. Because poor racial and ethnic minorities are more likely to live in larger cities, poverty is more an urban problem than a rural one.
3. Because capital punishment leads people to give serious thought to the consequences before committing crimes, crime rates are much lower in states that have capital punishment than in those that do not.
4. Because males are more prone to violence than females, suicide rates are lower for girls than for boys.
5. Because we all know that death is approaching as we grow older, fear of dying increases with age.

Many other examples could be given, but these common sense ideas should illustrate our point. Although you may agree with all of them, research findings indicate that all of these statements are false. Following are data sources to refute the above false statements:

1. Key findings from a 2002 Safe School Initiative study conducted by the U.S. Department of Education and the U.S. Secret Service found that most perpetrators of school shootings had not previously been evaluated for psychological disorders, nor had they sought assistance from a behavioral agency (Lipton, Savage, & Shane, 2011).

*Macro-level analysis is concerned with large-scale structures and processes such as war, unemployment, and divorce. Micro-level analysis is concerned with how individuals, such as the unemployed, behave in social situations. (iStockphoto)*

2. Poverty is more prevalent in rural areas than in urban communities. According to Lief Jensen (2006) approximately 7.3 million persons living in rural communities are poor. In 2005, 15.1% of the rural population was living in poverty, compared to 12.5% of persons living in urban communities.
3. The empirical evidence suggests there is very little relationship between the rate of murder and other crimes, and the use of capital punishment. The murder rates in states with the death penalty are not consistently lower than the rates in states without it. In general, the death penalty is *not* a deterrent to murder or other crimes.
4. While suicide rates (Table 1-1 and Figure 1-1) are higher for males than for females in most countries, including the United States, there are some countries where the rates between males and females are strikingly different, some where they are similar, and at least one (China) where they are higher for females (World Health Organization). Sociology prompts us to ask questions: Why are the various trends found in Table 1-1 taking place? What social and cultural factors among different groups have an effect on suicide rates?
5. A *Los Angeles Times* poll (Pinkus, Richardson, & Armet, 2000) found that only 7% of people over age 65 think about and fear death while 20% of 18- to 28-year-olds are afraid of dying.

These examples illustrate that although some popular observations may be true, many others are not supported by empirical data. Without social science research, it is extremely difficult to distinguish what is actually true from what our common sense tells us should be true. Many people have suffered enormous losses in personal relationships and business deals because they acted on the basis of what they considered "common sense" about what they believed was the truth. We believe that the knowledge you gain from sociology will help to improve the quality of your personal and professional life. Even if this is the only sociology course you ever take, we hope that after completing it you will have a far greater understanding of yourself, of your society, and of human behavior—as well as an increased ability to question many of the popular observations

**Figure 1-1** Distribution of Suicide Rates per 100,000 by Gender and Age, 2000

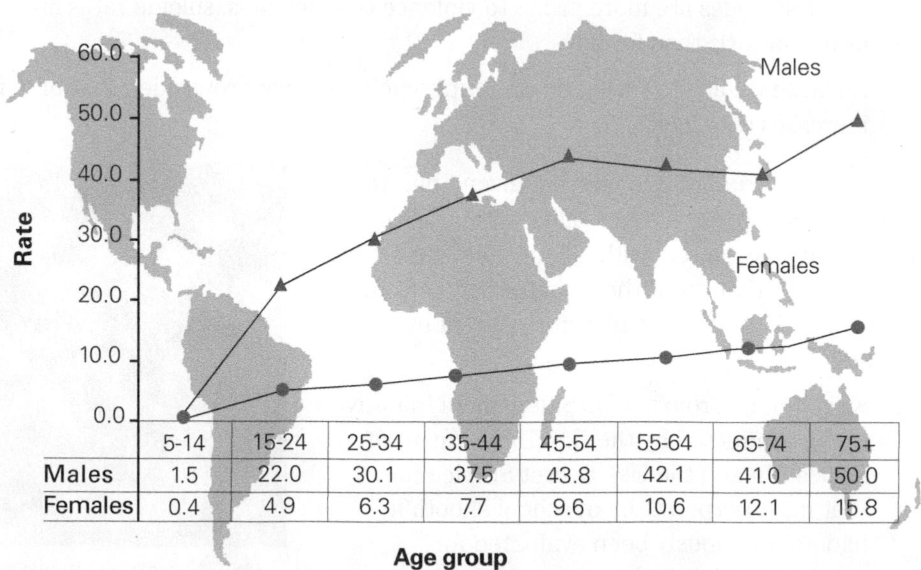


| | 5-14 | 15-24 | 25-34 | 35-44 | 45-54 | 55-64 | 65-74 | 75+ |
|---|---|---|---|---|---|---|---|---|
| Males | 1.5 | 22.0 | 30.1 | 37.5 | 43.8 | 42.1 | 41.0 | 50.0 |
| Females | 0.4 | 4.9 | 6.3 | 7.7 | 9.6 | 10.6 | 12.1 | 15.8 |

Adapted from "Distribution of Suicides Rates (per 100,000) by Gender and Age, 2000," World Health Organization. Retrieved from http://www.who.int/mental_health/prevention/suicide/suicide_rates_chart/en/, on March 06, 2013.

**Table 1-1** Suicide Rates per 100,000 by Country, Year, and Sex

Most recent year available; as of 2011

| Country | Year | Males | Females | Country | Year | Males | Females |
|---|---|---|---|---|---|---|---|
| Albania | 03 | 4.7 | 3.3 | Kuwait | 09 | 1.9 | 1.7 |
| Antigua and Barbuda | 95 | 0.0 | 0.0 | Kyrgyzstan | 09 | 14.1 | 3.6 |
| Argentina | 08 | 12.6 | 3.0 | Latvia | 09 | 40.0 | 8.2 |
| Armenia | 08 | 2.8 | 1.1 | Lithuania | 09 | 61.3 | 10.4 |
| Australia | 06 | 12.8 | 3.6 | Luxembourg | 08 | 16.1 | 3.2 |
| Austria | 09 | 23.8 | 7.1 | Maldives | 05 | 0.7 | 0.0 |
| Azerbaijan | 07 | 1.0 | 0.3 | Malta | 08 | 5.9 | 1.0 |
| Bahamas | 05 | 1.9 | 0.6 | Mauritius | 08 | 11.8 | 1.9 |
| Bahrain | 06 | 4.0 | 3.5 | Mexico | 08 | 7.0 | 1.5 |
| Barbados | 06 | 7.3 | 0.3 | Netherlands | 09 | 13.1 | 5.5 |
| Belarus | 07 | 48.7 | 8.8 | New Zealand | 07 | 18.1 | 5.5 |
| Belgium | 05 | 28.8 | 10.3 | Nicaragua | 06 | 9.0 | 2.6 |
| Belize | 08 | 6.6 | 0.7 | Norway | 09 | 17.3 | 6.5 |
| Bosnia and Herzegovina | 91 | 20.3 | 3.3 | Panama | 08 | 9.0 | 1.9 |
| Brazil | 08 | 7.7 | 2.0 | Paraguay | 08 | 5.1 | 2.0 |
| Bulgaria | 08 | 18.8 | 6.2 | Peru | 07 | 1.9 | 1.0 |
| Canada | 04 | 17.3 | 5.4 | Philippines | 93 | 2.5 | 1.7 |
| Chile | 07 | 18.2 | 4.2 | Poland | 08 | 26.4 | 4.1 |
| China (selected rural & urban areas) | 99 | 13.0 | 14.8 | Portugal | 09 | 15.6 | 4.0 |
| China (Hong Kong SAR) | 09 | 19.0 | 10.7 | Puerto Rico | 05 | 13.2 | 2.0 |
| Colombia | 07 | 7.9 | 2.0 | Republic of Korea | 09 | 39.9 | 22.1 |
| Costa Rica | 09 | 10.2 | 1.9 | Republic of Moldova | 08 | 30.1 | 5.6 |
| Croatia | 09 | 28.9 | 7.5 | Romania | 09 | 21.0 | 3.5 |
| Cuba | 08 | 19.0 | 5.5 | Russian Federation | 06 | 53.9 | 9.5 |
| Cyprus | 08 | 7.4 | 1.7 | Saint Kitts and Nevis | 95 | 0.0 | 0.0 |
| Czech Republic | 09 | 23.9 | 4.4 | Saint Lucia | 05 | 4.9 | 0.0 |
| Denmark | 06 | 17.5 | 6.4 | Saint Vincent and the Grenadines | 08 | 5.4 | 1.9 |
| Dominican Republic | 05 | 3.9 | 0.7 | Sao Tome and Principe | 87 | 0.0 | 1.8 |
| Ecuador | 09 | 10.5 | 3.6 | Serbia | 09 | 28.1 | 10.0 |
| Egypt | 09 | 0.1 | 0.0 | Seychelles | 08 | 8.9 | 0.0 |
| El Salvador | 08 | 12.9 | 3.6 | Singapore | 06 | 12.9 | 7.7 |
| Estonia | 08 | 30.6 | 7.3 | Slovakia | 05 | 22.3 | 3.4 |
| Finland | 09 | 29.0 | 10.0 | Slovenia | 09 | 34.6 | 9.4 |
| France | 07 | 24.7 | 8.5 | South Africa | 07 | 1.4 | 0.4 |
| Georgia | 09 | 7.1 | 1.7 | Spain | 08 | 11.9 | 3.4 |
| Germany | 06 | 17.9 | 6.0 | Sri Lanka | 91 | 44.6 | 16.8 |
| Greece | 09 | 6.0 | 1.0 | Suriname | 05 | 23.9 | 4.8 |
| Grenada | 08 | 0.0 | 0.0 | Sweden | 08 | 18.7 | 6.8 |
| Guatemala | 08 | 5.6 | 1.7 | Switzerland | 07 | 24.8 | 11.4 |
| Guyana | 06 | 39.0 | 13.4 | Syrian Arab Republic | 85 | 0.2 | 0.0 |
| Haiti | 03 | 0.0 | 0.0 | Tajikistan | 01 | 2.9 | 2.3 |
| Honduras | 78 | 0.0 | 0.0 | Thailand | 02 | 12.0 | 3.8 |
| Hungary | 09 | 40.0 | 10.6 | TFYR Macedonia | 03 | 9.5 | 4.0 |
| Iceland | 08 | 16.5 | 7.0 | Trinidad and Tobago | 06 | 17.9 | 3.8 |
| India | 09 | 13.0 | 7.8 | Turkmenistan | 98 | 13.8 | 3.5 |
| Iran | 91 | 0.3 | 0.1 | Ukraine | 09 | 37.8 | 7.0 |
| Ireland | 09 | 19.0 | 4.7 | United Kingdom | 09 | 10.9 | 3.0 |
| Israel | 07 | 7.0 | 1.5 | United States of America | 05 | 17.7 | 4.5 |
| Italy | 07 | 10.0 | 2.8 | Uruguay | 04 | 26.0 | 6.3 |
| Jamaica | 90 | 0.3 | 0.0 | Uzbekistan | 05 | 7.0 | 2.3 |
| Japan | 09 | 36.2 | 13.2 | Venezuela | 07 | 5.3 | 1.2 |
| Jordan | 08 | 0.2 | 0.0 | Zimbabwe | 90 | 10.6 | 5.2 |
| Kazakhstan | 08 | 43.0 | 9.4 | | | | |

Adapted from "Suicide Rates per 100,000 by Country, Year and Sex (Table)," World Health Organization, 2002. Retrieved from http://www.who.int/mental_health/prevention/suicide_rates/en/, on March 06, 2013.

widely accepted as truth by the press and by our fellow citizens. In addition, part of what is needed to develop your sociological perspective and to comprehend "the truth" is the realization that we live in a global world and we are but one part of the big picture. Media stereotypes often lead to misconceptions about other cultures or social issues within and outside our society.

## 1.1c Sociology and the Other Social Sciences

All branches of science attempt to discover general truths, propositions, or laws through methods based on observation and experimentation. Science is often divided into two categories: the social sciences and what are often referred to as the natural sciences. The natural sciences include (a) the *biological sciences*: biology, eugenics, botany, bacteriology, and so forth, which deal with living organisms, both human and nonhuman; and (b) the *physical sciences*: physics, chemistry, astronomy, geology, and so on, which deal with the nonliving physical world. The word "natural" must be applied to these sciences with caution, however. The topics covered by the **social sciences** are just as natural as those that the natural sciences embrace. Sociology, like other social sciences, applies the scientific method to studying human behavior. For example, the organization of cities, the collective action of a football team, and the patterns of interaction in a family system are just as natural as electricity, magnetism, and the behavior of insects and can be studied using a scientific approach.

Sociology is a social science, but it is important to realize that a complete understanding of a society or of social relationships would be impossible without an understanding of the physical world in which societies exist and an understanding of the biological factors that affect humans. Like the other social sciences—psychology, anthropology, economics, and political science—sociology deals with human relationships, social systems, and societies. Although the boundaries among the various social sciences are sometimes hazy, each tends to focus on a particular aspect of the world and tries to understand it.

**Anthropology** is, probably, the social science that has the most in common with sociology. Anthropology is a broad and varied discipline that includes physical anthropology, archaeology, cultural history, social linguistics, and social and cultural anthropology. *Physical anthropologists* attempt to understand both **traditional indigenous** and modern cultures by studying physical traits, such as the shape and size of skulls; artifacts, such as pottery and weapons; and genetic mutations of both human and nonhuman forms of life. The work of *cultural* or *social anthropologists*, on the other hand, is very similar to that of sociologists. Like sociologists, they are concerned with social systems and institutions, patterns of organization, and other aspects of society.

**Economics** is the study of how goods, services, and wealth are produced, consumed, and distributed within societies. **Political science** is the study of power, governments, and political processes. **Psychology** is concerned primarily with human mental processes and individual human behavior. Frequent areas of study include learning, human development, behavior disorders, perception, emotion, motivation, creativity, personality, and a wide range of other mental and behavioral processes. In addition to being studied by psychologists, some of these areas are also studied by sociologists and by members of a field known as **social psychology**.

*Sociology applies the scientific method to studying human behavior, such as the collective action of a football team. (iStockphoto)*

**Social science**
A science that has human behavior, social organizations, and society as its subject matter

**Anthropology**
The study of the physical, biological, social, and cultural development of humans, often on a comparative basis

**Traditional indigenous**
Refers to ethnic groups who are native to a land or region

**Economics**
The study of how goods, services, and wealth are produced, consumed, and distributed

**Political science**
The study of power, government, and political processes

**Psychology**
The study of human mental processes and individual human behavior

**Social psychology**
The study of how individuals interact with other individuals or groups and how groups influence the individual

**History** is considered either a social science or one of the humanities and provides a chronological record and analysis of past events. **Geography**, often considered a natural science, is concerned with the physical environment and the distribution of plants and animals, including humans. The *physical geographer* investigates climate, agriculture, the distribution of plant species, and oceanography. *Social* and *cultural geographers*, like sociologists, may be interested in how the distribution of people in a particular area influences social relationships. Sometimes, *urban geographers* and *urban sociologists* work together on such problems as how various types of housing affect family life and how a given transportation system affects employment and productivity. Although physical geography usually is not considered a social science, social geography clearly shares many areas of interest with the other social sciences.

# 1.2 THE DEVELOPMENT OF SOCIOLOGY

The study of sociology is a recent development in social history. Philosophers such as Aristotle and Plato had much to say about society and human relationships—but it wasn't until the late nineteenth century that a writer that we know of could appropriately be considered a sociologist. In fact, the label *sociologist* was not even applied to the early practitioners of the field in their own time—they have been identified as such only in retrospect.

Most early writers were interdisciplinary in orientation, drawing their ideas from philosophy, as well as from the physical and biological sciences. Actually, as a result of developments in the natural sciences, much of the early writing in sociology was based on the assumption that laws of human behavior could be discovered in the same way that laws of nature had been discovered by astronomers, physicists, and other natural scientists. These early writers also had great faith in the power of reason, assuming that it could be used to formulate laws that could be applied to improve social life and to eliminate or diminish social problems.

The discipline of sociology as we know it today emerged from the changes brought on by the Industrial Revolution in the nineteenth century. With the Industrial Revolution, people began migrating to towns and cities for factory jobs, which brought about such social problems as harsh child labor practices. (Library of Congress)

These assumptions were rapidly put to a test as the Industrial Revolution in Europe presented new challenges and social problems. People began to migrate to towns and cities for factory jobs. With many of these jobs came low wages, long working hours, harsh child labor practices, housing and sanitation problems, social alienation, social conflict, encounters with crime, and a variety of other social problems that provided an abundance of conditions for concern, study, and solution. The Industrial Revolution that began in England, the social revolution in France under Napoleon, and the political upheavals throughout Europe—all provide the backdrop for the emergence of the discipline known today as sociology. Thus, sociology originally developed as a practical discipline intended to address social problems (Turner & Turner, 1990).

We can begin to understand this discipline by briefly examining a few of the early writers who were influential in its development. Certainly, these are not the only important European thinkers who helped shape sociology; however, their work was seminal in shaping the foundations of the discipline.

**History**
The study of the past; social history is concerned with past human social events.

**Geography**
The study of the physical environment and the distribution of plants and animals, including humans

## 1.2a Auguste Comte

Auguste Comte (1798–1857) was born in southern France. He was educated in Paris where his studies were concentrated in mathematics and the natural sciences. Comte is usually credited with being the "father of sociology" because he coined the term *sociology.* He first called this new social science "social physics" because he believed that society must be studied in the same scientific manner as the world of the natural sciences. Comte said that sociology, like the natural sciences, would use empirical methods to discover basic laws of society, which would benefit humankind by playing a major part in the improvement of the human condition.

(Wikimedia Commons)

Comte is best known for his **law of human progress** (or law of the three stages), which basically states that society has gone through three stages: (1) the theological or fictitious, (2) the metaphysical or abstract, and (3) the scientific or positivist. In addition, a specific type of social organization and political dominance accompanies each mental age of humankind. In the first stage, the theological, everything is explained and understood through the supernatural. The family is the prototypical social unit (the model or standard to which others conform); priests and military personnel hold political dominance. In the second stage, the metaphysical, abstract forces are assumed to be the source of explanation and understanding. The state replaces the family as the prototypical social unit; and as in the Middle Ages and the Renaissance, the political dominance is held by the clergy and lawyers. In the third and highest stage, the scientific laws of the universe are studied through observation, experimentation, and comparison. The whole human race replaces the state as the operative social unit, and industrial administrators and scientific moral guides hold the political dominance. It was Comte's assertion that the scientific stage of human knowledge and intellectual development was just beginning in his day. According to Comte, sociology, like the natural sciences, could henceforth draw on the methods of science to explain and understand the laws of progress and the social order.

A related concept originated by Comte was the view that society was a type of "organism." Like plants and animals, society had a structure consisting of many interrelated parts; and it evolved from simpler to more complex forms. Using this organic model as a base, he reasoned that sociology should focus on **social statics**, the structure of the organism, and on **social dynamics**, the organism's processes and forms of change. Comte believed that sociology was the means by which a more just and rational social order could be achieved.

Comte was primarily interested in applying scientific principles of social life to affect social situations. That social actions are governed by laws and principles—just as physical actions are—is a significant fact that is useful to others besides academic social scientists. Whether in our personal lives or in our occupations, if we believe that individual personalities alone or fate alone can explain why problems occur, we might look in the wrong places for solutions or become powerless to solve them. In a discussion about Comte's ideas, social theorist Lewis Coser (1977) states, "As long as [people] believed that social actions followed no law and were, in fact, arbitrary and fortuitous, they could take no concerted action to ameliorate them."

**Law of human progress**
Comte's notion that society has gone through three stages: the theological, the metaphysical, and the scientific

**Social statics**
Comte's term for the stable structure of a society

**Social dynamics**
Comte's term for social processes and forms of change

Although Comte wrote primarily for the intellectual social leaders of his day, his ideas were useful to many people. His belief that society should be studied scientifically is the basis for all sociological research. Sociologists do not merely speculate, philosophize, or use opinions to formulate theories about social behavior; rather, they rely heavily on the scientific principles emphasized by Comte: observation, experimentation, and comparison. To explain the rate and/or causes of school shootings in the United States, for example, a sociologist might first formulate hypotheses to test. Perhaps the researcher believes the cause of school shootings is directly related to the learning behaviors of the shooter, who learned violent behavior from an abnormal or dysfunctional home life. The sociologist might then collect data that would enable him or her to compare the characteristics of school shooters: familial history, childhood behavioral problems, discipline style used by parents, etc.

## 1.2b Herbert Spencer

Herbert Spencer (1820–1903) was born in England and received, as did Comte, considerable training in mathematics and the natural sciences. One of Spencer's major concerns was with the evolutionary nature of changes in social structure and social institutions. He believed that human societies pass through an evolutionary process similar to the process Darwin explained in his theory of natural selection. It was Spencer who coined the phrase "survival of the fittest"—and he was the first to believe that human societies evolved according to the principles of natural laws. Just as natural selection favors particular organisms and permits them to survive and multiply, those societies that have adapted to their surroundings and can compete are the ones to survive. Those that have not adapted and cannot compete will encounter difficulties and will, eventually, die.

(Wikimedia Commons)

Spencer's theory paralleled Darwin's theory of biological evolution in other ways. He believed that societies evolved from relative homogeneity and simplicity to heterogeneity and complexity. As simple societies progress, they become increasingly complex and differentiated. Spencer viewed societies not simply as collections of individuals but as organisms with a life and vitality of their own.

In sharp contrast to Comte, the idea of survival of the fittest led Spencer to argue for a policy of noninterference in human affairs and society. He opposed legislation designed to solve social problems, believing it would interfere with the natural selection process. He also opposed free public education, assuming that those who really wanted to learn would find the means. Just as societies that could not adapt would die out, Spencer contended, individuals who could not fit in did not deserve to flourish.

As you can imagine, Spencer's ideas had the support of people of wealth and power. His theories strengthened the position of those who wanted to keep the majority of the population impoverished and minimally educated. His ideas also tended to support a discriminatory policy: Was it not a natural evolutionary law that kept people unequal? Spencer thought that conflict and change were necessary parts of the evolutionary process (like Marx, as discussed in the next section). Unlike Marx, however, he believed that planned change would disrupt the orderly evolution of society, which he thought would eventually improve the social order. (His goals are a radical departure from those of Marx in other respects, too, of course.)

Those familiar with contemporary politics in the United States will recognize a resurgence of ideas similar to those espoused by Spencer. How could a politician, a political science major, or a citizen gain insight for interpreting some policies implemented under some conservative political administrations? For example, Ronald Reagan, who became president of the United States in 1980 and who died in 2004, will be remembered largely for the dictum of "getting government off the backs of the people." This dictum was manifested in policies that led to lower taxes, less government regulation of environmental pollution, cutbacks in federal aid for college loans and to colleges in general, reduction in aid for social service programs, and deregulation of many industries. Americans were told that the rationale for such noninterference was to give people more freedom; this would, theoretically, stimulate the economy. This policy was reinforced again under the administration of George W. Bush and became a central value among many conservative politicians, especially within the Tea Party. The year 2011 was the centennial of Ronald Reagan's birth, and many of the ceremonies that honored his life also paid homage to his views on government non-interference. As an aside, it is interesting to note that unemployment rates in the mid-1980s (when Reagan gained support for his views about "non-government interference") peaked at 10.8% and then declined to around 3.8% by 2000 (U.S. Misery Index, 2010). At the end of 2009, the unemployment rates had again climbed to 10.1% and were still at around 8% just prior to the 2012 presidential election. This is around the time that the Tea Party began to gain strength and become a noticeable political force. Is this coincidental, or does this suggest that there is a connection between social theory, political views, and economic conditions? If so, why do you think a Spencerian philosophy of government noninterference becomes more popular during periods of high-unemployment?

The Tea Party, a powerful political force in the 2012 presidential election, espoused views of less government, which can be linked to Spencer's ideas about noninterference in social problems. (AP Wide World Photo)

Today few sociologists accept his ultraconservative theory of noninterference in social change. There is, however, widespread acceptance of the idea that societies grow progressively more complex as they evolve; and an increasing recognition that evolutionary processes seem to operate in certain areas, such as population change or the selection by the stratification system of the "socially most fit" for particular types of education and positions.

## 1.2c Karl Marx

Karl Marx (1818–1883) was born in Germany. As a young man, he moved to Paris and met the leading intellectuals of the radical movements of Europe, solidifying his conversion to socialism. During this time he also began his lifelong friendship with Friedrich Engels, with whom he wrote the now-famous *Communist Manifesto* (1969, originally published in 1847).

(Wikimedia Commons)

The theme common to all the writings of Marx and Engels was a profound sense of moral outrage at the misery produced in the lower classes by the new industrial social order. Marx concluded that political revolution was a vital necessity in the evolutionary process of society and that it was the only means by which the improvement of social conditions could be achieved.

**Social conflict**
A view of Karl Marx that social conflict—class struggle due to economic inequality—is at the core of society and is the key source of social change

**Economic determinism**
The idea that economic factors are responsible for most social change and for the nature of social conditions, activities, and institutions

**Bourgeoisie**
The class of people who own the means of production

**Proletariat**
The group in capitalist societies that does not own the means of production and has only labor to sell

Marx was a major social theorist and contributor to economic and philosophical thought. He believed that economics was the dominant institution in the shaping of a society. He argued that **social conflict**—struggle and strife—was at the core of society and the source of all social change. He asserted that all history was marked by **economic determinism**—the idea that all change, social conditions, and even society itself are based on economic factors—and that economic inequality results in class struggles. Marx believed society was comprised largely of two social classes: **bourgeoisie** (the owners and rulers) and the **proletariat** (the industrial

## sociology**atwork**

### Helping Migrant Farm Workers

Sandy Smith-Nonini is a former journalist, turned anthropologist. She earned her PhD in anthropology from the University of North Carolina at Chapel Hill. Smith-Nonini's work is an example of how Marx's theories can be used to explain the origins of inequities in the workplace.

Smith-Nonini has been studying migrant farmworkers and meat packers in North Carolina and working with advocacy groups defending their labor rights. These workplaces, which now depend heavily on immigrants, have unusually high rates of injuries and even deaths. Yet many citizens have little knowledge of new immigrants, much less of the working conditions within companies that stock the counters of our grocery stores. For this reason, Smith-Nonini has worked with a Unitarian-Universalist committee on a documentary project on farmworker conditions. The goal of her research and documentary is to raise awareness among the general public and among the farmworkers themselves, many of whom are not aware they have rights to fair labor conditions.

In 2004, when President Bush proposed a new legal status for immigrant workers, Smith-Nonini noted that many hoped for an end to the administration's "close the border" mentality. However, when she looked closer at the new proposals, Smith-Nonini became concerned. Under the plan, Mexican workers would be granted temporary visas to work in a specific job for an employer who participates in a "guest worker" program. The visas would be for 3-year periods and could be renewed with the same employer. Having studied the existing federal guest worker program, known as H2A, Smith-Nonini realized the new proposal was likely to replicate some of the worst abuses now affecting H2A workers.

In a news article criticizing the Bush plan, she noted the problems "derive from the fact that the employer is also the de facto immigration officer, with the power to deport those who grumble about work conditions or pay." From a Marxian perspective, the employers are clearly the owners of the means of production and able to create working conditions that the farmworkers have no choice but to accept.

"For example," Smith-Nonini states, "farmworkers employed by the North Carolina Growers Association (NCGA), the largest H2A farm labor brokerage in the country, routinely complain that workers who leave their assigned farm or who anger their farmer employer end up on a blacklist maintained by the NCGA." These workers, then, are not rehired. Smith-Nonini continues, "Abuses such as the blacklist, long contract period, and the inability of workers to change employers are possible only in a dual-labor market of the kind that is created by guest worker programs where a class of workers lacks full citizenship and labor rights. If employers had to compete in the general market for workers, they would be forced to improve conditions to attract workers."

Migrant workers play a role in strengthening the economy in many areas of the United States. One study, at North Carolina State University, estimated that each farmworker's labor contributed $12,000 to the state's agricultural profits. Smith-Nonini's research and advocacy raise the question of whether it's fair for the larger community to benefit so handsomely from this cheap labor while the workers themselves are not reaping a fair share of the rewards and are often suffering grave injustices in the process.

*(AP Wide World Photo)*

workers of his day). These conflicts between the rich and the poor, the owners and the workers (also referred to as the haves and have-nots), lead to feelings of *alienation*, a feeling among the workers of frustration and disconnection from work and life. The recognition among workers that society is stratified and that they share the same plight is known as **class-consciousness**, which according to Marx leads ultimately to revolution. It was Marx's belief that conflict, revolution, and the overthrow of capitalism were inevitable.

Karl Marx's ideas are used in practically every area of sociology. To simplify one of Marx's tenets, there is a fundamental inequality in social relationships between those who have assets (land, money, jobs, equipment, prestige, etc.) that provide them with power and those who do not. This inequality allows those who have power to dominate and exploit those who do not. Thus, all social relationships contain the elements of conflict between "haves" and "have-nots."

Many sociologists use this idea as a premise for interpreting a variety of social relationships regarding gender and race relations, marriage, economics, politics, employment, education, religion, justice, and other matters. In developing a theory about school shootings, for example, a Marxian analyst may focus on the conflict between students who feel powerless and those who seem to be in control (teachers, principals, and other, more popular students). In trying to explain education, the focus might be on the inherent conflict between faculty (the ones who control the grades) and students, or administration (the ones who control jobs and salaries) and faculty.

Today, regardless of whether they agree or disagree with Marx's ideas, few sociologists deny the importance of the contributions he made. Sociologists are still trying to understand the influence of economic determinism, social conflict, social structure, and social class.

## 1.2d Emile Durkheim

Emile Durkheim (1858–1917) can be considered the first French academic sociologist. In 1892, the University of Paris granted him its first doctorate in sociology. Six years later he was appointed chair of the first Department of Social Sciences at the University of Bordeaux and later was named chair of the Department of Education and Sociology, thus providing sociology the opportunity to be recognized as a science. In addition to teaching, Durkheim wrote critical reviews and published important papers and books. His best known books include *The Division of Labor in Society*, *The Rules of Sociological Method*, *Suicide*, and *The Elementary Forms of Religious Life.*

Durkheim is responsible for several important ideas. For one, he refused to explain social events by assuming that they operated according to the same rules as biology or psychology. To Durkheim, social phenomena are **social facts** that have distinctive social characteristics and determinants. He defined social facts as "every way of acting, fixed or not, capable of exercising on the individual an external constraint" (1893, p. 13). Since these facts are external to the individual, they outlive individuals and endure over time. They include such things as customs, laws, and the general rules of behavior that people accept without question. Stopping at traffic lights, wearing shirts, and combing one's hair are behaviors most people perform without dissent. In short, individuals are more the products of society than the creators of it.

Although an individual can come to know and be a part of society, society itself is external to the individual. For this reason, Durkheim concentrated on examining characteristics of groups and structures rather than individual attributes. Instead of looking at the personal traits of religious believers, for example, he focused on the cohesion or lack of cohesion of specific religious groups. He was not so concerned with the religious experience of individuals, but rather with the communal activity and the communal bonds that develop from religious participation (Coser, 1977).

Such communal interaction gives rise to what Durkheim called a **collective conscience**—a common psyche (spirit), which results from the blending together of

**Class-consciousness**
Awareness among members of a society that the society is stratified

**Social facts**
Reliable and valid pieces of information about society

**Collective conscience**
A collective psyche that results from the blending of many individual mentalities, but exists above any one individual

many individual mentalities yet that exists over and above any individual. Although the collective conscience is socially created, it is a powerful reality that comes to control us and cannot be denied. From this perspective, for example, whether God exists as a supernatural being is secondary to the fact that God exists as a result of people sharing and demonstrating their belief in God. To those sharing that belief, God is unquestionably and undeniably real, and thus an inescapable force. It is no longer a matter of a personal belief, but is now a social belief that becomes a force outside of any one of us.

Durkheim's work *Suicide* (1951) deserves special attention for several reasons. It established a unique model for social research; and it clearly demonstrated that human behavior, although it might seem very individual, could be understood only by investigating the social context in which the behavior took place. After looking at numerous statistics on different countries and different groups of people, Durkheim concluded that suicide was a social phenomenon, related to the individual's involvement in group life and the extent to which he or she was part of some cohesive social unit. Durkheim's central thesis was that the more a person is integrated into intimate social groups, the less likely he or she is to commit suicide. Durkheim used his thesis about integration into society to develop four explanations of suicide: egoistic, altruistic, anomic, and fatalistic (Durkheim, 1951). One of Durkheim's main points is that unlike popular (and common sense) explanations that explain suicide primarily as a personal act and a result of psychological conditions, he explains suicide in terms of peoples' connections to (or integration with) society and social groups and how organized or disorganized social conditions are. **Egoistic suicide** is a result of not being sufficiently integrated into society or meaningful social groups. When this occurs, one does not have strong social ties. Thus, an individual is left not only feeling alone but also without the bonds that could help him or her through a troubled period. For example, men and unmarried people have higher suicide rates than women and married people. **Altruistic suicide** is the opposite. This is when a person is overly connected to society or a social group to the extent that the group takes on more meaning than that person's personal life, and he or she lives for the group. The terrorists who were responsible for the 9/11 jet crashes into the World Trade Center in New York were on a suicide mission. Their fundamentalist religious convictions and their adherence to the values of al Qaeda were largely responsible for their involvement in these missions. The difference between egoistic and altruistic suicide is easy to remember if you simply think of the words. Egoism means a focus on the self. Without sufficient ties to society or social groups, this type of suicide is more likely to occur. Altruism means a concern for others. This may be more likely to occur when one is connected to groups that are strongly present in one's life.

(Wikimedia Commons)

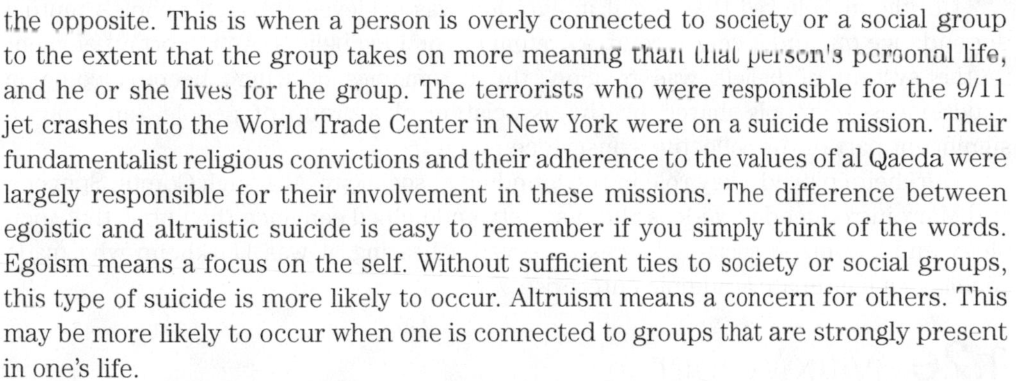

According to Durkheim, a third type of suicide, **anomic suicide**, occurs when an individual is faced with sudden social disorganization or a disruption in the social conditions that guide the individual's life. With such sudden changes, the values, goals, and rules for living (or norms) may suddenly lose their meaning, thus leaving the individual without guidance or patterns or regulations, and feeling alienated from life. He called this condition "anomie." While this may appear to be a psychological state, it is important to understand that "anomie" or "normlessness" is the result in the disruption of social patterns, thus leaving an individual disconnected from social regulations that guide his or her life. A sudden downturn in the economy (or a stock market crash) that results in a once wealthy individual becoming relatively impoverished (or, at least, losing the identity and lifestyle associated with extreme wealth) or the sudden loss of a spouse or domestic partner after 30 years of living together could result in a sudden lack of a compass to guide one's life—and thus to anomic suicide. The regulations that guided one's life suddenly become meaningless.

Finally, **fatalistic suicide** may occur when a person is faced with oppressive social conditions with such a high degree of regulation over his or her life that the person feels

**Egoistic suicide**
Suicide that results from lack of social integration into meaningful groups, leaving the individual with a sense of being isolated

**Altruistic suicide**
Suicide that results from being overly integrated into groups and the group meaning taking on more importance than the individual

**Anomic suicide**
Suicide that results from sudden changes in society or in one's life, leading to a disruption in the patterns that guide one's life

**Fatalistic suicide**
Suicide that results from oppressive social conditions that lead one to a fatal sense of hopelessness

Emile Durkheim believed religion to be an important element in the system of beliefs through which social integration was achieved. The ceremonies and symbols associated with religion became common and shared experiences and were, thus, a part of the collective conscience. (AP Wide World Photo)

there is no hope or possibility of pursuing their personal interests. Because of certain social conditions—for example, a society that fosters slavery—individuals may feel that they have been condemned to their fates, and thus be more inclined to suicide.

Durkheim believed that social integration was achieved through people's mutual dependence on, and acceptance of, a system of common beliefs. An important element in the system of beliefs was religion, the ceremonies of which become common experiences—symbols shared by the association of a group of people—and thus a significant part of the collective conscience.

Durkheim played a key role in the founding of sociology. Although Comte, Spencer, and Marx introduced new ideas about society and helped convince the public that sociology and the other social sciences deserved a hearing, it was Durkheim who made sociology a legitimate academic enterprise.

## 1.2e Max Weber

Max Weber (1864–1920; pronounced *Vay-ber*) was born in Germany. He was trained in law and economics, receiving his doctorate from the University of Heidelberg at age 25. His best-known works in sociology include *The Protestant Ethic and the Spirit of Capitalism*, *The Sociology of Hinduism and Buddhism*, *Theory of Social and Economic Organization*, and *Methodology of the Social Sciences.*

Weber's mixed feelings toward authority, whether familial or political, are reflected in his writings on the topic of power and authority. Weber discussed why men claim authority and expect their wishes to be obeyed. (Typically during his period, women were not considered.) His approach to sociology, however, has probably been as influential as his ideas. His predecessors considered societies in terms of their large social structures, social divisions, and social movements. Spencer based his studies on the belief that societies evolved like organisms; Marx considered society in terms of class conflicts; and Durkheim was concerned with the institutional arrangements that maintain the cohesion of social structures. These theorists assumed that society, although composed of individuals, existed apart from them.

Weber was concerned with value-free sociology. He did not believe that society could be studied value-free because sociologists would always interject their own values and beliefs when studying society or even when choosing what to study. Weber believed that sociologists must study not just social facts and social structures but also *social actions*—external objective behaviors as well as the internalized values, motives, and subjective meanings that individuals attach to their own behavior and to the behavior of others. The goal, Weber believed, was to achieve a "sympathetic understanding" of the minds of others. He called this approach **verstehen** (pronounced "*ver-shtay-en*"): understanding human action by examining the subjective meanings that people attach to their own behavior and to the behavior of others. Once values, motives, and intentions were identified, Weber contended, sociologists could treat them objectively and scientifically. Weber's concept of "verstehen" is a vital tool for academic and applied social researchers. As mentioned, Weber explained social class not just in terms of how much power, wealth, and prestige people have but also in terms of how they see and feel about their power, wealth, and prestige. So, for example, in conducting research on inequality between upper-class and middle-class groups, academic researchers need to find out not only what differences exist due to power and wealth but also how people in each group feel about their own self-worth and the worth of others.

*(Wikimedia Commons)*

This approach is evident in Weber's interpretation of social class. Whereas Marx saw class as rooted in economic determinism, particularly as related to property ownership, Weber argued that social class involves subjective perceptions of power, wealth, ownership, and social prestige, as well as the objective aspects of these factors.

## 1.2f Harriet Martineau

Harriet Martineau (1802–1876) was a significant contributor to the early development of sociology. Almost completely deaf by adulthood, Martineau immersed herself in reading and self-education. She studied social life in Great Britain and traveled, in 1834, to the United States to examine American social life for 2 years. She published her findings in *Society in America* in 1837 and in *Retrospect of Western Travel* in 1838. Due to her gender, much of her original research was ignored by the male dominated discipline. However, she was acknowledged for translating Comte's work, *Positive Philosophy*, into English in 1851, condensing his six-volume work into two volumes. Today, Martineau is recognized for her contributions to sociology and is considered to be one of the earliest founders of sociological thought and research.

*(Wikimedia Commons)*

Besides the scholars just discussed, other European thinkers—including Georg Simmel, Henri de Saint-Simon, Vilfredo Pareto, Ferdinand Toennies, and Karl Mannheim—contributed to the development of sociology. With rare exceptions, they viewed society as a social unit that transcended the individual or was greater than the sum of individuals. It was for this reason, in part, that they did not investigate the means by which individual humans come to accept and reflect the fundamental conditions and structures of their societies—a question that was an important concern of some early American sociologists.

**Verstehen**
Understanding human action by examining the subjective meanings that people attach to their own behavior and the behavior of others

# 1.3 THE DEVELOPMENT OF SOCIOLOGY IN AMERICA

The earliest sociologists were Europeans, but much of the development of sociology took place in the United States. The first department of sociology was established in 1893 at the University of Chicago, and many important early figures of the discipline were associated with that institution. At the time sociology was developing, rapid social change was occurring within America. Industrialization, urbanization, and immigration were three factors contributing to this change as the economy was shifting from agricultural to industrial. As people began to migrate to the cities, the increase in population created tremendous social problems including overcrowding, pollution, and crime, as well as many others. In addition, massive waves of immigrants were arriving in the United States which only intensified the problems, as their cultures often clashed with those of other immigrants and Americans. By the beginning of the twentieth century, communities were looking toward universities to find the answers to problems within the cities. Much like their European forerunners, American sociologists were concerned with social problems and social reform, in part because of the rapid social changes taking place in this country. Some of these early scholars (such as Robert Park, Ernest Burgess, Albion Small, Jane Addams, and W. E. B. DuBois) focused on urbanization and urban problems—ghettos, prostitution, drug addiction, juvenile delinquency, immigration, and race relations. Others—such as George Herbert Mead, W. I. Thomas and Charles Horton Cooley—helped lay the foundations for the understanding of social interaction.

In the 1940s, the center of sociological research shifted from Chicago to other schools such as Harvard and Columbia. Talcott Parsons (1902–1979), who was affiliated with Harvard, rapidly became the leading social theorist in America, if not the world. Drawing heavily on the work of European thinkers such as Weber and Durkheim, he developed a very broad "general theory of action" (Parson & Shils, 1951).

Robert K. Merton (1910–2003), a student of Parsons, began his teaching career at Harvard but moved in 1941 to Columbia University. Although his general orientation was similar to Parsons', Merton was much less abstract and much more concerned with linking general theory to empirical testing. This approach came to be known as the **middle-range theory**. His contributions to our understanding of such concepts as social structures, self-fulfilling prophecies, deviance, and bureaucracies place him among the leading American social theorists. C. Wright Mills, Peter Blau, Erving Goffman, Herbert Blumer, Ralf Dahrendorf, Randall Collins, and Jessie Bernard were other scholars who greatly contributed to sociology's development in reaching its present state. Much new work on the elderly, gender roles, popular culture, globalization, and peace studies is being undertaken. In addition, the methodological tools and procedures and the range of theories to explain social phenomena are more diverse today than ever before.

# 1.4 THE MAJOR THEORETICAL PERSPECTIVES IN SOCIOLOGY

Theories are explanations offered to account for a set of phenomena. *Social theories* are explanations of social phenomena, such as why people choose to marry as they do or why people behave differently in different social situations. Theories (to use the term in its broadest sense) help us explain and predict a wide variety of events. For example, if asked why juvenile violence occurs, you will likely have an opinion on the cause or causes of such crimes. A scientist will use a **theory**, a set of interrelated statements or propositions, to attempt to answer the question about juvenile crime or any other social phenomenon. Theories are based on a set of assumptions, self-evident truths, and research; and they include definitions and describe the conditions in which the phenomenon exists.

**Middle-range theory**

A set of propositions designed to link abstract theory with empirical testing

**Theory**

A set of logically and systematically interrelated propositions that explain a particular process or phenomenon

While sociological theories exist to explain everything from childrearing to automobile sales, a small number of basic theories are predominate in the field. We will examine these theories and how each can be applied in work settings and in your personal life. They are also described in more detail and applied to specific settings throughout this book.

## 1.4a Structural Functional Theory

**Structural functionalism** has its roots in the work of the early sociologists, especially Durkheim and Weber. Among contemporary scholars, it is most closely associated with the work of Parsons and Merton. Structural functionalists use a macro-level analysis to explain society and social structures.

**BVT*Lab***

Flashcards are available for this chapter at **www.BVTLab.com.**

Structural functionalism is sometimes referred to as "social systems theory," "equilibrium theory," "order theory," or simply "functionalism." The terms *structure* and *function* refer to two separate, but closely related, concepts. *Structures* can be compared to the organs or parts of the body of an animal, and *functions* can be compared with the purposes of these structures. The stomach is a structure; digestion is its function. In the same way, healthcare organizations and the military are social structures (or **social systems**), and caring for the sick and defending governmental interests are their functions. Like a biological structure, a social system is composed of many interrelated and interdependent parts or structures.

If you were to visit any society in the world, from the largest to the smallest, you would find that most societies, if not all, are comprised of five major structures: family, religion, education, economy, and government. According to structural functionalism, the overall function of a society is dependent on each structure performing its required duties. Those advocating this theory believe that all structures are interrelated and interdependent on each other. When working properly, a social system performs specific functions that make it possible for society and the people who comprise that society to exist. Therefore, each structure serves a function that leads to the maintenance or stability of the larger society. The educational system is intended to provide literary and technical skills; the religious system is intended to provide emotional support and to answer questions about the unknown; families are intended to socialize infants and children, and so on. The functionalist perspective assumes these social systems have an underlying tendency to be in equilibrium or balance; any system failing to fulfill its functions will result in an imbalance or disequilibrium. In extreme cases, the entire system can break down when a change or failure in any one part of the system affects its interrelated parts.

According to Merton, a social system can have both **manifest functions** and **latent functions**. *Manifest functions* are intended and recognized; *latent functions* are neither intended nor recognized. One manifest function of education systems is to teach literary and technical skills. They also perform latent functions, such as providing supervision for children while parents work and providing contacts for dating and even for marriage. Correctional institutions have the manifest functions of punishment and removing criminals from social interaction within the larger society. They may also perform the latent functions of providing criminals with advanced training in other criminal behaviors.

Merton recognized that not all consequences of systems are functional—that is, they do not all lead to the maintenance of the system. Some lead to instability or the breakdown of a system. He termed these consequences **dysfunctions**. Families have a manifest function of rearing children. The intensity of family interactions, however, can lead to the dysfunction, or negative consequence, of domestic violence and child abuse. Dysfunctions such as these may lead to the disruption of relationships within the family system or even to the total breakdown of the system.

Sociologists who adhere to the functionalist perspective examine the parts of a given system and try to determine how they are related to one another and to the whole. They

**Structural functionalism**

The theory that societies contain certain interdependent structures, each of which performs certain functions for the maintenance of society

**Social system**

A set of interrelated social structures and the expectations that accompany them

**Manifest functions**

The intended consequences of a social system

**Latent functions**

The unintended consequences of a social system

**Dysfunctions**

In structural functional theory, factors that lead to the disruption or breakdown of the social system observe the results of a given cluster or arrangement of parts, attempting to discover both the intended (manifest) and the unintended (latent) functions of these parts. In addition, they analyze which of these consequences contribute to the maintenance of a given system and which lead to the breakdown of the system. However, what may be functional in one system may be dysfunctional in another. For example, a function that is good for corporate profits may not be good for family solidarity, or one good for religious unity may not be good for ethnic integration.

According to the functionalist perspective, social systems exist because they fulfill some function for the society. Functionalists focus on order and stability, which has led some critics to argue it supports the status quo. With the emphasis on equilibrium and the maintenance of the system, the process of change, critics say, receives little attention.

## APPLYING STRUCTURAL FUNCTIONAL THEORY

Structural functional theory is one of the most generally applicable perspectives in social science. It is used by academic sociologists to study and analyze every form of social system, including families, prisons, governments, communities, schools, sports teams, and many others.

Just as structural functionalism is broadly applicable to problems of interest to academic sociologists, so is it a useful tool for almost every type of applied sociological problem. It can be particularly useful as a means of identifying and analyzing the components and goals of a system and of ensuring that those goals are met. When we try to solve problems in any type of social system—whether it is a society, a corporation, a family, a sorority, or a sports team—we must answer some central questions. What are the parts of the system? What functions do the parts actually serve? What functions are they intended to serve? How do the parts influence each other?

A structural functionalist exploring the phenomenon of school violence may look toward the family structure for explanation. During the past 40 to 50 years, the structure of the family has changed considerably. Many women, once expected to stay home and raise children, have entered the paid workforce instead of becoming stay-at-home wives and mothers. Even when a woman wants to stay home, the cost of raising a family today generally requires both parents to provide a paycheck to make ends meet. In addition, divorce is more common today than when your parents were children, and thus the number of single parent families in society has increased. From a functionalist perspective, these issues could create dysfunction in the family. Children left home alone may spend time involved in deviant behavior, such as vandalism, shoplifting, drug or alcohol use, etc. One of the intended (manifest) functions of the family is for parents to supervise the behavior and activities of their children and to socialize them about respecting the law. A latent function of families can be social isolation due to the increasing amount of independence given to children. Continuous separation from family and friends, unsupervised activities on the computer, and the belief in personal space without parental interference, may create socialization problems for a child struggling to fit in somewhere. If he or she feels like an outsider at school, other children may respond with ridicule, teasing, and bullying. In a rare situation, the child may respond with violence toward those he or she believes are responsible for the problems experienced at school.

**Functional alternatives**
Meeting functions of the system in ways other than initially intended

Robert Merton's theory of **functional alternatives** provides one way to avoid dysfunctions such as school violence. *Functional alternatives* are other ways to achieve the intended goal. Perhaps the family could provide an alternative for the child left alone, such as staying with a relative, attending an after school or sports program, or being involved in a community organization. It is imperative that parents recognize the problems experienced by their children, instead of dismissing them, and find solutions that work for everyone. This functional alternative would, hopefully, meet the needs of the child and lessen the chance of there being an episode of school violence.

The functional perspective can also be applied to tensions among the various parts of a system. The expectations or actions of the different parts of a system may fail to mesh. A building-supply store selling a variety of construction materials, for example, may have some employees who receive commissions from in-store sales and others who receive commissions from outside sales. Suppose that you are hired as an outside sales representative and you develop a large clientele of building contractors through contacts made while on the road. However, when one of those customers decides to purchase material directly from the store, an inside salesperson takes credit for the sale. Who should get the commission for the sale? The conflict arises not because of poor performance on the part of the salespeople but because of a systemic dysfunction. This lack of clarity and confusion over the store's specific goals and the goals of each of its parts can cause serious personnel conflicts that could undermine the business. In this situation, some type of explicit goal-setting or value-clarification process would be appropriate. These examples demonstrate how, by focusing on the functions of the parts of a system, we might be able to discover solutions to a problem.

## 1.4b Conflict Theory

**Conflict theory**, which also had its origins in early sociology—especially in the work of Karl Marx—has among its more recent proponents C. Wright Mills, Lewis Coser, Ralf Dahrendorf, and others. These sociologists share the view that society is best understood and analyzed in terms of conflict and power. Like structural functionalism, conflict theory entails macro-level analysis.

**BVT *Lab***

Flashcards are available for this chapter at **www.BVTLab.com.**

Karl Marx began with a very simple assumption: Society is constructed around its economic organization, particularly the ownership of property. Marx argued that society basically consists of two classes: those who own the means of production (bourgeoisie) and those who provide the labor (proletariat). These two groups are in opposition of one another and experience, as a result, ongoing class conflict. While the proletariat provide the labor that creates the wealth for the bourgeoisie, they (the proletariat) are never paid what they are worth. The profits made from their labor remains primarily in the hands of those who own the means of production. According to Marx, in any economic system that supports inequality, the exploited classes eventually recognize their submissive and inferior status and revolt against the dominant class of property owners and employers. The story of history, then, is the story of class struggle between the owners and the workers, the dominators and the dominated, the powerful and the powerless. Ultimately, conflict theory is about the exploitation of one class of people by another class.

Contemporary conflict theorists assume that conflict is a permanent feature of social life and that, as a result, societies are in a state of constant change. Unlike Marx, however, these theorists rarely assume conflict is always based on class or that it always reflects economic organization and ownership. Conflicts are assumed to involve a broad range of groups or interests—young against old, male against female, or one racial group against another—as well as workers against employers. These conflicts occur because such things as power, wealth, and prestige are not available to everyone; they are limited commodities, and the demand exceeds the supply. Conflict theory also assumes those who have or control desirable goods, services, and other resources will defend and protect their own interests at the expense of others.

In this view, *conflict* does not mean the sort of event that makes headlines, such as war, violence, or open hostility. It is, instead, regarded as the struggle occurring day after day as people try to maintain and improve their positions in life. Neither should conflict be regarded as a destructive process leading to disorder and the breakdown of society. Theorists such as Dahrendorf and Coser have focused on the integrative nature

**Conflict theory**

A social theory that views conflict as inevitable and natural and as a significant cause of social change of conflict, its value as a force contributing to order and stability. How can conflict be a constructive force? Basically, the answer is people with common interests join together to seek gains that will benefit all of those sharing these common interests. By the same token, conflict among groups focuses attention on inequalities and social problems that might never be resolved without conflict. Racial conflicts, for example, may serve to bind people with common interests together and may also lead to constructive social change, actually lessening the current conflict among groups.

There is an obvious contrast between the views of the functionalists, who regard society as balanced and in a state of equilibrium, and the views of conflict theorists, who assume that society is an arena of constant competition and change. Functionalists believe the social process is a continual effort to maintain harmony; conflict theorists believe it is a continual struggle to "get ahead." Functionalists view society as basically consensual, integrated, and static; conflict theorists believe it is characterized by constraint, conflict, and change. Whereas functionalists have been criticized for focusing on stability and the status quo, conflict theorists have been criticized for overlooking the less controversial and more orderly aspects of society.

## APPLYING CONFLICT THEORY

Like structural functionalism, sociologists use conflict theory to explain the relationship between the parts of a social system and the inequalities that exist among these parts. In recognizing conflict as a permanent feature of the life of any social system, conflict theory can be used to discover and explain the sources of the conflict. In addition to discovering and explaining the sources of conflict, conflict theory may be used to help create techniques to deal with conflict or to use it constructively in the workplace and in your personal life. Sociologists working as therapists or counselors in juvenile detention centers recognize that if conflicts in relationships are not resolved, problems will likely manifest and ultimately lead to a worse impact on the child, family, and community.

In dealing with any situation, whether it is running a business, coaching a basketball team, teaching a class, presiding over a group, maintaining a family, or organizing a labor union, conflict theory tells us to look for the hidden strains and frustrations, particularly between those in power who make the decisions (bosses, managers, owners, administrators, teachers) and those who carry out these decisions (workers, players, students). Even when those involved do not express dissatisfaction, there may still be conflict. Conflict in relationships is not always explicit, nor do individuals always express it. Nonetheless, some clues might help you to recognize conflict.

Conflict in relationships is not always explicit and individuals do not always express it. However, certain clues can indicate inequalities in position between such relationship members as husbands and wives. (Shutterstock)

When sociologists or counselors are looking for answers to conflict, they often look to clues that indicate inequalities in position between schools and students, husbands and wives, or between managers and workers. Some of these clues, or expressions of power differentials, may include covert signs of anger (e.g., overeating, boredom, depression, illness, gossip); *passive aggression* (sarcasm, nitpicking, chronic criticism); *sabotage* (spoiling or undermining an activity another person has planned); *displacement* (directing anger at people or things another person cherishes); devitalization of the relationship (a relationship that has become lifeless, equivalent to "emotional divorce"); or violence, resulting from unreleased pressures and tensions (Lamanna and Riedmann, 2009). These same consequences are likely to occur in families or in any other relationship in which conflict is denied. Realizing this, a sociologist—or anyone working with a group—might try to build into the group's activities some approved and expected ways of airing conflicts among members. Perhaps a basketball coach would initiate weekly "gripe sessions" where each member of the team is expected to discuss things that bother him or her about other players or about the coaches.

Conflict theory helps us realize that because conflict is normal and usually inevitable, it is okay to express it. In fact, some clinicians go so far as to recommend that their clients—whether they are married couples, universities, occupational groups, or sports teams—periodically engage in conflict to release tensions and initiate emotional interactions. For example, faculty members within university settings are represented by a president who is nominated and voted on by the body of the faculty at the university. The faculty president presides over the faculty senate comprised of members from each department within the university. The student body at the university has a similar structure where they elect a student body president and senate. To resolve conflict between the university and the students, the president of the student body will attend faculty senate meetings and express the concerns of the students. The faculty senate will listen to the concerns and vote on issues brought forth by the student body president. For example, a student body president is approached by a disabled student who is concerned over smoking areas close to the entrances to classroom buildings. She is confined to a wheelchair and at the level where a cigarette being tossed or "flicked" by a smoker could possibly injure her. The student body president listens to her concern and takes it to the student body senate; they vote to ban smoking on university property. However, they have to take this vote to the faculty senate, and the faculty senate, too, must vote to pass the smoking ban. If it passes, the bill would be sent to the president of the university for review and final approval. These organizations within the university and other settings are not meant to prescribe all-out war within groups but rather to encourage people with conflicts to develop explicit procedures to deal with differences in a rational and constructive way, instead of pretending they don't exist or will disappear on their own.

---

**thinking** SOCIOLOGICALLY

1. How would structural functional theory and conflict theory address the issue of gender discrimination within the workplace? How would each of these theories explain the selection process for fraternities and sororities?
2. To what extent is conflict inherent in the university setting? Is conflict primarily between student and university, student and faculty, or between student and student? Explain your answer.

## 1.4c Symbolic Interaction Theory

**Symbolic interaction theory**, although influenced somewhat by early European sociologists, was developed largely through the efforts of George Herbert Mead, W. I. Thomas, and Charles Horton Cooley—all who belonged to the Chicago School. The key difference between this perspective and those discussed earlier is the size of the units used in investigation and analysis. The previous two theories use a macro-level analysis to study societies; symbolic interaction theory, on the other hand, uses a micro-level approach. This theory studies individuals within societies, particularly the definitions and meanings attached to situations, rather than focusing on the large-scale structures.

**Symbolic interaction theory**
The social theory stressing interactions between people and the social processes that occur within the individual that are made possible by language and internalized meaning

The question of how individuals influence society and how society influences individuals is central to sociology. As you recall, early sociologists (Spencer, Durkheim, and Marx, for example) regarded society as an entity existing apart from the individual. Symbolic interactionists, however, assume society exists within every socialized individual; and its external forms and structures arise through the social interactions taking place among individuals at the symbolic level.

What does "symbolic level" mean? It can be explained this way. Suppose you are driving down the road in your car, and you see a brick wall closing off the entire road. You stop, of course, because you have learned you cannot pass through a physical object. If, however, you are riding down the same road and you come to a stoplight, once again, you stop—but why? No physical object prevents you from progressing. Your reason for stopping is that you have learned the red light is a *symbol* that means, "stop." The world around us can be said to consist of these two elements: physical objects and abstract symbols. Language is a system of symbols. It represents physical objects or concepts used to communicate.

According to George Herbert Mead, who played an important role in the development of symbolic interactionism, it is the ability of humans to use symbols that sets us apart from other animals and that allows us to create social institutions, societies, and cultures. People in a society share an understanding of particular symbols (the stoplight, for example). Social learning takes place at both symbolic and non-symbolic levels. By interacting with others, we internalize social expectations, a specific language, and social values. In addition, we learn to share meanings and to communicate symbolically through words and gestures. As humans, we can interact at both a physical (e.g., a slap) and a symbolic (e.g., showing a fist or making a verbal threat) level. Since we can relate symbolically, we can carry on conversations with ourselves. We can also imagine the effects of different courses of action. We can imagine what would happen if we were to throw a rotten tomato in the face of a police officer. By thinking through alternative courses of action, we can choose those we believe to be the most appropriate for a given situation. The fact that others share similar expectations makes life patterned and relatively predictable. Those who fail to recognize that a red traffic light means stop will have trouble getting any place safely in their cars.

*The world around us can be said to consist of two elements: physical objects and abstract symbols. A red stoplight is a symbol that we have learned means "stop." (Shutterstock)*

The interactionist perspective examines patterns and processes of everyday life that are generally ignored by many other perspectives. It raises questions about the self, the self in relationships with others, and the self and others in the wider social context. Why do some of us have negative feelings about ourselves? Why is it we can relate more easily with some persons than with others? Why do we feel more comfortable around friends than among strangers? How is it possible to interact with complete strangers or to know what to do in new situations? How are decisions made in families? Symbolic interactionists try to answer such questions by examining the individual in a social context. The starting point of this examination is the social setting in which an individual is born and the interactions he or she has with parents, siblings, teachers, neighbors, or others. From these interactions, we learn what is proper or improper, whether we are "good" or "bad," who is important, and so forth. A more complete explanation of this perspective is given in other sections throughout the book.

## APPLYING SYMBOLIC INTERACTION THEORY

The symbolic interactionist perspective emphasizes that people act on the basis of their interpretation of the language and symbols in a situation, and not the situation in and of itself. This perspective is useful, in that it points to the necessity of having people achieve at least a minimal agreement about the definition or meaning of a situation. One potential problem to develop in any relationship—whether on the job or in the home is the lack of consensus in people's definitions of a situation. The lack of consensus may be the result of a disagreement or a misunderstanding. The confusion may be about the roles individuals develop for themselves, the goals they think should be pursued collectively, or the ways in which resources (such as money or power) should be distributed. This could lead to a breakdown of a relationship altogether or to confusion, tension, strife, and general unhappiness, at the very least, within the relationship or social system. Some examples may show how the definition of a situation can be at the core of some interpersonal problems and how symbolic interaction theory can be used.

Imagine that you are the manager of a retail jewelry store, and you hire two salespeople. The salespeople are told their salaries will be partly straight pay and partly commission generated by their sales. Person A defines the situation as one in which potential customers should be divided equally between the two employees because they both work in the same place. Person B sees the situation as one of competition among the employees for sales. Both interpretations are possible and quite feasible. As a result, Person A sees Person B as aggressive, money-hungry, and cutthroat. Person B sees Person A as uncompetitive, complacent, and not sales-oriented. The tension mounts, and each salesperson believes the other has a personality problem. The problem, though, may be due not to personalities but to a lack of clarity about how each person defines what he or she has been employed to do. As the manager, how could your knowledge of symbolic interaction theory help you to resolve this problem? Symbolic interaction theory alerts us to the importance of effective communication among people so they can understand each other's perspectives. If this occurs, they may be able to coordinate their actions better. According to Johnson (1986), "the ultimate outcome is not only reinforcement of appropriate role performance but also the creation of a more supportive and satisfying atmosphere" (p. 60).

It is also important to understand that various individuals' definitions of a situation are related to their definitions of what constitutes a problem. Another person may not see what one person considers a problem as a problem. A male boss who continuously flirts with his female secretary through physical contact (arm touching, back rubbing, and so on) or sexually suggestive comments may think he is creating a friendly, supportive work atmosphere. He may be unaware that the secretary sees his actions as sexual overtures and feels harassed and exploited by his "friendliness."

Addressing the issue of school violence, a student who feels like an outsider, both at home and at school, may internalize the perceptions of others as hate or being unwanted. As a result he turns the perceptions of others inward and begins to see himself in the same way. Others in this individual's life may not have this perception at all but simply be focused on their own problems, completely unaware that the troubled youth perceives feelings of hate and being unwanted.

In each of these examples, open communication is needed so the definition of the situation can be clarified. Often a mediator, perhaps a sociologist but not necessarily, is needed to help explain each side to the other, in the hope of helping the parties to achieve at least a minimal agreement about the definition of the situation.

---

While the previous three theories are often cited as the major perspectives within the field of sociology, you should be familiar with some others that have made tremendous contributions to the study of society, social groups, and human behavior.

### **thinking** SOCIOLOGICALLY

Discuss how a symbolic theorist would explain "classroom conformity." Why do students, when asked questions by the professor, not respond, even when they know the answers?

## 1.4d Exchange Theory

Although symbolic interaction theory is the most widely used and recognized interaction perspective, exchange theory also falls within this general orientation. **Exchange theory** has a diverse intellectual heritage from sources in economics, anthropology, and psychology, as well as sociology. This perspective is based on the belief that life is a series of exchanges involving rewards and costs. In economic exchanges, people exchange money, goods, and services, hoping to profit or at least break even in the exchange. In anthropological, psychological, and sociological exchanges, the items of exchange include social and psychic factors. Consider the following: In return for your companionship, I'll invite you to my house; in return for your positive teacher evaluation, I'll work extra hard to be a good instructor. Work, gifts, money, affection, and ideas—all are offered in the hope of getting something in return.

Social exchange theory seeks to explain why behavioral outcomes such as marriage, employment, and religious involvement occur, given a set of structural conditions (age, race, gender, class) and interaction possibilities. Women, for example, marry men of a higher social status more frequently than men marry women of a higher social status. Exchange theorists would attempt to explain this finding by examining the desirable qualities men and women have to exchange. In the United States, for men to have money or a good job is viewed as desirable; for women to be physically attractive is viewed as desirable. Thus, we might expect that very attractive lower-status women could exchange their beauty for men of a higher economic and occupational status, which seems to be what happens.

Exchange theory assumes that people seek rewarding statuses, relationships, and experiences, and they try to avoid costs, pain, and punishments. Given a set of alternatives, individuals choose those from which they expect the most profit, rewards, or satisfaction; and they avoid those not profitable, rewarding, or satisfying. When the costs exceed the rewards, people are likely to feel angry and dissatisfied. When the rewards exceed the costs, they are likely to feel they got a good deal (unless they got it through exploitation or dishonesty, in which case, they may feel guilty and choose to avoid further interactions). Both parties are more likely to be satisfied with the interaction if there is perceived equity in the exchange, a feeling on the part of both that the rewards were worth the costs.

**BVT Lab**

Flashcards are available for this chapter at **www.BVTLab.com.**

Although people may work selflessly for others with no thought of reward, it is quite unusual. The social exchange perspective assumes that voluntary social interactions are contingent on rewarding reactions from others. When rewarding reactions cease, either the actions end or dissatisfaction results.

There are two different schools of thought in the exchange theory perspective. George Homans, the theorist responsible for originating exchange theory, represents a perspective consistent with that of behavioral psychologists, who believe that behavior can be explained in terms of rewards and punishments. Behaviorists focus their attention on actual behavior, not on processes that are inferred from behavior but cannot be observed. In exchange theory, the rewards and punishments are the behavior of other people, and those involved in exchanges assume their rewards will be proportional to their costs.

Peter Blau is the advocate of a different school of exchange theory, one that is consistent with symbolic interactionism. Blau does not attempt to explain all exchanges in terms of observable behavior. He argues the exchange is more subjective and interpretive and exchanges occur on a symbolic level. As a result, money may be a just reward only if the receiver defines it as such; and psychic rewards of satisfaction with doing a good job or of pleasing someone may be as important as money, gifts, or outward responses of praise.

**Exchange theory**

A theory of interaction that attempts to explain social behavior in terms of reciprocity of costs and rewards

Both Homans and Blau agree that what is important is that each party in the exchange must receive something perceived as equivalent to that which is given (to Homans, "distributive justice"; to Blau, "fair exchange"). All exchange involves a mutually held

**Table 1-2** Major Perspectives in Sociology

| Theory | Level of Analysis | View of Society | Major Concepts | Pros and Cons of Theory |
|---|---|---|---|---|
| Functionalism | Macro | Society consists of interdependent parts, each fulfilling certain functions. | Structure, function, manifest and latent function, dysfunction | **Pros:** examines structures within society; examines the "big picture"; emphasizes the impact that structures have in relation to consequences for society<br>**Cons:** does not emphasize the interactions between individuals |
| Conflict | Macro | Society consists of conflict between diverse groups within society competing for valuable and scarce resources. | Means of production, proletariat, bourgeoisie, social class, scarce resources | **Pros:** examines stratification and inequality and the reasons that they exist; examines who benefits from existing social relationships<br>**Cons:** does not explore competition within society as potentially beneficial |
| Interactionism | Micro | Interactions between people in society are negotiated using symbols, gestures, and communications, including non-verbal ones. | Symbols, social construction, definition of the situation | **Pros:** examines day-to-day interactions between people; examines the relationship between identity and social interaction<br>**Cons:** does not emphasize the ways in which large-scale structures affect interaction |
| Exchange | Micro | Actions are determined by weighing rewards and costs. | Exchanges, rewards, costs, benefits, negotiation | **Pros:** examines day-to-day interactions between people in terms of rewards and costs<br>**Cons:** does not emphasize the way in which large-scale structures affect interaction |
| Evolutionary | Macro | Social systems evolve naturally from simple to complex. | Organism, social arrangements, social systems, simple, complex, survival of the fittest | **Pros:** looks at society as evolving naturally over time; brings in the possibility of social evolution as connected with biological evolution<br>**Cons:** does not emphasize the potential negativity of "survival of the fittest" concept |

expectation that reciprocation will occur. If resources or exchange criteria are unequal, one person is at a distinct disadvantage; and the other has power over and controls the relationship. As a result, in marriage, unequal exchanges between husband and wife are likely to result in dominance of one over the other or may even end the relationship. In employment, if employee and employer do not recognize a fair exchange of rewards and costs, dissatisfaction may result. The employee may quit, or the employer may dismiss the employee.

In exchange theory, then, social life is viewed as a process of bargaining or negotiation, and social relationships are based on trust and mutual interests. In recent years, some sociologists have criticized exchange theory as overly adhering to economic and mathematical models that do not put enough emphasis on the human elements or content of a situation (Zafirovsky, 2003).

## thinking SOCIOLOGICALLY

1. Select a group or organization in which you are involved and explore it in terms of structural functionalism, conflict theory, symbolic interactionism, and exchange theory. What types of things would each perspective be interested in finding out? What types of answers might each perspective reach? Which theory or theories do you think most accurately explain the group or organization you selected? For help with this, review Table 1-2 (Major Perspectives in Sociology) and look especially at each of the theories' "views of society" and "major concepts." These should help you think about the types of questions each theory might generate.
2. Select a contemporary social problem and examine it using the Exchange Theory.

## 1.4e Evolutionary Theory

The evolutionary approach is associated with biological concepts and concerned with long-term change. **Evolutionary theory** suggests that societies, like biological organisms, progress through stages of increasing complexity. Like ecologists, evolutionists suggest that societies, also like organisms, are interdependent with their environments.

Most of the early sociologists and some recent ones adhere to an evolutionary view. Early sociologists often equated evolution with progress and improvement, believing natural selection would eliminate weak societies and those that could not adapt. The strong societies, they believed, deserved to survive because they were better. It was for this reason that early theorists, such as Spencer, opposed any sort of interference protecting the weak and interfering with natural evolutionary processes.

Contemporary evolutionists, on the other hand, rarely oppose all types of intervention. They tend to view evolution as a process resulting in change, but they do not assume changes are necessarily for the better. Almost all would agree that society is becoming more complex, for example; however, they might argue that complexity brings about bad things as well as good. The telephone is a good illustration of a technological improvement making our lives more complex. Surely it is an improvement—it permits us to be in contact with the whole world without stirring from our homes—but a contemporary evolutionist might point out a phone can also be an annoyance, as students trying to study and harried office workers can attest. Early evolutionists, on the other hand, would have been more likely to regard the telephone as a sign of progress and, hence, an unmixed blessing.

Evolutionary theory provides us with a historical and cross-cultural perspective from which to judge a wide range of social influences. If its basic premises of directional change and increasing complexity are valid, it should provide better comprehension of current trends and even help us to predict the future.

Although each of the theoretical perspectives has been discussed separately with regard to how they can be applied, it is important to note that in most cases, more than one can be used; and some may even be used in conjunction with each other. It should also be noted that even though some of the applications discussed might not be exactly what the people who originally devised the theories had in mind, this does not lessen the validity of these applications. On the contrary, using scientific theories in ways that extend beyond their original purpose demonstrates the significance of the theories. A number of additional theoretical orientations are discussed briefly to conclude this section.

**Evolutionary theory**

A theory of social development that suggests that societies, like biological organisms, progress through stages of increasing complexity

## 1.4f Additional Theoretical Perspectives and the Future of Sociological Theory

The reader should not be led to think that structural functionalism, conflict, symbolic interaction, exchange, and evolutionary theories compose all of the theories or theoretical perspectives in sociology. From the 1950s through the 1970s, sociology could have been more easily described in terms of these five theories with structural functionalism reigning supreme in the 1950s and conflict theory taking a strong foothold in the 1960s. However, by the mid-1980s, sociology began a proliferation of new theoretical perspectives (Turner, J. H., 2006). Ritzer (1999), sees this as a time of theoretical synthesis: an integration of micro and macro ideas, an integration of Marx's ideas into structural functionalism, a joining of exchange and structural theories into a new network theory, and so forth.

An example of an older, interdisciplinary, theoretical linkage can be seen in *sociobiological* orientations. You may have noted that Spencer's ideas of the survival of the fittest, described earlier in this chapter, had a biological base. Today, sociobiological theories link social behavior (crime, drinking, aggression, and so forth) to genetic or biological factors. For example, a sociobiologist would probably explain male sexual dominance or female nurturance by the differing genetic makeup of the sexes. If male-female differences are biologically determined, it could be expected that social influences would not greatly modify behavior. It could also lead to justifying sexual and racial inequalities because "that's the way things are," and little can be done to change them. Yet sociologists note, in spite of biological predispositions toward a particular behavior pattern, wide variations exist in sexual domination, nurturance, and other behaviors generally assigned to one sex or the other. Beliefs that human behaviors can be changed led to other theoretical linkages, such as the two examples that follow: humanistic and feminist theories.

*Humanistic* theories, consistent with ideas expressed by Marx, reject the positivist position that social science can or should be value free. This perspective is based on the following beliefs and practices: Sociologists or other social scientists should be actively involved in social change; efforts should be made toward achieving social justice and equity for everyone irrespective of gender or race; the mind has "free will"; and humans are in charge of controlling their own destiny. As Chapter 11 makes clear, secular humanism (the solving of problems by humans through their own efforts) disputes the religious focus on a god or on supernatural powers. Sociologists often take a humanistic perspective with a goal of using the knowledge, skills, and tools of sociology to improve social conditions and the lives of those less fortunate.

*Feminist* theories and perspectives hold the belief that gender is basic to all social structure and organization. The impetus for contemporary feminist theory involves a simple question: How do women interpret and experience the world differently from men? Answers to this question are based on beliefs that gender should not be the basis of social inequality, nor should men be more valued in the political arena (as more effective leaders of the country), in the home (as heads of the house), or in the workplace (where they sometimes make more money than women). Early waves of the feminist movement focused on equal rights. Contemporary feminist perspectives include multicultural, liberal, and socialist perspectives, and examine the interlocking systems of racism, sexism, and class. This "third wave" movement is marked by a desire for personal empowerment.

**BVT*Lab***

Flashcards are available for this chapter at www.BVTLab.com.

**thinking** SOCIOLOGICALLY

**Discuss the humanists' idea that sociologists should use their knowledge and skills to improve social conditions and the feminists' idea that gender is basic to all social organization and interaction.**

# CHAPTER 1 Wrapping it up

## Summary

1. Sociology is the study of society, social life, and the causes and consequences of human social behavior. The terms *society* and *social life* encompass interpersonal relations within and among social groups and social systems. Sociologists study a wide range of behavior—from small groups (families) to large ones (bureaucracies)—question the obvious, seek patterns and regularities, and look beyond individuals to social interactions and group processes.
2. Sociological imagination is the ability to see the world from a sociological point of view. Using sociological imagination, an individual is able to analyze a social phenomenon from a sociological perspective. This perspective can be applied both to microsociology, which considers problems at the level of interpersonal and small-group processes, and to macrosociology, which considers large-scale problems, structures, social organizations, and social systems.
3. Although many people believe the structure and workings of society are a matter of common knowledge, countless sociological findings disprove popular conceptions and provide surprising insights.
4. Sociology is one of the social science disciplines that tries to systematically and objectively understand social life and predict how various influences will affect it. Each social science attempts to accumulate a body of knowledge about a particular aspect of society and the social world. Other social sciences include economics, political science, anthropology, psychology, history, and geography.
5. Compared with the other sciences, sociology is of recent origin. Not until the 1880s was a scientific methodology applied to social phenomena. The Industrial Revolution and political upheavals in Europe encouraged various scholars to try to explain social change and the social order. Five theorists who had an especially important influence on the development of sociology are Comte, Spencer, Marx, Durkheim, Weber, and Martineau.
6. In the early 1900s, the development of sociology in America grew rapidly, drawing heavily from earlier European scholars. The Chicago School of thought focused on micro-level approaches with important contributions made by sociologists—such as Cooley, Mead, and Thomas—who stressed the importance of social interaction and the influence of society on human thought and action.
7. Not until the 1930s did sociology shift from the University of Chicago to other major educational institutions. In the eastern United States, Parsons, Merton, Mills, Coser, Homans, and Blau were influential in the development of social theory.
8. A social theory is a systematically interrelated proposition that seeks to explain a process or phenomena. Five major theories—three at the macro level and two at the micro level—have had an important influence on contemporary sociology: structural functional theory, conflict theory, symbolic interactional theory, exchange theory, and evolutionary theory.
9. Structural functional theory focuses on the parts of a system, the relationships among these parts, and the functions or consequences of social structures. These functions can be either manifest (intended and recognized) or latent (unintended and unrecognized). Some consequences are dysfunctional, in that they lead to the instability and breakdown of the system. Structural functional theories assume that systems have a tendency toward equilibrium and balance.
10. Conflict theory assumes that conflict is a permanent feature of social life and a key source of change. The Marxist orientation toward conflict assumes that it is rooted in a class struggle between the employers and the workers or between the powerful and the powerless. Many conflict theorists assume that conflict serves an integrative function and acts as a source of constructive change.

11. Symbolic interactionism, a micro-level theory, emphasizes relationships among individuals and between individuals and society. According to this theory, society is based on shared meanings, language, social interaction, and symbolic processes. It is the mind that differentiates humans from nonhumans and permits people to develop a social self, to assume the roles of others, and to imaginatively consider alternative courses of action.
12. Exchange theory assumes that social life involves a series of reciprocal exchanges consisting of rewards and costs. Exchange theories endeavor to explain why particular behavioral outcomes result from a given set of structural conditions and interaction possibilities.
13. Evolutionary theory suggests that societies, like biological organisms, go through transitions or stages and are interdependent with the environment or world around them.
14. Other theoretical perspectives or orientations include sociobiology, humanism, and feminism. The latter two both reject a positivist notion of total objectivity and noninvolvement and stress instead the need for active involvement in social change.

## Discussion Questions

1. Explain the sociological perspective, and discuss how it changes the way we look at societies that are different from our own.
2. What is the difference between macrosociology and microsociology? How would each examine police corruption?
3. Explain why common-sense knowledge is not the best source of information. With this in mind, discuss why women who are victims of domestic violence stay in abusive relationships.
4. Discuss what the social sciences have in common. How is each unique or different from the others?
5. What influenced the development of sociology both in Europe and in America?
6. The contributions of women and minorities in early sociology were largely overlooked. Explain what factors contributed to their lack of recognition by the field.
7. Why did early sociologists use natural science terms and methods to describe society? Discuss some shortcomings in following this approach.
8. Spencer's idea of "survival of the fittest" led to his belief in noninterference in human affairs. Explain how Spencer's beliefs would influence today's welfare system in the United States.
9. How might conflict theory apply to male and female workers in a field dominated primarily by men, such as construction work?
10. From a symbolic interactionist perspective explain why burning the American flag creates anger among most U.S. citizens. In your discussion, consider the significance of symbols and their meanings.
11. Apply social exchange theory to the interaction between you and your parents or your best friend. What are the costs and rewards of these relationships? What happens when the social exchanges are not defined as equitable?

U.S. Census
Helping You Make Informed Decisions

CHAPTER 2

# Methods of Studying Sociology

## SYNOPSIS

### The Research Process

- State and Define the Problem
- Conduct a Literature Review
- Develop Research Questions or Hypotheses
- Determine the Research Design
- Reliability and Validity
- Collect Data
- Analyze the Data
- Implications, Conclusions, Posing Future Questions, and Sharing the Results

### Types of Sociological Research

- Exploratory Research
- Descriptive Research
- Explanatory Research
- Evaluative Research

### Ethical Issues in Sociological Research

### Occupational and Personal Uses of Sociology

- Academic Sociologists
- Professional Sociologists in the Workplace
- Non-Sociologists in the Workplace
- Non-Sociologists in Society

**In this chapter,** we consider the use of scientific methods in sociology. We also examine standards of scientific inquiry, types of sociological research, research methods, and the process of research. In addition, we examine ethical issues within the field and how students can use sociology in their personal and occupational lives.

We hope that after reading this chapter, you will see the relevance of research methods in all areas of your life. All persons in society are affected by their knowledge (or lack of it) of the basic principles of research methods. To know nothing about the scientific method is to be a victim of false claims about products and ideas when exposed to advertising in newspapers, on TV, or from any other source. It is also important to know where and how to gain access to legitimate research results when making personal decisions and choices.

## Focal Point

### ARE TATTOOS A SIGN OF DEVIANCE, OR A CULTURAL FAD?

What does it mean to have a tattoo? Are those with tattoos rebellious and deviant? Does a tattoo provide us with any information about the character of the person who has it?

Suppose you were told that college students with tattoos are more sexually promiscuous than students without tattoos. Would you believe it? If you were thinking about getting a tattoo, would it cause you to question whether or not to get one? Would you be less likely to socialize, date, or even marry someone with a tattoo if you believed tattoos were a sign of sexual promiscuity? What if your doctor believed that persons with tattoos and body piercings were more likely to engage in other risky behaviors?

Due to the of the rise in popularity of body modification, researchers are looking to determine if those receiving tattoos, piercings, and other forms of modifications are engaging in a deviant act, and more likely to engage in other deviant or rebellious behavior, or if tattoos are simply a cultural fad.

Before deciding into which research to put our trust, we need to understand the research process. To do this, we must ask four questions about each research study: What is the purpose of the study? What methods did the researchers use to collect the data? What were the results of their study? What did they conclude from their study?

Let's apply these questions to one study.

***Study:*** *Tattooing and Body Piercing as Indicators of Adolescents Risk-Taking Behavior* (Carrol, Riffenburgh, Roberts, & Myhre, 2002)

***Purpose:*** The study assessed whether tattoos and body piercings serve as markers of risk-taking behaviors in adolescents.

***Methods:*** The researchers used the 58-question 1997 Centers for Disease Control and Prevention Youth Risk Behavior Survey. The survey was offered to all adolescents who came to the adolescent clinic. The survey contained standard Youth Risk Behavior Survey questions that inquire about eating behavior, violence, drug abuse, sexual behavior, and suicide. The researchers added questions about tattoos and body piercing. A total of 484 adolescents between the ages 12 to 22 were surveyed.

***Results:*** The researchers found that adolescents with tattoos and/or body piercings were more likely to have engaged

## 2.1 THE RESEARCH PROCESS

When a sociologist decides to conduct research, it is usually after he or she has become curious about some phenomenon. Sociologists do not reject authority, experience, cultural tradition, faith, or the media as sources of knowledge. However, most rely heavily on methods considered empirical or scientific. Empirical methods focus on observable phenomena, meaning that others should be able to observe the same phenomena and check our observations for accuracy. Unlike the common sense observations made as part of our daily experience, researchers using empirical methods strive to be objective. As they explore the problem, they identify a number of questions that need to be answered; and these usually lead to more questions. In an attempt to find answers, they will conduct scientific research. While there may be some variations among researchers, typically there are nine steps in the research process. Following are discussions of each of the steps.

### 2.1a State and Define the Problem

**Concept**
An abstract system of meaning that enables us to perceive a phenomenon in a certain way

The first step of the research process is to discuss the purpose of the study. This is where the researcher clearly articulates the problem under investigation and defines the concept(s) being studied. A **concept** is an abstract system of meaning that enables us to perceive a phenomenon in a particular way. Concepts are simply tools that permit in risk-taking behaviors and had greater degrees of involvement than those without either. Risk-taking behaviors included: disordered eating behavior, gateway drug use, hard drug use, sexual activity, and suicide. With regard to violence, the study found an association with males who had tattoos and with females who had body piercings. Gateway drug use was associated with those at a younger age, for both tattooing and body piercing. Hard drug use was associated with number of body piercings. The researchers found that suicide was associated with females having tattoos and being of a younger age for both tattooing and body piercing. Both tattoos and body piercings were found to be more common in females than males.

***Conclusions:*** Patients that come into the office with tattoos and/or body piercings may be involved in other risk-taking behaviors; and thus such body modifications should alert the practitioner to take preventive measures, including counseling. In addition, tattoo and body piercing discovery should be an important part of adolescent healthcare.

Based on the information provided from the study, can we assume that tattoos are equivalent to deviance? If you read this study, what would be your thoughts about its reliability? Tattoos have historically been viewed as a stigma associated with marginalized groups within society (sailors, prostitutes, bikers, gangs). Is it possible that the researchers were biased about adolescents with tattoos and piercings prior to initiating the study—which could influence the outcome? Were the methods used and the interpretations done in a scientific, unbiased way as to yield accurate, generalizable results?

*Research has found that adolescents with tattoos and/or body piercings are more likely to have engaged in risk-taking behaviors.* (iStockphoto)

Research findings are often used to make policy or other changes within organizations, settings, or groups. In the above study, the researchers concluded, "When doctors see a teenager who has a piercing [or tattoo], they should ask whether they smoke, ask about their friends, and maybe spend a little more time asking about their sexual behavior. Seeing a pierced or tattooed body part should help a doctor decide how to spend his or her time with a patient." Do you know enough about the research process to feel comfortable with the recommendations of the researchers?

us to share meanings. Most of the terms in the glossary are sociological concepts: norm, status, stratification, group, mob, folkway, and so on. The concept of "stratification," for example, represents a particular type of inequality that exists in society. Developing the concept made it possible for people to think and communicate about the social differentiation of people by wealth, gender, age, social position, and other characteristics. Concepts can mean different things to different people at different times. Therefore, care must be taken to define them precisely.

When concepts have two or more degrees or values, they are referred to as **variables**. For example, *husband* is a concept, and *years married* is a variable. *Dollar* is a concept; *level of income* is a variable. *Years of marriage* and *level of income* can both vary, but the meanings of the words *husband* and *dollar* remain constant.

Some concepts or variables are much easier to measure than others. We may all agree on how to measure the number of males and females in a room because we know how to measure quantities of people and how to determine gender. How would we, however, proceed with a study of the relationship between gender and happiness? *Happiness* is an abstract term that means different things to different people, and opinions would vary on how to measure it.

**Variable**
A characteristic such as age, class, or income that can vary from person to person; a concept that can have two or more values

The process of arriving at a means of measuring a concept or variable is referred to as *operationalization*. In this procedure, the sociologist selects indicators of an abstract concept, determining what will be observed and how it will be measured. In the preceding example, this would involve determining some criteria for assessing

**Table 2-1** Steps in the Research Process

| Steps in the Research Process |
|---|
| Statement of the Problem |
| Review of the Literature |
| Development of Hypotheses or Statement of Research Objectives |
| Choice of Research Design |
| Triangulation of Research Methods |
| Collection of Data |
| Analysis and Interpretation of Data |
| Development of Conclusions |
| Posing of New Research Questions |

happiness. We might decide that happiness is whatever the individuals themselves think it is and simply ask them whether they are happy or not, or ask them to rate their own happiness on a five-point scale. On the other hand, we might decide that factors such as absence of depression, high levels of self-esteem, or the ability to function successfully are indicators of happiness and attempt to measure those. Although opinions may differ on whether the criteria selected actually reflect happiness, the operationalization of the definition ensures that we understand the term *happiness* and thus know what it is that we are measuring. An **operational definition**, then, is a definition of a concept or variable such that it can be measured during research. Therefore, operationalization makes an abstract variable measurable and observable.

**BVT*Lab***

Flashcards are available for this chapter at www.BVTLab.com.

## 2.1b Conduct a Literature Review

The second step in the research process is to demonstrate that you have a significant understanding of the problem being examined. To accomplish this, you must conduct a literature review. In this step, the researcher attempts to find out as much information as possible about his/her topic of study. One of the best ways to do this is to examine the work of other scholars in the discipline. For social science research, such as that done in sociology, the literature refers to what has been published in academic books and journals. By understanding what has already been done, the researcher avoids the possibility of duplicating someone else's work; instead, they use other works to build onto their own existing knowledge base.

Also found in the literature review is a theory about the topic that is being studied. By using a theory, researchers attempt to find patterns and consistencies in what they are studying. Good theories are key sources of ideas for researchers to test; the information they discover through testing may be used, in turn, to modify and refine the theory. A good theory should be stated in abstract terms and should allow predictions to be made.

We want to emphasize the importance of conducting a thorough literature review as one of the first steps in conducting research. Consider this metaphor. Have you ever been involved in a deep, ongoing conversation with someone or with a group of friends when someone enters the conversation late, without any prior knowledge about what has been discussed so far? When that happens, have you ever noticed that the person entering the conversation late may bring up topics irrelevant to the conversation or things that have already been discussed? Then, as a result, the conversation gets a bit derailed? If that has ever happened to you, have you felt like saying to the newcomer, "You need to get up to speed about what we are talking about first before spouting out irrelevant ideas or things we spoke about a while ago"? If that sounds familiar, think of research as a conversation among scientists or other academics, a conversation that has

**Operational definition**
A definition of a concept or variable such that it can be measured

been taking place since long before you began your research. In order for your research (or your contribution to the "conversation") to be relevant, worthwhile, and valued, it is essential that you have a good foundation in what has already taken place within that "conversation" or the topic that you are investigating.

## 2.1c Develop Research Questions or Hypotheses

Once a thorough review of the literature has taken place, the researcher will pose either research questions or hypotheses, usually depending on the type of method he or she intends to use in the research. Sociological research involves two types of methods: qualitative and quantitative. Qualitative methods will typically utilize research questions and quantitative methods will utilize hypotheses.

**Qualitative methods** are used to determine the essential characteristics, properties, or processes of something or someone. Rather than desiring to count how many, how much, or how often, qualitative researchers may attempt to study conditions or processes such as how police make a decision to arrest someone, the reactions or responses of a spouse or parent to the loss of a loved one, or the processes used in obtaining illegal drugs.

**Quantitative methods** generally use propositions rather than questions. A **proposition** is a statement about the nature of some phenomenon. It generally consists of a statement about the relationship between two or more variables. The statement "Social activity is related to student grades" would be a proposition. If this proposition is formulated so that it can be tested, it is considered a **hypothesis**. A testable hypothesis would be "Students who attend more than one social activity per week have higher grade point averages than those who do not." Thus, hypotheses are propositional statements that indicate how the stated relations can be tested. In this example the hypothesis states that if social activity goes up, grade point averages will go up. This hypothesis is known as a **direct relationship** because it states that if a variable changes in one direction, a predictable change will occur in the same direction of the other variable. **Inverse relationships** are also possible. For example, "As social activity goes up, grade point averages go down." Hypotheses that involve direct or inverse relationships are *directional hypotheses*. *Null hypotheses*, which state that there is no relationship between the variables of interest, can also be formulated: "There is no relationship between social activity and grade point averages."

In scientific studies, the variable that is presumed to cause a change or an effect is known as the **independent variable**. The variable that is presumed to be affected by the independent variable is the **dependent variable**. Thus, in the above example, grade point average is the dependent variable or the effect; the cause of the change in GPA—social activity—would be the independent variable. One of the goals of scientific research is to establish a cause and effect relationship between variables. To establish a cause-effect relationship, researchers must establish an association between two variables. Variables that are not associated cannot be causally related.

## 2.1d Determine the Research Design

This step in the research process outlines the methods used by the researcher to test his/her hypotheses or answer the research questions. **Methodology** refers to the rules and guidelines followed in sociological research. As previously mentioned, there are two means to choose from—qualitative or quantitative research designs—each with a variety of methods to use in order to collect information or gather facts.

In a qualitative study, the researcher can use various methods to collect data, including observational methods. In **observational research**, the researcher or research team watches what is happening and makes no attempt to control, modify, or influence the ongoing activity.

**Qualitative methods**
The gathering and reporting of non-numerical data used to determine the essential characteristics, properties, or processes of something or someone

**Quantitative methods**
The gathering of numerical data that is usually used to test a hypothesis or examine the relationship between variables

**Proposition**
A statement of the relationship between two or more concepts or variables

**Hypothesis**
A statement about the relationship between variables that can be put to an empirical test

**Direct relationship**
A relationship between two variables in which an increase in one variable is accompanied by an increase in the other; compare with inverse relationship

**Inverse relationship**
A relationship between two variables such that an increase in one variable is accompanied by a decrease in the other; compare with direct relationship

**Independent variable**
A variable that causes a change or variation in a dependent variable

**Dependent variable**
A variable that is changed or influenced by another variable

**Methodology**
The rules and guidelines outlined and followed in social research

**Observational research**
Research in which the researcher watches what is happening and makes no attempt to control or modify the activity being observed

Participant observation occurs when the researcher is an active participant in the event being studied. Anthropologists frequently use this method to study a particular community or subculture. Sociologists have been participant observers in studies of nudist camps, bars, prisons, the drug trade, rock groups, tattoo parlors, and almost anywhere you can imagine. As a full participant observer, the researcher becomes directly involved in the group or community activities. For example, Laud Humphreys (1975) took on the role of the "lookout" in his Tearoom Trade research of homosexual behavior in roadside public restrooms. (There are ethical considerations that must be addressed in conducting research, and Humphreys' research is a good example of ethical violations that can occur. You will read more about this later in the chapter in the section "Ethical Issues in Sociological Research.") As participants, researchers may learn about some of the subtleties involved in personal interactions. The researcher may, therefore, acquire a deeper understanding of the emotions and beliefs that bind the group together than would be possible if a person not participating in the group made observations. Most participant observation research takes the form of a case study, in which a detailed study of an individual person, group, community, or activity is undertaken.

Survey research involves systematically asking people about such things as their attitudes, feelings, ideas, and opinions. *(iStockphoto)*

Suppose a researcher wants to study an entire culture or subculture of people. Then he or she can conduct **ethnographic research**. Ethnography has always been the primary form of investigation in anthropological research, and it has been a valued method of research for sociologists as well. Ethnography is a method of studying the social and cultural dimensions of human interaction. It is a form of research focusing on the sociology of meaning through close observation of sociocultural phenomena. Its goal is to understand communities and cultures from an insider's perspective, and then translate that understanding to outsiders. Ethnographic researchers will use a variety of techniques to gather information, including participation, observation, and interviewing.

Quantitative methods are designed to obtain numbers or amounts of something—the median age at marriage, the range of incomes or crime rates, for example. This type of research design often involves methods such as surveys, experiments, or secondary analysis.

The most common quantitative method is **survey research**. This method involves systematically asking people about their attitudes, feelings, ideas, opinions, behaviors, or anything else. Usually, the researcher uses a questionnaire to guide the questioning.

Surveys have a number of advantages over many other data-gathering procedures. They are usually easy to administer and often permit researchers to gather data on identical variables from many people simultaneously. Unlike most observation studies, which may take months or years, surveys provide a lot of information within periods ranging from a few minutes to several weeks.

There are problems with surveys, too, of course. First, if questions concern personal information about age, income, sex life, or criminal activities, for example, the respondents may not answer honestly. Second, if the questions or responses are highly structured, the results of the survey may not reflect the actual beliefs of the people being questioned, but rather the researcher's conceptions of how the questions should be asked and what people's answers are likely to be. To give an exaggerated example, a survey question about attitudes toward abortion would not yield valid information if it listed as the only possible answers either "I think abortion should not be allowed under any circumstances" or "I think abortion is permissible in situations involving rape or danger to mother's health." Third, surveys may fail to assess areas that are difficult to examine, and people's beliefs may be far more complex than a survey indicates. Despite these problems, survey research is widely used by social scientists.

**Ethnographic research**

A form of descriptive research focusing on the sociology of meaning through close observation of sociocultural phenomena

**Survey research**

A quantitative research technique that involves asking people questions about the subject being studied

Another method used in quantitative research is **secondary analysis**—the use of existing information that was gathered by others or that exists independently of your research. Secondary materials may include *personal documents*, such as letters, diaries, e-mail, internet blogs and forums, autobiographies, and speeches; *public records*, such as health, school, police, marriage, death, and divorce records; news sources, such as radio, TV, newspapers, magazines, books, professional journals, and reference materials available in most libraries; and *actual research data* gathered from other studies and available in existing data banks, such as at the National Opinion Research Center (NORC) in Chicago or the Roper Public Opinion Research Center in Massachusetts. One of the most widely used secondary data sources is the United States Census, which provides quantitative data on many aspects of peoples' lives such as race, religion, age, income, number of children, education level, and more.

The classic procedure used in scientific research is the **experimental design**, used to determine cause-effect relationships in carefully controlled situations. In an ideal experiment, it is possible to control all relevant factors and to manipulate, statistically or in the society itself, one variable to determine its effect.

To carry out an experiment, two matched groups of subjects are selected. In the **experimental group**, an independent variable is introduced; and it is the effect of this variable that is tested. The **control group** is identical to the experimental group in every respect, except that the variable is not introduced to this group. If we were studying the effects of dim lighting on social interaction, for example, we might randomly choose two groups of students. The experimental group would be placed in a dimly lit room, whereas the control group would be in a normally lit room. All other aspects of these settings would be identical (e.g., furnishings, size, time of day). The researcher would note differences in the behavior of the two groups: frequency of interaction, level of noise, number of subgroups formed, and other behaviors considered germane. Differences in the social behavior of the two groups would presumably be due to the influence of the independent variable, dim lighting; however, we should be cautious about concluding the association because another unidentified variable may have influenced the outcome.

*Industrial research professor Elton Mayo conducted a work-productivity study in 1939 that resulted in the "Hawthorne Effect."* (AP Wide World Photo)

When experiments are done in a laboratory setting, it is easier to control conditions than it is in a natural or field (non-laboratory) setting, thereby making it easier to establish causation. It has been argued, however, that laboratory settings are artificial and yield distorted results.

Like other methods, there are problems with experimental techniques, particularly when studying human behavior. How is it possible to conduct experiments with humans in either a laboratory or non-laboratory setting? We cannot lock people in rooms, withhold food, punish them, or remove them from friends and family. Doing this would by highly unethical and most likely unlawful. Instead we can study populations that already exist in the social world: prisoners, starving people, families who abuse their children, nursing homes that isolate people from their loved ones, and incarcerated juveniles placed in solitary confinement. The social world also contains populations of well-fed people, families that do not abuse their children, and so forth. It is often possible to find existing experimental and control groups that have all the characteristics in common, except the independent variable chosen for observation.

Another problem that can occur with sociological experiments is called the "Hawthorne Effect," which is when people's behavior changes because they realize they are being studied. Many years ago, one of the best-known experiments in sociology resulted in the "Hawthorne Effect" occurring. Before World War II, at the Hawthorne plant of Western Electric, Elton Mayo separated a group of women (the experimental group) from the other workers and systematically varied their lighting, coffee breaks,

**Secondary analysis**
The use of existing information that was gathered or exists independently of one's own research

**Experimental design**
A scientific procedure in which at least two matched groups, differing only in the variable being studied, are used to collect and compare data

**Experimental group**
In an experiment, the group to which an independent variable is introduced, with that variable not being introduced in the control group

**Control group**
In an experiment, the group not exposed to the independent variable that is introduced to the experimental group

lunch hours, and other environmental factors (Roethlisberger & Dickson, 1939). In the control group, work conditions went on as usual. Much to the amazement of the researchers, the productivity of the experimental group (the dependent variable) increased regardless of the variables that were introduced, including returning the workers to their original conditions. Obviously the desired result, increased productivity, was not being caused by a specific independent variable. On the one hand, the experiment seemed to be a success—the experimental group differed from the control group when independent variables such as lighting and coffee breaks were introduced. On the other hand, the experiment appeared to be a failure, in that one independent variable seemed to have as much influence as another. The researchers concluded that the women were trying to please the researchers and enjoyed the attention they were getting. The very presence of the researchers contaminated the experiment to the point that they became a significant independent variable and caused a change in the dependent variable—work productivity.

## 2.1e Reliability and Validity

In addition to choosing the method of data collection, the researcher must also outline the steps involved in measuring data. **Reliability** is the extent to which repeated observations of the same phenomenon yield similar results. The scientific standard of replication asserts that research should be conducted and reported in such a way that someone else can duplicate it. The use of similar subjects and measuring procedures under similar conditions should produce results virtually identical to those of the original study.

In the social sciences, the problems of replication are compounded by human factors. Some studies may be impossible to duplicate because of the nature of the problems studied. It would not be possible, for example, to duplicate studies of the reactions of East and West Germans on the day the Berlin Wall was opened and came down, or to duplicate studies of the residents of a particular town destroyed by flood or fire. It is possible, however, to perform studies on the residents of other communities or on other citizens who are granted freedom from a particular type of governmental or social repression and to note patterns in psychological adjustment, points of greatest stress, changes in kin and child relationships, or other conditions. The principle of replication of studies is based on the conviction that similar conditions and circumstances should produce highly similar results.

**Validity** is the extent to which observations actually yield measures of what they are supposed to measure. For example, if a bathroom scale registers different weights each time you step on it, it is not reliable. If it gives the same weight each time but it is not an accurate measure, the bathroom scale may be *reliable* (same results each time) but not *valid* (inaccurate weight). A common problem with research validity is that critics question whether the measurement instrument actually measures what it is supposed to measure. For example, on the bathroom scale, if the scale reliably and accurately determined your height, it would not be valid as a measurement of your weight. For a measure of your weight to be considered a fact, the scale must be both reliable (consistent) and valid (accurate measure of the factor or characteristic).

**Reliability**
The extent to which repeated observations of the same phenomena yield similar results

**Validity**
The extent to which observations actually measure what they are supposed to measure

## 2.1f Collect Data

After determining our research design, we begin the data-collecting step where we identify the group of people to be studied. The group might be doctors, students, taxpayers, voters in a given election, or any selected group that can provide the information needed to prove or disprove the hypotheses. This group is usually called the "population." Since we can rarely study all doctors, students, or taxpayers due to such factors as cost and time, we must pick an appropriate sample. A **sample** is a group of people chosen from the population who are thought to represent that population. The sample is questioned, and their answers are expected to reflect the beliefs of the population as a whole.

Samples are chosen by a variety of methods. A **random sample** is chosen by chance, so that every member of a group has an equal chance of being selected. Because

**Sample**
A number of individuals or cases drawn from a larger population

**Random sample**
A sample selected in such a way that every member of a population has an equal chance of being chosen

it is usually impossible to place all names in a hat, sociologists often assign a number to each name and use a table of random numbers to select which persons should be included. They may also use a method known as **systematic sampling**, in which a specific pattern of selection is followed, such as selecting every 20th name. A third method is **stratified sampling**, in which the population is divided into groups and then chosen at random from within those groups. If our population were students, we might stratify them by class rank, sex, or race and then randomly select from each of these groups. Regardless of how the sample is chosen, if every person has an equal chance of being chosen, it should be representative—it should reflect the attitudes of the total population.

Studies of the reaction of Germans to the opening of the Berlin Wall are impossible to duplicate. (AP Wide World Photo)

## 2.1g Analyze the Data

After we have performed all the steps to collect the data, analyzing it requires us to consider, again, the type of research method used. Using qualitative data collection techniques requires the researcher to look for patterns, themes, or trends during the analysis of the data.

Quantitative data analysis involves converting the data to numbers in order to run statistical tests. The researcher might want to include some descriptive data about each of the variables. For example, if a researcher wants to provide the average age of students enrolled in her Introduction to Sociology course, she can provide measures of central tendency This statistical technique provides averages using three possible ways. For the purpose of our example, let's say there are 11 students enrolled in the course with the following ages: 45, 40, 27, 25, 20, 20, 19, 19, 19, 18, and 18. If we want to know the most frequent response to our age question, the **mode** will provide us with the answer. However, if we want to know the midpoint, above which are one-half the students and below which are one-half, we would use the **median**. We could also determine the average, the **mean** sum of all the ages of students in our class, by dividing the total combined age of all the students by the number of people involved. Therefore, looking back on the ages of students enrolled in the class, the most frequent age of student in the class would be 19 years of age; therefore, this is our mode. The age at which half the students are below and half are above is 20 years, and it represents the median age. Finally, the average age is 24.5 years—the sum (270) divided by 11. As you can see, each one gave us a different answer; therefore, we must use caution when choosing which average to use.

Another frequently chosen statistical analysis is correlation, the degree to which the variables being measured can be connected to each other. A correlation exists if, when one variable increases, another variable either decreases or increases in a somewhat predictable fashion. For example, if our variables are income and education, we could determine the degree of association between the two. Suppose we find a strong correlation—as education increases so does income. We could suggest that level of education is related (correlated) to level of income. We have to be careful with our interpretations of correlations by not assuming that a relationship means one variable causes another to occur. Suppose we examined the relationship between smoking and pregnancy. We conduct a survey about smoking before and during pregnancy, and our sample consists of pregnant women at a low-income clinic. Upon analyzing our data we find a correlation between smoking and pregnancy;

**Systematic sampling**
Obtaining a sample from a population by following a specific pattern of selection, such as choosing every 10th person

**Stratified sampling**
Sampling in which a population is divided into groups and then subjects are chosen at random from within those groups

**Mode**
The most frequent response in a body of data

**Median**
A measure of central tendency, in which half the figures fall above and half the figures fall below; also known as the midpoint

**Mean**
A measure of central tendency computed by adding the figures and dividing by the number of figures; also known as the average

the more women who smoked, the more who became pregnant. Can we conclude that smoking causes pregnancy? What looks like a correlation is actually misleading or spurious when no meaningful relationship exists between the variables. While there is the appearance of causality, it would be foolish to think smoking causes pregnancy. However, there may be a true correlation between smoking and income.

There are some data that can be analyzed using either quantitative or qualitative methods. Take for example **content analysis** and focus groups—these two data gathering techniques could be analyzed using either method. Content analysis refers to the procedure of systematically extracting data from a wide range of communications—including newspapers, journals, books, television and so on. In analyzing the data, the researcher may look at quantifying it, such as how many times aggressive behavior occurs in children's cartoons, or qualitatively assessing whether the cartoons represent violence significant to a specific time period—say Bugs Bunny versus Power Rangers. Along these same lines, focus group data can be analyzed using quantitative or qualitative methods. Focus groups usually involve no more than 10 persons who are led by a moderator in a discussion concerning the participant's attitudes about some event, product, etc. For example, suppose we want to examine the attitudes of college students toward coed dormitories. Using a quantitative approach, we could simply measure the negative and positive comments made by the group, or we could separate their statements into themes, such as safety, personal space, etc., for a qualitative analysis. The type of method chosen by the researcher is guided by their research objectives.

*Interpreting a correlation between two variables—such as smoking and pregnancy—must be done carefully, as other factors may contribute to the relationship.* (Shutterstock)

## 2.1h Implications, Conclusions, Posing Future Questions, and Sharing the Results

After the data has been collected and analyzed, the next step is to determine what it all means. Simply reporting the findings is not enough; the researcher must also discuss what the findings imply. If you are using qualitative research methods, you will want to discuss patterns, themes, characteristics, or trends. If using quantitative methods, statistical findings will be discussed and generalizations proposed. Generalization refers to the extent we can apply our findings beyond the sample group. Generalization is a necessary part of the conclusion to our research.

The discussion and conclusion section is also where the researchers will tie their findings back to the theory proposed in the literature review and discuss how their findings contribute to the overall theoretical base. In addition, this section will explain any limitations or problems the researchers may have encountered while conducting the study.

All good research should be shared with others, particularly the scientific community. Research studies are found in professional journals, monographs, or discussed in books. In addition, research is cyclical, meaning it offers new questions for future researchers. Tying the findings back to the theory is part of the research because theories serve as important sources of new research.

**Content analysis**
The procedure of systematically extracting thematic data from a wide range of communications

**thinking** SOCIOLOGICALLY

1. Using the Social Science Index or another sociological library database, find one article, on any topic that personally interests you, that uses quantitative research and one that uses qualitative research. Summarize the methods used in each article.
2. Based upon the article you found that uses quantitative methods, formulate a quantitative research study. Follow the research process described, and provide an outline for each step.
3. Based upon the article you found that uses qualitative methods, formulate a qualitative research study. Can these same steps be followed? Why or why not? Discuss.

# 2.2 TYPES OF SOCIOLOGICAL RESEARCH

Now that you understand the steps in the research process, a further distinction between scientific and unscientific sociology can be clarified by examining the four most common types of research designs used in sociological studies. The four basic types—exploratory, descriptive, explanatory, and evaluative—will be discussed.

## 2.2a Exploratory Research

**Exploratory research** is typically used to explore some new social phenomenon, possibly allowing the researcher to examine a new program, group, process, activity, situation, etc., and to determine how those involved in the interaction process get along. Exploratory research usually answers the question "what" and provides information for future research.

Since very little is known about a new social issue or topic, exploratory studies can be challenging, with frequently changing goals and arbitrary guidelines. When conducting a literature review, a researcher may find few empirical studies related to their study. Therefore, theory development is often a goal of exploratory research, as well as methods and procedures.

For example, a criminal justice student may be interested in exploring the rising number of crimes identified as cyberstalking. Remember that exploratory studies answer the question "what"; therefore, the researcher is likely to learn that as the number of young people using the Internet continues to increase, so does the need to prevent them from becoming the target of online stalkers. In addition, in this example, the researcher would seek to define the concept of cyberstalking and perhaps explore some of the social ramifications, such as the problems faced by police departments in trying to prevent it.

**Exploratory research**
Research that attempts to answer the question "what" by explaining a new social phenomenon

## 2.2b Descriptive Research

**Descriptive research** describes social reality or provides facts about the social world. There are many different types of descriptive studies, which cover many different topics and are used in many different ways. However, all of them answer questions regarding who, what, where, when, how often, and how many. Who is victimized by particular types of wrongdoing? What needs would be met by a new park in a particular community? Where do people prefer to shop? When are people most likely to watch TV? How

**Descriptive research**
Research that describes social reality or provides facts about the social world

often do people buy a new car? How many people favor a particular presidential candidate? What is the level of morale of employees in an organization?

All descriptive studies share the goal of providing data on *social facts*, which are reliable and valid items of information about society. A *fact* could be a *behavior* (John scored three touchdowns), an *attitude* (women want equal pay for equal work), a *law* (the speed limit is 55 mph), or even a *statistic* (the median married-couple income in 2001 was $30,116). Descriptive research can be used by academic sociologists in helping to develop new theories, as well as non-sociologists who may use this type of research in their profession or business.

## 2.2c Explanatory Research

**Explanatory research** attempts to explain why things do or do not happen. Why do people with prison records have trouble finding jobs? What factors are related to students using drugs? Questions such as these are concerned with the problem of causation. What factors make a designated phenomenon happen or change? What is the cause of a given effect?

Explanatory (or analytical) studies and descriptive studies are similar, in that they both provide useful information about social reality. The primary difference between them is that explanatory studies are also concerned with answering the question "Why?" Explanatory research answers the question "Why?" by discovering the independent variable (the cause or event that precedes the behavior in question). For example, it may be true that the divorce rate is higher in some regions of the country than in others, but what are the variables associated with divorce that vary from region to region? Do some regions have more people of a certain age, religion, income level or political party affiliation?

*Descriptive research describes social reality, such as whether people who have served time in prison have more trouble finding jobs than people who have not served time. (AP Wide World Photo)*

Like descriptive studies, explanatory studies are the essential material out of which academic sociologists construct their theories. Suppose that explanatory research was conducted to find out the socioeconomic position of people who supported a particular presidential candidate. This information could help academic sociologists to construct general theories and explanations about the relationship between social class and voting behavior in general. However, this information is also useful for those involved in planning political campaigns. Does this mean that applied social research (research studies conducted by professional sociologists in the workplace) and academic (basic) research are exactly the same? At times, yes. The same studies could be used in different ways. However, a major difference between academic research and applied research is that sociologists doing research in the workplace are focusing on variables that are of specific interest to specific clients. The primary goal of professional sociologists in the workplace is to help a particular client find out what leads to or what is the result of particular actions or situations.

There are many types of descriptive and explanatory studies. Although it is not very likely that most of you will become sociologists, it is very likely that most of you will do or use descriptive and explanatory research as part of your job or in your personal life. As a sales representative for a beverage distributor, you will need to know where to find the highest rates of soft-drink consumption. As a display manager in a department store, you will need to find out what stimulates customers to remain in a store. As a physician opening up a new practice, you will have to find the locations that have the highest rates of illness in your specialty, and to discover what makes people feel at ease in a medical office.

**Explanatory research**
Research that attempts to explain why things do or do not happen by examining the relationship between social variables

## 2.2d Evaluative Research

**Evaluative research** measures how well a program or project works in relation to its goals. It determines the extent to which the intended goals are being met and provides a basis for deciding to continue, alter, or eliminate a program. Would stricter gun control measures curtail violence? Does prohibiting the use of cell phones while driving really prevent accidents? Do mandatory seat belt laws save lives? Evaluative studies may precede the implementation of a program, project, or policy to help determine whether it will produce the intended results.

There are four steps involved in systematic evaluative research: specification, measurement, analysis, and recommendation. Specification is the first and most important step. It means defining or identifying the goals to be met by the program, policy, or project. If, for example, the goal of sex education programs us to reduce teen pregnancies, then the basis for evaluating these programs must be the degree to which the programs reduce the rate of teen pregnancies and not whether teens continue to engage in premarital sex. It is imperative that the goal of the program being evaluated be understood before going any further in the research.

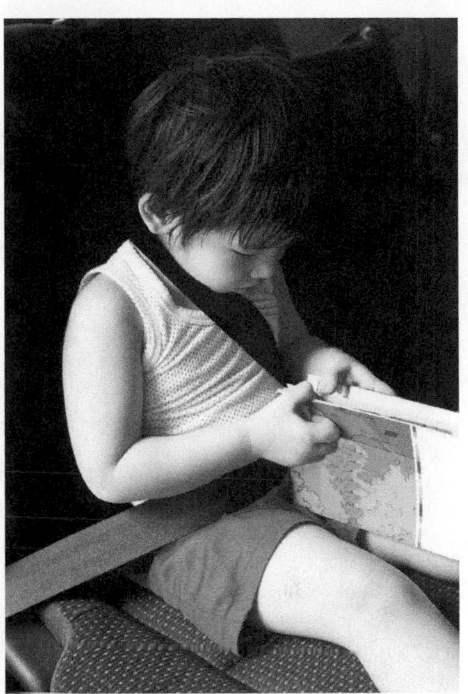

Evaluative research measures how well a program, such as the mandatory seatbelt law, works in relation to its goals. (Shutterstock)

The *measurement* is the way in which the researchers collect the information needed to evaluate the specified goal. For example, to measure the rates of teen pregnancies, a researcher might compare city hospital records on this subject for the years before and after a citywide sex-education program went into effect. Perhaps a survey of teens that asks them whether they regularly use birth control could be done in order to compare high schools with sex-education programs to those without.

*Analysis* is the use of the information collected in the measurement stage to draw conclusions. Methods of analysis range from simple to complex, depending on the specific research involved and the data obtained. Suppose that, in our evaluation of sex-education programs, we found that teen pregnancies in some participating schools increased while decreasing in others. It would probably be necessary to determine whether there were other variables that account for the teen pregnancy rate—such as age of students in the school, socioeconomic status, or religion. However, if it turned out that the number of teen pregnancies declined in every school that had a sex-education program and went up in every school that did not have such a program, it would be fairly safe to assume that the program works without doing any complex statistical analysis.

*Recommendation* is the final stage of evaluative research. Should the program continue as is? Are there particular changes that should be made? Should the program be eliminated altogether? An analysis of the sex-education program might find that teen pregnancies are reduced most when birth control devices are actually brought into class and students are instructed in how to use them, but that in programs where such devices are merely discussed or described, there is no change in the number of pregnancies. In this case, the researcher might recommend that all sex-education courses include exposure to actual birth control devices and specific instructions on how to use them.

Practically all of the human and public service fields regularly use evaluative research such as, but not limited to, social service organizations, government agencies, city planning departments, schools, and hospitals. However, the results of the research are used also by many non-sociologists—such as college administrators, politicians, social workers, hospital administrators, medical practitioners, teachers, advertisers, and others. Evaluative research is also used in the commercial world. For example, an advertising company needs to know whether its campaigns are attracting the clientele they are after. It is likely that at some point you will conduct some evaluative research of your own in your occupation. Do your innovative teaching techniques actually help

**Evaluative research**
Research that measures how well a program or project works in relation to its goals

students learn, or do they intimidate them? As a dentist, does your informal attire in the office make your patients feel at ease or lead them see you as unprofessional? As an auto salesperson, does your personal approach lead your customers to trust or mistrust you?

Evaluative research might also benefit you in your personal life. Although this might not be as formal or as methodologically sophisticated as that done by professional sociologists or by someone as part of his or her job, you will still probably need to do it at some point. For example, you may do it to evaluate your educational plans, career plans, investment strategies, or even the way you are raising your children. Clearly, there are many ways that you will use evaluative research in your personal life. You may have thought of many others already.

**thinking** SOCIOLOGICALLY

**Select a topic for study, such as cohabitation, female employment, or busing. What types of questions could be answered with exploratory, descriptive, explanatory, and evaluative research?**

# 2.3 ETHICAL ISSUES IN SOCIOLOGICAL RESEARCH

When conducting research, a number of ethical issues should be considered. Ethics require persons to follow the guidelines or rules regarding the standards of conduct for their specific profession or group. In the field of sociology, there are both general ethical guidelines and specific guidelines to follow, particularly when conducting research.

There is a general understanding among social scientists regarding the following: 1) Participation is voluntary. 2) There will be no harm to the participants. 3) Participants are informed of all risks associated with the study. Basically what this means is that anyone who participates in research should do so voluntarily, and the researcher will make certain the participants are not harmed in any way. Finally, there is informed consent, whereby the researchers have explained all the possible risks involved and the participants consent to participate in the study. However, while most research abides by the general guidelines, there is controversy within the field regarding the plausibility of absolute adherence to the rules. Are there studies that make it difficult to obtain voluntary participation?

**BVT** ***Lab***

Flashcards are available for this chapter at **www.BVTLab.com.**

One of the most controversial research studies within the field of sociology involved the dissertation of a graduate student. Laud Humphreys was attending Washington University in St. Louis when he became interested in sexual relations occurring between men in public restrooms. Humphreys began researching what he referred to as "Tearoom Trade," the act of sexual behaviors between two anonymous men in public restrooms. He wanted to understand why it occurred and who the men were who met in these public places. Humphreys knew that if asked to voluntarily participate in the study, the men would say no; and he would not be able to move forward with his work. Because Humphreys was determined to learn as much as possible about the practice he decided to become an insider so that he could study their behaviors. Focusing primarily on restrooms in public parks, Humphreys made himself a regular when the men were engaged in sexual activities; and he offered to be a lookout and warn the participants when others were entering the restroom. Wanting to track the men he encountered, Humphreys followed the men from the restroom and jotted their license plate numbers down. He then went to the police department and filed a false police report on each vehicle, which allowed him to get the personal information of each man. He persuaded the investigators of another study on men's health to include his participants in their study and to allow him to be the interviewer. Humphreys donned a different disguise and went to the men's houses to interview them about their health, including their sexual behavior. Humphreys observed 134 men, in all, in the public restroom and interviewed 100 of them, either in the restroom or through the health study. Through his research, Humphreys discovered that over 50% of the men he encountered in the restroom did not see themselves as homosexual; they were happily married men with children who worked in respectable jobs. They wanted to have quick sexual encounters without commitment or conversation, but considered themselves heterosexual. In addition, the men he met were more likely to hold conservative beliefs and values both politically and socially which acted as a veil of protection against suspicion.

Critics argued that Humphreys observed and interviewed participants without fully disclosing his intent to conduct research. He also manipulated information by writing down the vehicle tag numbers to obtain home addresses and used these, later, to interview participants again. The potential for harm was great for the participants who could have been "outed" if their identities were discovered during the research process.

One of the main problems that existed during the time of Humphreys' "Tearoom Trade" study was the absence of **Institutional Review Boards (IRB)** in higher education. Institutional Review Boards are ethical review committees whose main duties are to approve, monitor, and review research studies involving human subjects. Members of the committees are typically colleagues of the researcher or even members of the community. The role of the IRB is to be the overseer of research and to protect the rights and welfare of individual research subjects. Any agency that receives federal funding and conducts research using human subjects is required to have IRB committees to oversee the process. The goals of IRB committees are to ensure the following:

1. Subjects are selected fairly
2. Risks to subjects are minimal and reasonable
3. Risks of participation are fully disclosed to participants
4. Vulnerable subjects (easily coerced or influenced) are protected
5. Informed consent is reasonably obtained from subject or his/her legal guardian
6. Informed consent is appropriately documented
7. Safeguards are in place to protect the privacy and confidentiality of the subjects
8. Protection of data is outlined and monitored

Data collected from research studies are usually kept for 3 years in a secured and locked location to protect research subjects. Before researchers can undertake a study involving human subjects, the IRB has to give approval—and only after the above requirements are met. In addition, research studies are reviewed on an annual basis to make certain the rules continue to be followed.

**Institutional Review Boards (IRBs)**
Committees on college/university campuses and in research organizations that provide oversight of research that is conducted on human subjects

Now that you have learned, in these first two chapters, about the birth of sociology, as well as some of the theories and methods used within the field, how could a student benefit by taking courses in sociology? The next section provides you with some of the uses of sociology in both your personal and professional lives.

**thinking** SOCIOLOGICALLY

1. Discuss the pros and cons of the "Tearoom Trade" research. Consider how the data could have been gathered differently than through the methods used by Humphreys.
2. What is the purpose of Institutional Review Boards in university settings? How can IRB committees protect participants from becoming victims of poor research practices?

# 2.4 OCCUPATIONAL AND PERSONAL USES OF SOCIOLOGY

Beginning students of sociology often ask a number of related questions. Some of the more common ones are: (a) "Why should I take sociology? If I'm not interested in a sociological career, what use will it be to me?" (b) "What is the value of sociology to society? Why should this field be supported?" (c) "What do sociologists do? If I decided to become one, what career options would be open to me?" These are important questions that we continue to address throughout this book. One of our goals for this book is to demonstrate how the subject matter in each chapter can be used in occupations and in daily personal life. For now, however, we look briefly at four applications of sociology: (1) academic sociologists, (2) professional sociologists in the workplace (nonacademic), (3) nonsociologists in the workplace, and (4) nonsociologists in society.

## 2.4a Academic Sociologists

More sociologists are employed as teachers than in any other capacity. There are more than 15,000 sociologists in the United States today, and at least two-thirds of them consider teaching to be their primary responsibility. Most teaching sociologists also serve other functions—researcher, administrator, or social critic, for example. Increasingly, sociologists are being hired in the professional schools of such fields as medicine, nursing, law, social work, business administration, theology, and education.

Of the more than 15,000 sociologists in the United States today, at least two-thirds of them consider teaching to be their primary responsibility. (iStockphoto)

In addition to teaching, most academic sociologists do research. The research function is often regarded as contributing to the society at large by providing new knowledge about society. Most researchers engage in basic or pure research—the acquisition of knowledge for its own sake, with little thought about how the results will be used. For example, the basic researcher may seek information about the causes of crime, its prevalence, and its distribution by age, gender, or geography, but not be overly concerned with how this knowledge will be used.

## 2.4b Professional Sociologists in the Workplace

Peter H. Rossi and William Foote Whyte (1983), two prominent applied sociologists, suggest that sociology can be applied to the workplace in three major ways: applied social research, social engineering, and clinical sociology. Collectively, this type of work is referred to as applied sociology, practical sociology, or sociological practice.

## Applied Social Research

Many companies, government agencies, and other groups employ professional sociologists to collect and interpret research data on a variety of social issues or problems that the group may face. Applied social research is the use of sociological knowledge and research skills to obtain information for groups and organizations—such as banks, insurance companies, public utilities, retail stores, government agencies, schools, community service organizations, childcare centers, hospitals, and mental health centers, among others. An insurance company, for example, might employ sociologists to find out who the company's prospective customers are, as well as the types of insurance the prospective customers will need, their income levels and lifestyles, their values and beliefs, and the ways in which they determine which types of insurance they need.

The questions that organizations need to have answered by sociologists are endless. There are many types of applied social research, and it would not be practical to try to discuss all of them here. However, all of the types of research described previously in this chapter—exploratory, descriptive, explanatory, and evaluative—can be used as applied research. For example, in designing its first-year curriculum, a college might conduct exploratory research to gain a sense of the types of activities in which students like to engage before it designs its new student center. It might use descriptive research to find out how many first-year students fail out of college in their first year, as well as their ages, genders, races and types of extracurricular activities in which they were involved. It might use explanatory research to see if U.S. colleges that allow first-year students to pledge fraternities and sororities have a higher dropout rate than colleges that don't allow it. It might even conduct evaluation research to see if a policy requiring class attendance actually has an effect on the dropout rate. Of course, there are hundreds of other uses for applied research, and this is only one to which you might relate.

## Clinical Sociology

Clinical sociology is the use of sociological perspectives, theories, concepts, research, and methods for consulting and providing technical assistance to individuals, groups, or organizations. The Sociological Practice Association (which changed its name from the Clinical Sociology Association) defines clinical sociology as sociological intervention—using sociology to help in specific situations.

Clinical sociology is similar to another area of sociology, social engineering, which is attempting to change the way a society, organization, institution, or group is arranged to achieve a particular goal. Both have to do with social intervention, and it is sometimes difficult to see the difference between them. Social engineering is concerned with large-scale social planning, whereas clinical sociology is concerned more with advising on specific social settings and situations. Social engineering is likely to be involved with designing policies, laws, programs, and projects, whereas clinical sociology involves consultation, counseling, therapy, and conflict mediation. It is social engineering, for example, to develop a statewide basic education program to improve the quality of education that students receive; it is clinical sociology to counsel teachers in a particular high school about how to better communicate with students in the classroom. It is social engineering to create a nationwide project that would encourage corporations to offer onsite childcare for working parents; it is clinical sociology to offer group

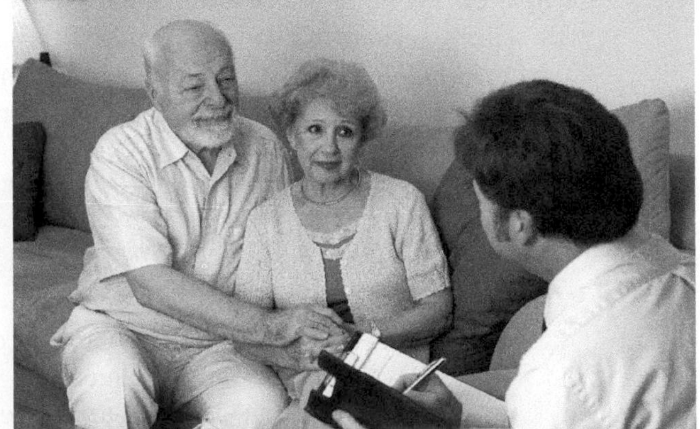

*Clinical sociologists are engaged in such careers as community healthcare.* (Shutterstock)

sociology**at**work

## Research Analyst

Jean Brittain Leslie is a research analyst at the Center for Creative Leadership in Greensboro, North Carolina. Prior to her current position, she was a research project manager at the *Greensboro News and Record*, a major daily newspaper in North Carolina. She received her BA in sociology from Elon University and her MA in sociology at the University of North Carolina at Greensboro.

Jean Leslie is one of those people who happened to stumble into sociology and fall in love with it. "I would like to say that I aspired to become a sociologist, but that is not the case. I, like many students, did not know what I wanted to do when I 'grew up' so I took many introductory courses. Sociology was one of them. Needless to say, I enjoyed it so much that I decided to major in it. In retrospect, sociology as compared to other majors most closely fits my personal orientation toward the world. A sociology degree … offers an intellectually stimulating framework to address the world." She says that sociology encourages her to objectively approach her work "or at least be aware of how my own values infiltrate my perspectives. Sociology has taught me to question what appears to be reality and to not take for granted shared meanings." Besides obviously benefiting from an understanding of symbolic interactionism and knowledge about how different cultures operate, Jean feels that the macro-level perspective that sociology offers is invaluable to her when studying organizations.

Jean credits her degree in sociology with helping her obtain her current position at the Center for Creative Leadership. "I am a researcher by occupation. My employer was looking for someone with skills similar to the ones I acquired through studying sociology." She says that courses such as research methods, statistics, sociological theory, and cultural anthropology provided her with a basic understanding of human behavior that is pertinent to her job. "I am working for an organization that studies managers and leaders from diverse organizations and cultural regions. Every time I go into a new project, I must read literature from other academic disciplines (for example, business, psychology, and counseling)." Jean notes that she often finds sociological perspectives in works from other disciplines. "It is not uncommon to find popular sociologists cited in non-sociological journals or presentations at Academy of Management meetings. Having attended both business and sociological professional conferences, I can tell you that both disciplines are facing similar quality research issues."

When thinking about a career, Jean thinks that there are some skills that all employers would prefer their employees have, which you can gain from sociology courses. "Writing abilities are a premium, the ability to communicate with others is another plus, and above all one must learn how to survive in a world where norms are often implicit. These things can be exercised through sociology if the student believes them to be important." Additionally, she feels that the perspective that sociology teaches is not duplicated in other academic disciplines. "Sociology offers a unique analytical approach to the world that can be applied in any career and organizational setting … The most obvious difference between sociology and other academic disciplines is the macro orientation. The unit of measurement for most of my coworkers is the individual. Due to my sociological orientation, I am able to bring a much more global perspective to our work. I do quite a bit of cross-cultural research in which sociology (as opposed to other disciplines) has the opportunity to shine."

therapy to working parents to help them overcome their conflicting loyalties, anxieties, and everyday problems.

Clinical sociologists are engaged in careers such as legislative consultation, law and criminal justice, corporate marketing, social work, psychiatric healthcare, community healthcare, child guidance, student counseling, and family therapy. Governments, businesses, and communities often seek clinical sociologists out to offer suggestions or advice. Their services have been requested in court decisions on busing, in neighborhood programs for crime prevention, in the development of personnel policies for insurance companies, in discrimination cases involving automotive companies, and in the creation of community mental health centers. Sociologists seldom work as full-time consultants, however. They are used in specific situations, such as offering methodological advice to groups doing evaluative studies, assisting in data analysis, or explaining the probable consequences of a set of alternative courses of action.



### thinking SOCIOLOGICALLY

1. Select a social phenomenon about which you are curious—such as a specific group, organization, or activity—and use as much information in this chapter as possible to discuss how you might investigate it from a sociological perspective. On what would you focus? What types of questions would you want to answer? What types of explanations would you expect to discover? How could the results of your study be useful professionally and personally?
2. What are some ways that the four types of applied research could be used in a profession or occupation that you are considering entering?

## 2.4c Non-Sociologists in the Workplace

Although it is usually necessary to have a graduate degree (MA or PhD) to be employed as a professional sociologist, sociology offers knowledge and skills that can be used by non-sociologists in a multitude of careers and occupations. Even if you are not interested in a career in sociology, the study of sociology offers valuable preparation for other types of careers. You do not even have to major in sociology to take advantage of its applications within most occupations. For example, if your interests lie in business, law, education, medicine, architecture, politics, or any profession dealing with people, social life, or social organization, sociology can be useful because it provides a wealth of knowledge that can be applied to any of these fields. Besides the specific theories, concepts, and perspectives that can be useful in and of themselves in occupational settings, sociology students develop research skills, critical-thinking and problem solving skills, interpersonal skills, and communication skills. In recent years, several studies have found that these skills are necessary for success in many careers and occupations.

### Research Skills

Research skills involve basic investigative capabilities. Essentially, they include quantitative (numerical) and qualitative (non-numerical) data-collection methods. The sociology student may develop skills in survey techniques (in-depth interviews and questionnaire construction), empirical observation, participant observation, experimentation, and library research. Lawyers, physicians, advertisers, market analysts, clerks, administrative assistants, publishers, and many others use these skills.

In business, information must often be gathered quickly. A newly employed investment banker must be able to find out very quickly who may be potential clients in a particular region. The manager of a retail store could either go with a hunch that a costly investment will pay off or could conduct a consumer survey to reduce the probability of making a financial blunder. Since research is basic to sociology, even a brief introduction to the field will acquaint you with a range of research techniques and methods you can use. Whether we use simple observation, formal structured interviews, content analysis, experimental designs, or elaborate statistical computations, an understanding of the variety of research techniques should be useful in many occupational settings and situations.

## Critical-Thinking and Problem-Solving Skills

Research skills and knowledge of sociological theories and concepts can add to your critical-thinking and problem-solving skills. To possess critical-thinking skills means to have the ability both to analyze a situation or information and to arrive at careful, precise judgments. With theory and research, you can investigate and carefully arrive at some solutions to problems faced in many occupations. For example, a physician who is having personnel problems with office staff might attribute the conflict to clashes in personalities. A knowledge of small-group processes, along with the ability to find and analyze models of successful organizational or personnel relationships, would be more useful than continually hiring and firing staff members. A lawyer must be able to critically evaluate the terms of a settlement and to find solutions to problematic areas in that settlement to ensure the protection of the client's interests. Two young chiropractors may need to figure out how to establish their practice and develop clientele in a city where they have no existing personal connections or sources of patient referral.

The ways in which sociology must be learned, which determine the nature of most sociology textbooks, facilitate the development of critical-thinking and problem-solving skills. The key to understanding sociological theories and concepts is not memorization, but rather involves careful analysis of the meanings and implications of these abstractions and coming up with concrete examples. Most sociology textbooks, particularly at the advanced levels, do not merely present theories; they usually evaluate the merit of those theories as compared to other ones. This type of learning forces the student to think critically. The assignment of term papers in which sociological theories and concepts must be applied to particular situations or events helps students to sharpen their problem-solving skills. Sociology students also learn other analytical skills, such as constructing and testing hypotheses, discovering explanatory factors, and reading tables. It would be hard to think of an occupation in which the ability to think critically and solve problems is not needed.

## Interpersonal Skills

Interpersonal skills are techniques that help you to efficiently manage yourself and others within an organization or in other interaction settings. These skills include management, leadership, interaction, diplomatic skills, and the ability to facilitate and coordinate group activities. Competence in setting goals, the ability to plan projects, and knowledge of how organizations work are also important interpersonal skills. Unclear objectives or poorly designed work programs could result in poor teamwork performance. For example, the business manager who is unable to coordinate the goals of the product-development staff (who stress innovation at any cost) with the goals of the accounting department (which values cutting expenses wherever possible) is bound to have problems.

Interpersonal skills can be developed through an understanding of sociological theories and concepts that focus on interpersonal and group relationships. Some of these theories and concepts concern culture, race and ethnic relations, gender relations, social stratification, socialization, social interaction, and social organization. For example, suppose that you are an elementary school teacher who wishes to increase the involvement of your Hispanic students' parents in your school. You might choose to do this by organizing a special club for those Hispanic parents. The knowledge that child rearing is traditionally the primary responsibility of mothers in Hispanic cultures might help give you some ideas for bringing such a group together. Health professionals might find it useful to know that people from different cultures respond to pain and symptoms in very different ways and, thus, might develop different ways of dealing with them. Both the factory managers and the union managers would be interested in knowing which aspects of the work environment different types of factory workers consider most important. The list goes on and on. For almost every job, knowledge of sociology would be a valuable tool that could be used to enhance interpersonal skills.





### Communication Skills

Perhaps the most important skill you need to have is the ability to communicate well. Without this ability, your other skills may not be apparent. As a student of sociology, you will have to develop both oral and written skills. Most assignments in sociology, written or oral, are concerned not only with giving correct answers but also with developing and presenting the argument clearly in order to get your point across. It is necessary not only to think clearly but also to express yourself clearly so that your argument can be understood. The perpetual interplay of ideas between students and professor—via class discussions and critical analyses—provides practical experience with "thinking on your feet" and with communicating your thoughts and ideas to others. Again, this is a skill that must be developed to be successful in any career.

Sociological insight plays an important role in effective communication. Sociology tells us, for example, that people from different cultures and social groups interpret language and other symbols in different ways and that language influences a person's perception of a given situation. With this in mind, middle-aged professors would find it useful to know the jargon of the various student groups at a college (jocks, punks, preps, honors students, etc.) to reach each of them emotionally and intellectually. Advertisers and salespeople would benefit if they could quickly find out the needs and wants of their clients through the subtle messages found in their conversations. The transplanted New Yorker who is recruited to be the director of a childcare center in North Carolina needs to understand why Southern parents might not trust "fast-talkin' Yankees." There are hundreds of other examples of how sociology can help us in our day-to-day communication problems. By now, you have probably thought of some examples of your own.

## 2.4d Non-Sociologists in Society

Since it is concerned with every aspect of social life, sociology should interest every social being. Just as we should have an understanding of sickness without having to be physicians and an understanding of money without having to be economists, an understanding of sociological principles can be useful in our daily lives because they involve an enormous range of events. Sociologists may study topics as diverse as the intimacy between husband and wife and the dynamics of mob violence. Violent crime may be the subject of one study, the communion of persons in a religious institution the subject of another. One investigator may be concerned with the inequities of race, age, and gender, while another may investigate the shared beliefs of common culture. Sociology is interested in both the typical or normal, and the unusual or bizarre.

Sociology can teach us to consider perspectives other than our own and to look beyond the individual in our efforts to understand individual behavior. It encourages us to look not merely at how people and events are unique and different, but also at how people share perceptions and how events occur in patterns. It familiarizes us with a range of theoretical explanations of how people think and act, of how societies' structures change, and of how society operates.

Perhaps most importantly, though, sociology can help us to understand ourselves. Humans are social animals, and people can understand themselves only in the context of the society in which they live. Knowledge of the social constraints that bind us can be frustrating—we may feel trapped, angry about our inability to control our lives, and disappointed at the social inequities that surround us. Only through understanding our society, however, can we truly understand ourselves.

C. Wright Mills (1956) wrote that the "sociological imagination" enables us to distinguish between "personal troubles" and "public issues." By understanding how societies and groups are organized, we may well come to realize that problems that we thought

**BVT*Lab***

Flashcards are available for this chapter at www.BVTLab.com.

we had caused ourselves might, in fact, be problems that result from social forces. Think of all the times you came down hard on yourself—or someone else—because of a problem you faced. If you knew how social forces generated the problem, you might be better able to deal with it. This one sociological idea alone—and there are hundreds of others—has implications for many of your social relationships. Consider, for example, how parents might handle a problem with their child if they could understand the cultural, structural, institutional, and group forces acting on the child instead of focusing solely on the child's problematic behavior.

Sociology is useful for more than just helping us with our problems. It also can help us with most of our important personal decisions, such as whether to get married, how many children to have, whether to buy a home, how much education to get, what kind of career to pursue, and when to retire.

Although "personal uses of sociology" have been discussed last, this is perhaps the most important section of the chapter for many of you. The author of *College: The Undergraduate Experience in America*, a report issued by the Carnegie Foundation for the Advancement of Teaching, states, "We found on most campuses a disturbing gap between the college and the larger world .... We feel compelled to ask: How can the undergraduate college help students gain perspective and prepare them to meet their civic and social obligations in the neighborhood, the nation, and the world?" (Boyer, 1986, p. 16). This report is as relevant in 2012 as it was in 1986.

Sociology has always been one of the disciplines best able to help meet such a challenge. In light of the Carnegie Foundation's recent findings, sociology is now more relevant to a college education than ever before. This book introduces you not just to sociology as a science, but also to sociology as a tool for improving the quality of your life and the lives of those around you.

# CHAPTER 2 Wrapping it up

## Summary

1. Although we also learn about society from everyday experiences, authority, faith, and tradition, sociology depends heavily on empirical research that uses the scientific method.
2. There are certain standards of inquiry basic to science, whether it is a natural or social science. Objectivity involves excluding personal values, beliefs, and biases from the research process, findings, and interpretations. The standard of replication requires that research be undertaken and reported such that someone else can replicate it. The standard regarding precision in measurement requires that whatever is studied be measurable and that measurements be precise, reliable, and valid.
3. Sociological research is of four basic types: exploratory, descriptive, explanatory, and evaluative. *Exploratory research* is typically used to study a new phenomenon. *Descriptive research* provides reliable, valid data on social facts. *Explanatory research* goes beyond description to determine why a particular social situation occurs and to discover cause-effect relationships.
4. Sociological methods are often categorized into two types: qualitative and quantitative. *Qualitative* methods are used to determine the essential characteristics, properties, or processes of something or someone. These methods often include case studies, laboratory observations, field observations, and participatory observations.
5. *Quantitative* methods are designed to determine the amounts or numbers of something: how many, how often, how statistically significant, and so forth. Experimental research and surveys are generally quantitative methods.
6. *Surveys*, the most frequently used method of sociological research, involve systematically asking people about their attitudes or behaviors, which is usually accomplished with the use of questionnaires. Choosing an appropriate sample and wording questions carefully are crucial parts of the survey method.
7. The *experimental method* involves the use of two or more similar groups. An independent variable is introduced into the experimental group but withheld from the control group.
8. Valuable data are often found in public records and secondary sources. *Content analysis* is one procedure used to critically examine this material.
9. Research generally involves a sequence of tasks that include formulating the problem, reviewing the literature, developing hypotheses for testing, choosing a research design, collecting data, analyzing the findings, drawing conclusions, and disseminating the results.
10. There are often many different ways to categorize data, formulate tables, and use statistical measures—such as the mode, median, mean, range, and variance. When data analysis is finished, conclusions are drawn and the results are made available to the public.
11. Ethics in sociology are meant to guide researchers in meeting the needs of human subjects involved in their studies. Among other things, maintaining integrity and protecting the confidentiality of subjects are paramount to sociological research.
12. Research methods are not only important and useful for sociologists, but also an integral part of many occupations and used often in our daily lives.

## Discussion Questions

1. Are music and art sciences? Are physics and biology sciences? Is any social science discipline, including sociology, a science? Why or why not?
2. Formulate two general propositions. Can you operationalize them—that is, reformulate them in terms of testable hypotheses?
3. Why are reliability and validity important in social research? Give examples to illustrate each.
4. Compare and contrast the advantages and disadvantages of qualitative and quantitative research. Give examples of where each type could be used and where one type could be more appropriate than the other.
5. What do you think of the idea that quantitative research represents masculine characteristics and qualitative research represents feminine characteristics?
6. List examples where observation research would be appropriate. What are its strengths and weaknesses?
7. Can sociologists utilize experimental designs? Give examples.
8. After reading about the Hawthorne effect, illustrate how researchers themselves might influence or contaminate the results.
9. Suppose that you want to study police brutality. What methods could you use? What are some ethical and political issues that you should consider? Should unpopular or undesirable results or findings not be made public?
10. An instructor says that she is going to grade on a curve. She returns your exam results with a score of 50. What types of additional data do you need to know to assess whether 50 is a good or a poor grade?

*Then I began to think, that it is very true which is commonly said, that the one-half of the world knoweth not how the other half liveth.*

François Rabelais

# PART TWO

# INDIVIDUALS WITHIN SOCIETY

Individuals create and are shaped by the society in which they live. While individuals don't agree on everything, there are overarching patterns of agreement that enable societies to function. These patterns of agreement are continually evolving. Collectively, these agreements form culture. Culture permeates every aspect of our lives. Intertwined with culture, we live our lives within social structures that include groups and organizations. Some of these groups and organizations are essential to what we are as individuals; and some are not as essential to our individuality, but they affect us, nevertheless. We are not born understanding and embracing the facets of our cultures, groups, and organizations. Rather, we learn them through socialization—a process that begins at birth and continues in all areas of our lives and throughout our entire lives. However, socialization does not create exact replication of one another and does not always result in conformity. At times, people deviate from the agreed upon patterns of our cultures, groups, and organizations. Various social control mechanisms come into play for those patterns that are essential to the overall functioning of a society.

CHAPTER 3

# Culture and Society

## SYNOPSIS

**Defining Culture**

**Elements of Culture**

- Symbols
- Language
- Values
- Beliefs
- Norms
- Technology and Material Culture

**The Web of Culture**

**Cultural Diversity**

- Subcultures
- High Culture, Folk Culture, and Popular Culture
- Countercultures
- Ideal and Real Culture
- Idiocultures

## 3.1 DEFINING CULTURE

The term culture means different things to different people. Many people use the words culture and society interchangeably; however, they are different in their meanings. To a sociologist a **culture** is a system of ideas, values, beliefs, knowledge, norms, customs, and technology shared by almost everyone in a particular society. In other words, culture is a society's entire way of life. A **society** is a group of interacting persons who live in a specific geographical area, who are organized in a cooperative manner, and who share a common culture. Neither culture nor society can exist without the other; there can be no society without a culture, and likewise, no culture without a society. A culture is a society's system of common heritage. Each of us has a culture because we were all raised in a society. We express our culture continuously in our dress, food, work, language, recreation, and other activities. We learn our culture from those within our society. Our families, friends, schools, and others teach us; and then we pass it on to future generations.

**Culture**
A system of ideas, values, beliefs, knowledge, norms, customs, and technology shared by almost everyone in a particular society

**Society**
A group of interacting people who live in a specific geographical area, who are organized in a cooperative manner, and who share a common culture

A comprehension of the elements of culture is vitally important to all interpersonal relationships, from personal life to occupation. In most discussions of culture, it is assumed that the various groups of people within a society share some expectations

Focal Point

## BILINGUAL EDUCATION

The rapidly increasing percentage of non-native English speakers in the United States has called increasing attention to the issue of bilingualism—the use of two or more languages—especially with regard to education. Hispanics constituted nearly 17% of the U.S. population in 2013 (U.S. Census, 2013) and are estimated to constitute 30% of the U.S. population by 2050 (Infoplease, 2007). The Bilingual Education Act of 1968 led to implementation of bilingual education programs in communities with large numbers of people who qualified for limited English proficiency (LEP). As of 2009, more than five million public school students had LEP; and the number is increasing (Jost, 2009). Although some bilingual education programs are designed to maintain the native language and culture of the child (maintenance programs), most are aimed at providing a transition to English and to mainstream American culture (transitional programs) (Hakuta, 1986). Today, the minority language predominantly at issue is Spanish. This is becoming increasingly true as the U.S. continues its rapidly increasing shift in the racial make-up of the youth population (under age 18) and involves important issues of identity, learning, and assimilation (Saulny, 2011). Whites are now a minority of the youth in ten states. Not surprisingly, immigration and bilingual education issues create the highest tensions in some of these states.

Advocates of bilingual education claim that because federal policy has been responsible for the presence of a large part of the LEP population in the United States—for example, through the acquisition of territory (such as Puerto Rico) and through wars (such as Vietnam and the Mexican-American Wars)—there should be continued federal policy for bilingual education (Hakuta, 1986). The crux of their argument is that teaching students in their native languages builds a stronger foundation for success in English and academics (Crawford, 2009). They advocate that when students receive lessons in their native language, the teachers can teach at the same level that they teach English-speaking students, rather than having to simplify it in English to make it understandable to LEPs. Thus, the more the students develop their cognitive and literary skills overall, the more likely they are to acquire English-speaking skills. Proponents of bilingual education say that it provides the best chance for LEP students to partake fully in the opportunities of American life (Berstein, 1990, p. 48). The National Association for Bilingual Education (NABE), for example, has argued that bilingual education programs have led to "improved academic achievement test scores, reduced rates of school dropout and student absenteeism, increased community involvement in education, and enhanced student self-esteem" for LEP students. NABE suggests that this overall improvement in the effectiveness of education benefits not only minority group members but also the future economic productivity of the United States as a whole. Additionally, it lays the foundation for improving the linguistic competencies of all Americans and enhances their understanding, tolerance, and appreciation for other cultures (Hakuta, 1986)

On the other side, opponents of bilingual education who support English immersion contend that bilingual education delays students' mastery of English (Jost, 2009). They feel that research on English immersion shows better academic gains for students. Further, and perhaps at the center of their argument, is their emphasis on assimilation into U.S. culture and belief that English is necessary for economic success in the United States (Hakuta, 1986). Supporters of English immersion also feel that teaching students in their native language through bilingual programming could lead parents to the conclusion that English may not be necessary, after all, in order to succeed. Interestingly, some opponents of bilingual education are immigrants who had to learn English and assimilate quickly upon coming to the United States at a young age. They insist that a bilingual education would have impeded their integration into American society (Romaine, 1989; Porter 2009). Many opponents feel that bilingual education leads to cultural pluralism, rather than assimilation, and thus has negative consequences for members of minority groups and for the nation as a whole.

Clearly, the controversy over bilingual education is more than a debate about language. It is a debate about cultural pluralism versus cultural assimilation and the values of each, as well as about the most effective ways of learning how to speak English. It also highlights the importance of language, as both a determinant and result of culture, and how it relates to the overall functioning of society.

about how it works and how its members should behave. In America, people live in houses or apartments. We buy food in a supermarket or grow it ourselves, we have jobs, and we generally expect our spouses to be sexually faithful to us. In traditional Eskimo culture, by contrast, people lived for part of the year in houses made of snow. They hunted for food because no one had "jobs" in our sense of the word. In some circumstances, sexual infidelity was not merely tolerated but was even encouraged through a practice of "wife lending." Since behaviors of these types vary from one group or society to another, they are viewed as products of culture rather than as basic aspects of human nature. In other words, these behaviors are not programmed genetically, as in most other animal life—they are determined by culture.

Culture is one of the most complex sociological and anthropological concepts, and one of the most central concepts to understanding human behavior. Every society is made up of both material and nonmaterial culture. Material culture includes all tangible things within our society. Houses, architecture, art, clothes, toys and tools are all examples of our material culture. All objects created within a particular society are a part of that society's material culture. Nonmaterial culture is comprised of mostly nontangible items within a culture. Laws, language norms, values, beliefs, ideas, and customs are all components of nonmaterial culture.

*Material culture includes all objects created within a particular society, such as this statue of the Buddha.* *(iStockphoto)*

Culture manifests itself in everything humans do—from birth to death we experience culture. The clothes we place on our newborns, the way we wear our hair, our dating rituals, and our funeral and burial practices—all are parts of our culture. Culture is learned and shared with others within our society. Most people spend their entire lives in the culture in which they were born and often take for granted the way things are done. This is reinforced when visiting another country, where it is not uncommon for people to experience culture shock—a feeling of confusion, disbelief, or outrage by something found "normal" in another culture that is completely at odds with what is practiced in one's own culture. Culture shock can range from mild to extreme. While traveling in Spain, you may be somewhat dismayed because your shopping routine is disrupted by the fact that many of the stores are closed in the middle of the day. You might become extremely disturbed while traveling in South Africa when witnessing the extreme juxtaposition between the poverty-stricken who are living in family groups in one-room, open shacks in close vicinity to upper-class mansions.

Sometimes culture shock stems from ethnocentrism. **Ethnocentrism** is the attitude that our own culture is superior to others; that our own beliefs, values, and behaviors are more correct than others; and that other people and cultures do things wrong compared to our own culture. Ethnocentrism was defined by William Graham Sumner as "that view of things in which one's own group is the center of everything and all others are scaled and rated with reference to it." (1980, p. 13)

Most groups in any society tend to be ethnocentric. Religious groups believe that they know the "truth" and are more moral than others. Scientists are equally likely to believe their methods are the best way to approach problems. Most Americans believe that monogamy is more "proper" than polygamy and that capitalism is far superior to communism. Many of us are likely to consider people who scar their bodies to be masochists. We are likely to believe that people who refuse to drink milk are ignorant

**Ethnocentrism**
The view that one's own culture is superior to others and should be used as the standard against which other cultures are judged

and that people who walk around half-naked are shameless. However, we think it quite natural that American women paint their lips and hang jewelry from their ears; that men tie a strip of cloth around their necks; and that people eat corn, which is considered chicken food in many cultures.

The opposite of ethnocentrism is xenocentrism, the belief that what is foreign is best—that our own lifestyle, products, or ideas are inferior to those of others. The strange, distant, and exotic are regarded as having special value. Cars made in Japan, watches made in Switzerland, beer brewed in Germany, fashions created in France, silks imported from India and Thailand, and gymnasts from Eastern European countries—all are believed to be superior to our own. In some instances, feelings of xenocentrism are so strong that people reject their own group.

Another form of cultural bias is temporocentrism, the belief that our own time is more important than the past or future. Accordingly, historical events are judged not in their own context but on the basis of contemporary standards. Our tendency toward temporocentrism leads us to assume that current crises are more crucial than those of other periods; therefore problems need to be solved now before it is too late. An associated belief is that actions taken now will have an enormous impact on life in the future. Temporocentrism is most prevalent among people who lack historical perspective. Even people with extensive educational training and a strong grasp of history tend to focus on the present, however.

**BVT*Lab***

Flashcards are available for this chapter at www.BVTLab.com

Social scientists who study other cultures attempt to view all behaviors, lifestyles, and ideas in their own context. The practice of examining cultures on their own terms and in relationship to their institutions and environment, rather than by the standards of another culture, is called **cultural relativism**.

According to the cultural relativistic perspective, an act, idea, form of dress, or other cultural manifestation is not inherently right or wrong, correct or incorrect. These things should be examined only in the context in which they occur; what is appropriate in one culture or context may be inappropriate in another. Nudity in the shower or at a nudist colony is appropriate, but nudity in the classroom is inappropriate. In some hunting societies, being fat may have survival value and may serve as a source of admiration. In America, however, fatness is regarded as unhealthy and rarely serves as a source of admiration. The point is that any aspect of a culture must be considered within its larger cultural context.

Cultural relativity does not mean that a behavior appropriate in one place is appropriate everywhere, nor does it mean that all behaviors are condoned simply because they make sense in a cultural context. It is not a license to do as one would wish. Even though having multiple wives makes sense for many Saudi Arabian men, killing female infants makes sense in a Brazilian tribe, and wearing loincloths makes sense to African Bushmen, these behaviors are not acceptable to most Americans. They make sense in some societies because they are part of a larger belief and value system and are consistent with other norms appropriate to that cultural setting.

**Cultural relativism**

The belief that cultures must be judged on their own terms rather than by the standards of another culture

## thinking SOCIOLOGICALLY

1. Provide a behavior that is seen as "normal" in the United States, but likely seen as a culture shock by people from another country.
2. Explain a time when you have experienced culture shock within your own society.

## APPLYING CULTURAL RELATIVISM

The worth of cultural relativism goes beyond analyzing or judging other societies. That aspect is important for social scientists, but the cultural relativistic perspective is also important for anyone who comes into contact with people from different cultures. Consider, for example, teachers in the United States who are faced with the growing number of students from minority cultures and the prospect of teaching within bilingual education programs. Many teachers have been taught to judge students by the norms of white, middle-class children (See & Strauss, 1985).

However, **norms** are different from culture to culture. For example, a Native American student might pause two or three seconds before answering a question as a courtesy to the questioner. A Hawaiian student might interrupt a questioner because such behavior displays interest. Hispanic and Asian children might not maintain eye contact with the teacher because they were raised in cultures in which it is disrespectful to maintain eye contact with someone of higher status. In these situations, it is possible that the teachers might interpret such children's actions as signs of being unprepared, inattentive, or disrespectful—and will treat them accordingly. This ethnocentrism on the part of the teachers could decrease their effectiveness.

Cultural relativism is important in any type of situation that involves people with different cultural backgrounds. As sociologists See and Strauss note, "Utilizing the cultural [relativistic] approach in the practice of counseling, education, public administration, and the healthcare and service professions means that special attention is placed on how the individual one is dealing with analyzes situations given their particular cultural backgrounds, social characteristics, and group affiliations." (1985, p. 69)

The approach also makes good business sense. The would-be entrepreneur from New York who visits the South and notices the lack of Jewish delicatessens might think she has stumbled upon a "gold mine." Assuming that a commodity that is highly valued in one cultural region will be just as "hot" in another region might lead to a financial disaster.

**Norms**
Formal and informal rules of conduct and social expectations for behavior

**Symbol**
Something that is used to represent something else, such as a word, gesture, or object used to represent some aspect of the world

# 3.2 ELEMENTS OF CULTURE

## 3.2a Symbols

The existence of culture depends on people's ability to create and understand symbols. A **symbol** is something that is used to represent something else. Words, numbers, flags, crosses, and kisses are symbols. During World War II, raising the middle and index fingers of one hand was the symbol "V" for victory; in other countries, it's a rude gesture. During the 1960s, the same gesture came to symbolize "peace." Raising the middle finger, or putting thumbs up or thumbs down, or spreading one's thumb and little finger ("hang loose" in Hawaii)—all convey particular meanings. In the same way, a stop sign is a symbol meaning "halt" and a cross is a symbol of Christianity.

*Symbol, such as flags, are an integral part of culture; and a culture's existence depends on the ability of that culture's members to understand them. Symbols are arbitrary designations in that a connection between a symbol and what it represents may not necessarily exist. (iStockphoto)*

Symbols are arbitrary designations. There is nothing inherent in the act of holding one's thumb up that indicates we approve of something. Neither is there anything inherent in an "A-Okay" gesture, signaled by forming a circle with the thumb and forefinger and holding up the other three fingers. Many people in the United States use it to signify that "all is fine." However, to use that same symbol in France and Belgium would convey a message that a person is of little or no worth. In Greece and Turkey, it would suggest an insulting sexual invitation. In parts of Italy, it would be an offensive reference to one part of the female anatomy. It's no wonder that interpersonal relationships among people from different cultures are influenced by an awareness of the meanings attached to symbols.

It is important to realize that symbols are collective creations. Many advertising agencies realize the importance of cultural symbols and distinguish between *general marketing*, which is aimed at the total population, and *segmented marketing*, which is aimed at specific ethnic, racial, or other groups. Segmented marketing uses symbols such as speech patterns (accents, slang), music, clothing, objects, hand signals, and other symbolic elements that are thought to be characteristic of the group the advertisers are trying to attract. Our success or failure in many relationships, from personal to professional, often depends on our ability to communicate symbolically.

## 3.2b Language

The most important set of symbols is **language**. Language, among humans, is the systematized usage of speech and hearing (including signing for the deaf) to convey or express feelings and ideas. It is through language that our ideas, values, beliefs, and knowledge are transmitted, expressed, and shared. It permits us to share our experiences from the past and present, to convey our hopes for the future, and to describe dreams and fantasies that may bear little resemblance to reality. Some scientists have questioned whether thought is even possible without language. Language is the chief factor in our ability to transmit culture.

Language is used to convey feelings and ideas; it is the most important set of symbols in a culture. Although not all societies are able to read and write their language, all societies possess a spoken language. (iStockphoto)

Cultures develop not only a verbal and written language but also a nonverbal language of gestures, expressions, mannerisms, and even the use of space. Latin American and North American (Canadian and the U.S. American) cultures, for example, use space between people differently during conversation. For Spanish speakers, standing close conveys cordiality and sincerity, whereas for English speakers it conveys pushiness. The distance that English speakers see as proper for conversations, Spanish speakers see as cold. Knowledge of another culture's nonverbal or "silent" language is invaluable for any type of interaction that involves people from different cultures, such as international businesspeople, lawyers, politicians, or diplomats. Business deals and international agreements often rely heavily on the private interaction of a few high-powered individuals. A deal might easily be soured if one party interprets the other's normal speaking distance as pushy or standoffish.

Suppose that you are a lawyer hired by an American electronics company that relies on Japanese parts. Part of your job entails securing a long-term contract to ensure that the company can continue to import the parts it needs for its products. It might help, in your negotiations with the lawyers that represent the Japanese firm, to learn about the nonverbal language used by Japanese people in their conversations and to learn how they interpret some of our nonverbal language. What do they consider to be polite standing or sitting distance between people? Are there any American gestures that we tend to use in our communication with others that might be offensive to Japanese people? What are some Japanese gestures that convey warmth, trust, and honesty?

**Language**
The systematized use of speech and hearing to communicate feelings and ideas

In the late 1920s and 1930s, the anthropologist Edward Sapir and his student Benjamin Whorf examined how language influenced behavior in different cultures. They concluded that language does influence the way we perceive things and how we behave, and contended that societies with different languages actually perceive the world differently. This idea is known as the **Sapir-Whorf hypothesis**.

As examples, note how words such as *snow* or *banana* create a certain mental image. What do you see when you hear those words? Would you see something different if a precise word or symbol existed for snow, depending on whether it was falling, drifting, frozen, fresh, compacted, in a cone, and so on? Would you behave differently (drive your car, go skiing, eat it, build a snowman), depending on your perception? Is a banana just a banana? Or, as to most Filipinos, do bananas differ in their size, colors, and uses, thus requiring precise words or symbols to convey the banana desired? Interpreters of languages such as Hebrew, Russian, or German often find that no parallel word exists in English for the word they are trying to translate. Thus, they can only try to convey in English the "reality" of the word they are translating. Our perceptions of reality seem to be greatly influenced by our language.

There has been great debate in recent years about the validity of the Sapir-Whorf hypothesis and whether or not our native language actually constrains our ability to understand a concept, such as time or space. Current research suggests that one's language does not prevent one from being able to understand something, but that language does shape how often and how deeply we think about certain things, and perhaps even our attitudes or feelings toward something (Deutscher, 2010). For example, one thing that differentiates English from languages such as French, Italian, or German is that nouns in English are not gender specific. If an object is gendered because of language (for example, *la* or *el* in Spanish), it may be possible that the gendering affects our perceptions, our attitudes, or even the way we use an object.

Regardless of how and why the connection between perception and language exists, the Sapir-Whorf hypothesis helps us to realize the necessity of studying foreign languages. Learning a foreign language is important not only because it allows us to speak to non–English speaking people but also because it allows us to see their view of reality and what they deem as important. For those whose work involves interaction with people from different countries—foreign diplomats, ambassadors, politicians, international businesspeople and lawyers, social workers, or others—being able to speak directly, rather than through an interpreter, is essential for complete understanding.

### thinking SOCIOLOGICALLY

1. Relate the Sapir-Whorf hypothesis to your personal life or academic field of study. Show how the language or the specific terminology in your discipline influences your perceptions of reality and your experiences.
2. Pick any group of which you are a member and identify the words that group uses that may have special meaning to members of that group. Think about how those same words may mean different things to non-group members and how the word has special connotations that only members of the group fully appreciate and understand. How do those words influence the way that people in the group interpret certain events?

**Sapir-Whorf hypothesis**
The hypothesis that societies with different languages perceive the world differently because their members interpret the world through the grammatical forms, labels, and categories their language provides

**Values**
Ideas and beliefs shared by the people in a society about what is important and worthwhile

## 3.2c Values

**Values** are ideas shared by the people in a society regarding what is important and worthwhile. Our values are the basis of our judgments about what is desirable, beautiful, correct, and good—as well as what is undesirable, ugly, incorrect, and bad. Most values have both positive and negative counterparts, which are reciprocally related. If you place a high positive value on fighting for your country, for example, you probably place a high negative value on those who refuse to fight. If you value marital sexual exclusiveness, you probably disapprove of those who engage in extramarital sexual relationships. Values are often emotionally charged because they stand for things we believe to be worth defending. Since values indicate what is proper or improper, they tend to justify particular types of behavior and to forbid others.

Sometimes, our stated values and our behavior are inconsistent. We may place a high value on freedom of the press but want to censor Communist writings. We may place a high value on individualism but want to punish people whose behavior is inconsistent with our definition of appropriate behavior. Our true values are often reflected more by what we do than by what we say. If we say we value education but have no interest in attending classes or paying for public schools, or if we say that we value simplicity but spend money conspicuously to display our wealth, our actions expose our real values.

Since values are learned cultural products, they differ from one society to another. Americans, for example, tend to be individualistic, using personal characteristics and achievements to define themselves, while societies such as Japan and the Israeli kibbutzim focus more on group harmony, unity, and loyalty. North Americans tend to see themselves as dominant over nature, while societies such as the Chinese or subcultures such as the Navajo see themselves as living in harmony with nature. Residents of Canada and the United States are more conscious of being "on time" than those in Asia and the Middle East.

Most cultures, despite diversity in their populations, tend to share certain value patterns. In American society, sociologist Robin M. Williams (1970) described 15 value orientations important in United States American life that are still at the core of U.S. American culture today:

1. *Achievement and Success* We stress personal achievement, especially secular, occupational achievement.
2. *Activity and Work* Every able-bodied person should work and not expect handouts.
3. *Moral Orientation* People should know the difference between right and wrong.
4. *Humanitarian Motives* We should help others who are in a crisis.
5. *Efficiency and Practicality* We should strive to be as efficient and thrifty as possible.
6. *Process and Progress* Our society favors technology and innovations.
7. *Material Comfort* Through hard work, we can use our money to buy a house, cars, and other material possessions.
8. *Equality* Everyone has an equal opportunity to succeed.
9. *Freedom* We believe in freedom to pursue our goals.
10. *External Conformity* Everyone should adhere to similarity and uniformity in speech, manners, housing, dress, recreation, politically expressed ideas, and group patterns.
11. *Science and Rationality* We know that science can solve problems, and we have faith in those who strive to make life better for us.
12. *Nationalism* We believe in the American system—its institutions, government, and education.
13. *Democracy* Our system advocates majority rule.
14. *Individualism* We believe in personal responsibilities.

**Table 3-1** The Elements of Culture

| | Nonmaterial |
|---|---|
| Symbols | Objects or events that represent other objects or events only because people agree as to their meaning |
| Values | Subjective reactions to experiences expressed in terms of good or bad, moral or immoral, the ideals that people look up to but do not necessarily achieve or pursue |
| Beliefs | The ideas people hold about what is true and/or real |
| Norms | Shared rules that define how people are supposed to behave under particular circumstances |
| Emotions | Inner reactions to experiences; societies enculturate (teach) their members to associate certain emotions with specific situations and to experience these emotional states at various intensities depending on the context |
| Attitudes | Likes and dislikes, and general preferences for certain experiences over others |
| Laws | Norms defined by political authorities as principles that members of a society must follow |
| Perceptions | Interpretations of cultural phenomena which may vary from person to person due to his or her unique experience as a member of society |
| Aspirations | Ambitions and goals that are valued and desired within a culture |
| Technological Knowledge | Human knowledge of the techniques and methods for subsistence (how one makes a living, acquires the calories for survival) and/or control of and adaptation to the cultural and natural environment |
| | **Material** |
| Artifacts | The material products of culture, past and present |
| Technology | The tools and products used for subsistence and/or control of and adaptation to the cultural and natural environment |

Adapted from "The Elements of Culture," by Basirico, L., & Bolin, A., in *Understanding the global experience: Becoming a responsible world citizen* by Arcaro, T., & Haskell, R. 2010, p. 39.

15. *Racism and Group Superiority* We evaluate people based on group performance and placement within society.

It must be kept in mind that these are general themes in American values, which change constantly. They are often in conflict, and they are not all exhibited in a single person's behavior. Sometimes, they even appear to be inconsistent. How can we value both independence and conformity, or equality and racial differentiation? Some of the explanations for these inconsistencies lie in whether the value is applied generally or specifically. A person might say, for example, "Our society believes strongly in freedom of the press, but I don't want my town library to carry novels with explicit sex in them." Other explanations may reflect the beliefs of different regions of the country.

William's states that most conflicts between value systems in the United States occur between those centering on individual personalities and those organized around categorical themes or conceptions. Group discrimination and racism, as categorical themes, are contrary to other central values of the society. Each of these values has a historical base and a complexity far greater than is evident in this brief discussion. Evidence does suggest, however, a decline in racist beliefs over several decades. Legislation has forced movements away from enforced segregation and public discrimination; and Congress has passed Civil Rights Acts and a series of laws that forbid discrimination because of race, sex, religion, nationality, place of birth, or place of residence. Thus, while a central value may continue

*As this photo shows, racial segregation was still in existence in the twentieth century. (Library of Congress)*

to exist which grants privilege based on group or racial affiliation, some evidence suggests that this particular theme may be fading.

An understanding of value systems can be useful for many people in their work. In a discussion of how to manage organizational conflict, for example, Hampton, Summer, and Webber (1982) emphasize the importance of being able to recognize that competing value systems are often the source of the conflict. They state the following:

> Instances of inadequate sharing of values and of competing goals are numerous. Individual self-actualization versus collective will is one value conflict that has been and will be fought on many battlefields. At a business level, salespeople value company responsiveness to the customer, while production personnel value equilibrium and predictability; engineers value ingenuity and quality, while finance values the profit margin; marketing emphasizes gross income, while the credit department values minimum credit loss, and so on. (p. 635)

A way to deal with these competing value systems is to try to create common values. Some experts on how to manage corporations suggest that successful organizations do this by developing stories, slogans, myths, and legends about the corporation (Kanter, 1983; Peters & Waterman, 1982). These help to decrease conflict and create a greater sense of mutuality. The "human relations school of management" relies heavily on the notion that sharing values is important for members of large corporations.

### thinking SOCIOLOGICALLY

1. Critique the values suggested by Williams. What differences do you believe exist between the ones he suggested more than 40 years ago and the ones we have today? Discuss why you think values have changed or have stayed the same.
2. To what extent do people have the right (or obligation) to impose their values on others (parents on children, a religious group on those of other religions, a culture on a subculture, etc.)? Illustrate with specific examples.
3. In thinking about a group, culture, or subculture of which you are a member, identify some central values. Discuss how they may be reciprocally related to other elements of culture that are listed in Table 3-1 ("The Elements of Culture").

## 3.2d Beliefs

**Beliefs** are views that people share about what is true or what really exists. This may at first seem to be an odd statement because what people contend "really" exists is perceived as facts, rather than unstated agreement. Of course we perceive these agreements as fact; otherwise a belief would have no strength to help. Beliefs can underlie almost any social situation or social institution. (We will talk extensively about social institutions in Part 4 of this book.) People may "believe" or agree on what it means to be a family. They may agree on what constitutes an appropriate form of government. They may agree on what constitutes an appropriate economic system that benefits society. Often, we think of beliefs as pertaining to our conceptions of a supernatural or creative force, what is at the basis of our existence, or what we think of as religion.

Let's take the example of religion. This is a social institution about which people have very strong beliefs. Again, it's difficult at first to think of the tenets of our religion as agreements rather than absolute. Indeed, if we thought of them as agreements, these tenets would be difficult to follow. However, consider the indigenous Australian Aborigine conceptions of the basis of life. For Australian Aboriginal peoples, life can

**Beliefs**
Views that people share about what is true or what really exists

be traced to a period known to them as The Dreaming. This is a period before written history or any direct human remembrance. The belief, or shared collective view, is that during that period creative spirits roamed the earth in the manifestation of non-human creatures: birds, snakes, lizards, turtles, and other animals. As they roamed the earth, they imbued it with their essence, their spirituality. The areas in which they roamed and imbued their spirituality are called "tracks" and are the mappings for Aboriginal peoples' "walkabouts." A "walkabout" is a spiritual encounter, not simply a walk in the outback. Thus, for Aborigines, the earth is sacred. This is a core belief, or shared view about reality, for them.

It is important to note that beliefs do not simply emerge from nothing and are not completely arbitrary. They develop out of people's relationship to things that are essential to their survival, be they land, the environment, resources, social arrangements, and so on.

Now, think back to the previous section on values. Think about how a society's or a culture's values are reciprocal, both stemming from and reinforcing that society's or culture's beliefs. What we collectively feel is good or bad, right or wrong, just or unjust, is related to what we collectively feel really exists. In the next section we talk about norms. As you read about norms, think, too, how these are reciprocally related to beliefs.

## 3.2e Norms

Norms are elements of nonmaterial culture and are rules of conduct or social expectations for behavior. These rules and social expectations specify how people should and should not behave in various social situations. They are both *prescriptive* (they tell people what they should do) and *proscriptive* (they tell people what they should not do).

**BVT*Lab***

Visit www.BVTLab.com to explore the student resources available for this chapter.

Whereas values are abstract conceptions of what is important and worthwhile, social *norms* are standards, rules, guides, and expectations for actual behavior. Norms and values are likely to be conceptually consistent, but values are less situation-bound and are more general and abstract. Norms link values with actual events. *Honesty* is a general value; the expectation that students will not cheat on tests is a norm. Most norms permit a range of behaviors—that is, some kinds or degrees of over-conformity and under-conformity are expected and tolerated, particularly in some settings or situations. We would not criticize a starving man for lying to get food, for example.

Early U.S. American sociologist William G. Sumner (1840–1910) identified two types of norms, which he labeled "folkways" and "mores." They are distinguished not by their content but by the degree to which group members are compelled to conform to them, by their degree of importance, by the severity of punishment if they are violated, or by the intensity of feeling associated with adherence to them. **Folkways** are customs or conventions. They are norms, in that they provide rules for conduct; but violations of folkways bring only mild censure. In the United States, most adults are expected to eat vegetables with a fork rather than a spoon or knife or chopsticks, and most students attend classes in pants or skirts rather than gowns or bathing suits. If you eat vegetables with a spoon or attend class in a gown or bathing suit, the chances are you will not be arrested or beaten; however, you may receive some smiles, glances, or occasional comments from others. Why? It may be easier to use a spoon for eating vegetables, and on hot days a bathing suit may be more comfortable attire. The reason that people would express mild disapproval is that these behaviors violate folkways that exist in the United States.

Like other norms, folkways are learned through interaction with others and are passed down from generation to generation. Folkways change as culture changes or when we enter different situations. Our tendency is to accept the folkways as appropriate without question. Why do suburbanites fertilize lawns and keep them trimmed? Why do people avoid facing one another in elevators? Why are people expected to chew food quietly and with their mouths closed? No written rules are being violated in these situations, and no one is being physically harmed. These are simply the folkways of our culture, the set of norms that specify the way things are usually done; and people who violate these norms are punished only mildly if at all.

**Folkways**

Norms of conduct of everyday life that bring only mild censure or punishment if they are violated

**Mores** are considered more important than folkways, and reactions to their violation are more serious. They are more likely than folkways to involve clear-cut distinctions between right and wrong, and they are more closely associated with the moral values a society considers important. Violations of mores inspire intense reactions, and some type of punishment inevitably follows. The punishment may involve expulsion from the group, harsh ridicule, imprisonment, or in some cases even death. Why don't people have sex in public? Why don't physicians end the life of elderly people who have terminal illnesses? Why don't people betray their country's well-being for money? Actions such as these violate cultural mores. Mores that prohibit something, that state, "Thou shalt not," are **taboos**. To love and care for one's children is a **mos** (the Latin singular of *mores*); to commit incest (marry or have intercourse) with them or neglect them is a taboo. In the United States, people who murder, commit treason, or engage in incest are widely regarded as sinful and wicked. They violate the mores of society by engaging in taboo behaviors.

Certain norms about which a society feels strongly may become laws, which are formal, standardized expressions of norms enacted by legislative bodies to regulate particular types of behaviors. **Laws** do not merely state what behaviors are not permitted; they also state the punishment for violating the law. Ideally, the punishment should reflect the seriousness of the crime or civil offense and should be carried out by a judicial system. This system legitimizes physical coercion and is above the control of any individual member of a society. Within the boundaries of their duties, members of a judicial system can use physical force and imprisonment, or even kill without retaliation. Laws, therefore, are formalized legislated norms that are enforced by a group designated for that purpose. In contrast, only the members of society themselves—not a separate group designated as enforcers—enforce folkways and mores (unless they are made into laws).

When a law does not reflect folkways and mores, its enforcement is likely to be ignored or given low priority. Although certain actions may be formally defined as illegal in certain communities (shopping on Sundays, smoking marijuana, having sex outside of marriage), enforcement is ignored because of changing folkways or mores that grant a degree of social approval to the behavior. This suggests that conformity to the norms of society comes not from formal law-enforcement officials but from the informal interaction of members of society. Members of society follow most norms, but adherence is not rigid. Adaptations to changing conditions are possible, and a certain degree of deviation from existing norms is both possible and beneficial for the effective functioning of society.

However, it is important to realize that cultural norms (folkways and mores) are not always beneficial for a society, group, or individual. Some norms may actually be harmful—what Erich Fromm (1965) calls the "**pathology of normalcy**." Thus, we can follow cultural norms when they do not harm us, but we do not always have to follow them. You might be able to improve the quality of your life if you analyze the costs and benefits of the norms you are expected to follow by society or by your peer group. As one clinical sociologist notes,

> Is it part of your peer subculture to take the easy way through school rather than to read, research, study, learn basic skills, and treat teachers and others with respect even while you disagree with them? The benefit of following peer-group norms of little work might be a degree with "no sweat," but the costs may be educationally empty school years, boredom, a bad conscience, a lack of pride in oneself, few solid accomplishments, and lifelong deficits in skills such as reading, writing, and critical thinking. Researching and analyzing the student subculture may show a pathology of normalcy. (Cohen, 1985, p. 46)

In this case, you might decide to deviate from the norms in order to maximize your gains. The process of violating norms beyond the range of group acceptability is called "deviance," and the process of applying sanctions to obtain social conformity is known as "social control."

**Mores**
Norms of conduct associated with strong feelings of right or wrong, violations of which bring intense reaction and some type of punishment

**Taboos**
Mores that prohibit something

**Mos**
Singular form of *mores* (from the Latin)

**Laws**
Formal, standardized expression of norms enacted by legislative bodies to regulate certain types of behavior

**Pathology of normalcy**
The concept that cultural norms are not always beneficial for a society, group, or individual

## 3.2f Technology and Material Culture

In addition to the nonmaterial aspects of culture—symbols, language, values, norms, and laws—societies use certain material techniques and products to maintain their standards of living and their lifestyles. The practical production and application of these techniques and products is a culture's **technology**. Technology applies the knowledge gained by science in ways that influence all aspects of culture. It includes social customs and practical techniques for converting raw materials to finished products. The production and use of food, shelter, and clothing, as well as commodities and physical structures, are also aspects of a society's technology. These physical products are **artifacts**. A society's artifacts can be very diverse: beer cans, religious objects, pottery, art, pictures, typewriters, computer terminals, buildings and building materials, clothes, books, and even contraceptive devices. Material artifacts reflect the nonmaterial culture—symbols, beliefs, values, norms, and behaviors—shared by the members of a society.

*An Ethiopian woman makes dough from banana stems. Such production and use of food is part of her material culture, which helps maintain her society's standard of living and lifestyle. It also reflects her society's technology—the knowledge gained and applied by its members.* (iStockphoto)

Artifacts provide clues to a society's level of technological development. Americans, especially those of European descent, take great pride in their level of technology. The ability to perform heart transplants, to split atoms, and to produce sophisticated patriotic missiles, supersonic jets, computers, and environmentally controlled living and working conditions leads us to perceive our type of culture as superior, advanced, and progressive. This perception is often accompanied by a belief that cultures with a low level of technological development are inferior and not progressive.

These are subjective perceptions, however, not scientific criteria for evaluating cultures. A more objective evaluation of what some call "less-developed" cultures indicates that they possess an amazing degree of skill and ingenuity in dealing with the environment. Many apparently crude techniques are based on fundamental principles of engineering. Today, people marvel at the rice terraces built several thousand years ago on mountainsides in Asia, which included water distribution systems that seem difficult to improve on today. These rice fields produced food for generations of families and communities without the aid of diesel tractors, complex machinery, or hybrid rice plants; many are still in use. Anthropologists know of countless instances of the survival of people under conditions that few members of "highly developed" cultures could endure. The adobe huts of Native Americans, the igloos of the Eskimos, or the bamboo houses of rural southeast Asia—none of which have indoor plumbing, heating, or air conditioning—would be inadequate homes for most members of more technologically advanced cultures. Yet these people's technology is suited to and perfectly adequate for their particular lifestyles. It could be argued that in more developed nations, the technology is developed by a handful of specialists; thus, the general population is less technologically proficient than members of so-called primitive groups. It is a mistake to dismiss a culture's technological system because it appears less developed or complex than our own.

A common phenomenon that all societies face at times is a disconnect between material culture and nonmaterial culture. The tendency for material culture (in particular, technology) to outpace nonmaterial culture (especially norms, values and beliefs) is called **cultural lag**. William F. Ogburn (1922) noted this phenomenon. An example of cultural lag in contemporary Western societies is that we have the technology to keep people alive through life support systems when, in some cases, a person's brain has deteriorated to the point where he/she may not be able to function. While the technology

**Technology**
The application of nonmaterial and material knowledge by a society to maintain its standard of living and lifestyle

**Artifacts**
Physical products or objects created through human actions

**Cultural lag**
The tendency for nonmaterial culture to lag behind material culture

exists to keep people alive in those instances, our norms and values pertaining to death have not evolved to the point where we are clear about what we should do.

**thinking** SOCIOLOGICALLY

Think about and discuss the cultural lag that exists between computer technology, in the forms that we use every day (such as laptops, smartphones, and tablets), and our norms and values in everyday life regarding such things as personal relationships and education.

# 3.3 THE WEB OF CULTURE

Where does culture come from? This is a question that sociologists and anthropologists (especially) have been examining since the birth of these disciplines. One answer is that cultures arise from agreements between people within a social system (be it among people within a geographic region, such as a country, or an organization) about things that are essential to their survival (Babbie, 1977, 1980) and in response to environmental factors. Social systems develop mechanisms and sets of rules to meet basic survival needs such as how reproduction practices are regulated, how we ensure that children are cared for, how we regulate power, how we ensure that basic material needs are met, how knowledge is disseminated, how we provide for spiritual nourishment, and more. Some of the things that are necessary for a social system to survive are universal, and some are distinct to particular organizations. Sociologists refer to these sets of rules as **institutions** (Basirico & Bolin, 2010, p. 42). Some of the universal institutions found throughout the world include family, economics, politics, religion, healthcare, and education. These certainly are not the only institutions that exist. You will learn more about these institutions in Part 4 of this book. Culture, then, refers to all of those ways of life (practices and what we think) that both stem from and shape social institutions. It is important to understand the relationship between culture and institutions because without that understanding, it is easy to become judgmental of other cultures.



Basirico and Bolin refer to a "web of culture" and emphasize that it is difficult to understand the elements of culture (refer back to Table 3-1) without understanding the relationship between the elements of culture and institutions. They use the analogy of a rubber band ball to illustrate the relationship between the elements of culture and institutions:

> "Think of the separate rubber bands as elements of culture—values, beliefs, norms, symbols, technology, and so on. Now, think not just of one value, one belief, one symbol, and so on but think of the hundreds of examples of values, beliefs, norms, symbols, and so forth in a particular place. Imagine that each rubber band represents one value, belief, symbol, norm, etc. Further, imagine that other rubber bands represent social institutions—the family, the economy, politics, religion, education, healthcare, and so forth. Think of how intertwined the strands of a rubber band ball are and how they create something solid, real, and tangible that is much more than the individual strands. The relationship between the elements of culture and institutions is a little like that ball in that they create a whole culture that is greater than the individual parts." (2010, p. 43)

**Institutions**

A stable cluster of values, norms, statuses, and roles that develops around a basic social goal

In order to help understand the relationship between the elements of culture and institutions within any particular culture, Basirico and Bolin suggest using a matrix to analyze your observations of that culture (see Table 3-2). They provide an instructive example of how you might analyze a wedding ceremony in the United States. First, think

sociologyatwork

## Teen Girls Help FBI Nab Cyber Stalkers

In 2008, there were an estimated 220 million Internet users in the United States, representing over 72% of the population. According to Nielsen Online Data (2008), the average person spends over 37 hours per month on the Internet and views an average of 1,489 web pages during that time. While adults access the Internet regularly, the number of children online continues to grow. Children use personal computers for numerous reasons, including school assignments, often requiring them to access information from several online sources. In addition to doing schoolwork, young persons are using the Internet to play games and to socialize. According to the view of the Pew Internet and American Life Project (2011, 2012), over 90% of young people between ages 12 and 17 access the Internet regularly. In 2011, an estimated 80% of them had a profile on a social networking site such as Facebook or MySpace, and 47% admitted to uploading personal pictures onto their profile for others to view.

The fear of children becoming the victims of online predators continues to grow in conjunction with the number of young people accessing the Internet. Parents, law enforcement, and advocacy groups search for new ways to lessen the possibility that children will fall victim to pedophiles skilled in the behaviors of young people online. The FBI estimates that at any given time 20,000 sexual predators are lurking online to persuade children to provide personal information about themselves, or even worse, to meet them outside their homes.

According to the Center for Missing and Exploited Children, the number of incidents of predators communicating with children is increasing. The Federal Bureau of Investigation (FBI) began trying to learn as much as they could about the behavior of young people online to combat the possibility that they would be convinced to meet a predator offline. However, the agents were not familiar with the sites or language used by young Internet users; and pedophiles caught on quickly, lessening the chances they would be caught.

The FBI decided to enlist the help of young people to train agents in the online culture of children. An agent sought the help of his daughter and some of her friends who regularly used the Internet and were familiar with the behaviors of other young people. When the girls first arrived, they administered a multiple choice and true/false test to measure the agents' knowledge of teen culture. Every agent failed the test. According to 14-year-old Mary, one of the trainers, "They, like, don't know anything." Her friend Karen, another 14-year-old, rolled her eyes and added, "They're, like, do you like Michael Jackson?"—obviously indicating how outdated the agents were in their understanding of young people.

By 2005, the girls had trained over 500 FBI agents from around the country on music, movies, and computer language, particularly the abbreviations used by young Internet users. As a result, within the first few years, the FBI arrested over 2,600 online sexual predators. The agents continue to receive regular training; however, Mary and Karen are no longer the trainers because, at age 16, they are too old. To stay on top, the FBI makes certain their training comes from young persons knowledgeable in the culture of teenagers who regularly use the Internet.

(AP Wide World Photo)

of what you might observe at such a ceremony. For example, you might notice who is performing the ceremony (priest, minister, rabbi, justice of the peace), what the bride is wearing, rings, invoking the use of the word "God," a limousine, a father "giving away" the bride, and many other things. Next, try to place each of these observations in the "web of culture" matrix. Notice that you might be able to place some of your observations in more than one box. Now, think a little more conceptually about the relationship between each of the elements of culture that you observed and the institutions and how they may reinforce each other.

Imagine taking this analytical approach to examine entire cultures in detail. Imagine again using this method to examine a culture that is very different from yours, perhaps even one that may seem deviant, and how it would help you to understand that culture in a non-judgmental way. The web of culture approach is one way that you can understand cultures in a culturally relativistic manner.

# 3.4 CULTURAL DIVERSITY

The complexity and diversity of a culture can be better understood by examining various units of a culture, such as subcultures, countercultures, idiocultures, the ideal and real cultures, and social institutions.

## 3.4a Subcultures

It is rare to find a society that has a single culture shared equally by all its members. Most societies include groups who share some of the cultural elements of the larger society yet also have their own distinctive set of norms, values, symbols, and lifestyles. These units of culture are **subcultures**. Subcultures exist within the confines of a larger culture. There are many subcultures within a society, and all of us belong to several at any given time. For example, in college you may be a member of a sorority or fraternity, young Democrats or Republicans, men or women's athletic team, chemistry or social work club, or some others. More often, subcultures reflect racial or ethnic differences, such

**Subcultures**

Group of people who share in the main culture of a society but also have their own distinctive values, norms, and lifestyles

**Table 3-2** Web of Culture

| | Nonmaterial Culture | | | | | | Material Culture | |
|---|---|---|---|---|---|---|---|---|
| Structures/Institutions | Symbols | Values | Beliefs | Norms | Emotions | Laws | Artifacts | Technology |
| Family Kinships | | | | | | | | |
| Educational Systems | | | | | | | | |
| Government/Political Systems | | | | | | | | |
| Religious/Magical Systems | | | | | | | | |
| Sex & Gender Systems | | | | | | | | |
| Healthcare Systems | | | | | | | | |
| Military Systems | | | | | | | | |
| Arts and Leisure Systems | | | | | | | | |
| Non-Kinship Association/ Interest Groups | | | | | | | | |

Adapted from "The Web of Culture" by Basirico, L., & Bolin, A., in *Understanding the global experience: Becoming a responsible world citizen* by Arcaro, T., & Haskell, R. 2010, p. 45.

as those found among black, Polish, or Chinese Americans. Other subcultures develop around occupations: corporate, military, medical, or factory work. The Mormons, Amish, Muslims, and other groups form religious subcultures. Some are based on geography, such as those found in the South and New England; others are based on wealth and age. There are also drinking, drug, reggae, and homosexual subcultures. Every society that has diverse groups of people has subcultures. All subcultures participate in the larger, dominant culture but possess their own set of cultural elements.

At times, the dominant culture and the subculture may conflict to such a degree that tremendous stresses occur and a crisis results. Members of the subculture may be required by the dominant culture to register for the military even though they value pacifism. The subculture may value the use of particular drugs but be forbidden by the dominant culture to obtain them. Also, note how subcultural differences are at the heart of the policy issue selected for this chapter: bilingualism. Can or should Spanish, Japanese, or Arab immigrants to the United States be able to retain their native language in their places of work? Can or should children in public schools be given reading materials and exams in their native language when that language is not English? Subcultural differences and the rights of specific religious, ethnic, or other minority groups are central to many legal and policy debates. An understanding of subcultures makes us realize the importance of differences, not merely between cultures, but between individuals within a culture as well.

**thinking** SOCIOLOGICALLY

Use the knowledge about culture presented in this chapter to discuss why and how the controversy over bilingual education is much more than a debate about language usage in schools.

## 3.4b High Culture, Folk Culture, and Popular Culture

Herbert Gans (1974) identified three "taste cultures" within the larger culture: high culture, folk culture, and popular culture. **High culture** or elite culture reflects the tastes of the wealthy, affluent, or upper classes. Individuals of high culture may distinguish themselves from those considered "beneath them" through language, education, housing, etc. They will often see themselves as more "cultured" than ordinary people. Members of high culture will attend the finest restaurants, operas, ballets, and socialize with others who belong to their inner circles. Folk culture is distinctively different from high culture. **Folk culture** reflects the tastes of the working class or ethnic groups. Craft fairs, bluegrass or jazz festivals, NASCAR—all are examples of folk culture. **Popular culture** tends to reflect the tastes of the masses within a society. Music, art, dance, radio, linguistic trends, and literature produced and consumed by members of society are part of popular culture. For example, Santa Claus, the Easter Bunny, Halloween, Monday Night Football, soap operas, and baseball games are part of popular culture in the United States. In this case, culture is constructed by, and shared among, common persons such as you and me.

**High culture**
The materials and ideas of wealthy, affluent, or upper classes (in contrast to popular culture)

**Folk culture**
The culture of the working class or ethnic groups

**Popular culture**
Trends, social activities, and shared experiences of everyday people (in contrast to elite culture)

## 3.4c Countercultures

A **counterculture** is a subculture that adheres to a set of beliefs and values that are in opposition to the dominant culture of which it is part. Because they accept such beliefs and values, members of a counterculture may behave in such radically nonconformist ways that they may drop out of society. Dropping out may mean either physically leaving

**Counterculture**
A subculture that adheres to a set of norms and values that sharply contradict the dominant norms and values of the society of which that group is a part

or ideologically and behaviorally leaving, by rejecting the dominant values and working to change them.

Delinquent gangs, some religious sects, hippies of the 60s, and some political extremists can all be classified as countercultures. The norms and values of each of these groups sharply contrasted with those held by the dominant culture. Often, these values are not merely different from those of the dominant culture but are, also, in opposition to them. Delinquent gangs may grant prestige and social approval for law-breaking, violence, theft, or the use of drugs to achieve their goals of dominance and material success. The youth movement of the 1960s—which included political activists, dropouts, and hippies—actively challenged the dominant cultural norms of hard work, financial success, conformity of dress, sexual restrictiveness, military superiority, and white supremacy. Perhaps the pendulum has swung away from countercultural trends among youth to countercultural trends among extreme right-wing adults. Today some right-wing religious groups are behind the bombing of abortion clinics, while less extreme groups have made efforts to legalize corporal punishment, mandate prayer in the public schools, and demand the inclusion of creationism in the school curriculum. With the destruction of the World Trade Center in New York, a greater awareness of terrorist countercultures exists within the United States. The individuals behind these deadly attacks, both domestic and foreign terrorists, disagreed with governmental policies and chose to take revenge on the citizens of our society.

*Auto racing is an example of folk culture, which reflects the tastes of the working class or ethnic groups.*
*(iStockphoto)*

## 3.4d Ideal and Real Culture

In most cultures, differences exist between what people are supposed to do and what they actually do. The **ideal culture** consists of the norms and values people profess to follow; the **real culture** is the culture they actually do follow. If you were asked to tell a foreign visitor about the norms and values of Americans, for example, you would probably describe the ideal culture, mentioning such topics as freedom, democracy, equal rights, monogamy, marital fidelity, and educational opportunity for all. The actual culture differs considerably from the ideal, however. The very poor are less likely to get a good education, marital infidelity is common, and many people have several spouses during their lives. The speed limit may be 55 mph, but many people drive at speeds of 65 or higher. Honesty in the classroom may be the norm, but cheating can be widespread. The point is that stated cultural norms and values are not always practiced.

**Ideal culture**
The norms and values that people profess to follow

**Real culture**
The norms and values that people actually follow and practice, which may or may not be the same as the ideal culture

**Cultural universals**
Aspects of culture that are shared by all people, such as symbols, shelter, food, and a belief system

Although cultures vary in their symbols, language, and behavior—and in their subcultures, countercultures, real and ideal cultures—all share some basic concerns known as **cultural universals**. People in all cultures must have food, shelter, and protection. All people face illness and death, and every society has a kinship system with taboos on incest. Like American suburbanites, African Bushmen and Mongolian nomads socialize and train their members in the ways of the culture, provide for work and leisure activities, and establish leaders and rulers.

## 3.4e Idiocultures

Gary Fine (1979) has argued that every group forms its own culture to a certain extent and he called these created cultures **idiocultures**. An *idioculture* is a system of knowledge, beliefs, behaviors, and customs created through group interactions. Members of a group share particular experiences and recognize that other members will understand references to a shared experience. Members of one group, for example, might roar with laughter whenever the word *cashew* is mentioned because it triggers a memory of a shared humorous experience. All small groups have a culture that is unique to themselves but that is, nevertheless, part of a larger cultural pattern. The group itself forms the group's idioculture; thus, idiocultures do not exist when a group is first formed. They are created from the opening moments of group interaction when people begin to learn names and other information about one another. With time, rules are established, opinions expressed, information exchanged, and events experienced together.

**Idioculture**
The system of knowledge, beliefs, behaviors, and customs that is unique to a given group

# CHAPTER 3 Wrapping it up

## Summary


1. A *culture* is a society's social heritage, the system of ideas, values, beliefs, knowledge, norms, customs, and technology that everyone in a society shares.
2. A *society* is a group of people who share a common culture. Some of the most significant elements of a culture are symbols, language, values, norms, and technology.
3. Societies consist of material and nonmaterial culture. *Material culture* includes all things tangible within society while *nonmaterial* culture involves all intangible aspects of society, such as norms and values.
4. When we encounter a culture different from our own, we may experience culture shock. This is often the result of our own ethnocentrism where we judge another culture based on our own.
5. The idea of *cultural relativism* suggests that cultures must be judged on their own terms, not by the standards of another culture. Acts, ideas, and products are not inherently good or bad; they must be judged in the cultural context in which they happen.
6. *Symbols* are arbitrary representations of something. The use of symbols is a human capability that allows us to make sense of reality, transmit messages, store complex information, and deal with an abstract world.
7. Our most important set of symbols is language, which enables us to transmit and store our social heritage.
8. It has been demonstrated that language influences how we perceive and experience the world. The Sapir-Whorf hypothesis suggests that the use of different languages by different societies causes them to perceive the world very differently. Rather than simply seeing the same world with different labels, they actually perceive different realities.
9. *Values* are conceptions about what is important and of worth. They are learned and shared cultural products that justify particular types of behavior. People in the United States tend to value achievement, success, work, a moral orientation, and humanitarian concerns, among other things.
10. Values indicate what is important, whereas norms are rules of conduct—the standards and expectations of behavior. Norms are of two types: *folkways*, which are customs or conventions that provoke only mild censure if violated, and *mores*, which are far more important and provoke severe punishment if violated. Laws are the formalized and standardized expressions of norms.
11. In addition to the nonmaterial aspects of culture such as these, there are material and technological aspects as well.
12. *Subcultures* are groups within a society that share the common culture but have their own distinctive set of cultural complexes. A *counterculture* is a type of subculture adhering to a set of norms and values that sharply contradict the dominant norms and values of the society of which the group is a part. To a certain extent, all groups possess localized cultures of their own, which are known as *idiocultures*.
13. The culture a society professes to follow (its ideal culture) differs from the culture it actually does follow (its real culture).
14. Understanding the various elements of culture is useful in a variety of occupational settings, including health professions, service organizations, politics, public administration, education, business, and others, as well as in your personal life. Sociologists have come to be used as cultural translators who help to lessen misperceptions and increase understandings among people from diverse cultural settings.

## Discussion Questions



1. Make a list of leisure activities that might be considered high culture. Do the same for folk and popular culture. How might you explain why you participate in some of these activities and not in others?
2. How many examples can you give of symbols using only your hand and fingers? Can you think of any that mean different things in different contexts or to people of different cultures? Have any of these changed over time?
3. Discuss the significance or accuracy of the statement, "Societies with different languages actually see or perceive the world differently."
4. How would an understanding of the Sapir-Whorf hypothesis help politicians to evaluate whether the United States should promote bilingual education programs?
5. Joe listens to his music (quietly, with earphones, of course), and Mary reads her *New York Times* in their sociology class. Is this illegal, forbidden, or harmful behavior? Why is the professor likely to disapprove of such behavior?
6. Discuss ways in which existing student norms may not be beneficial, or may even be harmful, to students.
7. Using the concepts of ethnocentrism and cultural relativism, discuss the impact that a bilingual education might have on understanding other cultures.
8. Think about the subcultures, countercultures, or idiocultures of which you are a member. Differentiate these, and explain the differences.
9. Differentiate between real and ideal cultures. Why are they seldom one and the same?

PRO

CHAPTER 4

# Social Structure, Social Groups, and Social Organizations

## SYNOPSIS

### Components of Social Structure

- Status and Role
- Role Ambiguity, Role Strain, and Role Conflict
- Roles as Relationships: Pattern Variables

### Groups

- Limited and Non-Social Groups
- Social Groups
- Primary and Secondary Groups
- In-Groups and Out-Groups
- Peer Groups
- Reference Groups

### Group Size

- Social Networks

### Formal Organizations

- The Importance of Formal Organizations
- The Goals of Formal Organizations

### Bureaucracy

- Bureaucracy as an Ideal Type and Its Functions
- Dysfunctions of Bureaucracies
- Voluntary Associations

Focal Point

## PREVENTABLE DISASTERS

On April 20, 2010, there was an explosion one mile below the surface of the Gulf of Mexico on a rig owned by the British Petroleum Oil Company (BP). This led to the largest accidental oil spill in history. Nearly 5 million barrels (later estimated by independent researchers to be approximately 185 million gallons) of oil spewed into the Gulf of Mexico before the Macondo well was finally capped successfully, 86 days after the explosion. The oil spill caused catastrophic amounts of environmental damage and financial losses to tourism and fishing industries in Louisiana, Mississippi, Alabama, and Florida. Many of the areas affected were small, sleepy coastal communities that rely on the income provided by the natural resources that the Gulf of Mexico offers.

In the months following the disaster, a presidential panel studied the accident. The panel's conclusion was that the accident was preventable and was the result of BP, Haliburton, Transocean, and several other contractors having taken hazardous timesaving steps without adequate consideration for the potential risks. Surveys of workers on the Deepwater Horizon, the oil rig that exploded, revealed that many of them had concerns about safety practices prior to the explosion; however, they feared reprisals if they had said anything. Many key components in the oil rig had not been inspected since 2000, even though requirements call for inspections every 3–5 years. Investigators also revealed concerns about the quality of cement that was used in the construction of the oil well after discovering that Haliburton and BP knew weeks before the explosion that the cement mixture they had planned to use to seal the bottom of the well was unstable (Broder, 2010). In December 2010, the United States Department of Justice filed a lawsuit against BP and eight other companies that were involved with the construction of the oil well (http://www.nytimes.com, 2011).

The repercussions of the oil spill were disastrous enough, but matters were made even worse by the fact that it occurred as the United States was in the midst of one of its worst economic crises since the 1930s Great Depression. The housing market, the unemployment rate, the bank closings, and other indicators signified one of the bleakest economic periods in United States history. Particularly hard hit by the economic downturn, and the least likely to bounce back quickly, were the very people who depended upon the resources from the Gulf of Mexico to sustain a livelihood. How could such a preventable disaster occur? How could decisions have been made that might have led to enormous gains by BP (had the oil rig not exploded) that entailed risks to the livelihood of millions of others so dependent upon the Gulf of Mexico? While this chapter does not discuss the answers to these questions specifically, it does provide discussions of sociological concepts necessary for understanding the ways in which groups and organizations are formed and maintained. On the other hand, how do members of groups and organizations develop their ways of thinking, often at times to protect their own interests at the expense of others? What are the intended functions of bureaucratic procedures? How, also, can bureaucracy become a series of rituals that loses sight of the initial organizational goals, and thus leads to potential negative consequences? After reading this chapter, you should return to this vignette about the oil spill to see if you can use your knowledge about social structure, groups, and organizations to help explain why preventable catastrophes sometimes occur.

*An explosion one mile below the surface of the Gulf of Mexico on a rig owned by the British Petroleum Oil Company (BP) was the largest accidental oil spill in history.* (AP Wide World Photo)

# 4.1 COMPONENTS OF SOCIAL STRUCTURE

Social structure means that society is organized in a way that makes human behavior and relationships predictable. It means that human behavior is socially patterned. Social structures provide us with familiarity in everyday life, thus allowing us to make sense of our social interactions and to predict patterns. For example, we can assume a great deal about people simply by knowing their occupation. Suppose you are at a social gathering, and the person with whom you are speaking tells you she is a medical doctor. How does that influence what you think about her? What does her information imply about her character? What if she said she was a restaurant server? Would it change your perception of her? During the process of social interaction, a person's position in society often influences how we act toward them. In addition, we come to expect certain behaviors and actions based on a person's position. Social structure is composed of social statuses, roles, groups, organizations, and institutions. With the exception of institutions, these components are examined in this chapter.

## 4.1a Status and Role

When we hear the word **status**, we often think of prestige; status in sociological terms is different, however. Status is a socially defined position that an individual occupies. While a status does not mean prestige, a position (status) held by an individual can imply esteem standing, such as that of judge, doctor, or bank executive. On the other hand, if a person is a janitor, we may consider his occupation to be less prestigious. Judge, doctor, bank executive and janitor are all statuses within society. They exist independently from the people who occupy them.

An individual will, generally, occupy several statuses at one time. The **status set** is the combination of all the statuses any individual holds at a given time. You, for example, are a student if you are enrolled in a school, a son or daughter to a parent, a brother or sister if you have a sibling, a friend or acquaintance to your peers, and a citizen of some country. A status set including student, daughter, sister, friend, and citizen guides what you do and enables others to predict much of your behavior. Students behave differently from teachers (and are expected to), just as children behave differently from adults.

There are two ways that a person acquires a status: it is either ascribed or achieved. **Ascribed status** is obtained involuntarily or without effort on the part of the individual. Ascribed statuses can be acquired at birth—such as age, race, or sex. For example, being a sister, daughter, woman, white, or poor are statuses that can be given to you at birth without willingness on your part. An **achieved status** is one you choose voluntarily or attain through effort or ability. Examples of achieved statuses include husband, athlete, coach, parent, or deviant. Typically, statuses are obtained through a combination of both ascription and achievement.

Sometimes, a particular status stands out among all the others you occupy and may lead people to ignore other statuses in your status set. A **master status** takes priority over all the others in your social identity. Depending upon the social context, a few examples of a master status might include things such as celebrity, professional athlete, and ex-convict. One's race and occupation are often the source of a master status. It is important to realize that social context may help determine a master status. The child of a celebrity attending your college may be seen primarily in terms of her celebrity status. That celebrity status might not hold as much weight when the same person is walking across a Hollywood set.

Any given status in your status set has a dynamic aspect, a set of expectations and behaviors associated with it in a given group or society; these are **roles**. Status and role, like structure and function, parent and child, or student and teacher, are reciprocal concepts. Different roles (expectations for behavior) are associated with different statuses (positions). A useful way to think about this is that you occupy a status,

**Status**
The socially defined position an individual occupies

**Status set**
The combination of all the statuses any individual holds at a given time

**Ascribed status**
A status obtained involuntarily or without effort on the part of the individual

**Achieved status**
A status that you choose voluntarily or attain through effort or ability

**Master status**
A particular status in one's status set that takes priority over the others

**Role**
The social expectations or behaviors associated with a particular status

Although Angelina Jolie and Brad Pitt occupy many statuses, such as spouse, parent, and social activist, it is their status as movie actors that serves as a master status and determines how most people see and treat them. (AP Wide World Photo)

but you play a role. A role is a collection of expectations associated with a status. Figure 4-1 oversimplifies the complexity of statuses and roles, but it does illustrate the relationship between the two concepts. Multiple roles attached to individual statuses are **role sets**. These role expectations and behaviors are learned through the socialization process. Learning what to expect from others who occupy given statuses and what behaviors are appropriate for our own statuses are basic aspects of life as a social being. We learn to expect different behaviors from persons who occupy different statuses. For example, what is the role of a mother within our culture? The expected behavior of a mother is that she love, nurture and care for her children. The roles or expectations of the father are different. He is expected to provide for his family financially and to present himself as a strong and secure man.

**Role set**
Multiple roles that are attached to individual statuses

**Role ambiguity**
A situation in which the expectations associated with a particular social status are unclear

**Role strain**
A situation that occurs when differing and incompatible roles are associated with the same status

## 4.1b Role Ambiguity, Role Strain, and Role Conflict

**Role ambiguity** exists when the behavior or actions expected from us, within a particular status, are unclear. We may find ourselves asking, "What am I supposed to be doing?" "How am I supposed to act?" We may experience role ambiguity in a variety of situations, such as in a new job or on a date.

**Role strain** results from a single role overload or from contradictory demands placed on a given status. Despite our best efforts, the expectations may exceed the time and energy we have available to fulfill them. If your parents expect you to get A or B grades, and you cannot meet their expectations because of other demands on your time that are part of your role expectations as a student—such as school work-study, social fraternity or sorority clubs, athletic teams, residence hall meetings, or because of

**Figure 4-1** Statuses and Roles

(iStockphoto)

the difficulty you have in understanding the material—you are probably experiencing role strain.

**Role conflict** occurs when the demands or expectations associated with two or more statuses interfere with each other or are incompatible. Your status as student may require that you attend class on Friday morning. Your status as boyfriend may require that you meet your girlfriend at the airport when she arrives at the same time that your class is in session on Friday. Your job and schooling may get in the way of each other in terms of demands on your energy and scheduling and may create role conflict regarding expectations. A student who is an athlete or a performing artist may face a conflict between meeting the expectations of being at practice or rehearsal and also being expected to attend an event for a class that afternoon. These are time and energy role conflicts.

Other role conflicts can result not only from competing demands on the time and energy required to fill different roles but also because of different value expectations that may be built into a single status. Can parents be expected to discipline their children at the same time that they are expected to show them love and affection? Can Christians both love their enemies and shoot them during war? These are *value role conflicts.*

*Each status a person holds is associated with an expected role related to that status, and we learn to expect different behaviors from people occupying different statuses. A mother, for example, is expected to provide love and care for her child.* (Shutterstock)

To sum up, then, role ambiguity results from uncertainty over the expectations of a given role. Role strain results from a role overload or the inability to carry out or live up to the expectations of a given status. Role conflict arises from the need to conform to incompatible expectations (time and energy or values) of the same or differing roles.

Role ambiguity, role strain, and role conflict seem particularly prevalent in industrialized societies where people assume complex status sets with multiple and often unclear and incompatible role expectations. Yet it would be totally misleading to conclude that roles are a negative and troublesome characteristic of human behavior. On the contrary, the role expectations that accompany social statuses are the means by which behavior is made predictable, human relationships become patterned, and society is organized.

## APPLYING KNOWLEDGE OF ROLES

Although strict adherence to prescribed role expectations is rare, the power of roles to shape human behavior should not be underestimated. Does the individual shape the role or does the role shape the individual? Do we often find corruption in high government positions because corrupt people are elected to those positions, or is it because the nature of the role and the power it bestows lead to corruption? Do people have maternal and paternal instincts by nature, or does the role of parent lead one to become nurturing and authoritarian? Are college students "party animals" by nature, or does one become a member of that species because of expectations that students at a particular college should be that way?

Some researchers have found strong evidence that we take on or accept the roles we are playing. For example, Phillip Zimbardo's (1971) famous prison experiment demonstrates the power of social structure and roles over personality. Zimbardo set up a mock prison at Stanford University and hired students to simulate the roles of prisoners and guards in order to help gain an understanding of prison systems and role relationships. He had to cancel his experiment prematurely because of how the students—"the cream of the crop of their generation"—had internalized the roles of guards and prisoners that they were assigned to play.

**Role conflict**
A situation that exists when differing expectations are associated with the same role or when two or more of an individual's roles have differing expectations

Zimbardo's research is still relevant today. His conclusions were cited in a *Time Magazine* article as an explanation for the behavior of American soldiers mistreating Iraqi prisoners of war in Abu Ghraib. The Bush administration had blamed the abusive behavior on a "few bad apples"; however, a look at the backgrounds of the soldiers implicated suggests otherwise. Israeli psychiatrist Dr. Ilan Kutz notes, "During actual wars, if there isn't any particular command figure in charge who puts a stop to it, [torture and sadism by prison guards] can spread like a psychological epidemic." In prisons, Zimbardo concluded, abuse is virtually guaranteed if three key components are not present: clear rules, a staff that is well trained in those rules, and tight management that includes punishment for violations. At Abu Ghraib, the conditions for conforming to the role of abuser were present (McGeary, 2004).

How is the knowledge that role expectations play a powerful part in shaping behavior useful to us? Primarily, it alerts us to the possibility that personal and interpersonal behavior is more than a matter of individual personalities or predispositions. This fact, in itself, has important practical implications. Clinical sociologists, for example, are often hired to conduct training programs in stress management in hospital, business, and educational settings. Training programs that teach managers how to restructure work environments and role relationships are usually more successful in reducing stress than programs that focus exclusively on dealing with the psychological problems of individuals (Goldman, 1984).

Realizing the importance of role relationships and social structure, applied sociologists have actually helped some industries overcome problematic situations. A classic example is William Foote Whyte's work (1949) in the restaurant industry. Whyte found that role ambiguity among waiters, waitresses, and kitchen workers—not personality conflicts—accounted for the friction, anxiety, and emotional outbursts in many restaurants. His solution relied mainly on creating clear, specific roles for each of the different types of workers in the restaurants. It seems obvious to us now that this is the best way to run a restaurant; however in 1949, Whyte's solution had a major impact on the entire restaurant industry.

All of us—sociologists or not—can use what we know about roles and behavior to our advantage. Administrators and managers might examine how roles are structured—instead of examining individual personalities—to increase efficiency in their organization. In our personal lives, parents might first try to understand the roles outside the family that their children are expected to play before they try to shape their behavior through a series of rewards and punishments.

---

**thinking** SOCIOLOGICALLY

1. Make a diagram of your statuses and roles. Which of your statuses are ascribed, and which are achieved?
2. Describe a time in your college or work career when you have experienced role ambiguity, role strain, and/or role conflict.

## 4.1c Roles as Relationships: Pattern Variables

Another way to help you understand the concept of roles is to think of roles as guidelines for our behavior within relationships. For example, in my status of professor, I have role relationships with students, other professors, the dean, parents, and so forth. In your status of student, you have role relationships with other students, professors, your advisor, members of organizations in which you participate, and so on. While we often act out our roles when we are alone, for the most part a role usually implies a reciprocal

**BVT*Lab***

Flashcards are available for this chapter at www.BVTLab.com

relationship such as parent-child, professor-student, husband-wife, doctor-patient, judge-defendant, coach-player, minister-congregant, and hundreds more.

To more fully explain the nature of roles and how they may regulate our interactions, Talcott Parsons (1960; 1951) developed the concept of pattern variables. **Pattern variables** are sets of contrasting expectations that pertain to every role we enact in our lives. In carrying out any role, there are patterns that regulate how we judge people, how much emotion we are expected or allowed to express, the extent to which we are concerned with our own well-being or the well-being of the group, the depth or scope of the relationship, and whether or not we respond to people based upon their ascribed or their achieved statuses.

The first pattern variable is **universalism versus particularism**. This pattern variable pertains to the criteria on which we judge or evaluate each other. In some role relationships, we are expected to evaluate each other based upon objective criteria. This is called universalism. Some examples are professor-student or judge-defendant relationships. If I give an exam, it is my responsibility to use the same standards to evaluate all my students. Whether or not you are my friend, come from my home state, or share my political or religious beliefs must have no bearing on how I evaluate you. I am expected (indeed, required) to use objective standards to evaluate students. However, in other role relationships, such as parent-child or husband-wife, we are expected to be very partial in our judgment or evaluation of one another. This is called particularism. When your kindergarten-age child brings home her first painting, you will automatically say how beautiful it is, even if it is filled with scribble; and you will not use some standards of fine art to judge her work. When your significant other asks, "How do I look in these jeans," it's fairly safe to assume that if you took out some fashion guide, you would not win any points with that person.

The second pattern variable is **affective neutrality versus affectivity** (or instrumentalism versus emotion). This pattern variable pertains to the extent to which expression of emotion should be part of a relationship. In some role relationships, such as doctor-patient or judge-defendant, the expression of emotion has no place in how we should be interacting with each other. Imagine how uncomfortable you would feel if your doctor overtly expressed his or her emotions towards you during an examination. It's simply not acceptable. While there is a certain amount of caring that is appropriate for a "bedside manner," crossing that line into personal expressions of emotion is inappropriate. On the other hand, in some role relationships we are expected to be very expressive with our emotions, such as in a parent-child, friend-friend, or significant other role relationship. Indeed, lack of sufficient emotional expression in a marriage could result in the termination of the relationship.

The third pattern variable is **specificity versus diffuseness**. This focuses on the depth, scope, or purpose of a role relationship. In some role relationships, the purpose is very narrowly defined. For example, a student-professor role relationship has a very specific, narrow scope. The purpose of your interactions is for learning. Your relationship with a professor has nothing to do with your personal life, what you do on weekends, helping you fix your car, deciding on where you will go on vacation, or going to the movies. While your professor may casually talk about your personal lives on a superficial level, if that relationship crosses too much into areas beyond the scope of the course material, it could lead to confusion about expectations and potentially lead to unfairness. Contrarily, however, in role relationships between parents and children or friends and friends, there is an expectation that you will interact for a large variety of reasons. Can you imagine how you would feel if you asked your friend for help with a problem and your friend replied with something like, "Sorry. Call me when you want to make plans about going out to have fun"? It's not a leap of imagination to think that that person is not a "true" friend and that you would react negatively to such a comment.

The fourth pattern variable is **self-orientation versus collective-orientation**. This pattern variable focuses on expectations regarding how much we should be focusing on our own self-interests or the interests of the group (or those in the role

**Pattern variables**
Sets of contrasting role expectations regarding judgement, emotions, depth of the relationship, self or collective focus and the extent to which ascribed or achieved statuses guide the relationship

**Universalism versus particularism**
A pattern variable that pertains to expectations about how we should judge or evaluate each other in role relationships

**Affective neutrality versus affectivity**
A pattern variable that pertains to expectations about the extent to which emotions are part of role relationships

**Specificity versus diffuseness**
A pattern variable that pertains to expectations about the scope or breadth of role relationships

**Self-orientation versus collective-orientation**
A pattern variable pertaining to whether or not we should be focused on our own self-interests or the interests of the group within role relationships

relationship). When you shop for a new car, it's completely understandable that both the salesperson and the customer will each try to maximize their own self-interests. In fact, sometimes when a salesperson says that he or she is really trying to help us and that she or he is losing money, it leads us to question his/her sincerity. When you are competing with athletes on an opposing team or in a competitor-competitor role relationship, you are expected to be out for yourself. If you tell your coach that you intentionally lost the game because you felt that everyone should have a chance of winning, it's likely you wouldn't be on the starting team for the next match. By contrast, in a role relationship with your family members you are expected to be more concerned for the well-being of the group. The family member that reaches for the last piece of chocolate cake, while not everyone has had a slice, is scolded for not sharing. The member of the basketball team who "showboats" to try to garner attention for himself or herself, rather than being a "team player," is taken out of the game.

Finally, the fifth pattern variable, **ascription versus achievement** pertains to whether a role relationship should be guided by our achieved or ascribed statuses. In your role-relationship with your sociology professor, your gender, race, age, or any other ascribed statuses should have no bearing on how you interact with each other. If either of you refers back to those statuses as the basis of your relationship, it would be highly inappropriate. The basis of your relationship with your professor is your achieved status and your role as student and his or her role as professor. However, think of a parent's relationship with a child. Whether or not that child is a student or the president of her sorority or has become a lawyer should not be the determinant of how you interact. It is the fact that that person is your child or your parent that guides the relationship. What your parents do for a living, whether or not they are employed, or how much money they make is not likely to determine the basis of your relationship. I suspect that some children don't even know what their parents do for a living.

### thinking SOCIOLOGICALLY

1. Make a list of all of the statuses in your status set. For each status, list the role set or all of the role relationships that are part of each status. Next, make a list of what some of these role relationships entail. Finally, think about the types of role conflicts that may naturally occur in your life as a result of the complexity of your status sets and role sets.
2. Discuss how the pattern variables can help to explain role conflict.

## 4.2 GROUPS

While statuses and roles are important in society, another major component of social structure is the social group. Groups can be classified as either non-social or social, with the degree of social interaction ranging from none to constant.

Humans are social animals. Even those who think of themselves as loners participate in many groups; and groups, for most of us, are a major source of satisfaction. You may eat with a particular group of friends every day, belong to a drama club, or play tennis every week with your gym class. You probably depend on social groups, social organizations, and social systems for most of your psychological and physical needs. Research indicates that we are influenced, not only by the groups to which we currently belong and with which we identify, but also by those with which we associated in the past and potentially by those with which we may identify in the future.

**Ascription versus achievement**

A pattern variable that pertains to whether interactions within a role should be guided by the ascribed or the achieved status of those who are interacting in a particular relationship

## 4.2a Limited and Non-Social Groups

Throughout this chapter we focus our discussion on *social groups*—those in which people physically or socially interact. However, there are non-social and limited social groups recognized by sociologists as well. These include statistical and categorical groups, aggregates, and associational or organizational groups.

**Statistical groups** are not formed by group members but by sociologists and statisticians, primarily for record keeping and analysis. For example, in 2010, some 74.7 million children younger than age 18 were living in the United States (Families and Living Arrangements, 2010). The group of women between 5 feet 1 inch and 5 feet 5 inches tall would be another statistical group. Some sociologists do not consider groups of this sort to be groups at all because the members are unaware of their membership and there is no social interaction or social organization (see Table 4-1).

An example of an organizational group is a band. (iStockphoto)

**Categorical groups** are those in which a number of people share a common characteristic. We all belong to categories and share common characteristics with others within society. Blondes, the homeless, single mothers, children, students, and tall people are all categorical groups. Categorical groups are not social groups because the members do not interact with other members who share common characteristics. They are important, however, in the common identity member's share with others like them.

An **aggregate** is a group consisting of a collection of people who are together in one place and socialize very little. People standing in line for movie tickets, individuals waiting for the bus, and drivers stuck in a traffic jam—all share a common space but may not see themselves as belonging to a group.

**Associational** or **organizational groups** consist of people who join together in some organized way to pursue a common interest, and they have a formal structure. Most of us belong to a number of groups, and they can be formed for almost any conceivable purpose. The university, a volleyball team, a Rotary Club, the Democratic Party, General Motors Corporation, and Protestant churches—all are associational groups.

As you can see, a number of different kinds of groups are recognized; and their boundaries are not easy to state clearly. Like other classification schemes, the one we have suggested makes use of some criteria but ignores others that may in some circumstances be equally important. Groups might also be classified on the basis of social boundaries between members and nonmembers, adherence to a special set of norms, awareness not only of kind, as in Table 4-1, but also of membership or a variety of other factors.

**Statistical group**
A group formed by sociologists or statisticians in which members are unaware of belonging and have no social interaction or social organization

**Categorical group**
A group of people who share a common characteristic but do not interact or have any social organization

**Aggregate**
Any collection of people together in one place that interact briefly and sporadically

**Associational (or organizational) group**
A group of people who join together to pursue a common interest in a organized, formally structured way

**Social group**
A group in which people physically or socially interact

## 4.2b Social Groups

A **social group** involves the following: (a) some type of interaction; (b) a sense of belonging or membership; (c) shared interests or agreement on values, norms, and goals; and (d) a structure—that is, a definable, recognizable arrangement of parts. Thus, the sociological use of group involves interaction, a consciousness of membership, shared interests, and a definable structure. From the above discussion, associational or organizational groups are social, but less intimate, and limited in the amount of interaction.

Social groups are important because they provide us with a social identity, serve as a key to understanding social behavior, link the self with the larger society, and help us understand social structure and societal organization.

**Table 4-1** A Classification of Non-social and Limited Social Groups

| Type of Group | Awareness of Kind | Social Interaction | Social Organization | Example |
|---|---|---|---|---|
| Statistical | No | No | No | Average family size |
| Categorical | Yes | No | No | Redheads |
| Aggregate | Yes | Limited | No | Football crowd |
| Associational | Yes | Limited | Yes | Democratic Party |

## 4.2c Primary and Secondary Groups

The term **primary group** was coined by Charles H. Cooley (1909) to refer to small, informal groups of people who interact in a personal, direct, and intimate way. Members of our primary group, according to Cooley, were the most important in shaping the human personality. Primary groups involve intimate face-to-face association and interaction; and their members have a sense of "we-ness," involving mutual identification and shared feelings. Their members tend to be emotionally attached to one another and involved with other group members as whole people, not just with those aspects of a person that pertain to work, school, or some other isolated part of one's life. Your family, close friends, girlfriend or boyfriend, and some neighbors are likely to be members of your primary group. A primary group tends to remain intact for a long time, and its members are often considered irreplaceable.

*Your family, close friends, girlfriend, or boyfriend, and some neighbors are likely to be members of your primary group. (Shutterstock)*

A **secondary group** is a group in which members interact in an impersonal manner, have few emotional ties, and come together for a specific practical purpose. Like primary groups, secondary groups may be small, but they also can be large and may involve face-to-face contacts and cordial or friendly interactions. Secondary group interactions are more formal than primary group interactions; however, they are just as important. Most of our time is spent in secondary groups—committees, professional groups, sales-related groups, classroom groups, or neighborhood groups. As a student, you come together with other students at specified times to learn sociology. While you have the class in common with many others, it is unlikely that you will develop a close relationship with all the individuals enrolled in the course. In fact, it is quite likely you would not recognize many of your classmates if they passed you in the hallways.

The key difference between primary and secondary groups is in the quality of the relationships and the extent of personal intimacy and involvement (Table 4-2). Primary groups are person-oriented, whereas secondary groups tend to be goal-oriented. We allow those with whom we have a close relationship to occupy more of our personal space than members of secondary groups. A primary group conversation usually focuses on personal experiences, feelings, and casual, open sharing, whereas a secondary group conversation is more apt to be impersonal and purposeful.

**Primary group**
A small, informal group of people who interact in a personal, direct, and intimate way

**Secondary group**
A group in which the members interact impersonally, have few emotional ties, and come together for a specific, practical purpose

Primary and secondary groups are important both to individuals and to society. Primary groups are particularly important in shaping the personality, in formulating self-concepts, in developing a sense of personal worth, and in becoming an accepted member of society. They are also an important source of social control and social cohesion. Such famous scholars as Erich Fromm (1965) and Lewis Mumford (1962) contend that the strength and vitality of primary groups are the basis of the health of a society. In an increasingly impersonal world, they are sources of openness, trust, and intimacy.

**Table 4-2** Characteristics of Primary and Secondary Groups

| Primary Groups | Secondary Groups |
|---|---|
| Informal | Formal |
| Smaller in number | Larger in number |
| Intimate | Less intimate |
| Person-oriented | Goal-oriented |
| Longer in duration | Shorter in duration |

People who are not members of some primary group—a marriage, friendship, or work relationship—experience greater health problems and other difficulties.

Although primary groups are vital to the health of individuals and society, secondary groups are also important because they tend to meet specific goals. They help societies function effectively and permit people who do not know one another intimately to perform their jobs more effectively. Most formal organizations such as schools, corporations, hospitals, and unions comprise many secondary groups and relationships.

## 4.2d In-Groups and Out-Groups

An **in-group** is a social category to which persons feel they belong and in which the members have a consciousness or awareness of kind. One of the key characteristics of an in-group is the members' sense of belonging. Those who belong think of one another as forming a social unit. This unit has boundaries that separate "us" from "them," that differentiate those who are "in" from those who are "out." Members believe they share a common fate, adhere to a common ideology, come from a common background, or otherwise resemble the other members. In-groups may be primary groups, but are not necessarily so. We can feel "in" with people we have never met or shared personal intimacies with—members of our alumni group, religious group, or veterans group, for example. University of California graduates, Buddhists, or Iraq War veterans may experience feelings of comradeship or a sense of togetherness.

*We can feel "in" with people with whom we have never met or shared personal intimacies, such as members of our alumni group. (Shutterstock)*

As we feel the we-ness among our group, an **out-group** is one to which we feel we do not belong. Out-groups are made up of those who do not share an awareness of kind. We do not identify or affiliate ourselves with members of out-groups, and we feel little allegiance to them. We treat most members of out-groups with indifference; at times, however, we may feel hostile toward them because of our tendency toward ethnocentrism—the predisposition to perceive our own in-group as superior to others. The out-group, being inferior, does not deserve the same respect as the in-group. Thus the members of an in-group—friends, classmates, doctors, and industrialists—may defend other in-group members even when it does an injustice to those who are "out."

**In-group**
A social group to which people feel they belong and with which they share a consciousness of kind

**Out-group**
A group to which people feel they do not belong, with which they do not share consciousness of kind, and with which they feel little identity

The difference between in- and out-groups is sociologically important for at least two reasons. First, in-group members tend to stereotype out-group members as they notice and compare the differences between their own group and out-groups. The way we interact with others is often based upon prejudices we have towards groups we consider as out-groups. For example, we tend to avoid members of out-groups when the out-group is a group to which we attribute a negative stereotype (Wyner, 2010).

Second, when we perceive threats from out-groups, it heightens our in-group solidarity. Strange as it may seem, an attack on our in-group can have positive effects. After the 9/11 terrorist attacks on the World Trade Center, for example, citizens of diverse backgrounds united as "Americans"; and ideological, political, and racial differences within the country were diminished. American flags and other displays of support and patriotism were evident everywhere. Similarly, economic hardships may bring the members of a family closer together—just as flood destruction may bring a community closer together.

After the September 11, 2001, attacks on the World Trade Center, the country united as an in-group of "Americans." (Shutterstock)

In turn, members of in-groups may overreact toward out-groups in times of crises. When the Alfred P. Murrah Federal Building in Oklahoma City was blown up on April 19, 1995, killing 167 people, we immediately began searching for a member of an out-group. After one of the worst acts of terrorism in America, we quickly discovered that the perpetrator was a member of our own in-group when Timothy McVeigh, a veteran, was arrested for the bombing. Later we learned that he was a member of a radical anti-government militia group in the U.S., and he was placed into an out-group category.

Knowing that out-group threats often increase the solidarity of members of an in-group is useful for anyone helping a group overcome conflict among its members. A therapist, for example, may work with a group of rehabilitated alcoholics by discussing ways in which they can begin to see drinkers as an out-group rather than an in-group as they had previously done. Similarly, in an effort to overcome the conflict among workers in an industrial plant, a labor union leader may call the workers' attention to the common enemy they face in management. If you were a coach of a high school softball team having difficulty with arguments and competition among the team players, how could you use what you know about out-groups to make the players feel closer to one another? Our affiliation with a particular in-group may provide us with an identity and a sense of belonging, but it also induces conflict and restricts our relationships and interactions with others.

## 4.2e Peer Groups

One type of group from which in- and out-groups draw their members is the **peer group**, an informal primary group of people who share a similar status and who usually are of a similar age. The unique factor in peer groups is equality. In most groups, even small ones such as marriages or committees, one person or more have a higher status or a position of dominance; however, in peer groups the members are roughly equal in importance.

Although peer groups are most often discussed in connection with young people, they are found in all age groups. Most friendships, regardless of the friends' ages, share the characteristics of a peer group: they are informal, primary relationships, and the participants are of equal rank and often of the same sex.

**Peer group**

An informal primary group of people who interact in a personal, direct, and intimate way

**Reference group**

A group with which people identify psychologically and to which they refer in evaluating themselves and their behavior

## 4.2f Reference Groups

**Reference groups** are the groups with which we identify psychologically. They serve as sources of self-evaluation (comparative reference groups) and influence how we think and act and what we believe (normative reference groups). People need not belong to a group for it to be a reference group for them; groups we aspire to belong to might also be reference groups.

Comparative reference groups are an important source of information about our performance in a given area. Just as cultures tend to assess themselves on the basis of their own standards, individuals assess themselves in accordance with the standards of their reference group. Receiving a grade of B may be a source of pride to students if their peer reference group did worse; but it may be a source of disappointment to a family reference group if they expected an A from their child. A professor's income may be good relative to an assistant professor's income, but it may be poor relative to the income of someone employed in industry. In brief, we tend to judge our worth, accomplishments, and even our morality in comparison with groups of reference.

Normative reference groups serve not only as sources of current evaluation but also as sources of aspiration and goal attainment. A person who chooses to become a professional baseball player, a lawyer, or a teacher begins to identify with that group and is socialized to have particular goals and expectations associated with that group.

Having knowledge of people's reference groups can sometimes help us understand why they behave as they do. It may explain why a teenager who never smokes or drinks at home will do so with a school group, or why politicians may vary their stances on an issue, depending on the audiences they are addressing. Our aim is to please and to conform to the expectations and behaviors of the groups that are important to us.

## APPLYING KNOWLEDGE OF REFERENCE GROUPS

The concept of reference groups also helps us understand why some people are unhappy or dissatisfied with their condition. People often feel deprived, not necessarily because of the objective conditions they face, but because they compare themselves to a reference group. This is known as **relative deprivation**. Sociological research has turned up many instances of groups that have experienced relative deprivation. Thomas Pettigrew (1964), for example, found that the economic and social conditions for black Americans improved greatly after World War II (for example, life expectancy increased, civil-service jobs increased, income increased, and college attendance increased). Yet blacks became progressively more dissatisfied. Pettigrew pointed out that this was because when compared to whites, a reference group, blacks were and still are considerably lacking equality in many areas. Indeed, the economic and social conditions improved much more for whites, leaving blacks to experience relative deprivation. Relative deprivation has been found to explain many areas of life including health, mortality, suicide bombings, and others. For example, Pham-Kanter (2009) found that people tend to report certain types of illnesses—such as ulcers, diabetes and cardiovascular problems—at higher rates in very low-income groups and at lower rates in very high-income groups. Sayre (2010) found evidence that relative deprivation helps to explain the phenomenon of Palestinian suicide-bombings. There is ample research that supports the idea that reference groups indeed have an impact on our social and psychological well-being and on our actions.

Sociologists and economists are finding that employers and administrators would do well to pay attention to relative deprivation when they make decisions about salaries, bonuses, benefits, and other working conditions that affect various groups within an organization (Stark, 1990). They could increase their ability to relate to the employees and treat them more fairly if they could understand the reference groups to which their employees compare themselves.

For example, pretend that you are the owner of a construction company, and your staff and your employees are dissatisfied with their wages. Before you consider giving an across-the-board 10% raise to all employees, you might first consider the impact of such a raise. The employees making higher salaries to begin with will receive bigger raises in terms of real dollars. So, in effect, you might be giving more money to those who need it the least and less money to those who need it the most. If you do this, do you think that the problem of worker dissatisfaction will be solved? Probably not. Instead, you might consider looking at to whom the various work groups compare themselves and trying to determine some fair amount that would bring each group more in line with the others or with groups at similar levels in different companies.

**Relative deprivation**
A feeling of being deprived, not because of objective conditions, but because of comparison to a reference group

On a personal level, the concept of relative deprivation helps us to understand our own feelings of inadequacy and might help us to realize the sources of some of our frustrations. Many of us are happy with our lot in life—or with our car, clothes, stereo equipment, and so on—until we see members of our reference groups with something better. If we could realize that we are experiencing a relative deprivation—not an objective one—we might be able to deal with our feelings of inadequacy.

# 4.3 GROUP SIZE

Group size has an effect on many of our social interactions, such as in the family, at work, on a jury, or while participating in a protest. First, size affects group membership interactions. The smallest group, a *dyad*, consists of two people. When just two people are involved, each of them has a special responsibility to interact—if one person withdraws, the group no longer exists. With the addition of a third person, the dyad becomes a *triad* and the interactions change drastically. If one person drops out, the group can still survive. In a group of three, one person can serve as a mediator in a disagreement or alternatively side with one person and then the other. A third person, however, can also be a source of conflict or tension. The phrase "two's company, three's a crowd" emphasizes the dramatic shift that takes place when dyads become triads. When a triad adds a fourth or fifth member, two subgroups can emerge. As group size increases, the stability of the group decreases. It may be more difficult to choose a leader, arrive at an agreement or consensus, or decide who will perform particular tasks.

*The size of a group has a dramatic effect on how its members interact. A dyad is the smallest group size, and its existence depends on the interaction of both members. In a triad, such as in this photo, the group can survive even if one of its members drops out. Further, one person in a triad may serve as a mediator between the other two and maintain the group's cohesiveness. iStockphoto)*

A second consequence is that as size increases, so does the division of labor. If the group is small, all the members may engage in the same activities. As size increases, however, activities tend to become specialized.

The third consequence is that increases in group size result in an increasingly rigid and formal structure. Whereas small groups are likely to operate informally according to unwritten rules, large groups usually conduct meetings in accordance with Robert's Rules of Order or some other standard formula. Also, small groups are more apt to emphasize personal and primary characteristics. A small grocery store run by a family, for example, may reflect the tastes of the family members. Jobs may be delegated to various people on the basis of their preferences, and work schedules may be drawn up to accommodate one person's going to college or another person's social life. Large groups, on the other hand, emphasize status and secondary characteristics. In a large supermarket chain, committees make decisions. Chairpersons, division heads, or managers are selected; the problems of bureaucratic red tape begin. In contrast to small groups, employees are expected to conform to the demands of their jobs rather than changing their jobs to meet their personal preferences.

The fourth is that as the size of a group increases, so does the need for a more formal type of leadership. With increasing size come complex problems relating to the coordination of activities and decisions; this leads to the emergence of group leaders—persons who have the authority, the power, or the potential ability to direct or influence the behavior of others. In small groups, decisions may be made informally, in a spirit of mutual sharing and agreement, with no designated leader. In large groups, the leadership becomes more formal and decision-making is more constraining.

A fifth consequence of an increase of group size is a change in communication patterns. In large groups, the leaders tend to dominate the discussions. They talk the most and are addressed the most because the discussion and comments of other members are directed toward them. Although similar patterns of communication may exist in small groups, members who never join the discussion in a large group may do so in a small one.

Sixth, as size increases, cohesion decreases. A group is considered cohesive when members interact frequently, when they talk of "we," when they defend the group from external criticism, when they work together to achieve common goals, and when they are willing to yield their own personal preferences for those of the group. Membership stability is important for cohesion because a high turnover rate has a negative effect. Conformity is also important—failure to abide by group norms and decisions lessens cohesiveness. Social scientists have found that cohesiveness within groups generally improves group performance. Group cohesiveness tends to reduce the anxieties of group members and leads to greater cooperation. A statement such as this suggests that the ability to create cohesion (for example, by reducing group size) can be an important tool for managers and administrators. The adage "many hands make light work" may not apply to all situations.

## 4.3a Social Networks

Each of us is involved in numerous groups of the types just described: primary, secondary, large, small, peer, reference, and so forth. Through these groups, we develop linkages or ties to a total set of relationships: a **social network**. Social networks link people. Think, for example, of your social network. It probably includes your family, your friends, your neighbors, classmates, members of social clubs, people you work with, and others.

**BVT*Lab***

Visit www.BVTLab.com to explore the student resources available for this chapter.

Unlike close personal networks, many of our social networks include linkages with people with whom we have little in common and only occasional contact. These may be people whom we only know of or who only know of us. These "weak" ties, however, can be extremely important in getting a job or a "good deal" on a purchase. Perhaps this can be illustrated by the frequently heard phrase, "Who you know is as important as what you know." This is social networking. Evidence of the increasing importance of networking in everyday life can be found in the growing popularity of websites such as Facebook, MySpace, Twitter, and others.

Social networks do not just happen. Over time, we build and establish ties to others, some strong, some weak. Strong ties may be characterized by emotional involvement and are sustained in a variety of ways, including calls, visits, letters, cards, attendance at particular events, and—as suggested by Cheal (1988)—through gifts. Marsden (1987) found that the average individual had only three strong ties with individuals with whom they could discuss important matters.

The ties to people in social networks do not have to be strong to have an important impact on our lives. Indeed, Malcolm Gladwell in his best-selling book *The Tipping Point: How Little Things Make a Big Difference* (2000) uses the findings of sociologist Mark Granovetter (1974) to explain how it is that the networks that have weak ties can have some of the most profound effects on our lives. For example, Granovetter found that when finding a job, weak ties are more important than strong ties. We are more likely to have strong ties to close friends, people in our neighborhood, people we work with, members of our church congregation, and so on. They occupy a world that is very similar to ours. However, people who are only acquaintances, rather than close friends, are more likely to inhabit social worlds that are quite different than ours, thus allowing us to cast our net of contacts to places outside of what is immediately accessible to us.

There is little question of the importance of social networks. Social networks do make a difference in professional advancement, as well as in developing a sense of self-worth and integration into the society and culture of which we are a part.

**Social network**

The linkage or ties in a set of relationships

## thinking SOCIOLOGICALLY

1. Provide examples of some of your groups and examine the importance of each in your life.
2. How can you begin, early in your college career, to establish social networks that would increase your chances of getting job offers after graduation?
3. Are you a subscriber to any social networking websites such as Facebook, MySpace, or Twitter? If so, provide some examples of how networking through any of these websites has affected your personal life or professional opportunities.

# 4.4 FORMAL ORGANIZATIONS

Social organization refers to the stable patterns within our society: its norms, mores, roles, values, communication patterns, social institutions, and the like. One form of social organization is the **formal organization**, a large social group deliberately constructed and organized to achieve some specific and clearly stated goals. The *Encyclopedia of Associations* (2008) provides details of more than 22,200 national professional societies, labor unions, trade associations, fraternal and patriotic organizations, and other types of structured groups in the United States alone, which consist solely of voluntary members. More than 135,000 entries are listed when international organizations—as well as regional, state, and local—are included.

*A church is a formal organization created to meet a specific goal.* *(iStockphoto)*

Organizations tend to be stable, often keeping the same structure and continuing to exist for many years. Those who belong to an organization generally feel a sense of membership. Industrial corporations, professional sports (including leagues, teams, and fans), country clubs, trade unions, schools, churches, prisons, hospitals, and government agencies are formal organizations created to meet specific goals. All groups have goals of some sort; however, they are often latent, unstated, and general. Group members may even have conflicting goals; but in an organization, the goals are specific, clearly stated, and usually understood precisely by the members.

Consider the case of a family and a school. Both have as goals the education of children. The parents in a family may read to the youngest children and provide the older ones with books, magazines, and newspapers. They may also encourage children to play learning games or take them to museums and concerts. In a formal organization such as a school, however, the education program is much more highly structured. The teachers, administrators, and other staff members have been trained to teach a particular subject to a single group or to meet some other specific goal. The overall educational goals of the school, although perhaps subject to disagreement, are stated and understood more clearly than those of the family. The same holds true with factories (see Figure 4-2) and all other formal organizations, including voluntary associations, which are described at the end of this chapter.

## 4.4a The Importance of Formal Organizations

**Formal organization**

Large social group deliberately organized to achieve certain specific, clearly stated goals

Every day, we deal with some sort of formal organization in connection with work, food, travel, healthcare, police protection, or some other necessity of life. Organizations enable people who are often total strangers to work together toward common goals. They create levels of authority and channels of command that clarify who gives orders,

***Figure 4-2*** Hierarchy Structure of Mid-Sized University

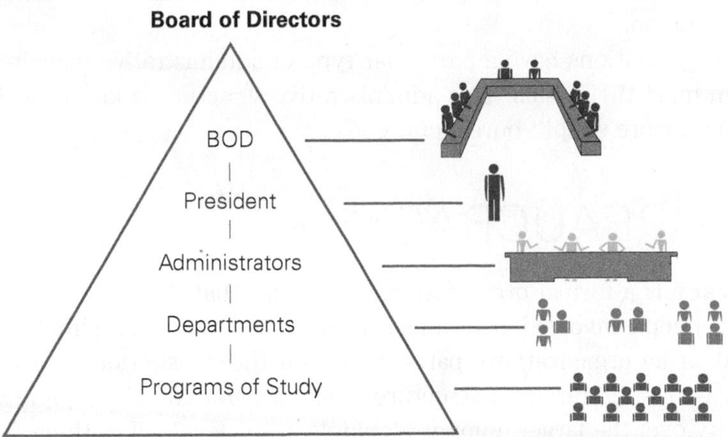


who obeys them, and who does which tasks. They are also a source of continuity and permanence in a society's efforts to meet specific goals. Individual members may come and go, but the organization continues to function. Thus, formal organizations make it possible for highly complex industrialized societies to meet their most fundamental needs and to pursue their collective aspirations.

*Formalization* is the process by which the norms, roles, or procedures of a group or organization become established, precise, and valid and by which increasing attention is given to structure, detail, and form. The formalization of organizations is the characteristic that distinguishes complex societies from small tribal societies.

## 4.4b The Goals of Formal Organizations

As you can well imagine, the goals of different organizations vary widely. Businesses are interested chiefly in making a profit. Service organizations assist people with problems such as unemployment or illness. Some organizations, such as unions or stamp collectors, exist to promote the interests of their own group; other organizations, such as governments, the military, and prisons, are established to provide services to the general public.

Given this diversity of goals, it is not surprising that some formal organizations are in conflict with each other. The goals of right-to-life and right-to-choice organizations such as the National Organization for Women (NOW), for example, are very different; and conflict between the two is evident. Conflict also exists regarding employee drug testing. The goals of some organizations, such as the Department of Transportation, favor this activity, while the goals of other organizations focus on the right to privacy and the noninterference in our personal matters.

Conflicts appear both between organizations and within them. Universities must determine whether the primary goal of their faculty is teaching or research. Medical organizations must decide whether their chief function is to aid and protect the physician or to improve the healthcare given to the public. Sometimes, an organization's apparent primary goal (e.g., service) is used to conceal its actual primary goal (e.g., profit). A private mental institution, for example, may emphasize the quality of the care it gives in its literature, but decisions about whether to provide a particular service to its clients may always be made on the basis of profitability.

There are often conflicts between the goals of an organization's administration and those of its employees or the clients or public it serves. In a university, for example, the main priority for the administration may be to balance the budget. The aim of the faculty may be to do research and publish papers. The students may be most concerned with receiving a good education through exceptional teaching and the use of outstanding library and laboratory facilities, which may conflict with cost-saving measures and cut into professors' research time. Finally, some influential alumni may consider all these goals less important than having an outstanding football team, which brings the school national recognition.

Formal organizations have a particular type of administrative machinery designed to help them meet their goals. This administrative structure is known as bureaucratic organization or, more simply, bureaucracy.

## 4.5 BUREAUCRACY

A **bureaucracy** is a formal organizational structure that directs and coordinates the efforts of the people involved in various organizational tasks. It is simply a hierarchical arrangement of an organization's parts, based on the division of labor and authority (see Figure 4-2). A hierarchical structure is like a pyramid—the people at each level have authority over the larger number of people at the level below them. The authority resides not in a person but in the office, position, or status within the organization. In other words, the responsibilities and authority associated with a particular job in the hierarchy remain essentially the same, regardless of the person occupying the position. Merton (1968) defines bureaucracy as "a formal, rationally organized social structure involving clearly defined patterns of activity in which, ideally, every series of actions is functionally related to the purposes of the organization" (p. 195).

### 4.5a Bureaucracy as an Ideal Type and Its Functions

One of the pioneers of sociology, Max Weber (1864–1920), authored the classical work on bureaucracy. Weber dealt with bureaucracy as an **ideal type**, which is a model of a hypothetical pure form of an existing entity. In other words, he did not concern himself with describing a specific bureaucracy; rather, he examined a great many bureaucracies in an attempt to discover the general principles that govern how they operate. An ideal type, then, is not to be thought of as a perfect entity in the usual sense of the word ideal. As this chapter later shows, bureaucracies are often far from perfect. As Weber (1914–1947) suggests, bureaucracies typically have the following characteristics:

- *Division of Labor and Specialization* Each member or worker is trained for a specific job. Each member has carefully described responsibilities, and each job is designed to meet a specific need.
- *Hierarchy of Authority* Organizations are run by a chain of command—a hierarchy of bosses and workers who are, in turn, the bosses of other workers. All officials are accountable to those at a higher level for their own responsibilities and for those of subordinates (refer back to Figure 4-2).
- *Impersonality* Employees are expected to maintain integrity and to separate their personal lives from their professional lives. The office and the organization's written files are in a separate location from the employees' homes, and families and are not subject to their influence. The organization's money and equipment belong to the organization, not to individuals; its activity is separate from the activity of private life.
- *Qualifications* Organizations select personnel on the basis of merit, using standardized criteria such as civil service examinations or educational training rather than friendship or political or family connections.
- *Career Pattern* Employees are expected to devote themselves completely to the business of the organization and to recognize that people work their way to the top. As one moves up in the hierarchy, job security and

**Bureaucracy**

A hierarchical, formally organized structural arrangement of an organization based on the division of labor and authority

**Ideal type**

A model of the hypothetical, pure form of an existing entity salaries improve. Seniority is recognized, valued, and rewarded. Whether the organization is the U.S. Army, General Motors, or the Catholic Church, increasing time with the organization and adequate job performance are supposed to bring promotions, higher pay and status, and stronger tenure or job security.

- *Written Rules* The operation of the organization is governed by a consistent set of rules that define the responsibilities of various positions, assure the coordination of tasks, and encourage the uniform treatment of clients. Written rules are used rather than informal communication; the larger the organization, the more rules are used to cover almost every possible situation.

A hierarchical organization, division of labor, and the other attributes of the bureaucratic ideal type are essential to efficient functioning in a bureaucracy. As we all know, however, bureaucracies have their shortcomings. Most of us associate them with red tape, mountains of forms to complete, and endless lines. How and why do bureaucracies get so bogged down?

## 4.5b Dysfunctions of Bureaucracies

Robert Michels (1876–1936), a colleague of Weber, believed that, inevitably, formal organization would be dominated by a small self-serving group of individuals at the top. He coined the term "the **iron law of oligarchy**" in 1911, in reference to his theory. Michels argued that simple power in the hands of those at the top of the pyramid allowed them an opportunity to promote their own self-interests.

Weber focused on many of the positive accomplishments of bureaucracies: precision, coordination, reliability, efficiency, stability, and continuity. Merton (1968) was the most important writer on the dysfunctions of bureaucracy. He observed that people in bureaucracies tend to develop what Veblen called **trained incapacity**, which occurs when the demands of discipline, rigidity, conformity, and adherence to rules render people unable to perceive the end for which the rules were developed. In Merton's words, "Adherence to the rules, originally conceived as a means, becomes transformed into an end-in-itself" (p. 199). This condition is similar to *ritualism*, which is discussed in another chapter.

We have all had experiences in which an obsessive adherence to procedures and rules kept us from meeting goals. In corporations, for example, employees are often required to routinely send copies of memos, emails, and letters to people who do not look at them and perhaps would not know what the correspondence meant if they did. It would be much more efficient simply to stop sending them. Often, our training, habits, or traditional ways of behaving blind us to alternatives that might be far more effective than the ones to which we are accustomed.

A second dysfunction comes about when hiring and promotions are based on a rigid set of formal qualifications—5 years' experience or a college degree, for example—rather than skill or performance. In one instance, a woman with 10 years' experience in her company and an excellent work reputation was passed over for promotion to supervisor because her company's policy dictated that supervisors must have a college degree. There are also instances in which excellent college teachers are denied tenure because they do not have a sufficient number of publishing credits. In bureaucratic organizations, formal qualifications may supersede performance in hiring and promotion.

A third dysfunction of bureaucracy with which we are all familiar is the runaround. Who among us has not called an organization and had our call transferred to two or three other departments, only to be returned to the first person to whom we spoke, with the problem still unresolved? Recall that bureaucracies have rules defining the duties and responsibilities of various offices. The legal department handles legal matters, the personnel office handles recruitment, rank, and salary matters, and the

**Iron law of oligarchy**
The perspective that a formal organization would be dominated by a small self-serving group of people who achieve power and promote their own interests

**Trained incapacity**
The situation that exists when the demands of discipline, conformity, and adherence to rules render people unable to perceive the end for which the rules were developed

payroll department issues checks, withholds money for benefits, and pays taxes. Other departments handle other matters. Now, which one would you get in touch with about a lawsuit concerning the payment of salary? The difficulty is that actual problems do not always fit neatly into the compartments designed to handle them. If a problem does not clearly fall within a department's area of responsibility, or if it involves several departments, the runaround is likely to begin.

Understanding the dysfunctions of bureaucracy may help administrators, managers, and entrepreneurs assess whether the positive aspects of this form of organizational structure outweigh the negative. Bureaucracy as an organizational form is not for every situation. The mom-and-pop grocery store, for example, may attract large numbers of customers precisely because of its friendly, informal, "homey," nonbusiness-like atmosphere. Running that business according to bureaucratic principles would probably lead to its demise. Some professional and educational settings where efficiency and production are less important than high-quality interpersonal relationships are also better off without rigid bureaucratic procedures. The large-scale "student processing" that efficiently pushes students through a university system and hands them a diploma in 4 years would be dysfunctional in the small liberal arts college. The physician who boasts "family care in a caring way" would probably see a decline in business if she decided that seeing patients without appointments was an inefficient way to run her practice. In situations such as these, the manifest function of the organization might possibly be distorted—and failure might result—if the principles of bureaucracy are applied.



### thinking SOCIOLOGICALLY

1. Based upon what you have learned about bureaucracies in this chapter, describe how the dehumanization process takes place within an organization with which you are familiar. Consider how statuses and roles within the organization contribute to dehumanization.
2. Discuss how the university you attend is bureaucratic. Using your knowledge of social structure, groups, and organizations, discuss how the college would be different if it became less bureaucratic and more bureaucratic, respectively.

## 4.5c Voluntary Associations

**Voluntary associations** are organizations that people join because they share their goals and values and voluntarily choose to support them. People join many formal organizations because they are forced to or because they need the income, protection, or training that these organizations offer. Examples include schools, the armed services, insurance companies, and places of work. Voluntary associations, however, are joined out of personal interest, to participate in some social program, or as a channel for political action.

Voluntary associations are instances of associational or organizational groups, which were discussed earlier in this chapter. They typically involve awareness of kind, social interaction, and formal organization. Awareness of kind is central to our voluntary involvement because we share the interests and goals of the membership, whether the group is the League of Women Voters, Boy Scouts of America, National Rifle Association (NRA), National Association for the Advancement of Colored People (NAACP), the Baptist Church, or the American Sociological Association. We enjoy socially interacting with other members because of our common focus of attention and shared interests. Since these associations are formally organized, they have officers and bylaws or a constitution. Some associations are small and highly informal; others are large, formal, and bureaucratically organized, demanding dues and conformity to

**Voluntary associations**

An organization people join because they share the organization's goals and values and voluntarily choose to support them established procedures. Membership is voluntary rather than by ascription; members can leave if they become dissatisfied.

In studies covering several decades, sociologists have learned a good deal about voluntary associations. We know that they are class-limited, meaning that members in any given association usually come from similar socioeconomic levels. Bowling club members are unlikely to join golf clubs; members of a wealthy businessmen's club are unlikely to join the Ku Klux Klan. Churches are voluntary associations that cover the class and wealth spectrum, but those living at poverty level seldom attend the same church as the affluent. Although people of all ages and socioeconomic levels join voluntary associations, middle-aged people of high social status and education are the most frequent participants. Men are more likely to join than women, but American women are more likely to join associations than women in most other countries.

# CHAPTER 4 Wrapping it up

## Summary

1. Society is socially structured. It is composed of many parts, including social statuses, roles, groups, organizations, and institutions. Statuses are socially defined positions that individuals occupy. A combination of statuses held by a person is a *status set*. Statuses can be ascribed or achieved, but usually involve a combination of the two. Sometimes a particular status, *a master status*, takes priority over all the others.
2. All statuses have sets of expectations and behaviors associated with them. These are roles and role sets. What a role prescribes, the perception of it, and the behavior that is actually performed may all be very different. Commitment to the role, the flexibility it permits, and competing demands from other roles may clarify these differences.
3. Three difficulties can result from roles: *role ambiguity*, in which the expectations are not clear; *role strain*, in which contradictory demands or the ability to live up to the expectations of the role produces stress; and *role conflict*, in which inconsistent expectations are associated with the same role, or there are conflicting expectations between roles. However, roles are basic to social structure and social behavior, making them predictable, patterned, and organized.
4. Social groups are so fundamentally a part of our existence that it is difficult to imagine life without them. Most social groups involve interaction, a sense of belonging or membership, shared interests and values, and some type of structure.
5. Members of statistical and categorical groups, often formed for comparative and research purposes, share common characteristics but are not social groups, in that they do not interact with one another.
6. *Aggregates* are social collections of people who are in physical proximity to one another. They are loosely structured groups that are short-lived and involve little interaction. Members of associations and *organizational groups* interact, are aware of their similarity, and are organized to pursue a common goal.
7. *Primary groups* are small and informal and emphasize interpersonal cohesion and personal involvement. *Secondary groups* are less personal and intimate, and they are more goal-oriented and purposeful.
8. *In-groups* are those to which people feel they belong. The in-group shares a common allegiance and identity, tends to be ethnocentric, and stereotypes members of the *out-group*. In-group cohesion is intensified by out-group threats.
9. *Peer groups* are informal primary groups of people who share a similar status and usually are of similar age. *Reference groups* provide self-evaluation and direct aspirations. They are the groups we use to assess our own performance, even if we do not actually belong to them.
10. Groups are also differentiated by size. The addition of even a few people changes group interactions considerably; as size increases, there are generally changes in the division of labor, formality, leadership, communication, and cohesion.
11. Formal organizations are deliberately organized to achieve specific goals. They are particularly important in industrialized societies, in which many relationships are impersonal. Formal organizations are sources of authority and of continuity in our efforts to meet basic societal and personal goals, but conflict within and between organizations is common.
12. *Bureaucracy* is a type of administrative structure found in formal organizations. It is a hierarchical arrangement of the parts of an organization, based on a division of labor and authority. Roles in the hierarchy are based on position or office, not on individual characteristics. Bureaucracies operate in a location separate from the homes and families of their employees. They also operate according to objective rules, hire and promote people on the basis of merit, and encourage workers to rise in the hierarchy through hard work. They can

have a positive influence on efficiency, precision, coordination, stability, and continuity.

13. Bureaucracies have dysfunctions as well. Trained incapacity, the bureaucratic runaround, and impersonality appear to be negative characteristics of bureaucracies. The iron law of oligarchy refers to a small group of self-serving people, generally at the top of the bureaucratic pyramid, who promote their own interests.
14. *Voluntary associations* are organizations that people join because they share the goals and values of these organizations and choose to support them. Since membership is voluntary, members can resign if their interest wanes.

## Discussion Questions

1. What is meant by the statement, "Society is socially structured"?
2. Answer the question, "Who am I?" in terms of your status set. List several social expectations (roles) that are generally attributed to statuses within the set. From this, discuss the various role conflicts that are part of your life.
3. List some of your primary and secondary groups. Describe the ways you act in each of these. Compare the criterion by which you are judged by others in each of these groups.
4. Discuss some of the most important reference groups in your life. How do they affect how you think about things and about yourself, and how you act? Do you belong to any reference groups of which you are not a member? If so, explain.
5. Illustrate how group processes and outcomes or consequences are influenced by the size of the group.
6. In relation to social networks discuss the statement, "Who you know is as important as what you know."
7. Must bureaucracies be impersonal? Is it possible to have a bureaucracy that maintains close social relationships? Why or why not?
8. Discuss some problems that primary groups in an organization might encounter when faced with increasing bureaucratization.
9. How are statuses and roles in a group, organization, or community affected by bureaucratization?
10. Why do people join voluntary organizations?

CHAPTER 5

# Socialization and Social Interaction

## SYNOPSIS

Focal Point

## TRANSGENDER SOCIALIZATION AND IDENTITY: THE CASE OF JOHN/JOAN

Bruce Reimer (who later changed his name to David) was an identical twin boy born in August 1965. At around eight months of age, both boys were brought in to their doctor to be circumcised. Rather than use a scalpel, which was the more typical method for circumcision, the physician opted to use an electric cauterizing needle to remove Bruce's foreskin because Bruce happened to be brought to the operating room first. Because of complications with the procedure, Bruce suffered severe burns to his penis that resulted in dismemberment within a few day (Money & Tucker, 1975; Westheimer & Lopater, 2005).

Needless to say, the parents were devastated. Several months later—while they were still considering what course of action to take to help their child live a life in which he could normally fulfill his bodily functions and obtain satisfaction as an adult—their doctor referred them to Johns Hopkins University Medical Center. Concurrently, Dr. John Money, a psychologist who specialized in working with transsexual people (gender reassignments) and had a clinic at Johns Hopkins, was receiving a great deal of publicity. Money presented the Reimers with the option of reconstructing their son's genitals and his undergoing treatments that would ultimately make him biologically a female. Gender reassignment through genital reconstruction up until that time had been rare, although not unprecedented; and gender reconstruction for hermaphrodites (children born with ambiguous genitals) did exist as a viable medical alternative. Today, gender reconstruction of intersexes at birth is highly controversial as it is not clear with which gender the individual will identify as an adult. At the time, however, the Reimers' choice to begin transgender procedures did not seem unreasonable to them. Bruce was 22 months of age when he began the process. It is important to mention, however, that until that time he had been socialized as a boy during the period of life in which, arguably, some of the most profound gender imprints on our identity are formed.

On July 3, 1967, Bruce became Brenda; the Reimers were instructed to never discuss or doubt their decision to have their son undergo gender reconstruction. The transformation to a female was to be absolute and unequivocal. From that moment on, the Reimers raised their child as a girl. Not only did they socialize her as a girl, she also embarked on a series of hormonal treatments through early adolescence that would result in female physical characteristics, such as the development of breasts. In 1997, John Colapinto revealed through an article in *Rolling Stone Magazine* the truth about Brenda, who at age 14 had stopped living as a girl (prior to having the surgery that would have created an organ that simulated a vagina). "Brenda" eventually changed his name to David. The story became known as the "case of John/Joan."

As Colapinto discovered, "Brenda" had never fully embraced "her" identity as a female. She continuously tried to exhibit the same type of masculine behavior as her twin brother. Dr. Money, however, was insistent on maintaining a strict regime of feminine gender role socialization in order to achieve what he felt would be a complete gender transformation. Ultimately, when he was 14-years-old, Bruce's parents told him the truth about his past, and he began to try to live his life as a male.

Bruce eventually had a prosthetic device implanted to simulate a penis, changed his name to David, and married. His marriage lasted for 14 years. However, the trauma of his childhood continued to plague him as an adult, and he committed suicide in 2004.

The case of John/Joan is important because it demonstrates the interplay and complexity of biology and socialization on the development of gender identity.

# 5.1 WHAT IS SOCIALIZATION?

**Socialization**
The process of learning how to interact in society by learning the rules and expectations of society

**Socialization** is the lifelong process through which people are prepared to participate in society at every level: individual, interpersonal, group, organizational, and institutional. It shapes our identities and the skills, norms, values and beliefs that underlie our actions and interactions. This learning occurs in all interactions from the minute a baby is born. Individuals must learn about their culture, including the rules and expectations of the culture. In the United States, most people learn to speak the English language and to eat with a fork. They learn that cereal, bacon, and eggs are breakfast foods and that sandwiches are appropriate for lunch. They find out that some people do work that is defined as important and that those who do not or will not work are of less value. They discover that particular countries and people are friendly and others are hostile. Women learn to smile when they are tense and to cry at good news as a release of tension. Men learn that they should not cry, although some still do so at times.

It would be misleading and an oversimplification to suggest that socialization can be directly understood as resulting only from obvious social forces such as family, age, gender, peer groups, race/ethnicity, socioeconomic status, and others. Socialization includes the complex interplay of social, cultural, psychological, and biological processes and is a concept that has been undergoing change and refinement within the fields of sociology and psychology since it was first developed (Morawski & St. Martin, 2011).

*Socialization is a lifelong process that begins the moment a baby is born. It is believed that physically healthy children cannot develop normal social behavior without social interaction. (Shutterstock)*

Sociologists believe that even physically healthy children cannot develop normal social behavior without social interaction. The controversy over the extent to which behavior results from predetermined biological characteristics or from socialization is known as the **nature-nurture debate**. This debate has continued for centuries, but it has drawn more interest recently as a result of the new science of sociobiology.

## 5.1a Sociobiology and the Nature-Nurture Debate

**Sociobiology** is the study of the biological and genetic determinants of social behavior (Wilson, 1975). Sociobiologists are biologists by training, although some sociologists and other social scientists support their views. Sociobiologists believe that social behavior is determined by inborn genetic traits, which influence human behavior in much the same way that animals are influenced by their genetic inheritance. An example would be that sexual preference is determined genetically and that humans have a genetic tendency to have only one or a very few mates (Van den Berghe, 1979). Sociobiologists also believe, for example, that altruistic behavior (behavior performed to benefit others without regard for oneself) and warlike behavior are biologically based, although these and other behaviors may be modified by social experience.

Most sociologists criticize the sociobiological viewpoint on the grounds that behavior varies greatly from culture to culture. Sexual behavior, for example, whether with the same sex or the opposite sex, varies enormously. As for warlike behavior, it is completely absent in many societies. According to Hoffman (1985), a specialist in the study of socialization, geneticists do not pay enough attention to environmental and socialization factors in their studies. Thus, when they draw conclusions from their studies, they do not know what effects the environment or socialization might have had.

In addition to the doubts of sociologists, many physiologists believe that there is no genetic basis for human behavior. Biological drives or **instincts**, which are patterns of reflexes that occur in animals, are very powerful. Insects and birds perform many complex behaviors even when they have been reared in isolation. Honeybees perform complicated dances to show other bees where food is located, and birds build intricate nests in the same manner as others of their species, each without having had any environmental opportunities for learning. So far, no powerful, fixed drives or instincts have been discovered in human beings.

**Nature-nurture debate**
A longstanding debate over whether behavior results from predetermined biological characteristics or from socialization

**Sociobiology**
The study of the biological and genetic determinants of social behavior

**Instincts**
Biological or hereditary impulses, drives, or behaviors that require no learning or reasoning

Sexual behavior in human beings, long thought to be a biological drive, varies so much from society to society and from time to time that researchers are now convinced that it is greatly shaped by social learning. Lauer and Handel (1983), for example, report some of the variations. For instance, in the Victorian era, it was assumed that women did not enjoy sexual intercourse, and men were sometimes advised not to have intercourse more than twelve times per year. Today, women who were studied in an Irish community expressed no sexual desire and engaged in intercourse only as a duty. Men in the community avoided intercourse before hard work because they thought it sapped them of their energy. On the other hand, young men in some South Pacific cultures have intercourse several times a night. Appropriate sexual behavior, then, is learned in the context of a particular culture.

Researchers believe social learning shapes sexual behavior in humans. *(iStockphoto)*

There is a resurgence of interest among a growing faction of sociologists in the sociobiological approach. Arcaro and Kilgariff (2002), for example, argue that incorporating evolutionary psychology with traditional sociological perspectives is essential for developing a unified body of sociological theory. Sanderson (2001), a contemporary social theorist, feels that if sociologists ignore the importance of biology as an explanation of behavior, "they are going to look increasingly foolish both within the academy and to the larger educated public."

Money (1980), a physiologist and a psychologist, believes that the nature-nurture controversy is based on an illusion. He believes that environmental factors become part of our biology when we perceive them. When a piece of information enters our minds, it is translated into a biochemical form. Although we do not fully understand the workings of the brain, we do know both that the brain stores information permanently and that information in the brain can cause physiological changes in other parts of our bodies. Money contends that the information in our brains shapes our behavior and that distinctions between nature and nurture are irrelevant.

## 5.2 THE DEVELOPMENT OF A SELF

How do we know who we are? If asked to describe yourself, what would you say? Are you pretty, smart, skinny, witty, funny? Perhaps you see yourself as just the opposite—ugly, dumb, fat, dull, or boring. What factors contribute to the development of our identities? Do we care what others think about us? Scholars such as George Herbert Mead and Charles Horton Cooley contributed to the study of the importance of early socialization on the individual.

### 5.2a George Herbert Mead: Mind, Self, and Society

The students of George Herbert Mead were so impressed with his insights about human interaction that after his death they compiled his lectures and published a book, *Mind, Self and Society from the Standpoint of a Social Behaviorist* (1934). Mead demonstrated that the unique feature of the human mind is its capacity to use symbols, and he discussed how human development proceeds because of this ability. Through language and human interaction an individual develops a **self**. According to Mead, "The self is

**Self**
The sense of one's own identity as a person

something which has a development; it is not initially there, at birth, but arises in the process of social experience and activity, that is, develops in the given individual as a result of his relations to that process as a whole and to other individuals within that process" (1935, p. 135). Language is the key to the development of self. Words in a language have meaning; we use language symbols when we think or talk to ourselves, and when we talk to other people. When we see another person in the street, we do not simply react to the person instinctively. We interpret the situation by giving meaning to the other person's behavior. We think, "Is this someone I know, or a stranger? Do I want to know this person, ignore her, say hello to her?" If we say "hello" to the other person, we are using a symbol that means, "I wish to greet you in a friendly manner." The other person knows the meaning of the symbol. This is an example of **symbolic interaction**, the social process that occurs within and among individuals as a result of the internalization of meanings and the use of language.

Mead recognized how important it is for people to interact with others in the development of the self. When infants are born, they cannot differentiate among all the objects they see. The world appears as a kaleidoscope of color and movement. Very soon, however, they learn to distinguish important objects, such as the source of nourishment and the parent who brings it. Infants also eventually learn to differentiate themselves from their surroundings and from other persons. For example, as a father repeatedly brings a bottle to his daughter, she becomes aware that she is the object of her father's attention. She learns to differentiate herself from the crib and other objects. She learns that she is a separate object receiving both the bottle and her father's attention. Infants also develop expectations about their parents' behaviors and about their parents' roles. They expect their parents to bring the bottle.

## 5.2b Role-Taking: Significant Others and Generalized Others

Mead used the term **role-taking** to describe the process of figuring out how others will act. The ability to take a role is extremely important to children. In fact, **play** is a way of practicing role-taking. Children often play "house" or "school," taking the role of **significant others**—mother, father, or any other person important to them. By taking the roles of these significant others, children can better understand their own roles as children, students, sons, or daughters.

Mead believed that children develop role-taking skills during play and ultimately learn to take the role of others through the process. He identified three stages in which the self emerges through play, and he labeled them: preparatory, play and game. In the *preparatory stage*, children are only capable of imitating the people in their lives. They are not yet aware of their sense of self but are learning to become social through meaningful interaction with others. In Mead's second stage, the *play stage*, children begin to take the role of others significant in their lives. Children enjoy playing dress up and may pretend to be mother, father, fireman, teacher, etc. In the *game stage*, the child is older and is capable of understanding, simultaneously, not merely one individual but also the roles of several others. The child now has the ability to put himself in the place of others and act accordingly. Once the child can do this, Mead contends, he or she can "take the role of the generalized other."

*In the play stage, children may enjoy playing dress up and may pretend to be mother, father, etc. (Shutterstock)*

**Symbolic interaction theory**

The social theory stressing interactions between people and the social processes that occur within the individual that are made possible by language and internalized meanings

**Role-taking**

Assuming the roles of others and seeing the world from their perspective

**Play**

According to Mead, a way of practicing role-taking

**Significant others**

Important people in the lives of children, especially with regard to socialization

By practicing the roles of others in play, children learn to understand what others expect of them and how to behave to meet those expectations. As adults, when we take roles, we figure out what others are thinking and how others will act; then we can act accordingly. Often, however, we do not have the opportunity to play out the role of others, except in our imagination.

A child who responds differently to each person in his or her life would never develop a sense of self. In order to develop a sense of self, the child learns to see others not as individuals but as **generalized others**, the organized community or social group that provides reference for his own conduct. Mead used the example of a baseball game to illustrate the concept of generalized other. A child playing baseball develops generalized expectations of each position on the team: pitchers throw, fielders catch, batters hit and run, regardless of the individuals playing those positions. These generalized expectations become incorporated into the child's sense of self.

## 5.2c The "I" and the "Me"

Once a child has an idea of the generalized other, he or she can begin to develop a personality, an individual way of behaving. The child learns to meet the expectations of the group in some situations but may argue with the group on other occasions. The child interprets the situation and then decides how to act. That is what makes each person unique.

To analyze each person's unique ability to respond to the generalized other, Mead theoretically divided the person into two parts: The "**I**" and the "**me**." The *I* represents the acting person, as in "I attend class." The *I* is not self-conscious. When taking a test in class, the *I* concentrates on the test, not on the self.

The *me* represents the part of self that sees self as an object, the part that is concerned with society's expectations of self, such as, "Society expects me to go to class." It is the *me*, seeing self as an object, which says after class, "You really did great on the exam!" or after the party says, "You really made a fool of yourself!" The socially constructed *me* spends a good deal of time talking to the *I*.

We use the generalized other to shape our own personality throughout life. We may decide, for example, that attending class is a waste of time or that multiple-choice tests are unfair. We may choose to go along with the norms, or we may choose to argue against them. To do either, however, we must understand the expectations of the generalized other—the school, in this case. We develop our own **mind**, our own ability to think, based on the expectations of the generalized other.

Mead believed that the human mind is entirely social and develops through interaction. Although we are born with a brain, Mead argued, we do not learn to use our mind to think and develop ideas until we have learned the expectations of our society. We learn these expectations mostly through language, and then we use language to talk to ourselves and to develop our own ideas. We get ideas about the usefulness of class attendance and multiple-choice tests. We also get ideas about what we are like, what we want to become in the future, or the relative attractiveness of the persons sitting next to us. It is easy to understand that we would not think about class attendance if there were no classes to attend. It is not as obvious, but just as true, that the relative attractiveness of the persons sitting next to us is based on what we have learned from society about attractiveness. We have learned what color of hair and skin, what size of nose, and what height and weight are valued by society. Based on this, we establish our own definition of attractiveness in others and in ourselves.

**Generalized others**
The assumption that other people have similar attitudes, values, beliefs, and expectations, and therefore that it is unnecessary to know a specific individual in order to know how to behave toward that individual

**I**
The acting, unselfconscious person

**Me**
The part of the self that sees self as object, evaluates self, and is aware of society's expectations of self

**Mind**
The process of using a language and thinking

## APPLYING MEAD'S ROLE-TAKING

Although many of Mead's theories are useful in providing an understanding of how our self develops, understanding this concept is also important to our personal and professional relationships. For clinical sociologists, therapists, and other counselors who help people deal with problems, role-taking is an important *verstehen* technique. *Verstehen* is Max Weber's concept referring to a deep imagining of how things might be and feel for others. For example, a client undergoing drug counseling may explain his or her fears and feelings of inadequacy to the therapist; however, unless the therapist can see things from a drug user's point of view, the therapy might be cold and meaningless to the client.

Clinicians, counselors, and therapists may also ask their clients to engage in role-taking as part of their treatment. Marriage counselors sometimes help husbands and wives confront their marital problems by having them switch roles temporarily so that they can feel what it is like to be in the other's position. By having the husband take the role of wife and the wife take the role of husband, each spouse may learn to see himself or herself the way the other spouse does. Each spouse's role-taking might help in developing more sensitivity to the partner's needs.

In your career or occupation, engaging in role-taking can improve how you relate to, organize, and lead other people. As a teacher, you might find examples to which students can relate better if you can imagine how the students see the subject matter. For example, teachers sometimes show movies explaining serious topics; however, if a particular movie is old, the students may find the fashions dated and the movie quaint, thus missing the point of the movie. As a physician, you might develop a better "bedside manner" if you can put yourself in the place of the cancer patient you are treating. All of us find it difficult to understand the feelings, attitudes, and ideas of every person with whom we interact, so we find more efficient ways to deal with people. We develop a sense of self and a generalized other.

## 5.2d Charles Horton Cooley: The Looking-Glass Self

Charles Horton Cooley (1864–1929), like Mead, theorized that the idea of the self develops in a process that requires reference to other people, a process he called the **looking-glass self**. According to Cooley, the looking-glass self has three components: (1) how we think our behavior appears to others, (2) how we think others judge our behavior, and (3) how we feel about their judgments. We know that we exist—that we are beautiful or ugly, serious or funny, lively or dull, intelligent or stupid—through the way other people treat us. We never know exactly what other people think of us, of course; but we can imagine how we appear to them and how they evaluate our appearance. Ultimately, the looking-glass self concept is based on perception and effect—the perception we believe others have of us, and the effect those perceptions have on our self-image.

Our imagination about our own looking-glass self may or may not be accurate. If it is not accurate, we may think we are clumsy when other people think we move very gracefully. We may think we speak clearly when others think we mumble. We may think we are shy even when others admire our confidence. Whether our ideas about ourselves are accurate or not, we believe them; we often respond to these imagined evaluations with some feeling, such as pride, mortification, or humiliation.

Cooley noted that when we refer to ourselves, we are usually referring to our looking-glass self, not to our physical being—such as our heart, lungs, arms, and legs. We usually refer to our opinions, desires, ideas, or feelings (I think, I feel, I want); or we associate the idea of the self with roles (I am a student, an athlete, a friend). This sense of self exists in relation to other people. We compare and contrast ourselves with others; our own sense of uniqueness is based on that comparison. Even the language we use to refer to ourselves must be learned from other people.

In sum, both Mead and Cooley pointed out that the major difference between social theories of the self and psychological theories of the self is that social theories emphasize that society exists first and that the individual is shaped by society. Psychological

**Looking-glass self**
A process occurring in social interaction and having three components

theories emphasize individual development apart from social processes; that is, the individual develops and then responds to society based on preexisting tendencies to behave in particular ways. (See Jean Piaget, Sigmund Freud, Lawrence Kohlberg.)

## APPLYING COOLEY'S "LOOKING-GLASS SELF"

One common manifestation of Cooley's theory is the **self-fulfilling prophecy**, a concept developed by Robert Merton. A self-fulfilling prophecy is a prediction that causes us to act as if a particular definition of others, a situation, or ourselves were true—even if it is not true; and as a result, it becomes true because of our actions. The "self-fulfilling prophecy" concept is related to an idea known as "Thomas Theorem," stemming from the work of the sociologist W. I. Thomas. Thomas stated that "if [people] define situations as real, they are real in their consequences." This does not mean that events simply come into being because we will or imagine them. Rather, it means that people act in accordance with how they define situations, and through their actions certain events come about. A classic example of a self-fulfilling prophecy—and how defining a situation as real can lead to events that bring that definition to fruition—is a bank failure. Banks operate under the reasonable assumption that all the depositors will not want all of their money back at the same time. Banks do not merely keep our money in a vault; rather, they invest it so that they can pay us interest and also make a profit. However, if all the depositors at the First International Bank believe a rumor (or a prediction) that the bank does not have enough money to give back to them, they might all rush to get their money from the bank at the same time. The resultant bank failure would not be due to any economic or management problems, but due solely to a sociological, self-fulfilling prophecy.

We now look at the self-fulfilling prophecy and see how it relates to the looking-glass self. If we imagine that others think we are a particular kind of person (even if we are not), we may believe that their perceptions are true. As a result, we may act in a manner that results in our becoming the way that they perceive. Suppose, for example, that you imagine that others think you are a funny person. It does not matter whether they really think you are funny; what matters is that you imagine that they think you are funny. Because you believe that you are a funny person, you may make an extra effort to become funny by learning and telling new jokes, doing amusing things at parties, and generally cultivating your sense of humor. ("Because I am a funny person, I am the kind of person who knows a lot of good jokes, so I had better be prepared.")

The knowledge that the looking-glass self often becomes a self-fulfilling prophecy may be useful in a variety of ways. First, it might be applied in some occupational settings. How, for example, could this knowledge improve your effectiveness as a teacher? If you are aware that people see themselves as they think others (especially significant others) see them, you might try to be especially sensitive to how you react to students when they ask questions in class, when you speak to them in your office, or when you make comments on their papers. If students think that they are being put down or are perceived as unintelligent, they may prematurely give up on learning a subject. Conversely, if students develop positive views of themselves because they think you, as the teacher, see them as intuitive, creative, and interesting, they may strive to cultivate those qualities even further; and it may play an important part in their interaction with others. As a parent, as well as a teacher, the implications of the looking-glass self on adolescent self-approval are significant (Gamble & Yu, 2008).

**Self-fulfilling prophecy**
A prediction that comes true because people believe it and act as though it were true

## 5.2e Erving Goffman: The Presentation of Self

Throughout life, our socialization influences the way we interact with each other. Erving Goffman (1959) was interested in the process of interaction once a self has been developed. Every interaction, Goffman believed, begins with a **presentation of self**. The way we present ourselves gives other people cues about the type of interaction we expect. In formal situations, we usually greet friends with a handshake or a remark, whereas in informal situations, we may greet friends with a hug or a kiss. If we are with friends, we talk and laugh; but on a bus or in an elevator, we do not speak to strangers, and we keep a social distance even when space is crowded and we cannot keep physically distant. Psychologists refer to our manner of presentation as "body language." We give cues about ourselves in the way we present and use our bodies in interaction.

In an attempt to analyze how interaction takes place, Goffman (1959) compared social interaction to a drama on stage—a comparison known as the **dramaturgical approach**. Whenever we interact, we prepare ourselves backstage and then present ourselves as if onstage, according to what we have learned in the socialization process. Goffman believed that all behavior, even the most routine, is neither instinctual nor habitual—it is a presentation. Most Americans prepare to present themselves by showering, washing their hair, and using deodorant—in our society, cleanliness and a lack of odor are important. Complexions must be smooth—so men shave, women put on makeup, and adolescents use cosmetics to cover up acne. Suitable clothing is selected so that we can present ourselves formally in formal situations and casually in casual situations. A formal setting such as a church, a more informal setting such as a classroom, and a casual setting such as a basketball arena—all require very different presentations. In some settings, one can race for a front-row seat, talk loudly, wave to friends, and eat and drink. In other settings, these behaviors would be quite inappropriate.

In illustrating the dramaturgical approach, Goffman described a character, called "Preedy," as he presented himself on a beach on the Riviera. Preedy very consciously tried to make an impression on the people around him. It was his first day on vacation, and he knew no one. He wanted to meet some people, but he did not want to appear too lonely or too eager; so he presented himself as perfectly content in his solitary state.

The following excerpt from Goffman (1959) describes Preedy's behavior:

> If by chance a ball was thrown his way, he looked surprised; then let a smile of amusement lighten his face (Kindly Preedy), looked round dazed to see that there were people on the beach, tossed it back with a smile to himself and not a smile at the people, and then resumed carelessly his nonchalant survey of space.
>
> But it was time to institute a little parade, the parade of the Ideal Preedy. By devious handlings he gave any who wanted to look a chance to see the title

**Presentation of self**
The way we present ourselves to others and how our presentation influences others

**Dramaturgical approach**
An approach to the study of interaction in which interaction is compared to a drama on stage; the importance of setting and presentation of self are emphasized

*Erving Goffman believed every interaction, such as the greeting of friends, begins with a presentation of self.* *(Shutterstock / iStockphoto)*

of his book—a Spanish translation of *Homer*, classic thus, but not daring, cosmopolitan, too—and then gathered together his beach-wrap and bag into a neat sand-resistant pile (Methodical and Sensible Preedy), rose slowly to stretch at ease his huge frame (Big-Cat Preedy), and tossed aside his sandals (Carefree Preedy, after all).

The marriage of Preedy and the sea! There were alternative rituals. The first involved the stroll that turns into a run and a dive straight into the water, thereafter smoothing into a strong splashless crawl towards the horizon. But of course not really on the horizon. Quite suddenly he would turn on to his back and thrash great white splashes with his legs, somehow thus showing that he could have swum further had he wanted to, and then would stand up a quarter out of water for all to see who it was.

The alternative course was simpler, it avoided the cold-water shock and it avoided the risk of appearing too high-spirited. The point was to appear to be so used to the sea, the Mediterranean, and this particular beach, that one might as well be in the sea as out of it. It involved a slow stroll down and into the edge of the water—not even noticing his toes were wet, land and water all the same to him—with his eyes up at the sky gravely surveying portents, invisible to others, of the weather (Local Fisherman Preedy). (p. 5)

Notice how much Preedy could say about himself without uttering a word. Whether anyone enters the water in as calculated a manner as Preedy is questionable, but whoever watches someone like Preedy will form an opinion of him from his presentation. As Henricks (2012) notes with regard to Goffman's explanation, there "is the tension between the understandings that other people and groups have of us (our identity) and how we understand that same person (our self)" (p. 66). The example of Preedy illustrates this tension and the intentionality of our actions in trying to maintain a certain image to others and to ourselves. Henricks further notes, "Goffman's work ... is mostly about the ways in which people create and sustain focused lines of action. As actors in situations, we want to see ourselves—and be seen by others—in certain agreed upon ways" (p. 67).

The dramaturgical approach helps us understand that how one appears is at least as important as what one actually does or says—and often, it is more important.

## 5.2f Maintaining the Self

Once we have presented ourselves in a particular role and have begun to interact, we must maintain our presentation. In class, a student cannot begin to shake hands with fellow students, wander around the room, or write on the blackboard. It would not only disrupt the class but would also spoil the presentation of that student, who would be considered disruptive, strange, or worse. If students or others want to maintain the definitions others have of them, they must maintain a performance in accord with the definition.

Sometimes we inadvertently do not maintain our performance, so we try to **account** for or to excuse our behavior (Scott & Lyman, 1968; Simon & Manstead, 1983). If we are late and want to avoid giving the impression that we are always late, we make excuses: "I am usually very prompt, but my car ran out of gas." "I thought the meeting was at eight o'clock, not seven o'clock."

**Account**
An effort at maintaining the self by explaining the reasons for or facts surrounding the behavior

**Disclaimers**
An aspect of maintaining our presentation of self in which we deny behavior that contradicts how we wish to be viewed

We also try to maintain our presentations by using **disclaimers**—that is, disclaiming a role even while we are acting in that role. "I usually don't drink, but this punch is so good" disclaims the role of drinker. Examples of phrases that tell the audience that the self is not what it appears to be are "I'm not prejudiced, but ..." followed by a racist remark, or "I'm no expert, but ..." followed by a remark only an expert could make.

Often, the audience accepts a person's accounts or disclaimers, and the interaction proceeds smoothly. Sometimes, however, the drama does not work out so well. We may present ourselves in the role of someone who knows how to act in social situations but not live up to those claims. We may fall down a flight of stairs as we make our grand entrance. We may stand up at a meeting to give a report, claiming to be an expert, but our trembling hands and factual errors will not support these claims. The speaker and those in the audience may attempt to ignore the errors; but at some point, the speaker may get too flustered to continue the pretense of living up to the role or may become embarrassed and laugh, cry, faint, or blush. When a group can no longer support the claims made by an individual, the whole group may become embarrassed or angry (Goffman, 1967).

Implicit in interactions is the assumption that presentations will be maintained. Each person agrees to maintain the self and to support the presentations of others. If people's presentations are not supported by the people themselves or by others, this may be followed by an emotional response. For example, in some situations, I may become embarrassed; if my presentation is ridiculed, I may get angry. In another situation, if someone seems to fill your image of the ideal romantic love, you may fall in love with that individual. If the person then is cruel, unfaithful, or behaves in some other way that tarnishes your image of him or her, you may grow angry and eventually fall out of love.

Not only do we learn behavior in the process of socialization and interaction, we also learn appropriate feelings about others and ourselves. We learn self-esteem by understanding how others evaluate us; we learn when to be embarrassed, when to be angry, and both when to fall in love and with what type of person. If we are angry with someone who deserves our respect, we feel guilty about our feelings. If we love someone whom others define as entirely inappropriate, we become confused. Again, we have expectations about maintaining these performances of self—both our own and others'—and we respond emotionally when these expectations are not met. This happens in all of our roles and in whatever groups in which we act.

**BVT *Lab***

Flashcards are available for this chapter at www.BVTLab.com

**thinking** SOCIOLOGICALLY

1. What is required for babies to develop into full human beings? What are the components that make us human?
2. Think of times you have seen your looking-glass self inaccurately. How has this shaped your actions?
3. Think of a time when your presentation of self was not maintained. How did you respond emotionally?

# 5.3 MAJOR AGENTS OF SOCIALIZATION

Socialization is found in all interaction, but the most influential interaction occurs in particular groups referred to as "agencies of socialization." Among the most important are family, schools, peer groups, and the mass media.

## 5.3a Family

The family is considered the primary agency of socialization. It is within the family that most children encounter the first socializing influence, and this influence affects them for the rest of their lives. For example, families give children their geographical location, as Easterners or Westerners, and their urban or rural background. The family also determines the child's social class, race, religious background, and ethnic group. Each of these factors can have a profound influence on children. They may learn to speak a particular dialect, to prefer particular foods, and to pursue some types of leisure activities.

Families also teach children values that they will hold throughout life. Children frequently adopt their parents' attitudes about the importance of education, work, patriotism, and religion. Even a child's sense of self-worth is determined, at least in part, by the child's parents.

One of the values instilled in the children of most American families concerns the worth of the unique individual. We are taught that we possess a set of talents, personality characteristics, and strengths and weaknesses peculiar to ourselves—and that we are responsible for developing these traits. Our parents tell us that we can be all that we want to be, as long as we work hard and want something badly enough. Ultimately, we are responsible for our successes and failures. This view of the value of the individual is not found in all cultures, however. Many people who emigrated from southern Europe, for example, believe that one's primary responsibility is to the family, rather than to oneself. The son of a European farm family, for example, is expected to be loyal and obedient to the family, to work for its benefit, and eventually, to take over the management of the farm when the parents are old. In our culture, however, staying with the family is often regarded as a sign of weakness or of lack of ambition on the part of young adults; when adult children return home to live, both they and their parents often feel uncomfortable (Clemens & Axelsen, 1989; Schnaiberg & Goldenberg, 1989). Some cultures, such as China's, place an emphasis on inculcating both individualist and collectivist values; this indicates that modern and traditional values are part of family socialization of children (Lu, 2009).

*The family is considered the primary agency of socialization. It can determine social class, religious belief, language, and how the family members view themselves. This influence will affect them for the rest of their lives.* iStockphoto)

## 5.3b Schools

In some societies, socialization takes place almost entirely within the family; but in highly technical societies, children are also socialized by the educational system. Schools in the United States teach more than reading, writing, arithmetic, and other basic academic skills. They also teach students to develop themselves: to test their achievements through competition, to self-discipline, to cooperate with others, and to obey rules, all of which are necessary if a youngster is to achieve success in a society dominated by large organizations.

Schools teach sets of expectations about the work children will do when they mature. The children begin by learning about the work roles of community helpers such as firefighters and doctors; later, they learn about occupations more formally. They take aptitude tests to discover their unique talents; with the help of teachers and guidance counselors, they set occupational goals.

Schools also teach citizenship in countless ways. They encourage children to take pride in their communities; to feel patriotic about their nation; to learn about their country's geography, history, and national holidays; to study government, explain the role of good citizens, urge their parents to vote, and pledge allegiance to the U.S. flag; to become informed about community and school leaders; and to respect school property. At times, what a child is taught in school may conflict with the values taught within the home. For example, a child who is taught to believe that religion is central to his or her life will find it difficult to understand the separation of church and state in public education. Schools can provide the first occasion when children are challenged to question their family's beliefs.

Most school administrators and teachers reinforce our cultural emphasis on the uniqueness of individuals. Thus, they try to identify the unique talents of students through comparison and competition with other students and then attempt to develop these talents so that they will become useful to the larger society. Japanese schools, operating in a less individualistic society, assume that all students will be able to meet whatever standards the schools set.

## 5.3c Peer Groups

Young people spend considerable time in school, and their **peer group** of people their own age is an important influence on their socialization. Peer-group socialization has been found to have an impact on so many values, attitudes and behaviors concerning things such as dating, sexuality, ethnic/racial interactions, delinquency, risk taking, overall adjustment, and many other issues of central importance in the lives of young people (Poteat, 2007; Rivas-Drake & et al., 2009; Ellis & Zarbatany, 2007; Higins & et al., 2010; Criss & et al., 2009). Teenagers' most intimate relationships are often those they have with their peers, rather than those with parents or siblings; they influence one another greatly. In fact, some young people create their own unique subcultures. Coleman and his colleagues (1974), who refer to these groups simply as "cultures," list as examples the culture of athletic groups in high schools, the college campus culture, the drug culture, motorcycle culture, the culture of surfers, and religious cultures. In part because teenagers are often unsure of themselves, they may prize the sense of belonging that they get from their subculture, although the pressures to conform to group expectations can be quite severe.

*Peer groups are an important influence on young people's socialization. (iStockphoto)*

Peer groups can be a strong influence on a young person's life. A sense of belonging is important to school-aged children and can influence how they react toward themselves. Clothing styles, music, and dating habit preferences are beginning to form during the teen years; those teens who fail to conform to their group's behavior may be seen as "outsiders," which in turn can lead to feelings of rejection.

## 5.3d Religion

All societies have some form of religion, and how one practices or doesn't practice religion is dependent upon the individual's social interaction with others. Religion can be an extremely powerful influence on a person's social self. Children whose parents encouraged them to attend church early in life are more likely to rely on faith and prayer throughout much of their adult life, as well. Children learn the language of their religion and ideas about what is and is not acceptable behavior, particularly regarding morality.

## 5.3e The Mass Media

The American **mass media**—television, popular magazines, and social network websites and other forms of communication intended for a large audience—play a major role in teaching Americans to consume goods. They devise programs that attract a particular audience and then sell products to that audience. American children spend more than 53 hours a week watching TV or using video games, cellphones, and computers (Kaiser Family Foundation, 2010). While most advertising takes place on TV, almost all of these other portable devices are vehicles for some form of advertising. Thus, younger children urge their parents to buy the cereals, snack foods, and toys that they see advertised. An average of 200 junk food ads are shown in 4 hours of children's Saturday morning cartoon programming (Herr, 2007). Teenagers listen to their favorite

**Peer group**
An informal primary group of people who share a similar or equal status and who are usually of roughly the same age

**Mass media**
Forms of communication—such as television, popular magazines, and radio—intended for a large audience

music on the radio or the Internet and buy the products advertised there. At the very least, the mass media teach people what products are available. In addition, by age 13, the average American has seen 200,000 acts of violence on television, 40,000 of these being murders (Herr, 2007).

The mass media also teach values and needs. An advertisement may teach you, for example, that thoughtful, sensitive children send their parents Hallmark cards on special occasions or just to convey, "I love you." You may learn that "people on the go," like you, drink Pepsi "uh-huh;" or you may learn that intelligent, frequent travelers should not leave home without their American Express cards.

The mass media also teach viewers something about what life is like, although the view presented may be an idealized version. For example, people learn from television comedy shows that the American family is very happy. Everyday problems of living—such as dented automobiles, lackluster sex lives, occupational failures, trouble with juggling two careers and childcare, or a shortage of money—are treated as abnormalities on television, or at least as items for comedy or curiosity. Viewers may develop unrealistic expectations about the quality of their own lives. If we can understand that our conception of what is normal is one that we have been socialized to accept by the media, perhaps we would not have such unrealistic expectations of our spouses, our children, and ourselves. With more realistic expectations, perhaps we could become more tolerant of ourselves and of others.

### thinking SOCIOLOGICALLY

1. How have your parents influenced your development of a self? What are some of the values and beliefs taught to you that remain an important component of your life today?
2. Discuss the importance of education on the development of a self. How did education either enhance or contradict what was taught to you by your parents?

# 5.4 SOCIALIZATION OF GENDER ROLES

Socialization plays an especially important part in determining what children believe to be acceptable behaviors for members of their own sex. Even though the situation has begun to change, our environment bombards both men and women with subtle and not so subtle suggestions that some types of behavior are acceptable for women and other types of behavior are acceptable for men. People who diverge significantly from expected gender roles often meet with resistance from individuals and from the social system. The same sources of socialization that influence people in other areas of their lives—home, school, the mass media, and interactions with others—also affect the socialization of gender roles.

**Instrumental role**

A role that emphasizes accomplishment of tasks—such as earning a living to provide food and shelter—and is traditionally associated more with men than with women

**Expressive role**

A role that emphasizes warmth and understanding rather than action or leadership—and is traditionally associated more with women than with men

## 5.4a Infant and Childhood Experiences

Gender-role socialization in our society begins at birth. When a baby is born, he or she is wrapped in a blue or a pink blanket; from that moment on, parents respond to the infant on the basis of its gender (Bem & Bem, D., 1976). Boys tend to be socialized to grow up to play **instrumental roles**, performing tasks that lead to goals they have set for themselves. Girls tend to be socialized to be more verbal, more expressive, more emotional, and when they grow up, more interested in interpersonal relationships—characteristics that have been labeled the **expressive role** by sociologists (Zelditch, 1955).

Research has shown that infants are viewed differently depending on these future role expectations. Infant boys are often described as big, athletic, strong, or alert; however, infant girls are usually described as tiny, dainty, sweet, pretty, delicate, inattentive, or weak. Parents tend to notice the dainty fingernails of the baby girl, even though those of the baby boy look identical. Boy and girl infants are also treated differently. Boys are handled roughly and tossed around playfully; girls are held more, cuddled, talked to, and treated as if they were very fragile. Even the tone of voice used is different. Boys are talked to in loud voices, whereas girls are spoken to gently. Parents also give their children different surroundings, toys, and games, based on gender. However, traditional gender roles do not necessarily have to be the outcome of childhood socialization. A study of NCAA Division 1 female athletes revealed that parental influence was a significant influence in both the athletes' desire to participate in and their success in sports. This form of socialization included role modeling on the part of parents, the opportunities and the expectations provided by parents, and the various ways of leading females to interpret sports as a meaningful and realistic pursuit (Dixon & et al., 2008).

Other research shows that infants respond differently to early variations in treatment (Pridham, Becker, & Brown, 2000). Children who are touched and talked to cling to their mothers and talk to them more, regardless of their gender; because girls are held and talked to more than boys, they tend to reciprocate with this kind of behavior (Goldberg & Lewis, 1969; Moss, 1967).

Parents teach their boys and girls different techniques for solving problems. When doing a puzzle, for example, parents give girls specific advice, but they try to help boys learn problem-solving techniques (Frankel & Rollins, 1983). Toys selected for boys are either constructive (pieces are added to build or change the toy, such as railroads) or aggressive (such as guns), while toys for girls are more nurturant or attractive, such as dolls (Lorber, 2003).

**BVT** ***Lab***

Visit www.BVTLab.com to explore the student resources available for this chapter.

Gender socialization also results in how children's emotions develop. Parents tend to encourage the expression of sadness more for girls than for boys. Gender socialization is not only affected by the gender of the children but also by the parents as well. Fathers tend to inhibit the expression of sadness in their children more than do mothers (Cassano & Perry-Parrish, 2007).

Today, parents are beginning to have different role expectations for their daughters. More and more parents realize that their daughters will have to compete in the work force. In Sweden, where the government has long been active in discouraging differential treatment of boys and girls, Lamb et al. (1982) found that parents treated their infant sons and daughters alike. However, the two parents differed from one another. They treated their children the way that they had been treated as children. Mothers smiled, cooed, and cuddled their infants more than fathers did; fathers were more playful. These children experienced both types of socialization. As would be expected, the educational and occupational aspirations of boys and girls differ according to whether they are raised by traditional or feminist parents (Blakemore & Hill, 2008).

## 5.4b Gender-Role Socialization in Schools

Children continue to learn gender-role behavior in nursery school (Ornstein, 1994). Classroom observations of 15 nursery schools showed that the teachers (all women) treated boys and girls differently. Teachers responded three times more often to disruptive behavior by boys than by girls. The boys usually got a loud public reprimand, whereas the girls were given a quiet rebuke that others could not hear. Disruptive behavior is often an attempt to gain attention; because the boys received the attention they were seeking, they continued to behave disruptively. When the teacher paid less attention to the boys, this behavior diminished. Teachers were also more willing to help the boys find something to do. The girls who were not doing anything were ignored and received attention only when they were literally clinging to the teacher's skirts.

The teachers spent more time teaching boys. In one instance, the teacher showed boys how to use a stapler; but when a girl did not know how to use it, the teacher took the materials, stapled them herself, and handed them back to the girl. Both problem-solving and analytical abilities are related to active participation, but girls were not given the opportunity to try things as often as boys were. Boys are also praised more for good work and are encouraged to keep trying. Girls are praised for appearance but left in the dark about their academic performance (Sadker & Sadker, 1994).

Teachers also evaluate boys differently from girls. If the preschool child is a boy, the teacher evaluates him no differently whether he is compliant or not. However, compliance is a significant factor in evaluating girls. Less compliant girls are viewed as less intellectually competent (Gold, Crombie, & Noble, 1987).

Schools teach gender roles in other ways as well. Most elementary school teachers are women, but principals and superintendents are most often men. Women teachers are more likely to teach young children; yet as subject matter becomes more sophisticated and specialized, more men are found teaching. Children receive subtle messages about the capability of men and women as they observe the jobs they hold. School counselors also encourage children to follow expected gender roles. Career counselors will define girls who want to enter masculine occupations or boys who want to enter traditionally feminine occupations as in need of more extensive guidance. Efforts are sometimes made to steer them into more "appropriate" occupations.

## 5.4c Gender-Role Socialization in Peer Groups

Children play mainly in same-sex groups, and this contributes to their socialization. Macoby (1998) notes that children segregate themselves into same-sex playgroups whenever they have a choice of playmates. This tendency begins at the preschool ages and increases until the children reach puberty. Furthermore, this tendency to segregate is stronger when adults do not interfere—in other words, children are more segregated in the cafeteria than they are in the classroom.

Although it is not clear why children segregate themselves in playgroups, at least part of the explanation is that children in mixed groups will be teased for liking or loving a member of the opposite sex (Macoby, 1998). Children who have ongoing friendships with members of the opposite sex often go into hiding about these friendships by age 7. They will not acknowledge each other in public and only play together in the privacy of their own homes. To the extent that children segregate themselves to avoid teasing, they are responding to the behavior of older members of the society. They are being socialized to play in same-sex groups.

The result of playing in same-sex groups is that girls are socialized to act like girls and boys are socialized to act like boys (Greenwald, Hedges, & Laine, 1996). Macoby (1998) found that the children did not form groups based on like interests. Whether the girls were passive or aggressive, they played with other girls; the same was true of boys. Once in the playgroup, however, girls learn to act in socially binding ways while boys act competitively. In conversation, for example, girls acknowledge each other, agree with each other, and pause frequently to give others a chance to speak. Boys more often use commands, interrupt, boast, heckle each other, tell jokes, and engage in name-calling. When engaged in taking turns, boys use physical means to get a turn, such as pushing and shoving, while girls use conversational means, persuading others to let them have a turn. As they learn how to get along with others of the same sex, girls especially are less interested in playing with those of the opposite sex because their socially binding norms are less influential and powerful than the competitive norms of boys (Maccoby, 1988); when girls do play with boys, girls become passive.

Psychologist Carol Gilligan argues that as young girls progress through early socialization, they end up "hitting the wall." In other words, all the negative messages they have received from society about their image, abilities, worth, etc., come flooding back to influence their perceptions of themselves. The gender socialization that begins at birth and continues throughout life has consistently emphasized a male dominated society where power is less likely to be in the hands of females. When girls fail to conform to the standards set for them by society, the blame will fall on their shoulders. They will be viewed as "tomboy," "oddball," "manly," or some other term situated on their unwillingness to act the way they are supposed to. Gilligan suggests that gender related stereotypes are harmful to the socialization of girls. For example, the words of former Harvard President Lawrence Summers in 2005 drew enormous criticism when he suggested at an academic conference on economics that innate differences between men and women might be one reason fewer women succeed in science and math careers. Summers also suggested that discrimination and socialization are not what creates the low number of female professors in science and engineering. He argued that "the real issue is the overall size of the pool," not the size of the pool that was "held down by discrimination."

**thinking** SOCIOLOGICALLY

**How do the theories of socialization presented in this chapter help to explain Gilligan's notion that as young girls progress through early socialization they end up "hitting the wall"?**

## 5.4d Mass Media and Socialization of Gender Roles

From childhood on, Americans spend thousands of hours watching television, which has a strong tendency to portray gender-role stereotypes. In children's television programming, male characters are more often portrayed as aggressive, constructive, and helpful, whereas female characters are more often passive and defer to males. Many children and adults watch adult programs, especially the situation comedies. *I Love Lucy*, which was originally produced in the 1950s and is still seen in reruns, featured Lucille Ball as a consistently inept housewife who had to be rescued by her harassed but tolerant husband. Every episode revolved around Lucy's getting into some sort of trouble. Current situation comedies are a little subtler.

*Television programs, such as I Love Lucy, tend to portray gender-role stereotypes. Lucille Ball's character was portrayed as an inept housewife who had to be rescued by her harassed but tolerant husband. (AP Wide World Photo)*

Advertising on television and in the press also tends to stereotype both men and women or to portray roles that are impossible to fulfill. Career women are portrayed as superwomen who combine a successful career, motherhood, and a terrific marriage with cooking a gourmet meal for a small dinner party of 10. At the other extreme, women are portrayed as beautiful, bewildered homemakers, even when they work outside the home. These ads show the woman arriving home from work to cook the family meal or do the family wash, but apparently overwhelmed by indecision about what to serve or how to get shirt collars really clean. A male voice heard in the background tells the woman how to solve her problem. Men in ads are stereotyped as forceful, athletic, involved in business of some kind, or at least actively watching a ball game, and always knowing exactly what they want or which beer has more gusto.

News reporting has generally followed the stereotypes established by society when discussing issues related to women. During the 2008 presidential election the focus was on women, particularly with Hillary Clinton as a presidential candidate, Sarah Palin as a vice-presidential candidate, and Nancy Pelosi as the Speaker of the House. For example, the New York journalist Amanda Fortini wrote, "In the grand Passion play that was this election, both Clinton and Palin came to represent—and, at times, reinforce—two of the most pernicious stereotypes that are applied to women: the bitch and the ditz." Another example came from Contessa Brewer, a female anchor for *MSNBC Live*, who wondered on air if Pelosi's "personal feelings [were] getting in the way of effective leadership"—a problem she suggested would not surface in "men-run leadership posts"—and whether men were "more capable of taking personality clashes" (Millican, 2006).

## APPLYING GENDER-ROLE SOCIALIZATION

Understanding that gender-role stereotypes are a product of socialization is important for you in your work life and in your personal life. One important problem in the workplace that results from gender-role stereotypes is discrimination against women. This has taken a variety of forms, including unfair hiring practices, lower wages, sexual harassment, and many others.

Some companies hire consultants to develop training programs to help employees at all levels understand the sources of these gender-related tensions in the workplace. Employees can be made aware of how stereotypes are generated through media and other agents of socialization. Also, exercises may be used to help men and women employees understand each other's work experience a little better. One way is to have the men and women engage in role-reversal role-playing. This can help them to see situations from the other gender's point of view and to become more sensitive to each other's needs and attitudes. The key theme that runs through the training is to get beyond the gender stereotypes that people have learned in their previous socialization.

*As was seen in the treatment of Sarah Palin (above) and Hillary Clinton during the 2008 presidential election, news reporting generally follows established gender stereotypes.* *(AP Wide World Photo)*

Stereotypes generated through gender-role socialization may also create problems in your intimate relationships. In her book *Intimate Strangers*, Lillian Rubin (1983) discusses how our **gender identity** as males or females often prevents people of the opposite sex (husbands and wives, boyfriends and girlfriends, or just close friends) from developing true intimacy. That is, as a result of gender-role socialization, males often learn to see themselves in terms of stereotypical instrumental traits (aggressive, unemotional, dominant, career-oriented, and so forth), and females often learn to see themselves in terms of stereotypical expressive traits (passive, emotional, subordinate, relationship-oriented, and so forth). Think of how these perceptions might interfere with the ability of men and women to develop close emotional bonds. Since you see yourself as a "real man," for example, you may find it difficult to express your emotions openly, to cry in front of others, or to be sensitive, even if these feelings tend to emerge. Because you see yourself as a "real woman," you may find it difficult or confusing to have an equal say in your relationship, to take charge of a situation, or to be aggressive, even though you may want to. The realization that gender roles and gender identities are learned through socialization and are not an inherent part of our biological makeup can help both sexes to overcome many barriers to intimacy and to relate to each other as whole individuals.

**Gender identity**
The social construction of boys and girls, men and women, as opposed to their biological characteristics

**thinking** SOCIOLOGICALLY

**In the discussion of how the news media portrays female candidates, both journalists were themselves female. Explain why women are likely to criticize other women and to reinforce gender stereotypes.**

# 5.5 SOCIALIZATION IN ADULTHOOD

The knowledge we acquire as children shapes the meanings we give to ourselves and to the world, and it can continue to influence us for the rest of our lives. We never stop learning new things, however; every day, we have new experiences, learn new information, and add the meanings of these new facts to what we already know. Adult socialization occurs when we learn new roles that are expected from us as we get older. Although new knowledge may be different from knowledge acquired as children, the same agencies of socialization are at work.

## 5.5a College and Marriage

Like children, adults are socialized by their families. Adult socialization also occurs in schools. Colleges teach adults of all ages, and the move from home to college can be a period of intense socialization. College freshmen must adapt to their new independence from the family and make their own decisions about health, food, sleep, class attendance, study habits, exercise, and social relationships. They must learn to live in crowded situations and to compete with peers. Some avoid these decisions by going along with the crowd. Others drop the values they learned in the family and adopt a new set of values, whereas some continue to maintain family values in the new setting. Each choice entails some socialization.



Single people must be socialized when they marry in order to live intimately with their spouses and to share living arrangements. Each person is socialized toward marriage based on their own set of experiences and social interactions while growing up. Once married, a young couple must decide how to define their marriage based on their own expectations rather than those of others.

## 5.5b Parenthood

When a couple has children, they learn the role of parent and will probably rely on the knowledge of childcare that they acquired from their own parents. Because the two parents were themselves brought up by different sets of parents, they will have learned different child-rearing techniques and therefore will have to socialize each other to reach an agreement about childcare practices. As the children grow up, the parents must be socialized to allow their children to become independent after years of dependency. All of this learning is a part of adult socialization.

Children are often very active socializers of their parents. As infants, they let their parents know when they need attention. Beginning at about 2 years of age, they become aware of themselves, learn to say "no," and begin to let their parents know when they need some independence. This process of demanding both attention and independence continues as long as the children are at home. It can result in serious conflicts in some youths, particularly those who rebel, fight, take drugs, or run away from home. The socialization of parents can be quite dramatic, but it is often successful. A questionnaire given to mothers and fathers of college students (Peters, 1985) found that the parents had learned different attitudes and behaviors about sports, leisure, minority groups, drug use, and sexuality from their children.

## 5.5c Career

Another type of adult socialization is occupational training, which teaches the attitudes and values—as well as the skills—associated with an occupation. Acquiring a new job involves taking on new statuses and roles. A new employee in an office has to learn how to conform to the expectations of the other workers and to the business's written and unwritten rules. During this socialization, the employee will discover the answers to many questions: Are men and women expected to wear suits, or is less formal clothing acceptable? Do employees address one another by their first names? Is rigid adherence to established procedures expected? Are some department heads more accommodating than others?

## 5.5d Resocialization

Major adaptations to new situations in adulthood may sometimes require **resocialization**. The changes people undergo during this period are much more pervasive than the gradual adaptations characteristic of regular socialization. Resocialization usually follows a major break in a person's customary life; this break requires that the person adopt an entirely new set of meanings to understand his or her new life. Divorce, retirement, or the death of a loved one usually involves the process of resocialization. Retirement from work is sometimes an easy process of socialization to a new situation, but it often requires a great deal of resocialization. Retired people often lose at least part of their income, so they may have to adapt to a new standard of living. With the loss of work, new sources of self-esteem may have to be developed; society may help in this process by providing education on financial management, health, and housing. Employers may also provide counseling services and support groups for retired persons, especially when they want employees to retire.

Besides loss of income and self-esteem, retirement creates another resocialization problem. Most roles involve social expectations and provide rewards for meeting those expectations. However, there are few social expectations associated with retirement other than the loss of a previous role; as a result, the satisfactory performance of the retirement role goes unrecognized. To compound the problem, the retired person's spouse often dies during this period, so he or she must relinquish the family role, as well as the work role. Nonetheless, if the retired person has enough money to buy nice clothes, enjoy hobbies, and afford travel for social events or volunteer work, then he or she can create a new role that is rewarding.

**Mortification of self** (Goffman, 1961), the most dramatic type of resocialization, occurs in such institutions as the armed forces, prisons, and mental hospitals. People entering these institutions are totally stripped of their old selves. Physically, they are required to strip, shower, and don institutional clothing. All personal possessions are taken away; they must leave behind family, friends, and work roles. They must live in a new environment under a new set of rules and adopt a new role as a military person, prisoner, or mental patient. Their previous learning must be completely redefined.

Whether dealing with socialization or with resocialization, the human mind is very complex. People learn varied sets of meaning during their lives, and they interpret each situation on the basis of their own biography and their own definition of the situation. How a person presents the self and maintains interactions depends on his or her unique interpretation of self, others, and the situation. It is this ability to interpret that makes socialization and social interaction such a varied, interesting, and challenging area of study.

**Resocialization**

Socialization to a new role or position in life that requires a dramatic shift in the attitudes, values, behaviors, and expectations learned in the past

**Mortification of self**

Stripping the self of all the characteristics of a past identity, including clothing, personal possessions, friends, roles and routines, and so on

# CHAPTER 5 Wrapping it up

## Summary

1. Socialization is the process of learning how to interact in society. Infants must interact in order to survive; as they interact, they learn about society.
2. Sociobiologists believe that inborn genetic traits direct human behavior just as they direct the behavior of animals. They contend that sexual, altruistic, and warlike behaviors occur in humans because we are predisposed to them in our genetic makeup. Most biologists and social scientists, however, sidestep the nature-nurture debate by believing that people's behavior is determined by their biological capacity to learn socially.
3. Human beings are unique because they learn a symbol system—language. Through linguistic interaction, we develop a self—an idea of who we are.
4. Mead used the term role-taking to describe the process of figuring out how others think and perceive us. According to Mead, children take the role of only one other person at a time at first. Children practice role-taking in play and learn to generalize in team games. The I acts, but the me sees the self as an object. The interplay between the two allows the self to act freely while aware of social reactions.
5. Charles Horton Cooley used the term looking-glass self to describe how people learn about themselves; he argued that our identities are heavily influenced by our perceptions of how others view us. We see ourselves not as we are, and not as others see us, but as we think others see us.
6. Goffman compared interaction to a drama on stage. We present ourselves as we want other people to define us. Once we have presented ourselves, everyone involved in the interaction is expected to maintain that presentation. We justify our discrepant behavior by making excuses or disclaimers. If we cannot maintain our presentations, we will respond to our failure with emotion, often embarrassment or anger.
7. Some of the important agencies of socialization are the family, schools, peer groups, and mass media.
8. From birth, males and females are socialized differently. Men are expected to be instrumental, active, and task-oriented, whereas women are expected to be expressive, nurturing, and people-oriented.
9. Resocialization may be necessary when a person's life changes dramatically and abruptly, such as when he or she goes to prison or retires.

## Discussion Questions

1. How could the ideas of Mead and Cooley be used to discuss your own gender-role socialization?
2. Using Cooley's looking-glass self concept, discuss how your perception of how others see you influences the way you think about yourself. What effect does this have on you?
3. Discuss things you do in college that you believe are important because your peers tell you they are important. Are these messages from your peers making you a better student?
4. Discuss things you do in college that you believe are important because the mass media tell you they are important. Are these messages from the mass media making you a better student?
5. Imagine that you are putting on a skit about getting ready to go to class (or put on such a skit, if possible). What impression are you going to make on professors? On classmates?
6. How does your backstage preparation for class differ from your performance onstage?
7. Think back to your most recent casual conversation, perhaps at lunch. What disclaimers were used in the course of this conversation?
8. Use Goffman's ideas about social interaction to develop an explanation of socialization.

# Deviance and Social Control

## SYNOPSIS

### What Is Deviance?
- Positive Functions of Deviance
- Dysfunctions of Deviance

### Deviance and Social Control
- Positive Internal Controls of Deviance
- Informal and Formal External Controls of Deviance

### The Relative Nature of Deviance
- Variation by Time
- Variation by Place
- Variation by Situation
- Variation by Social Status

### Theories Explaining Deviance
- Psychological Theories of Deviance

### Sociological Theories Explaining Deviance
- The Structural Functionalist Perspective
- Conflict Theory
- The Symbolic Interactionist Perspective
- Labeling Theory

### Social Consequences of Deviance
- Deviance and Crime
- Types of Crime
- Measuring Crime in the United States
- Criminal Justice System
- The Future of the Criminal Justice System

Focal Point

# PRESCRIPTION DRUG ABUSE

What is drug abuse? Every United States president since Richard Nixon has had the "war on drugs" as a priority. In the past 40 years, the war on drugs has cost the U.S. over $1 trillion and hundreds of thousands of lives (CBSNews, 2013). Combating drug abuse remains one of the United States' most important domestic and foreign policy issues.

President George W. Bush's anti-drug campaign focused on a law-enforcement model that attacked the "supply-side" of the illegal drug industry—traffickers, smugglers and users (Katel, 2006). President Obama's anti-drug strategy shifted from the "supply-side" approach to a policy that treated illegal drug use as a public health issue, putting more resources into prevention and treatment (Hernanel, 2010).

Regardless of the various tactics used, there are still many public misconceptions about the drug abuse problem. One misconception is that the word "drugs" refers only to illegal drugs such as marijuana, cocaine (and derivatives such as "crack"), methamphetamine (and derivatives such as MDMA and ecstasy), phencylidine (PCP), and LSD and other hallucinogens (Coleman & Cressey, 1990). However, alcohol and tobacco are also drugs, and they can be more dangerous than illegal drugs and are readily accepted in many social circles. The Institute of Medicine reported in 2007 that tobacco kills more people in the U.S. annually than AIDS, alcohol, cocaine, heroin, homicides, suicides, car accidents and fires combined (Oral Cancer Foundation, 2011).

One of the most problematic drug problems today is prescription (legal) drug abuse. While we hear news regularly about celebrities who have died or have suffered from abusing prescription drugs, celebrities are not the only ones who suffer from medication abuse. In 2005, more people ages 45 to 54 died from prescription drug overdoses than in car crashes (CQ Researcher, 2009). Yet, many people still believe that prescription drugs are safer than illegal drugs. This misconception is an important part of the drug abuse problem today.

Rates of death from overdoses (accidental or intentional) from prescription opioids (such as Vicodin, Oxycontin and other sedatives) are 4 to 5 times more than during the heroin epidemic of the 1970s (Clemmit, 2009). The use of legitimate painkillers and stimulants (such as Ritalin and Adderall) to treat ADHD (attention deficit hyperactivity) has increased significantly in the last few decades; with this increase in prescriptions and availability has come an increase in abuse. Prescription drug overdoses are now more common than deaths from heroin and cocaine combined. Deaths from prescription opioids increased 150% in the U.S. between 1999 and 2004.

All this raises the question of who and what should be the focus of the "war on drugs." Recently, the Drug Enforcement Administration has been focusing on pharmacies as possible perpetrators (albeit, unknowingly) of drug abuse. In 2012, one major supplier of OxyContin and Percocet cut off its supply to pharmacies after the supplier was accused by the DEA of ignoring signs that pharmacies in Florida were dispensing the drugs in such a way that they might be feeding "street demand" for these narcotics (Meier, 2012). This type of crackdown on drugs is a very different approach than cracking down on illegal dealers and raises questions about the direction of drug policies in the United States. Should the federal Drug Enforcement Administration enact tighter controls? Does the pharmaceutical industry bear any responsibility, and do they profit excessively? Do physicians prescribe drugs too freely? Should there be more of a focus on combating the availability of drugs on the Internet? Should drug education be re-designed to focus on

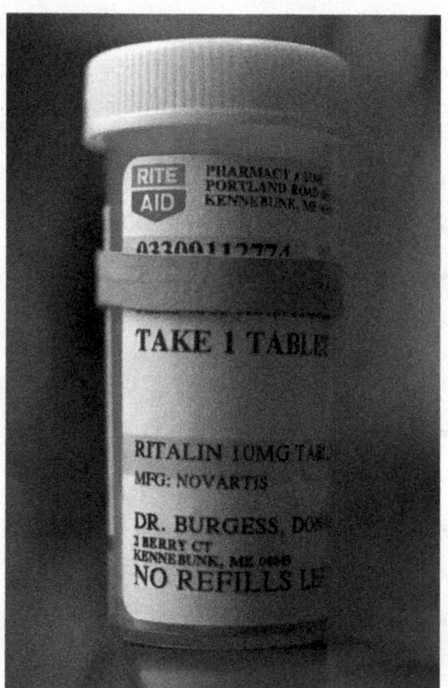


*The use of painkillers and stimulants (such as Ritalin and Adderall) to treat ADHD (attention deficit hyperactivity) has increased in use significantly in the last few decades.* (AP Wide World Photo)

prescription drugs rather than on "street" drugs? Have the social expectations for achievement and success from parents and schools led to an increase in drug use to combat feelings of inadequacy or to the use of performance-enhancing drugs? These are only questions, not blame.

Sociology does not focus on individual blame to understand social problems; rather, it explores the structural and cultural factors that create social problems. For example, while it does not deny that some people may be more or less biologically or psychologically prone to drug abuse, it is more concerned with understanding the social nature of the drug world and the wider social environment, and the ways in which they can affect people's tendencies toward drug use. The issue of prescription drug use illustrates how sociological theories of deviance can be used to reconceptualize social problems in ways that might help solve them.

## 6.1 WHAT IS DEVIANCE?

Deviance is universal because people everywhere violate social norms. It exists in all societies, wherever people interact and live in groups. Deviance means different things to different people. The definition we use influences our explanations of its causes and our attempts to control it. Does deviance reside in the individual? Is it a particular type of act or behavior? Is it defined socially? Are some groups of people immune from being labeled deviants? Our answers to questions such as these will influence how we analyze deviance and whether we ultimately understand it.

We define **deviance** as variation from a set of norms or shared social expectations and deviants as the people who violate these shared expectations. Deviance involves a social audience that defines particular people and behaviors as going beyond the tolerance limits of social norms. The opposite of deviance is conformity, when people follow the norms of their social group or society. Social norms, rules, and expectations about appropriate and inappropriate behavior exist in all societies.

All societies permit variations in the behavior demanded by the norms. Where variations are possible, people will test their range; some will inevitably exceed the boundaries of permissible and approved behavior.

### 6.1a Positive Functions of Deviance

While deviance may be viewed negatively by society at times, it may have positive effects, as well. Deviance is part of the nature of all social systems and is traditionally regarded as evidence of social disorganization. However, many deviant subcultures—such as gangs, organized crime, prostitution, or police corruption found in highly organized societies—may be highly organized themselves. As early as 1894, Durkheim pointed out that deviations should be regarded as a normal part of a society (Kelly, 1979). It appears that deviance performs various social functions.

Deviance helps to *define the limits of social tolerance*. Indicating the extent to which norms can be violated without provoking a reaction helps to clarify the boundaries of social norms and the limits of behavioral diversity. Methods of social control—such as arrests, psychiatric counseling, criminal trials, and social ostracism—help to define these limits. Arrests and trials indicate to the public the seriousness of some deviations and the extent to which violations of norms are tolerated. For many years, bullying was tolerated as a typical behavior of school children, particularly boys; however, with the current attention given to school violence (both in the U.S. and other countries), most schools today have implemented "bullying" policies (Farrington & Ttofi, 2009; Hilton, Angela-Cole, & Wakita, 2010). Police may tolerate a person driving a couple of miles

**Deviance**
Variation from a set of norms or shared social expectations

over the speed limit; but if that person is in a school zone, he will likely be stopped and ticketed. By observing societal reactions to deviance, members learn the limits of acceptable variation from norms.

Deviance can *increase the solidarity and integration of a group*. Such a label can unite the people who share it. Most people find emotional support and a sense of community among others who share their values and behavior patterns. If the group is considered deviant by society, members of the group tend to defend and protect one another and derive their identities from their group. By the same token, highly integrated groups may form in an attempt to defeat or eliminate deviants because having a common enemy tends to unite group members.

Deviance can serve as a *"safety valve" for social discontent*. When people desire things that the social norms do not permit them to have, they may become frustrated and angry, attacking norms or even attempting to destroy the social system. Some types of deviance permit people to escape from conventional norms and rid themselves of frustration without disrupting the social system as a whole. Cheating on paying income tax may be an outlet for frustration with government spending on wasteful projects or with being underpaid. The use of illegal drugs may be a safety valve against job frustrations or an unhappy marriage. Cheating on income tax and drug use involve risk to individuals, but may prevent expressions of frustration more injurious to society. Some deviances tend indirectly to support such basic institutions as marriage, the economy, and the government by funneling off anger and discontent.

*Bullying was tolerated for many years as a typical behavior of school children. Today most schools have implemented a "bullying" policy. (Shutterstock)*

Deviance can *indicate defects or inadequacies in the existing social organization*. High rates of some kinds of deviance may expose problems in the social order. Large numbers of parking violations may indicate that there are not enough parking spaces. Outbreaks of violence in prison serve as a warning that the system is inadequate. Activities such as freedom marches by blacks in the South or the Occupy Wall Street demonstrations were organized acts of defiance (and deviance) intended to force leaders and the public to address perceived problems in the social system.

Deviance can *set in motion steps that lead to social change*. Such change can involve modifications to the existing structure, modifications of behavior, or changes in the definitions of deviance. Until the early 1960s, a black person who tried to sit in the front of a bus in Alabama was regarded as deviant. Following bus boycotts, court cases, and rulings against segregation, this behavior is no longer considered deviant. As social norms change, so do their definitions; folkways and mores may be modified as a consequence of deviant acts.

## 6.1b Dysfunctions of Deviance

Some consequences of deviance are dysfunctional. Deviances can disrupt, destabilize, or even lead to the complete breakdown of a social system. Given the range of tolerance of norm violations, isolated instances of deviance generally have little effect on the stability of systems. Widespread, long-term, and more extreme norm violations can impair the functioning of groups or of entire systems.

Deviance can *disrupt the social order*. Violations of norms can disturb the status quo, make social life unpredictable, and create tension and conflict. Teachers who refuse to teach, parents who ignore their children, or workers who fail to perform their appointed tasks can keep the system from functioning smoothly. The effect of an alcoholic father on a family system is a good example. The family's income may decrease, the wife may have to assume full responsibility for raising the children, and the children may be ashamed to bring friends home. Deviance is, thus, often dysfunctional because it disrupts the order and predictability of life.

Deviance can *disrupt the will of others to conform*. If norm violations are unpunished or if members of society refuse to obey established rules, the desire to conform is decreased. Studying for an exam may seem pointless if you know that other students are going to cheat. Obeying the speed limit can be frustrating if other drivers blow their horns to get you out of the way so that they can speed by. To work hard when others are lazy, to be honest when others are dishonest, or to obey the rules when others ignore them—the effort can seem pointless. When deviance and conformity are not differentiated, the act's deviant definition disappears. If they receive the same response or reward, what is the motivation to conform? Conformity to a given norm, rule, or law makes sense only if (1) others conform as well, (2) those who conform are differentiated from those who do not in some way, and/or (3) norm violators receive some type of punishment.

Deviance can *destroy trust*. Social life is based in part on the assumption that other people are honest and trustworthy. When interpersonal trust decreases, people become more dependent on the legal system to define, interpret, support, and enforce the law. If all car dealers (or car buyers) were honest, written contracts would not be necessary; a few judges and lawyers would be out of work. In this sense, deviance is functional for the legal system, but it is dysfunctional to the society as a whole. Widespread deviance destroys our confidence and trust in others, just as it disrupts the will to conform.

**BVT*Lab***

Flashcards are available for this chapter at www.BVTLab.com

Deviance can *divert resources* into social rehabilitation and control efforts—resources which otherwise could be used elsewhere. It may be functional in that it provides thousands of jobs for those who rehabilitate and control criminals, drug addicts, the mentally ill, and others; however, it is dysfunctional in that the money and other resources used to deal with deviance cannot be used for other constructive and productive purposes. Criminal activities alone cost billions of dollars every year. Most would agree that these funds could be used more profitably elsewhere.

Clearly, deviance is neither all good nor all bad. Some of its consequences lead to the stability and maintenance of the system while others tend to disrupt it.

## 6.2 DEVIANCE AND SOCIAL CONTROL

The fact that deviance is universal and sometimes has positive social functions does not eliminate the need to control it. If societies are to survive, they must have ways of manipulating people into conforming to social norms. The influences can be internal or external, negative or positive, and formal or informal. The norms of society are maintained both by encouraging conformity and by discouraging deviance.

Conformity to social norms is generally explained in terms of two social control processes: (1) **Internal means of control** occur when members conform to the norms because they believe they should, even when other members of the group are not present. (2) **External means of control** are the responses of others to a member's behavior. Others in the group will utilize pressures or sanctions to attempt to control an individual's behavior. The two types of control tend to operate interactively.

Groups will typically rely on sanctions to control the behaviors of members. **Sanctions** are rewards and punishments used to encourage proper behavior or to discourage deviant conduct. **Positive sanctions** are actions that encourage individuals to continue a behavior while **negative sanctions**, such as a frown, are utilized to stop a behavior from being repeated. In addition, the type of sanction used can be either formal or informal. Formal sanctions generally occur in a public setting, whereas informal sanctions are spontaneous acts used by other group members to control behaviors.

**Internal means of control**
Learned patterns of control that exist in the minds of individuals and make them want to conform to social norms

**External means of control**
Pressures or sanctions that are applied to members of society by others

**Sanctions**
Rewards and punishments that are used to encourage proper behavior

**Positive sanctions**
Actions that encourage individuals to continue a behavior

**Negative sanctions**
Actions that discourage individuals from a particular behavior

## 6.2a Positive Internal Controls of Deviance

Internal controls are those that exist within the particular individual's moral and social codes of behavior. They include a wide range of factors: positive self-image, self-control, ego strength, high frustration tolerance, and a sense of social responsibility, among others. The workings of internal controls can be explained, in part, by socialization theories. These theories explain how we internalize norms, learn what others expect of us, and develop a desire to conform to those expectations. Some types of deviance, such as criminality and mental illness, are widely believed to be caused by inadequate socialization, especially in the years of early childhood.

Most social control is directly related to a person's *social self*—our definitions of who we are in relation to the society in which we live. Internal motivations to conform result not because people fear being caught or fear punishment but because people have been socialized to see themselves in a certain way and to believe that stealing, cheating, murder, and some other behaviors are wrong. Again, the looking-glass self and the self-fulfilling prophecy are relevant here, and both could be used in personal and professional relationships. The manager of a large department store, for example, might have a problem with employee theft of goods in the store. Instead of threats of punishment, the manager might try to get the employees to see themselves as part of a team working together toward a common goal. College teachers who have a problem with students not doing their reading assignments might treat the students as if they were mature, responsible individuals and commend their positive actions. It is true that rewards or punishments might work at times. However, when people act *only* out of fear of punishment or desire for a reward, and the reward or punishment is the only reason for conforming to the desired behavior, people may no longer conform if the reward or punishment is removed.

Robert Burck, the "Naked Cowboy" performs in New York City. Although some may call his behavior deviant, the positive sanctions he receives from passersby encourage him to continue. (AP Wide World Photo)

Parents might use the knowledge that people tend to act in a manner consistent with their view of themselves in a positive way to influence and socialize children. Instead of trying to control their behavior with rewards or punishments, parents might try to instill a sense of high self-esteem and self-respect in their children through the way they act toward them. If children are constantly ridiculed and put down, they may come to have a low self-esteem and low self-respect; thus, the children may act accordingly. On the other hand, if children are often praised or corrected in a more positive way, their positive self-images may motivate them to adopt more positive social values and to act in accordance with these values.

Feelings about right and wrong are sometimes referred to as "conscience." The saying, "Let your conscience be your guide" assumes that you have internalized some notions about deviant and nondeviant behavior. For most people, the conscience develops as a direct result of socialization experiences in early childhood and later in life. Social institutions, such as the family and religion, significantly aid in the internalization of social norms. Once social norms are internalized, deviations produce feelings of guilt, remorse, or conflict. The relatively high prevalence of conformity in comparison to deviance is largely due to internal controls.

## 6.2b Informal and Formal External Controls of Deviance

External controls are those that come from outside an individual. They can be either informal or formal. **Informal external controls** involve peers, friends, parents, or the other people with whom we associate regularly; these people apply pressure to encourage us to obey the rules and conform to social expectations. The same techniques can be used to encourage conformity to deviant norms.

Informal social controls may be used to control the behaviors of persons within our racial, ethnic, family, or peer group. For example, why are some ethnic groups more prone to problems with alcoholism than others, or more likely to be involved in athletics? Glassner and Berg (1980) found that American Jews avoid alcohol problems through protective social processes such as childhood socialization, adult relationships, and avoidance techniques. These same techniques could be used in African American communities to promote athletics over gangs, drugs, or other deviant behaviors. **Formal external controls**, the systems created by society specifically to control deviance, are probably the least influential. Courts, police officers, and prisons are formal external controls. Unlike internal controls and informal external controls, formal controls are supposed to be impersonal and just. In actuality, however, the legal system tends to favor some groups of people, just as conflict theory suggests. Even in prisons, guards tend to overlook rule violations by some prisoners and to enforce the rules with others. The discretionary power of police officers, prosecutors, judges, and other officials in arresting, prosecuting, and convicting people is often used arbitrarily. It may be highly dependent on factors other than deviance per se. Age, race, sex, social status, known prior deviations, and other factors—all have been shown to affect the nature and outcome of formal control mechanisms.

# 6.3 THE RELATIVE NATURE OF DEVIANCE

Cultural relativism is the assumption that behaviors, ideas, and products can be understood or evaluated only within the context of the culture and society of which they are a part. In the same way, a **relativistic view** suggests that deviance can be interpreted only in the sociocultural context in which it happens. Is a person who is seven feet tall a deviant in the context of professional basketball? Is a person without a bathing suit a deviant at a nudist beach? Is taking opiate drugs to treat excruciating pain deviant? Is killing deviant in the context of war? Context influences all of these determinations.

If deviance is relative rather than absolute, an act that is deviant in one context may not be deviant in another. A behavior considered "sick" in one society could be thought of as healthy in a different society. An act that might be statistically deviant in one culture might not be in another. Thus, as is generally true of cultural relativism, acts that are defined as deviant in some places are not defined as such everywhere. By the same token, however, the fact that an act is defined as nondeviant in one situation does not mean that it is nondeviant everywhere. Deviance does not consist merely of acts or behaviors but also of the group responses, definitions, and meanings attached to behaviors; we can expect, therefore, that definitions of deviance will vary with differing circumstances. Some of the most important variations that affect these definitions concern time, place, situation, and social status.

## 6.3a Variation by Time

An act considered deviant in one time period might be considered nondeviant in another. Cigarette smoking, for example, has a long history of changing normative definitions.

**Informal external controls**
Positive and negative controls—such as smiling, frowning, and high-fives—used to influence behavior

**Formal external controls**
Generally occur in a public setting such as a courtroom

**Relativistic view**
The view that deviance can be interpreted only in the sociocultural context in which it occurs

Nuehring and Markle (1974) note that in the United States, between 1895 and 1921, 14 states completely banned cigarette smoking, and all other states except Texas passed laws regulating the sale of cigarettes to minors. In the early years of this century, stop-smoking clinics were opened in several cities; antismoking campaigns were widespread. Following World War I, however, cigarette sales increased and public attitudes toward smoking changed. Through the mass media, the tobacco industry appealed to women, weight-watchers, and even to health seekers. States began to realize that tobacco could be a rich source of revenue, and by 1927, the 14 states that had banned cigarettes had repealed their laws. By the end of World War II, smoking had become acceptable; and in many contexts, it was considered to be socially desirable.

In the 1950s, scientists found that smoking could cause a variety of diseases, including lung cancer and heart disease. In 1964, the surgeon general published a landmark report on smoking and health; soon thereafter, some states began passing anticigarette legislation again. Laws were passed requiring a health warning on cigarette packages, and in 1973, the National Association of Broadcasters agreed to phase out cigarette advertising on television (Markle & Troyer, 1979). Another surgeon general's report in 1986 crystallized and pushed this concern to a new level: smoking not only harms the health of those who choose to smoke, but it is also hazardous to those who must breathe residual smoke while in physical proximity of someone who is smoking.

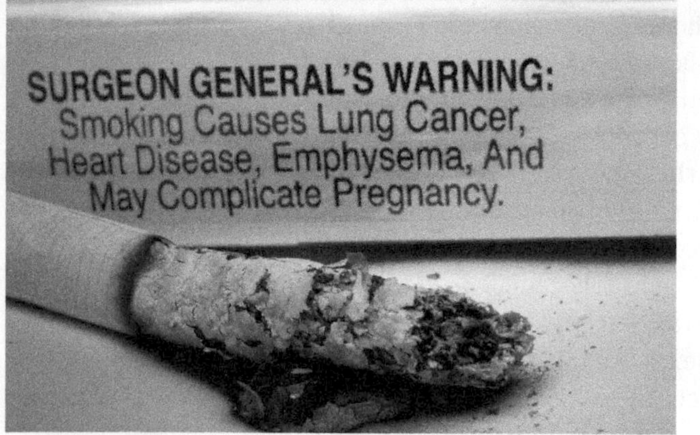


*An act that is considered nondeviant in one time period—such as cigarette smoking, which was acceptable during the middle part of the last century—might be considered deviant in another. (iStockphoto)*

The result was that by the 1990s, airlines, restaurants, and other public places either prohibited smoking totally or designated segregated sections for smokers and nonsmokers. By the beginning of 2009, 23 of the 50 states, plus Washington, DC, had banned smoking in most public places, including restaurants and bars. Some states have banned smoking within 1,000 feet of schools and other areas, such as recreational facilities, where children would likely be without adult supervision. All of these actions suggest that smoking is increasingly being considered a deviant behavior. Many other examples could be given to illustrate how behaviors defined as deviant change over time, such as the use of intoxicating products (see the Volstead Act), various other psychoactive drugs, appropriate bathing attire, nonmarital sexual behavior, and so forth.

## 6.3b Variation by Place

Behaviors viewed as deviant in one location, society, or culture may be considered nondeviant in others. In most African cultures, having more than one wife is a sign of wealth, prestige, and high status. In the United States, however, having more than one wife at a time is a punishable offense. Topless bathing is common on certain public beaches in Southern Europe, but is defined as immoral, criminal, or delinquent in American society. Bullfighting in Spain and Mexico and cockfighting in the Philippines are festive, legal gambling activities that produce income; however, they are forbidden in the United States. On the other hand, American dating practices, divorce rates, crime rates, and the widespread acceptance and practice of capital punishment are considered shocking by much of both the Western and non-Western world. For example, the United States remains the leader, in comparison to other countries, in incarceration rates (Walmsley, 2009).

Figure 6-2 provides data on the incarceration of women in six countries, including the United States. Note that the U.S. is double that of the country with the next largest number, and more women are incarcerated in the U.S. than all the other countries listed on the chart, combined.

**Figure 6-1** World Prison Population List

- More than 10.1 million people are held in penal institutions throughout the world, mostly as pretrial detainees/remand prisoners or as sentenced prisoners. Almost half of these are in the United States (2.29m), Russia (0.81m) or China (1.65m sentenced prisoners). In addition more than 650,000 are in 'detention centres' in China; if these are included the overall Chinese total is over 2.3 million and the world total more than 10.75 million.
- The United States has the highest prison population rate in the world, 743 per 100,000 of the national population, followed by Rwanda (c. 595), Russia (568), Georgia (547), U.S. Virgin Islands (539), Seychelles (507), St. Kitts & Nevis (495), British Virgin Islands (468), Belize (439), Dominica (431), Bermuda (428), Grenada (423), and Curacao (422).
- More than half of the other countries and territories (54%) have rates below 150 per 100,000.
- The world population at mid-2010 was estimated at 6.9 billion (United Nations); if set against the world prison population of 10.1 million this would produce a world prison population rate of 146 per 100,000 (156 per 100,000 if set against a world prison population of 10.75 million).
- Prison population rates vary considerably between different regions of the world, and between different parts of the same continent. For example:
  - in Africa the median rate for western African countries is 47.5 whereas for southern African countries it is 219;
  - in the Americas the median rate for South American countries is 175 whereas for Caribbean countries it is 357.5;
  - in Asia the median rate for south central Asian countries (mainly the Indian sub-continent) is 42 whereas for eastern Asian countries it is 155.5;
  - in Europe the median rate for western European countries is 96 whereas for the countries spanning Europe and Asia (e.g. Russia & Turkey) it is 228.
  - in Oceania (including Australia and New Zealand) the median rate is 135.
- Prison populations are growing on all five continents. Updated information on countries included in previous editions of the World Prison Population List shows that prison populations have risen in 78% of countries (in 71% of countries in Africa, 82% in the Americas, 80% in Asia, 74% in Europe, and 80% in Oceania).

Adapted from "World Prison Population List" by Roy Walmsley, International Centre for Prison Studies. Retrieved from http://www.idcr.org.uk/wp-content/uploads/2010/09/WPPL-9-22.pdf

There are variations in definitions of deviance within cultures as well as among them. Take, for example, the smoking issue, used in illustrating variation of deviance over time. Compared to the United States, countries in Africa are very lenient toward the use of tobacco among their youth. There are only 5 countries, out of 46 in the region,

**Figure 6-2** Comparative Rates of Incarcerated Women

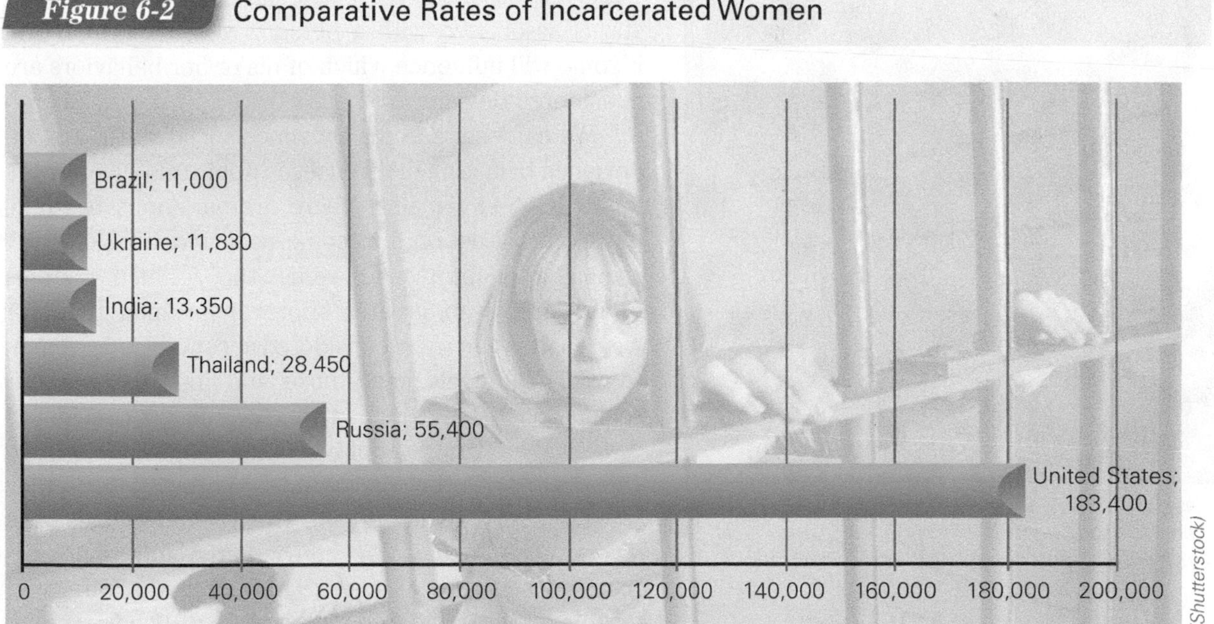


SOURCE: Christopher Hartney (2009). U.S. Rates of Incarceration: A Global Perspective. Oakland, CA: National Council on Crime and Delinquency. Available online at www.nccdglobal.org

which have advertisement bans on tobacco. In addition, no country in Africa requires age verification at the time of tobacco sales.

## 6.3c Variation by Situation

Behavior that is defined as deviant in one situation may not be in another, even in the same time period and geographical area. A man who dresses in women's clothes to act in a play would be considered normal, but a man who dresses in women's clothes in the audience would not. Sex between husband and wife in the home is granted social approval, but sex by the same husband and wife at a public beach or on the church altar might land them in jail or in a mental hospital.

When is it okay to lie? As children, we are taught not to tell a lie, but our society actually encourages us to lie in certain situations. In fact, there are occupations that are built around the art of deceit—lawyers, car salesmen, etc. Most lies are meant to prevent a negative reaction rather than the other way around. Have you ever told someone they looked good when they did not, or said a particular food item was tasty when it was horrible? There are over 500 million Facebook users worldwide. Think of how people can manipulate the way they present themselves or information about their lives on Facebook and other social network websites. Is it OK to "lie" about where we happen to be in order to protect our homes or ourselves? With Facebook, we have the opportunity to present select things about ourselves, including aspects of our biography and even the way we look. Is it wrong to control that image so that it is not a complete representation of who we really are?

While many might argue and agree that cheating is always wrong, the social relativity of deviance reminds us that we must carefully select the time, place, and situation in which to behave in particular ways. The identical behavior by the same individual may be appropriate at one time, place, or situation yet not at others.

## 6.3d Variation by Social Status

Deviance also varies with social status both ascribed and achieved. Until recently, both women and minority members wouldn't have publicly aspired to be the president of the United States as such an open aspiration might have been considered deviant. On the other hand, wealthy, educated white males were encouraged to participate in politics. The status associated with a person's sex, race, age, and income will influence which of his or her behaviors are considered deviant.

We can examine the influence social status has on deviance by noting differences in appropriate behaviors for males and females. There are variations by time, place, and situation; but some behaviors are generally given greater approval for women than for men, whereas others are given greater approval for men than for women. It is generally considered acceptable for women to wear high heels, panty hose, and lipstick; yet in our society, such behaviors in men would be considered deviant. Men can go topless to any beach, but women who do so would be considered deviant.

*Until recently, women and minority members who aspired to be the president of the United States would have been considered socially deviant. (AP Wide World Photo)*

The relativistic perspective acknowledges the diversity of behaviors, convictions, and sanctions that can be found in society, as well as the variety of meanings and definitions attributed to behaviors and sanctions. This view also recognizes the potential for conflict, both in a large society and in a single person who attempts to conform to the norms of different groups. A teenager may be encouraged to drink alcohol by peers but not by parents. A Catholic couple may wish to use only what are considered "natural" contraceptive methods to coincide with church norms, yet want to use more artificial methods to conform to their own norms and those of their friends and society.

## APPLYING THE RELATIVISTIC VIEW OF DEVIANCE

From the relativistic perspective, deviance is not assumed to reside exclusively either in people or in actions. It is, rather, an interactive process involving people's behavior, an audience, societal norms or subgroup norms and definitions, and society as a whole. The view that deviance can be interpreted only in the sociocultural context in which it occurs has important implications for the creation, implementation, and evaluation of many social policies that deal with social problems such as poverty, teen pregnancies, homelessness, drug addiction and alcoholism, and the spread of disease, among many others. However, it is incorrect to categorically explain the existence of particular social problems (for example, poverty) as the result of people's failure to conform to societal norms.

It is easy to say that people have problems because their behavior is atypical. This type of reasoning, known as **blaming the victim**, implies that the people facing social problems cause them. The way that policymakers (politicians, legislators, and the people who vote for them) explain social problems directly influences how they propose to deal with them. If you feel that a group is to blame for its situation, you may try to change the group rather than to search for other causes of the problem or to examine the social context or circumstances in which the problems take place.

Governments do not formulate policies exclusively. You probably will formulate policies in your job and even in your personal life, so you, too, may benefit from using the relativistic view of deviance. For example, the value of this view may help you if you are, or decide to become, a parent. As a parent, you will find yourself constantly making policies that you want your children to obey. Will you forbid your daughter to ask a boy out on a date because that type of behavior might have been considered immoral in your grandparents' day? Will you prohibit your son from growing his hair long or from wearing an earring because that was considered a sign of rebellion at one time? Both of these behaviors, considered deviant at one time, are acceptable behaviors in contemporary society. Parents may improve their relationship with their children if they keep in mind the relativistic view of deviance.

**Blaming the victim**
A type of reasoning that implies that social problems are caused by the people facing them

### thinking SOCIOLOGICALLY

1. Why are women more likely to be incarcerated within the United States than other countries? Explain how social views concerning women may lead to higher rates of incarceration.
2. Why do you think the incarceration rate, in general, is higher in the United States than in other countries? Does this fact suggest that people in the United States are more criminal, that we have different approaches to defining deviance, that we place more efforts on crime control, that there is less tolerance for deviation, or other explanations?

# 6.4 THEORIES EXPLAINING DEVIANCE

Scientists have developed a variety of theories to explain deviance, but the fact that many theories exist does not mean that one is correct and the others incorrect. Theories often reflect the discipline from which they were developed. Biological theories tend to focus on genetic, anatomical, or physiological factors. Psychological theories tend to emphasize personality, motives, aggression, frustration, or ego strength. Sociologists usually emphasize sociocultural, organizational, environmental, or group factors.

## 6.4a Psychological Theories of Deviance

Some psychological theories are based on the idea that the causes of behavior are rooted in a person's physiological or genetic makeup: instincts, needs, drives, and impulses. Social psychologists often consider the social context of behavior in addition to these factors.

Psychological theories often associate deviance with a sickness and argue that deviance results from a psychological abnormality, a psychopathic personality, or a mental illness. This explanation assumes that deviant behaviors—such as alcoholism, child abuse, and crime—are the consequences of mental illness. While mentally ill people may commit deviant acts, this theory does not account for deviance among people who are not otherwise considered mentally ill, nor does it explain why some mentally ill people do not engage in deviant behaviors.

### Psychoanalytic Theory

Sigmund Freud spent his entire life attempting to explain human behavior. Freud believed that all human behavior is motivated by the desire to feel pleasure, based on two instincts—sexuality and aggression. Although Freud's theories have come under criticism, his psychoanalytic approach to working with clients, the patient/doctor conversation, is still very popular today among clinicians, psychologists, psychiatrists, and others.

According to Freud, the human personality is made up of three components: the id, the superego, and the ego. The *id*, present at birth, is our pleasure seeking principle, constantly seeking immediate gratification. The *superego* refers to the internalized norms of society, what we typically think of as our "conscience" or "the morality principle." The *ego*, sometimes referred to as the "reality principle," mediates between the innate drives of the individual (id) and the demands of society (superego), enabling the individual to postpone immediate gratification at times when it may be socially unacceptable.

Sigmund Freud believed the human personality is made up of three components: the id, the ego, and the superego. (AP Wide World Photo)

Because we are all born with an id, we have the potential to be deviant. If our id dominates the other two components, we are more likely to exhibit deviant behavior. On the other hand, if our superego is the dominating component, we are likely to be rigid in our behavior. The ego acts to balance the two others and maintain social conformity.

Freud also believed we have three layers of psyche: the conscious, preconscious, and subconscious. The *conscious* part of the mind is what we are most aware of and contains our wants, needs, and desires. Our *preconscious* mind is just below the surface of our conscious mind and can be brought to the surface through a memory or experience. The last component is the one that can cause us the most problems. Our *subconscious* mind is likely to keep painful memories repressed and to hold our biological desires and urges well below the surface. This component of our psyche could contribute to irrational thinking.

Other psychological theories suggest that deviance is a learned behavior much like any other behavior. Through experiences, we will enhance or alter our behavior in order to obtain a desired response from others. Bandura

Figure 6-3 The Iceberg Metaphor of the Mind

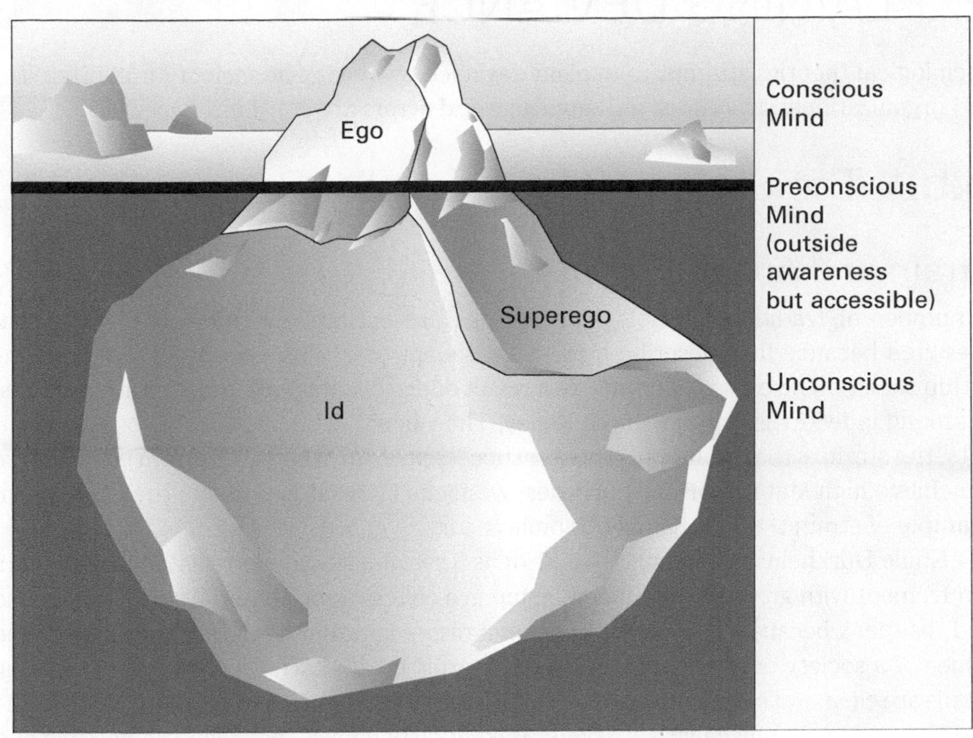


and Walters (1959) argued that people are not born with the ability to act violently, but learn to be aggressive through life experiences. A child can learn violent behavior by observing someone acting aggressively and receiving a desired reward for their behavior. For example, a drug dealer in an impoverished neighborhood may be seen as a positive figure if he has money, cars, clothes, and other things generally unattainable when living in poverty. Children may learn to act aggressively by observing domestic disputes within the home. Young boys and girls are more likely to become abusers or marry abusers when they witness violence between their parents.

Some psychological explanations suggest that deviance results from frustration and aggression. When needs are not fulfilled, frustration results, which in turn leads to aggression and often to antisocial, deviant behaviors—the greater the frustration, the more extreme the aggression. Frustration over lack of money, the loss of a job, or a failure in love can lead to aggressive acts: speeding, child abuse, robbery, or even murder. One difficulty with this explanation is that frustration is defined so broadly that it includes almost any behavior. Another problem is that it does not account for people who are frustrated but do not act deviantly.

In general, psychological explanations based on frustration, aggression, unconscious needs, instincts, guilt, weak egos, personality traits, and so forth have generated much research but have resulted in very inconclusive results. Many theories or ideas, such as those involving instinct and unconscious needs, are extremely difficult—if not impossible—to test empirically. Explanations based on frustration and aggression or on illness fail to differentiate the deviant from the nondeviant. Another major difficulty with most biological and psychological theories is that they ignore the relative nature of deviance—the influence of social context, variations in rates of deviance, and social responses to deviance. Several sociological theories, some of which incorporate psychological components, consider factors other than acts and actors.

# 6.5 SOCIOLOGICAL THEORIES EXPLAINING DEVIANCE

Sociological theories attempt to explain deviance by looking at sociocultural processes and organizational structures, although acts and actors are considered as well.

## 6.5a The Structural Functionalist Perspective

### Strain and Anomie Theory

A number of traditional sociological theories are collectively referred to as **strain theories** because they describe how people adapt to strains experienced by persons within society. The causes of crime are a result of disadvantages within cultures, groups, or among individuals (Agnew, 1985; Kelley, Thornberry, & Smith, 1997). To some theorists, the strain is the inability to realize a success goal. To others, the strain is the failure to achieve high status. For our purposes, we focus on what is perhaps the best-known example of strain theory—namely, anomie theory.

Emile Durkheim concluded that suicide is a social phenomenon related to a person's involvement with group life and membership in a cohesive social unit. Anomic suicide, he said, happens because of social and personal disorganization. People feel lost when the values of a society or group are confused or norms break down. Under most conditions, norms are clear and most people adhere to them; but during times of social turmoil, people find themselves in unfamiliar situations. Making distinctions—between the possible and the impossible, between desires and the fulfillment of those desires—becomes impossible. This condition of social normlessness is termed **anomie**. In an anomic society, the rules for proper behavior are not present, creating confusion or other problems.

Merton (1968) extended Durkheim's explanation of anomie and applied it to the study of crime. His strain theory suggests that deviance arises from the struggle society has between its culturally defined goals and the socially approved means by which they are met. In the United States the goals are to obtain wealth, power, and success while the legitimate means of reaching these goals include education, hard work, and deferred gratification. Such groups as the poor, teenagers, racial minorities, and blue-collar workers are constantly informed through education, the media, and friends that material success is an important goal; yet legitimate means for achieving it are often unavailable. Thus, deviance is the result of a strain between a society's culture and its social structure; between culturally prescribed goals and the socially approved ways of achieving them.

Merton listed five ways in which people adapt to the goals of a culture and the institutionalized means of achieving them (see Table 6-1). Only *conformity* to both the goals and the means is nondeviant. The other four methods of adaptations—innovation, ritualism, retreatism, and rebellion—are all varieties of deviant behavior. *Innovators* accept social goals, but reject the acceptable means of achieving them. Students who want to get good grades are adhering to widely held values; but if they cheat, they are violating a norm for achieving that goal.

A third mode of adaptation is ritualism. *Ritualists* follow rules rigidly without regard for the ends for which they are designed. The office manager who rigidly adheres to all the rules and makes sure employees come to work on time and follow all the policies of the company is a ritualist. By focusing on petty rules, he or she loses sight of the real goal of the office. Ritualists conform to traditions and never take chances. Merton suggests that lower-middle-class Americans are likely to be ritualists when parents pressure their children to compulsively abide by the moral mandates and mores of society. This form of adaptation is not generally considered a serious form of deviant behavior. People cling to safe routines and institutional norms, thereby avoiding dangers and frustrations that they feel are inherent in the competition for major cultural goals.

**Strain theories**

Theories of deviance suggesting that the experience of socially induced strain, such as anomie, forces people to engage in deviant activities

**Anomie**

When deviance arises from the incongruence between a society's emphasis on attaining certain goals and the availability of legitimate, institutionalized means of reaching those goals

**Table 6-1** Merton's Typology of Modes of Individual Adaptation

| Modes of Adaptation | Culture Goals | Institutionalized Means |
|---|---|---|
| I. Conformity | + | + |
| II. Innovation | + | – |
| III. Ritualism | – | + |
| IV. Retreatism | – | – |
| V. Rebellion | ± | ± |

*Note.* In this typology, Merton used the symbol + to signify "acceptance," – to signify "rejection," and ± to signify "rejection of prevailing values and substitution of new values."



Retreatism is a more drastic mode of adaptation. *Retreatists*, such as prostitutes, alcoholics, and drug addicts, reject both the cultural goals and the institutional means. These people are truly aliens; they are in the society but not of it. They are members of their society only in that they live in the same place. Retreatism is probably the least common form of adaptation, and it is heartily condemned by conventional representatives of society. Retreatist deviants are widely regarded as a social liability. According to Merton (1968, p. 155), this fourth mode of adaptation "is that of the socially disinherited who, if they have none of the rewards held out by society, also have few of the frustrations attendant upon continuing to seek these rewards."

The fifth and final mode of adaptation is rebellion. *Rebels*, such as members of revolutionary movements, withdraw their allegiance from a society they feel is unjust and seek to bring into being a new, greatly modified social structure. Military militia groups such as the one Timothy McVeigh belonged to prior to bombing Oklahoma City's Murrah Building would be considered rebels. This category is seen as the one most likely to be deviant and to reject most societal goals. Merton suggests that it is typically members of a rising class, rather than the most depressed strata, who organize the resentful and the rebellious into a revolutionary group.

*Retreatists, such as alcoholics, adapt by being in society but not of it; they reject both the cultural goals and institutional means. (iStockphoto)*

Merton's theory has been criticized on a number of different grounds (Thio, 1988). Some critics argue that it erroneously assumes that a single system of cultural goals is shared by the entire society. It has also been faulted for failing to explain why some people choose one response while others choose a different one. Another weakness is that some types of deviance—for example, rape or domestic violence—do not neatly fall into any of his five modes of adaptation. Other critics argue that Merton's theory ignores the influence of societal reactions in the shaping of deviance and the fact that much perceived deviance involves collective, rather than individual, action. Finally, much criticism has been leveled at Merton's underlying assumption that deviance is disproportionately concentrated in the lower socioeconomic levels.

There are strengths to anomie theory, as well. It provides a framework for examining a wide range of social behavior; it has stimulated many research studies; and it has raised the social consciousness of deviance analysts. This last mentioned point is particularly true for some members of the new generation of sociologists. These theorists have devised conflict theories of deviance that emphasize the widespread social oppression and basic contradictions found at the heart of our socioeconomic system.

## 6.5b Conflict Theory

Conflict theorists are the major critics of the assumption made by the functionalist and anomie theories that a society shares a single set of values. **Conflict theory** contends that most societies contain many groups that have different, often conflicting, values and that the strongest groups in a society have the power to define the values of weaker groups as "deviant." Conflict theorists emphasize the repression of the weak by the powerful, the exploitation of the masses by strong interest groups, and the influential and often wealthy groups who use laws, courts, and other agencies to oppose the interests and activities of lower socioeconomic groups and minorities.

Most businesses exist to make a profit. If in making a profit, they also (intentionally or unintentionally) provide jobs, raise the level of personal gratification, and improve the community, little conflict may result. However, if high taxes, high wages, fringe benefits, safety requirements, or pollution control disrupt profits, then lobbying groups, political contributions, and media campaigns are used to influence legislation, taxation, and controls. Part-time workers may be used extensively to eliminate the cost of fringe benefits. Members of minority groups, particularly new immigrant groups, may be hired at lower wages than those paid to others. Community tax incentives may be granted to sustain businesses or industries at the expense of the individual. The powerful exploit those with less power, and this exploitation by the elite produces inequality and institutionalized violence. The conflict between the powerful and the weak, therefore, influences both the creation of deviance and our response to it.

*A weakness in Merton's theory is that some types of deviance, such as domestic violence, do not neatly fall into any of his five modes of adaptation. (Shutterstock)*

People tend to assume that the law is based on the consensus of citizens, that it represents the public interest, and that it treats citizens as equals and serves the best interests of society. Conflict theorists, however, argue that the law means that legal authorities *ought* to be fair and just but are actually unfair and unjust, favoring the rich and powerful over the poor and weak. This condition exists, they say, not because law enforcement officials are cruel or evil, but because they would antagonize members of the middle and upper classes if they arrested them for their white-collar offenses. These classes might then withdraw their support from law-enforcement agencies, thus leading to loss of law-enforcement jobs. Later in this chapter, we discuss white-collar crime. White-collar crime, such as fraud in the world of investments, is an example of how the rich and powerful can often get away with egregious crimes that have devastating individual and social consequences and yet go unnoticed and often unpunished. While one of the most famous white-collar criminals of recent times, Bernie Madoff, was convicted of defrauding investors and received a 150-year-prison sentence, many who contributed to the economic meltdown that occurred in 2008 were completely untouched by the criminal justice system and received exorbitant incomes in the years following the crisis (Pontell & Geiss, 2010). This is partially because they were protected either by Security Exchange Commission (SEC) policies or a failure of the SEC to adequately police investment brokers.

Quinney (1979) and Spitzer (1975), who agree that deviance and deviants are defined and controlled by the powerful, go a step further and blame the lack of justice directly on the capitalist system. Drawing heavily from Karl Marx, Spitzer contends that populations are considered deviant by capitalists when they disturb, hinder, or question any of the following: (1) capitalist modes of appropriating the products of human labor, (2) the social conditions under which capitalist production takes place, (3) patterns of distribution and consumption in capitalist society, (4) the socialization of productive and nonproductive roles, or (5) the ideology that supports capitalist society.

**Conflict theory**

A social theory that views conflict as inevitable and natural and as a significant cause of social change

According to the conflict perspective, the dominant class—for the most part—determines definitions of deviance. Rates of deviance are determined primarily by the extent to which the potentially deviant behaviors threaten dominant class interests, while control of deviance is largely determined by the extent to which the powerful can socialize and reward those who follow their demands. Many conflict theorists perceive their theory as a call for political action to raise a revolutionary consciousness and end the oppression of the powerless by the powerful.

Like other theories, conflict theory has its critics that fault it for not searching for the causes of deviant behavior. They also say it does not explain the crimes and deviances that are basically nonpolitical (vices or trivial deviations, such as outlandish forms of dress or goldfish-swallowing contests). In addition, conflict theorists have been criticized for assuming that in the utopian communist society murder, robbery, rape, and other crimes will disappear after the power to criminalize them is abolished.

## 6.5c The Symbolic Interactionist Perspective

Theories that fall under the interactionist perspective are micro level in analysis and focus on sociocultural learning—the processes through which deviant acts are learned and the conditions under which learning takes place. Deviant behaviors are learned through essentially the same processes as other behaviors. Unlike functionalist and conflict theories, interactionist theories emphasize the groups to which people belong and the ways in which they learn the norms prescribed by those groups. In other words, people grow up in groups and situations in which deviance is the norm, and thus it is learned. Three of these theories focus specifically on deviance: cultural transmission theory, differential association theory, and social learning theory.

**Cultural transmission theory** suggests that when deviance is part of a subculture's cultural pattern, it is transmitted to newcomers through socialization. According to this theory, when there is a tradition of deviance in a subculture, the gang, peer group, or the playgroup passes on the norms of that subculture during interaction with newcomers. As a result they become deviant, also—not only by violating larger cultural norms but also by conforming to the norms of the subculture.

People learn not only from gangs or peer groups but also from other agents of socialization—parents, teachers, church leaders, business colleagues, and others. A person could learn deviant attitudes by observing that people throw away parking tickets, keep incorrect change from a supermarket, or find ways to avoid paying taxes. One primary source of learning about deviance may be institutions designed to correct deviance, such as juvenile homes, detention centers, reformatories, prisons, and mental hospitals. Even people within these subcultures, however, are exposed to and learn conforming behaviors. So why are some people attracted to deviant behaviors while others are not?

To answer this question and explain how deviance and crime are culturally transmitted, Edwin Sutherland (1939) devised the differential association theory (Sutherland & Cressey, 1970). Sutherland attempted to determine why crime rates vary among different groups of people. Why is the crime rate higher in the city than in the country and higher in impoverished areas than in other areas? Why do more males than females and more young people than older people commit crimes? Sutherland also wanted to explain why some individuals become criminals and others do not.

**Differential association theory** suggests that deviance results when individuals have more contact with groups that define deviance favorably than with groups that define it unfavorably. Sutherland contended that criminal behavior is learned rather than inherited or invented and that it takes place through verbal and nonverbal communications, primarily in intimate groups. Learning a criminal behavior involves acquiring a set of motives, drives, rationalizations, and attitudes, as well as specific techniques for committing the act itself. Sutherland did not believe that contact with criminals was necessary for a person to become deviant. Exposure to definitions favoring deviance

**Cultural transmission theory**
The theory that a community's deviance may be transmitted to newcomers through learning and socialization

**Differential association theory**
The theory that deviance results when individuals have more contact with groups that define deviance favorably than with groups that define it unfavorably

would be sufficient, and the influence and frequency of these exposures vary from person to person. According to this theory, deviance is a learned behavior, a set of behaviors transmitted to people through their interactions with others.

**Social learning theory** is a revision of Sutherland's differential association theory, in accordance with the principles of behavioral theory (Akers, R. L., 1977; Akers et al., 1979). Social learning theory suggests that deviant and conforming behaviors are determined by the consequences—rewards or punishment—that follow them. This is known as *operant* or *instrumental conditioning* (concepts first developed by psychologists Edward Thorndike and B.F. Skinner), whereby behavior is acquired through direct conditioning or through imitating the modeled behavior of others. A behavior is strengthened by rewards (positive reinforcement) or the avoidance of punishment (negative reinforcement) and weakened by aversive stimuli (positive punishment) or loss of rewards (negative punishment). Akers and his colleagues (1979) state that the acquisition and persistence of either deviant or conforming behavior are functions of what particular behaviors have been rewarded or punished, which is known as **differential reinforcement**. The norms and attitudes people learn from others, especially peers and family, are also influential.

Akers and his colleagues found that alcohol use was positively correlated with exposure to and association with users. (iStockphoto)

For example, Akers and his colleagues (1979) assessed the social learning theory of deviant behavior with data on factors that influenced the drinking (alcohol) and other drug use of 3,000 adolescents. They found that alcohol and other drug use were both positively correlated with exposure to users and association with users. They also found that the use of drugs such as alcohol increased when use was reinforced more than punished and when use was defined positively or neutrally. Although differential association accounted for most of the adolescents' variations in alcohol and other drug use, differential reinforcement, definitions, and imitation were also influential.

**Sociocultural learning theories** focus on how deviance is learned. Critics argue that these theories do not explain how deviance originated or how some behaviors came to be defined as deviant. It has also been argued that these theories do not deal adequately with those who commit deviant acts in isolation, rather than as part of a group. Furthermore, these theories are often difficult to test empirically without engaging in circular reasoning—deviance is caused by a tradition of deviance, caused by earlier deviance. Another weakness is that it is very difficult to determine precisely what stimuli or learning experience cause a person to initially commit a deviant act instead of a conforming act. Nevertheless, sociocultural learning theories have contributed to our understanding of the nature of deviance.

**Social learning theory**
The view that deviant and conforming behaviors are strongly influenced by the consequences that follow them

**Differential reinforcement**
The view that the acquisition and persistence of either deviant or conforming behavior is a function of what behaviors have been rewarded or punished

**Sociocultural learning theories**
Theories that deal with the processes through which deviant acts are learned and the conditions under which learning takes place

**Labeling theory**
A theory that emphasizes how certain behaviors are labeled "deviant" and how being given such a label influences a person's behavior

## 6.5d Labeling Theory

The theories of deviance discussed so far have focused on deviant people, deviant acts, the process of learning deviance, and the causes of deviance. **Labeling theory** is concerned primarily with how some behaviors are labeled "deviant" and how being given such a label influences a person's behavior.

Most labeling theorists interpret deviance in terms of symbolic interaction processes. Like other behaviors, deviant behavior is not regarded as a particular type of act undertaken by a person in isolation. It is, rather, a result of human interactions, as well as people's interpretations and definitions of their own actions and those of others. As Kitsuse (1962) stated it, "Forms of behavior *per se* do not differentiate deviants from nondeviants; it is the responses of the conventional and conforming members of the society who identify and interpret behavior as deviant which sociologically transform persons into deviants" (p. 253).

Note that, according to this perspective, deviance is a relative condition. It is not a specific type of act; rather, it is the consequence of applying a particular label. As noted several decades ago by Becker, "Social groups create deviance by making the rules whose infraction constitutes deviance and by applying those rules to particular people and labeling them as outsiders" (Becker, 1974). Thus, if two people commit the same act, one might be labeled a deviant and the other might not, depending on the meaning given to the act by their social groups.

Edwin Lemert (1951), one of the first labeling theorists, identified two categories of deviance. *Primary deviance* involves behavior that violates social norms but is temporary and sporadic. Individuals who are involved in primary deviance do not regard themselves as deviant, nor are they regarded as such by those around them. *Secondary deviance* involves habitual violation of norms by individuals who not only consider themselves deviant but also are labeled as deviant by others. Secondary deviance becomes a routine, resulting in a label that leads to further deviance. The behavior, for example, of a student who buys one term paper to turn in to a history professor might be primary deviance. However, if this student consistently cheated on tests and turned in papers that she had not written herself, her behavior would be considered deviant by her peers, her professors, and herself; and it would, therefore, constitute secondary deviance. Sociologist Erving Goffman also believed that when one is labeled, one can assume a "retrospective labeling," which is a re-interpretation of a person's past based on present deviance (Macionis, 2004).

What are the consequences of labeling? According to this theory, being labeled as deviant has negative consequences because labeled people tend to see themselves as deviant, which leads them to continue their so-called deviant behavior. Thus, we have the development of a deviant career and a label that becomes a master status—cheat, prostitute, liar, and so on. Getting so labeled leads others to view one in terms of that deviant status, overlooking other qualities or statuses. Beyond that, labeled people may no longer be treated as respectable parents, teachers, or community members; they may lose their jobs, be rejected by friends, or be sent to a prison or a mental hospital. Responses of this sort often push labeled people further into the deviant activity. Ex-convicts who cannot get legitimate jobs may return to robbery or drug dealing. Those labeled as mentally ill lose many of the social supports necessary for mental health. Drug addicts, alcoholics, and prostitutes may turn to others who share the same label for support and companionship, which leads them to organize their lives around their deviance.

Who labels whom? Of labeling, Becker (1974) says, "A major element in every aspect of the drama of deviance is the imposition of definitions—of situations, acts, and people—by those powerful enough or legitimated to be able to do so" (p. 62). The labelers, therefore, would include such social control agents as police, judges, prison guards, and psychiatrists, whereas the labeled would include criminals, delinquents, drug addicts, prostitutes, mental patients, and others. Consistent with the conflict theory described earlier, rich, white, or powerful people are more likely to apply the labels; poor, black, and otherwise powerless people are more likely to be labeled. A poor or minority person is more apt to be arrested, prosecuted, and convicted than a rich or white person for committing the same act.

Data from the Bureau of Justice Statistics, for example, show that in 2007, over 7.3 million people were on probation, in jail or prison, or on parole. This number declined by 1.3% to 7.1 million in 2010 (Glaze, 2011). The estimated number of sentenced prisoners varies greatly between gender and racial groups. An important question is whether or not the differential number of people in prison and sentenced is related to social statuses such as gender, race and socioeconomic level. Table 6-2, for example, compares rates of incarceration by gender and race and Hispanic/Latino origin.

Although many sociologists accept it, labeling theory has its critics. It does not explain the causes of deviance, nor can it be used to predict who will be labeled and in what contexts. Like other symbolic interaction theories, labeling theory is difficult

Table 6-2 Estimated Number of Inmates Held in Custody in State or Federal Prisons or in Local Jails per 100,000 U.S. Residents, by Sex, Race and Hispanic/Latino Origin, and Age, June 30, 2010



| | | Male | | | | Female | | | |
|---|---|---|---|---|---|---|---|---|---|
| Year | Total | Total[a] | White[b] | Black[b] | Hispanic/Latino | Total[a] | White[b] | Black[b] | Hispanic/Latino |
| Total[c] | 732 | 1,352 | 678 | 4,347 | 1,775 | 126 | 91 | 260 | 133 |
| 18–19 | 829 | 1,508 | 762 | 4,192 | 1,580 | 100 | 72 | 144 | 135 |
| 20–24 | 1,538 | 2,728 | 1,269 | 8,008 | 3,298 | 253 | 199 | 408 | 284 |
| 25–29 | 1,696 | 3,018 | 1,437 | 8,932 | 3,892 | 293 | 224 | 535 | 317 |
| 30–34 | 1,798 | 3,215 | 1,629 | 9,892 | 3,896 | 344 | 271 | 647 | 323 |
| 35–39 | 1,581 | 2,813 | 1,509 | 9,100 | 3,197 | 336 | 272 | 663 | 268 |
| 40–44 | 1,355 | 2,435 | 1,375 | 7,689 | 2,713 | 279 | 201 | 603 | 240 |
| 45–49 | 1,000 | 1,848 | 972 | 6,048 | 2,416 | 173 | 116 | 391 | 165 |
| 50–54 | 642 | 1,213 | 637 | 4,032 | 1,736 | 93 | 66 | 194 | 115 |
| 55–59 | 386 | 750 | 414 | 2,486 | 1,249 | 44 | 29 | 85 | 87 |
| 60–64 | 212 | 420 | 250 | 1,350 | 789 | 21 | 14 | 49 | 30 |
| 65 or older | 70 | 155 | 100 | 485 | 306 | 5 | 4 | 8 | 8 |

*Note.* Based on the total incarcerated population on June 30, 2010, and the U.S. resident population estimates for July 1, 2010, by sex, race and Hispanic/Latino origin, and age. Rates may be different than those reported in appendix table 2 due to different reference dates. Detailed categories exclude persons who reported two or more races.

[a] Includes American Indians, Alaska Natives, Asians, Native Hawaiians, other Pacific Islanders, and persons identifying two or more races. [b] Excludes persons of Hispanic or Latino origin. [c] Includes persons under age 18.

Adapted from "Correctional populations in the United States, 2010" by L. E. Glaze. The Bureau of Justice Statistics is the statistical agency of the U.S. Department of Justice.

to test empirically. Another criticism is one that also applies to conflict theory: If the powerful create and impose the deviant label, how is it possible that powerful people are also sometimes labeled as deviant? Critics have also questioned the extent to which the labeling of deviance encourages deviant behavior rather than deters it. Finally, are all persons in prisons or mental hospitals there simply because someone chose to label them, or are some behaviors so disruptive that severe sanctions such as institutionalization must be imposed to maintain social order? Other social consequences of deviance are discussed in the next section.

## thinking SOCIOLOGICALLY

1. Select one of the theories discussed above and explain why deviant behavior occurs among teenagers within the United States.
2. Discuss what you believe to be the pros and cons of prison. In addition, discuss the functions and dysfunctions of using prison, instead of community-based sentencing, for non-violent offenses.
3. Examine Table 6-2, and discuss possible reasons for the different rates of incarceration among gender, racial, and Hispanic/Latino origin groups.

# 6.6 SOCIAL CONSEQUENCES OF DEVIANCE

## 6.6a Deviance and Crime

We have defined deviance as variation from a set of norms or shared social expectations. A **crime** is a violation of criminal statutory law, and a specific punishment applied by some governmental authority generally accompanies the violation. Many types of deviance, such as rape, robbery, and murder, are criminal acts in most states; other types of deviance—such as bizarre behaviors related to mental disorders, wearing unusual clothes, cussing in public, and shouting at strangers passing by—are not. Just as definitions of deviance differ from group to group, criminal activities and crime rates vary in different legal jurisdictions, with accompanying differences in rates of enforcement. For example, prostitution (illegal in most states) is legal in Nevada. A decade ago, it was legally impossible for a man to rape his wife. Today, many states have amended their rape laws to make the relationship between the rapist and the victim irrelevant.

## 6.6b Types of Crime

Crimes are most often separated as violent or non-violent offenses. Violent crimes are those we most refer to as street crimes, usually involving a victim. The most common form of violent crime is assault. Violent crime includes four crimes: homicide, forcible rape, aggravated assault, and robbery. These crimes, including robbery, involve a victim because there is a threat or use of force against the victim.

Property crimes are committed with the intent of gaining property without the threat or use of force. Property crimes include larceny-theft, burglary, motor-vehicle theft, and arson. Arson is included because it involves the destruction of property. Crimes are also classified in the U.S. as felonies and misdemeanors. *Felonies* are crimes that are punishable by 1 year or more in a state prison. *Misdemeanors* are less serious crimes, usually punishable by a fine and/or up to 1 year in a county jail.

Some crimes are seen as victimless crimes, usually associated with a society's moral values and beliefs. Some view victimless crimes as not harming anyone except the persons committing the crimes. Included in victimless crimes are prostitution, vagrancy, gambling, public drunkenness, etc. Who are the victims of these crimes? Do they violate public decency? There is much debate over the impact victimless crimes have on society.

White-collar crime was a term coined by Edwin Sutherland in 1939 to refer to those, generally seen as respectable, individuals who break the law in the course of their employment for the purpose of personal or organizational gain. These individuals are usually corporate or government employees. The FBI investigates billions of dollars of white-collar crime annually. White-collar crime often takes the form of fraud in healthcare, mortgage, insurance, mass marketing, banking, investments and many other areas. (FBI, 2011). The case of Bernie Madoff, for example, involved taking an estimated $65 billion from investors in a Ponzi scheme (named after con man Charles Ponzi in 1920) over a 40-year period (Pontell & Geiss, 2010). In the largest scam in U.S. history, Madoff—former chairman of the NASDAQ stock exchange—convinced investors he could make a quick return on their money. His clientele involved nearly 5,000 investors, including endowments from non-profit organizations. On March 12, 2009, Madoff pleaded guilty to 11 counts, including securities fraud, and faced a sentence of up to 150 years in prison. Other examples of white-collar crimes include embezzlement, insider trading, bribery, and kickbacks.

**Organized crime** consists of groups expressly organized to carry out illegal activities such as the distribution of drugs, the operation of a gambling business, or loan sharking (lending money at excessively high rates). Some consider organized crime to be the tightly knit national organization variously called the "Mafia," the "Cosa Nostra," the "syndicate,"

**Crime**

A violation of a criminal statutory law accompanied by a specific punishment applied by some governmental authority

**Organized crime**

Groups expressly organized to carry out illegal activities

or the "mob"; others use the term more loosely to cover any group of organized professional criminals who maintain control of a large-scale illegal business enterprise.

In either case, the organization has a strict hierarchy, ranging from the "lords of the underworld" (who make the important decisions and direct the activities) to those at the lower levels (who follow the orders). Those at the lower levels, who deal directly with the public, are the ones who get caught; however, some may get released through the leader's connections with the police, judges, or relevant professionals. Organized crime groups maintain control within their group or organization through threats, intimidation, bribery, and—when they deem it necessary—violence.

Bernie Madoff pleaded guilty in 2009 to the white-collar crime of bilking investors out of an estimated $65 billion. (AP Wide World Photo)

Another category of crime is juvenile crime, involving those under the age of 18. Juvenile crimes refer to the age of the offender rather than types of crimes committed; therefore, juvenile crimes can involve anything from a felony to a status offense. Status offenses are crimes only because the individual is under age, such as truancy and running away. The most common juvenile crime is theft-larceny, whereas for adults the most common offenses involve drugs. Recidivism (repeating criminal behavior after previous punishment) has been a concern for juvenile offenders. Research suggests the high rate of status offenses contributes largely to the rates of juvenile recidivism.

## 6.6c Measuring Crime in the United States

Accurate estimates of crime rates are difficult to make because a high percentage of crimes go undetected and unreported. Official data on crime in the United States typically come from two sources: the Uniform Crime Report and the National Crime Victimization Survey. In addition, self-report surveys provide information on prevalence and types of offenses committed by offenders.

The Uniform Crime Report (UCR) is the official source for statistical data on crimes committed in the United States. Collected by the Federal Bureau of Investigation and published in a yearly volume entitled *Uniform Crime Reports*, the statistics are gathered from law-enforcement agencies around the country. The crimes recorded in the FBI reports are divided into *violent crimes* and *property crimes*. Approximately 13 million property crimes are known to be committed each year. The famous FBI "Crime Clock" for 2011, shown in Figure 6-4, is one dramatic way of illustrating how frequently some offenses are committed.

As with most data collection methods, the UCR has its share of problems. First, it does not provide a clear picture of crime in the United States because only crimes that are recorded by the police are provided and only 50% of violent crimes were reported to the police in 2011. Second, each police department creates its own set of statistics and may report biased information regarding the level of crime in the city. Third, only the most serious offense is recorded when multiple crimes occur.

Like the UCR, the NCVS has problems, including over-reporting or under-reporting of information. A person may believe he or she was the victim of theft, when he or she simply misplaced a piece of property. Memory is another concern with getting accurate information on the NCVS. It is not unusual for victims of crime to have problems with dates, times, and locations all of which can lead to survey mistakes.

Another method of collecting data on crime is self-report surveys. This type of survey is given to offenders, usually juveniles or prison inmates, and asks them to voluntarily report whether they have committed various criminal acts. Self-report surveys also tend to show the incidence of crime to be much higher than the officially reported incidence; again, the data should be used with caution.

**Figure 6-4** Crime Clock, 2011

The crime clock should be viewed with care. Because it is the most aggregate representation of *Uniform Crime Reports (UCR)* data, it is designed to convey the annual reported crime experienced by showing the relative frequency of occurrence of the index offenses. This mode of display should not be taken to imply regularity in the commission of offenses; rather, it represents the annual ratio of crime to fixed time intervals.

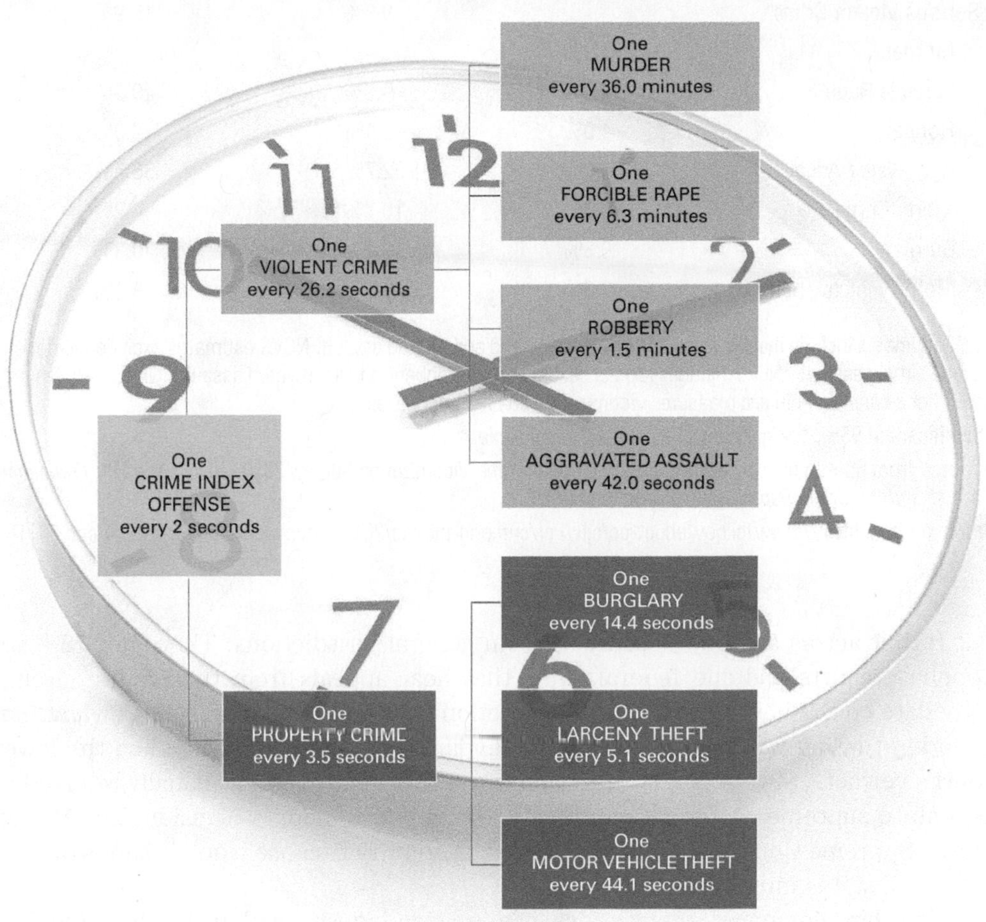


Retrieved from http://www.fbi.gov/about-us/cjis/ucr/crime-in-the-u.s/2011/crime-in-the-u.s.-2011/offenses-known-to-law-enforcement/crime-clock

## 6.6d The Criminal Justice System

The criminal justice system consists of our police, courts, and corrections—each equally important in reducing the incidence of crime within the United States.

Policing can be divided into four broad categories: local, county, state, and federal agencies. In the United States, policing is mainly the responsibility of local and county agencies, such as city police and county sheriff's departments. State level policing typically involves highway patrols and/or agencies such as the Texas Rangers. At the federal level, law enforcement agencies—such as the Drug Enforcement Agency and the Bureau of Alcohol, Tobacco, and Firearms—assist local, county, and state law enforcement when they are needed.

Another component of the criminal justice system is the court system, which has the authority to hear and decide cases within jurisdictional areas. In the United States, there is a dual court system comprised of federal and state level courts. Each state maintains its own state level court system with approximately 12,000 general jurisdiction courts across the United States. Appellate courts do not hear new cases

**Table 6-3** Percent Changes in the Number of Crimes Reported in the UCR and the NCVS, 2010–2011

| Type of Crime | UCR | NCVS | |
|---|---|---|---|
| | | Total | Reported to the Police |
| Violent Crime[a] | –4.0% | 17.6%* | 12.8% |
| Serious Violent Crime[b] | ~ | 9.3% | 16.9% |
| Murder | –1.9% | ~ | ~ |
| Forcible Rape[c] | –4.0% | –9.2% | –49.9%* |
| Robbery | –4.0% | –2.1% | 12.9% |
| Aggravated Assault | –4.0% | 22.7%** | 36.5%* |
| Property Crime | –0.8% | 10.7%* | 4.2% |
| Burglary | 0.3% | 13.8%* | 0.3% |
| Motor Vehicle Theft | –3.3% | 3.5% | 3.1% |

[a]UCR estimates include murder, forcible rape, robbery, and aggravated assault. NCVS estimates exclude murder and include simple assault. [b]NCVS includes rape or sexual assault, robbery, and aggravated assault. [c]NCVS includes rape and other sexual assault, and measures victimization against both sexes.

*Significant at 95%. **Significant at 90%. ~ Not applicable.

Adapted from Bureau of Justice Statistics, "National Crime Victimization Survey, 2010–2011"; and FBI, *Preliminary Annual Uniform Crime Report,* January–December 2011.

Retrieved from http://www.fbi.gov/about-us/cjis/ucr/crime-in-the-u.s/2011/preliminary-annual-ucr-jan-dec-2011

but rather act as a reviewer of those from general jurisdictions. There are 12 state appellate courts and one federal court that hear appeals from the federal circuit. Appellate courts have a great deal of discretion with regard to their rulings which can include ordering a new trial, allowing defendants to go free, or upholding the lower court's verdict. However, all 50 states have a "court of last resort," usually referred to as a state supreme court that can review the appellate court's decision. The United States Supreme Court is the highest law in the country because when it hands down a ruling, all states must abide by it.

The third component, corrections, is a growing industry within the United States, with a population of over 2 million persons either incarcerated in prisons or on some type of community corrections, such as probation or parole. In addition to probation and parole, other community corrections ordered by the courts include home confinement and restitution. Probation is widely used and involves a sentence of imprisonment that is suspended by the court, provided the convicted person abides by the rules of the court. Parole occurs when a parole authority releases an inmate before his or her sentence has expired. The released prisoner must report to a parole officer and follow the protocol established upon reentry into society. Home confinement or house arrest is sometimes ordered when a person is not a serious offender and he or she has a job. The individual must be in the home at all times except when working and is monitored using an electronic device usually placed on the ankle. A court may also order a person to pay restitution to his or her victim or volunteer services to the community.

*When community corrections are not an option, an inmate may be sent to a jail, prison, or private prison.*

*(iStockphoto)*

When community corrections are not an option, an inmate may be sent to a jail, prison, or private prison. There were more than 1.6 million inmates in the U.S. in 2010. The majority of jail inmates are pre-trial

**Table 6-4** Rate and Percent Change of Violent Victimization, by Demographic Characteristics of Victim, 2002, 2010, and 2011, per 1,000 People

| Demographic Characteristic of Victim | Violent Crime | | | | | Serious Violent Crime[a] | | | | |
|---|---|---|---|---|---|---|---|---|---|---|
| | Rates[b] | | | Percentage Change[c] | | Rates[b] | | | Percentage Change[c] | |
| | 2002 | 2010 | 2011 | 2002–2011 | 2010–2011 | 2002 | 2010 | 2011 | 2002–2011 | 2010–2011 |
| Total | 32.1 | 19.3 | 22.5 | –30%* | 17%* | 10.0 | 6.6 | 7.2 | –28%* | 9% |
| **Sex** | | | | | | | | | | |
| Male | 33.5 | 20.1 | 25.4 | –24%* | 27%* | 10.4 | 6.4 | 7.7 | –26%* | 20% |
| Female | 30.7 | 18.5 | 19.8 | –36* | 7 | 9.5 | 6.8 | 6.7 | –30* | -2 |
| **Race/Hispanic origin[d]** | | | | | | | | | | |
| White[e] | 32.6 | 18.3 | 21.5 | –34%* | 18%* | 8.6 | 5.8 | 6.5 | –24% | 13% |
| Black[e] | 36.1 | 25.9 | 26.4 | –27* | 2 | 17.8 | 10.4 | 10.8 | –39* | 4 |
| Hispanic | 29.9 | 16.8 | 23.8 | –20* | 42* | 12.3 | 6.7 | 7.2 | –42* | 7 |
| American Indian/ Alaska Native[e] | 62.9 | 77.6 | 45.4 | –28 | –42** | 14.3! | 47.3! | 12.6! | –12 | -73* |
| Asian/Native Hawaiian/ other Pacific Islander[e] | 11.7 | 10.3 | 11.2 | –4 | 9 | 3.4! | 2.3! | 2.5! | –25 | 12 |
| Two or more races[e] | — | 52.6 | 64.6 | — | 23 | — | 17.7 | 26.2 | — | 48 |
| **Age** | | | | | | | | | | |
| 12–17 | 62.7 | 28.1 | 37.7 | –40%* | 34%* | 17.0 | 11.7 | 8.8 | –48%* | -25% |
| 18–24 | 68.5 | 33.9 | 49.0 | –28* | 45* | 24.7 | 17.0 | 16.3 | –34* | –4 |
| 25–34 | 39.9 | 29.7 | 26.5 | –34* | –11 | 12.3 | 7.1 | 9.5 | –22** | 34 |
| 35–49 | 26.7 | 18.2 | 21.9 | –18* | 21** | 7.6 | 5.6 | 7.0 | –8 | 24 |
| 50–64 | 14.6 | 12.7 | 13.0 | –11 | 3 | 4.4 | 3.7 | 4.3 | –4 | 15 |
| 64 or older | 3.8 | 3.0 | 4.4 | 17 | 48 | 1.8 | 0.9 | 1.7 | –9 | 91 |
| **Marital status** | | | | | | | | | | |
| Never married | 56.3 | 31.8 | 35.5 | –37%* | 11% | 16.1 | 11.9 | 11.7 | –27%* | –2% |
| Married | 16.0 | 7.8 | 11.0 | –31* | 40* | 5.7 | 2.2 | 3.7 | –34* | 70 |
| Widowed | 7.1 | 6.7 | 3.8 | –46** | –43 | 4.4 | 3.0! | 0.7! | –85* | –78* |
| Divorced | 44.5 | 35.2 | 37.8 | –15 | 7 | 10.9 | 11.2 | 9.2 | –15 | –18 |
| Separated | 76.0 | 60.2 | 72.9 | –4 | 21 | 34.8 | 18.8 | 26.4 | –24 | 40 |

[a]Includes rape or sexual assault, robbery, and aggravated assault. [b]Per 1,000 persons age 12 or older. [c]Calculated based on unrounded estimates. [d]The collection of racial and ethnic categories changed in 2003 to allow respondents to choose more than one racial category. [e]Excludes persons of Hispanic or Latino origin.

*Significant at 95%. **Significant at 90%. ! Interpret with caution. Estimate based on 10 or fewer sample cases, or coefficient of variation is greater than 50%. — Less than 0.5.

Adapted from Bureau of Justice Statistics, "National Crime Victimization Survey, 2002, 2010, and 2011." Retrieved from http://bjs.ojp.usdoj.gov/content/pub/pdf/cv11.pdf

detainees waiting for their day in court. If an inmate is sent to one of the country's 1,325 state prisons or 84 federal prisons, the inmate may encounter some overcrowding with nearly 1.5 million other inmates. In 2001, it cost nearly $60 billion to run the prisons within the United States (Schmallager & Pittaro, 2008). Private prisons are becoming increasingly popular to ease the burden of overcrowding. State governments contract private firms to provide correctional services for inmates. In 2010, there were 1.6 million state and federal prisoners in the U.S. More than 8% (approximately 128,000) were housed in privately owned prisons. That was a 39% increase between 2002 and 2009. Thus, with significant financial incentives, the detention industry has become a big business (Lee, 2012).

## 6.6e The Future of the Criminal Justice System

In the future, it is expected that the focus of criminal justice will be on globalization and the effects international and transnational crimes have on our system. Globalization refers to the idea that the world is getting smaller and crimes committed in other countries will have an effect on the United States. Louise Shelley, director of the Transnational Crime and Corruption Center, suggests that transnational crime will be as much a defining issue for twenty-first century policymakers as was the Cold War for the twentieth century (Fairchild & Dammer, 2005). Transnational crimes such as terrorism, computer crimes, sea piracy, drug and human trafficking, money laundering, and corruption will influence the United States criminal justice system in many ways. Police will need specialized training to deal with specific crimes. For example, the most widely trafficked and most widely abused drug is cannabis, with seizures reported in 98% of all countries and territories. Courts will have concerns over jurisdiction and nation sovereignty, as the U.S. Department of Treasury estimates that as much as $100 billion is laundered annually in the U.S. and anywhere from $300–$500 billion worldwide (Fairchild & Dammer, 2005). As police and courts work to combat crime, the corrections industry continues to expand with the number of persons incarcerated showing steady growth.

# CHAPTER 6 Wrapping it up

## Summary

1. Deviance is universal, and every society has people who commit acts defined as exceeding the tolerance limits of social norms.
2. Deviance can influence social systems in several different ways. Some of the consequences are *functional*. Specifically, they can help to define the limits of social tolerance, increase the solidarity and integration of groups, serve as a safety valve for future deviance, indicate inadequacies in the system, and bring about constructive change. Other consequences are *dysfunctional*. For example, deviance can disrupt the social order, decrease the will of others to conform, destroy trust, and divert resources that otherwise could be used elsewhere in social rehabilitation and control efforts.
3. The mechanisms of social control are used to maintain conformity. Control of deviance is generally explained in terms of two factors: internal controls and external controls. *Internal controls*, which are exerted by individuals on themselves, involve such factors as self-concept, ego strength, high frustration tolerance, and conscience. These controls are believed to be acquired through socialization. *External controls* include both informal interactions with people, such as family and friends, and formal controls, which are carried out by the agencies designated by society to maintain law and order.
4. The *relative nature of deviance* assumes that deviance can be defined only in the context of the society or group in which it takes place. Deviance is not thought to be a particular type of act. It is, rather, a relative condition that varies according to time, place, situation, and social status. This view takes into account the great diversity of meanings that can be associated with people or acts in different situations.
5. Psychological theories emphasize such factors as personality, motivation, willpower, frustration, aggression, and ego strength.
6. Sociological theories focus on the interaction, organization, and social normative factors through which people learn definitions of deviance. These factors also determine people's behavior, which a social audience labels as either deviant or nondeviant.
7. Functionalist theories, such as *strain* and *anomie theories*, link deviance to conflicts between culturally valued goals and the institutionalized means of achieving them. Innovation, ritualism, retreatism, and rebellion are deviant modes of adaptation.
8. *Conflict theories* contend that definitions of deviance are devised by the powerful to repress and exploit the weak. An influential, wealthy elite is assumed to oppose and control the powerless, the poor, and minorities.
9. *Interactionist theories*, which are based on sociocultural learning, examine both social and psychological influences, but emphasize the processes through which deviant acts are learned and the types of conditions under which they are learned. *Cultural transmission theory*, sometimes called "subculture theory," explains the continuity of crime and deviance in some geographical areas as the result of the transmission of deviant norms from one generation to the next.
10. *Differential association theory* contends that deviance is learned through verbal and nonverbal communication, by associating differentially with deviant or nondeviant individuals or groups. The social learning theory of deviance, which draws heavily on differential association theory, suggests that operant (instrumental) conditioning and imitation play important roles in the learning of behaviors. Differential rewards and punishments, as well as exposure to conforming or deviant models, greatly influence whether we develop deviant or conforming attitudes and behaviors.
11. *Labeling theory*, rather than emphasizing acts or individuals in isolation, focuses on why some people and acts are singled out as deviant and also on the effects of being labeled deviant. This approach, which is based on the principles of

symbolic interaction, assumes that the definition of deviance and other behaviors is a collective process. People in social contexts define and interpret their own behavior and that of others and apply labels on the basis of their definitions. These labels have a significant effect on the continuation of deviant behavior for both those defined as deviant and the audience who labels them.

12. The social consequences of deviance include crime, in that *crimes* are violations of criminal statutory law. Types of crime include violent and non-violent crimes, property crimes, victimless crimes, white-collar crimes, organized crimes, and juvenile crimes.
13. Rates of criminal activity are measured using two primary sources of data. The UCR measures the amount of crime reported to police, and the NCVS gauges those crimes that go unreported. In addition, self-report surveys are used to appraise crimes as reported by the offenders.
14. The criminal justice system includes police, courts, and corrections. Police can be divided into local, county, state, and federal law enforcement. Courts include state and federal level systems with the authority to hear cases based on jurisdiction. Corrections include incarceration and community sentences such as probation, parole, house arrest, and restitution.
15. The future of the criminal justice system will increasingly focus on globalization and the influence of transnational and international crimes on the United States.

## Discussion Questions

1. How do you define deviance? Explain what it means to say that deviance is socially defined.
2. Evaluate why women kill their children. If the mother is found guilty of killing her daughter, which theory most likely explains why the mother committed the murder?
3. How would you explain the variation in the rates of women incarcerated around the world? Can it be explained using the relativistic view? How do social responses differ in each country?
4. What are the similarities and differences among the anomie, conflict, interactionist, and labeling theories of deviance?
5. How can the definition of some types of behavior as being deviant (regardless of their sociocultural context) result in misguided social policies? Give some examples other than the ones shown in this chapter.
6. What are some types of behavior that are commonly explained in terms of psychological theories of deviance? Is it possible to explain these in terms of sociological theories? If so, how?
7. Compare the usefulness of the psychological theories of deviance with that of the sociological theories of deviance.
8. How does being labeled a "deviant" influence interaction patterns? Does "truth" (i.e., accuracy, correctness) matter? Is it ever okay to tell a lie?
9. Discuss some ways in which deviance has positive functions in society. Give examples.
10. Use the sociological theories of deviance to discuss the internal and external controls of deviance.

*All animals are equal, but some animals are more equal than others.*

GEORGE ORWELL

# PART THREE

## SOCIAL INEQUALITY

We live in a globalized world that brings together people of diverse backgrounds and life experiences. Our diversity exists in many forms: gender, gender identity, race, ethnicity, socioeconomic standing, sexual orientation, age, religion, political viewpoints, and physical and psychological ability or disability. When we embrace and appreciate our differences, it is this very diversity that is a foundation of the richness of our humanity. At the same time, our diversity can also result in differential treatment within society, with some receiving unequal benefits and others being faced with the unequally difficult challenges because of the nature of their diversity. One of the central areas of sociology is the exploration and explanation of differentiation.

cebook

CHAPTER 7

# Social Differentiation and Stratification

## SYNOPSIS

Focal Point

## HURRICANES KATRINA AND SANDY: NATURAL DISASTERS AND INEQUALITY

(Shutterstock)

In August 2005, one of the worst and costliest hurricanes, Katrina, hit New Orleans and caused catastrophic damage and loss of life. The images shown by the media were of poor, mainly black, citizens of New Orleans trapped by the floodwaters. As the nation watched, people were forced to confront the issues of racism, poverty, and inequality within the United States. Even though the mayor had called for mandatory evacuations, most of the poor were unable to leave on their own; no coordinated efforts by the government were put in place to address this problem. However, the attitudes of many Americans were not of empathy but of media bias. Blaming the victim is a common phenomenon in America. Many people believe that everyone has some means, however small, to "make it" when catastrophe occurs—whether it is the help of family and friends or any other means necessary. We fail to realize that most Americans live from paycheck to paycheck; having the means to leave our house, job, school, etc., is not an immediate option for most of us.

Grusky and Ryo (2006) examined the opinions of Americans after Katrina and suggested that disaster had the potential to re-adjust the mind-set of society toward the poor and poverty in the United States. Their report indicated that while 70% of Americans tuned in to hear news about Katrina, not everyone's opinions about poverty were changed by the events. Of those tuned in to the effects of Katrina, 40% still felt that there is nothing the government can do to address poverty and inequality or reveal that it is a major problem in the United States. Grusky and Ryo examined what is referred to as "the dirty little secret hypothesis," which says that disasters often reveal injustices that exist in society as a result of inequality. For example, many in the public news media felt that Hurricane Katrina would call attention to how inequality is largely responsible for the devastating effects of natural disasters (due to things such as lack of an adequate infrastructure or slow response rates after the disaster); as a result of the exposure of that "dirty little secret," U.S. Americans would support a renewed war on poverty to combat the injustices of inequality. Only partially was this effect borne out after Hurricane Katrina. Activists who already understood the ramifications of inequality prior to Katrina were hardened in their approach that further steps to eradicate social inequality should take place. Non-activists remained opposed to stepping up government efforts to eradicate inequality and tended to feel that the "dirty little secret" being exposed was being presented as such as a result of a liberal news bias. How is it that people can see the same images, yet draw vastly different opinions about those affected? If the trapped group had been mainly white and middle class, would the response of those watching have been different?

In 2012, Hurricane Sandy struck the Northeast and Middle Atlantic regions of the United States. It was the largest hurricane ever to hit that region, causing record flooding and destruction to homes and businesses. When comparing size, intensity, and number of people affected, Sandy was at least as potent as—if not more potent than—Katrina (Wallace & Kaleem, 2012). Yet, the government and public response, as well as the media assessment, were radically different for each storm. After Katrina, the government reaction was slow and was highly criticized by the media. With Sandy, the government response was swifter and the media reactions to the recovery much more positive. Some—economist Paul Krugman, for example—feel that the difference was due to having a Republican administration in office when Katrina hit; Republicans typically tend to be anti–government involvement in affairs, as opposed to a Democratic administration, which tend to be pro-government as was seen when Sandy struck (Krugman, 2012). Krugman argues that FEMA (the Federal Emergency Management Agency) was less effective under the Bush administration than it was under the Obama administration. Others have argued that the government response was swifter in the aftermath of Sandy because the storm struck a few weeks before the presidential election and that it was a political maneuver by the Democrats. Possibly other factors may also have come into play in explaining the different response rate. The areas affected by Sandy included more economically important areas with much larger populations and a bigger industrial base (Irwin, 2012). Yet even in the NY area, there were accusations that the cleanup cleaved along class lines, with areas of Manhattan receiving help prior to the less affluent areas of the Rockaways (Nir, 2012). Without having an objective analysis of the recovery operations, it would be difficult to provide the real reasons for why assistance happens more quickly in some regions than in others. However, what all of these speculations suggest is that there are many social factors involved that revolve around inequalities that determine the impact of catastrophic natural events on people's lives.

*Natural disasters, such as the one depicted here, have different effects on people depending upon their position in the stratification system.* (AP Wide World Photo)

How does class status affect one's life chances? How are other factors—such as race, gender, and age—related to social class? As you read this chapter, think about the importance of class to those who experience natural disasters. Does race or economic status influence how we see victims? What other factors influence what we see?

# 7.1 UNDERSTANDING SOCIAL STRATIFICATION

Americans emphasize a commitment to equality and a belief in the American middle-class lifestyle, yet seldom do they realize how incredibly wealthy a few are and how extremely poor others are. A relatively few people control great wealth and power, living in luxury beach houses in the summer and mansions in the winter. Meanwhile, as many as 2 or 3 million Americans eat in soup kitchens (when they eat), have no homes at all, and without a home are not qualified to vote. In reality, people are not created equal, nor do they experience equality in their lives.

**Inequality**—the unequal access to scarce goods or resources—is found in most, if not all, societies. In some countries, some goods and resources are hard to come by. For example, we have a tendency to believe water is plentiful, whereas in many African countries it is extremely scarce. Land is a scarce resource in some areas of the world; in others, it is so plentiful that no one bothers to claim ownership. In societies where there are not enough workers, child labor becomes a valuable resource. From their youth, people work to contribute to the family income, instead of going to school.

**Inequality**
Differences between groups in regard to wealth, status, or power

Of course, people differ in other ways as well. Some people have blue eyes, and some have brown eyes. Some people live and work on the East Coast, and some on the West Coast. Some people travel in their work, and others prefer to work at a desk. Some people like to work with people, and others prefer solitary work. This is **social differentiation**—how people vary according to social characteristics. Usually, we do not rank people as high or low based on these differences.

**Social differentiation**
The difference or variation of people based on selected social characteristics such as class, gender, race, or age

Rather, people are ranked according to their ability to access scarce resources. Wealth, **power** and prestige are scarce, but valuable, resources within the U.S. Wealth includes money, stocks, and property, while power and prestige include education, respect, and membership in political and philanthropic organizations. The ranking of people according to their wealth, power, or prestige is known as **social stratification**.

**Power**
The ability to control or influence the behavior of others, even without their consent

**Social stratification**
The ranking of people according to their wealth, prestige, or party position

Water is extremely scarce in many African countries. (iStockphoto)

Our ranking in the stratification system influences every part of our lives: where we live, access to education, what jobs we work, what we eat, how or if we vote, whom we marry, our sexual behavior, sports, hobbies, and health.

## 7.2 TYPES OF SOCIETIES AND SOCIAL DIFFERENTIATION

In simple societies, there is little division of labor—all people perform similar tasks and possess similar wealth. As a result, there is little social differentiation. In complex societies, there are wide divisions of labor, with a wide array of social positions. Stratification develops as we rank these positions in order of importance. Lenski (1966) found that stratification generally increases as societies grow in wealth and become more complex. He differentiated five basic types of societies, as described below.

**Hunting-and-gathering societies** consist of about 50 people, or even fewer, who live on what they can find to eat. They are often nomadic, moving from place to place in search of food. They are usually very poor and must share what they find to eat in order to survive. No one can be excused from work. Surpluses of food or supplies are not accumulated, so no one can become wealthy. Some people may gain special respect because of their age, wisdom, skill in hunting, or magical abilities; but they do not derive any power from their status because there is no area to exercise their authority and little to do except work. With so little differentiation in these societies, there is little stratification.

**Hunting-and-gathering societies**
Small, often nomadic societies that have no agriculture and live on food that is found

**Simple horticultural societies**
Societies that grow food using very simple tools, such as digging sticks

**Division of labor**
The assignment of interrelated specialized tasks within a social system in order to accomplish a goal

**Advanced horticultural societies**
Societies with irrigation systems and other advanced farming practices

**Agrarian societies**
Complex societies with farming, armies, merchants, and a concentration of wealth in the hands of a few people

In **simple horticultural societies**, people farm using a digging stick as their basic tool. They have a fairly reliable source of food and may even have a surplus from time to time. Thus, they can remain in one location, build shelters, and make tools. A surplus of food and supplies allows them some leisure time, which they use for sports and ceremonial activities. They also occasionally fight wars to protect their land. A **division of labor** develops when some people take on certain specialized occupations—warriors, and ceremonial and political leaders, for example. Ceremonial leaders are sometimes paid for performing ceremonies, especially those involving healing, and they may become wealthy. Political leaders, with the assistance of warriors, can capture slaves and enforce their edicts. As labor is divided among different groups and wealth and status accumulate, a stratification system develops.

**Advanced horticultural societies** farm with irrigation, terracing, and fertilization. These techniques increase the food supply, so the size of the population can grow. Societies at this level have learned how to work metals. This increases the variety of material goods, as well as the variety of occupations. As the size and wealth of the populations increase and a greater variety of occupations develops, stratification increases. Political leaders in advanced horticultural societies become very wealthy and powerful as they increase the size of their armies and slave labor. Social differentiation and stratification are much greater in these societies than in simple horticultural societies.

**Agrarian societies**, such as those found in Europe during the Middle Ages, have far more sophisticated technology than horticultural societies. This advanced technology increases the development of centralized power in two ways. First, as defenses and weapons are improved, arming a warrior with the materials needed to win battles becomes an expensive proposition. By supplying the weapons, the rich are able to develop armies that they use to conquer land and slaves and to control farmers, who then become the serfs of the society. Second, as the variety of goods grows, a merchant class develops to trade those goods. The more powerful rulers tax the wealth accumulated by the merchant class and become extremely rich.

As wealth and power become concentrated in the hands of very few people, society becomes severely stratified. During the Middle Ages, the rulers and governing classes in agrarian societies probably received income of about a quarter to a half of the national income (Lenski, 1966).

In simple horticultural societies, people use a digging stick as a farming tool. (iStockphoto)

**Industrial societies**, such as the United States and Western European countries, have the greatest division of labor, the most wealth, and therefore the most stratification—at least at the beginnings of industrial revolutions. Industrialization, which is structured on the factory system of production and the assembly line, requires workers to perform very specialized tasks. Workers specialize in operating a particular piece of equipment, packing a manufactured product, driving a truck to market, advertising the product, selling the product, and so on. Workers do not produce goods for personal consumption. Instead, they do a specific job in exchange for money and then buy personal goods with that money.

Durkheim (1893) argued that in preindustrial times the division of labor created **mechanical solidarity**, a situation in which people do similar work but are not very dependent on each other. Most people farmed and were self-sufficient. He believed that the division of labor could create **organic solidarity** because as each person specializes in one phase of production, he or she becomes dependent on others to produce other products. As a result, Durkheim believed, society would become more integrated and people would become more equal. However, Durkheim's predictions did not come about. Industrial societies have developed a wide gap between those at the top and those at the bottom. The surplus of goods produced, when accumulated in the hands of just a few people, make those people very wealthy compared with others.

Irrigation is one technique of successful farming. (iStockphoto)

## 7.3 SYSTEMS OF STRATIFICATION

Systems of stratification range from open to closed. In **open systems**, individual accomplishments are encouraged and advancements in the things that count—typically wealth, power, prestige. Equality is not influenced by gender, race, age, etc., since status is based on achievement. A class system, such as exists in the United States, is an open system—at least in principle. In a **class system**, social status is defined in terms of wealth and income. There are no legal definitions of class, so the system is an open system. Classes are fluid—that is, there is unlimited social mobility between one class and another. Anyone can move to a higher or lower ranking by either gaining or losing wealth; as a result, class societies are highly competitive, and power has become increasingly important to maintain a high position in the stratification system.

**Industrial societies**
Societies with great division of labor, highly specialized work, and a great concentration of wealth

**Mechanical solidarity**
The idea of Durkheim in which people do similar work but are not very dependent on one another (in contrast to organic solidarity, in which people are very dependent on others)

**Organic solidarity**
Durkheim's term for the integration of society that results from the division of labor

**Open system**
A system of stratification in which it is possible to move to a higher or lower position

**Class system**
A system of stratification found in industrial societies in which one's class is determined by one's wealth and in which vertical social mobility is possible

In **closed systems**, status is determined at birth and social mobility is based on a person's social position. Individual achievement is not rewarded because status is determined by law or through inheritance. Closed systems include caste, estate, and slave systems. In a **caste system**, a person's social status is ascribed at birth. Worth is judged on the basis of religious or traditional beliefs about the person or the person's family. India, where there are some 3,000 castes, provides the best example of a caste system. Status is determined by religion rather than race. In 1949, India officially outlawed the caste system, yet it remains deeply embedded in the culture and is practiced routinely in rural areas. The 2008 Academy Award-winning movie *Slum Dog Millionaire* highlighted the influence India's caste system has on the status, identity, education, and employment of individuals within society.

An **estate system** was very similar to a caste, in that status was ascribed and social mobility limited. Law and membership through inheritance determined the identity of a person. An example of an estate system was during the Middle Ages in Europe, where three estates existed. The *first estate* was comprised of nobility, wealthy families, and powerful landowners. Their status allowed them great privilege and opportunities, including the right to not work since labor was believed to be beneath them. The *second estate* was made up of clergy from the Roman Catholic Church. Highly powerful, the church owned land and collected taxes. The *third estate* was comprised of commoners, or laborers, particularly those of the land. Serfs, as they were called, could only move out of their estate if they were knighted or performed a remarkable deed for the king.

The **slave system** of stratification has been less recognized, but is equally important to this discussion. In a slave system, there existed a basic belief in the ownership of humans as labor. A debtor could enslave a person who owed him a debt, and that person's labor could be used as a form of repayment. When a person committed certain types of crimes, that person could be sentenced to slavery and required to work for the family of his victim. The first slaves in the American colonies were purchased from a Dutch ship in 1619 and initially considered as indentured servants who would work for a specific period of time to repay their passage debt. However, when labor demands exceeded the supply of workers, the United States turned to chattel slavery.

**Closed system**

A system of stratification in which there is no movement from one rank to another

**Caste system**

A system of stratification in which one's social position is ascribed at birth, one's value is assessed in terms of religious or traditional beliefs, and in which upward social mobility is impossible

**Estate system**

A system of stratification in which one's social position is ascribed by law or through inheritance

**Slave system**

A system of stratification in which there exists a basic belief in the ownership of humans as labor

**Social class**

A category of people who have approximately the same amount of power and wealth and the same life chances to acquire wealth

**Life chances**

The opportunities a person has to improve his or her income and lifestyle

# 7.4 DIMENSIONS OF A CLASS SYSTEM

Class systems are commonly economically based societies where a person's wealth determines his/her classification. Marx was the first to describe class system as a form of stratification. Weber (1946) pointed out that as the class system develops in industrial civilizations, class, status, and power become scarce resources for which people compete within society.

## 7.4a Social Class

**Social class** is a ranking generally based on a person's wealth. A number of things contribute to one's wealth—such as income and occupation, power derived from wealth, and the "life chances" to acquire wealth. **Life chances** are opportunities people have to improve their social class status such as education, health, and autonomy. For example, members of a first generation immigrant farm family will have fewer life chances than subsequent generations.

Social classes typically share similar characteristics such as occupation, education, lifestyle, attitudes and behaviors. In the United States, three classes exist: upper class, middle class, and lower class. However, throughout the years we have increasingly included a working class, as well as a further stratified middle class. According to the Pew Research Center (Morin, 2008), America is home to four middle classes: top middle, satisfied middle, anxious middle, and struggling middle. As shown in Figure 7-1, in 2011

**Figure 7-1** Percentage Distribution of Adults, by Income Category, 1971–2011

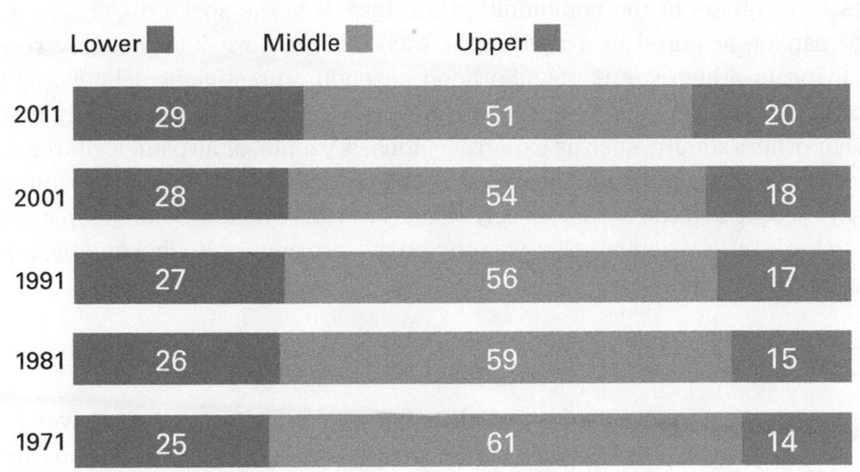


*Note.* Adults are assigned to income categories based on their size-adjusted household income in the calendar year prior to the survey year (e.g., 2010 income is from the 2011 survey).

Adapted from Pew Research Center tabulations of the Current Population Survey, "Pew Research Social & Demographic Trends," 1971–2011.

Retrieved from http://www.pewsocialtrends.org/2012/08/22/the-lost-decade-of-the-middle-class/

the middle income tier of U.S. Americans included 49% of adults compared with 53% in 2008 and 61% in 1971 (Pew Research Center, 2012).

**Table 7-1** Dimensions of Stratification of the High School Elite

| Class (wealth or skills for the marketplace) |
|---|
| Wealthy students |
| Most likely to succeed |
| Valedictorian |
| Best athletes |
| Honor society members |
| Best actors and actresses |
| **Status (honor and respect)** |
| Most popular |
| Best dressed |
| Best looking |
| Members of sororities and fraternities |
| Most poised |
| Prom queens |
| **Power (leadership activity)** |
| Student body officers and delegates |
| Club officers |
| Newspaper editors |
| Class officers |
| Sorority and fraternity officers |

## 7.4b Social Status

**Social status**, according to Weber, is the amount of honor and prestige a person receives from others in the community; therefore, it is the social dimension of class. Prestige can be acquired in a number of ways—being born into a highly respected family, living in a high-status neighborhood, attending prestigious schools, or joining high-status groups or clubs. People also gain prestige by being able to buy consumer goods that others admire, such as expensive houses, yachts, or airplanes. Status can also be gained by holding respected positions in the community, such as clergy member or professor. People's status is very closely related to their wealth. Some people use their wealth to buy status whereas other wealthy people are content to live quietly, relatively unknown in the community.

## 7.4c Power

**BVT Lab**

Flashcards are available for this chapter at www.BVTLab.com

Power is another component of social class within the United States. Power is about having authority and respect, usually within an organization in which decisions are made to reach the group's goals—such as to win an election, change a law, revise the banking system, educate children, or any other goal. A person can gain power in the community by being politically active in national, state, or local politics, or active in special interest groups, in influential clubs, or in any other type of organization in which decisions are made to reach broad-based societal goals. By developing power, people can increase their social status through winning respect and can increase their social class through reaching goals that are profitable to them.

Class, status, and power are often closely interrelated. Status and power can be used to increase wealth. Wealth can be used to buy consumer goods and increase status or to join prestigious clubs and increase political power. These three sources of status do not always go together, however. Wealthy people who are criminals, who live reclusive lives, or who are otherwise atypical have low status if no one respects them. Priests, ministers, college professors, and community leaders may be poor but still have a high status. Powerful leaders who use their position to increase their wealth sometimes do so in such a way that they lose status and the respect of others. Table 7-1 provides examples of the dimensions of stratification among high school students.

### thinking SOCIOLOGICALLY

1. Think of ways in which you could gain power if you had great wealth.
2. If you have high social class and status, will you also have increased power? Explain.
3. Discuss the ways in which life chances contribute to having wealth, power, and success.

## 7.4d Socioeconomic Status

It is difficult to place individuals in a particular social stratum because class, status, and power can all influence where they might be placed. Is the widower of a distinguished scholar who lives on a small retirement income in the same class as a mail carrier or a shoplifter who has the same income? Does a rural doctor who serves the poor and receives a small income have the same class position as a suburban doctor who serves the rich and has a large income? As you can see, class boundaries can be difficult to determine. A person who has a high position in one category may have a low position in a different category. Where, then, should that person be placed?

**Social status**

The amount of honor and prestige a person receives from others in the community; also, the position one occupies in the stratification system

To resolve this problem, sociologists have developed the concept of **socioeconomic status (SES)**. This concept considers income, education, and occupation when assessing a person's status. Someone who earns $50,000 will be ranked higher than a person earning $10,000; a college graduate will be ranked higher than a high school graduate; and anybody in a professional or management occupation will be ranked higher than a laborer. Usually there is a consistent pattern among these three rankings of status. People with many years of education tend to hold occupations that afford high status and high incomes. One of the more interesting problems sociologists study is how to categorize people who have "status inconsistency"—an advanced education but a very low income, for example.

**Socioeconomic status (SES)**

An assessment of status that takes into account a person's income, education, and occupation

# 7.5 SOCIAL CLASS IN THE UNITED STATES

Access to a specific social class in the United States is based on several factors—including family background, wealth, education, occupation, and a variety of other characteristics. The best way to understand the class system is to look at each one separately.

The earliest studies of stratification in America were based on people's opinions of other people. A study completed in "Middletown" during the Great Depression (Lynd & Lynd, 1929, 1937) found differences between the business class and the working class. When the study was originally done, the business class lived in larger and better quality housing than did the working class. The very wealthy had elaborate mansions with indoor plumbing and central heating, whereas working-class homes were much smaller and often lacked indoor plumbing; water had to be carried in from an outdoor well. A wood or coal stove provided heating.

In another study, Caplow et. al. (1982) found that it had become more difficult to identify classes among the population in "Middletown." The working class now lives in houses that are only slightly smaller than those of the business class, and they contain all of the amenities that modern society provides—enjoying not only indoor plumbing and central heating but also self-cleaning ovens, dishwashers, and other labor saving devices. The wealthy are likely to live relatively modestly in town while spending more of their money less conspicuously out of town. Today, the perceived boundaries between social classes are not always clear.

*John D. Rockefeller was considered old money upper class.* (Library of Congress)

## 7.5a The Upper Class

The upper class is those individuals who have considerable wealth. Wealth consists of personal property: liquid assets (cash in bank accounts), real estate, stocks, bonds, and other owned assets. This class has net worth in the millions or billions and controls as much as they possess. By owning many shares of the major corporations, they influence not just their own fortunes but also those of many others. The Rockefeller family, for example, dominates key banks and corporations and has been known to control assets of more than fifteen times their personal wealth.

There is generally one of two categories into which the upper class fit, old money or new money. In the past, most of those in the upper class inherited wealth that had been passed down from generation to generation. The Rockefeller and DuPont families would be considered *old money* upper class. *New money* is a fairly new phenomenon as the dot-com industry increased the wealth of many. Individuals, such as Bill Gates, made their millions either starting Internet companies or investing in them. Others, such as Oprah Winfrey and professional athletes, earned their wealth using creative talents. More recently, some individuals have become very rich by winning a lottery and changing their lives virtually overnight. While lottery winners may be considered wealthy by income standards, access to the realm of upper class involves more than money. It is unlikely they would be invited to rub elbows with the Hiltons, Rockefellers, and others.

## 7.5b The Middle Class

As mentioned previously, 51% of Americans now consider themselves part of the middle class, the largest of all the classes. However, unlike the lower and upper classes that seem to be clearly distinct and identifiable classes in terms of income, lifestyle, and opportunities, the middle class covers a broad range of differences. Thus, it is difficult to define precisely who is in the middle class and what it is like to be "middle class." Politicians toss the term around as if is a clearly defined concept that defines people with many similarities. In reality, the differences in income, lifestyle, and opportunity of people within the lower and higher ranks of the middle class are vast. Most sociologists stratify middle class further into upper middle and lower middle. Interestingly, in 2008 the Pew Research Institute argues that the middle class itself is stratified into four distinct groups: top, satisfied, anxious, and struggling (Morin, 2008). Even though the data are now more than 4 years old, it is worth taking a look at the Pew Research distinction for the purposes of helping to understand the variability within the middle class. At the highest point on the stratum is the *top middle* class, the largest of the four groups, with 39%. Income levels for the top middle class range between $50,000 and $100,000, and they are more likely to have a college degree. White males between the ages 30 to 49 make up the majority of this level, and 46% acknowledge having a high satisfaction with life. Nearly 70% of the class is married, and 46% believe the lives of their children will be better than their own.

**BVT*Lab***

Visit www.BVTLab.com to explore the student resources available for this chapter.

The *satisfied middle,* comprised of 25% of those identifying as middle class, are more likely to be white women between the ages of 18 and 29 or age 65 and over. They have an income generally between $30,000–$49,000 and less than a college education. Members are more likely to be unmarried, which is not uncommon for their age group. They see their quality of life as high and believe the lives of their children will be higher.

The *anxious middle* class make up 23% of the overall middle class and have higher incomes and education than those in the satisfied group. This group is less optimistic about their futures, even with incomes between $50,000 and $99,000 and some degree of college education. They are more likely to be white, married, and between ages 30 to 40. They rank their level of satisfaction as either low or medium and see the outlook of their children's lives as less hopeful than the other three groups.

The bottom group is the *struggling middle* class, with incomes of $20,000 or less. This group has more minority members than the other three categories, but whites still make up 56% of the struggling middle class. Group members are likely to be unmarried and to have a high school degree or less. They have a low satisfaction with life, but an equal number identified themselves as either being medium or highly satisfied with their financial fate. In addition, the majority believes their children will have a better life than theirs in the future.

One of the problems with the Pew classification is that it bases its categories solely on income level (see Table 7-2). In reality, people making less than $20,000 are not living what most of us would consider a middle class lifestyle and are probably close to being in, if not already in, the lower class; those making more than $120,000 certainly are not living an upper class life style and are barely upper middle class (depending upon the size of one's family).

## 7.5c The Lower Class

The lower class consists of individuals who generally have the least amount of education and the most difficulties with employment. The working poor, the displaced, and

**Table 7-2** Who Is Middle Income?

| Year | Middle-Income Range |
|---|---|
| 2010 | $39,418 to $118,255 |
| 2000 | $42,185 to $126,554 |
| 1990 | $37,546 to $112,637 |
| 1980 | $33,538 to $100,613 |
| 1970 | $29,896 to $89,689 |

*Note.* Incomes are adjusted for household size and then scaled to reflect a three-person household.

Adapted from the Pew Research Center tabulations of the Current Population Survey, Annual Social and Economic Supplements, 1971–2011.

Retrieved from http://www.pewsocialtrends.org/2012/08/22/the-lost-decade-of-the-middle-class.

the unemployed are members of the lower class, with women and children increasingly overrepresented. While income distribution is used to identify members of social classes, self-identification as a member of the lower class is less likely. The term "low class" conjures up images of someone who is impoverished, uneducated, lazy, and other derogatory visions of people unwilling to pull themselves up and take advantages of life's opportunities.

## 7.5d Poverty

**Poverty** is defined as having fewer resources than necessary to meet the basic necessities of life—food, shelter, and medical care. The U.S. Department of Health and Human Services has developed a measure of poverty that takes into account the size of the family, the number of children, and whether the family lives on a farm. The Social Security Administration first used the Poverty Index in the 1960s to determine how much a family of four would need to survive on a basic diet. In 2011 the poverty index for a family of four was $22,350, compared to $17,600 in 2001, $13,400 in 1991, and $9,280 in 1981 (U.S. Department of Health and Human Services, 2012). The government reports that in 2009, 14.3% of the population was living in poverty, compared to 11.1% in 1999, 12.8% in 1989 and 10.4% in 1979 (see Figure 7-2 and Figure 7-3).

Counting the poor has been a difficult task for governmental agencies. First, the government assumes that living on a farm costs less than living in the city; therefore, the poverty index is different for each. Second, no distinction is made between geographical locations of urban cities. For example, a family of four living in New York City is considered no different than a family of four residing in Tulsa, Oklahoma—each would be based on the same poverty index. In reality, there is a difference between absolute and relative poverty. Absolute poverty occurs when people fall below a minimum subsistence level and are unable to function. They don't have the basic necessities such as food, water, and shelter to survive. Relative poverty, on the other hand, occurs when people lack resources relative to others within their economic income level and the overall standards of society. Going back to the previous example, a family of four surviving on $25,000 a year in New York City will suffer relative poverty compared to a family of four living in Tulsa, Oklahoma, and having the same income.

Low paying jobs for poor people would not solve the problems of poverty. Of the adult poor, about 40% work at jobs that pay so little that they fall below the poverty line even though they work. The adults who are poor and not working are retired, ill or disabled, going to school, or keeping house. Approximately one-third of the poor in the United States are children. Most adults who could be working, and are not, are unemployed because they cannot find work; they are not unemployed by choice (Eitzen & Zinn, 2007).

**Poverty**
Having fewer resources than are required to meet the basic necessities of life, according to rates based, usually, on a government index of income relative to size of family and farm/non-farm residence

**Figure 7-2** Number in Poverty and Poverty Rate, 1959–2011

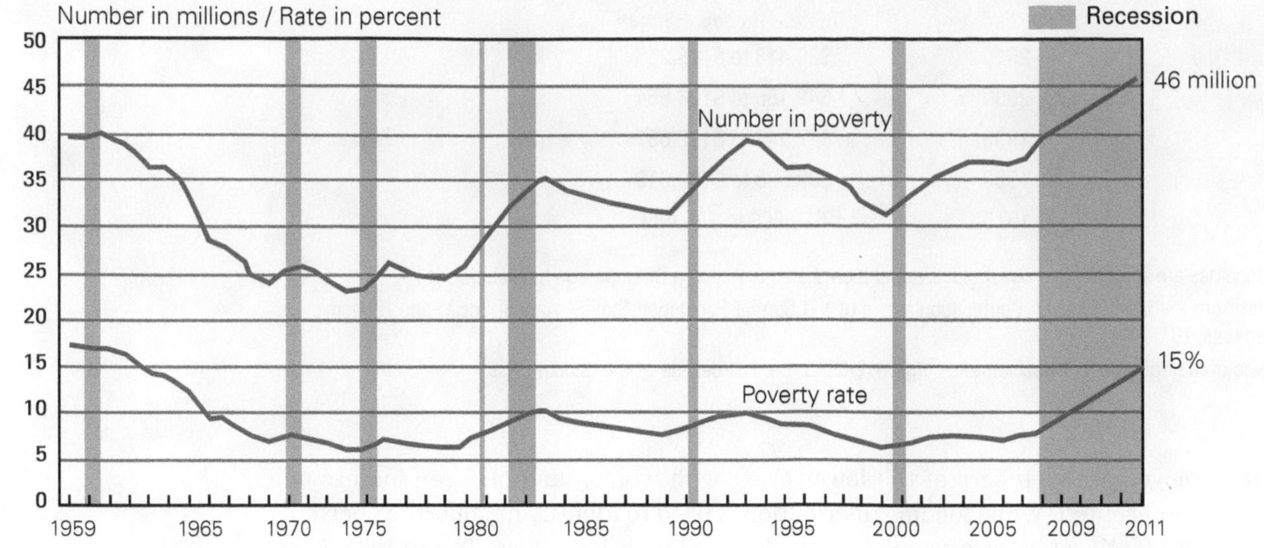


*Note.* The data points are placed at the midpoints of the respective years.

Those most likely to live in poverty in the United States are women and children. Referred to as the *feminization of poverty*, increasingly the poor include unwed, separated, and divorced mothers who serve as the heads of households. In 2009, 32.5% of female-headed households were living in poverty. Today, women head more than half of all families living in poverty, and many of them receive little support from the fathers of their children.

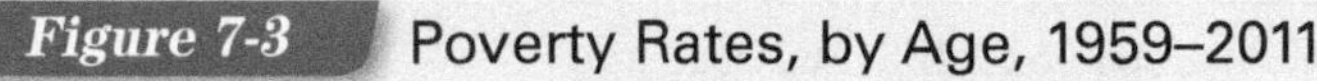

**Figure 7-3** Poverty Rates, by Age, 1959–2011

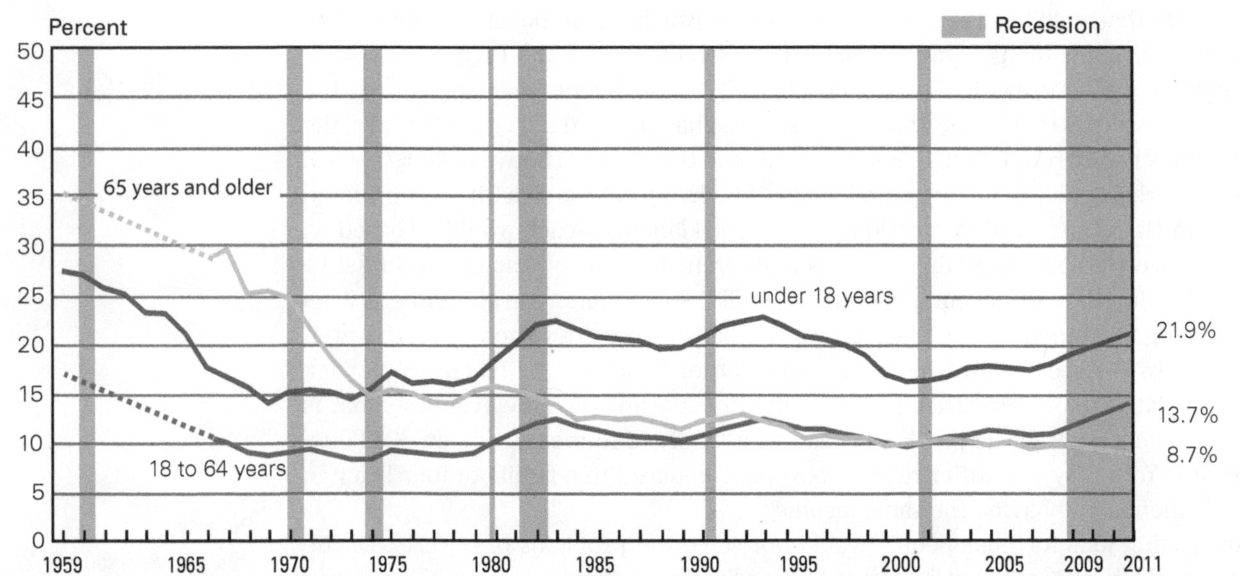


*Note.* Data points are placed at the midpoints of the respective years. Data for people aged 18–64 and 65 and older are not available from 1960 to 1965.

## 7.5e Inequalities in the United States

### Class-Consciousness

*Class-consciousness* is the awareness that different classes exist in society and that people's fates are tied to the fate of their whole class. Americans tend not to be very class conscious because they believe in social mobility, the possibility of moving upward to a higher class. However, the upper class is more likely to maintain class-consciousness and to recognize the boundaries between themselves and the middle or lower classes. The upper class will send their children to the same private schools, attend the same social functions, and vacation in the same luxury resorts as others in their class.

### Income Inequalities

Wealth is not evenly distributed within the United States. G. William Domhoff (2013) has spent most of his career studying the relationship between income inequality and power in the United States. Interestingly, a recent study showed that most Americans are unaware of how concentrated the wealth is in the United States (Norton & Ariely, 2011). The top 1% of households own nearly 35% of the privately held wealth (total net worth) and the next 19% own 50%, leaving 15% of the wealth to be shared by the bottom 80% of households (Wolff, 2010). Put another way, the top 1% has more than double the cumulative wealth of the bottom 80%. If you look at financial wealth (total net worth minus the value of one's home), the inequality is even greater with the top 1% having almost 43% of the wealth and the bottom 80% sharing 7% (see Table 7-3).

*Protesters picket the bonuses and bailout provided to AIG in 2009. With government assistance such as tax breaks to large corporations and salary increases, it's easy to see how income inequalities are likely to occur.* (AP Wide World Photo)

In 2011, the median income in the United States for people with full-time jobs was $48,202 for men and $37,118 for women (*Current Population Survey*, 2011). (The *median* is the amount at which half of a given population falls above and half falls below.) The median household income was $50,054 in 2011, down from its peak of $50,831 in 2010 (DeNavas-Walt, Proctor, & Smith, 2012).

Problems on Wall Street, in 2009, placed a spotlight on the inequalities of income. American International Group (AIG), for example, received billions of dollars from the government to assist the company financially. A short time later it was determined that $165 million of the government's bailout money was given as bonuses to AIG's top executives. A total of 298 top executives received bonuses of $100,000 or more. Add to this type of government assistance the tax breaks for large corporations and salary increases and it is easy to see how income inequalities are likely to occur.

# 7.6 LIFE CHANCES

## 7.6a Occupations

For most people, the most important life chance in a society such as the United States is the opportunity to have a successful and respectable occupation or career that provides an adequate income. The upper middle class holds the majority of professional positions—those of doctors, lawyers, business managers, and other high-ranking workers in large organizations. Many people think of the professional person as the typical

**Table 7-3** Share of Wealth Held by the Bottom 99% and Top 1% in the United States, 1922–2007

| Year | Bottom 99% | Top 1% |
|---|---|---|
| 1922 | 63.3 | 36.7 |
| 1929 | 55.8 | 44.2 |
| 1933 | 66.7 | 33.3 |
| 1939 | 63.6 | 36.4 |
| 1945 | 70.2 | 29.8 |
| 1949 | 72.9 | 27.1 |
| 1953 | 68.8 | 31.2 |
| 1962 | 68.2 | 31.8 |
| 1965 | 65.6 | 34.4 |
| 1969 | 68.9 | 31.1 |
| 1972 | 70.9 | 29.1 |
| 1976 | 80.1 | 19.9 |
| 1979 | 79.5 | 20.5 |
| 1981 | 75.2 | 24.8 |
| 1983 | 69.1 | 30.9 |
| 1986 | 68.1 | 31.9 |
| 1989 | 64.3 | 35.7 |
| 1992 | 62.8 | 37.2 |
| 1995 | 61.5 | 38.5 |
| 1998 | 61.9 | 38.1 |
| 2001 | 66.6 | 33.4 |
| 2004 | 65.7 | 34.3 |
| 2007 | 65.4 | 34.6 |

*Note.* 1922–1989 data from Wolff (1996); 1992–2007 data from Wolff (2010), in Domhoff (2011).

American worker—educated, earning a comfortable living, owning a home, and sending children to college. Most people in the ordinary ranks of business management, however, need a second worker in the family to afford this higher standard of living.

The majority of people in the United States are considered working class by sociologists—skilled laborers, clerical workers, labor supervisors, and unskilled laborers in industry, or service workers who provide cleaning, maintenance, and other services to those industries. These jobs have much in common—routine work, low wages and strict supervision.

Some working-class occupations pay considerably less than others. For one thing, many blue-collar workers—especially construction workers—typically are laid off at some point during the year, which reduces their total annual income. Also, these workers make less than the median income even when there are no layoffs. Many low-paid, working-class people fall below the poverty line and enter the class that has come to be called the "working poor." Most of these people work at jobs that do not pay enough money to bring them out of poverty. The minimum wage in the United States provides income to one person working full-time year-round—well below the poverty line for a family of four people.

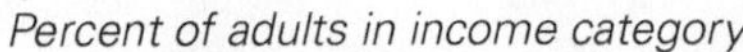
Figure 7-4 Income Status of Adults, by Age, 1971–2011

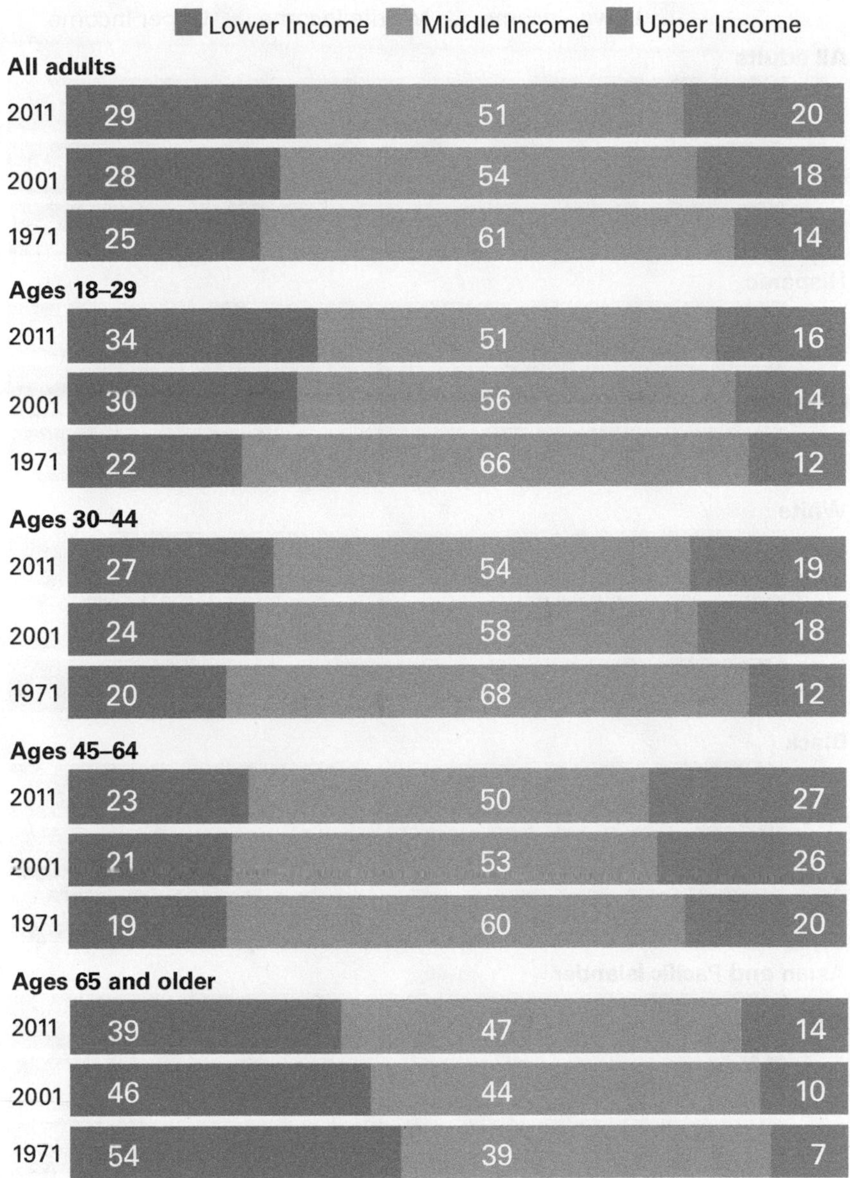


*Note.* Households are assigned to income categories based on their size-adjusted income in the calendar year prior to the survey year (e.g., 2010 income is from the 2011 survey).

Adapted from Pew Research Center tabulations of the Current Population Survey, Annual Social and Economic Supplements, 1971–2011.

Retrieved from http://www.pewsocialtrends.org/2012/08/22/the-lost-decade-of-the-middle-class/

## 7.6b Housing and Lifestyle

The very rich often own several luxurious homes. They spend their leisure time with their wealthy friends and neighbors, and they work together on the boards of banks and corporations. They manage their business affairs with much mutual respect and close cooperation (Domhoff, G. W., 2005, 1967). Their children usually marry the children of other wealthy families; thus, rich families are often related to other rich families, and their wealth remains in the same group. Their housing provides a lifestyle that enables them to know other wealthy people, thereby giving them numerous opportunities to increase their wealth further.

**Figure 7-5** Income Status of Adults, by Race and Ethnicity

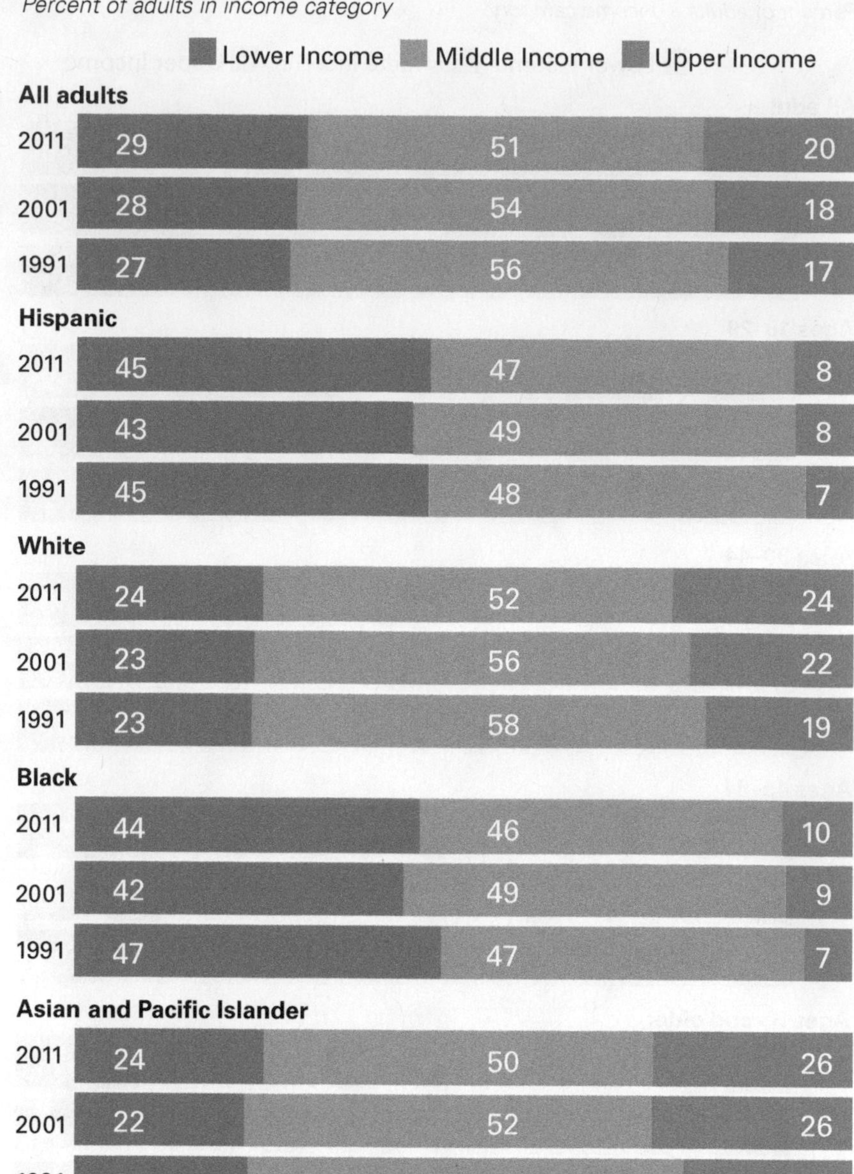


*Note*: Households are assigned to income categories based on their size-adjusted income in the calendar year prior to the survey year (e.g., 2010 income is reported in the 2011 survey). Hispanics are of any race, whites, blacks, Asians and Pacific Islanders are non-Hispanic, single-race-only groups.

SOURCE: Pew Research Center tabulations of the Current Population Survey, Annual Social and Economic Supplements, 1971–2011 http://www.pewsocialtrends.org/2012/08/22/the-lost-decade-of-the-middle-class/

*An estate of the very rich (iStockphoto)*

Upper-middle-class managers and professionals, who are near the top 20% of earners, are more likely to own homes in the suburbs. Their homes may sometimes be in gated communities or in specific suburban areas. Security alarms, manicured yards, swimming pools, entertainment rooms, and other luxuries are commonly found in the homes of the upper-middle class. In addition to providing a nice place to live, owning a home has proved to be a good investment because homes increase in value with inflation. The mortgage interest on homes also provides income tax deductions.

**Figure 7-6** Income Status of Adults, by Gender, 1971–2011

*Percent of adults in income category*

| | Lower Income | Middle Income | Upper Income |
|---|---|---|---|
| **All adults** | | | |
| 2011 | 29 | 51 | 20 |
| 2001 | 28 | 54 | 18 |
| 1971 | 25 | 61 | 14 |
| **Men** | | | |
| 2011 | 26 | 52 | 21 |
| 2001 | 24 | 56 | 20 |
| 1971 | 22 | 63 | 15 |
| **Women** | | | |
| 2011 | 32 | 49 | 19 |
| 2001 | 31 | 52 | 17 |
| 1971 | 28 | 59 | 13 |

*Note.* Households are assigned to income categories based on their size-adjusted income in the calendar year prior to the survey year (e.g., 2010 income is reported in the 2011 survey).

Adapted from Pew Research Center tabulations of the Current Population Survey, Annual Social and Economic Supplements, 1971–2011.

Retrieved from http://www.pewsocialtrends.org/2012/08/22/the-lost-decade-of-the-middle-class/

Lower-middle or working-class people are likely to live in the suburbs, but they are less apt to own their own homes. Those who do own homes live in modest neighborhoods and tend to their own yards on the weekends. Those who rent houses or apartments do not have financial buffers from inflation or benefit from homeowner tax deductions. Instead, as prices go up, their rents go up; they may find it very difficult to maintain their standard of living.

*Those in the upper-middle class tend to own their homes. (iStockphoto)*

The lower class often finds it very difficult to get adequate, affordable housing. They may live in substandard housing in rural areas or in urban slums, and they often pay high rents for housing. Their neighborhoods may be run down, with little pride in the upkeep of properties, and crime ridden. Sometimes two or more families share the same overcrowded apartment in order to meet the rent payments.

The poorest people in the United States do not have access to housing, living in shelters or on the street. The number of street people is not known, but it is estimated that there are as many as 3 million homeless in the United States. The homeless have either lost contact with their families or have no families. Some of them may work on a day-to-day basis, but they do not earn enough money to rent a place to live. Others have no income. They sleep

**Figure 7-7** Income Status of Adults, by Education, 1971–2011

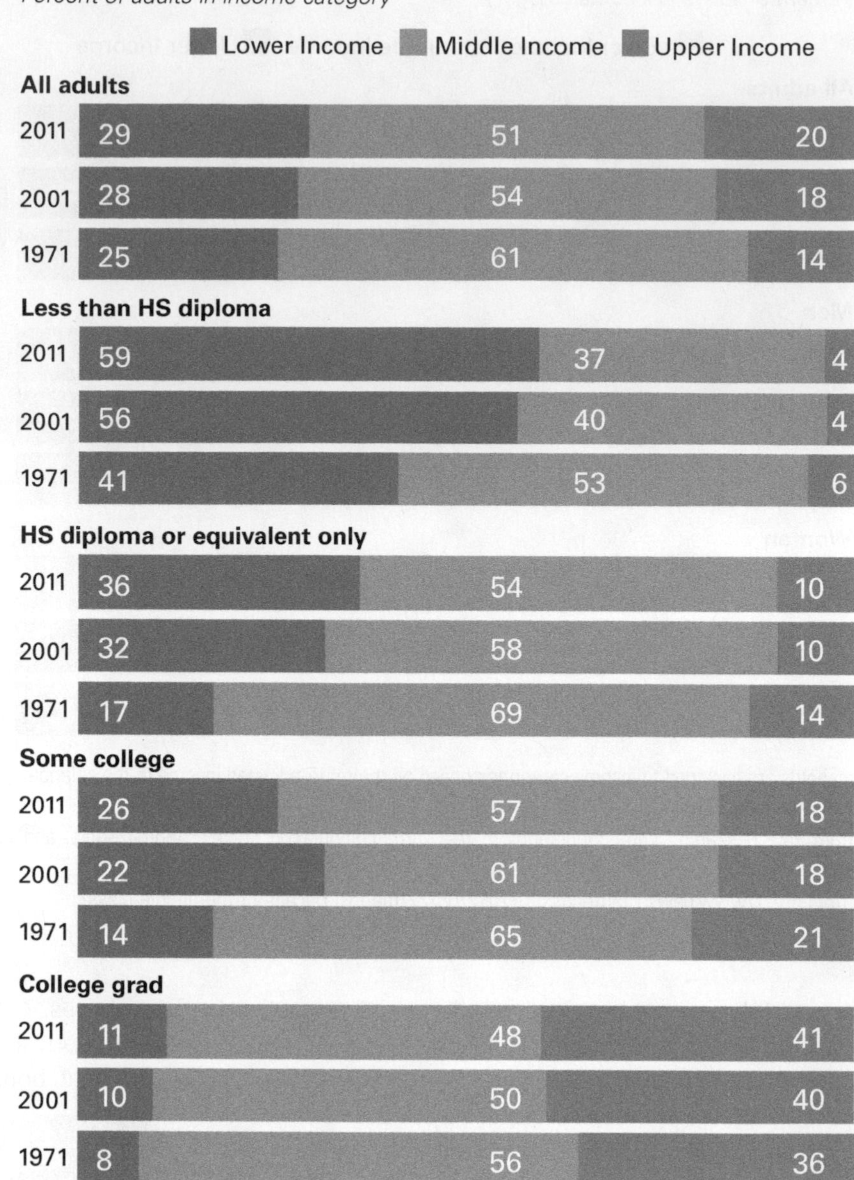


*Note.* Households are assigned to income categories based on their size-adjusted income in the calendar year prior to the survey year (e.g., 2010 income is reported in the 2011 survey).

Adapted from Pew Research Center tabulations of the Current Population Survey, Annual Social and Economic Supplements, 1971–2011.

Retrieved from http://www.pewsocialtrends.org/2012/08/22/the-lost-decade-of-the-middle-class/

in subways, doorways, or on park benches. They are more likely to be the victim of rape or assault, and in winter, they sometimes freeze to death.

In addition, children under the age 18 account for 39% of the homeless population, 500,000 children live in foster homes, and another 130,000 are waiting to be adopted (National Coalition for the Homeless, 2009). Many others are in hospitals, mental health facilities, and detention centers because they have no homes or families who can take care of them.

Homeless children exhibit high degrees of social isolation which is, in turn, related to emotional health concerns such as depression and social anxiety (Anooshian, 2003).

**Table 7-4** Distribution of Net Worth and Financial Wealth in the United States, 1983–2007

| Total Net Worth | | | |
|---|---|---|---|
| | Top 1% | Next 19% | Bottom 80% |
| 1983 | 33.8% | 47.5% | 18.7% |
| 1989 | 37.4% | 46.2% | 16.5% |
| 1992 | 37.2% | 46.6% | 16.2% |
| 1995 | 38.5% | 45.4% | 16.1% |
| 1998 | 38.1% | 45.3% | 16.6% |
| 2001 | 33.4% | 51.0% | 15.6% |
| 2004 | 34.3% | 50.3% | 15.3% |
| 2007 | 34.6% | 50.5% | 15.0% |
| **Financial Wealth** | | | |
| | Top 1% | Next 19% | Bottom 80% |
| 1983 | 42.9% | 48.4% | 8.7% |
| 1989 | 46.9% | 46.5% | 6.6% |
| 1992 | 45.6% | 46.7% | 7.7% |
| 1995 | 47.2% | 45.9% | 7.0% |
| 1998 | 47.3% | 43.6% | 9.1% |
| 2001 | 39.7% | 51.5% | 8.7% |
| 2004 | 42.2% | 50.3% | 7.5% |
| 2007 | 42.7% | 50.3% | 7.0% |

From Wolff (2004, 2007, & 2010), in Domhoff, 2011.

Children between kindergarten and 6th grade who live in homeless shelters believe academic is virtually unattainable. A recurring theme among shelter parents and children is that their lower social status negatively influences the attitude of school officials toward them (Marcus, 2002).

The poor suffer in personal, perhaps not so obvious ways, as well. For example, insurance companies have developed the concept of "moral hazards" to justify requiring deductibles from the insured. The idea behind this insurance company practice is that full payment to the insured (without having to pay a deductible) for disasters such as fires or automobile accidents would induce anti-social behavior such as being careless around the home or driving dangerously, thus serving as a "moral hazard." Policy makers have applied the concept of "moral hazards" to issues such as public assistance, unemployment insurance, and other efforts used to combat unemployment and poverty. Unfortunately, in situations that are completely beyond the control of victims—such as the catastrophic storms Katrina and Sandy—the poor suffer the most consequences. This negative effect of the "moral hazards" approach has led S. M. Miller (2007) to coin the term "immoral hazards"—the harming of people through governmental or corporate neglect.

*The lower class may live in substandard housing. (iStockphoto)*

## 7.6c Education

The children of the rich are the group most likely to go to private preparatory schools and elite colleges, regardless of their grades. They not only earn credentials that are useful in business but also make more valuable contacts with influential people who can help them get high-paying positions. Middle-class children ordinarily graduate from public or parochial high schools, and they have an excellent chance of going to college. Working-class children usually complete high school, but only those who achieve very high grades are likely to attend college. Poor children tend to drop out of high school and often live in neighborhoods with poor schools, in which they may not even learn to read and write. Moreover, when they see that high school graduates often have trouble getting jobs, they become discouraged and quit as soon as they are old enough because there is no apparent advantage to staying in school. Thus, education is a life chance very closely associated with family wealth.

## 7.6d Medical Care



Medical care is not distributed equally. The rich and the middle classes are usually covered by medical insurance through their employers. Insurance covers most medical expenses, and members of these classes generally receive good medical care. Nearly 51 million people in the United States were without health insurance in 2009 (United State Census Bureau, 2012). The less income you make, the less likely you are to have health insurance. Case in point: 27% of people who made less than $25,000 in 2009 did not have health insurance, compared to 9% of those who made more than $75,000.

In all modern industrialized societies except the United States and South Africa, everyone in the society is covered by a national health system that meets their health needs. As a result, infants are born with full medical care, children are immunized from childhood diseases, and the diseases of adults are treated promptly, usually at no cost to the patient.

On March 23, 2010, President Obama signed into law legislation that would extend healthcare coverage to 32 million people who were not covered. Yet, the attorneys general from more than 20 states sought to stop the law from going into effect, and every Republican in Congress opposed the law (Clemmit, 2010). The plight of the poor to receive adequate healthcare will likely continue for some time.

## 7.6e Criminal Justice

Herbert Gans (1971) argues that the poor are punished and identified as deviant more than members of the middle class. The poor are overrepresented within the criminal justice system. Those living in poverty are less likely to be able to afford legal representation and lack the political power to change their fate. The United States incarcerates more people than any other country, with the majority of inmates coming from poverty or low-income homes.

# APPLYING KNOWLEDGE OF INEQUALITY AND LIFE CHANCES

Knowledge of the different life chances available to members of different social classes can be used in a number of practical ways. Clinical sociologists and other therapists may use this knowledge to gain a greater understanding of clients from different social classes. As we have seen, people from different social classes have different types of problems and different perspectives on those problems.

Politicians and legislators may rely on this information to help them develop meaningful, relevant, and workable social policies to help the underprivileged. Differences in occupational opportunities, living arrangements, education, and medical treatment may strongly influence a person's psychological makeup. This fact has important implications for what type of policies will or will not succeed. Consider, for example, policies regarding welfare. A welfare program that increases the number of jobs for the poor may look very attractive to someone in the middle or upper class. However, to assume that the mere availability of jobs will enable the downtrodden to compete in the same manner that members of the middle class do is to assume that people from all classes are the same. A welfare program may need to include some type of counseling for recipients to help them gain the confidence and self-esteem necessary for success in a competitive market. Other measures might include education and career training, housing reforms, and improved medical care.

Teachers may also benefit from knowledge of different life chances. The crowded living conditions of some lower-class families may inhibit lower-class students from spending the necessary amount of solitary homework time it takes to understand some subjects. Because their parents may not have experienced the rewards that a good education can bring, lower-class students may not receive the same reinforcement about the importance of studying and achieving good grades that middle-class students do. Lower-class students may not have role models who have achieved upward mobility due to a good education and may have a difficult time seeing the value in schoolwork, as a result.

Teaching upper-middle-class students and lower-class students, therefore, may require very different teaching strategies. Teachers of lower-class students may need to spend as much time helping their students understand the value and importance of an education as they do with the course material itself; and they may need to explain difficult material more slowly, more intensively, and in more ways during class time rather than expect students to master the material at home.

These examples are only a few ways in which knowledge of how life chances relate to position in the stratification system can he used. Consider how you could use this knowledge in a career that you are thinking about entering. Also consider how you can use this knowledge to understand how to get ahead. Are people more or less stuck in their social strata, or can they get ahead?

---

## thinking SOCIOLOGICALLY

1. Social class influences the life chances of individuals in what ways? Choose one of the middle class categories identified by the Pew Research Center, and discuss the life chances of a member if he/she lived in your city. Discuss the following: income, neighborhood, work, play, school, church, healthcare, and so on. Use specific examples from your city to illustrate the specific class.
2. Develop an explanation for the inequalities found with public education school systems.
3. Discuss the pros and cons of having a national healthcare system where all members of society are covered by insurance, regardless of their social class ranking.
4. Examine the income differences by age, gender, race/Hispanic origin, and education in Figures 7-4, 7-5, 7-6, and 7-7. What differences do you notice in changes of income among these different groups? Discuss what you think accounts for these differences? How are the life chances of members of each of these groups affected by these changes?

# 7.7 SOCIAL MOBILITY IN THE UNITED STATES

Social mobility—changing social position—can occur in a variety of ways. A change to a job of higher rank or marriage to a person of higher rank is **upward mobility**, and a movement to a job of lower rank is **downward mobility**. Sometimes, marrying someone of a lower rank can produce downward mobility.

Persons who change class or status within their own lifetimes experience **intragenerational mobility**. Mobility between generations, or **intergenerational mobility**, is traditionally measured by comparing the social positions of parents and children. If sons or daughters have higher positions than their parents had, they are upwardly mobile; if the younger generation's position is lower, they are downwardly mobile. Both the social structure and individual characteristics influence upward and downward mobility.

**Upward mobility**
Movement in the stratification system to a position of greater wealth, status, and power

**Downward mobility**
A move to a position of lower rank in the stratification system

**Intragenerational mobility**
A change of social position or rank, up or down, within one's own lifetime

**Intergenerational mobility**
A change of social position or rank, up or down, from one generation to the next, such as when children have a higher status than their parents

**Split labor market**
A labor market in which some jobs afford upward mobility and others do not

## 7.7a Structural Characteristics of Mobility in the United States

Mobility in this country is influenced by numerous factors: (a) growth of large corporations; (b) increased standard of living; (c) growth of urban areas; (d) maintenance of a split labor market, which splinters the labor pool in ways that minimize mobility; and (e) advanced technology, such as reliance on computers and robots.

The growth of large corporations has influenced the wages people are paid. Those who work in large organizations often earn more than those who work in small firms. People in supervisory positions earn a percentage more than the people they supervise, and their earnings generally increase as the number of people they supervise increases. Thus, as corporations grow larger, supervisors earn more. Many qualified people in large organizations never have the opportunity to be supervisors, however; despite their high qualifications, they will never be able to earn the income of the supervisor.

The increasing standard of living over the past century has improved the lives of most workers in the United States, even though their relative class or status remains unchanged. This improvement is especially true for factory workers, whose wages and living conditions have improved dramatically since the turn of the century.

The growth of urban areas, where the cost of living is higher, has led to higher wages for city dwellers. Equally qualified people doing the same work are apt to earn more money in the city than in the country. Doctors, for example, earn considerably more in large metropolitan areas than in rural areas.

A split labor market is one in which some jobs afford upward mobility while others do not. The job market is split between manual and non-manual work and is further segmented within these spheres. White-collar workers cannot move into higher-level manual work or into the professions, which normally require extensive educational certification. Manual workers cannot be promoted into the skilled crafts or into white-collar positions. Farmers are completely outside the main sphere of upward mobility.

*Increased technology has expanded the number of white-collar clerical and service jobs. (Shutterstock)*

The **split labor market** provides even greater obstacles for women, the poor, and minority groups, who mostly occupy the lowest ranks of manual and non-manual occupations. Their jobs often have no career paths at all, and the poor rarely get the opportunity for professional training or apprenticeships in the skilled crafts. In recent years, robots do more and more manual jobs (or corporations have moved such jobs overseas where labor is cheaper). Not only is there no mobility in manual work, but also the number of manual-labor jobs is shrinking. Thus, increased technology has eliminated some jobs involving manual labor and has increased the number of white-collar clerical and service jobs.

# 7.8 THEORIES OF SOCIAL STRATIFICATION

Why are societies stratified? How is it that some people have more of the scarce resources society has to offer? This question was widely debated by early sociologists. As mentioned in Chapter 1, Spencer believed that superior people would educate themselves and become leaders, whereas inferior people would remain in the bottom ranks of society. Society, he said, developed through an evolutionary process, and those who profited from natural selection—"survival of the fittest"—came out on top. This process of natural selection was good for social progress, he argued, and society should not interfere with it.

Marx, who argued that stratification would eventually cause revolution, formulated the opposing view. The upper class in industrial society hired the proletariat to work in their factories, exploited them for profit, and drove them into poverty. As the proletariat became poorer, Marx contended, they would become aware of their plight and would revolt. The theories of these early European writers have had a strong influence on modern theories of stratification and have resulted in the structural functional theory and the conflict theory.

## 7.8a Structural Functional Theory

Structural functionalists have refined Spencer's notion that society, like any other organism, is self-regulating and self-maintaining. It consists of interrelated parts that serve a function in maintaining the system as a whole. When they recognized that stratification was a persistent force in society, they argued that it must serve some function. They hypothesized that because modern society is so complex, people with strong leadership skills are needed to organize and run the complex businesses and industries. People with strong leadership abilities need advanced training and must be willing to work very hard and assume a great deal of responsibility. Society must encourage these efforts by rewarding leaders with wealth and status—scarce resources that in turn can be used to gain power.

In terms of inherent worth as a human being, Davis and Moore (1945) acknowledged that an artist or a teacher might be equal to a corporate executive. The talents of artists and teachers, however, are not as scarce and therefore not as valuable to the society, according to Davis and Moore. Thus, corporate executives who have the talent to lead business and industry are more highly rewarded, not because they are more worthwhile human beings but because they are making greater contributions to the functioning of society. This theoretical perspective permits a belief in human equality at the same time that it explains inequality. If society had an equal need for all types of work, then all its members would be equal in the stratification system.

## 7.8b Conflict Theory

Conflict theorists reject the functional viewpoint (Duberman, 1976), arguing that inequality develops as a result of people's desire for power and that close-knit groups compete with one another to gain possession of the scarce resources that are a source of power. According to this view, resources are not rewards for talent or for assuming difficult tasks—they are acquired through inheritance, coercion, or exploitation. Inequality results when one group acquires more resources than other groups.

Once a dominant group gets power, according to conflict theorists, the group **legitimates** its power and makes it acceptable by appealing to the values of the masses.

**Legitimate**
To make the power of the dominant group acceptable to the masses so they let the dominant group rule without question

Politicians often use democratic values, a mandate from the people, to legitimate their stance on issues. The powerful may point to progress as a value to gain support for everything from expenditures for scientific research to acceptance of a polluted environment. Corporations may appeal directly to patriotic values to justify their opposition to a raise in corporate taxes—what is good for the corporation is good for the nation; or they may appeal to the value of equal opportunity, arguing that such a raise would cost jobs. These beliefs and perceptions, when accepted by the masses, become the prevailing **ideology**. *Ideology* refers to a set of cultural beliefs, values, and attitudes that legitimate the status quo as well as attempt to change it.

If the masses are influenced by elite ideology, they are said to have **false consciousness**—a lack of awareness of their own interests and an acceptance of elite rule. If, on the other hand, the masses are aware that people's fates are tied to the fate of their own class, they are said to have **class-consciousness**. For example, if people realize that which neighborhood school they attend is determined by how much money they have, they have class-consciousness.

Theories of social stratification are important not only because they help us to understand why some basic social inequalities exist, but also because they provide a basis on which politicians and legislators may develop social policies. For example, whether a politician favors increased government spending on social services (such as welfare, Medicaid, food stamps, and shelters for the homeless) may have to do with his or her understanding of why people need such services. A politician who believes that poverty exists because of individuals' unwillingness or lack of motivation to work hard may oppose government spending. Conversely, a politician who believes that poverty exists because of basic inequities in the system may support government spending. Issues such as these often have no clear answers, but theories of social stratification can offer politicians important insights for dealing with them and can prevent politicians from relying solely on their own values and beliefs.

## 7.8c Attempts at Synthesis

Some sociologists have tried to reconcile the functional and conflict theories of stratification (Dahrendorf, 1951; Lenski, 1966; Tumin, 1963). Accumulating research suggests that stratification has a wide variety of causes—some based on conflict, some on cooperation. A stratification system based on religion, for example, may emphasize feelings of community and selflessness. Others, based on land ownership or accumulation of money, may emphasize competition and the efforts of individuals. As our understanding of the nature and development of stratification improves, it is becoming increasingly apparent that stratification is influenced by a great many different factors: how food is grown, how supplies are manufactured and distributed, how much wealth accumulates, and how people use their leisure time, to name only a few. Neither functional nor conflict theory offers us a full understanding of how stratification systems develop.

There is, however, widespread agreement that all stratification systems are based on the consensus among members of the society that inequality is good, fair, and just. People may accept stratification because they value the achievements of the wealthy or because the media have misled them. Whatever the reason, acceptance of the stratification system confers power on those of high rank.

**Ideology**

A set of ideas about what society is like, how it functions, whether it is good or bad, and how it should be changed

**False consciousness**

Lack of awareness of class differences and acceptance of upper-class rule

**Class-consciousness**

Awareness among members of a society that the society is stratified

# CHAPTER 7 Wrapping it up

## Summary


1. Inequality develops as a result of the unequal distribution of scarce resources. People are differentiated, but not usually ranked, on the basis of many criteria: hair color, height, hobbies, or region of the country in which they live.
2. People are ranked, or stratified, on the basis of their possession of or access to scarce resources.
3. Very simple societies have little division of labor and little stratification. Agrarian and industrial societies have more wealth, greater division of labor, and more stratification.
4. There are four types of stratification systems that have existed in the world: (1) In *caste systems*, positions are assigned at birth, according to the position of the caste, and a person's caste is fixed for life. (2) In *estate systems*, position is determined by law or through inheritance. (3) In *slave systems*, position typically is assigned at birth. (4) In *class systems*, found in industrial societies, a person may be able to move into higher or lower strata. Sources of power in a class-based society include class position, status, and party position.
5. Determinants of class position within the United States include social class, social status, and power. Many sociologists are using socioeconomic status to determine class position.
6. Most people identify themselves as middle class; however, lifestyles of Americans vary widely—most importantly in terms of occupation, housing, healthcare, and educational opportunity—even within the middle class.
7. Life chances for occupations, housing, education, and medical care vary in relation to a person's place in the stratification system.
8. Upward mobility is most influenced by structural changes in the workplace. The proliferation and increasing size of large corporations has improved the standard of living for many workers. The segmented or split labor market has limited upward mobility for lower-class people.
9. Structural functionalists believe that systems of stratification develop because societies need scarce leadership skills and reward those who are willing to assume the responsibility of leadership.
10. Conflict theorists contend that stratification develops because some groups gain a monopoly over scarce resources through either inheritance or conflict, and they use those resources to maintain their high positions.


## Discussion Questions

1. Discuss the functions of the stratification system in American society. Discuss its dysfunctions.
2. Look through your campus newspaper, and find ways that groups legitimate their political positions.
3. Discuss the extent of class-consciousness that you would expect to find on your campus and in your community. Do you think people are very aware of class? Would the people you know use the same categories of class used in the Jackman and Jackman study?
4. What people have the most power in your community? Do they have power because of their wealth, their status, or their position in an organization? Explain.
5. Has the quality of your education been influenced by the amount of money your family has?
6. Discuss how poverty affects those involved with the criminal justice system. Are those living in poverty more likely to be victims or offenders? Explain.
7. How does the split labor market lead to further separation between the rich and the poor?

CHAPTER 8

# Racial and Ethnic Differentiation

## SYNOPSIS

### Racial, Ethnic, and Minority Groups

- Race and Racial Groups
- Ethnicity and Ethnic Groups
- Minority Groups

### Attitudes, Behaviors, and Their Influence

- Stereotypes
- Prejudice
- Discrimination
- Racism

### Patterns of Racial and Ethnic Relations

- Integration and Assimilation
- Pluralism
- Segregation
- Mass Expulsion
- Genocide

### Ethnic Stratification

- Ethnic Antagonism

### Racial and Ethnic Groups in the United States

- Hispanic Americans
- African Americans
- Asian Americans
- Native Americans
- WASPs and White Ethnic Americans
- Jewish Americans

### The Future

Focal Point

# MARK ALL THAT APPLY

In 1790 the United States conducted its very first census, counting the number of people living within the 13 colonies. Approximately 650 U.S. marshals rode on horseback, using only pencil and paper to count the heads of households and other persons living in their homes. It took the marshals 18 months to count the 3.9 million people living in America at that time. The first census was relatively easy with only six questions. They included the name of the head of household and the number of people living in the household—free white men over age 16, free white men under age 16, free white women, other free people, and slaves.

Since that first census over 200 years ago, one has been conducted every 10 years with alterations to the questions occurring nearly as frequently. For example, racial categories have changed almost regularly, with some groups expanding while others were excluded altogether. Indians were excluded from the first census, and blacks were considered only three-fifths of a person. During the 1850 census, racial categories included the rising number of racially mixed people. Racial classification included white, black, and Mulatto (mixed race)—with blacks and Mulattos further categorized as either free or slave. It wasn't until later that censuses included persons other than whites and blacks. The 1870 Census reflected the end of slavery, but added Chinese and Indian to the racial categories. The Tenth Census in 1890 further quantified mixed race persons by adding Quadroon (one-quarter black) and Octoroon (any degree up to one-eighth black) to the Mulatto (one-half black) category. While quantifying black racial categories may appear to have benefited persons with mixed race heritage, the distinction was designed, in fact, to limit their access to resources. Not long after slavery ended, the United States entered a period of Jim Crow segregation where persons with any degree of black blood were considered black, regardless of their skin color. These categories stayed in place until the 1930s; but new categories of race were also added, such as "Mexican," which was removed at the next census in 1940. Today, Mexicans are not classified as a race at all, but rather are ethnically lumped together with other groups under the "Hispanic" category.

The biggest change to racial classifications occurred in 2000, when persons were allowed for the first time in history to mark more than one race. The 2000 Census questionnaire contained 15 race options, including an option for "Some other race." On a questionnaire item separate from race identification, individuals were asked to indicate whether their ethnicity is "Hispanic or Latino" or "Not Hispanic or Latino."

According to the U.S. Census, this new change reflects the growing number of interracial children and the increasing diversity throughout the country. After the data was tabulated, 2.4% of the population had identified themselves as belonging to two or more races. Of those, 4% were children under age 18. Among the population of persons who marked two or more races, 93% identified themselves as only two races. The largest group of two races was "White and Other" with over 32%, followed by "White and Native American" with 15.86%, and "White and Asian" with 12.72%. The percentage of those people that chose "White and Black" as their race was 11.5 percent. Hawaii was the state with the largest population of persons who identified themselves as multiracial (24.1%).

How we define race changes over time. The way race was defined in 2000 will likely change in 20 or 30 years. In addition, other cultures may see race differently than we do in the United States. For example, in the former South African system of racial separation, there were four legally defined racial categories—white, black, Colored, and Indian. Established in 1950, those racial categories defined how people were treated—including what schools they went to, whom they could marry, whether they could vote, and much more. In 1991, South Africa officially abolished their system of racial separation.

The arbitrary categories of race found on the censuses throughout the history of the United States suggest that race is socially constructed, rather than biologically. Race is defined and redefined to reflect the beliefs of our society at any given time. How will adding the "Mark all that apply" instruction to the census change our definition of race in the future?

(Shutterstock)

# 8.1 RACIAL, ETHNIC, AND MINORITY GROUPS

The terms *racial*, *ethnic*, and *minority* are often used interchangeably and rather loosely. Although they may be treated as equivalent or overlapping concepts, it is important to differentiate these terms before we discuss the more substantive issues of race and ethnic relations.

## 8.1a Race and Racial Groups

The term "race" has only been around for a short period of time and is one of the most arbitrary and misunderstood concepts used by our society. A **racial group** is a socially constructed category of people who are distinguished from each other by select physical characteristics. These traits typically include basic physical attributes such as facial features, body type, skin color, hair texture, and so on. Definitions of race can include biological, physical, and social meanings.

The essential question is whether there are significant variations in the physical traits of different populations of humans. The focus of investigation has ranged from obvious characteristics, such as skin and hair coloring, to less obvious traits, such as blood type and genetically transmitted diseases.

The effects of climate have complicated classification of peoples by skin color. It has been found that varying degrees of exposure to sunlight causes variations in skin shading. Asians and Africans have darker coloring because they live in more tropical climates. Classification by skin color is further complicated by biological mixing—for example, the Creoles of Alabama and Mississippi, the Red Bones of Louisiana, the Croatians of North Carolina, and the Mestizos of South America. Whether members of these groups have Native American or African American ancestors is a matter of dispute.

In reality, truly objective criteria of racial groups based strictly on physical or biological characteristics do not seem to exist. Sociologists and anthropologists have concluded that race is primarily a social construct rather than a biological one. That is, it is a concept that has been defined to help make distinctions about humans based upon inherited physical characteristics. The trend in current thinking among social scientists and many natural scientists is that we cannot.

What may be of more importance is how and why race has been defined over the years. Some feel that the concept of race was developed by the dominant groups in the world as a mechanism to prejudge, divide, rank and control populations that were different from themselves. The concept of race distorts our ideas about differences among groups throughout the world and contributes to myths about their behaviors and characteristics, and also contributes to the perpetuation of inequality between dominant groups and minority groups (American Anthropological Association, 1998; Morning, 2009).

**Racial group**

A socially constructed category that distinguishes by selected inherited physical characteristics

The concept of race found popularity in the United States during slavery and Jim Crow segregation. In the mid-1600s, the fear of a degenerative race led many colonies to create laws forbidding marriage between blacks, Native Americans, and whites. After slavery, a one-drop rule was put in place that required any person with one-drop of African blood to identify as black. The case of Susie Guillory Phipps, for example, highlights the problems generations of children encountered even after the one-drop rule was ended. In 1982, Phipps went to the Department of Vital Records in Louisiana to get a birth certificate. Upon receiving it she noticed the race box on her certificate was marked "black," rather than "white." Phipps, thinking a mistake had clearly been made, brought it to the attention of the employee. The agency informed Phipps that no mistake was made and that she was correctly identified as black even though her parents, grandparents, and great-grandparents were white. Phipps took her case all the way to the Louisiana Supreme Court, which upheld the lower court's ruling that Ms. Phipps was indeed legally "black." During the trial, the government produced a family tree tracing eleven generations of her family that included a black slave and white plantation owner. At the time of Phipps' birth, the legal one-drop rule was still in place, identifying her as black, regardless of her social identity.

*In the 1600s, many U.S. colonies had laws forbidding marriage between people of different races. (Shutterstock)*

Social and cultural conceptions of race, regardless of their lack of biological basis, have probably the most important meaning with regard to the individual being labeled. A person will typically associate with those who validate his/her racial identity. For example, people who are of mixed black and white heritage and who identify themselves as black will likely want to authenticate their identity to others including their social circle, peers, class, etc. In 2000, the U.S. Census—which relies on self-definition—for the first time allowed individuals to mark "all that apply" with regard to race. As a result, 6.8 million people, or 2.4% of the population, identified themselves as multiracial. In the case of Susie Phipps, legally she was black; however, her social identity remained white as a result of how she and society perceived her race. In 2010, 9 million people identified themselves as multiracial, or 2.9% of the population.

In review, social definitions far outweigh biological definitions of race; however, these social definitions are based on some combination of some inherited physical traits, regardless of any evidence that there are clear and distinct physical differences or that any such differences can explain human behavior. Some physical traits—such as hair color, height, and size of feet—may be inherited; yet, these are rarely used to differentiate people into one racial category or another, where as other physical traits—such as skin color—may be used. Taking these considerations into account, biological differences per se do not constitute racial differences. Rather, a racial group is a socially defined group distinguished by selected physical characteristics, even though these characteristics are difficult to ascertain.

## 8.1b Ethnicity and Ethnic Groups

The concept of ethnic groups originally referred to group membership based upon nationality (country of origin), but now also includes religion, language, or region. In this sense, for example, Jews, Mormons, Latinos, and White Southerners can be considered **ethnic groups**. As with race, the concept of ethnicity may be loosely based on selected physical characteristics, but is primarily a social construction that includes unique cultural traits, ascribed membership, sense of community, ethnocentrism, and territoriality.

**Ethnic group**
Group of people characterized by cultural traits that reflect national origin, religion, and language

Unique cultural traits may include manner of dress, language, religious practices, or speech patterns. Ethnic groups are often seen as subcultures, distinguished by their cultural traits from the dominant group. However, cultural traits alone will not set one group apart from the other.

Ascribed membership means the person's ethnic characteristics were ascribed at birth. When an individual is born into an ethnic group, it is unlikely he/she will leave unless there are unusual circumstances. For example, a person may be born into the Jewish culture, but choose to leave and adopt the culture of another group, such as Christianity or Catholicism.

Sense of community exists when an ethnic group displays a sense of common association among its members. Sociologist Milton Gordon (1964) suggests that the ethnic group serves as a social-psychological reference for creating a "sense of peoplehood." This sense of we-ness is derived from a common ancestry or origin when people sense a community, an awareness of belonging to a group. However, the common ancestry does not have to be authentic, as long as the ethnic group (or others) perceive themselves as a community. Therefore, just like race, ethnicity is socially created and maintained.

Ethnocentrism is another common characteristic among ethnic groups. When a group has a sense of peoplehood, they have a tendency to judge other groups by the standards and values of their own. Group solidarity serves as a source of ethnocentrism, or the belief that one's own group is superior to others. The norms, values, beliefs, attitudes, and behaviors of one's own group are perceived as natural or correct while other groups are seen as unnatural or incorrect.

Territoriality refers to the idea of "nations within nations," where groups occupy distinct territories within the larger society. Enclaves of ethnic groups can be found in larger communities where they have some degree of autonomy away from the dominant culture. Stores, restaurants, community centers, and other facilities accommodate or are owned by members of the ethnic group.

In the United States, the largest identified ethnic group is Hispanic. However, within this category are a number of other ethnic groups including Mexicans, Spaniards, Puerto Ricans, Cubans, and others. Each has a distinctive culture in America, which can create problems when they are classified as a single ethnic group.

**BVT*Lab***

Flashcards are available for this chapter at www.BVTLab.com

## 8.1c Minority Groups

The concept of a **minority group** refers to a group's access to power and status within a society. A minority group's size is insignificant to its being labeled as a subordinate category of people. Women, for example, are a numerical majority in American society, yet they have historically held a minority status within society. In the Republic of South Africa, whites comprise less than one-fifth of the total population, but are considered the dominant majority group. A *minority group* tends to have less control or power over their own lives than do the members of a dominant or majority group and to experience a narrowing of life's opportunities for success, education, wealth, and the pursuit of happiness. In other words, a minority group does not share, in proportion to its numbers, in what a given society defines as valuable (Schaefer, R. T., 2005).

In the United States, the most highly valued norms have historically been those created by White Anglo-Saxon Protestant (WASP) middle classes. The extent of a group's departure from the norms established by the dominant group will define their social status within society. Thus, the elderly, poor people, poor people in Appalachia, Southern Whites, disabled persons, gays and lesbians, and members of most diversity populations are minority groups in the United States.

**Minority group**

A group that is subordinate to the dominant group in terms of the distribution of social power, defined by some physical or cultural characteristics, and is usually—but not always—smaller in number than the dominant group

**thinking** SOCIOLOGICALLY

1. To what extent is race based solely on biological, legal, or social criteria in the U.S. today?
2. Using the ideas of interactionist theory, explain the social significance of racial, ethnic, or minority categories.

# 8.2 ATTITUDES, BEHAVIORS, AND THEIR INFLUENCE

One of the most serious problems faced by most racial and ethnic groups in America and around the world is how they are perceived and treated by others. For a number of reasons, people tend to treat those they perceive to be different in ways that they would not treat members of their own group. As a result, rising inequalities have increased societal strains and tensions among different groups. To pursue ideals of equality, we must understand how the attitudes underlying unfair practices are formed.

## 8.2a Stereotypes

**Stereotypes** are exaggerated beliefs usually associated with a group of people, based on race, ethnicity, gender, religion, or sexual orientation. Stereotypes generally begin with a particular belief about an undesirable characteristic of a member of a group. Through interaction with others, the socially constructed belief will persist and be generalized to the entire group, thus creating a stereotype. Stereotypes often, but not always, develop out of fear, or when the dominant group feels threatened by a particular group.

Within many racial and ethnic stereotypes there exists a "kernel of truth" in a perceived belief. In other words, there may be group members who possess the characteristic used as the foundation of the stereotype; however, it does not apply to the entire group, and it may be an exaggeration of that "kernel of truth." Needless to say, stereotypes do not begin to address the great variety of behavior that exists among members of diverse populations.

The media plays a significant role in the establishment and persistence of stereotypes about racial and ethnic groups. Consider the stereotypes that were reinforced about Italian Americans by the TV show *The Sopranos* that aired for eight years (1999–2007). In 2004, Italian American groups confronted Dream Works SKG about the ethnic slurs and stereotypes that were perpetuated by the movie *Shark Tale*, especially since the intended audience of the movie was children. In the movie, Don Lino is the godfather of great white sharks. The Italian American groups who protested felt that "The movie introduces young minds to the idea that people with Italian names—like millions of Americans across the country—are gangsters" (Rose, 2004).

Stereotypes are rarely used to create positive images of a racial or ethnic group; instead, they are used to tear down the social value of a particular group within society. When stereotyped group members themselves begin to internalize the belief, they will act toward themselves accordingly. Several researchers have focused on how children form racial identities (Clark & Clark, 1939; Spencer, 1985), as well as how children form attitudes about others based on race (Van Ausdale & Feagin, 1996). The Clark and Clark study (1947) examined how black children see themselves during play. Provided with identical black and white dolls (except for the color), black children were more likely to see the "white" doll as more positive, pretty, nice, etc., while identifying the "black" doll as bad, negative, or ugly. In a similar vein, Radke and Trager's (1950) early

**Stereotypes**
Widely held and oversimplified beliefs about the character and behavior of all members of a group that seldom correspond to the facts

studies of black children support the idea that members of a stereotyped minority tend to internalize the definitions attached to them. In their study, the children were asked to evaluate "black" and "white" dolls and to tell stories about black and white persons in photographs. The children overwhelmingly preferred the white dolls to the black ones; the white dolls were described as good, the black dolls as bad. The black individuals in the photographs were given inferior roles as servants, maids, or gardeners. In 2006 Kiri Davis, a young filmmaker, recreated the Clark and Clark study and found black children are still influenced greatly by the stereotype that white is socially accepted more than black. In her 7 minute video, Davis asked the children to "pick the doll that is nice," with 15 out of 21 black children choosing the "white" doll.

Another effect of stereotypes that has become controversial in recent years is the practice of racial and ethnic profiling. Profiling is the practice of subjecting people to increased surveillance or scrutiny based on racial or ethnic factors, without any other basis (Chan, 2011). For example, black citizens undergo significantly more repeated motor vehicle stops by police than white citizens. Growette-Bostaph (2008) found that this was not the result of differences in driving behavior but rather the result of being members of different population groups.

*Japanese Americans suffered prejudicial treatment after the battleship USS* Arizona *was bombed by the Japanese in a surprise attack at Pearl Harbor on December 7, 1941.* (AP Wide World Photo)

## 8.2b Prejudice

**Prejudice** is an attitude, usually negative, that is used against an entire group and often based on stereotypes of racial or ethnic characteristics (Schaefer R. T., 2005). It involves thoughts and beliefs that people harbor which, in turn, lead to categorical rejection and the disliking of an entire racial or ethnic group. A variety of theories have been offered to explain prejudice.

*Economic theories of prejudice* are based on the supposition that both competition and conflict among groups are inevitable when different groups desire commodities that are in short supply. These theories explain why racial prejudice is most salient during periods of depression and economic turmoil. In California, for example, from the 1840s through the depression of the 1930s, economic relations between European and Chinese Americans were tolerant and amiable as long as the Chinese confined themselves to occupations such as laundry and curio shops. When Chinese Americans began to compete with European Americans in gold mining and other business enterprises, however, violent racial conflicts erupted. Japanese Americans had a similar experience during their internment in camps after the bombing of Pearl Harbor.

The exploitation variant of economic theory argues that prejudice is used to stigmatize a group as inferior, to put its members in a subordinate position, and to justify their exploitation. The exploitation theme explains how systems under capitalism have traditionally justified exploiting recent immigrants who have little money, few skills, and difficulties with English.

*Psychological theories of prejudice* suggest that prejudice satisfies psychic needs or compensates for some defect in the personality. When people use **scapegoating**, they blame other persons or groups for their own problems. Another psychological strategy involves **projection**, in which people attribute their own unacceptable traits or behaviors to another person. In this way, people transfer responsibility for their own failures to a vulnerable group, often a racial or ethnic group. **Frustration-aggression theory** involves a form of projection (Dollard, Miller, Doob, Mower, & Sears, 1939). In this view, groups who strive repeatedly to achieve their goals become frustrated after failing a number of times. When the frustration reaches a high intensity, the group seeks an outlet for its frustration by displacing its aggressive behavior to a socially approved

**Prejudice**
A preconceived attitude or judgment, either good or bad, about another group that usually involves negative stereotypes

**Scapegoating**
A psychological explanation of prejudice that involves blaming another person or group for one's own problems

**Projection**
A psychological explanation of prejudice that suggests that people transfer responsibility for their own failures to a vulnerable group, usually a racial or ethnic group

**Frustration-aggression theory**
The theory that prejudice results when personal frustrations are displaced to a socially approved racial or ethnic target

target, often a racial or ethnic group. Thus, it has been argued that Germans, frustrated by runaway inflation and the failure of their nationalist ambitions, vented their aggressive feelings by persecuting Jews. Poor whites, frustrated by their unproductive lands and financial problems, drained off their hostilities through antiblack prejudices. Schaefer (2005) adds a theory called *normative theory* that emphasizes socialization as an explanation for prejudice. The theory maintains that peers and social influences either encourage tolerance or intolerance toward others. In other words, a person from an intolerant household is more likely to be openly prejudiced than someone from a tolerant household.

The **authoritarian personality theory** argues that some people are more inclined to prejudice than others, due to differences in personality. According to this theory (Adorno, Frenkel-Brunswik, Levinson, & Sanford, 1950), prejudiced individuals are characterized by rigidity of outlook, intolerance, suggestibility, dislike for ambiguity, and irrational attitudes. They tend to be authoritarian, preferring stability and orderliness to the indefiniteness that accompanies social change. Simpson and Yinger (1972) questioned whether these traits cause prejudice and suggested that they may, in fact, be an effect of prejudice or even completely unrelated to it. In addition, this theory reduces prejudice to a personality trait in individuals.

## APPLYING THEORIES OF PREJUDICE

Gordon Allport (1954), in *The Nature of Prejudice*, noted that interracial interaction would reduce prejudice only when the groups are of equal status, they have common goals, and their interactions are sanctioned by authorities. Allport's notion is congruent with the economic theory that says that competition and conflict can heighten prejudice. Using these ideas, a classroom program known as the "jigsaw technique" was developed by Aronson and his associates. Weyant (1986) offers a description of that technique:

> The jigsaw technique involves dividing the class into small groups of usually about five to six students each. Each child in a group is given information about one part of a total lesson. For example, a lesson on Spanish and Portuguese explorers might be divided such that one child in the group is given information about Magellan; another student receives information about Balboa, another about Ponce de Leon, etc. The members of the group then proceed to teach their part to the group. Afterward, the students are tested individually on the entire lesson. Just as all the pieces of a jigsaw puzzle must be put into place to get the whole picture, the only way any one student can master the entire lesson is to learn all the pieces of information from his or her peers. Equal status is attained because every student has an equally important part. The common goal is to put together the entire lesson. (pp. 108–109)

Evaluation studies of the jigsaw technique found very positive results, including increased attraction of classmates to one another and higher self-esteem. These results also helped alleviate some of the causes of prejudice suggested by psychological theories. Furthermore, the results were obtained with only a few hours of "jigsawing" a week, so the goals of desegregation were met without a major restructuring of the schools.

Techniques to reduce prejudice do not have to be confined to the classroom. Community leaders such as local politicians, businesspeople, and ministers might help eliminate racial tensions in a neighborhood by developing programs that require citizen participation. A church, for example, might sponsor a food drive to help the needy. In organizing a committee to run such a drive, the pastor or director could create racially and ethnically integrated committees to handle the various responsibilities necessary to make the drive a success. These might include committees for advertising and publicizing, collection, distribution, setup, and cleanup. Like the classroom, people of

**Authoritarian personality theory**
The view that people with an authoritarian type of personality are more likely to be prejudiced than those who have other personality types

different minority groups would work with and depend on each other in a cooperative rather than a competitive situation—thus having an opportunity to overcome some of their prejudices.

Your knowledge of how prejudice occurs could lead to many other programs to help eliminate this serious social problem. For example, as a parent, how do you think you could use what you have learned in this chapter to prevent your children and their friends from developing prejudice against minority groups?

---

**thinking** SOCIOLOGICALLY

1. What are some dysfunctional aspects of prejudices and stereotyping? What are some functional aspects?
2. How could the information contained in the section "Applying Theories of Prejudice" be used to make social action programs more effective?

## 8.2c Discrimination

Prejudice is a judgment, an attitude. **Discrimination**, on the other hand, is overt behavior or actions. It is the categorical exclusion of members of a specific group from certain rights, opportunities, and/or privileges (Schaefer R. T., 2005). According to the conflict perspective, the dominant group in a society practices discrimination to protect its advantages, privileges, and interests.

**BVT** *Lab*

Improve your test scores. Practice quizzes are available at www.BVTLab.com

Most of us can understand discrimination at the individual level. A person may engage in behavior that excludes another individual from rights, opportunities, or privileges simply on the basis of that person's racial, ethnic, or minority status. For example, if I refuse to hire a particular Japanese American to type this manuscript because he or she does not read English, I am not engaging in prejudicially determined discrimination. On the other hand, if I refuse to hire a highly qualified typist of English because he or she is Japanese American, that is discrimination.

Merton designed a classification system to examine four ways that prejudice and discrimination can be defined.

1. *Unprejudiced non-discriminators (all-weather liberals)* are individuals who are not prejudiced, and they don't discriminate against other racial groups. They believe that everyone is equal. However, they usually won't do anything to stop others from being prejudiced or discriminating.
2. *Unprejudiced discriminators (fair-weather liberals)* are people who are not prejudiced, but will not speak out against those who are. They will laugh nervously when a racist joke is told. Their main concern is to not hurt their own position.
3. *Prejudiced non-discriminators (fair-weather bigots)* are individuals who don't believe that everyone is equal; but because we live in a "politically correct" society, they will not disclose their prejudice unless they believe they are among like-minded people. They don't act on their prejudices.
4. *Prejudiced discriminators (all-weather bigots)* are the hardcore racists. They don't believe races are equal and will share their beliefs with anyone willing to listen. They will openly discriminate against persons due to their race or ethnicity.

**Discrimination**

Overt unequal and unfair treatment of people on the basis of their membership in a particular group

Individual discrimination has become more insidious than in the past. Outward acts of discrimination, such as when James Byrd was dragged to his death behind a truck in Texas simply because he was black, are uncommon today. Instead, individual discrimination is harder to recognize, but still prevalent. Today, a black family may be turned down for a rental house because the owner does not like blacks, or a Mexican worker won't be hired because the manager thinks all Mexicans are lazy. Even though these practices are illegal based on the Civil Rights Act, they are still a common problem for racial and ethnic groups. According to the Southern Poverty Law Center, there were 1,002 hate groups in the United States in 2010, up 12.8% from 888 in 2007. Hate groups have beliefs and practices that attack or malign a class of people, typically for what are perceived to be inherent, unchanging characteristics. Hate group activities include things such as criminal acts, marches, rallies, meetings, and publications (Southern Poverty Law Center, 2012).

Discrimination also operates at the institutional level when prejudices are embedded in the structures of our social institutions. Rothman (2005) defines the institutionalization of inequality at the structural level: the collection of laws, customs, and social practices that combine to create and sustain the unequal distribution of rewards based on class, minority status, and gender (Rothman, 2005). Therefore, **institutional discrimination** is the continuing exclusion or oppression of a group as a result of criteria established by an institution. In this form of discrimination, individual prejudice is not a factor; instead, groups are excluded based on prejudices that are entrenched in the structure of the institution. Laws or rules are not applied with the intent of excluding any person or group from particular rights, opportunities, or privileges; however, the outcome has discriminatory consequences. Grodsky and his colleagues (2008, p. 386) conducted research on how "standardized testing in American education has reflected, reproduced, and transformed social inequalities by race/ethnicity, social origins, and gender." Testing does not intentionally contribute to social inequalities; because some have access to or are denied education that better prepares them for standardized testing, however, inequality is perpetuated.

*Stella and James Bryd, Sr. arrange flowers around the headstone of their son, James Bryd, Jr. Bryd was dragged to death in 1998 in Texas simply because he was black.*
*(AP Wide World Photo)*

Suppose, for example, that a school requires, for admission, a particular minimum score on a standardized national exam based on middle-class white culture. Individuals outside of that culture will find the exam to be more difficult. In such a case, no bias against any particular racial or ethnic group may be intended—anyone who meets the criteria can be admitted. However, the result is the same as if the discrimination were by design. Few members of minority or ethnic groups could meet the requirements for admittance to the school or club, and the benefits of belonging would apply mainly to the white students who could pass the test. This would tend to continue existing patterns of educational and occupational deprivation from one generation to the next.

A similar process operates in our criminal justice system. Suppose that individuals from two different ethnic groups are arrested for identical offenses and given the same fine. If one can pay the fine but the other cannot, their fates may be quite different. The one who cannot pay will go to jail while the other one goes home. The result is institutional discrimination against the poor. Once a person has been imprisoned and has probably lost her or his job, that individual may find that other jobs are harder to find.

**Institutional discrimination**

The continuing exclusion or oppression of a group as a result of criteria established by an institution

**Racism**

The belief that one racial group is superior to others, typically manifested through prejudice and discrimination

## 8.2d Racism

**Racism** is the belief that one racial group or category is inherently superior to others. It includes prejudices and discriminatory behaviors based on this belief. Racism can be regarded as having three major components. First, the racist believes that her or his own race is superior to other racial groups. Racism often entails racial prejudice and ethnocentrism.

The second property of racism is that it has an ideology, or set of beliefs, that justifies the subjugation and exploitation of another group. According to Rothman (1978), a racist ideology serves five functions:

1. It provides a moral rationale for systematic deprivation.
2. It allows the dominant group to reconcile values and behavior.
3. It discourages the subordinate group from challenging the system.
4. It rallies adherence in support of a "just" cause.
5. It defends the existing division of labor.

The third property of racism is that racist beliefs are acted upon. Many examples of racist actions in this country could be highlighted. The lynching of blacks in the U.S. South and the destruction of entire tribes of Native Americans, who were regarded as little more than animals, are two of the more extreme instances.

Racism is the belief that one racial group or category is inherently superior to others. The Ku Klux Klan, shown here, holds such a belief concerning whites. (AP Wide World Photo)

Racism, like discrimination, can be of two types. Individual racism originates in the racist beliefs of a single person. Racist storeowners, for example, might refuse to hire black employees because they regard them as inferior beings. **Institutional racism** occurs when racist ideas and practices are embodied in the folkways, mores, or legal structures of various institutions.

The policy of apartheid in the Republic of South Africa is, in many ways, one of the most notorious examples of institutional racism. This policy calls for biological, territorial, social, educational, economic, and political separation of the various racial groups that compose the nation. Only in the past few years have the media brought the South African racial situation to the conscious attention of most Americans. As a result, many schools, foundations, and industries have removed from their investment portfolios companies that have a major investment in that country. Others have taken public stands against the institutionalized racism that supports different rules, opportunities, and activities based on the color of one's skin.

Richard Schaeffer identifies six ways that racism is dysfunctional, or disruptive to the stability of a social system, even to the dominant members of the society (Schaefer, 2005). They are as follows:

1. A society that practices discrimination fails to use the resources of all individuals. Discrimination limits the search for talent and leadership to the dominant group.
2. Discrimination aggravates social problems such as poverty, delinquency, and crime; it places the financial burden of alleviating these problems on the dominant group.
3. Society must invest a good deal of time and money to defend the barriers that prevent the full participation of all members.
4. Racial prejudice and discrimination undercut goodwill and friendly diplomatic relations between nations.
5. Social change is inhibited because change may assist a subordinate group.
6. Discrimination promotes disrespect for law enforcement and for the peaceful settlement of disputes.

**Institutional racism**
Racism that is embodied in the folkways, mores, or legal structures of a social institution

# 8.3 PATTERNS OF RACIAL AND ETHNIC RELATIONS

When different racial and ethnic groups live in the same area, widespread and continuous contact among groups is inevitable; however, it rarely results in equality. Generally, one group holds more power and dominates the other groups. In some cases, assimilation, pluralism, segregation, expulsion, or genocide will occur. Whatever the form of group interaction, relations among groups is strongly influenced by their rankings in the stratification system.

## 8.3a Integration and Assimilation

**Integration** occurs when ethnicity becomes insignificant and everyone can freely and fully participate in the social, economic, and political mainstream. All groups are brought together. **Assimilation** occurs when individuals and groups forsake their own cultural tradition to become part of a different group and tradition. With complete assimilation, the minority group loses its identity as a subordinate group and becomes fully integrated into the institutions, groups, and activities of society.

Assimilation in the United States appears to focus on one of two models: the **melting pot** and **Anglo conformity**. The following formulations differentiate these two terms (Newman, 1973):

Melting pot: A + B + C = D

Anglo conformity: A + B + C = A

In melting-pot assimilation, each group contributes a bit of its own culture and absorbs aspects of other cultures such that the whole is a combination of all the groups. Many sociologists in the United States view the melting-pot model as a popular myth, with reality better illustrated by the Anglo conformity model. *Anglo conformity* is equated with "Americanization," whereby the minority completely loses its identity to the dominant WASP culture.

The degree to which assimilation takes place is different for different ethnic and racial groups. There are two important mechanisms that help to determine the extent to which a group assimilates (and, thus, the extent to which its members retain or lose their cultural identity). The first, and most important, is the group's ownership of society's resources. The more ownership of resources that a group has, the less likely it is that the group will have to assimilate in order to succeed. The second most important mechanism that affects assimilation is whether or not a group has been cut off from its mother society. In cases where the immigrant population still has strong ties with its mother society, such as with Mexicans and Puerto Ricans, assimilation has been retarded because the groups can maintain their cultural practices. Simply put, groups who have been able to resist domination by the country to which they have migrated are more likely to resist assimilation (Barber, 2007).

Integration is a two-way process. The immigrants must want to assimilate, and the host society must be willing to have them assimilate. The immigrant must undergo *cultural assimilation*, learning the day-to-day norms of the WASP culture pertaining to dress, language, food, and sports. This process also involves internalizing the more crucial aspects of the culture, such as values, ideas, beliefs, and attitudes. **Structural assimilation** involves developing patterns of intimate contact between the guest and host groups in the clubs, organizations, and institutions of the host society. Cultural assimilation generally precedes structural assimilation, although the two sometimes happen simultaneously.

Cultural assimilation has occurred on a large scale in American society although the various minorities differed in the pace at which they were assimilated. With

**Integration**

The situation that exists when ethnicity becomes insignificant and everyone can freely and fully participates in the social, economic, and political mainstream

**Assimilation**

The process through which individuals and groups forsake their own cultural tradition to become part of a different group and tradition

**Melting pot**

A form of assimilation in which each group contributes aspects of its own culture and absorbs aspects of other cultures, such that the whole is a combination of all the groups

**Anglo conformity**

A form of assimilation in which the minority loses its identity completely and adopts the norms and practices of the dominant WASP culture

**Structural assimilation**

One aspect of assimilation in which patterns of intimate contact between the guest and host groups are developed in the clubs, organizations, and institutions of the host society white ethnics of European origin, cultural assimilation went hand in hand with **amalgamation** (biological mixing through large-scale intermarriage). Among Asian ethnics, Japanese Americans seem to have assimilated most completely and are being rewarded with high socioeconomic status. In contrast, Chinese Americans, particularly first-generation migrants, have resisted assimilation and have retained strong ties to their cultural traditions. The existence of Chinatowns in many cities reflects this desire for cultural continuity.

Assimilation involves more than just culture borrowing because immigrants want access to the host's institutional privileges. The issue of integration is particularly relevant in three areas: housing, schooling, and employment.

## 8.3b Pluralism

Are the elimination of segregation and the achievement of integration the only choices in societies with racial and ethnic diversity, or can diverse racial and ethnic groups coexist side by side and maintain their distinctive heritages and cultures? This issue is what Lambert and Taylor (1990) address as "the American challenge: assimilation or multiculturalism" and what Lieberson and Waters (1988) state as "melting pot versus cultural pluralism."

The existence of Chinatowns in many cities, such as this one, reflects the desire of many Chinese immigrants for cultural continuity. (iStockphoto)

*Multiculturalism* or **cultural pluralism** can be defined as a situation in which the various racial, ethnic, or other minority groups in a society maintain their distinctive cultural patterns, subsystems, and institutions. Perhaps this can be illustrated by the following formula:

Cultural pluralism: A + B + C = A + B + C

Whereas those who support assimilation and integration seek to eliminate ethnic boundaries, a pluralist wants to retain them. Pluralists argue that groups can coexist by accepting their differences. Basic to cultural pluralism are beliefs that individuals never forget or escape their social origin, that all groups bring positive contributions that enrich the larger society, and that groups have the right to be different yet equal.

Several authorities believe that assimilation and pluralism are happening simultaneously in American society. Glazer and Moynihan (1970), in their seminal work on assimilation, *Beyond the Melting Pot*, perceive the process of becoming what they call "hyphenated" Americans as involving cultural assimilation. Thus, a Russian American is different from a Russian in Russia, and an African American is not the same as an African in Africa. On the other hand, they perceive the emergence of minority groups as political interest groups as a pluralistic trend. Gordon (1978) contends that assimilation of minorities is the prevailing trend in economic, political, and educational institutions, whereas cultural pluralism prevails in religion, the family, and recreation.

Cultural pluralism results in separate ethnic communities, many of which are characterized by a high degree of institutional completeness; that is, they include institutions and services that meet the needs of the group—such as ethnic churches, newspapers, mutual aid societies, and recreational groups. These ethnic enclaves are particularly attractive to recent immigrants who have language problems and few skills. Schaefer (2003) compared ethnic communities to decompression chambers.

Today, we are witnessing a resurgence in interest of various ethnic groups in almost forgotten languages, customs, and traditions. This is characterized by people's increased interest in the culture of their ethnic group, visits to ancestral homes, their increased use of ethnic names, and their renewed interest in the native language of their own group.

**Amalgamation**
The process by which different racial or ethnic groups form a new group through interbreeding or intermarriage

**Cultural pluralism**
The situation in which the various ethnic groups in a society maintain their distinctive cultural patterns, subsystems, and institutions

The general rule has been for American minorities to assimilate, however. Most ethnic groups are oriented toward the future, not on the past. American ethnics are far more interested in shaping their future within the American structure than in maintaining cultural ties with the past. However, as Rothman (2005) contends, the importance of a multicultural model is accelerated by the recognition that whites will probably be a numerical minority sometime after the year 2050.

## 8.3c Segregation

**Segregation** is the physical and social separation of groups or categories of people. It results in ethnic enclaves such as Little Italy, Chinatown, a black ghetto, and a Hispanic barrio. The most significant division, however, is between whites in the suburbs and blacks and other minorities in the inner cities. At the institutional level, segregation can be attributed to discriminatory practices and policies of the federal housing agencies and of mortgage-lending institutions. Suburban zoning patterns that tend to keep out poorer families are also influential. At the individual level, segregation is the result of the refusal by some whites to sell their houses to non-whites or the desire of minorities to live in their own ethnic communities.

Segregation was common in the U.S. through the 1950s. This photo was taken at the Illinois Central Railroad in 1956. (AP Wide World Photo)

The city-suburb polarization of blacks and whites continues through the early part of this millennium. This pattern of segregation continues in spite of a 1965 federal law that prohibits discrimination in the rental, sale, or financing of suburban housing. Based on this law, all banks and savings and loan associations bidding for deposits of federal funds were requested to sign anti-redlining pledges. *Redlining* is the practice among mortgage-lending institutions of imposing artificial restrictions on housing loans for areas where minorities have started to buy. Despite these and other advances, American society has a long way to go in desegregating housing patterns.

School segregation was brought to national attention with the 1954 decision in *Brown v. the Board of Education of Topeka, Kansas*, in which the U.S. Supreme Court ruled that the assignment of children to schools solely because of race—called **de jure segregation** (meaning segregation by law)—violates the U.S. Constitution and that the schools involved must desegregate. For decades prior to the *Brown* decision, particularly in the South, busing was used to keep the races apart even when they lived in the same neighborhoods and communities.

In the past few decades, attention has shifted to the North and West, where school segregation resulted from blacks and whites living in separate neighborhoods, with school assignment based on residence boundaries. This pattern, which is called **de facto segregation** (meaning segregation in fact), led to legislation in many cities that bused blacks and whites out of their neighborhood schools for purposes of achieving racial balance. Defenders of the legislation argue that minority students who are exposed to high-achieving white middle-class students will do better academically. They also contend that desegregation by busing is a way for whites and minority groups to learn about each other, which may diminish stereotypes and racist attitudes.

It is not always clear whether segregation is de facto or de jure. School districts may follow neighborhood boundaries and define a neighborhood school so that it minimizes contact between black and white children. Is that de facto segregation (resulting from black and white neighborhoods) or de jure segregation (resulting from legally sanctioned assignment of children to schools based on race)? Regardless of what it is, the vast majority of black children in Atlanta, Baltimore, Chicago, Cleveland, Detroit, Los Angeles, Memphis, Philadelphia, and many other cities today attend schools that are predominantly black.

**Segregation**
The separation of a group from the main body usually involving separating a minority group from the dominant group

**De jure segregation**
The legal assignment of children to schools solely because of race

**De facto segregation**
School assignment based on residence boundaries in which blacks and whites live in separate neighborhoods

## 8.3d Mass Expulsion

**Mass expulsion** is the practice of expelling racial or ethnic groups from their homeland. The United States routinely used expulsion to solve conflicts with Native Americans. In an incident known as "The Trail of Tears," the Cherokees were forced out of their homeland in the region where Georgia meets Tennessee and North Carolina. The removal was triggered by the discovery of gold in the Georgia mountains and the determination of European-Americans to take possession of it. The exodus went to the Ohio River and then to the Mississippi, ending in what is now Oklahoma. Of the 10,000 Cherokees rounded up, about 4,000 perished during the exodus.

Racist thinking and racist doctrine were rampant between 1850 and 1950, which is aptly called "the century of racism." Since 1950, it has declined in many parts of the world; however, there is no question that it still exists.

## 8.3e Genocide

**Genocide** is the practice of deliberately destroying a whole race or ethnic group. Raphael Lemkin coined the term in 1944 to describe the heinous crimes committed by the Nazis during World War II against the Jewish people, which is the supreme example of racism. Of the 9,600,000 Jews who lived in Nazi-dominated Europe between 1933 and 1945, 60% died in concentration camps. The British also solved race problems through annihilation during their colonization campaigns overseas. Between 1803 and 1876, for example, they almost wiped out the native population of Tasmania. The aborigines were believed by the British to be a degenerate race, wild beasts to be hunted and killed. One colonist regularly hunted natives to feed to his dogs.

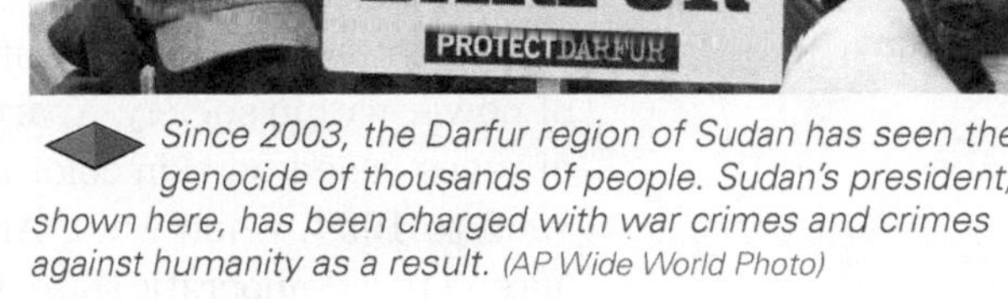


Since 2003, the Darfur region of Sudan has seen the genocide of thousands of people. Sudan's president, shown here, has been charged with war crimes and crimes against humanity as a result. (AP Wide World Photo)

Lemkin (1946) defined genocide as the "crime of destroying national, racial or religious groups." As early as 1717, the U.S. government was giving incentives to private citizens for exterminating the so-called troublesome (American) "Indians," and Americans were paid generous bounties for natives' scalps. Through the processes of displacement, diseases, removal, and assimilation, the Native American population was reduced to meager numbers, less than 1% of the U.S. population today.

In the 1990s, the world witnessed the genocide in Rwanda that left over a million men, women, and children dead and many more displaced from their homeland. Today, we are once again witnessing the tragic events of genocide taking place in the Darfur region of Sudan. Since 2003, the conflict in Darfur has left over 400,000 dead and 2.5 million people displaced. Tens of thousands of people are being raped and killed based only on their ethnicity. In March 2009, the International Criminal Court charged Sudan's president, Omar Hassan al-Bashir, with seven counts of war crimes and crimes against humanity.

Because of its moral distinctiveness, genocide has been called the "crime of crimes" (Schabas, 2000; Lee , 2010). While international concern about genocide subsided after World War II, events in Rwanda, Darfur, and other areas have led to a justification and resurgence of international humanitarian military intervention.

**Mass expulsion**
Expelling racial or ethnic groups from their homeland

**Genocide**
The deliberate destruction of an entire racial or ethnic group

# 8.4 ETHNIC STRATIFICATION

As we discussed in Chapter 7, **stratification** is structured social inequality. It is the ranking of entire groups of people that perpetuates unequal rewards and power in a society (Schaefer R. T., 2005).

Donald L. Noel (1975) contends that three conditions are necessary for ethnic stratification to occur in a society: ethnocentrism, which is the tendency to assume that one's culture and way of life are superior to all others (Schaefer R. T., 2005), competition for resources, and inequalities in power. The inevitable outcome of ethnocentrism is that other groups are disparaged to a greater or lesser degree, depending on the extent of their difference from the majority. Competition among groups occurs when they must vie for the same scarce resources or goals, but it need not lead to ethnic stratification if values concerning freedom and equality are held and enforced. According to Noel, it is the third condition, inequality in power, which enables one group to impose its will upon the others. Power permits the dominant group to render the subordinate groups ineffectual as competitors and to institutionalize the distribution of rewards and opportunities to consolidate their position.

The rankings of people based on race, nationality, religion, or other ethnic or minority affiliations is clearly not unique to the United States. South Africa serves as an example of ethnic stratification, unmatched by any other society (Marger, 2003). White South Africans of European decent created a system of apartheid (white supremacy) that had caste-like elements. Blacks were seen as inferior in every way to whites, and a formal system of racial classification defined the status of all others. Ethnic categories during apartheid included whites, Coloreds, Asians, and Africans. While whites made up only 10% of the population, they controlled all other aspects of society. Coloreds were those who had a mixture of white and black parentage; while treated differently from whites, they held more privileges than Africans. Asians were mainly indentured servants brought in from India. Their treatment was similar to the Coloreds during apartheid; once their servitude had ended, they could establish themselves within society. Over 75% of the population of South Africa was black African, yet they held the least amount of power within society. Apartheid was legal segregation that allowed for the separation of races based on skin color alone. This system of discrimination stayed in effect from 1948 to 1994, when white Afrikaners (The Nationalist Party) relinquished power and agreed to a democratic state. History is full of examples where race, ethnicity, or religion has been the dominant factor in the treatment of human beings.

What positions do ethnic and racial groups occupy in the stratification system of the United States? Tables 8-1, 8-2 and 8-3 provide a historical perspective on measures of stratification between groups.

## 8.4a Ethnic Antagonism

**Ethnic antagonism** is mutual opposition, conflict, or hostility among different ethnic groups. In the broadest sense, the term encompasses all levels of intergroup conflict—ideologies and beliefs such as racism and prejudice, behaviors such as discrimination and riots, and institutions such as the legal and economic systems. Ethnic antagonism is closely linked to the racial and ethnic stratification system. The best-known theory of ethnic antagonism is that of the split labor market, as formulated by Edna Bonacich in a series of articles in the 1970s (1972; 1975; 1972).

A central tenet of split-labor-market theory is that when the price of labor for the same work differs by ethnic group, a three-way conflict develops among business managers and owners, higher-priced labor, and cheaper labor. Business—that is, the employer—aims at having as cheap and docile a labor force as possible. Higher-priced labor may include current employees or a dominant ethnic group that demands higher wages, a share of the profits, or fringe benefits that increase the employer's costs.

**Stratification**

The structured ranking of entire groups of people that perpetuates unequal rewards and power in a society

**Ethnic antagonism**

Mutual opposition, conflict, or hostility among different ethnic groups

**Table 8-1** Poverty Rates for Selected Race and Ethnic Groups in the United States, 2007–2011

| | Poverty | | | | |
|---|---|---|---|---|---|
| Race | 2007 | 2008 | 2009 | 2010 | 2011 |
| Whites (non-Hispanic) | 8.2 | 11.2 | 12.3 | 9.9 | 9.8 |
| Blacks | 24.5 | 24.7 | 25.8 | 27.4 | 27.6 |
| Asians | 10.2 | 11.8 | 12.5 | 12.2 | 12.3 |
| Hispanics | 21.5 | 23.2 | 25.3 | 26.5 | 25.3 |
| National Average | 12.5 | 13.2 | 14.3 | 15.3 | 15.9 |

SOURCE: U.S. Bureau of the Census, Income, Poverty, and Health Insurance Coverage in the United States: 2007, 2009, 2011. *Current Population Reports.* (DeNavas-Walt, Proctor, & Smith, 2012) and U.S. Census Bureau Poverty 2010 and 2011, Alemayehu Bishaw, September 2012, http://www.census.gov/prod/2012pubs/acsbr11-01.pdf

Cheaper labor refers to any ethnic group that can do the work done by the higher-priced laborers at a lower cost to the employer.

Antagonism results when the higher-paid labor groups, who want to keep both their jobs and their wages (including benefits), are threatened by the introduction of cheaper labor into the market. The fear is that the cheaper labor group will either replace them or force them to lower their wage level. This basic class conflict then becomes an ethnic and racial conflict. If the higher-paid labor groups are strong enough, they may try to exclude the lower-paid group. **Exclusion** is the attempt to keep out the cheaper labor (or the product they produce). Thus, laws may be passed that make it illegal for Mexicans, Cubans, Haitians, Chinese, Filipinos, or other immigrants to enter the country; taxes may be imposed on Japanese automobiles, foreign steel, or clothes made in Taiwan.

**Exclusion**

Attempts to keep cheaper labor from taking jobs from groups that receive higher pay

Bonacich claims that another process, **displacement**, is also likely to arise in split labor markets. Capitalists who want to reduce labor costs may simply displace the higher-paid employees with cheaper labor. They can replace workers at their present

**Displacement**

A process occurring in split labor markets in which higher paid workers are replaced with cheaper labor

**Figure 8-1** Real Median Household Incomes by Race and Hispanic Origin: 1967 to 2011

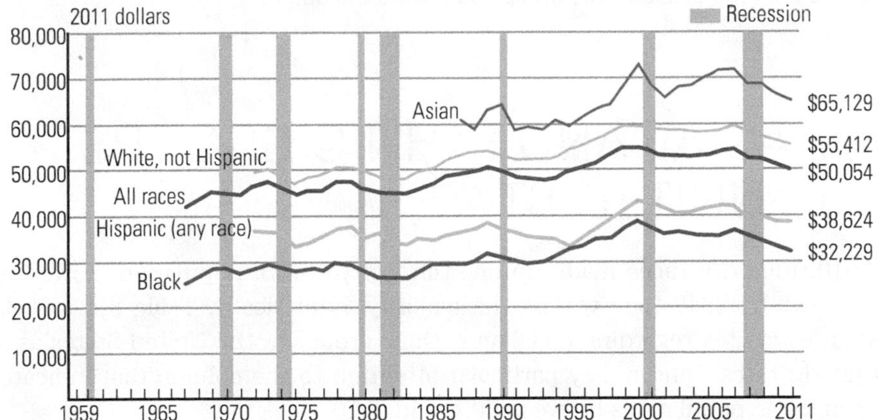


*Note.* Median household income data are not available prior to 1967. Implementation of 2010 Census population controls beginning in 2010. For information on recessions, see Appendix A.

Adapted from U.S. Census Bureau, *Current Population Survey,* 1968 to 2012, Annual Social and Economic Supplements. http://www.census.gov/prod/2012pubs/p60-243.pdf

**Table 8-2** Median Family Income and Earnings by Race, 2007–2011

(iStockphoto)

| Race | 2007 | 2008 | 2009 | 2010 | 2011 |
|---|---|---|---|---|---|
| White (non-Hispanic) | 24,920 | 55,319 | 54,461 | 53,340 | 25,214 |
| Black | 34,091 | 34,088 | 32,584 | 33,137 | 32,229 |
| Hispanic | 38,679 | 37,769 | 38,039 | 38,818 | 38,624 |
| Asian | 65,876 | 65,388 | 65,469 | 66,286 | 65,129 |

Adapted from U.S. Bureau of the Census, "Civilian Population: Employment Status by Race, Sex, Ethnicity 1970–2007"; U.S. Bureau of the Census, "Income and Earnings Summary Measures by Selected Characteristics: 2008 and 2009."

location or move their factories and businesses to states or countries where the costs are lower. This is evident in auto parts, clothes, and other products with tags or labels such as "made in Mexico," or "made in Korea," or made in any other country where labor costs are considerably lower than in the United States.

An alternative to the split labor market is what Bonacich terms **radicalism**, in which labor groups join together in a coalition against the capitalist class and present a united front. When this occurs, Bonacich claims, no one is displaced or excluded. Anyone who gets hired comes in under the conditions of the higher-priced labor. Bonacich believes that as long as there is cheap labor anywhere in the world, there may not be a solution to a split labor market within a capitalist system.

**thinking** SOCIOLOGICALLY

1. Can you identify five ethnic groups in the United States and stratify them? What criteria do you use? What social significance can you attach to the ranking you have given a particular group?
2. Discuss the pros and cons of split labor market theory from the perspective of both the higher-priced worker and the lower-priced worker. How does this influence the opinions one group has toward the other?

## 8.5 RACIAL AND ETHNIC GROUPS IN THE UNITED STATES

As of 2010, minority races made up one-third of the U.S. population; however, it is expected that by 2042 they will be the majority, numerically. Table 8-4 reflects the population estimates regarding racial and ethnic groups in the United States as of the 2010 United States Census. Pay particular attention to the column that indicates the changes in these populations between 2000 and 2010.

One reason it is important to understand the extent to which the racial and ethnic population of the United States is changing is its impact on the political climate, especially elections. In 2012, in what was initially expected to be a much closer presidential race, President Barack Obama won a decisive victory over former Governor Mitt Romney.

**Radicalism**

Labor groups joining together in a coalition against the capitalist class

## Table 8-3 Educational Attainment Percentages by Race and Hispanic Origin, 1970–2010

| Year | Total[1] | White[2] | Black[2] | Asian and Pacific Islander[2] | Hispanic[3] |
|---|---|---|---|---|---|
| **High School Graduate or More[5]** | | | | | |
| 1970 | 52.3 | 54.5 | 31.4 | 62.2 | 32.1 |
| 1980 | 66.5 | 68.8 | 51.2 | 74.8 | 44.0 |
| 1990 | 77.6 | 79.1 | 66.2 | 80.4 | 50.8 |
| 1995 | 81.7 | 83.0 | 73.8 | (NA) | 53.4 |
| 2000 | 84.1 | 84.9 | 78.5 | 85.7 | 57.0 |
| 2005 | 85.2 | 85.8 | 81.1 | [6]87.6 | 58.5 |
| 2006 | 85.5 | 86.1 | 80.7 | 87.4 | 59.3 |
| 2007 | 85.7 | 86.2 | 82.3 | 87.8 | 60.3 |
| 2008 | 86.6 | 87.1 | 83.0 | 88.7 | 62.3 |
| 2009 | 86.7 | 87.1 | 84.1 | 88.2 | 61.9 |
| 2010 | 87.1 | 87.6 | 84.2 | 88.9 | 62.9 |
| **College Graduate or More[5]** | | | | | |
| 1970 | 10.7 | 11.3 | 4.4 | 20.4 | 4.5 |
| 1980 | 16.2 | 17.1 | 8.4 | 23.9 | 7.6 |
| 1990 | 21.3 | 22.0 | 11.3 | 39.9 | 9.2 |
| 1995 | 23.0 | 24.0 | 13.2 | (NA) | 9.3 |
| 2000 | 25.6 | 26.1 | 16.5 | 43.9 | 10.6 |
| 2005 | 27.7 | 28.1 | 17.6 | [6]50.2 | 12.0 |
| 2006 | 28.0 | 28.4 | 18.5 | 49.7 | 12.4 |
| 2007 | 28.7 | 29.1 | 18.5 | 52.1 | 12.7 |
| 2008 | 29.4 | 29.8 | 19.6 | 52.6 | 13.3 |
| 2009 | 29.5 | 29.9 | 19.3 | 52.3 | 13.2 |
| 2010 | 29.9 | 30.3 | 19.8 | 52.4 | 13.9 |

NA = not available.

[1]Includes other races not shown separately. [2]Beginning 2005, for persons who selected this race group only. The 2003 Current Population Survey (CPS) allowed respondents to choose more than one race. Beginning 2003, data represents persons whom selected this race group only and excluded persons reporting more than one race. The CPS in prior years only allowed respondents to report one race group. See also comments on race in the text for section 1. [3]Persons of Hispanic origin may be any race. [4]Includes persons of other Hispanic origin not shown separately. [5]Through 1990, completed 4 years of high school or more and 4 years of college or more. [6]Starting in 2005, data are for Asians only, excludes Pacific Islanders.

Adapted from U.S. Census Bureau, Statistical Abstract of the United States, Table 229, 2012.

Retrieved from http://www.census.gov/population/www/socdemo/edu-attn.html

Many political analysts feel that Obama's victory was largely due to the failure of the Romney campaign to consider the impact of an electorate that was 28% non-white in 2012, up from 20% in 2000. In spite of capturing 59% of the non-Hispanic white vote, Romney still lost the election. Winning most of the vote of women, another minority group increasing in the electorate (23% of voters in 2012 compared with 19% in 2000), was also a significant factor in Obama's victory. Regardless of their political differences, Obama strategists may have been better at understanding and anticipating the impact of demographic changes in the United States. According to Howard University sociologist Roderick Harrison, the Obama campaign strategists "put together a coalition of populations that will eventually become the majority or are marching toward majority status in the population [in terms of size], and populations without whom it will be very

**Table 8-4** Population by Hispanic or Latino Origin and by Race for the United States, 2000 and 2010

| Hispanic or Latino Origin and Race | 2000 | | 2010 | | Change, 2000 to 2010 | |
|---|---|---|---|---|---|---|
| | Number | Percentage of the Population | Number | Percentage of the Population | Number | Percent |
| **Hispanic or Latino Origin and Race** | | | | | | |
| Total Population | 281,421,906 | 100.0 | 308,745,538 | 100.0 | 27,323,632 | 9.7 |
| Hispanic or Latino | 35,305,818 | 12.5 | 20,447,594 | 16.3 | 15,171,776 | 43.0 |
| Not Hispanic or Latino | 246,116,088 | 87.5 | 258,267,944 | 83.7 | 12,151,856 | 4.9 |
| White alone | 194,552,774 | 69.1 | 196,817,552 | 63.7 | 2,246,778 | 1.2 |
| **Race** | | | | | | |
| Total Population | 281,421,907 | 100.0 | 308,745,538 | 100.0 | 27,323,632 | 9.7 |
| One Race | 274,595,678 | 97.6 | 299,736,465 | 97.1 | 25,140,787 | 9.2 |
| White | 211,460,626 | 75.1 | 223,553,265 | 72.4 | 12,092,639 | 5.7 |
| Black or African American | 34,658,190 | 12.3 | 38,929,319 | 12.6 | 4,271,129 | 12.3 |
| American Indian and Alaska Native | 2,475,956 | 0.9 | 2,932,248 | 0.9 | 456,292 | 18.4 |
| Asian | 10,242,998 | 3.6 | 14,674,252 | 4.8 | 4,431,254 | 43.3 |
| Native Hawaiian and Other Pacific Islander | 398,835 | 0.1 | 540,013 | 0.2 | 141,178 | 35.4 |
| Some Other Race | 15,359,073 | 5.5 | 19,107,368 | 6.2 | 3,748,295 | 24.4 |
| Two or More Races | 6,826,228 | 2.4 | 9,009,073 | 2.9 | 2,182,845 | 32.0 |

*Note.* In Census 2000, an error in data processing resulted in an overstatement of the Two or More Races population by about 1 million people (about 15%) nationally, which is almost entirely affected by race combinations involving some other race. Therefore, data users should assess observed changes in Two or More Races population and race combinations involving Some Other Race between Census 2000 and the 2010 Census with caution. Changes in specific race combinations not involving Some Other Race, such as White and Black or African American, or White and Asian, generally should be more comparable.

Adapted from U.S. Census Bureau, Census 2000 Redistricting Data (Public Law 94-171) Summary File, Tables PL1 and PL2; and 2010 Census Redistricting Data (Public Law 94-171) Summary File, Table P1 and P2

difficult to win national elections and some statewide elections, particularly in states with large black and Hispanic populations" (Benac & Cass, 2012).

## 8.5a Hispanic Americans

As of 2010, there were nearly 50.5 million Hispanics living in the United States, up from 33.3 million in 2000. That is an increase of 43%. This category includes those who classify themselves as Mexican American, Puerto Rican, Cuban, Central American, South American, and other Hispanic or Latino. Our discussion focuses on Mexican Americans, who constitute approximately 65.5% of the Hispanic-American group.

Over 1 million Mexican Americans are descendants of the native Mexicans who lived in the Southwest before it became part of the United States, following the Mexican American war. They became Americans in 1848, when Texas, California, New Mexico, and most of Arizona became U.S. territory. These four states plus Colorado contain the largest concentrations of this group today.

Other Mexican Americans have come from Mexico since 1848. They can be classified into three types: (1) *legal immigrants*; (2) *braceros*, or temporary workers; and (3) *illegal aliens*. The Mexican Revolution caused large-scale migration in the early

1900s because of unsettled economic conditions in Mexico and the demand for labor on cotton farms and railroads in California. Before the minimum wage law was passed, agricultural employers preferred braceros to local workers because they could be paid less; the braceros were not a burden to the federal government inasmuch as they returned to Mexico when their services were no longer needed.

The number of illegal aliens from Mexico is not known; estimates range from 1 to 10 million. Immigration policy concerning legal and illegal Mexican immigrants generally varies with the need for labor, which in turn depends on economic conditions. When the demand for Mexican labor was high, immigration was encouraged. When times were bad, illegal aliens were tracked down, rounded up, and deported. They were scapegoats in the depression of the 1930s and again in the recession of the early 1980s.

Strong family ties and large families characterize traditional Mexican American culture. The extended family is the most important institution in the Chicano community. The theme of family honor and unity occurs throughout Mexican American society, irrespective of social class or geographical location. This theme extends beyond the nuclear family unit of husband, wife, and children to relatives on both sides and persists even when the dominance of the male becomes weakened. It is a primary source of emotional and economic support and the primary focus of obligations.

Minorities such as women, blacks, and some Hispanics often hold jobs of lower status and power and receive lower wages. (iStockphoto)

Mexican families tend to be larger than U.S. American families. In 2006, 22.5% of Hispanic families had five or more people. About twice as many Hispanic families had five or more members compared to non-Hispanics. Families of this size, when linked with minimal skills and low levels of income, make it difficult for the Mexican American to enjoy life at a level equal to the dominant groups in American society. The median family income for non-Hispanic white families in 2009 was $54,461 compared to $38,039 for Hispanic families. Combining a large family size with a low income makes life very hard for most Hispanic Americans.

To improve the educational and income level of the Mexican American family, several Mexican American social movements have emerged over the past three decades. One movement was directed at having bilingual instruction introduced at the elementary level. Bilingualism emerged as such a politically controversial issue that in 1986 California passed a resolution (joining 6 other states) making English the state's official language. Today, 30 states have English-only laws, and more are considering legislation.

Cesar Chavez, one of the best-known Chicano leaders, led another movement. In 1962, he formed the National Farm Workers Association (later the United Farm Workers Union) and organized Mexican migrant farm workers, first to strike against grape growers and later against lettuce growers. The strikes included boycotts against these products, which carried the struggles of low-paid Chicano laborers into the kitchens of homes throughout America. Primary goals of Chicano agricultural and political movements, in addition to increasing wages and benefits for migrant workers, included increasing the rights of all workers and restoring pride in Mexican American heritage.

The Hispanic population is fairly young, with the average age around 27 years for both men and women. Education is perhaps the most influential factor creating income gaps for Hispanic workers. As Table 8-3 indicates, the percentage of Hispanics with less than a high school degree is the largest among all racial groups. This, along with a young workforce and low-skilled or semi-skilled labor, creates economic hardships for Hispanic families.

## 8.5b African Americans

African Americans comprise the second largest racial minority in the United States. Because of such unique historical experiences as slavery, legal and social segregation, and economic discrimination, many African Americans have lifestyles and value patterns that differ from those of the European-American majority. Relations between whites and blacks have been the source of a number of major social issues in the past several decades: busing, segregation, job discrimination, and interracial marriage, to mention a few.

Perhaps these issues can be understood more fully by examining five major social transitions that have affected or will affect African Americans (Eshleman & Bulcroft, 2006). The first transition was the movement from Africa to America, which is significant because of three factors: color, cultural discontinuity, and slavery. *Color* is the most obvious characteristic that sets whites and blacks apart. *Cultural discontinuity* was the abrupt shift from the culture learned and accepted in Africa to the cultural system of America. Rarely has any ethnic or racial group faced such a severe disruption of cultural patterns. *Slavery* was the singular motivation for bringing many Africans to American, at that time. Africans did not come to this country by choice—most were brought as slaves to work on Southern U.S. plantations. Unlike many free African Americans in the North, slaves in the South had few legal rights. Southern blacks were considered the property of their white owners, who had complete control over every aspect of their lives. Furthermore, there were no established groups of blacks to welcome and aid the newly arrived Africans, as was the case with other immigrant groups.

(Shutterstock)

A second major transition was from slavery to emancipation. In 1863, a proclamation issued by President Lincoln freed the slaves in the Union, as well as in all territories still at war with the Union. Although the slaves were legally free, emancipation presented a major crisis for many African Americans because most were faced with the difficult choice of either remaining on the plantations as tenants with low wages or none at all for their labor, or searching beyond the plantation for jobs, food, and housing. Many men left to search for jobs, so women became the major source of family stability. The shift to emancipation from slavery contributed to the third and fourth transitions.

The third transition was from rural to urban and from Southern to Northern communities. For many African Americans, this shift had both good and bad effects. Cities were much more impersonal than the rural areas from which most blacks moved; however, cities also provided more jobs, better schools, improved health facilities, a greater tolerance of racial minorities, and a greater chance for vertical social mobility. As of 2001, 23 million African Americans lived in a metropolitan area and 13.5 million lived within a central city (Annual Demographic Survey, 2002). Blacks are no longer confined to the inner cities, but are active participants in large metropolitan areas.

The job opportunities created by World War I and World War II provided the major impetus for the exodus of African Americans from the South to the North, a trend that continued through the 1960s. In 1900, 90% of all African Americans lived in the South. By 1980, this figure had dropped to 53%, but increased to 55.3% by 2002 (Burton, 2011). Today, there are more black people in New York City and Chicago than in any other cities in the world, including African cities, and these cities have retained their top rankings for 30 years. Atlanta and Washington, D.C. are the cities with the third and fourth largest African American population. New York and Florida rank first and second, respectively, among states with the highest African American population.

The fourth transition was from negative to positive social status. The African American middle class has been growing in recent years and resembles the European American middle class in terms of education, job level, and other factors. In 2008, 40% of blacks had household incomes of $50,000 or more, up from 29.4% in 1980. An even greater advance can be seen in the number of blacks who have made $100,000 or more:

13.4% made more than $100,000 in 2008, up from 4.5%. That is nearly a 300% increase. However, it must be pointed out that the percentage of blacks reaching the middle and upper middle classes is still noticeably lower than for whites, even when comparing the 2008 figures for blacks to the 1980 figures for whites (see Table 8-5). A high proportion of African Americans remain in the lower income brackets, because of the prejudice,

**Table 8-5** Money Income of Families—Percent Distribution by Income Level in Constant (2008) Dollars, 1980 to 2008

| Year | Number of Families (in 1,000s) | Percent Distribution | | | | | | | Median Income (dollars) |
|---|---|---|---|---|---|---|---|---|---|
| | | Under $15,000 | $15,000 to $24,999 | $25,000 to $34,999 | $35,000 to $49,999 | $50,000 to $74,999 | $75,000 to $99,999 | $100,000 and Over | |
| **ALL FAMILIES[1]** | | | | | | | | | |
| 1990 | 66,322 | 8.7 | 9.4 | 10.3 | 15.6 | 22.5 | 14.6 | 19.1 | 54,369 |
| 2000[2] | 73,778 | 7.0 | 8.6 | 9.3 | 14.3 | 19.8 | 15.1 | 26.2 | 61,083 |
| 2008 | 78,874 | 8.4 | 9.2 | 9.9 | 13.7 | 19.3 | 14.2 | 26.0 | 61,521 |
| 2009[3] | 78,867 | 8.7 | 9.1 | 10.0 | 13.8 | 19.4 | 13.5 | 25.6 | 60,088 |
| **WHITE** | | | | | | | | | |
| 1990 | 56,803 | 6.6 | 8.7 | 10.0 | 15.8 | 23.3 | 15.4 | 20.4 | 56,771 |
| 2000[2] | 61,330 | 5.7 | 7.9 | 9.0 | 14.2 | 20.1 | 15.8 | 27.7 | 63,849 |
| 2008[4,5] | 64,183 | 76.8 | 8.5 | 9.5 | 13.4 | 19.8 | 15.0 | 27.5 | 65,000 |
| 2009[3,4,5] | 64,145 | 7.2 | 8.4 | 9.5 | 13.8 | 19.9 | 14.1 | 27.0 | 62,545 |
| **BLACK** | | | | | | | | | |
| 1990 | 7,471 | 23.9 | 14.7 | 12.5 | 14.4 | 17.5 | 8.8 | 8.2 | 32,946 |
| 2000[2] | 8,731 | 15.1 | 14.0 | 12.8 | 15.8 | 18.7 | 10.3 | 13.0 | 40,547 |
| 2008[4,6] | 9,359 | 18.2 | 14.4 | 12.8 | 15.3 | 16.6 | 9.8 | 13.4 | 39,879 |
| 2009[3,4,6] | 9,367 | 18.0 | 14.5 | 13.3 | 15.2 | 16.4 | 10.6 | 12.1 | 38,409 |
| **ASIAN AND PACIFIC ISLANDER[7]** | | | | | | | | | |
| 1990 | 1,536 | 8.1 | 7.8 | 8.2 | 11.6 | 21.2 | 15.0 | 28.5 | 64,969 |
| 2000[2] | 2,982 | 6.2 | 6.4 | 6.4 | 11.7 | 17.3 | 15.5 | 37.0 | 75,393 |
| 2008[4,7] | 3,494 | 7.7 | 7.2 | 7.6 | 12.8 | 16.0 | 13.0 | 36.6 | 73,578 |
| 2009[3,4,7] | 3,592 | 6.9 | 7.0 | 7.9 | 10.4 | 17.7 | 12.3 | 37.7 | 75,027 |
| **HISPANIC ORIGIN[8]** | | | | | | | | | |
| 1990 | 4,981 | 17.0 | 16.3 | 13.6 | 17.3 | 19.1 | 8.5 | 8.2 | 36,034 |
| 2000[2] | 8,017 | 12.8 | 14.6 | 13.0 | 18.1 | 19.4 | 10.5 | 12.0 | 41,469 |
| 2008 | 10,503 | 15.5 | 14.6 | 14.1 | 16.8 | 17.2 | 9.6 | 12.5 | 40,466 |
| 2009[3] | 10,422 | 15.2 | 14.7 | 14.3 | 16.0 | 17.9 | 9.5 | 12.4 | 39,730 |

[1]Includes other races, not shown separately. [2]Data reflect implementation of Census 2000-based population controls and a 28,000 household sample expansion to 78,000 households. [3]Median income is calculated using $2,500 income intervals. Beginning with 2009 income data, the Census Bureau expanded the upper income intervals used to calculate medians to $250,000 or more. Medians falling in the upper open-ended interval are plugged with "$250,000." [4]Beginning with the 2003 Census Population Survey (CPS), the questionnaire allowed respondents to choose more than one race. For 2002 and later, data represent persons who selected this race group only and exclude persons reporting more than one race. The CPS in prior years allowed respondents to report only on race group. See also comments on race in text for Section 1. [5]Data represent white alone, which refers to people who reported white and did not report any other race category. [6]Data represent black alone, which refers to people who reported black and did not report any other race category. [7]Data represent Asian alone, which refers to people who reported Asian and did not report any other race category. [8]People of Hispanic origin may be any race.

Adapted from U.S. Census Bureau, *Income, Poverty and Health Insurance Coverage in the United States: 2008*, Current Population Reports, P60-236(RV), and Historical Tables—Table F-23, September 2009. See also http://www.census.gov/hhes/www/income/income.html> and <htpp://www.census.gov/hhes/www/income/data/historical/families/index.html

segregation, and discriminatory practices endured by them throughout most of their time in this country; only in the past 30 years have they achieved a measure of equality. Previously, they were routinely denied equal protection under the law, equal access to schools and housing, and equal wages.

The final transition was from negative to positive self-image. A basic tenet of the symbolic interaction approach is that we develop self-image, our identities, and our feelings of self-worth through our interactions with others. Throughout most of our history, African Americans have been the last to be hired and the first to be fired. It would be understandable if blacks' self-esteems were lower than those of whites; yet studies have shown that blacks' self-evaluations are equal to or higher than those of whites, and their rate of suicide is about one-half that of whites. Unfortunately, one major consequence of cuts in social programs that took place under the Reagan and George H. W. Bush administrations is that the cuts may have conveyed a message to all minority groups in the United States that they are of little importance, compared with the interests of the dominant white middle and upper classes.

## 8.5c Asian Americans

The Asian American community in the United States is a highly diverse group, even more so than the Hispanic community. Asian immigration to the United States has consisted of two distinct parts: the "Old Asians" and the "New Asians" (Marger, 2003). The first group consisted of Chinese immigrants arriving in the middle of the nineteenth century and spanning to the early twentieth century. Japanese, Korean, and Filipino workers—mainly recruited for hard labor like low-income construction jobs—followed the Chinese. The next wave of Asian immigrants to enter the U.S. is the most recent group, comprising a more diverse cultural heritage. This group is distinct from the first group in that the educational levels, occupational skills, and social class status of the second group has been much higher. While the most numerous groups within the Asian population are those with Chinese, Filipino, and Japanese heritages, Asian Indians, Koreans, Hawaiians, and Guamanians are also included in this category. In the past decade, more immigrants have come from the Philippines, China, Vietnam, Korea, and India than from any other country outside of North and South America. Other groups represented in the large amounts of immigrants to America come from Africa, Iran, Cambodia, and the United Kingdom, with recent increases from Poland and Laos.

(iStockphoto)

As mentioned, the Chinese were the first Asians to enter this country in large numbers. Mostly single males, Chinese workers intended to return home after working in the United States. In 1882, due to the fear of white workers that Chinese men would take their jobs, an anti-Chinese movement began that culminated in a ban on immigrants from China. The Chinese Exclusion Act was made permanent in 1907 and began a series of restrictions by the United States on other immigrant groups. In 1943, the ban was lifted, but life for Chinese immigrants suffered as a result. The Chinese have historically resisted assimilation and tend to uphold traditional values, such as filial duty, veneration of the aged and of deceased ancestors, and arranged marriages. Chinese American families tend to be male-dominated, and an extended family pattern is the rule. In 1965, large-scale immigration from China to the U.S. occurred and increased their population.

Today, most Chinese Americans live in large urban enclaves in Hawaii, San Francisco, Los Angeles, and New York in areas known as Chinatowns. While the sights, sounds and smells in Chinatowns seem exotic, there is often overcrowding, poverty, poor health, rundown housing, and inadequate care for the elderly. Yet not all Chinese live in Chinatowns. Those who have "made it" live in the suburbs.





Like the Chinese, most early Japanese immigrants were males imported for their labor. For both groups, employment was at low-prestige, physically difficult, and low-paying jobs. Both groups were victims of prejudice, discrimination, and racism. As time went by, a large percentage of Japanese immigrants turned to farming, instead of construction, and honed their farming skills mainly in California (Marger, 2003). Other important differences between the Chinese and Japanese that promoted diverse outcomes were noted by Kitano (1991). For example, the Japanese came from a nation that was moving toward modernization and an industrial economy, while China (during the time of major emigration) was an agricultural nation that was weak and growing weaker. This meant that the Japanese had the backing of a growing international power, while the Chinese were more dependent on local resources. Another difference focused on marriage and family life. The Japanese men sent for their wives and families almost immediately. In contrast, many Chinese men left their wives in China or remained as bachelors primarily as a result of the Chinese Exclusion Act of 1882, which closed the door to Chinese immigrants. One consequence of this was the birth and presence of children for the Japanese, which meant facing issues of acculturation and a permanent place in the larger community. This process was delayed among the Chinese because they had so few children. Japanese Americans are today more fully integrated into American culture and have higher incomes than the Chinese or other Asian groups.

During World War II, European Americans feared that there might be Japanese Americans working against the American war effort, so the federal government moved most of them to what they called "relocation camps." Families were forced to pack up whatever possessions they could and to move to camps in Utah, Arizona, California, Idaho, Wyoming, Colorado, and Arkansas, abandoning or selling at nominal prices their land and their homes and severely disrupting their lives. Many were incensed at the suggestion that they were not loyal Americans capable of making valuable contributions to the American war effort. Many also noted that German Americans were not similarly relocated. In addition, some of the relocated families even had sons serving in the U.S. armed forces. Altogether, more than 110,000 people of Japanese ancestry, 70,000 of them U.S. citizens by birth, were moved. After the war, the Japanese were allowed to return to their homes; but even with the token monetary compensation recently awarded them, they have never been compensated adequately for the time, businesses, or property lost during their internment.

## 8.5d Native Americans

The Native American population is actually a varied group of tribes having different languages and cultures. At the time of the European invasion of America, there were perhaps 200 distinct groups that traditionally have been grouped into seven major geographical areas (Feagin & Feagin, 2002):

1. Eastern tribes, who hunted, farmed, and fished
2. Great Plains hunters and agriculturists
3. Pacific Northwest fishing societies
4. California and neighboring area seed gatherers
5. Navajo shepherds and Pueblo farmers of the Arizona and New Mexico area
6. Southwestern desert societies (e.g., Hopi) of Arizona and New Mexico
7. Alaskan groups, including the Eskimos

Estimates of the number of Native Americans in the United States at the time of the European settlement range from 1 to 10 million. By 1800, the native population had declined to 600,000; and by 1850, it had dwindled to 250,000 as a result of starvation,

**BVT Lab**

Visit www.BVTLab.com to explore the student resources available for this chapter.

deliberate massacre, and diseases such as smallpox, measles, and the common cold. Since the turn of the century, however, their numbers have increased dramatically. In the 1970s, the Native American population exceeded the 1 million mark for the first time since the period of European expansion; by 2010, it reached an estimated 3 million (including Eskimos and Aleuts), according to the U.S. Bureau of the Census.

By the 1960s, Native Americans were no longer regarded as nations to be dealt with through treaties. Most tribes were treated as wards of the U.S. government and lived isolated lives on reservations. Today, about half of all Native Americans live on or near reservations administered fully or partly by the Bureau of Indian Affairs (BIA). Many other Native Americans have moved to urban areas or have been relocated there by the BIA to help in their search for jobs and improved living conditions.

Native Americans are among the most deprived of American minority groups. Their unemployment rate is twice that of European Americans (Feagin & Feagin, 2002). Most hold jobs at lower occupational levels and have incomes far below the median for American families. Housing is often severely crowded, and two-thirds of their houses in rural areas have no plumbing facilities. The life expectancy is about two-thirds the national average. It appears that teenage suicide, alcoholism, and adult diabetes are more common among reservation-dwelling Native Americans than among any other group in the country. Studies suggest that Native Americans have the lowest school enrollment rates of any racial or ethnic group in the United States (Feagin & Feagin, 2002). The norms, practices, and even materials within public schools often are at variance with those of Native American groups. In the Southwest, at least, many of these public schools are actually boarding schools, removing children entirely from their families and homes. In either type of school, children are often pressured not to speak their native language or to practice their native traditions.

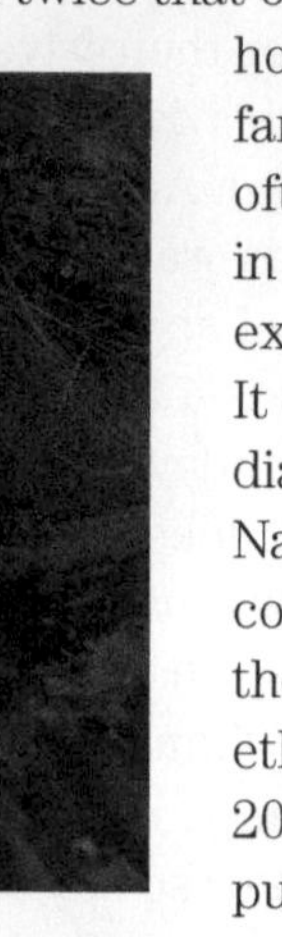

*(iStockphoto)*

One area in which Native Americans differ from the mainstream culture is in family structure. The Native American equivalent to the family is the band, which includes a number of related families who live in close proximity. The band is composed of kin people who share property, jointly organize rituals and festivals, and provide mutual support and assistance. Bands are egalitarian and arrive at decisions collectively.

Since the 1960s, many Native American tribes have united and formed organized collectives to demand a better life for their people. Several tribes have banded together to bargain more effectively with the federal government, and they have sometimes used militant tactics to get results. Nonetheless, Native Americans—the only group that did not immigrate to the United States—remain a subordinate group. Stereotyped as inferior, they have suffered exploitation and discrimination in all of our basic social institutions.

## 8.5e WASPs and White Ethnic Americans

Most of the white population in the United States today emigrated as a result of European expansionist policies over the past 350 years. Earlier immigrants were WASPs, who came mainly from northern and western European countries such as Britain, Ireland, Scotland, Sweden, Norway, Germany, France, and Switzerland. Although they are a minority group in terms of numbers within the U.S. population, they are not a minority in terms of political and economic power. Thus, they have pressured African Americans, Hispanic Americans, Native Americans, and other racial, ethnic, and other minority groups to assimilate or acculturate to the ideal of Anglo conformity, the ideal of Americanization, or the model of A + B + C = A.

Historically, WASP immigrants displayed what became known as the "Protestant ethic." This was an ethic of a strong belief in God, honesty, frugality, piety, abstinence, and hard work. As the majority group in terms of power, they were not subject to the prejudices and discrimination experienced by other, later, immigrants. The pressure on these other groups to be assimilated and integrated into American society meant, basically, to think and behave like the WASP.

The more recent European immigrants are today's white ethnics. They came largely from southern and eastern European countries, such as Italy, Greece, Yugoslavia, Russia and other former Soviet republics, and Poland. Schaefer (2003) states that white ethnics separate themselves from WASPs and make it clear that they were not responsible for the oppression of Native Americans, African Americans, and Mexican Americans that took place before their ancestors had left Europe.

The majority of these immigrants, although they did not totally discard their roots, adopted American norms and values. Many dropped their European names in favor of names that sounded more "American," and most white ethnics have successfully assimilated.

The emerging assertiveness of African Americans and other non-whites in the 1960s induced many white ethnics to reexamine their positions. Today, many American ethnic communities emphasize more of their folk culture, native food, dance, costume, and religious traditions in establishing their ethnic identities. They have sought a more structured means of expressing, preserving; thus, many have formed fraternal organizations, museums, and native-language newspapers in an effort to preserve their heritage (Lopata, 1976).

(Shutterstock)

## 8.5f Jewish Americans

One of the predominant religious ethnic groups is the Jewish American. America has the largest Jewish population in the world, estimated to be 6.5 million and exceeding the approximately 4 million Jews in Israel. They are heavily concentrated in the New York City metropolitan area and other urban areas.

Jewish Americans are basically ethnic in nature, in that they share cultural traits to a greater extent than physical features or religious beliefs. As a minority group, they have a strong sense of group solidarity, tend to marry one another, and experience unequal treatment from non-Jews in the form of prejudice, discrimination, and segregation. Although Jews are generally perceived to be affiliated with one of the three Jewish religious groups—Orthodox, Reform, or Conservative—many, if not the majority of Jews, do not participate as adults in religious services or belong to a temple or synagogue; yet, they do not cease to think of themselves as Jews. The trend in the United States seems to be the substitution of cultural traditions for religion as the binding and solidifying force among Jewish Americans.

Injustices to Jewish people have continued for centuries all over the world. The most tragic example of anti-Semitism occurred during World War II, when Adolf Hitler succeeded in having 6 million Jewish civilians exterminated—the terrifying event that has become known as the "Holocaust." Anti-Semitism in the United States never reached the extreme of Germany, but it did exist. As early as the 1870s, some colleges excluded Jewish Americans. In the 1920s and 1930s, a myth of international Jewry emerged that suggested Jews were going to conquer all governments throughout the world by using the vehicle of Communism, which was believed by anti-Semites to be a Jewish movement. At that time, Henry Ford, Catholic priest Charles E. Coughlin, and groups such as the Ku Klux Klan published, preached, and spoke about a Jewish conspiracy as if it were fact. Unlike in Germany or Italy, however, the United States government never publicly promoted anti-Semitism, and Jewish Americans were more likely to face issues of how to assimilate than how to survive.

Concern about anti-Semitism seemed to decrease drastically following World War II through the 1960s; but in the 1970s and continuing today, anti-Semitic sentiments and behaviors appear to be on the increase. Whatever the cause, racial or ethnic hostility tends to unify the victims against attackers and Jewish Americans are no exception.

### thinking SOCIOLOGICALLY

1 Using information found in this chapter (and other relevant chapters, if necessary), discuss the racial and ethnic hierarchy found within American society. What has led to, and continues to exacerbate, inequality among the various groups?

2. Examine your own family tree and compare your grandparents, great-grandparents, etc., to the early immigrant groups. How would life have been different for them during their generation?

## 8.6 THE FUTURE

What does the future hold for ethnic groups and integration in the United States? Will there be a time when Americans can get past racial and economic injustices and conquer the serious problems that we have yet to overcome? Racism continues to powerfully influence individual lives and the interactions of different ethnic groups, and each step in the integrative process presents new problems.

Despite the new problems that crop up and the frequent news stories of racial and racist incidents, there is reason for optimism. Just as few would argue that race relations are everything they should be in this country, few would refute the fact that progress has been made during the past 4 decades. A number of barriers to equality have been eliminated. Civil rights activism during the 1960s and 1970s brought about reforms in laws and government policies. In 1963, affirmative action policies were established; and President Kennedy issued an executive order calling for the disregard of race, creed, color, or national origin in hiring procedures, as well as in the treatment of employees. Affirmative action has since become a principal government instrument in eradicating institutional racism (Feagin & Feagin, 2002); its laws were later amended to include women, so that today, the laws also prohibit discrimination on the basis of sex.

The reduction of institutional racism has had both indirect and direct effects. According to the "contact hypothesis," interracial contact leads to reductions in prejudice with the following conditions: (1) The parties involved are of equal status, and (2) the situation in which the contact occurs is pleasant or harmonious. This hypothesis, reflecting an interactionist perspective, claims that these conditions cause people to become less prejudiced and to abandon previously held stereotypes. The importance of both equal status and pleasant contact cannot be overlooked. For example, a black employee being abused by a white employer (unequal status), or two people of equal status from different ethnic or minority groups competing for the same job opening (unpleasant contact) do little to promote interracial harmony and may lead to greater hostility, in fact.

Changes in the way that minorities are portrayed in the mass media have also influenced levels of prejudice. During the 1950s and 1960s, when blacks and other minorities were portrayed, it was usually in stereotyped roles as servants or other low-status workers. Today, although it could be argued that portrayals of minorities in the media still tend to reflect stereotypes, the situation has improved considerably.

Another cause for optimism is the frequent finding of research studies that better-educated people are more likely to express liking for groups other than their own. It may be that the educated have a more cosmopolitan outlook and are more likely to question the accuracy of racial stereotypes. It is to be hoped that the trend in this country toward a more-educated population, along with the other advances that have been made, will contribute to a reduction in prejudice and the more complete realization of the American ideals of freedom and equal opportunity.

Lastly, one needs to look no further than the 2008 and 2012 presidential elections and the forum of candidates who sought the highest office in the land. There has never been a time of such diversity within the political spectrum for president of the United States. This appeared to be the first time predicted front-runners in the election were from such diverse backgrounds. Hillary Clinton was a strong female candidate for the Democratic Party in 2008 and alongside her was Barack Obama, another strong contender who happened to be of mixed ancestry: African American and European American. The field of candidates also included Mitt Romney, a very strong prospect in the Republican Party who happens to be Mormon. As Barack Obama took the oath of office for president of the United States for the first time, it was a cold frigid afternoon when thousands and thousands of people lined the streets, courtyards, and Lincoln Mall to witness that historic occasion. We should recognize that these truly are steps toward equality for all.

# CHAPTER 8 Wrapping it up

## Summary

1. A race is a defined group or category of people distinguished by selected inherited physical characteristics. Throughout history race has been defined in biological, legal, and social terms. An *ethnic group* is a collection of individuals who feel they are one people because they have unique cultural traits, ascribed membership, and a sense of community, ethnocentrism, and territoriality.
2. Racial and ethnic groups are considered minorities when they are subordinate to another group in terms of power, social status, and privilege, and when their norms, values, and other characteristics differ from those that prevail in a society.
3. A stereotype is applied to entire groups of people based on a particular belief. *Prejudice* is a negative attitude toward an entire category of people. A variety of theories have been offered to explain prejudice, including economic and psychological ones. Prejudice often involves acceptance of ethnic *stereotypes*, widely held beliefs about the character and behavior of all members of a group.
4. Whereas prejudice is an attitude, *discrimination* is overt behavior on the part of individuals or institutions. It is the categorical exclusion of all members of a group from particular rights, opportunities, or privileges. Merton provides four categories of discriminators.
5. *Racism* includes prejudices and discriminatory behaviors based on three distinguishing characteristics: (1) the belief that one's own race is superior to any other race, (2) an ideology, and (3) actions based on racist beliefs. Genocide and mass expulsion are consequences of extreme forms of racism.
6. *Ethnic stratification* allocates status on the basis of ethnic or racial membership and is most evident in the different lifestyles and opportunities of different groups. Three conditions necessary for ethnic stratification to occur include ethnocentrism, competition, and inequalities in power.
7. Inequality may lead to ethnic antagonism. A leading theory of ethnic antagonism, the split-labor-market theory, suggests that conflict results among business ownership and management, higher-priced labor, and lower-priced labor. The basic fear of those in higher-priced labor is of being displaced by the lower-priced labor, which business owners view as one way of reducing costs.
8. Racial and ethnic inequalities can be resolved through either integration or pluralism. Integration involves assimilation, an event that occurs when individuals and groups forsake their own cultural traditions to become part of a different group or tradition. The extent to which integration and assimilation has or has not occurred represents *social distance*.
9. Two models of assimilation are the *melting pot* and *Anglo conformity*. The former means that different groups contribute something of their own culture and absorb aspects of other cultures, with an outcome different from any former groups. The latter, equated with Americanization, means that the minority loses its identity to the dominant WASP culture.
10. *Segregation* is the physical and social separation of groups or categories of people. It may be *de jure*, segregation by law, or *de facto*, segregation in fact.
11. *Cultural pluralism* refers to a situation in which various racial, ethnic, or minority groups exist side by side but maintain their distinctive cultural patterns, subsystems, and institutions. Resurgence of this idea is evident in the ethnic and other minority emphasis on their native language, customs, and traditions.
12. The major racial or ethnic groups in the United States are African Americans, Hispanic Americans, Asian Americans, Native Americans, and European ethnics. The largest of these groups is African American. African Americans, brought to the U.S. initially by the singular fact of slavery, have long been in the process of going through

a number of social transitions. Today, most live in metropolitan areas with high population concentrations in Northern cities.

13. Hispanic Americans include those who classify themselves as Mexican, Puerto Rican, Cuban, Central and South American, and other Hispanics from Spain or other Spanish-speaking countries. Mexican Americans, or Chicanos, are the largest Hispanic American group and are characterized by strong family ties and large families. A number of social movements have emerged over the past few decades to improve the status and living conditions of this group.
14. Numerous other ethnic and other minority groups exist in the United States today. Asian Americans include those with ties to China, Japan, the Philippines, India, Korea, Vietnam, and other Asian countries. Native Americans, the only nonimmigrant group, are often grouped into seven major geographical areas with distinct language patterns and tribal customs.
15. White Anglo-Saxon Protestant (WASP) groups came predominantly from northern and western European countries, while white ethnic groups came predominantly from southern and eastern European countries. Jewish-Americans are basically ethnic in nature, in that they share cultural traits to a greater extent than physical features or religious beliefs.
16. Although relations among ethnic groups are far from perfect in this country, some progress has been made during the past few decades. Government regulations have made discriminatory action illegal, and numerous affirmative action programs have been instituted in political, educational, and economic agencies throughout the country. The election of our first non-white president, changes in the portrayal of minorities in the media and the trend toward a better-educated population may lead to further progress in this area.

## Discussion Questions

1. Discuss the differences between the sociological concepts of racial, ethnic, and minority groups.
2. Do you believe that racial identity is based on biological, legal or social factors? Explain.
3. Select a racial, ethnic, or minority group other than your own, and compare it with your own.
4. Identify a prejudice that you hold, and use the theories of prejudice to discuss why you might have this prejudice.
5. Do you think that anyone has ever held a prejudice or discriminated against you? Why do you think so? Was this prejudice accurate?
6. What is the difference between de jure and de facto segregation? Can you identify either in your local community or state?
7. Differentiate between individual and institutional racism. Give specific examples.
8. Discuss the melting pot, Anglo conformity, and pluralism models described in the chapter. Show how your community or city would be different, depending on which model was most prevalent.
9. What is the significance of any of the social transitions that have occurred or are occurring for African Americans? For example, is the demographic shift from the rural South to the urban North significant? How?
10. Based on the increases in the African American, Hispanic American, and Asian American population in the United States, social demographers suggest that within the next quarter century, the number of these groups will surpass the number of white-ethnic and WASP Americans. Will white Americans then be the minority? Explain.

# Chapter 9

# Gender Differentiation

## SYNOPSIS

### Sex and Gender Differentiation

- Biological Bases of Gender Differentiation
- Social Bases of Gender Differentiation
- Adult Sex Differentiation

### Cross-Cultural Gender Differentiation

### Theories of Gender Differentiation

- Structural Functional Theory
- Conflict Theory

### Gender Differentiation and the Workplace

- Women in the Workplace
- Income
- The Split Labor Market
- Comparable Worth
- Upward Mobility
- Women's Work in the Family

### The Women's Movement

- The Women's Movement in the United States
- The Women's Movement in Europe

### The Consequences of Inequality

- Gender and Poverty
- Women's Self-Esteem
- Medical Care
- Sexual Harassment
- Family Violence
- Rape

### The Future of Gender Inequality

## Focal Point

# WOMEN IN AMERICA

In March 2011, the Office of Management and Budget along with the Economics and Statistics Administration within the Department of Commerce released the report, *Women in America: Indicators of Social and Economic Well-Being.* The report takes a comprehensive look at how women fare with regard to family life, income, employment, health, crime and violence. This was the first federal government report about the state of women since one produced in 1963 by the Commission on the Status of Women, established by President Kennedy. That such a comprehensive document has been created recently, and that so much time has elapsed since the previous report about the state of women in the United States, is an important message in itself. While the report does highlight some important gains for women, the extensive time lapse between the current report and the previous one suggests that some of these gains for women have taken a very long-time to achieve and also that there is still some distance to go for women to achieve full equality. In addition, the magnitude of the document is evidence that attention to women's status is a critical part of trying to insure a fully functional and egalitarian society. This report provides important information that will be explored further in this chapter as we discuss gender equality and inequality. Following are some highlights of the report:

### People, Families, and Income

- Females make up 51% of the U.S. population.
- Women continue to earn less than men for the same work. Women are two to three times more likely than men to live in poverty.
- Women are more likely than men to live without a spouse. The percentage of women who are married declined from 72% in 1970 to 62% in 2009, as compared to 84% and 66% for men, respectively.
- Almost twice as many women in 2008 as in 1970 have never had a child (18% compared to 10%).

### Education

- Women have made greater educational gains than men in recent decades, across all ethnic groups and in all developed countries.
- In 2008, the college enrollment rate for women was 72%, compared to 66% for men. As compared to males, white, black and Hispanic women had higher graduation rates and lower dropout rates at all levels of education, took more advanced placement exams, and earned more post-secondary degrees.
- Women still lag behind men in their mathematics assessment tests, but score higher than men in reading. In the United States and in other developed countries, the percentage of women entering natural science and technology fields is lower than that of men. In school, males are more likely to be subject to physical bullying, whereas females are more likely to be victims of electronic bullying.

### Employment

- The labor force participation rate for women in 1950 was 33% and was 66% in 2009, having held steady since 1999, as compared to 75% of men.
- Statistically, 51% of all persons employed in management, professional and related occupations in 2009 were women; however, they are more represented than men in the lower paying positions within these categories.
- Women still lag behind men in weekly earnings, but have made gains. In 1979, women earned 62% of what men earned as compared to 80% in 2009.
- Unemployment rates for women have risen less than for men in recent recessions.
- In dual income families in 2009, 87% of wives spent time on household activities as compared to 65% of husbands.

### Health

- Although the gender gap is closing the area of life span, women still live longer then men. Life expectancy for women in the United States is lower than in other industrialized countries.
- Mortality from heart disease, the leading cause of death among women, has decreased 68% since 1950; yet the mortality rate for cancer, the second leading cause of death for women, decreased only 17%. The lung cancer rate increased 500%. The maternal mortality rate in the United States is much lower than it was in the 1950s, but it is significantly higher than in many European countries.

- More women than men have chronic medical conditions such as asthma, emphysema, arthritis, or cancer. Men have a higher rate of heart disease and diabetes.
- The Caesarean section rate rose from 21% in 1996 to 32% in 2008.
- Approximately 15% of women and 26% of men have no regular source of healthcare.

Crime and Violence

- The rate of nonfatal violent crimes against women has declined from 43 per 1,000 women in 1993 to 18 per 1,000 women in 2008.
- The rate of sexual victimization and intimate partner violence affects women in more than five times the instances it affects men. In 2008, intimate partners were responsible for 5% of all violence against men, compared to 25% of all violence against females. While the rate of rape declined 60% between 1993 and 2000 (and has remained consistent since then, between 2004 and 2008, police were not notified in approximately half of all the incidents of rape. Women are much more likely than men to be victims of stalking. In 2006, the number of female victims was 20 per 1,000 women as compared to 7 per 1,000 men.
- While men commit more crimes—especially violent crimes—than women, the proportion of women arrested for crimes is increasing. Women represented 18% of all those arrested for violent felony crimes in 2008, up from 11% in 1990. During that same period, the percentage of women arrested for larceny increased from 25% to 35%.
- The number of women under some form of correctional supervision between 1990 and 2008 increased 121%.

Women have made important gains in the past half-century, but still suffer from inequality in a number of ways. This chapter explores reasons for some of the differences between men and women's behaviors, considering gender primarily as a social explanation rather than a biological one.

(Shutterstock)

# 9.1 SEX AND GENDER DIFFERENTIATION

**Sex** refers to biological characteristics—the genetic, hormonal, and anatomical differences between males and females. **Gender**, on the other hand, is a social status. It refers to social differences between the sexes, specifically to the cultural concepts of masculinity and femininity. Our culture traditionally associates masculinity with being strong, competent, rational, unemotional, and competitive. It associates femininity with being nurturant, caring, and able to deal with the emotional side of relationships.

**Sex**
The biological and anatomical characteristics that differentiate males and females

**Gender**
A social status that refers to differences between the sexes, specifically to differences in masculinity and femininity

**Gender roles** refer to the behaviors that are expected of men and women, behaviors assigned on the basis of the assumed characteristics of masculinity and femininity. They are roles required to fill the needs of the society. While we typically tend to think of masculine roles as instrumental and female as expressive, these expectations are not universal across all cultures.

**Gender roles**
The expectations for behavior deriving from culturally created definitions of masculinity and femininity

In order to understand the difference between biological sex and socially defined gender roles, we review some of the basic biological differences between men and women.

## 9.1a Biological Bases of Gender Differentiation

Males and females differ from the moment of conception, when sex is determined. The ovum of the mother always carries an X chromosome, one of which is needed to bear the genetic material to develop either a male or a female. The father's sperm may carry either an X or a Y chromosome. If the sperm carries a second X chromosome, the fetus will develop into a female. If the sperm carries a Y chromosome, on the other hand, testes develop that secrete a hormone that causes the embryo to develop as a male. Between birth and puberty, the hormones produced by males and females are the same; thus, other than the development of either male or female sex organs, these chromosome differences cause very few physical differences between boys and girls.

Physiologists and psychologists have been more interested in behavioral differences between males and females. They ask whether the sex hormones in the fetus affect the central nervous system, therefore influencing how males and females behave. In order to find answers to this question, they study infants and children.

The research literature is extensive on this point, but it gives no clear indication that boys and girls are born with a predisposition toward different behaviors. In a recent cross-cultural study, researchers observed aggression in 192 children between the ages of 3 and 9 years old. They observed children in naturalistic settings in Belize, Kenya, Nepal, and American Samoa. Results showed that boys exhibited aggression in approximately 10% of their social behaviors, girls in 6%; in all four cultures the aggression of boys was more frequent than that of girls (Munroe, Hulefeld, Rodgers, Tomeo, & Yamazaki, 2000). These differences could be explained as differences in socialization.

## 9.1b Social Bases of Gender Differentiation

Most people in nurturing roles—such as teachers, counselors, and parents—are unaware that they have a tendency to treat males and females in gender-biased ways in nurturing, counseling, and educational situations (Sadker & Sadker, 1985; 1986). It is profoundly important for people in these roles to understand that a person's gender characteristics may be determined as much by social conditions as by heredity. The concept of the self-fulfilling prophecy comes into play here. If children are treated as if they have (or do not have) particular characteristics, they may well develop (or fail to develop) those traits. Teachers play a significant role in shaping the potential of males and females, treating students—from kindergarten to graduate school—in terms of stereotypical gender traits. This occurs both in and out of the classroom.

If parents assume, for example, that females are by nature non-aggressive, they might directly discourage—or indirectly discourage by lack of attention or praise—their daughter from engaging in rough-and-tumble activities or contact games. As a result, the girl may not develop aggressive or competitive qualities—not because of her genetic makeup, but because she was never encouraged to develop them.

On the other hand, if parents assume that their son, because he is male, necessarily has good physical dexterity or analytical ability, they might encourage him to play with puzzles and to figure them out on his own. As a result, he may become adept at tasks that require physical coordination and analytical ability. The point is that children often develop the traits that we assume that they have by nature, as a result of the activities we provide for them.

One study, for example, found that in classrooms, boys were more likely than girls to get individual instruction on a task when they asked for it; they also received more tangible and verbal rewards for academic work (Serbin & O'Leary, 1975). Girls were responded to less than the boys—usually only when they were physically close to the teacher—and were rarely encouraged to work on their own. Boys received more attention whether they were close to the teacher or not, and they were encouraged to do independent work.

**BVT*Lab***

Flashcards are available for this chapter at www.BVTLab.com

It is important to point out that research on behaviors that contribute to the development of stereotypical gender traits—such as the differential treatment of boys and girls in educational settings—has become a political issue. Sadker (2000), a renowned scholar in the area of gender bias in educational settings, notes that ultraconservative "educational research" organizations have been created to discredit decades of studies documenting gender bias in schools. "In the past," Sadker (2000) notes, "the enemies of equity spoke more openly about the beliefs: the 'natural' roles of men and women the 'biological destinies' of each, even biblical references to the second class status of females." Because the Internet and the media do not evaluate research the same way that academic scholars do, politically funded and affiliated commentary is often seen by the public as valid "research," thus perpetuating gender bias and stereotypes that lead to inequity between females and males. By keeping in mind that we often unintentionally send hidden messages to males and females regarding their capabilities, teachers, counselors, and parents might develop more effective ways to give both genders an equal opportunity to excel in all academic areas and might develop ways to advise students (in terms of careers, choice of major, and other areas related to academics) based on their qualities and characteristics as individuals, and not on whether they are male or female.

**thinking** SOCIOLOGICALLY

Do you think any gender roles might really be sex roles—in other words, based on biological characteristics rather than social experiences?
Explain why or why not.

## 9.1c Adult Sex Differentiation

When children reach adolescence, they begin to produce sex hormones again; the secondary sex characteristics develop—facial hair on men and breasts on women, for example. Most of these secondary sex characteristics are of little importance in behavior. Men do develop more muscular builds than women, especially in the upper part of their body. As a result, men have more muscle strength and greater spurts of energy, and are able to lift heavier objects. Women have a larger proportion of fat on their bodies, particularly through the breast and hip areas. This enables them to have more endurance over long periods of time than men. Women also have greater finger dexterity and should tend to be better able to do fine work with their hands, such as surgery, needlework, or dentistry.

However, socialization to gender roles, rather than physical differences, shape adult behavior. In our society, for example, even though women have greater finger dexterity, most dentists and surgeons are men (but most dental assistants are women). Women's finger dexterity is valued primarily in low-paying factory work, where sewing or electronics work is assigned to women. Cross-cultural studies show that the variety of gender roles men and women play in societies depends on the norms of society, rather than on any physical characteristics.

# 9.2 CROSS-CULTURAL GENDER DIFFERENTIATION

In some cultures, men and women occupy roles in ways very unlike those typically found in the United States. In the Chambri (formerly called "Tchambuli") society of New Guinea, for example, the women are the workers. They do the fishing, weaving, planting, harvesting, and cooking—all the while they are carrying and caring for their children.

They are generally confident, laughing, brisk, good-natured, and efficient. They have a jolly comradeship that involves much rough joking. The men, on the other hand, are more involved in producing arts and crafts and in planning ceremonies. They tend to be more emotional than the women and also more responsive to the needs of others. The women typically have an attitude of kind tolerance toward the men, enjoying the men's games and parties but remaining rather remote emotionally (1935).

In many African societies, the women have traditionally owned much of the land. Europeans have often tried to impose their own system of ownership on these tribes, sometimes with dire consequences. When Europeans introduced modern farming methods to the Ibo tribe of Nigeria, they took the land from the women and gave it to the men. The men raised cash crops, which they sold, and the women were left without their traditional means of subsistence. In 1923, the Ibo women rioted; 10,000 women looted shops and released prisoners from jail. In 2 days of intense rioting, 50 people were killed and another 50 were injured. Later, the women became more organized and continued their revolt against land reforms and taxation with more riots, strikes, cursing, and ridicule (Leavitt, 1971).

*In the Chambri society of New Guinea, the women are the workers and do such tasks as weaving and fishing as well as child rearing.* *(AP Wide World Photo)*

## 9.3 THEORIES OF GENDER DIFFERENTIATION

The gender-role socialization of members of a society seems to differ with the type of society. In hunting-and-gathering societies, in which survival depends on the constant search for food, both males and females must be responsible for finding food; therefore, both are socialized to be assertive and independent. As societies grow wealthier and more complex, and as the division of labor increases and hunting is no longer necessary to provide food for people, gender-role differentiation increases. If both men and women are capable of meeting the demands of almost all positions or statuses without being constrained by biological factors, why does role differentiation increase? Why do women have lower status in modern society than men? Sociologists have explored these questions from several theoretical perspectives, including structural functionalism and conflict theory.

### 9.3a Structural Functional Theory

As mentioned in Chapter 1, structural functionalists believe that society consists of interrelated parts, each of which performs certain functions in maintaining the whole system. They assume, accordingly, that women have traditionally made important contributions to society. They raised children, maintained the home, and provided food, clean clothing, and other necessities of daily living. They played an expressive role, nurturing and providing emotional support for husbands and children returning home from work or school. The woman in the family created the atmosphere of close interpersonal relationships necessary to a worthwhile human experience, relationships lacking in the competitive workplace (Mann, Grimes, Kemp, & Jenkins, 1997; Parsons & Bales, 1955; Smith, 1993). Although these skills are vital to society, they do not command a salary outside of the home. According to this perspective, the traditional function of the male was to play the instrumental role of protecting and providing for his wife and children. He was the head of the household, controlling where the family lived, how money was spent, and making other decisions important to the survival of the family.

He also made political and economic decisions in the community by serving in powerful decision-making positions.

Structural functionalists might argue that many traditional family functions have moved from the family to other social institutions. Most families no longer find support through work at home. Instead, work is more likely to take place in the factory or office. However, it will be interesting to see how the advancement of telecommuting from home affects family functions in the future. The number of telecommuters has increased by 73% in the US between 2005 and 2011 (from around 1.8 million people to around 3.1 million) (Global Workplace Analytics and the Telework Research Network, 2012). Recreation has also moved away from the family and is sponsored by Little Leagues, tennis clubs, and other organizations at recreation centers. Structural functional theorists believe that, because of changing socialization practices and changing beliefs about work, play, and other functions of the family, the complementary roles of husbands and wives are changing to parallel roles, ones where roles of husbands and wives are similar. The change has been gradual, but both husbands and wives are now likely to work outside the home and both are increasingly sharing household duties. Most functionalists believe that the family will benefit as equality increases between men and women.

*Recreation has moved away from the family and is now sponsored by such organizations as Little League.*

*(iStockphoto)*

## 9.3b Conflict Theory

A conflict theory of gender differentiation focuses on the power and authority discrepancies between men and women. The conflict perspective views women's relative social status, domestic violence, rape, and disparities in wages as resulting from degradation and exploitation by men. Very early in the development of horticultural societies, military force was used to protect land and other valuable private property and also to capture women from other tribes. Women were prized possessions who could work for their captors to increase wealth, provide children who would grow into future workers, and increase the prestige of the men who owned them. It was not just as future workers that children were important. As they grew old, men needed children to look after the property and to inherit it when the men died. To know who his children were, a man needed to isolate his women from other men. Thus, women became the protected property of men, so that men could accumulate wealth and have children to inherit it. According to this perspective, from earliest times, men exploited women for the work they did and for the children they bore and reared.

The process of industrialization removed work from the family. However, conflict theorists argue, men were not willing to lose their control over the labor of women. They either tried to keep women out of the work force entirely or used them as a surplus labor force, moving them in and out of the lowest-paying jobs as the economy required. They passed laws regulating the kind of work that women could do and the hours they could work. They also passed laws regulating women's rights to income, property ownership, and birth control; and they made women exclusively responsible for domestic tasks. Men forbade women from joining unions and from entering professions. Legally and by tradition, they prevented women from gaining high positions in the work force. Men increased their position of power and dominance, while sustaining the dependence of women on them. Less powerful men were also hurt by the practice of keeping women in positions with low pay. The existence of a labor force of poorly paid women meant that lower-paid women could easily replace men who asked for higher wages.

As can be seen, these two theories of gender differentiation lead sociologists to diverse approaches in the study and understanding of the behavior and roles of men and women. According to a structural functional perspective, as industrial society develops, women should move into the work force and attain equality with men. According to a conflict perspective, as industrial society creates more wealth and power for men, men will use their wealth and power to improve their own position; and women will lag farther and farther behind. We now turn our attention to gender differentiation in the workplace, and more specifically, to women in the workplace.

# 9.4 GENDER DIFFERENTIATION AND THE WORKPLACE

## 9.4a Women in the Workplace

The status of women in the workplace is often treated as if it were a new issue. However, women have always played an important economic role in society, moving in and out of the work force as the economy required. Throughout much of history, women produced much of what was needed in the home and also made items for sale in the marketplace. With the growth of large cities during the Middle Ages, new options became available to them. They became traders and innkeepers and occasionally ran breweries and blacksmith shops. They often joined guilds (Bernard, 1981), which were a type of medieval trade union. Those who did not wish to marry could become **Beguines**, members of urban communes of seven or eight women who pursued such occupations as sewing, baking, spinning, and weaving.

Women from the upper class could join convents and become nuns. At that time, some convents had great wealth and beautiful furnishings, and nuns wore beautiful embroidered robes. Some convents also had great scholarly reputations and were political forces to be reckoned with.

When the plagues swept Europe and devastated the population, the powerful Catholic Church and the states of that time wanted women to stay home and have babies to increase the population. The states passed laws banning the Beguine communes, and the Church closed most of the nunneries. In those nunneries that remained open, the nuns were required to wear black habits and to serve the poor. Otherwise, family life was the only secure option for women and their income was from the goods, particularly textiles, that they could produce in the home.

The textile and other goods traditionally produced by women in the home were the first to be manufactured in factories at the beginning of the Industrial Revolution. Many women who were poor, young, and single went to work in the mills under deplorable working conditions and for very little pay. Married women could seldom leave the home for the 12-hour workdays required in the mills and still maintain their homes, so they lost their ability to earn income.

With increased population growth and industrialization, good farmland became increasingly scarce; so men also became available for factory work. Protective labor laws were passed that limited both the number of hours that women and children could work and the types of work they could do. By the nineteenth century, then, women had lost the few work options that had existed for them in earlier centuries. The only source of economic well-being was marriage.

**Beguines**

Communes existing during the Middle Ages that consisted of peasant women who chose not to marry and who took vows of celibacy

In the United States at the beginning of the twentieth century, many upper-class women received an education, and some worked in the professions. Poor women who worked were usually employed as servants. The vast majority of women, however, were married and worked in the home to meet the needs of their families. In fact, during the Great Depression in the 1930s, married women who took jobs were considered selfish and unpatriotic. Jobs were scarce. The unemployment rate rose to 25% and if a woman worked, she was seen as taking a job away from a man who needed it to support his family.

In 1941, the country went to war. Men were sent overseas, and women were told that it was now their patriotic duty to help out in the war effort by going to work. Women held every conceivable job and for many of them, it was their first opportunity to earn a good salary. They worked not only at white-collar jobs but also in factories, building the planes and ships needed for war. In fact, so many women went to work in defense plants that they inspired the creation of a mascot: "Rosie the Riveter."

So many women went to work in defense plants during World War II that they inspired the creation of a mascot: "Rosie the Riveter." (AP Wide World Photo)

After the war was over, men returned to their jobs; many women were seen as dispensable and were fired. Since many of these women had supported themselves and families on their salaries, it was a hardship to give up work. However, the economy shifted from the needs of wartime to peace, and it became the patriotic duty of women to go home and have babies. The country had experienced very low birth rates throughout the Great Depression and World War II, and it needed to build its population of future workers. Thus began the "baby boom," which continued until 1960 when the birth rate began to decline.

In the 1960s, there was a labor shortage because of the low birth rates during the depression and World War II. Unemployment was low, and salaries were high. Women were once again welcomed into the labor force, at least to fill low-paying jobs. From that time to the present, wages did not keep up with inflation, and more and more women were required to work to help pay family expenses. As of 2009, 59.2% of women were in the work force in the United States and they composed 46.8% of workers, projected to increase to 46.9% by 2018 (U.S. Department of Labor). While the increase in the percentage of women in the workforce by 2018 seems insignificant, this will account for 51.2% of the increase in total labor force growth between 2008 and 2018.

## 9.4b Income

The median income for women working full-time year-round in 2011 was $37,118—77% of the median for men, which was $48,202 (U.S. Census, 2011). In 1960, women earned 61% of what men made (a median income of $21,646 for women and $35,675 for men). During the 1960s and 1970s, the gap between men and women widened as more women moved into the work force and took low-paying jobs. By the late 1970s, women made only 59% of what men made. In 2009, women earned about 78% of what men earned. Clearly, this wage differential is now narrowing, largely because the mean income of men is decreasing. There are several reasons for the continuing gap in earnings:

1. More women than men are entering the work force in low-paying occupations, such as clerical, service, or blue-collar work. Often, these jobs have no career lines, so women cannot advance to higher positions.
2. Women are sometimes paid less than men, even though they hold equivalent jobs.

**Table 9-1** The 20 Most Prevalent Occupations for Employed Women in 2010

| Occupation | Number |
|---|---|
| Secretaries and administrative assistants | 2,963,000 |
| Registered nurses | 2,590,000 |
| Elementary and middle school teachers | 2,300,000 |
| Cashiers | 2,293,000 |
| Nursing, psychiatric, and home health aides | 1,700,000 |
| Retail salesperson | 1,582,000 |
| Waitresses | 1,470,000 |
| First-line supervisors/mangers of retail sales workers | 1,376,000 |
| Customer service representatives | 1,263,000 |
| Maids and housekeeping cleaners | 1,252,000 |
| Receptionists and information clerks | 1,188,000 |
| Childcare workers | 1,181,000 |
| Bookkeeping, accounting, and auditing clerks | 1,179,000 |
| First-line supervisors/managers of offices and administrative support workers | 1,035,000 |
| Managers, all other | 1,013,000 |
| Accountants and auditors | 989,000 |
| Teaching assistants | 892,000 |
| Personal and home care aides | 839,000 |
| Office clerks, general | 837,000 |
| Cooks | 790,000 |

Adapted from United States Department of Labor

3. People with low salaries receive smaller raises. A 10% raise on $20,000 is smaller than a 10% raise on $30,000, with the result that income differentials increase even as percentage increases remain equal.

Women have been steadily returning to work for 4 decades. Surely, many women have gained considerable education and work experience during this time, and the gap in earnings between men and women should be closing more rapidly than it is (see Tables 9-1 and 9-2). The question, then, is this: Why do women remain in low-paying occupations?

## 9.4c The Split Labor Market

One reason that women are not advancing is the split labor market. In a split labor market, there are two distinct and unequal groups of workers (Bonacich, 1972). The **primary labor market** is reserved for elites, people who will advance to high-level positions. Primary-labor-market jobs offer job security, on-the-job training, high wages, and frequent promotions. Corporate managers, professionals, and engineers belong to this labor market.

**Primary labor market**

The labor market reserved for people who will advance to high-level positions

In the **secondary labor market**, jobs pay poorly and there is little job security. There are many layoffs, but few promotions or salary increases. Most women work in the secondary labor force in secretarial, typing, and clerical jobs, as sales clerks or waitresses, or in manufacturing jobs. This inequality caused by the split labor market accounts for much of the inequality in earnings between women and men (Bose & Rossi, 1983; Marshall & Paulin, 1985).

**Secondary labor market**

The labor market in which jobs pay poorly, there is little job security, and there are few promotions or salary increases

The secondary labor market is growing in size, both in the United States and throughout the world. During the decade of the 1980s, unions worldwide lost power.

**Table 9-2** Top 20 Best Paying Jobs for Women in 2012

| Occupation | Median Yearly Income | Women as Percentage of Profession | Earnings as Percentage of Men's Earnings |
|---|---|---|---|
| Pharmacists | $99,000 | 56% | 95% |
| Lawyers | $85,000 | 34% | 87% |
| Computer and information systems managers | $80,000 | 26% | 97% |
| Physicians and surgeons | $79,000 | 36% | 79% |
| Chief executives | $76,000 | 25% | 69% |
| Nurse practitioners | $74,000 | 85% | N/A |
| Software developers | $72,000 | 18% | 86% |
| Operations research analysts | $65,000 | 44% | 105% |
| Human resource managers | $66,000 | 72% | 86% |
| Psychologists | $65,000 | 71% | N/A |
| Computer programmers | $64,000 | 20% | 93% |
| Physical therapists | $63,000 | 60% | 80% |
| Occupational therapists | $62,000 | 86% | N/A |
| Management analysts | $61,000 | 45% | 78% |
| Physical scientists | $61,000 | 38% | 79% |
| Medical and health service managers | $61,000 | 72% | 80% |
| Computer systems analysts | $59,000 | 35% | 81% |
| Medical scientists | $59,000 | 55% | 102% |
| Marketing and sales managers | $59,000 | 44% | 68% |
| Postsecondary teachers | $57,000 | 43% | 80% |

Adapted from "The 20 Best-Paying Jobs For Women In 2012" by J. Goudreau, 2012, *Forbes Magazine*, July 16, 2012.

As a result, there has been increasing pressure to weaken job security and to reduce or eliminate minimum-wage regulations. It is now easier for employers to dismiss midlevel managers or highly skilled manufacturing workers. The employer can automate the job, then, with robotic or other machinery or can divide it into simple, repetitive tasks, which can be done by temporary workers at very low wages. Such workers do not develop complex skills; they have no route into the primary labor force. They are not promoted; they do not receive any company benefits such as childcare, health insurance, or pensions, and often are not eligible for social security.

Shifts in union composition in recent years have led to new research about the changing nature of the split-labor market. Global markets have led to shifts in the power and balance in labor unions, with membership of workers in the upper tiers declining and increasing among those in the lower tiers. In the old split labor market, organized labor drew its strength from the upper tier of the organized workforce to help combat the sometimes unjust practices of employers. Today, we are seeing greater strength within the lower tiers to overcome assaults against labor unions. This movement has the potential to bring more fairness and justice to the most vulnerable members of society (Chun, 2008).

Nevertheless, women are still disproportionately poor as compared to men. Many of the jobs in the secondary labor force are being moved from industrialized countries to developing world countries, where labor is even cheaper. There, many rural women are being recruited to leave their homes and take jobs in the new urban industries. Leaving home to go to work is a greater sacrifice in Asian countries than it is in Western countries because in Asia the women are traditionally very sheltered. Often, once they leave home, they are no longer respectable; they are not welcome to return home, and they also lose their opportunity to marry. In some countries, the women compose almost half the work force. According to the Global Poverty Project (2012), "Women work two-thirds of the world's working hours, produce half of the world's food, but earn only 10% of the world's income and own less than 1% of the world's property. On average, women earn half of what men earn."

## 9.4d Comparable Worth

Some jobs are low paying simply because they are held by women, not because the job does not require considerable skill. For example, some office work requires many skills but is often paid less than maintenance work, a position traditionally held by men. Many women argue that pay scales should be based on **comparable worth**—work of equal value, requiring the same level of skill, should earn equal pay, even when the work is not identical. If clerical work, for example, is as necessary to an organization and requires the same level of skill as maintenance work, workers in these two occupations should receive equal pay. If the sale of women's clothing is of equal value and requires the same skill as the sale of men's clothing, it is argued that these two occupations should receive equal pay. Currently, they do not.

In the secondary labor market, most women work in such occupations as secretary or waitress. *(iStockphoto)*

The idea of comparable worth has met with a great deal of resistance because companies resist increasing salaries, and women have little bargaining power (O'Donnell, 1984). Legally, it is discriminatory to pay women less for their low-status jobs if the low status is conferred solely because of the gender of the worker. It is not considered discriminatory to pay a worker less if the job has low prestige.

## 9.4e Upward Mobility

As was noted in the beginning of this chapter, women make up about half of the labor force, yet women who reach management-level positions seem to confront a glass ceiling. Only 19 Fortune 500 companies (3.8%) and 40 Fortune 1000 companies (4%) have female CEOs or presidents (Catalyst, 2012). In 1995, 8.7% of corporate officers in Fortune 500 companies were women, peaking at 16.4% in 2005, and falling back to 15.7% as of 2009 (Catalyst, 2011) (see Figure 9-1). At the level of vice president or above in major companies, there has been no significant increase in the number of women in these positions during recent years.

Research has shown that in order to increase earnings and to get promoted into executive positions, a person needs experience in two areas: authority and autonomy (Spaeth, 1985). **Authority** consists of supervisory experience and experience in a decision-making position. **Autonomy** on the job means having the ability to decide how work will be done. People who decide for themselves how they will do a job are more committed to their work than people who are told what to do (Spaeth, 1985).

Women have less authority and less autonomy in their work than do men (Jaffee, 1989). The major reason is that most women work in female-dominated jobs—as nurses, teachers, and bank tellers—and these jobs do not generally offer either authority or autonomy. However, discrimination also plays a role in why women do not achieve these more powerful positions. When men enter a female-dominated work field, they often quickly move into one of the few positions that has authority and autonomy. For example, the majority of elementary school teachers are women, but most school superintendents are male.

**Comparable worth**
Evaluating and rewarding different occupations equally if the work in each occupation requires the same level of skill and is of equal value to the employer

**Authority**
Power accepted as legitimate by those it affects

**Autonomy**
The ability to decide how work will be done

**Figure 9-1** Fortune 500 Corporate Officer Positions Held by Women*

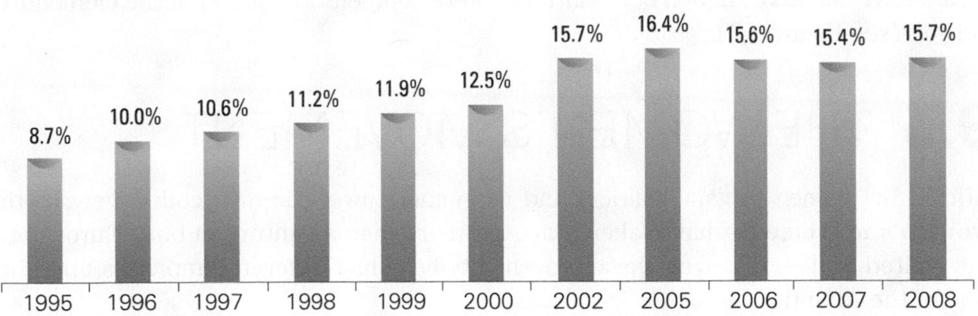


*In 2009, Catalyst instituted a methodology change that makes comparison to previous annual Corporate Officer statistics inappropriate.

Adapted from Catalyst, "2008 Catalyst Census of Women Corporate Officers and Top Earners of the Fortune 500" (2008); Catalyst, "2007 Census of Women Corporate Officers and Top Earners of the Fortune 500" (2007); Catalyst, "2005 Catalyst Census of Women Corporate Officers and Top Earners of the Fortune 500" (2006).

When women work in occupations in which the work force is mixed—male and female—women are still less likely than men to get the jobs with authority and autonomy. This lack of opportunity has been shown to occur even when education and work experience are equal, regardless of whether the woman has family responsibilities (Jaffee, 1989).

**thinking** SOCIOLOGICALLY

1. How could the material in this chapter be used to develop a strategy for parents, teachers, employers, and politicians that would help lead to greater equality between women and men in the workplace?
2. Use material (including theories, concepts, and facts) from this chapter to discuss why the glass ceiling exists for women.

## 9.4f Women's Work in the Family

It is generally recognized that women carry the greatest burden in the family, doing the unpaid but necessary labor of housework and childcare (Berk, 1985). Understanding spousal perceptions of fairness in housework is necessary because the division of household labor can be a source of dissatisfaction in many marriages, especially for wives. Wives who feel that household work is inequitable tend to be less happy in their marriages and personally, and have higher rates of depression than those who feel that housework is shared equitably (Rogers & Amato, 2000; Bird, 1999). One thing that contributes to wives' levels of satisfaction is how much housework their husbands share equally. Spousal housework hours mean more to wives' perception of fairness then their own housework hours. This is not only an American phenomenon but true in many other countries as well (Ruppanner, 2008). It is not just the amount of work that they each do that has to do with wives' happiness. When spouses share housework, wives feel more appreciated and recognized for their household contributions (Lee & Waite, 2010). As women enter the work force, they continue to carry this family burden. Working women spend less time on housework than women who do not work; however, working women spend more time on housework than their husbands, even when the wife works a 40-hour week and the husband is unemployed (Hochshild, 2003). When household chores increase, such as when a child is ill, women are more likely than men to increase their hours of work at home. In 2012, salary.com calculated that a stay-at-home mom would have earned $112,962 per year if she were compensated for all of the elements of her job (see Figure 9-2).

# 9.5 THE WOMEN'S MOVEMENT

Efforts by women to gain political and economic power—known collectively as the **women's movement**—have taken place for more than a century in both Europe and the United States. However, these movements have had different emphases on either side of the Atlantic.

## 9.5a The Women's Movement in the United States

**Women's movement**
The social movements led by women to gain political and economic equality

The women's movement in the United States, instead of seeking special privileges for women, has emphasized equal rights. In an attempt to unite all women behind the cause of equality, the movement has remained separate from any particular political party or union, for fear that such an alignment would divide women.

**Figure 9-2** What Is a Stay-At-Home Mom Worth?

**What Is a Stay-at-Home Mom Worth?**
Each year thousands of moms complete our salary.com Mom Wizard. We rely on mothers, both stay-at-home and working, to provide the number of hours spent performing their motherly duties each week. We consider the description as "hybrid" including 20 jobs that could make up the position of mom. Based off our mom feedback, we benchmark the median salaries for each job to the national median salary as reported by employers. The final salary is calculated by weighting the salaries and hours worked in each role. Find out your mom's salary at mom.salary.com.
**On average, stay-at-home moms juggle 94 hours of work per week.**

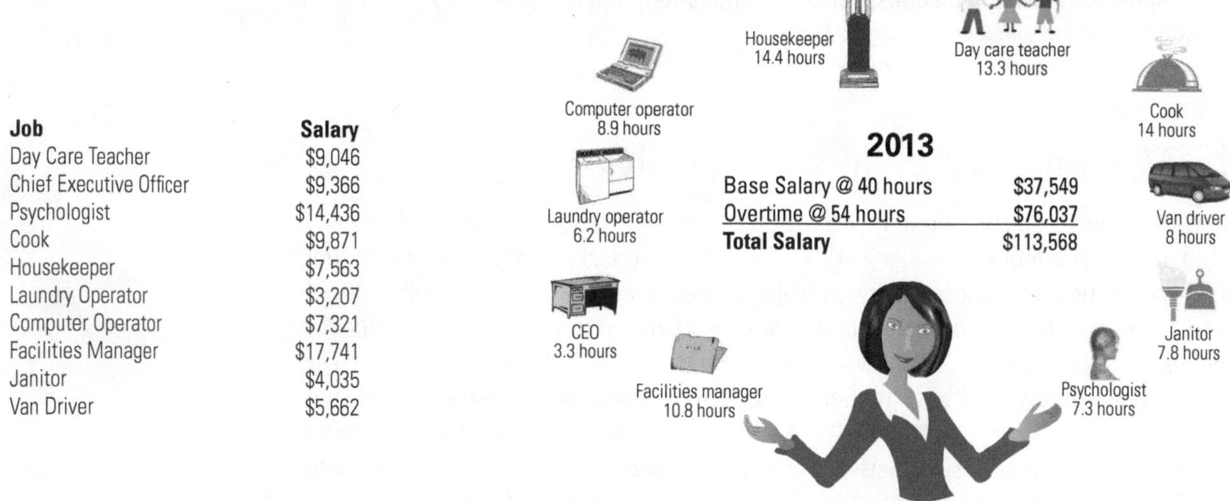

| Job | Salary |
|---|---|
| Day Care Teacher | $9,046 |
| Chief Executive Officer | $9,366 |
| Psychologist | $14,436 |
| Cook | $9,871 |
| Housekeeper | $7,563 |
| Laundry Operator | $3,207 |
| Computer Operator | $7,321 |
| Facilities Manager | $17,741 |
| Janitor | $4,035 |
| Van Driver | $5,662 |



**Historical Stay-at-Home Mom Salaries**

| 2012 | 2011 | 2010 | 2009 | 2008 |
|---|---|---|---|---|
| $112,962 | $115,432 | $117,856 | $112,732 | $116,805 |
| 94.7 hours | 96.6 hours | 98.9 hours | 96.4 hours | 94.4 hours |

Adapted from "What Is a Stay-At-Home Mom Worth," Salary.com, 2012.
Retrieved from http://www.salary.com/stay-at-home-mom-infographic/

**Figure 9-3** Weekly Hours of Basic Housework by Gender and Marital Status

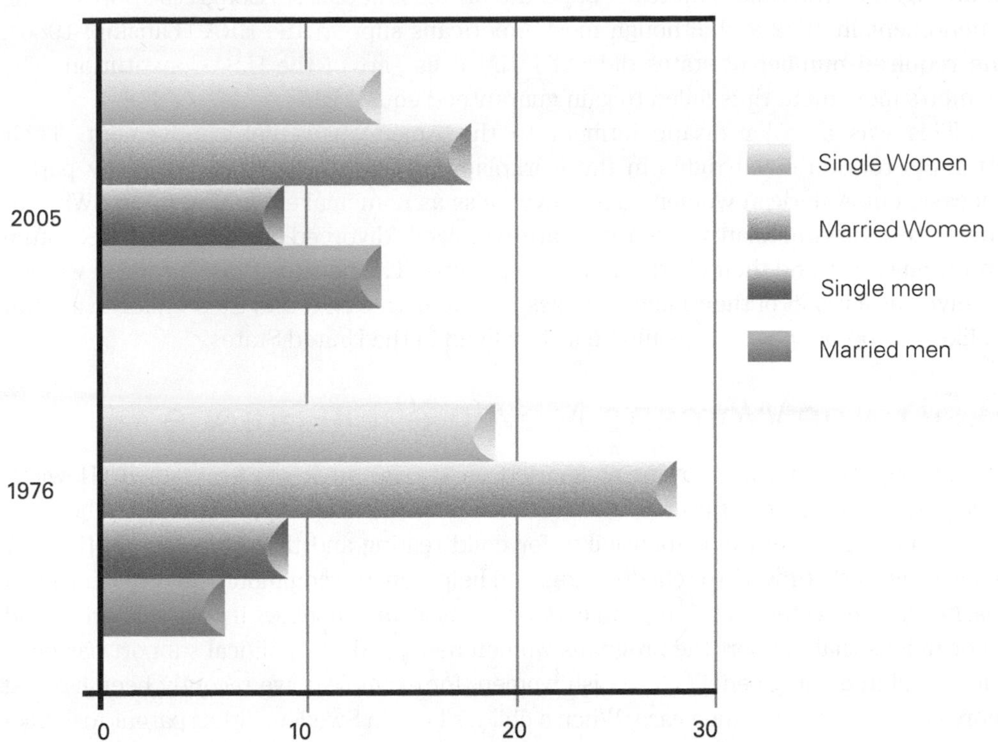


Adapted from "Panel Study of Income Dynamics." Product and distribution by the Institute for Social Research, Survey Research Center, University of Michigan, Ann Arbor, Michigan, 2013.

However, the cause of equality has divided women. The movement wants equality for women in the workplace and thereby plays down the importance of special treatment for women as homemakers. This has served to alienate women who give primary importance to their roles as homemakers and who want special support and protection in their homemaking roles. In general, the level of benefits that working mothers in this country can expect falls far below the norm for their European counterparts and they continue to have difficulty being recognized as fully committed workers.

The women's movement has succeeded in gaining many rights for women. Through the women's suffrage movement, women first gained the right to vote in the 1920s and they can now hold many jobs from which they previously were barred. Today, there are female bartenders, construction workers, and bus drivers, to mention just a few. Laws have been passed guaranteeing them equal pay for equal work, and they have gained the right to practice birth control and to obtain abortions. Except for the right to vote, however, these rights are not guaranteed under the U.S. Constitution and Congress could change the laws that grant these rights at any time (or their constitutional legitimacy could be changed through new U.S. Supreme Court rulings).

*Women suffragists march in New York City in 1915. (Library of Congress)*

The women's movement supported the **Equal Rights Amendment (ERA)**, a proposed amendment that would have guaranteed women equal rights under the Constitution. The ERA states simply, "Equality of rights under the law shall not be denied or abridged by the United States or any state on account of sex." Congress approved the amendment in 1972 and although most Americans support the ERA (Lansing, 1986), the required number of states did not ratify it as part of the U.S. Constitution. The women's movement thus failed to gain guaranteed equal rights.

This was a major disappointment to the American women's movement. Their attempts to gain equal rights in the workplace and in the law met with only partial success, but American women gained even less as homemakers and mothers. Without adequate pay, American women who are widowed, divorced, or never married often find themselves and their children living in poverty. The benefits that European women received as a result of their movement assures them that they and their children are not as likely to be poor as they would be if they lived in the United States.

### 9.5b The Women's Movement in Europe

In Europe, the women's movement focused on special privileges for women (Hewlett, 1986). Those involved in the movement believe that women have special problems because they assume most of the responsibility for child rearing and therefore need better pay when they work, time off for childbearing, and help from the community in providing child rearing. The movement in European countries has aligned itself with political parties and labor unions that support the programs women need, and this political support has been successful in gaining benefits. Swedish women, for example, have recently been earning more than 80% of what men earn. When a child is born in Sweden, either parent may take leave for one year and still receive 90% salary for 38 weeks of that year. In addition, state-supported childcare, noted for its excellence, is usually available for children when the parent returns to work. In Austria, women in manufacturing earn 82% of what men earn, and women receive 100% of their salaries while on leave for the birth of a child, although the leave granted is shorter than it is in Sweden. Although Sweden has the best benefits for women, almost all European nations pay women a higher proportion of men's earnings than women earn in the United States. In addition, these countries offer both childcare and paid leaves-of-absence for parenting.

## 9.6 THE CONSEQUENCES OF INEQUALITY

The most obvious result of gender inequality in the United States is the high level of poverty among women. However, the stratification system results in other notable gender differences as well. In this section, we discuss the problems of poverty, women's self-esteem, medical care, sexual harassment in the workplace, family violence, and rape.

### 9.6a Gender and Poverty

Given the many problems women face in the workplace, it is not surprising that in 2011 more than 30% of women who were heads of families with no husband present had incomes below the poverty line (DeNavas-Walt, Proctor, & Smith, 2012). Women are said to be *heads of families* if they have children to support. Persons in female-householder families are the most likely demographic group to be chronically poor. The U.S. Census, Bureau of Labor Statistics shows a steady trend of poverty, which primarily affects women and children in their care. This increase in the number of women who head families suffering in poverty continues and has been called the **feminization of poverty**. Black

**Equal Right Amendment (ERA)**
A proposed amendment to the Constitution of the United States, which was not ratified, that gave equal rights to women

**Feminization of poverty**
An increase in the proportion of women below the poverty line, particularly female heads of households

and Hispanic women have a much greater likelihood of living in poverty than white or Asian women.

In the older population, the increase in poor women is partly due to their longevity because men die at an earlier age than do women. Also, the death of a man can throw his widow into poverty by reducing the amounts of Social Security and pension she receives and also by reducing any savings she might have had, which were used to pay for medical and nursing care prior to his death.

Those most severely affected by poverty are women who are responsible for both the care and the financial support of children, and the children in their care. Children either reduce the hours that a mother can work or increase her childcare costs. Available new jobs tend to be low-paying and frequently do not provide the basics for mother and children. Researchers have identified a new family type in the United States, the "fragile family," that also contributes to economic hardships especially for single women with children (Kalil & Ryan, 2010). These families are the result of an increase in the rates of non-marital childbirth. These families consist of cohabiting couples as well as single mothers, but single mothers experience the most economic hardship. Public safety nets (such as food stamps, Medicaid, housing, and childcare) help. However, single mothers in fragile families increasingly have to turn to private safety nets (such as family and friends) to make ends meet; these are neither consistent nor dependable, nor do they significantly improve mothers' economic circumstances. Because the high rate of non-marital childbirth is likely to continue rise, and at a time when public assistance is coming increasingly under question, single mothers are likely to face economic hardship for some time to come.

*Women responsible for the care and financial support of children and children in their care are most severely affected by poverty.* (Shutterstock)

An additional cause of the feminization of poverty relates to single-parent families resulting from no-fault divorce and the rising divorce rate. No-fault divorce laws, first passed in California in 1970 and since adopted in some form by most states, do not require that anyone be blamed for the breakdown of the marriage (Weitzman, 1985); also, they do not require punitive payments to be paid by one spouse to the other. This is in sharp contrast to traditional divorce laws, in which one spouse—usually the husband—was considered to be at fault. As punishment, he was sometimes required to pay alimony to his wife and sometimes the family home was awarded to her. This could support her for the rest of her life. Under no-fault divorce, both husband and wife are expected to assume equal responsibility for themselves and for their children after the divorce. Alimony, if awarded, is usually awarded as a temporary measure to give the wife time to find a job and adjust to a new life. Usually, it is ordered that the family home be sold so that the proceeds can be divided equally. The child-support payments required of the husband are usually low because the courts assume that the wife will help to support the children. Little consideration is given to the fact that she may not be able to earn much money.

As a result of the no-fault divorce laws, a man who divorces his wife can expect a 42% increase in his standard of living (Weitzman, 1985). He is allowed to keep half of the family assets and most of his income. He is free from the burden of supporting his wife and needs only to contribute a small portion of his paycheck to his children while they are under age 18. In contrast, a woman who is divorced will experience a 73% decline in her standard of living (as will her children, if she has custody). The woman must provide a home, support herself, and support her children on what is usually a very small paycheck. In the time since no-fault divorce first went into practice in some states, not much has changed in terms of the long-term financial impact on women.

In addition, if a father sues for custody, the low earnings of a woman may be taken into account by the courts. In 70% of the cases where the father sues for custody, he will win because he has the financial means to support his children (Weitzman, 1985). Often, men threaten to sue for custody even when they do not want it, just to get women to negotiate smaller child-support payments (Weitzman, 1985); some women so fear losing their children that they will sacrifice future income rather than risk a custody battle. Thus, many women are receiving even smaller settlements than they are entitled to under the law, which increases the number of women (and their children) who have incomes below the poverty line.

## 9.6b Women's Self-Esteem

Most women are, sooner or later, housewives and mothers, at least for a time. Because our society gives so little respect and esteem to these roles, it is not surprising that women tend to give themselves little respect for accomplishments in these areas and they often find the demands of the role stressful. Gove and Geerken (1977), in trying to develop a theory to explain stress, argued that married women experience high rates of stress because the role of a married woman is not respected in American society. To test this theory, a study was conducted comparing American women of European descent with Mexican women (Ross, Mirowsky, & Ulbrich, 1983b). Since previous research had shown that the family is more highly valued in Mexico than it is in the United States, this research hypothesized that Mexican women would feel less stress because they were more valued as family members. It was found that Mexican women did, in fact, receive more support for their role in the family and suffer less stress.

In America, evidence supports the idea that many women have low self-esteem regarding their personal appearance. They are expected to be thin and beautiful and as a result, women spend more time, energy, and money than men on cosmetics, diet, and exercise products. Numerous examples exist of women who are extremely critical of their bodies and diet, to the point of malnutrition. In extreme cases, excessive dieting results in anorexia or bulimia, illnesses most often seen in women, and which sometimes result in death from starvation. It is important to point out that gender concern over body image and self-esteem varies across cultures. Whereas most research has found that women are more concerned with their appearance and experience greater body dissatisfaction, and thus lower self-esteem, than men, recent research has found that body image disturbances are of concern to Australian men (Mellor, Fuller-Tyskiewicz, McCabe, & Ricciardelli, 2010). This suggests that issues of body image and self-esteem are not inherent to gender in and of itself, but have much to do with the importance that different cultures and societies place on body image for men and for women.

Females at all ages in the United States also experience depression more often than men. *Women in America*, the government report document discussed at the beginning of this chapter, reports that in any two-week period, 8% of women and girls report experiencing clinically significant depression as compared to 5% of men and boys. Depression for females is found even more often for those living below the poverty line, blacks, and those between ages 40 and 59.

## 9.6c Medical Care

When men go to their physicians with complaints, they are likely to receive a very thorough physical. When women go to their physician with complaints, they are likely to receive a prescription for tranquilizers or antidepressants instead of a physical (Ehrenreich & English, 1979). Even when their symptoms are severe, women receive fewer diagnostic tests for heart disease and receive less treatment; although post-menopausal women have comparable rates of heart disease to men's rates, only half

**BVT Lab**

Visit www.BVTLab.com to explore the student resources available for this chapter.

as many women receive heart bypass operations as men. Women also receive only half the number of diagnostic tests for lung cancer (despite women's increasing rates of lung cancer) and are only half as likely to receive a kidney transplant (Trafford, 1991). According to Trafford, this indicates negligent healthcare for women. While women receive less care for the major diseases that kill people in this country, physicians have a tendency to interfere with and over treat the normal reproductive process (Schur, 1984). As a result, the following procedures are done routinely and are unnecessary in 90% of cases: fetal monitoring during labor; use of drugs to induce early labor; use of anesthesia, forceps, and related techniques in delivery; performance of *episiotomy* (surgical incision at the opening of the vagina during the birth process); and surgical delivery through Cesarean section. Cesarean sections have risen from 5% to over 30% of births in the past three decades. In 2009, the cesarean rate was the highest ever reported in the United States. (Reinberg, 2011). Recent research has shown that women use more health services and incur greater expenditures for healthcare than men. Women have significantly more annual care visits, diagnostic services, and total medical charges than men, even after controlling for health status and variables related to socioeconomic status and demographic factors such as age and ethnicity (Bertakis & Azari, 2010). This is especially problematic since, as noted in *Women in America*, the share of women without health insurance, ages 18 to 64 has increased. In 2009, 18% of non-elderly women lacked health insurance compared to 13% in 1984. (It should be noted that the percentage of uninsured also rose for men during the same time period, from 16% to 24%.)

Women also have an excessive number of *hysterectomies*, the removal of the uterus and sometimes of the other female reproductive organs. Physicians have argued that the female reproductive organs are not useful except to have children, and they perform this major abdominal surgery for any number of reasons, sometimes as minor as for the relief of menstruation. However, many women who have had hysterectomies report serious depression and difficulty in adjusting to sexual activity (Stokes, 1986).

In recent years, there has been increasing interest in new reproductive technologies. Although research continues to investigate the causes of infertility and birth defects, most research has concentrated on amniocentesis and artificial reproduction. Amniocentesis is early testing of the fetus, and the fetus is usually aborted if defective. The mother often feels little choice in whether to abort (Rothman, 1986a) because the social pressure to abort a defective baby is so strong. Reproductive technologies also include the work associated with so-called test-tube babies. Some hope that women eventually will be freed of the reproductive role; but others fear that women's status would be lowered further, and their bodies would become no more than a source of spare parts (Corea, 1985; Rowland, 1985).

Women in all types of jobs suffer from unwelcome sexual advances by coworkers or superiors. (iStockphoto)

## 9.6d Sexual Harassment

Women in all types of jobs suffer from **sexual harassment**, unwelcome sexual advances made by coworkers or superiors at work. Women who reject sexual advances may be denied a job, intimidated, given poor work evaluations, denied raises or promotions, or fired.

Sexual harassment is much more widespread than is generally realized. The first questionnaire ever devoted solely to this topic surveyed working women in 1975 (Farley, 1978). The results were startling: 92% of respondents cited sexual harassment as a serious problem, and 70% reported that they had personally experienced some form of harassment. Other more recent studies indicate that sexual harassment is also a major problem in colleges and universities, in offices of the United Nations, in the United States military, in civil service jobs, and in private industry.

**Sexual harassment**
Sexual advances made by coworkers or superiors at work

In deciding how to respond to sexual harassment, the victim must consider the economic necessity of keeping the job, opportunities for getting another job, the likelihood of obtaining decent work evaluations and future promotions, the possibility of being fired, and the attitudes of family and friends regarding her situation. The victim usually decides to quit, transfer to another job within the organization, or simply to do nothing and to suffer in silence because probably no one will believe her if she makes a complaint.

## 9.6e Family Violence

Family violence is a widespread problem in the United States. Indeed, "[U.S. American] women are more likely to be killed, physically assaulted, sexually victimized, hit, beat up, slapped, or spanked in their own homes by other family members than anywhere else, or by anyone else, in our society" (Gelles, 1995, p. 450). The Centers for Disease Control (2012) reports that each year women experience about 4.8 million intimate partner related assaults and rapes. Men are the victims of 2.9 million intimate partner related assaults. Intimate partner violence resulted in 2,340 deaths in 2007, of which 70% were female and 30% were male. Battery causes more injury to women than rape (including rape with battery), auto accidents, and muggings combined (Cleage, 1993). Nearly one in four women in the United States reports experiencing violence by a current or former spouse or boyfriend at some point in her life (www.endabuse.org).

*An estimated 4 million women are battered each year by their husbands or lovers. (Shutterstock)*

When a wife or child is being abused, the wife often does not leave the home or remove the child from the home. Sometimes, the wife believes she deserves to be beaten, but women frequently have no money of their own and no safe place to go (Chasin, 1997). It is likewise difficult for a woman to take her children out of her home when she has no means of support, no food, and no shelter. Thus, while the reasons for family violence are complex, one of the major reasons it continues is that women are unable to support themselves and their children and are therefore unwilling to leave home.

## 9.6f Rape

Rape is another form of violence that results in part from gender inequality. The FBI's Uniform Crime Reports show that 78,770 rapes were reported in 1982 and increased significantly to 109,593 one decade later. The number of reported rapes decreased in 2001 to 90,491, but once again increased 3.4% to 93,934 in 2006. Of women, 10.6% and 2.1% of men have experienced forced sex at some point in their lives—that is more than 11 million women and 2 million men (Basile, Chens, Black, & Saltzman, 2007). These numbers are estimates of actual rapes, which are likely two to three times higher than the number reported to authorities. Most sexual assault victimization is not disclosed (Kilpatrick, Edwards, & Seymour, 1992).

One myth about rape often believed by the public is that rape usually occurs between strangers. However, very often men know the women they rape. In the typical incidence of **acquaintance rape** or *date rape*, the man and woman have been dating for a long time, perhaps a year. In one study of rape on a college campus, 20% to 25% of female college students reported having been raped (Fisher, Cullen, & Turner, 2000).

Another myth about rape is that rape is sexually motivated. When men rape women, it is often an act of aggression. Men may rape because they hate women, they wish to be cruel or violent, or they seek revenge (Henslin, 1990). Nevertheless, because society believes that rape is a sexual act, they believe that women involved in rape have done something sexual to invite rape. Perhaps the women wore enticing clothing, appeared in public at late hours, drank too much, or did not resist the advances of men. Efforts are

**Acquaintance rape**
Rape by someone who is known to the person being raped (such as in date rape)

being made to reduce the tendency to blame the victim of the rape for her victimization. Nevertheless, should the rapist be caught and brought to trial, the reputation of the victim will come under scrutiny. It will be assumed that if she is sexually active, the rapist may have interpreted her behavior as an invitation for him to attack her (Hamlin, 2001).

Some feminists have argued that rape and other forms of violence are the end result of the norms of aggressiveness that men learn to display toward women. Pornography and some erotic literature have been severely criticized, not because they are sexual but because most pornography depicts women as passive victims of violent men. The message to readers of this type of pornographic literature is that the violent abuse of women is both masculine and normal (Lederer, 1980). A society that differentiates the sexes, gives one sex a lower status than the other, and provides little opportunity for mutual respect between the sexes is likely to continue to see violence against one sex by the other.

## 9.7 THE FUTURE OF GENDER INEQUALITY

Will gender differentiation decrease? Will women become economically and occupationally equal to men? If the structural functionalists are correct, women will gradually win promotions and pay increases that will move them into the upper echelons of the bureaucratic work world and that will win them equality with men. According to the U.S. Department of Labor and Statistics in its 2006 report, "At all levels of education women have fared better than men with respect to earnings."

**BVT *Lab***

Improve your test scores. Practice quizzes are available at www.BVTLab.com

Another alternative is also possible, one that combines aspects of the functionalist and conflict views. Upper-class women may use a college education as a stepping-stone into the primary labor market. Their educational credentials and their family background will help them get good positions, where, like upper-class men, they will be groomed for greater responsibility and will achieve higher and higher positions. Working-class women, without family connections and educational opportunity, are likely to remain in the secondary labor market and to fall farther and farther behind. In such a scenario, gender differentiation could diminish considerably even while class differences remained great. Complete equality between men and women requires an end to class, as well as gender, differentiation.

### thinking SOCIOLOGICALLY

1. Do you believe that women will progress through the glass ceiling? What factors explain why they may or may not?
2. If women made it through the glass ceiling, which of the consequences of inequality would disappear?

# CHAPTER 9 Wrapping it up

## Summary

1. Modern societies differentiate people on the basis of gender, gender roles, and our concepts of masculinity and femininity.
2. Males and females differ in anatomy, chromosomes, and hormones; however, research does not show important differences in behavior because of these sex differences. In fact, where one might expect to find differences in behavior based on physical characteristics, such as females having the most important jobs requiring finger dexterity, the opposite is true. Men have the jobs defined as most important, regardless of physical attributes.
3. In other cultures, the definitions of masculinity and femininity differ, so that men and women occupy roles very different from those found in the United States.
4. According to structural functionalists, women play an expressive role in society, nurturing the family while men play an instrumental role, providing financially for the family. These roles are changing rapidly, and men and women are sharing roles more often now.
5. According to conflict theorists, women have been exploited by men throughout history, kept out of the paid work force, or moved in and out of the lowest-paying jobs as needed by the economy.
6. Women have been pushed out of the work force when birth rates were low, so their only alternative would be to get married and have babies. Women have also been encouraged to enter the work force when there was a shortage of workers.
7. When women enter the work force, it is often to take positions in the growing secondary labor market, where salaries are low, work is often part-time or temporary, and fringe benefits are practically nonexistent.
8. Even when women have jobs requiring skills equal to men's jobs, they are not paid comparable amounts.
9. Upward mobility for women is limited first by the inability to move from the secondary work force to the primary work force, and then by the inability to move above the glass ceiling to executive positions. Women are not given positions that provide experience in authority and autonomy and therefore are not eligible for promotion.
10. Women who have families do most of the work at home, whether they are married or not. Their physical and mental health often suffers.
11. The women's movement in Europe fought for special privileges for women and made significant gains in women's salaries, childcare, and maternity leaves.
12. The women's movement in the United States fought for equality and gained the right to vote and to work at a wider variety of jobs, but it divided women because there was no support for women's family responsibilities.
13. As a result of all of these discriminating conditions, 34% of women in the United States suffer from poverty when they have children to support.
14. In *no-fault divorce*, the father is required to pay only a small portion of the cost of caring for his children because it is assumed that the mother will pay a share, even if she has custody of the children and a low-paying job.
15. Women in the United States suffer low self-esteem because they get little respect for their family responsibilities.
16. Women get less than adequate healthcare because women's reproductive organs are seen as problematic when they are not, and women's complaints about other organs are not taken seriously enough.
17. Women are more likely than men to be subjected to violence. It is more probable for women than men to be harassed at work, treated violently at home, and raped by acquaintances and strangers.

18. It is possible that women may gradually win promotions and get ahead, or they may be trapped in the secondary labor market. It is also possible that women of the upper classes will move ahead while women of the lower classes remain in the secondary work force, reinforcing two classes of women.

## Discussion Questions

1. Discuss the relationships among sex, gender, and gender roles.
2. Discuss how various explanations of gender differentiation can be used to account for the way that you have developed. In doing so, identify some experiences in your life in which you were treated in a particular way primarily because of your gender.
3. Use the knowledge of cross-cultural gender differentiation to evaluate the merits of social and biological explanations of gender differentiation.
4. How do structural functionalism and conflict theory account for the persistence of traditional gender roles? Use personal examples to illustrate each approach.
5. Why do you think that the status of women in the workplace is often treated as if it were a new issue? What are some factors that have affected women's status and role in the workplace throughout history?
6. Why is there a wage differential between women and men in the workplace?
7. How has the split labor market affected men and women differently?
8. Discuss some structural factors that make upward mobility easier for men than for women.
9. Compare the impact of the women's movement in Europe with the women's movement in the United States. Where do you think that women have the best chance for equality? Why?
10. What are some consequences of gender inequality for men and women in families and at work?
11. How are such issues as sexual harassment, family violence, and rape a result of gender inequality?

*The aim of education is the knowledge not of fact but of values.*

DEAN WILLIAM R. INGE

# PART FOUR

# SOCIAL INSTITUTIONS

Every society has basic needs that must be met in order for that society to survive and to perpetuate its ways of life. However, how each of these needs are met may vary based upon cultural, historical and environmental circumstances that are unique to that society and include the following:

- The replacement of members, regulation of sexual activity, determination of kinship, and providing for offspring
- Teaching and socializing new members of society and transmitting knowledge from one generation to the next, as well as creating new knowledge for the advancement of society's goals
- Insuring and regulating the production of goods and services so that society's material needs are met
- Regulating the legitimate use of power and preserving social order
- Establishing mechanisms to help provide a sense of morality, spirituality, and inter-connectedness and to help overcome anxieties related to mortality
- Assuring the physical and mental well being of its members

Social institutions are the systems that develop within each society to meet these basic needs for survival and perpetuation. This part of the book explores the social institutions of family, education, economy, government, religion and healthcare.

SCREEN ★ ACTORS
tbs

CHAPTER 10

# Family Groups and Systems

## SYNOPSIS

**What Is Family?**

**Variation in Kinship and Family Organization**

- Marriage and Number of Spouses
- Norms of Residence
- Norms of Descent and Inheritance
- Norms of Authority
- Norms for Choice of Marriage Partner

**A Functionalist Perspective on the Family**

- Socialization
- Affection and Emotional Support
- Sexual Regulation
- Reproduction
- Social Placement

**A Conflict Perspective on the Family**

**Other Perspectives on the Family**

- An Exchange Perspective
- An Interactionist Perspective
- A Developmental Perspective

**The American Family System**

- Marriage Rates and Age at Marriage
- Family Size
- Divorce

**Nontraditional Marital and Family Lifestyles**

- Nonmarital Cohabitation
- Childless Marriage
- One-Parent Families
- Dual-Career Marriages

## Focal Point

# A NEW AMERICAN FAMILY?

Until recently, families in the United States almost always consisted of a husband and wife, their children, and frequently their extended family. Divorce was rare until the middle of the twentieth century, and sex was a topic not widely discussed in public. However, today, most American families no longer fit the traditional mold. In fact, the modern American family is more diverse than ever. Moreover, tolerance of alternate family forms and family-related behavior is on the rise. To be sure, for the first time in history, same-sex marriage is legal in many parts of the United States. As of 2009, nearly half of all children in the United States are born out-of-wedlock (Ravitz, 2009). Cohabitation is also on the rise. Even polygamy is slowly gaining legitimacy (Hostin, 2008). If these trends continue, the American family will almost certainly appear fundamentally different by the turn of the next century. Consider the cases below.

Nadya Suleman is an unmarried mother with fourteen children living in California. In January 2009, Nadya gained national attention when she gave birth to octuplets even though she was already a mother of six, unmarried, and living on government money (Richards & Olshan, 2009). In 2008, Nadya had six embryos from previous in-vitro fertilizations implanted in her womb. Remarkably, two of the embryos split and all eight were fertilized. Public reaction to the octuplets was mixed. Many asked how an unemployed single-mother could ever raise fourteen children without going bankrupt. Others were dismayed that Nadya wouldn't identify the father. Still more were shocked that Nadya showed no signs of shame in having children out-of-wedlock. Many people only saw Nadya as a quick way to make money, however: in February 2009, Vivid Entertainment offered Nadya a million-dollar deal to star in a pornographic film (McKay, 2009). Two months later, Nadya sought to trademark her new nickname—the Octomom—for a television show and a line of diapers (Duke, 2009).

The second case involves Mary Cheney, the daughter of former Vice President Dick Cheney. Mary, a lesbian, received considerable media attention concerning her sexuality and delivery of a child out-of-wedlock in 2007. Since 1992, Mary has been cohabiting with her female partner Heather Poe. In December 2006, Mary reported that she was pregnant, but details of who the father was and how the baby was conceived were never released (Argetsinger & Roberts, 2006). While Vice President Cheney was reportedly elated about his daughter's pregnancy, many social conservatives were not. The Concerned Women for America, for example, denounced the pregnancy as "unconscionable" (BBC News, 2006).

The third example centers on the pregnancy of Bristol Palin, daughter of the former vice-presidential candidate, Sarah Palin. In 2008, Bristol became pregnant while unmarried (Saul, 2009). When news of the pregnancy broke out, Bristol claimed she was engaged to the father (Levi Johnston, a classmate) of the child-to-be and would soon get married. However, Bristol and Levi broke off their engagement several months after their son was born in December 2008 (Saul, 2009). That leaves Bristol today as a single mother with a child born out of wedlock.

Another example focuses on the connection between same-sex marriage and polygamy. While polygamy is still not prevalent enough today to threaten monogamy as the dominant form of marriage in the United States, many social conservatives are concerned that the legalization of homosexual marriage may change this (Zeitzen, 2008). Proponents of traditional marriage point out that the idea of same-sex marriage was unheard of just a generation ago. Because of pressure from the political left since the 1970s, however, gay marriage has been gaining legitimacy in the United States. Social conservatives argue that, should gay marriage become a federally protected form of marriage, the legalization of polygamy could very well become the next agenda for the political left. As evidence, they point out that in 2005, when the Canadians legalized gay marriage,

*Our traditional images of the 'normal' family consisting of mother, father, and children are gradually being expanded to include a variety of family forms, as this scene from the television show 'The New Normal' depicts.* (AP Wide World Photo)

Ottawa commissioned a series of reports on Canada's polyg amy laws to see if polygamy should be decriminalized in that country (Lak, 2009). While no one can say that legalizing gay marriage will definitely lead to the legalization of polygamy, the fact that people are even debating the possibility shows how much the American family is changing.

While the nation is still very much divided about the acceptability of same sex marriages, there has been a rapid shift in recent years towards approval. The majority of U.S. Americans now support gay unions. The November 2012 elections and a Supreme Court decision in June, 2013, more than doubled (to 13) the number of states authorizing gay marriages. (The New York Times, 2013).

The above cases underscore a core tenet of this chapter: family systems and the social expectations that go along with them are relative. The United States has traditionally encouraged monogamy and fidelity, while discouraging divorce and adultery. Powerful social and political forces have recently begun to whittle away at these traditions, however. As a result, the appearance of the American family in the years to come may be significantly different than the one Americans think of as usual today.

This chapter considers the family as a group, as a social system, and as a social institution. For most of us, the family serves as a primary social group; it is the first agency of socialization. Sociologists consider the family to be a *social system* because it is composed of interdependent parts, it has a characteristic organization and pattern of functioning, and it has subsystems that are part of the larger system. The family is considered a *social institution* because it is an area of social life that is organized into discernible patterns and because it helps to meet crucial societal goals.

## 10.1 WHAT IS FAMILY?

Although the answer may appear quite obvious to most of us, it becomes less obvious to judges who must make decisions on property settlements for cohabiting couples, social service workers who get adoption requests from unmarried persons or same-sex couples, or government agencies who must decide who is eligible for various benefits. Some definitions result in informal stigmatization and discrimination against families who do not meet the qualifications, such as a mother and her child, two men, or an unmarried man and woman. The **family** has traditionally been defined as a group of kin united by blood, marriage, or adoption, who share a common residence for some part of their lives, and who assume reciprocal rights and obligations with regard to one another. Today, however, the reality of childless marriages, stepparents, one-parent households, same-sex unions, and cohabiting couples has led sociologists to think about families in terms of a variety of types of intimate relationships, sexual bonds, and family realms. For example, a same-sex (lesbian or gay) couple or a heterosexual cohabiting couple, with or without children, would not be a family in traditional terms of blood, marriage, or adoptive ties. However, in terms of family-like relationships based on what families do (engage in intimate interactions, share household expenses and a division of labor, recognize other members as part of a primary intimate bonded unit), some same-sex or cohabiting partners are being viewed as families for purposes of property settlements, housing regulations for "families only," or employee benefit plans.

**Family**
A group of kin united by blood, marriage, or adoption who share a common residence for some part of their lives and assume reciprocal rights and obligations with regard to one another

There are tremendous variations in traditional family structures and processes that exist in our own culture and in others around the world. There exists recognition of differentiating families as conjugal, nuclear, families of orientation and procreation, as well as extended or modifications of an extended structure. The smallest units are called **conjugal families**, which must include a husband and wife but may or may not include

**Conjugal families**
Families consisting of a husband and wife, with or without children

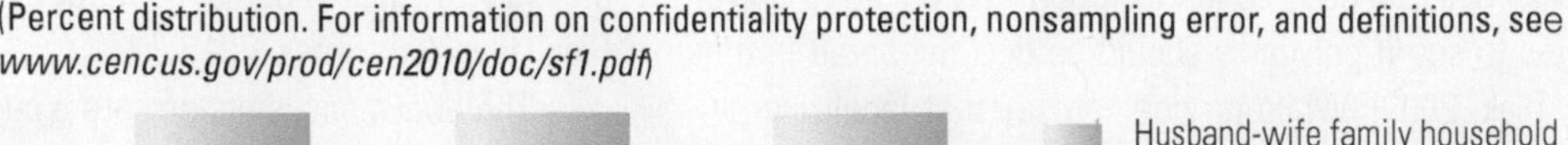

**Figure 10-1** Households by Type: 1990, 2000, 2010

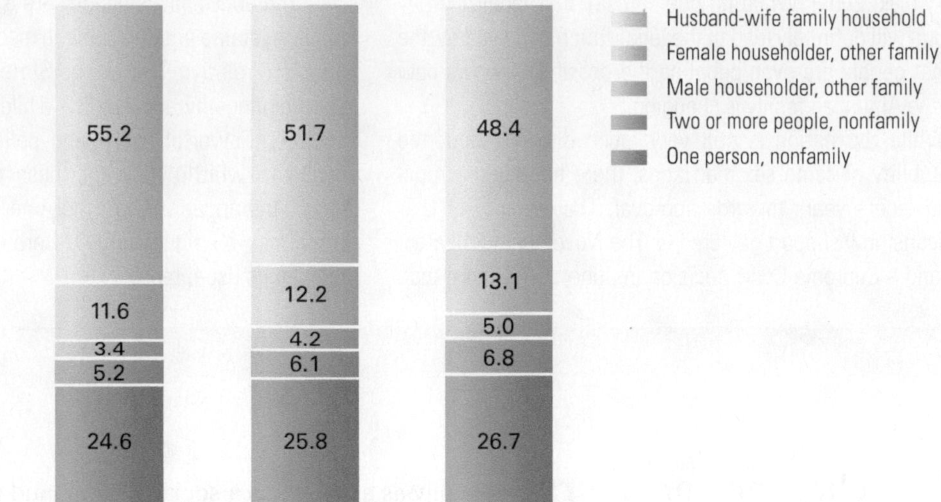


Adapted from U.S. Census Bureau, Census 2010 Summary File 1; Census 2000 Summary File 1; 1990 Census of Population, Summary Population and Housing Characteristics, United States (1990 CPH-1-1). Retrieved from http://www.census.gov/prod/cen2010/briefs/c2010br-14.pdf

children. **Nuclear families** may or may not include a husband and wife—they consist of any two or more persons related to one another by blood, marriage, or adoption who share a common residence. Thus, a brother and sister or a single parent and child would be nuclear families but not conjugal families.

The definition used in census reporting in the United States is the nuclear family. Family households are identified when the members of a household are related to the householder. The count of family units, regardless of whether the householder is in that family, is considered a family group. In 2010, there were 116.7 million family households. Of these, 56.5 million were husband-and-wife family households. The number of households in the U.S. increased by 10.7% (by a little over 11 million households) between 2000 and 2010. However, the percent of family households actually declined from 68.1% in 2000 to 66.4% in 2010. The number of unmarried couple households increased from around 5.5 million in 2000 to nearly 7.8 million in 2012, an increase of 41.4% (Lofquist, Lugaila, O'Connell, & Feliz, 2012).

**Nuclear families**
Families in which two or more persons are related by blood, marriage or adoption and who share a common residence

Approximately 90% of all Americans marry at some time in their lives (Zinn & Eitzen, 2005). In so doing, they become members of two different, but overlapping, nuclear families. The nuclear family into which a person is born and reared (consisting of the person, brothers, sisters, and parents) is termed the **family of orientation**. This is the family in which most basic early childhood socialization occurs. When a person marries, a new nuclear (and conjugal) family is formed, which is called the **family of procreation**. This family consists of the person, a spouse, and children. These relations are diagrammed in Figure 10-2.

**Family of orientation**
The nuclear family into which one was born and in which one was reared

**Family of procreation**
The nuclear family formed by marriage

In the world as a whole, conjugal and nuclear families as isolated and independent units are rare. In most societies, the norm is the **extended family**, which goes beyond the nuclear family to include other nuclear families and relatives, such as grandparents, aunts, uncles, and cousins.

**Extended family**
A family that goes beyond the nuclear family to include other nuclear families and relatives such as grandparents, aunts, uncles, and cousins

The typical family in the United States is not an isolated nuclear unit that is separate from extended kin contacts and support, nor is it an extended family in the traditional sense that extended family members share the same household. American families typically have what is called a **modified-extended family structure**, in which individual nuclear families retain considerable autonomy and yet maintain connections with other nuclear families through visits, calls, or the exchange of goods, services, or affective greetings. This type of family differs from the traditional extended family, in that its members may live in different parts of the country and may choose their occupations independently rather than following a parent's occupation.

**Modified-extended family structure**
The family structure in which individual nuclear families retain considerable autonomy yet maintain connections with other nuclear families in the extended family structure

## APPLYING DEFINITIONS OF FAMILY

It is important for many reasons to realize that there may be more than one acceptable definition of what a family is. Recognizing that there is a tremendous variety of types of family patterns is an essential part of helping social scientists to overcome their own ethnocentrism, stereotypes, and prejudices, which might get in the way of doing their objective research.

As suggested earlier, it is important for politicians who make policies that affect families to understand that because there are variations in types of families, strict definitions may be problematic. As Skolnick (1991) and many others who have explored the impact of policies upon the family have noted, how a family is defined has important consequences for the nature of policies and how they are carried out. Zoning laws, tax laws, welfare regulations, federally funded student loan guidelines, and many other policies often employ a particular definition of a family. Limiting the definition of a family to one type—or even a few—can have serious consequences for people's lives. Policymakers need to understand that families may not necessarily be limited

*In most societies, the norm is the extended family, which includes nuclear families and other relatives.* (iStockphoto)

**Figure 10-2** Families of Orientation and of Procreation

to the middle-class norm of mother, father, and their children residing together in a male-dominated household.

In a clinical setting, the therapeutic and counseling techniques used by marriage and family counselors may be determined largely by how the family is defined. Assuming that there is only one definition of the family could lead some therapists to look at families that fall outside that definition as pathological or troubled. Certainly, some families are in trouble, but not necessarily because they do not fit the norm of the white, middle-class nuclear family. In recognizing that there are many possible ways to live as a family, marriage counselors might be able to be more creative and flexible in what they have to offer their clients.

Finally, and perhaps most important for you, the recognition that there is more than one acceptable definition of a family can lead to more choices and freedom in your own life. This does not mean, however, that you have complete freedom to live the way you want to or that every family pattern will necessarily work. As this chapter shows later, many family and kinship patterns may be workable only in a particular social context that emphasizes the social creation and construction of family and kinship patterns. However, the options that are workable in a particular social context may not be as limited as they were once thought to be.

### **thinking** SOCIOLOGICALLY

1. Examine both traditional and nontraditional definitions of the family. How might family policies differ, depending on the definition used?
2. In terms of patterns of helping and assistance, visiting, or letter writing, to what extent do families in the United States (or your own family) resemble a modified-extended family?
3. Choose two family forms to compare. Discuss whether or not each can meet the basic tasks required of family units. What can you conclude about "what a family really is"?
4. Identify, through an Internet search, the Supreme Court cases involving gay marriage in 2012 and 2013, what the outcomes were, and discuss the implications for the future of family forms in the United States. Consider what impact this decision might have on the types of households illustrated in Figure 10-2.

## **10.2** VARIATION IN KINSHIP AND FAMILY ORGANIZATION

Family groups and systems are only one type of kinship association. **Kinship** is the web of relationships among people linked by common ancestry, adoption, or marriage. All societies have general norms for defining family and kin groups and how these relationships are organized. These norms concern such matters as who lives together, who is the head of the group, who marries whom, how mates are selected, which relatives in family and kin groups are most important, and how and by whom children are to be raised. Although some general norms tend to determine the statuses and roles of family members, other norms and the kinship systems they govern vary greatly.

**Kinship**
The web of relationships among people linked by common ancestry, adoption, or marriage

## 10.2a Marriage and Number of Spouses

Marital status (single, married, separated, widowed, divorced) and number of spouses (none, one, more than one) are two major variations in family organization. To most Americans, the most "proper" form of marriage is **monogamy**, in which one man is married to one woman at a time. This form of marriage is the only one universally recognized; it is the predominant form even in societies where other forms exist. However, only about 20% of the world's societies are strictly monogamous.

While the United States is strictly monogamous, Americans frequently have more than one spouse over a lifetime. This pattern of "marriage, divorce, and remarriage" is called **serial** or **sequential monogamy**. It is both legally and socially accepted to have more than one wife or husband as long as it is done sequentially and not simultaneously. It is illegal in every state in the United States to be married to more than one person at any given time.

There are a variety of alternatives to monogamy. Murdock (1957) investigated the frequency of **polygamy**, marriage to more than one spouse, in a sample of 554 societies from around the world. He found that **polygyny**, in which a man has more than one wife, was the norm in 77% of these societies, whereas **polyandry**, in which a woman has more than one husband, was culturally favored in less than 1%. **Group marriage**, in which several or many men are married to several or many women, has been practiced among selected groups in some societies; however, nowhere is it the dominant form.

One example of group marriage in the United States was that of the Oneida Community, the founding group of Oneida Corporation, which is listed today on the New York Stock Exchange. For about 30 years in the mid-1800s, John Humphrey Noyes preached that people were capable of living sinless lives based on a spiritual equality of all persons: materially, socially, and sexually. The outcome of this teaching was a group marriage structure where all adults were recognized as married to each other, all adults were parents to all children, and the total emphasis was on "we" rather than "I."

The fact that a society permits one to have several spouses does not necessarily mean that a large proportion of all marriages are polygamous. Except for group marriage, multiple spouses are possible on a large scale only when the ratio of the sexes is unbalanced. When polygamy is practiced, it is controlled by societal norms like any other form of marriage. Rather than resulting from strictly personal or psychological motives, it is supported by the values and norms of both sexes and is closely linked to the economic conditions and belief systems of the wider society.

Polygamy itself may take a variety of forms. The most common form of polygamy is polygyny. In many societies, having several wives is a mark of prestige and high status. The wealthy, the leaders, and the best hunters may get a second or third wife. Multiple wives may also be desired as a source of children, especially sons. Polygyny is very common in Africa, among Muslim groups in the Middle East and Asia, and in many tribal groups in South America and throughout the world. In the United States, some Mormon fundamentalists living in Utah and neighboring states practice polygyny. While the Mormon Church has officially rejected polygamy for over a century, Utah legalized polygamy in 2011 (Lake, 2011). Not surprisingly, people who know a polygamist, infrequent churchgoers, and older people tend to hold more positive views of polygamy (Nielsen, 2009).

Polyandry is quite rare. Where it is practiced, the co-husbands are usually brothers, either blood brothers or clan brothers who belong to the same clan and are of the same generation. Among the Todas, for example, a non-Hindu tribe in India, it is understood that when a woman marries a man, she becomes the wife of his

**Monogamy**
The marriage of one man to one woman

**Serial or sequential monogamy**
Marriage to a number of different spouses in succession, but only one at any given time

**Polygamy**
The marriage of one man or woman to more than one person of the opposite sex at the same time

**Polygyny**
The marriage of one man to more than one wife at the same time

**Polyandry**
The marriage of one woman to more than one husband at the same time

**Group marriage**
A form of marriage in which several or many men are married to several or many women

*Marital status is just one major variation in the family organization. (iStockphoto)*

Members of the Fundamentalist Church of Jesus Christ of Latter-Day Saints board a bus for relocation in Texas in 2008. (AP Wide World Photo)

brothers at the same time. This type of polyandry, where brothers are co-husbands, may also be referred to as **fraternal polyandry**.

## 10.2b Norms of Residence

When people marry, decisions about place of residence are typically dictated by societal norms and conform to one of three patterns. In Western societies, the residence norm is **neolocal**—the couple lives alone wherever they wish—but this pattern is rare in the rest of the world. Of the societies Murdock (1949) examined, only about 10% considered it appropriate for newlywed couples to move to a place of residence separate from both the husband's and the wife's families. This type of residence pattern seems to be linked with norms of monogamy and individualism. Nearly three-fourths of the societies studied by Murdock were **patrilocal**—the newlywed couple lived not just in the groom's community but also usually in his parents' home or compound. This type of residence is most common in polygamous hunting-and-gathering societies throughout Asia, Africa, and Latin America. In the United States, the Amish communities represent one example of a patrilocal system. A **matrilocal** residence pattern, in which the newly married couple lives with the wife's family, was the norm in about 15% of the societies Murdock studied and was generally found where women held title to the land.

**Fraternal polyandry**
A form of polyandry where brothers are co-husbands

**Neolocal**
A family norm that newly married couples should establish residences separate from those of both sets of parents

**Patrilocal**
A family norm that newly married couples should live with the husband's family

**Matrilocal**
A family norm that newly married couples should live with the wife's family

**Patrilineal**
A family system in which descent and inheritance are traced through the father's line

**Matrilineal**
A family structure in which descent and inheritance are traced through the mother's line

**Bilateral lineage**
A descent system in which influence, wealth, and power are assigned to both sides of the family

## 10.2c Norms of Descent and Inheritance

Children inherit two separate bloodlines at birth, the mother's and the father's. Most societies place more importance on one lineage or the other. The most common norms of descent are **patrilineal**, in which kinship is traced through the male kin, the father's lineage. In this type of descent system, offspring owe a special allegiance and loyalty to the father and his kin, who in turn protect and socialize the children and eventually pass to the sons their authority, property, and wealth. Under this system, the key ties are those among father, sons, and grandsons. The wife may maintain ties to her kin, and she contributes her genes to her children; however, she and her children are considered members of her husband's family.

In a **matrilineal** system of descent, descent and inheritance are traced through the mother's line. The mother's kin assume the important role among offspring. Matrilineal norms of descent are uncommon, but they do exist. Among the Trobriand Islanders, for example, kinship, wealth, and responsibility for support are traced through the female line.

In the United States, the norm is to assign influence, wealth, and power to both sides of the family. This system is referred to as **bilateral lineage**. Kinship lines are traced equally through the biological relatives of both the mother and the father, and inheritance is passed on in equal proportions to all children regardless of sex. One consequence of this descent system is that neither kin group exerts much power and influence over the children, which has a significant effect on social change: a newlywed couple coming from families with different values and lifestyles may choose to conform to neither and establish a lifestyle of their own. In addition, the likelihood of marrying someone with different values increases because the parents and kin groups in bilateral systems have relatively little influence over whom their sons or daughters marry.

## 10.2d Norms of Authority

All families and kinship systems have norms concerning who makes important decisions. These norms follow the pattern of other norm variations in that they are aligned with gender. Most societies are **patriarchal**—the men have the power and authority and are dominant. In Iran, Thailand, and Japan, the male position of dominance is even reflected in the law. In matriarchal societies, the authority rests with the females, especially wives and mothers. **Matriarchal** systems are rare, even among matrilineal societies such as that of the Trobriand Islanders, where the wives do not have authority over their husbands. It is important to note that, while authority in most families rests with the males, wives and mothers often have a strong impact on decisions as well.

The least common pattern of authority is the **egalitarian** model, in which decisions are equally divided between husband and wife. Some have argued that the United States is egalitarian because husbands and wives either make decisions jointly or assume responsibility for different areas of concern. The husband might make decisions related to his job, the automobile, or home repairs, whereas the wife might make decisions related to her job, the home, food, clothing, or the children. Many would argue that the family system in the United States is more patriarchal than egalitarian, however, because males generally control income and other family resources.

*Endogamous norms vary from one society to another. For example, marriages between members of different racial groups were considered improper at different times in America. (Shutterstock)*

## 10.2e Norms for Choice of Marriage Partner

Every society has norms concerning the appropriateness or unacceptability of some types of marriage partners. These norms can be divided into two categories: **exogamy**, in which people must marry outside of their own group, and **endogamy**, which requires that people considering marriage share particular group characteristics, such as age, race, religion, or socioeconomic status.

Some exogamous norms are almost universal. **Incest**—sexual relations with or marriage to close relatives—is forbidden in almost every society. One cannot marry one's mother, father, brother, sister, son, or daughter. Isolated exceptions to this taboo are said to have existed between Egyptian and Inca royalty. Most societies also forbid marriage between first cousins and between members of the same sex. Argentina, the Netherlands, Belgium, Canada, Iceland, Portugal, Spain, South Africa, and most recently Norway in 2008 and Sweden in 2009 now allow gay marriage. As of 2013, thirteen states have legalized same sex marriage: California, Connecticut, Delaware, Iowa, Maine, Maryland, Massachusetts, Minnesota, New Hampshire, New York, Rhode Island, Vermont and the District of Columbia.

Norms concerning endogamy and exogamy perform an important social function, but the nature of that function is widely debated. A number of authorities have suggested that the incest taboo, for instance, is a result of the dangers of inbreeding. Others contend that the taboo is instinctive, that prolonged associations with people during childhood precludes viewing them as a marriage partner or that marriage within a kinship group would lead to intense conflicts and jealousy. Murdock (1949) suggests that a complete explanation of the incest taboo must synthesize theories from the different disciplines that deal with human behavior.

There are also a number of explanations for endogamy. It is widely believed that members of similar groups—be they racial, socioeconomic or religious—share similar

**Patriarchal**
A society in which men have the power and authority and are dominant.

**Matriarchal**
A family structure in which the wife dominates the husband

**Egalitarian**
The norm of authority in the family in which decisions are equally divided between husband and wife

**Exogamy**
A marriage norm requiring a person to marry someone from outside his or her own group

**Endogamy**
A marriage norm requiring a person to marry someone from his or her own group

**Incest**
Socially forbidden sexual relationships or marriages with certain close relatives

values, role expectations, and attitudes, which results in fewer marital or kinship conflicts. Further, marriages between people of the same socioeconomic status keep the wealth and power within the social class. Although the norms of endogamy vary among and within societies such as the United States, all societies foster suspicion and dislike of groups whose values, behaviors, and customs are unfamiliar or seem strange. Both exogamy and endogamy, therefore, restrict the eligibility of available marriage partners for both sexes.

**thinking** SOCIOLOGICALLY

1. Polygyny is known to exist as a legitimate form of marriage in many societies around the world. Why does (or should) the United States not legally permit either polygyny or polyandry?
2. What are some consequences of a particular type of lineage system? Think of examples that illustrate whether families are patrilineal, matrilineal, or bilateral, and what difference it makes.
3. What factors aid in determining "appropriate" societal norms around marriage and family? How does determining these factors help us understand societal unrest around marriage and family in the United States?

# 10.3 A FUNCTIONALIST PERSPECTIVE ON THE FAMILY

The functionalist perspective emphasizes the structures of social systems and the functions of these parts in maintaining the society. Despite the many variations that exist in family structure around the world, families everywhere perform many of the same functions. Among the more important are socialization, affection and emotional support, sexual regulation, reproduction, and social placement.

## 10.3a Socialization

More than 60 years ago, Parsons and Bales (1951) suggested that the family has two essential functions: (1) the primary socialization of children so that they can become true members of the society in which they were born, and (2) the stabilization of the adult personalities of the society. The family teaches its members the rules, expectations, knowledge, skills, values, and norms of the society, culture and subculture within which the family resides. While families perform many functions, only the function of nurturant socialization of children is universal. However excellent hospitals, childcare centers, and nursery or elementary schools may be, none seems to perform the socialization and learning functions as well as the family (Elkin & Handel, 1989; Spitz, 1945). This emphasis on the infant and young child should not cause us to overlook the socialization function of the family on adults, however. Parents learn from each other, from their children, and from other kin as they interact in the intimate network bound by blood and marriage ties. This affective support is a second function provided by the family.

## 10.3b Affection and Emotional Support

The second function suggested by Parsons and Bales (1951)—the stabilization of the adult personalities of the society—seems to be just as important as the first. Although some individuals enjoy living alone, most people need others who care, show affection, share joys and sorrows, and give support in times of need. Although friends, neighbors, co-workers, and government agencies provide social support, none is as effective as the family at providing warm, supportive relationships.

The importance of this family function is evidenced in many different ways. Aging persons particularly exemplify this idea. In studies, they often indicated that good relationships with their children are a major source of gratification. In fact, people who have a network of family connections live longer than those who are single, widowed, or divorced.

## 10.3c Sexual Regulation

All societies approve of some sexual behaviors and disapprove of others. Marriage is the most universally approved outlet for sexual behavior. Societies control sexual activity in a number of ways. The chief means is by socializing sexual norms and attempting to enforce them. Secluding single women, for example, might enforce the norm of chastity. Society also differentiates sexual rights in accordance with various roles and statuses (male, female, single, married, priest, teacher) and places taboos on intercourse at some times in the reproductive cycle, such as during menstruation, pregnancy, or immediately following childbirth. The norms of most societies discourage practices such as incest, rape, child molesting, voyeurism, and the like. Sexual norms are concerned with more than just sexual intercourse; they also cover such behaviors as kissing and touching, as well as appropriate attitudes and values.

In the United States, the most pervasive socially approved sexual interest is heterosexual. Sexual relationships are generally defined in terms of the family and marriage, as premarital or extramarital relationships, for example. Other institutions—religion, education, economics, or politics—may also regulate sexual behaviors and attitudes, but it is not one of their primary tasks. Families have the chief responsibility in this area and because they regulate sexual activity, it seems logical that they also control the function of reproduction.

## 10.3d Reproduction

The family is the most widely approved social context for having children. Children are sometimes born outside the family, of course; if it is common, however, it is considered a social problem. According to the functionalist perspective, a society's reproductive practices should conform to institutional patterns and should be integrated with other societal functions, such as sexual regulation, physical and emotional support, and socialization. This view reflects the **principle of legitimacy**, formulated by Bronislaw Malinowski (1930) more than 70 years ago. The principle states that every society has a rule that every child should have a legitimate father to act as the child's protector, guardian, and representative in the society.

Those who are not functionalists may be disturbed by this explanation of the role of the family. It suggests that children born outside of the family are stigmatized in some way, that they are illegitimate. Even functionalists would concede that there are functional alternatives to a biological father; father substitutes can fulfill the essential social tasks and roles of a father. Interactionists would also argue that the biological link between parent and child is less significant than the social links—what are important to the child are role models, social support, and patterns of interaction that will enable the child to develop adequately and to function effectively in society.

Clinicians often deal with problems of adjustment between adopted children and their parents, who may have fears of rejection or inadequacy because they are not biologically related to their child. Counselors can help parents to realize the overriding significance of the social ties between parent and child, and thus help to allay the parents' fears. With today's high divorce rate (discussed later in this chapter), many of you will remarry and perhaps be involved in **blended families**—families composed of at least

**Principle of legitimacy**

Malinowski's idea that every society has a rule that every child should have a legitimate father to act as the child's protector, guardian, and representative in society

**Blended families**

Families composed of at least one formerly married spouse, the children of the previous marriage or marriages, and new offspring one formerly married spouse, the children of the previous marriage or marriages, and new offspring. Sometimes, stepparents feel guilty about not being able to instantly love their stepchildren. Other tensions may develop between biologically unrelated children. Realizing the essential significance of the social links between family members may help family members to overcome some of those tensions. Further, a more active approach by family members and counselors working with such families could involve finding ways to strengthen those links through activities that provide close interaction and communication.

Clinicians often deal with problems of adjustment between adopted children and their parents.
iStockphoto)

Although it is true that children may be born outside of a family unit, it is undeniably the family that universally fulfills the function of giving legal status and social approval to parenthood and reproduction.

### 10.3e Social Placement

The social placement of children is a family function closely associated with socialization and reproduction. Social placement involves determining what roles and statuses the child will occupy in society. As discussed elsewhere, some of the statuses that a person will occupy are ascribed at birth, such as age, sex, and social class position. Children generally assume the legal, religious, and political status of their family as well. Even statuses that are achieved, such as marriage, occupation, and education, are greatly influenced by one's membership in a particular family or kin network.

The family also performs functions other than the five mentioned (i.e., socialization, affection and emotional support, sexual regulation, reproduction, and social placement). It fulfills basic economic, protective, educational, recreational, and religious functions, as well.

## 10.4 A CONFLICT PERSPECTIVE ON THE FAMILY

Conflict theorists, like functionalists, recognize variations in family structure and accept the idea that the family provides basic social needs and goals. However, conflict theorists contend that social systems, including the family, are not static structures that maintain equilibrium and harmony among the parts. They argue, rather, that social systems are constantly in a state of conflict and change. They contend that conflict is natural and inevitable in all human interactions, including those between male and female, husband and wife, and parent and child, and that these conflicts are the result of a continual struggle for power and control. Marriage is one of many contexts in which each person seeks his or her rights. The struggles of parenthood involve not just rivalries among siblings but also between parents and children.

Conflict stems from the unequal distribution of scarce resources. In all systems, some have more resources than others, which gives them dominance and power over others. Feminist theories, like conflict theories, argue that inequalities exist not only in the economic and occupational realm but also in the family. Friedrich Engels (1902) claimed that the family, the basic unit in a capitalist society, serves as the chief means of oppressing women. The husband is the bourgeois and the wife is the proletariat. As general Marxist-feminist theory suggests, when women become aware of their collective interests, they will question the legitimacy of the existing patterns of inequality and will join together against men to bring about changes and the redistribution of resources: power, money, education, job opportunities, and the like. Conflict is as inevitable in the family as it is in society, and it leads to change.

Conflict theory assumes that economic organization, especially the ownership of property, generates revolutionary class conflict. In families, property ownership involves not just one's home and possessions but people as well. Coltrane and Collins (2001) argue that basic to the institution of sexual stratification is the notion of sexual property, the belief that one has permanent exclusive sexual rights to a particular person. In societies operating under a system of patriarchy that is dominated by males, the principal form of sexual property is male ownership of females, husband ownership of wives.

This pattern of male ownership and male dominance has a long history, stemming from laws in ancient Hebrew society and continuing through the twentieth century. The Hebrew laws stated, among other things, that if a man had sexual intercourse with an *unbetrothed* (not contracted for marriage) virgin, he was required to marry her and to pay her father the bride price. In many societies, women are closely guarded so they will not attract other men and lose their market value. These practices are reflected in such customs as wearing a veil and strict chaperonage. Even in the United States, women could not legally make contracts or obtain credit until recently, and women are still not guaranteed equal rights under the U.S. Constitution. The status of women is also evident in many wedding ceremonies, in which the father "gives away" some of his property—the bride—and the bride vows not just to love but also to honor and obey her new owner (the groom).

How can this inequality and the prevalence of male domination be explained? The most common theory relates power and domination to available resources. Men gain power over women through their physical strength and their freedom from the biological limitations of childbirth. The traditional resource of women, on the other hand, is their sexuality. Before and during marriage, women traditionally control men by giving or withholding sexual "favors."

Conflict theory suggests that the structure of domination shifts as resources shift. In general, those with greater occupational prestige, higher income, or more education have more power. Women who bear children, it could be argued, gain status, prestige, and power because they are fulfilling the important role of mother. However, realistically, exactly the opposite happens. A woman's power declines with the birth of a child and goes down even more with additional children. Why? Women with children are more likely to be confined to the home, with the primary responsibilities of childcare, and do not have the time or the liberty to acquire resources such as education, income, or the type of job that would increase their power. Logically, we can argue, we might expect women today to be in better bargaining positions relative to men because they are having fewer children and are more likely hold jobs. Being free from unwanted pregnancies and from childbirth, combined with increased education and income, lessens their economic dependence on husbands. The result today is that there seems to be a major trend, at least in the more industrialized nations, toward greater equality between the sexes, both within and outside of marriage and the family.

Conflict in families also occurs over issues other than inequality between men and women. It can arise over a variety of issues: place of residence, inheritance rights, decision-making, selection of mates, violence (especially rape), sexual relationships, and marital adjustment, to mention a few. In every instance, the issue is likely to involve an inequality of power, authority, or resources, which will lead to conflict. This means that these marital conflicts are not necessarily due to personality clashes but rather to inequality, a power imbalance in the relationship.

It is important for married people and marriage counselors to understand this in trying to work out troubled relationships. It may be more important to try to adjust the balance of power between spouses than to try to adjust personalities that are thought to be incompatible. These ideas may be useful for you even if you are not currently married. Consider your relationship with your boyfriend or girlfriend. Can you think

**BVT*Lab***

Flashcards are available for this chapter at www.BVTLab.com

of any ways in which an imbalance of power sometimes leads to disagreements? The disagreements do not necessarily mean that there is a loss of affection for one another—although there may be—but may instead reflect inequality in the relationship.

# 10.5 OTHER PERSPECTIVES ON THE FAMILY

## 10.5a An Exchange Perspective

All human interactions, including those between husbands and wives or parents and children, can be viewed in terms of social exchange. Social exchange theory assumes that people weigh rewards and costs in their social interactions. If the exchange is unequal or is perceived as unequal, one person will be at a disadvantage, and the other will control the relationship. In this regard, exchange theory parallels the conflict perspective. If people in a relationship give a great deal and receive little in return, they will perceive the relationship as unsatisfactory. These ideas can be illustrated with mate selection.

Everywhere in the world, selecting a mate involves trying to get the best spouse for what one has to offer. As you know from our earlier discussion of the endogamous and exogamous rules of marriage, selecting a mate is never a matter of completely free and independent choice. One must conform to societal norms.

Marriages may be arranged in several ways. At one extreme, they may be organized by the families of the people to be married; the prospective spouses may have no say in the matter at all. When this practice is followed, the criteria of the exchange involve such factors as money, prestige, family position, or power. When, on the other hand, the people to be married choose their mates themselves, the exchange criteria involve factors such as love, affection, emotional support, beauty, personality, prestige, and fulfillment of needs. The latter procedure is rare in the world as a whole, the United States being one of the few countries that practices it.

One of the most widely researched exchange theories of mate selection is the theory of **complementary needs**. Robert Winch believed that although mates tend to resemble each other in such social characteristics as age, race, religion, ethnic origin, socioeconomic status, and education, they are usually complementary rather than similar in respect to needs, psychic fulfillment, and individual motivation (1954; 1958). Rather than seeking a mate with a similar personality, one seeks a person who will satisfy one's needs. If both people are dominant, for example, the relationship will not succeed. However, if one is dominant and the other submissive, the relationship is complementary and the needs of both parties are met.

An earlier exchange theory of mate selection was Willard Waller's (1938) analysis of courtship conduct as a process of bargaining, exploitation, or both. In his words, "When one marries he makes a number of different bargains. Everyone knows this and this knowledge affects the sentiment of love and the process of falling in love" (p. 239). Although it is doubtful that only "he makes bargains" or that "everyone knows this," the fact that bargaining and exchanges take place for both males and females in the mate-selection process is today widely recognized and accepted. Good looks, athletic stardom, a sense of humor, clothes, and money are resources commonly perceived as valuable in the exchange process. In mate selection, as in other interaction processes, people rarely get something for nothing, although each person—either consciously or unconsciously—tries to maximize gains and minimize costs. Over the long run, however, actual exchanges tend to be about equal and if they are not, the relationship is likely to end.

**Complementary needs**

A theory of mate selection based on the idea that people marry those who provide the maximum need gratification when needs tend to be complementary rather than similar

Like conflict theory, exchange theory helps us to recognize the importance of equality in a marriage and may be a useful perspective in dealing with troubled marriages. If a relationship is in trouble, counselors or therapists might try to evaluate the balance of exchange that exists in a marriage. They might find that there is more of a balanced exchange than is apparent; if this is the case, they could explain to the couple the resources that each partner provides. If there were, indeed, an imbalance, the clinician would recognize that this is likely to be a major source of trouble and may help the couple to find ways to attain a balanced exchange. Here, again, is a perspective that you can use to examine some of your relationships even if you are not married.

## 10.5b An Interactionist Perspective

An interactionist perspective on the family uses a social-psychological approach to examine interaction patterns, socialization processes, role expectations and behaviors, and the definitions or meanings given to various family issues. This approach considers not just structural variations but also the interactional patterns and covert definitions associated with structural arrangements.

Few relationships are more enduring or more intense than marriage, and few reflect the principles of interactionism so comprehensively. Marriage exemplifies the central ideas of symbolic interaction: shared meanings, significant others, role expectations, role taking, definitions of situations, symbolic communication, and so on.

Marriage is dynamic—the needs of the married individuals and their role relationships change frequently. According to the interactionist perspective, husband and wife have a reciprocal influence on each other. Each partner continually affects the other, so adjustment is a process, not an end result. Good adjustment means "the individual or the pair has a good working arrangement with reality, adulthood, and expectations of others" (Waller & Hill, 1951, p. 362).

Each of us brings to a marriage certain ideas about what is proper behavior for our spouses and ourselves. Inevitably, as people interact, they find that some behaviors do not fit their preconceived definitions. Unless the definitions or the behaviors change, one spouse or both may be frustrated in attempting to fulfill their roles. Some argue that these frustrations are increasing because the roles of husband and wife are more flexible and diverse than they were in the past. Others maintain that today's increased flexibility and diversity decrease marital strain by allowing partners a greater range of options. In either case, what the interactionist considers important is that the couple share definitions, perceptions, and meanings. Also, disagreements may not lead to conflict if they involve issues considered unimportant. Suppose, for example, that a wife likes football but her husband does not. The situation will not lead to conflict if the husband defines football as important to his wife and accepts her behavior. In the same way, a husband's desire for only part-time employment or his wish to avoid cooking is a source of conflict only if the wife has different expectations. Adjustment is a result of shared expectations.

Married couples must continually redefine themselves in relation to each other; marriage counseling may help. (iStockphoto)

To maintain a satisfactory relationship, married couples must continually redefine themselves in relation to each other, which is often an unconscious process. When problems arise, marriage counseling may help by bringing unconscious definitions into consciousness, thus allowing the couple to examine how they influence the relationship.

The interactionist perspective stresses the importance of analyzing marriages and other relationships in the context in which they occur. A definition, role expectation, or behavior that is appropriate in one setting may be inappropriate in another. This perspective also emphasizes the notion that a successful marriage involves a process of adjustment, or continual adaptation to shifts in shared meaning.

Interactionism, thus, is a particularly useful perspective for marital therapy. The family is not simply a group of separate people independently performing separate functions. The interactionist perspective helps us to realize that family members act largely on the basis of how they interpret one another's actions. Using the interactionist perspective, clinicians may come to understand that each family has its own context that provides the basis for interaction and for interpretation of each family member's actions. This being the case, a clinician using this perspective might work on making sure that the individual family members understand clearly what the other family members intentions are, and might also help to clarify how each person defines the actions of the others.

### 10.5c A Developmental Perspective

The developmental perspective on the family suggests that families pass through a family life cycle, a series of different responsibilities and tasks. This perspective suggests that successful achievement at one point in the developmental process is essential in effectively accomplishing later tasks, whereas failure in earlier tasks leads to increased difficulty with later tasks. Just as individuals must learn to crawl and walk before they can run, new families must be able to perform various financial, sexual, and interpersonal tasks to maintain the family unit and meet later developmental goals.

During its life cycle, the family passes through a sequence of stages that require different interaction patterns, roles, and responsibilities. The number of stages identified depends on the intent of the researcher. There may be as few as two, but the most typical division is of seven stages. The transition points between stages most often center on the age of the oldest child.

The first stage typically begins with marriage and extends to the birth of the first child. For most couples, this stage involves defining the marital relationship, learning to communicate effectively, resolving conflicts, working out mutually satisfying and realistic systems for getting and spending the family income, deciding about parenthood, and dealing with adjustment to life as a married pair.

Stage two may include families with children. During this stage, the couple changes from a dyad of husband and wife to a triad of parents and offspring. The central tasks are adjusting to parenthood, dealing with the needs and development of the infant or young child, relating to parents and in-laws who are grandparents to the child, assuming and managing the additional housing and space needs, and continuing the communicative, sexual, and financial responsibilities described in stage one.

Stage three may extend from early school years to pre-teen. When children enter school, both parents and children face new relationships and responsibilities. In this stage, the family focuses on the education and socialization of children. The increasing significance of peer relationships, children's changing interests and activities, and the management of parent-child conflicts are added to the ongoing marital, work, and other responsibilities. A second or third child, the loss of a job, or the dissolution of the marriage modifies the responsibilities generally associated with this stage.

Stage four is the family with adolescents. Data suggest that at the adolescent stage, the family often undergoes economic problems. Medical and dental costs, food, clothing, transportation, entertainment, education, and other expenses often place a strain on the budget. For many families, such issues as drinking, drugs, and sex become additional sources of strain. New types of adolescent dance, music, dress, and jargon must also be accommodated. In addition, families in this stage begin to prepare their teenager to be launched from the home.

Stage five—the launching stage—begins when the oldest child leaves home. The young person's departure—to marry, to attend college, or to take a full-time job—creates a significant transition for both parent and child. This stage may be very brief, as with a one-child family in which the child marries upon graduation from high school, or it may extend over many years, as happens when there are several children or when an unmarried child remains in the home for many years, dependent on parents for support.

When the children have been launched, the family returns to the original two-person conjugal unit; at the same time, however, it may expand to include sons- or daughters-in-law and grandchildren.

Stage six—the "empty nest"—is the period when all the children have left home and continues until the retirement or death of one spouse. It may be very brief because of one or more children remaining in the home through their twenties or because of an early death of a spouse; or it may cover many years, as when the last child departs when the parents are in their late thirties or early forties and when the parents remain employed until age seventy or later. At this stage, the interpersonal focus is on the married couple, yet intergenerational family responsibilities can arise. The husband and wife in the middle years may have some responsibility for their retired and elderly parents and also for their married children and grandchildren, who may seek emotional and financial support from the middle generation from time to time.

The seventh stage generally begins with retirement and extends until the marriage ends with the death of one spouse. Because women live longer than men and are usually younger than their husbands, they are widowed more often than men. With the death of both spouses, the family life span for that family has ended, and the cycle continues with each successive generation.

### thinking SOCIOLOGICALLY

1. Apply an exchange perspective to several close relationships in your life. What did you have to offer, and in turn, what did you receive? Can you identify instances in which an unequal relationship led to the termination of the relationship?
2. Suppose that you are a sociologist who is called upon to testify as an expert witness in a child custody case. This is a case in which the father wants a joint custody arrangement, but the mother objects and wants sole custody of the child. Assume that there is no violence or any other urgent reason to keep the child away from the father. Develop an argument for or against joint custody, using any or all of the theories just covered.

## 10.6 THE AMERICAN FAMILY SYSTEM

The American family system emphasizes monogamy, neolocal residence, a modified-extended kinship linkage, bilateral descent and inheritance, egalitarian decision-making, endogamous marriage, and relatively free choice of mate. American families tend to be small and rather isolated when compared with families of other countries. Marital and family roles for women and men are becoming increasingly ambiguous. We tend to emphasize love in mate selection, and we are often sexually permissive prior to or outside of marriage. In addition, divorce is granted easily.

Table 10-1 shows the marital status of the population by sex and age. You can see that as of 2012, the population of the United States included nearly 120 million males and a little over 127 million females age 15 and over. Approximately 34.2% of the men and 28.4% of the women were never married. A relatively small number (around 2.9 million) of the men were widowers, compared with 11.2 million of the women who were widows. Much publicity is given to the breakup of marriages through divorce, but only 8.9% of the men and 11.1% of the women had a divorced status in 2012. Note how these figures vary by age. Very few older people are single, and very few young and middle-aged people are widowed. The divorced population is concentrated most heavily in the age 35 to 54 group.

**Table 10-1** Marital Status of People 15 Years Old and Over, 2012 (in Thousands, Except Percentages)

| All Races | Total (Number) | Married Spouse Present (Number) | Married Spouse Absent (Number) | Widowed (Number) | Divorced (Number) | Separated (Number) | Never Married (Number) | Total (Percent) | Married Spouse Present (Percent) | Married Spouse Absent (Percent) | Widowed (Percent) | Divorced (Percent) | Separated (Percent) | Never Married (Percent) |
|---|---|---|---|---|---|---|---|---|---|---|---|---|---|---|
| **BOTH SEXES** | | | | | | | | | | | | | | |
| Total 15+ | 247,573 | 122,095 | 3,568 | 14,058 | 24,911 | 5,668 | 77,273 | 100.0 | 49.3 | 1.4 | 5.7 | 10.1 | 2.3 | 31.2 |
| 15–17 years | 12,975 | 35 | 75 | 3 | 16 | 106 | 12,741 | 100.0 | 0.3 | 0.6 | 0.0 | 0.1 | 0.8 | 98.2 |
| 18–19 years | 8,255 | 110 | 49 | 14 | 25 | 67 | 7,989 | 100.0 | 1.3 | 0.6 | 0.2 | 0.3 | 0.8 | 96.8 |
| 20–24 years | 21,870 | 2,406 | 237 | 32 | 195 | 349 | 18,650 | 100.0 | 11.0 | 1.1 | 0.1 | 0.9 | 1.6 | 85.3 |
| 25–29 years | 20,889 | 7,377 | 295 | 43 | 768 | 447 | 11,958 | 100.0 | 35.3 | 1.4 | 0.2 | 3.7 | 2.1 | 57.2 |
| 30–34 years | 20,312 | 10,894 | 347 | 37 | 1,438 | 617 | 6,980 | 100.0 | 53.6 | 1.7 | 0.2 | 7.1 | 3.0 | 34.4 |
| 35–39 years | 19,132 | 11,780 | 338 | 118 | 1,968 | 681 | 4,246 | 100.0 | 61.6 | 1.8 | 0.6 | 10.3 | 3.6 | 22.2 |
| 40–44 years | 20,782 | 13,206 | 411 | 171 | 2,675 | 681 | 3,637 | 100.0 | 63.5 | 2.0 | 0.8 | 12.9 | 3.3 | 17.5 |
| 45–49 years | 21,567 | 13,577 | 360 | 323 | 3,248 | 788 | 3,271 | 100.0 | 63.0 | 1.7 | 1.5 | 15.1 | 3.7 | 15.2 |
| 50–54 years | 22,354 | 14,543 | 372 | 593 | 3,654 | 634 | 2,558 | 100.0 | 65.1 | 1.7 | 2.7 | 16.3 | 2.8 | 11.4 |
| 55–64 years | 37,944 | 24,615 | 572 | 2,068 | 6,413 | 854 | 3,423 | 100.0 | 64.9 | 1.5 | 5.4 | 16.9 | 2.2 | 9.0 |
| 65–74 years | 23,373 | 15,073 | 244 | 3,407 | 3,207 | 313 | 1,129 | 100.0 | 64.5 | 1.0 | 14.6 | 13.7 | 1.3 | 4.8 |
| 75–84 years | 13,117 | 6,996 | 184 | 4,260 | 1,091 | 101 | 486 | 100.0 | 53.3 | 1.4 | 32.5 | 8.3 | 0.8 | 3.7 |
| 85+ years | 5,003 | 1,482 | 86 | 2,989 | 213 | 31 | 203 | 100.0 | 29.6 | 1.7 | 59.7 | 4.3 | 0.6 | 4.1 |
| 15–17 years | 12,975 | 35 | 75 | 3 | 16 | 106 | 12,741 | 100.0 | 0.3 | 0.6 | 0.0 | 0.1 | 0.8 | 98.2 |
| 18+ years | 234,598 | 122,060 | 3,493 | 14,055 | 24,896 | 5,562 | 64,532 | 100.0 | 52.0 | 1.5 | 6.0 | 10.6 | 2.4 | 27.5 |
| 15–64 years | 206,080 | 98,544 | 3,055 | 3,403 | 20,401 | 5,224 | 75,454 | 100.0 | 47.8 | 1.5 | 1.7 | 9.9 | 2.5 | 36.6 |
| 65+ years | 41,493 | 23,551 | 513 | 10,655 | 4,511 | 444 | 1,819 | 100.0 | 56.8 | 1.2 | 25.7 | 10.9 | 1.1 | 4.4 |
| **MALES** | | | | | | | | | | | | | | |
| Total 15+ | 119,877 | 61,047 | 1,759 | 2,864 | 10,696 | 2,475 | 41,035 | 100.0 | 50.9 | 1.5 | 2.4 | 8.9 | 2.1 | 34.2 |
| 15–17 years | 6,664 | 8 | 30 | - | 8 | 54 | 6,565 | 100.0 | 0.1 | 0.4 | - | 0.1 | 0.8 | 98.5 |
| 18–19 years | 4,172 | 46 | 20 | 4 | 12 | 40 | 4,051 | 100.0 | 1.1 | 0.5 | 0.1 | 0.3 | 1.0 | 97.1 |
| 20–24 years | 10,982 | 879 | 88 | 9 | 70 | 135 | 9,800 | 100.0 | 8.0 | 0.8 | 0.1 | 0.6 | 1.2 | 89.2 |
| 25–29 years | 10,430 | 3,151 | 154 | 10 | 305 | 189 | 6,620 | 100.0 | 30.2 | 1.5 | 0.1 | 2.9 | 1.8 | 63.5 |
| 30–34 years | 10,028 | 5,087 | 176 | 8 | 602 | 230 | 3,924 | 100.0 | 50.7 | 1.8 | 0.1 | 6.0 | 2.3 | 39.1 |
| 35–39 years | 9,418 | 5,842 | 159 | 38 | 847 | 239 | 2,294 | 100.0 | 62.0 | 1.7 | 0.4 | 9.0 | 2.5 | 24.4 |
| 40–44 years | 10,252 | 6,414 | 241 | 27 | 1,212 | 302 | 2,057 | 100.0 | 62.6 | 2.3 | 0.3 | 11.8 | 2.9 | 20.1 |
| 45–49 years | 10,569 | 6,618 | 175 | 81 | 1,462 | 388 | 1,846 | 100.0 | 62.6 | 1.7 | 0.8 | 13.8 | 3.7 | 17.5 |
| 50–54 years | 10,894 | 7,296 | 188 | 127 | 1,631 | 296 | 1,356 | 100.0 | 67.0 | 1.7 | 1.2 | 15.0 | 2.7 | 12.4 |
| 55–64 years | 18,137 | 12,491 | 271 | 446 | 2,826 | 395 | 1,707 | 100.0 | 68.9 | 1.5 | 2.5 | 15.6 | 2.2 | 9.4 |
| 65–74 years | 10,980 | 8,199 | 126 | 690 | 1,278 | 146 | 541 | 100.0 | 74.7 | 1.2 | 6.3 | 11.6 | 1.3 | 4.9 |
| 75–84 years | 5,543 | 4,056 | 89 | 769 | 383 | 51 | 196 | 100.0 | 73.2 | 1.6 | 13.9 | 6.9 | 0.9 | 3.5 |
| 85+ years | 1,809 | 961 | 43 | 656 | 61 | 10 | 79 | 100.0 | 53.1 | 2.4 | 36.3 | 3.4 | 0.6 | 4.3 |
| 15–17 years | 6,664 | 8 | 30 | - | 8 | 54 | 6,565 | 100.0 | 0.1 | 0.4 | - | 0.1 | 0.8 | 98.5 |
| 18+ years | 113,213 | 61,039 | 1,730 | 2,864 | 10,688 | 2,421 | 34,471 | 100.0 | 53.9 | 1.5 | 2.5 | 9.4 | 2.1 | 30.4 |
| 15–64 years | 101,545 | 47,832 | 1,502 | 749 | 8,974 | 2,269 | 40,220 | 100.0 | 47.1 | 1.5 | 0.7 | 8.8 | 2.2 | 39.6 |
| 65+ years | 18,332 | 13,216 | 258 | 2,115 | 1,722 | 206 | 816 | 100.0 | 72.1 | 1.4 | 11.5 | 9.4 | 1.1 | 4.5 |
| **FEMALES** | | | | | | | | | | | | | | |
| Total 15+ | 127,695 | 61,047 | 1,809 | 11,193 | 14,215 | 3,193 | 36,238 | 100.0 | 47.8 | 1.4 | 8.8 | 11.1 | 2.5 | 28.4 |
| 15–17 years | 6,310 | 27 | 45 | 3 | 8 | 52 | 6,176 | 100.0 | 0.4 | 0.7 | 0.0 | 0.1 | 0.8 | 97.9 |
| 18–19 years | 4,083 | 65 | 30 | 11 | 14 | 26 | 3,938 | 100.0 | 1.6 | 0.7 | 0.3 | 0.3 | 0.6 | 96.4 |
| 20–24 years | 10,888 | 1,527 | 149 | 23 | 124 | 214 | 8,850 | 100.0 | 14.0 | 1.4 | 0.2 | 1.1 | 2.0 | 81.3 |
| 25–29 years | 10,459 | 4,226 | 141 | 33 | 463 | 258 | 5,338 | 100.0 | 40.4 | 1.3 | 0.3 | 4.4 | 2.5 | 51.0 |
| 30–34 years | 10,284 | 5,807 | 171 | 28 | 836 | 387 | 3,055 | 100.0 | 56.5 | 1.7 | 0.3 | 8.1 | 3.8 | 29.7 |
| 35–39 years | 9,714 | 5,939 | 179 | 80 | 1,122 | 442 | 1,953 | 100.0 | 61.1 | 1.8 | 0.8 | 11.5 | 4.5 | 20.1 |
| 40–44 years | 10,530 | 6,792 | 171 | 144 | 1,464 | 379 | 1,580 | 100.0 | 64.5 | 1.6 | 1.4 | 13.9 | 3.6 | 15.0 |
| 45–49 years | 10,999 | 6,960 | 185 | 243 | 1,786 | 400 | 1,426 | 100.0 | 63.3 | 1.7 | 2.2 | 16.2 | 3.6 | 13.0 |
| 50–54 years | 11,460 | 7,247 | 183 | 466 | 2,024 | 338 | 1,202 | 100.0 | 63.2 | 1.6 | 4.1 | 17.7 | 3.0 | 10.5 |
| 55–64 years | 19,808 | 12,123 | 300 | 1,622 | 3,588 | 458 | 1,716 | 100.0 | 61.2 | 1.5 | 8.2 | 18.1 | 2.3 | 8.7 |
| 65–74 years | 12,393 | 6,875 | 117 | 2,717 | 1,929 | 168 | 588 | 100.0 | 55.5 | 0.9 | 21.9 | 15.6 | 1.4 | 4.7 |
| 75–84 years | 7,574 | 2,940 | 95 | 3,491 | 708 | 50 | 290 | 100.0 | 38.8 | 1.3 | 46.1 | 9.3 | 0.7 | 3.8 |
| 85+ years | 3,193 | 521 | 43 | 2,332 | 152 | 21 | 125 | 100.0 | 16.3 | 1.3 | 73.0 | 4.8 | 0.6 | 3.9 |
| 15–17 years | 6,310 | 27 | 45 | 3 | 8 | 52 | 6,176 | 100.0 | 0.4 | 0.7 | 0.0 | 0.1 | 0.8 | 97.9 |
| 18+ years | 121,385 | 61,021 | 1,764 | 11,190 | 14,208 | 3,141 | 30,061 | 100.0 | 50.3 | 1.5 | 9.2 | 11.7 | 2.6 | 24.8 |
| 15–64 years | 104,535 | 50,712 | 1,553 | 2,654 | 11,427 | 2,955 | 35,235 | 100.0 | 48.5 | 1.5 | 2.5 | 10.9 | 2.8 | 33.7 |
| 65+ years | 23,160 | 10,335 | 255 | 8,540 | 2,789 | 238 | 1,003 | 100.0 | 44.6 | 1.1 | 36.9 | 12.0 | 1.0 | 4.3 |

Adapted from U.S. Census Bureau, Current Population Survey, 2012 Annual Social and Economic Supplement Internet Release Date: November 2012. Retrieved from http://www.census.gov/hhes/families/data/cps2012.html

## 10.6a Marriage Rates and Age at Marriage

*Rates of marriage* (the number of people who marry in a given year per 1,000 people or per 1,000 unmarried women age 15 and over) are influenced by a variety of factors. The rate characteristically falls during periods of economic recession and rises during periods of prosperity. The rate also tends to rise at the beginning of a war and after a war has ended. Variations in the age of the population are also influential.

In the United States prior to 1900, the rate was relatively stable, varying between 8.6 and 9.6 marriages per 1,000 people per year. Shortly after the beginning of the twentieth century, the rate rose until the Depression of the early 1930s, when it dropped to a low of 7.9. Marriage rates rose dramatically at the outset of World War II, as young men sought to avail themselves of the deferred status granted to married men or simply wanted to marry before going overseas. The end of the war and the return of men to civilian life precipitated another upsurge in marriages. In 1946, the marriage rate reached 16.4, an unprecedented and to-date unsurpassed peak. Subsequently, it dropped. While there have been fluctuations, it has declined steadily since 1970. In 2011, the marriage rate was 6.8 per 1,000 population (Centers for Disease Control and Protection, 2013).

In the United States, marriage rates have distinct seasonal and geographic variations. More marriages take place in June than in any other month, followed by August, May, and September. The fewest marriages are in January, February, and March. Interestingly, the favorite month for marriage varies by age group: teenage brides and grooms prefer June; brides ages 30 to 34 and grooms ages 45 to 54 most often choose December; and brides 35 to 54 and grooms 55 to 64 tend to select July. Most marriages take place on Saturday. Friday is next in popularity; Tuesdays, Wednesdays, and Thursdays are the least popular.

As an example of a use of sociological statistics, put yourself in the position of a business that has to do with marriage—a florist, bridal boutique, tuxedo rental store, caterer, limousine service, or travel agent. Knowing the times of year that people prefer to get married and what the specific age group preferences are could vastly help these businesses increase their success. This information could help businesses to plan when and where to advertise, when to have the most personnel available to help potential customers, how to decorate the showrooms and arrange displays to appeal to the age groups most likely to shop at a particular time of year, and so forth.

Suppose that you are a travel agent and you know not only that June is the most popular time to get married but also that young people prefer it most. You might decorate your showroom with travel posters with young rather than middle-aged people in them, have a large number of low-priced packages available, perhaps have a young travel agent on duty, and advertise during the preceding months in the magazines that young people are most likely to read.

Statistics about when people get married could also be very useful to you in planning your own marriage. If most marriages occur in June, for example, it will be more difficult to reserve the specific time and place you want for your ceremony and the rates for caterers, limousines, travel, flowers, and tuxedo rentals are likely to be higher then.

Most marriages in the United States are between people of roughly the same age. The median ages at first marriage in 1900 were 25.9 for males and 21.9 for females. The median age at first marriage in 2010 was 28.2 for men and 26.1 for women, a difference of 2.1 years (Table 10-2).

Recently, people have been postponing marriage until they are older, which reflects a decision on the part of young people to live independently as they pursue higher education or job opportunities. In the past two decades, there has been a rapid increase in the percentage of men and women who have never married. In 1970, one in every ten men (10.5%) and nearly one in every five women age 25 to 29 years had never married, but by 2012, this proportion had increased to 63.5% for men and 51% for women, as shown in Table 10-3 (U.S. Bureau of the Census Population Survey, 2005–2009).

## Table 10-2 Median Age at First Marriage, 1890–2012

The following table shows the median age of men and women when they were first married in the United States from 1890 to 2012. The median age for a man's first marriage was 28.2 years in 2010, up from 26.1 in 1990. The median age for a woman's first marriage was 26.1 years in 2010, up from 23.9 in 1990.

| Year | Males | Females | Year | Males | Females |
|---|---|---|---|---|---|
| 1890 | 26.1 | 22.0 | 1997 | 26.8 | 25.0 |
| 1900 | 25.9 | 21.9 | 1998 | 26.7 | 25.0 |
| 1910 | 25.1 | 21.6 | 1999 | 26.9 | 25.1 |
| 1920 | 24.6 | 21.2 | 2000 | 26.8 | 25.1 |
| 1930 | 24.3 | 21.3 | 2001 | 26.9 | 25.1 |
| 1940 | 24.3 | 21.5 | 2002 | 26.9 | 25.3 |
| 1950 | 22.8 | 20.3 | 2003 | 27.1 | 25.3 |
| 1960 | 22.8 | 20.3 | 2004 | 27.4 | 25.3 |
| 1970 | 23.2 | 20.8 | 2005 | 27.0 | 25.5 |
| 1980 | 24.7 | 22.0 | 2006 | 27.5 | 25.9 |
| 1990 | 26.1 | 23.9 | 2007 | 27.7[1] | 26.0 |
| 1993 | 26.5 | 24.5 | 2008 | 27.6 | 25.9 |
| 1994 | 26.7 | 24.5 | 2009 | 28.1 | 25.9 |
| 1995 | 26.9 | 24.5 | 2010 | 28.2 | 26.1 |

[1]The margin of error for 2007 is +/– 0.2 years

Adapted from U.S. Bureau of the Census. Retrieved from www.census.gov.

Teenage marriages are an issue of special concern in the United States. Married teenagers have an increased high school dropout rate and a high unemployment rate. The divorce rate for teenagers is estimated to be from two to four times the rate

## Table 10-3 Percent Never Married, 1970–2012

| Age | 1970 | 1999 | 2000 | 2002 | 2004 | 2008 | 2012 |
|---|---|---|---|---|---|---|---|
| **Male:** | | | | | | | |
| 20 to 24 | 35.8% | 83.2% | 83.7% | 85.4% | 86.7% | 86.9% | 89.2% |
| 25 to 29 | 10.5% | 52.1% | 51.7% | 53.7% | 56.6% | 57.6% | 63.5% |
| 30 to 34 | 6.2% | 30.7% | 30.0% | 34.0% | 33.4% | 32.4% | 39.1% |
| 35 to 39 | 5.4% | 21.1% | 20.3% | 21.1% | 23.4% | 23.0% | 24.4% |
| 40 to 44 | 4.9% | 15.8% | 15.7% | 16.7% | 18.5% | 16.9% | 20.1% |
| **Female:** | | | | | | | |
| 20 to 24 | 54.7% | 72.3% | 72.8% | 74.0% | 75.4% | 76.4% | 81.3% |
| 25 to 29 | 19.1% | 38.9% | 38.9% | 40.4% | 40.8% | 43.4% | 51.0% |
| 30 to 34 | 4.9% | 22.1% | 21.9% | 23.0% | 23.7% | 24.0% | 29.7% |
| 35 to 39 | 7.2% | 15.2% | 14.3% | 14.7% | 14.6% | 15.2% | 20.1% |
| 40 to 44 | 6.3% | 10.9% | 11.8% | 11.5% | 12.2% | 12.9% | 15.0% |

Adapted from "Statistical Abstract of the United States," U.S. Bureau of the Census. Retrieved from http://www.census.gov/hhes/families/data/cps2012.html

for marriages that begin after age 20. Many teenage marriages involve a pregnancy at the time of marriage, and data consistently show a higher divorce rate among marriages begun with a pregnancy (Teachman, 1983). In reference to his research on economically disadvantaged couples, Fein (2004) states: "Whereas the vast bulk of first transitions to parenthood among upper middle class couples *follow* first marriages, first births among disadvantaged newlyweds are far more likely to *precede* marriage." Furthermore, among couples who married in 1990, one-third of those in the bottom education category had their first child before marriage, compared with one-tenth of those in the top education category. Among African Americans, the fraction is even higher: over half (51%) married after their first transition to parenthood (Fein, 2004). Studies indicate that people who marry young, for a variety of reasons, are unprepared for the process of selecting a mate and assuming a marital role and are disproportionately represented in divorce statistics.

Most married couples have or want to have children. (iStockphoto)

## 10.6b Family Size

Throughout the world, most married couples have or want to have children. Voluntarily childless marriages are uncommon, although a pattern of childless marriages does exist. In the United States in 2000, 34.6 million married couples were without children. Measuring the number of births and the population growth in a country is usually done in terms of the "crude birth rate," usually referred to simply as the birth rate. The birth rate is the number of births during a year per 1,000 population. In 2000, the birth rate in the United States was 14.2 per 1,000 population. In 2008 it was 14.18 per 1,000 population, but in 2009 dropped to 13.82 per 1,000 population. While this does not seem like a big change, an examination of birth rates between 2000 and 2009 indicates that drop between 2008 and 2009 was precipitous when looked at comparatively (see Table 10-4). Rates, such as birth rates, do not have much meaning unless looked at comparatively. When significant variations occur, such as the change in the birth rate between 2008 and 2009, this indicates to social scientists that there are factors that led to the change that should be explored. Like marriage rates, birth rates fluctuate with wars, socioeconomic conditions, and other variables.

The "baby boom" period of the late 1940s and the 1950s produced an unanticipated but significant rise in the United States birth rate. It may have been caused by increases in the normative pressures on women to have children, the end

**Table 10-4** United States Birth Rate (Births/1,000 Population)

| Year | Birth Rate (Births/1,000 Population) | Year | Birth Rate (Births/1,000 Population) |
|---|---|---|---|
| 2000 | 14.20 | 2005 | 14.14 |
| 2001 | 14.20 | 2006 | 14.14 |
| 2002 | 14.10 | 2007 | 14.16 |
| 2003 | 14.14 | 2008 | 14.18 |
| 2004 | 14.13 | 2009 | 13.28 |

Adapted from "CIA World Factbook, 2009."

of the disruption brought about by war, postwar economic prosperity, or the long-term psychological effects of growing up during the Great Depression. Bean (1983) states that while social and cultural conditions during the era supported having families, increased costs tended to discourage couples from having large families. Thus, only a minor part of the baby boom can be attributed to families deciding to have three or more children.

In 2000, 19.5 million married couples had four or more children under age 18 (Current Population Reports, 2001). Improved methods of birth control, liberalized abortion laws, and a widespread acceptance of family planning measures have decreased the number of unplanned and unwanted births and have enabled couples to have the number of children they want. Over the last decades of the twentieth century, the size of U.S. families has declined very rapidly. Since 1970 the percentage of households containing five or more people has fallen by half. On the other hand, the number of single and two-person households has soared. One group of single households that has increased particularly fast is single women between age 30 and age 35 (Grier and Miller 2004). The increase in single households has been accompanied by an increase in the number of single households with children. In 1980 in the U.S., 19.5% of single parent households had children as compared to 29.5% in 2008. This type of increase is seen in many countries throughout the world (see Tables 10-5 and 10-6).

Because families are groups, the numbers of people in the group influences the behavior of its members. Perhaps the greatest difference in family interaction patterns comes with the birth of the first child because the transition to parenthood involves a major shift in parental role expectations and behaviors. A number of writers have called the early stages of parenthood a "crisis," a traumatic change that forces couples to drastically reorganize their lives (Hobbs, 1965; LeMasters, 1957). Later studies concluded, however, that for most couples, beginning parenthood is a period of transition but not a period of change so dramatic that it should be termed a crisis.

With the birth of the first child, the expectation exists that a second and third child should follow. One-child families have generally been viewed as unhealthy for parents and child alike. The "only" child has been described as spoiled, selfish, overly dependent, maladjusted, and lonely. Parents of a single child have been described as selfish, self-centered, immature, cold, and abnormal. Research findings, however, do not support these descriptions.

Findings generally tend to support those of Blake (1981; 1981b; 1989), who claims that single children are intellectually superior, have no obvious personality defects, tend to consider themselves happy, and are satisfied with the important aspects of life, notably jobs and health. In fact, Blake's research supports the *dilution hypothesis*, which predicts that, on average, the more children a family has, the less each child will achieve in such areas as educational and occupational attainment. That is, there is a dilution of familial resources available for children in large families and a concentration of such resources in small ones. These diluted resources include the parents' time, emotional and physical energy (including that of a mother who is frequently pregnant), attention, personal interaction, and material resources that allow for personal living space and privacy within the home, better neighborhoods surrounding the home, specialized medical and dental care, travel, and specialized instruction, such as music lessons.

These findings are extremely important for you to consider in planning your own families. Would you be more receptive to having just one child, knowing that "only" children do as well as—or better than—children with siblings? Would you be less willing to have a large number of children, knowing about the dilution hypothesis? Clearly, many factors enter into the decision of how many children you may personally want or actually have—such as age at marriage, religious orientation, effective use of contraception, career pattern, and so forth. Nonetheless, what is known about the consequences of having few or many children has important implications for personal decision-making and social policy as well.

Although a number of studies revealed no effect, positive or negative, to be associated with family size, very few exist that associate positive consequences with large families. It

**Table 10-5** Single Parent Households by Country 1980–2009

| Country and Year | Number (1,000) | Percent of All Households with Children | Country and Year | Number (1,000) | Percent of All Households with Children |
|---|---|---|---|---|---|
| **United States:** | | | **Germany:** | | |
| 1980 | 6,061 | 19.5 | 1991 | 1,429 | 15.2 |
| 1990 | 7,752 | 24.0 | 1995 | 2,496 | 18.8 |
| 2000 | 9,357 | 27.0 | 2001 | 2,274 | 17.6 |
| 2008 | 10,536 | 29.5 | 2008 | 2,616 | 21.7 |
| **Canada:** | | | **Ireland:**[2] | | |
| 1981 | 437 | 12.7 | 1981 | 30 | 7.2 |
| 1991 | 572 | 16.2 | 1991 | 44 | 10.7 |
| 2001[1] | 1,184 | 23.5 | 2002 | 50 | 17.4 |
| 2006 | 1,276 | 24.6 | 2006 | 78 | 22.6 |
| **Japan:** | | | **Netherlands:** | | |
| 1980 | 796 | 4.9 | 1988 | 179 | 9.6 |
| 1990 | 934 | 6.5 | 2000 | 240 | 13.0 |
| 2000 | 996 | 8.3 | 2009 | 310 | 16.0 |
| 2005 | 1,163 | 10.2 | **Sweden:** | | |
| **Denmark:**[2] | | | 1985 | 117 | 11.2 |
| 1980 | 99 | 13.4 | 1995 | 189 | 17.4 |
| 1990 | 117 | 17.8 | 2000 | 240 | 21.4 |
| 2001 | 120 | 18.4 | 2008 | 200 | 18.7 |
| 2009[1] | 165 | 21.7 | **United Kingdom:**[3] | | |
| **France:** | | | 1987 | 1,010 | 13.9 |
| 1982 | 887 | 10.2 | 1991 | 1,344 | 19.4 |
| 1990 | 1,175 | 13.2 | 2000 | 1,434 | 20.7 |
| 1999 | 1,494 | 17.4 | 2008 | 1,750 | 25.0 |
| 2005[1] | 1,725 | 19.8 | | | |

[1]Break in series. [2]Data are family-based, rather than household-based, statistics. [3]Great Britain only (excludes Northern Ireland)

SOURCE: U.S. Bureau of Labor Statistics, updated and revised from "Families and Work in Transition in 12 Countries, 1980–2001." *Monthly Labor Review,* September 2003, with national sources, some of which may be unpublished.

is not family size per se, however, that creates health problems or family difficulties. Large families heighten the complexity of intragroup relations, pose problems in fulfilling family needs, and influence how much money and attention can be devoted to each child.

## 10.6c Divorce

The United States has one of the highest divorce rates in the world. According to the Summary of Vital Statistics, the U.S. rate of divorce per 1,000 persons per year in 2008 was 5.2—compared with 3.5 in Germany, 3.5 in Sweden, 3.1 in Japan (in 2000), 3.0 in France (in 2000), and 1.3 in Italy (U.S. Census, 2012). Some contributing factors may be:

1. Individualism: Families are spending less and less time together and are more concerned with personal happiness.
2. Romantic love subsides. The excitement goes away.

### Table 10-6 Births to Unmarried Women by Country 1980 to 2008

Percent of all live births

| Country | 1980 | 1990 | 2000 | 2005 | 2006 | 2007 | 2008 |
|---|---|---|---|---|---|---|---|
| United States | 18.4 | 28.0 | 33.2 | 36.9 | 38.5 | 39.7 | 40.6 |
| Canada | 12.8 | 24.4 | 28.3 | 25.6 | 27.1 | 2.3 | (NA) |
| Japan | 0.8 | 1.1 | 1.6 | 2.0 | 2.1 | (NA) | (NA) |
| Denmark | 33.2 | 46.4 | 44.6 | 45.7 | 46.4 | 46.1 | 46.2 |
| France | 11.4 | 30.1 | 43.6 | 48.4 | 50.5 | 51.7 | 52.6 |
| Germany[1] | (X) | 15.1 | 23.4 | 29.2 | 30.0 | 30.8 | 32.1 |
| Ireland | 5.9 | 14.6 | 31.5 | 31.8 | 32.7 | (NA) | (NA) |
| Italy | 4.3 | 6.5 | 9.7 | 15.2 | 16.2 | 17.7 | (NA) |
| Netherlands | 4.1 | 11.4 | 24.9 | 34.9 | 37.1 | 39.5 | 41.2 |
| Spain | 3.9 | 9.6 | 17.7 | 26.6 | 28.4 | 30.2 | 31.7 |
| Sweden | 39.7 | 47.0 | 55.3 | 55.4 | 55.5 | 54.8 | 54.7 |
| United Kingdom | 11.5 | 27.9 | 39.5 | 42.9 | 43.7 | (NA) | (NA) |

*Note.* NA = Not available; X = Not acceptable.

[1]Data is for 1991 instead of 1990

SOURCE: U.S. Bureau of Labor Studies, updated and revised from "Families and Work Transitions in 12 Countries 1980–2001," *Monthly Labor Review,* September 2003, with national sources, some of which may be unpublished. Retrieved from www.census.gov/compendia/statab/2012/tables/12s1335.xls

3. Women are less dependent on men. They now have careers of their own.
4. Stressful relationships contribute, especially since both work outside of the home.
5. Divorce is now more socially acceptable.
6. Divorce is now easier to legally obtain (Macionis, 2012). Since 1970, many states have moved to a no-fault divorce system, in which marriages can be ended on the basis of what are commonly called "irreconcilable differences."

As stated earlier, the divorce rate in the U.S. in 2008 was 5.2 per 1,000 population; even though it is one of the highest rates in the world, it has decreased from 7.9 per 1,000 population in 1980. Like marriage rates, divorce rates tend to decline in times of economic depression and rise during periods of prosperity. They also vary by geographic and social characteristics. Geographically, the general trend in the United States is for divorce rates to increase as one moves from east to west. Demographic figures show that more than one-half of all divorces are among persons in their late 20s and early 30s. While the numbers are fewer, the divorce rate is exceptionally high among teenagers. Divorce is also most frequent in the first 3 years after marriage, and the incidence is higher among the lower socioeconomic levels. Whether education, occupation, or income is used as an index of socioeconomic level, the divorce rate goes up as the socioeconomic level goes down.

The National Center for Policy Analysis reported in 1999 that states in the Bible Belt lead the United States in divorces. In the southern states included, the divorce rates are roughly 50% above the national average (Cracy, 1999). Rates in the South still tend to be higher than the national average. Do Southerners just have a harder time getting along? A true sociological explanation will look for trends and patterns. Experts cite low household incomes, the tendency to marry at a younger age, and religious belief systems that allow divorce as major factors in producing such a high divorce rate. After 1999, the Center for Disease Control and the National Center for Health Statistics ceased to publish aggregated divorce counts for all 50 states due to four major states failing to report their statistics. The findings will continue in the U.S. Census Reports.

These variations in rate of divorce give us clues about its causes. The fact that rates are higher in the western United States indicates that divorce may be related to the liberality of the laws and the degree of cultural mixing. Financial problems and emotional immaturity may be factors in the high rates found among teenagers. Difficulties in adjusting to new relationships or discrepancies in role expectations may contribute to the divorce rates in the first 3 years after marriage. Money problems, lack of education, and working at a low-status job may account for the rates found in the lower socioeconomic levels. Although other factors are involved, and there are some exceptions to these general patterns, divorce is not merely a result of personal characteristics. These variations illustrate how social and cultural factors can influence the chances that a marriage will end in divorce. Since the mid-1990s, a few states have enacted laws providing for "covenant marriages." Couples who marry under the category of a covenant marriage are voluntarily choosing to make divorce more difficult to obtain in the future. Once a couple has chosen the covenant marriage option, they give up the right to divorce under the no-fault system in the state where they were married. In covenant marriages, cause for divorce is usually limited to domestic violence, a felony conviction with jail time, or adultery. The movement to create covenant marriages was heavily driven by evangelical Christians who were alarmed by the rising U.S. divorce rate. As of 2009, three states offer the covenant marriage option: Louisiana, Arkansas, and Arizona.

**thinking** SOCIOLOGICALLY

1. The research suggests many advantages of small families over large ones. Can you think of ways that large families may be advantageous over small ones?
2. How would you explain the tremendous variation in divorce rates in the following: (a) from one country or society to another; (b) between religious and ethnic groups in a given country such as the United States or Canada; and (c) over time?

# 10.7 NONTRADITIONAL MARITAL AND FAMILY LIFESTYLES

In the United States today, many people are choosing alternatives to the *traditional family* that consisted of a husband, a wife, and two or more children. The husband was the authority and primary, if not sole, wage earner, whereas the wife was submissive to the husband and served as primary child caregiver and homemaker. Now, however, the diversity of families in this country is greater than ever before, and changes are occurring rapidly. Four nontraditional approaches to family life are discussed here in more detail: (1) nonmarital cohabitation, (2) childless marriage, (3) one-parent families, and (4) dual-career marriages.

## 10.7a Nonmarital Cohabitation

**Nonmarital cohabitation**, or living together, occurs when two adults who are not related or married to each other occupy the same dwelling as a couple in an intimate relationship or partnership. The "What is a family?" reference, as mentioned earlier in this chapter, was made in relation to defining families in nontraditional ways. Examples used to illustrate families defined in terms of intimate relationships, sexual bonds, and

**Nonmarital cohabitation**
An intimate arrangement in which two unmarried and unrelated adults share a common household or dwelling

family realms included examples of both heterosexual and homosexual (lesbian and gay) cohabitation.

Both heterosexual and same-sex unions are attracting increasing attention among social researchers, as well as policymakers. A number of churches are recognizing the legitimacy of gay/lesbian unions. A number of businesses are extending spousal benefits to both heterosexual and homosexual cohabitants. A number of communities are accepting the civil registration of such relationships. State and national legislators are being forced to reexamine who is to be included or excluded from social policies covering a range of issues (family/parent benefits, adoption, surrogate parenting, housing, and others).

Most census data on unmarried couples have tended to focus on the heterosexual union. More than 7.5 million unmarried couples lived together in 2010 (U.S. Bureau of the Census Population Survey, 2005–2009), more than ten times the number in 1970. Although nonmarital heterosexual cohabitation is not just a college-student phenomenon, nor is it confined to the generation under age 25, most research on cohabitation has involved college student populations. In a review of this research, Waite and his colleagues (2000) found that non-married cohabitants are significantly less committed to each other than married couples. With regard to the division of labor, cohabiting couples tended to mirror the society around them and accept gender roles characteristic of other couples their age. The same was true for sexual exclusivity. Most believed in sexual freedom within their non-married relationship, but most voluntarily limited their sexual activity with outsiders.

Nonmarital heterosexual cohabitation does not appear to be a substitute for marriage, a cure-all for marital problems, or a solution to the problem of frequent divorce. Most cohabitating relationships are short-term and last only a few months; however, the longer that couples cohabit, the more likely they are to eventually marry. However, according to the National Marriage Project completed by Rutgers University in 2005 and titled, "The State of Our Unions," while the divorce rates in the U.S. may be declining, more men and women are cohabitating, many with children, rather than marrying. In cohabiting heterosexual couples, as in married couples, women do most of the housework.

Unmarried couples, whether of the same or the opposite sex, experience problems quite similar to those of married couples: concern over financial matters, the division of labor, and relationships with extended family members. Although unmarried cohabitation does not fall within acceptable value limits for everyone, it does appear to have functional value for an increasing number of adults of all ages. For many couples, it provides a financially practical situation (two together can live more cheaply than two separately); a warm, homelike atmosphere; ready access to a sexual partner; an intimate interpersonal relationship; and for some, a highly exclusive, long-term partnership.

## 10.7b Childless Marriage

In recent years, the subject of the voluntarily childless marriage as an acceptable marital lifestyle has gained increased attention for a number of reasons. First, it is inconsistent with myths about the existence of a maternal instinct—the notion that all women want to have, love, and care for a child or children. Second, it changes the functions of marriage and the family that deal with reproduction, nurturant socialization, and social placement. Third, the availability and reliability of contraceptives and of abortion make it possible for women and couples to have no children if they so choose.

Veevers (1975) conducted in-depth interviews with childless wives living with their husbands and found that they held a number of uncommon beliefs about parenting. Most of these women were married to husbands who agreed that children were not desirable. The wives defined parenthood in negative rather than positive terms and denied the existence of a maternal instinct. They dismissed the accusation that childlessness was abnormal. Pregnancy and childbirth were perceived to be at best unpleasant and at worst difficult and dangerous. They regarded childcare as excessively burdensome and unrewarding and as having a deleterious effect on a woman's life chances. Finally, they defined parenthood as a trap that interfered with personal happiness.

The childfree alternative may be an acceptable family form and lifestyle for a small proportion of families. Under some conditions, as in the dual-career marriages discussed later, childlessness may be conducive to both personal and marital satisfaction and adjustment.

## 10.7c One-Parent Families

One-parent families are those in which the mother or, more commonly, the father does not share the household with the children and the remaining parent. As shown in Table 10-7, 85.5% of Asian American, 77.5% of white non-Hispanic, 67% of Hispanic origin, and 39.2% of black children under age 18 years were living with both parents in 2010. In the traditional view, this is the way family "should be," the most appropriate family structure for the socialization of children. However, 12.4% of Asian American children, 19.3% of white non-Hispanic children, 29% of Hispanic-origin children, and 53.3% of black children were living with the mother only. Living with the father only were 3.4% of all children, 23.3% with their mother only and 4.1% of all children living with neither parent.

There are approximately 75 million families in the U.S. Approximately 56 million are married-couple families and nearly 14 million are female-headed households with no father present. Nearly 10% of all families are below the poverty level, 4.8% of married-couple families are below the poverty level, and nearly 29% of families without a father present are below the poverty level (U.S. Bureau of the Census Population Survey, 2005–2009). All of these families below the poverty level are likely to receive Medicare, school lunches, and food stamps, and live in subsidized housing. These are the families affected most harshly by efforts to cut welfare, by religious group efforts to forbid abortion, and by government policies that demand what is called "workfare" (i.e., programs requiring

**Table 10-7** Living Arrangements of Children by Race and Ethnicity: 2010 (in Thousands)

| | All Races | | White | | Black | | Asian | | Hispanic | |
|---|---|---|---|---|---|---|---|---|---|---|
| Living Arrangements | # | % | # | % | # | % | # | % | # | % |
| **Children** | 74,718 | 100 | 71,089 | 100 | 11,272 | 100 | 3,300 | 100 | 6,491 | 100 |
| Living with: | | | | | | | | | | |
| Two Parents | 51,823 | 69.4 | 31,859 | 77.5 | 4,424 | 39.2 | 2,658 | 85.5 | 11,345 | 67.0 |
| Married Parents | 49,106 | 65.7 | 30,835 | 67.5 | 3,911 | 34.7 | 2,777 | 84.1 | 10,046 | 60.9 |
| Unmarried Parents | 2,717 | 3.6 | 1,024 | 2.5 | 513 | 4.6 | 45 | 1.4 | 1,020 | 6.0 |
| One Parent | 19,857 | 26.6 | 7,938 | 19.3 | 6,007 | 54.4 | 408 | 12.4 | 4,919 | 29.0 |
| Mother only | 17,285 | 23.1 | 6,382 | 15.5 | 5,791 | 53.3 | 334 | 10.1 | 4,456 | 26.3 |
| Father only | 2,572 | 3.4 | 1,555 | 3.8 | 405 | 3.6 | 74 | 2.2 | 463 | 2.6 |
| No parent | 3,038 | 4.1 | 1,292 | 3.1 | 841 | 7.5 | 70 | 2.1 | 677 | 4.0 |
| Grandparents only | 1,655 | 2.2 | 692 | 1.7 | 523 | 4.6 | 23 | 0.7 | 303 | 1.9 |
| Other relatives only | 650 | 0.9 | 196 | 0.05 | 206 | 1.8 | 22 | 0.7 | 192 | 1.1 |
| Nonrelatives only | 595 | 0.8 | 334 | 0.8 | 92 | 0.8 | 14 | 0.4 | 126 | 0.7 |
| Other arrangement | 138 | 0.2 | 711 | 0.2 | 20 | 0.2 | 11 | 0.3 | 29 | 0.2 |
| At least 1 biological parent | 70,236 | 94.0 | 39,033 | 95.0 | 10,213 | 90.6 | 3,113 | 94.3 | 16,008 | 94.5 |
| At least 1 stepparent | 6,156 | 6.2 | 2,818 | 6.9 | 627 | 5.6 | 81 | 2.5 | 933 | 5.5 |
| At least 1 adoptive parent | 1,258 | 1.7 | 701 | 1.7 | 177 | 1.6 | 109 | 3.3 | 193 | 1.8 |

Adapted from U.S. Census Bureau, Housing and Household Economic Statistics Division, Fertility & Family Statistics Branch, "America's Families and Living Arrangements, 2010," Tables FG10, Family Groups; Table C9, Children 1/by Presence and Type of Parent(s), Race and Hispanic Origin/2. Retrieved from http://www.census.gov/population/www/socdemo/hh-fam/cps2010.html

welfare recipients to work full- or part-time in order to receive their below-poverty-level income). Members of such families often have disproportionate school dropout rates, few job related skills, high unemployment rates, irregular incomes, little dental or other healthcare, and little control over their own fates.

In a cross-cultural study, Bilge and Kaufman (1983) contend that one-parent families are neither pathological nor inferior. Stigmatizing them in this way, they claim, is a refusal to recognize the economic inequalities of our society. They say that, in combination with an extended network of concerned kin (grandparents, siblings, uncles, aunts, etc.), single parent families can offer emotional support and that they are a suitable alternative to the traditional family. Bilge and Kaufman also note that around the world, one-parent female-headed families are able to bring up children and provide emotional support.

What happens to children in American female-headed families? Cashion (1982) reviewed the social-psychological research pertaining to female-headed families published between 1970 and 1980. She concluded that children in these families are likely to have good emotional adjustment, good self-esteem (except when they are stigmatized), comparable intellectual development to others of the same socioeconomic status, and rates of juvenile delinquency comparable to other children of the same socioeconomic standing. The major problems in these families stem from *poverty* and from *stigmatization*. Poverty is associated with problems in school and juvenile delinquency. It also contributes to poor attitudes among mothers about their situations and impairs a mother's sense of being in control. Stigmatization is associated with low self-esteem in children. It results in defining children as problems even when they do not have problems. Cashion's general conclusion is that the majority of female-headed families, when not plagued by poverty, have children who are as successful and well-adjusted as those of two-parent families.

As of 2010, 11.9% of American households are categorized as female-headed households with children, but there is significant variation in the share of female-headed households by race and ethnicity. Mothers without a father present headed about 7.8% of white non-Hispanic and 5.9% of Asian households. In contrast, single mothers with children accounted for 29.3% of all black households and 18.4% of Hispanic households (U.S. Bureau of the Census Population Survey, 2005–2009). While the percentage of female-headed households with children increased particularly rapidly among blacks in the later stages of the twentieth century, this trend appears to have slowed by the early 2000s (AmeriStat, 2003).



## 10.7d Dual-Career Marriages

One of the important social changes since World War II has been the increase of women, generally, and of married women, more specifically, in the labor force. In 1940, despite a sharp increase in the number of working wives during the depression of the 1930s, only 15% of all married women living with their husbands held an outside job. By 1960, the proportion had risen to 32%, 58.4% by 1990, and 61.4% by 2009 (U.S. Bureau of the Census Population Survey, 2005–2009).

Women who have children are less likely to hold jobs than those who do not, although with each decade the presence of children decreases in importance as a factor in whether women are employed. The proportion of married women in the labor force is highest among those who have no children under age 6 years to take care of at home. However, even among the women who have one or more children under age 6, more than half are employed. Most of these employed women are in clerical or service work, with earnings well below those of their male counterparts. Arrangements of this type are called "dual-employed marriages." (It is assumed, sometimes incorrectly, that the husband is also employed.)

Although women have been taking jobs in increasing numbers, the "dual-career" marriage is a relatively recent development. The word career is used to designate jobs that are taken not just to produce additional income but also for the satisfaction involved. Careers typically involve a higher level of commitment than just "paid employment," and they progress through a developmental sequence of increasing responsibility. One study, conducted by Burke and Weir (1976), of one- and two-career families found that women in two-career families reported fewer pressures and worries, more communication with husbands, more happiness with their marriages, and better physical and mental health than women who did not work outside the home. In contrast, the men in the two-career families, as opposed to one-career families, were in poorer health and less content with marriage, work, and life in general. It seems that the husband of a career wife loses part of his support system when his wife no longer functions as a servant, homemaker, and mother. Wives who have careers, on the other hand, are able to expand into roles that have a more positive value for them.

Despite these rewards for women, most studies of dual-career marriages suggest that they involve certain strains. One of these strains, particularly for women, develops due to what Fox and Nichols (1983) refer to as "time crunch." Wives are often expected to perform the majority of household tasks whether they have careers outside the home or not. In addition, wives usually accommodate more to the husband's career than vice versa, and husbands and wives have differential gains and losses when both have a career. Although the professional employment of women is gaining increasing acceptance, sexual equality in marriage has not yet been achieved. Wives are, generally, expected to give up their own jobs for the sake of their husbands and to consider their families their first duty.

### thinking SOCIOLOGICALLY

Does an increase in nontraditional marital and family lifestyles signify a breakdown of the family?

In regard to one-parent families, discuss the following:

(a) the adoption of children by single persons

(b) the feminization of poverty

(c) the need for children to have two parents

CHAPTER

# 10 Wrapping it up

## Summary

1. The family serves a number of different purposes. It is the primary social group, a system of interdependent statuses and structures, and a social institution organized to meet certain essential societal goals.
2. The smallest family units—nuclear and conjugal families—consist of persons related by blood, marriage, or adoption who share a common residence. Sociologists also distinguish families of orientation, families of procreation, extended families, and modified-extended families.
3. Families throughout the world vary in many different ways, such as in number of spouses. A person may have one spouse (*monogamy*) or two or more (*polygamy*). In *group marriages*, there are several people of each sex. *Sequential monogamy* involves having several wives or husbands in succession, but just one at any given time. *Polygyny*, in which one man is married to more than one woman, is the most common form of polygamy. *Polyandry*, in which one woman has several husbands, is very rare.
4. Families vary in their norms of residence. Most cultures adhere to one of three patterns: *neolocal*, in which the couple is free to choose its own place of residence; *patrilocal*, in which the couple lives in the groom's community; and *matrilocal*, in which the couple lives in the bride's community. Worldwide, the patrilocal pattern is the most common.
5. Families have different norms of descent and inheritance. The *patrilineal* pattern, in which lineage is traced through the father's kin, is the most common; however, there are also *matrilineal* and *bilateral* patterns.
6. Families vary in their norms of authority and decision-making. Sociologists recognize systems of three types: patriarchal, matriarchal, and egalitarian. The *patriarchal* pattern of male dominance, power, and authority is the most widespread.
7. Norms vary with regard to the marriage partner considered appropriate. *Endogamous rules* state that a marriage partner should be from a similar group. *Exogamous rules* state that marriage partners should be from a different group. Incest and same-sex marriages are almost universally forbidden, whereas marriage to a person of the same race, religion, and socioeconomic status is widely encouraged.
8. Several theoretical perspectives are widely used to explain family structures, interaction patterns, and behaviors. *Functionalists* examine variations in family structures, such as those just described, in terms of the functions they perform. According to this perspective, the family has many major functions: socialization, affection and emotional support, sexual regulation, reproduction, and social placement.
9. According to the *conflict perspective*, family members continually struggle for power and control. Conflict, which stems from the unequal distribution of scarce resources, is a major force behind social change.
10. The *exchange perspective* assumes that there are rewards and costs in all relationships, including those in marriage and the family. This view suggests that when selecting a spouse, people try to get the best they can with what they have to offer. The *complementary needs theory* proposes that people seek mates who will meet their needs without causing conflicts.
11. The *interactionist perspective* emphasizes the influence of role expectations and how people define situations. In this view, marriage, like other relationships, is a dynamic process of reciprocal interactions.
12. The *developmental perspective* focuses on the time dimension. Change is analyzed in terms of the family life cycle, a series of stages that families go through from their inception at marriage through their dissolution by death or divorce.
13. The American family system emphasizes norms of monogamy, neolocal residence, modified extended kinship, bilateral descent and inheritance, egalitarian decision-making, endogamous

marriage, and relatively free choice of mate. In a number of respects, however, the American family is quite variable.

14. Rates of marriage vary widely in terms of time period, geographical location, economic conditions, and other factors. The number of marriages also varies by season and by day of the week. The age at marriage in the United States, which declined from the turn of the century until the mid-1950s, has since increased; marriages among teenagers are unlikely to last.
15. Norms concerning family size and parent-child relations are influenced by such variables as socioeconomic status, religion, education, urbanization, and female participation in the labor force. Although most married couples have or want to have children, younger women today generally plan to have small families, compared with earlier generations.
16. The United States has one of the highest divorce rates in the world. Like birth rates, rates of divorce vary with time period, geographical location, and socioeconomic level, and differing techniques of computing the divorce rate yield different figures about the rate of divorce. Variations in these rates illustrate how social and cultural factors influence the chances of marital dissolution.
17. Many marital and family lifestyles exist today that do not conform to the traditional model of two parents, two or more children, with the husband and wife performing fixed roles. The number of unmarried couples of all ages who live together, for example, is increasing dramatically.
18. Childless marriages are increasingly common, in part because of the availability and reliability of contraceptives and abortion.
19. The number of one-parent families is increasing sharply, and many of these families are below the poverty level.
20. Marriages in which both spouses work have been common for a long time, but the dual-career marriage is a relatively recent development. There are many strains in these marriages, but women who have careers report fewer life pressures and worries and more happiness in their marriages. The men involved in two-career marriages tend to be relatively discontent, however.

## Discussion Questions

1. Discuss the importance of definitions of the family with regard to child custody policies.
2. What types of norms for choice of marriage partner—endogamy or exogamy—exist for you? These norms are encouraged and enforced in what ways?
3. Why does the United States insist on monogamy when many countries of the world permit polygamy? Why is polygyny very common and polyandry very rare?
4. How have norms of residence, descent and inheritance, authority, and choice of marriage partner changed in the United States over the past century? What do you think has led to these changes?
5. What types of questions would you ask about parent-child relations, using functionalist, conflict, interactionist, exchange, and developmental perspectives?
6. How do you explain the rapid increase in the median age at first marriage over the past two decades in the United States?
7. What types of social conditions are likely to affect the size of families in the United States and around the world? How does size affect family interaction patterns, educational systems, or the economy?
8. Should divorce be made more difficult to obtain? Why or why not? Discuss the consequences of divorce for men, women, children, and the society at large.
9. Discuss the pros and cons of nonmarital cohabitation. How are these types of relationships similar to or different from marriages?
10. What kinds of problems are encountered in dual-career marriages that do not occur in marriages where only one spouse is employed?

# CHAPTER 11

# Religious Groups and Systems

## SYNOPSIS



Throughout the world, people meditate, pray, join communes, worry about "being saved," partake in rituals, bow to statues, burn incense, chant, offer sacrifices, torture themselves, and proclaim their allegiance to many gods or to a particular god. Anthropologists suggest that events, acts, and beliefs such as these are part of every society, both today and throughout history. Together, these behaviors constitute a society's religious system.

Focal Point

## POLITICAL ISLAM: THE CASE OF SAUDI ARABIA

Saudi Arabia is a theocratic monarchy with Islam as the official religion. The Saudi king holds executive, legislative, judicial, and religious powers. His official title is the Custodian of the Two Holy Mosques, and he is both the prime minister and supreme religious leader of Saudi Arabia. Even so, because the constitution of Saudi Arabia emanates from the Qu'ran, the power of the king is not absolute; rather, his power is constrained by the strictures of Islam. The king remains one of the most influential leaders on earth, however, with a fifth of the world's proven oil reserves under his control (CIA World Factbook, 2009).

The Saudi government strongly encourages and supports a highly fundamentalist branch of Islam that seeks to purify the Muslim religion of any innovations or practices that stray from the original teachings of the Prophet Mohammed. Because of this, Saudi Arabia has some of the strictest religious laws in the world. What's more, the Saudi government has no legal protection for religious freedom because freedom of religion violates Wahhabism. Infidels are forbidden from practicing religion in public, and non-citizens have to carry identity cards indicating whether they're Muslim or non-Muslim (U.S. State Department, Saudi Arabia, 2007).

The Saudi government censors the press, blocks Internet sites, and prohibits criticism of the royal family and Wahhabism. This policy is not only enforced inside Saudi Arabia but also reaches overseas to such Saudi-owned media outlets as *Al Hayat*, a major pan-Arab newspaper in Lebanon and Morocco (Sharp, 2004). While most local newspapers are privately owned in Saudi Arabia, the Saudi government can vet editors and dismiss journalists at any time without cause. Since 1999, the Saudi government has blocked more than 2,000 websites deemed unfit for Muslim viewing (Herminda, 2002).

A system of Islamic courts handles all judicial cases in Saudi Arabia. A judge with religious training presides over each court. There are no juries. The king represents the highest court of appeals and has the power to pardon. While the Saudi government officially sanctions five schools of Islamic legal doctrine, Saudi universities focus almost exclusively on the Wahhabi school (U.S. State Department, 2008). Accordingly, most judges in Saudi Arabia follow Wahhabism in carrying out justice.

In the Saudi judicial system, institutionalized discrimination against infidels is an acceptable practice. For religious reasons, Jews and Christians face less discrimination than other infidels. However, all infidels are treated with less respect than Muslims. To illustrate, consider how Saudi judges calculate accidental death or injury compensation for male infidels. When a male plaintiff is Jewish or Christian, he can only be awarded half of what a Muslim male would receive under the same circumstances. If a male plaintiff is Buddhist or Hindu, he can only receive a sixteenth of that to which a male Muslim would be entitled (U.S. State Department, 2008).

In Saudi Arabia, education revolves around Islam. Accordingly, public schools in Saudi Arabia are also religious institutions. What's more, all Saudi students receive compulsory instruction in Wahhabism. In accordance with Islamic law, girls and boys attend separate schools. In many cases, Saudi students are taught to demean different religions and non-Wahhabi Islam (Blanchard, 2008). Infidels may only attend secular private schools because religious schools of any kind are banned for non-Muslims (U.S. State Department, 2008).

To enforce Islamic law, the Saudi government utilizes a corps of religious police called the *mutaween*. The *mutaween* has over 10,000 patrolmen working throughout Saudi Arabia (MacLeod, 2007). The *mutaween* can arrest married women for talking to unmarried men. They can detain anyone displaying homosexual behavior and arrest women for driving. They can punish anyone for eating pork or drinking alcohol. They even have the power to confiscate consumer products deemed un-Islamic. Perhaps the most egregious incident attributed to the *mutaween* in recent years occurred in 2002 when they blocked 15 schoolgirls from escaping a burning building because the girls weren't wearing proper Islamic dress. All 15 girls perished as a result of the *mutaween's* actions (BBC News, 2002).

Understanding political Islam in Saudi Arabia is relevant to sociology and this chapter because it underscores how religion can influence society in profound and different ways. The United States, for instance, has no official religion while the Saudis are officially Muslim. The U.S. constitution protects religious freedom. The Saudi constitution forbids it. The point is that religion is not only a simple matter of spirituality and personal belief but also a multifaceted social force with major implications for society.

(iStockphoto)

Religion has always been the anchor of identity for human beings. Religious beliefs give meaning to life, and the experiences associated with them provide personal gratification as well as a release from the frustrations and anxieties of daily life. Ceremonies, formal acts, or rituals are essential for both personal identity and social cohesion. We have ceremonies to rejoice about the birth of an infant, to initiate a young person into adult society, to celebrate a new marriage, to bury the dead, and to fortify our belief that life goes on. Most of these ceremonies are linked to religion.

# 11.1 A SOCIOLOGICAL APPROACH TO RELIGION

## 11.1a What Is Religion?

One of the earliest writers on the sociology of religion was the French sociologist Emile Durkheim. In *The Elementary Forms of the Religious Life* (1915), Durkheim defined *religion* as "a unified system of beliefs and practices relative to sacred things, that is to say, things set apart and forbidden—beliefs and practices which unite into one single moral community called a church, all those who adhere to them" (p. 47).

Durkheim identified several elements that he believed to be common to all religions. He viewed the first element, *a system of beliefs and practices*, as the cultural component of religion. The *beliefs* are states of opinion; and the practices, which Durkheim termed "rites," are modes of action. These beliefs and practices exist within a social context, consistent with the values and norms of the culture.

The second element, *a community or church*, he saw as the social organizational component. A church, in this sense, is not a building or even a local group that gathers together to worship. Rather, it is a collective of persons who share similar beliefs and practices. He claimed that in all history, we do not find a single religion without a community of believers. Sometimes, this community is strictly national. A corps of priests sometimes directs it, and it sometimes lacks any official directing body; however, it always has a definite group at its foundation. Even the so-called cults satisfy this condition, for they are always celebrated by a group or a family. What the community does is to translate the beliefs and practices into something shared, which led Durkheim to think of these first two elements—the cultural and social components of religion—as being linked. Contemporary sociologists of religion do recognize a functional difference between the two, in that a person may accept a set of religious beliefs without being affiliated with a particular church.

The third element, *sacred things*, he saw as existing only in relation to the profane. The **profane** is the realm of the everyday world: food, clothes, work, play, or anything generally considered mundane and unspiritual. In contrast, the **sacred** consists of objects or ideas that are treated with reverence and awe: an altar, bible, prayer, or rosary is sacred. A hamburger, rock song, football, or sociology text is profane. However, Durkheim believed that anything could become sacred. Sacredness

**Profane**

That which belongs to the realm of the everyday world; anything considered mundane and unspiritual

**Sacred**

Objects and ideas that are treated with reverence and awe

is not a property inherent in an object. It exists in the mind of the beholder. Thus, a tree, a pebble, a ring, a scarf worn by Elvis Presley, or a baseball bat used by Babe Ruth may be considered sacred.

An African child holds a rosary. Emile Durkheim believed that a sacred object could be a rosary, an altar, or a bible. He also believed that sacredness is not a property inherent in an object, but rather that sacredness exists in the mind of the beholder. (iStockphoto)

Durkheim hypothesized that religion developed out of group experiences as primitive tribes came to believe that feelings about sacredness were derived from some supernatural power. As people perform certain rituals, they develop feelings of awe, which reinforce the moral norms of society. When they no longer feel in awe of moral norms, society is in a state of anomie or without norms. Informal social control is possible largely because people have strong feelings that they should or should not do certain things. When people no longer have such feelings, social control breaks down. We see an example of this in some of our cities, where church doors are locked to prevent robberies. In many societies, nobody steals from churches because they believe they will be punished or suffer some form of retribution from their god(s).

Other sociologists present somewhat different views of religion, but most would agree that a **religion** has the following elements:

1. Things considered sacred, such as gods, spirits, special persons, or any object or thought defined as being sacred
2. A group or community of believers who make religion a social, as well as a personal, experience, because members of a religion share goals, norms, and beliefs
3. A set of rituals, ceremonies, or behaviors that take on religious meaning when they express a relationship to the sacred, such as in Christian ceremonies, when bread and wine are sacred components of communion that symbolize the body and the blood of Christ
4. A set of beliefs—such as a creed, doctrine, or holy book—which may define what is to be emphasized and/or how people should relate to society, or what happens to persons after their death
5. A form of organization that reinforces the sacred, unites the community of believers, carries out the rituals, teaches the creeds and doctrines, initiates new members, and so on.

**Religion**
An organized community of believers who hold certain things sacred and follow a set of beliefs, ceremonies, or special behaviors

**Animism**
The religious belief that spirits inhabit virtually everything in nature and control all aspects of life and destiny

**Shamanism**
The religious belief that certain persons (shamans) have special charm, skill, or knowledge in influencing spirits

## 11.2 THE ORGANIZATION OF RELIGION

People have tried to understand the world around them throughout history, but we do not know exactly how or why they began to believe in supernatural beings or powers. Societies such as the Bushmen of Africa, who rely on hunting and gathering as their primary means of subsistence, often explain things in naturalistic terms. This type of religion is known as **animism**, which is the belief that spirits inhabit virtually everything in nature—rocks, trees, lakes, animals, and humans alike—and that these spirits influence all aspects of life and destiny. Sometimes they help, perhaps causing an arrow to strike and kill a wild pig for food. At other times, they are harmful, as when they make a child get sick and die. Specific rituals or behaviors, however, can sometimes influence these spirits and pleasing them results in favorable treatment.

Some groups, such as the Tapajos of Brazil, practice a form of religion known as **shamanism**, which revolves around the belief that certain individuals, called "shamans," have special skill or knowledge in influencing the spirits that influence processes and events in the environment. Shamans (spiritual leaders), most of whom are men, are called upon to heal the sick and wounded, to make hunting expeditions successful, to protect the group against evil spirits, and to generally ensure the group's well-being. Shamans receive their power through ecstatic experiences, which might originate from a psychotic episode, the use of a hallucinogen such as peyote, or deprivation such as fasting or lack of sleep. More than 10 million people in the world are identified as shamanists. All but about 250,000 of these are located in Asia.

Within the United States, Native Americans of the Pacific Northwest who live on reservations hold that ancestral spirits work for the good or ill of the tribe through shamans. The shaman is a very powerful spiritual leader among most of the 176 Native American tribes recognized by the federal government. However, most Native Americans today do not follow the shaman or tribal spiritual leader. Most are urban and most are Christian—primarily Roman Catholic. Many have become involved in The Native American Church Movement, started in the late 1960s, which serves as a compromise between traditional ceremonial practices and Christian beliefs.

Totems such as these usually represent something important to the community. It is believed that totemism was one of the earliest forms of religion. (iStockphoto)

A third form of religion among selected groups is **totemism**, the worship of plants, animals, or other natural objects, both as gods and ancestors. The totem itself is the plant or animal, which is believed to be ancestrally related to a person, tribe, or clan. Totems usually represent something important to the community, such as a food source or a dangerous predator, and the people often wear costumes and perform dances to mimic the totem object. Most readers are probably familiar with the totem poles used by North American Indians in Ketchikan, Alaska. These tall posts, carved or painted with totemic symbols, were erected as a memorial to the dead. Totemism is still practiced today by some New Guinea tribes and by Australian aborigines. Durkheim believed that totemism was one of the earliest forms of religion and that other forms of religious organization evolved from it.

Religions may be organized in terms of the number of gods their adherents worship. **Polytheism** is belief in and worship of more than one god. Hinduism, which is practiced mainly in India, has a special god for each village and caste. People believe that these gods have special powers or control a significant life event, such as harvest or childbirth. Monotheism, on the other hand, is belief in only one god. **Monotheism** is familiar to most Americans because the two major religious groups in this country—Christians and Jews—believe in one god.

**BVT*Lab***

Flashcards are available for this chapter at www.BVTLab.com

Most Westerners are less familiar with such major religions as Buddhism, Confucianism, Shintoism, and Taoism. These religions are neither monotheistic nor polytheistic because they do not involve a god figure. They are based, rather, on sets of moral, ethical, or philosophical principles. Most are dedicated to achieving some form of moral or spiritual excellence. Some groups, such as the Confucianists, have no priesthood. Shintoism and Confucianism both place heavy emphasis on honoring one's ancestors, particularly one's parents, who gave the greatest of all gifts—life itself.

**Totemism**
The worship of plants, animals, and other natural objects as gods and ancestors

**Polytheism**
The belief in and worship of more than one god

**Monotheism**
The belief in one god

## 11.2a Churches, Sects, and Cults

Religious systems differ in many ways, and sociologists have devised numerous ways for classifying them. We have already seen how Durkheim divided the world into the sacred and the profane. Another scheme of classification that is used is that of churches, sects, and cults. This scheme focuses directly on the relationship between the type of religious organization and the world surrounding it.

Max Weber (1930) was one of the first sociologists to clarify the interrelationships between people's beliefs and their surroundings. In his classic essay, *The Protestant Ethic and the Spirit of Capitalism*, he argued that capitalism would not have been possible without Protestantism because Protestantism stressed the importance of work as an end in itself, of personal frugality, and of worldly success as a means of confirming one's salvation and evidence of God's favor. In dealing with this relationship between religion and the economy, he identified two major types of religious leaders. One, the **priest**, owes authority to the power of the office. By contrast, the **prophet** holds authority on the basis of charismatic qualities. Priestly and prophetic leaders are often in conflict, for the priest defends and represents the institution or society in question and supports the status quo. The prophet, not bound to a given institution, is more likely to criticize both the institutions and the general society.

This contrast led Weber to suggest that different sectors of society would develop different types of organizations to accompany their different belief systems. The ruling class or leaders, the better educated, and the more wealthy would need a more formalized type of religion that accepts modern science and the existing social world. The laboring class, the less educated, and the poor would need a type of religion that emphasizes another world or life and an emotional, spontaneous experience to console them regarding their deprivation in this life.

**Priests**

Religious leaders who owe their authority to the power of their office

**Prophets**

Religious leaders who have authority on the basis of their charismatic qualities

**Mysticism**

The belief that spiritual or divine truths come to us through intuition and meditation, not through the use of reason or via the ordinary range of human experience and senses

A German theologian and student of Weber, Ernst Troeltsch (1931), continued this line of thinking. Troeltsch divided religions into three categories: mysticism, churches, and sects. **Mysticism** is the belief that spiritual or divine truths come to us through intuition and meditation, not through the use of reason or the ordinary range of human experience and senses. Mystics, persons who believe in mysticism, practice their beliefs outside of organized religion. They often pose problems for other religious groups because they purport to be in direct contact with divine power. Evelyn Underhill, a Christian mystic, defines mysticism in the following way: "Mysticism, according to its historical and psychological definitions, is the direct intuition or experience of God; a mystic is a person who has, to a greater or less degree, such a direct experience—one

**Table 11-1** Characteristics of Churches, Sects, and Cults

| Characteristics | Church | Sect | Cult |
|---|---|---|---|
| Membership based on: | Faith | Conversion | Emotional commitment |
| Membership is: | Inclusive, regional/national boundaries | Closely guarded and protected | Closely guarded and protected |
| Size is: | Large | Small | Small |
| Class/wealth is: | Middle/higher | Lower, limited | Varies by recruit |
| Organization is: | Bureaucratic | Informal organization of faithful | Loose, organization around leader |
| Authority is: | Traditional | Charismatic | Charismatic |
| Emphasis is on: | Brother/sisterhood of all humanity | The select and faithful | New and unusual lifestyle |
| Clergy are: | Highly trained, professional | Deemphasized, high lay participation | Divinely chosen, individualized |
| Salvation is through: | Grace of God | Moral purity and being born again | Adherence to leader/cult demands |
| Relationship to state is: | Compromising, closely aligned | Hostile | Ignored and avoided |
| Theology is: | Modernistic | Fundamentalistic | Innovative, unique, pathbreaking |
| Worship is: | Formal, orderly | Informal and spontaneous | Innovative, often radical |

whose religion and life are centered, not merely on an accepted belief or practice, but on that which the person regards as first-hand personal knowledge."

The church and the sect are differentiated in many ways but in particular by their relationships with the world around them (see Table 11-1). A **church** is an institutionalized organization of people who share common religious beliefs. The membership of churches is fairly stable. Most have formal bureaucratic structures with trained clergy and other officials, and they are closely linked to the larger society and seek to work within it. The majority of the religious organizations in the United States would be considered churches.

**Church**
An institutionalized organization of people who share common religious beliefs

**Ecclesia**
An official state religion that includes all or most members of society

**Denominations**
Well-established and highly institutionalized churches

**Sects**
Religious groups that have broken away from a parent church, follow rigid doctrines and fundamentalist teachings, and emphasize "otherworldly" rewards, rejecting or deemphasizing contemporary society

**Fundamentalism**
The belief that the Bible is the divine word of God and that all statements in it are to be taken literally, word for word

Two categories of churches that are sometimes differentiated are the **ecclesia** and the **denomination**. An ecclesia is an official state religion that includes all or most of the members of society. As a state church, it accepts state support and sanctions the basic cultural values and norms of the society. Sometimes, it administers the educational system as well. The Church of England in Great Britain and the Lutheran churches in the Scandinavian countries are two contemporary examples of national churches. The contemporary power of these churches, however, is not as great as was the power of the Roman Catholic Church in Western Europe during the Middle Ages or even its power today in Spain, Italy, and many Latin American countries.

Churches in the United States are termed denominations. They are not officially linked to state or national governments. In fact, various denominations may be at odds with state positions on war, abortion, taxes, pornography, alcohol, equal rights, and other issues, and no nation has more denominations than the United States. The U.S. Bureau of the Census lists approximately 80 denominations with memberships of 60,000 or more (Statistical Abstract, 2000), but the list would probably exceed several hundred if all of the small or independent denominations were added.

Whereas churches (ecclesia and denominations) are well established and highly institutionalized, **sects** are small groups that have broken away from a parent church and that call for a return to the old ways. They follow rigid doctrines and emphasize fundamentalist teachings. **Fundamentalism** is the belief that the Bible is the divine word of God and that all statements in it are to be taken literally, word for word. Incidentally, this is a position taken by about one-third of the United States population (Wood, 1990), most of whom are not members of sects but are affiliated with institutionalized churches that take very conservative views toward social issues. The creationism controversy, for example, stems from the fundamentalist position that the world was literally created in 6 days. Sect groups follow this type of literal interpretation of the Bible, although different groups focus their attention on different Bible scriptures. Their religious services often involve extensive member participation, with an emphasis on emotional expression.

*Jim Jones was the founder of the cult the Peoples Temple in Jonestown, Guyana.* (AP Wide World Photo)

There are many sects in the United States today including the Jehovah's Witnesses, Jews for Jesus, and a number of fundamentalist, evangelical, and Pentecostal groups. Although evangelical groups, like fundamentalist groups, maintain that the Bible is the only rule of faith, they focus their attention on preaching that salvation comes through faith as described in the New Testament. Pentecostal groups, usually both evangelical and fundamentalist, are Christian sects with a highly emotional form of worship experience. Some contrasting characteristics of churches, sects, and cults are shown in Table 11-1.

Another form—some would say "extreme form"—of religious organization is the **cult**, the most loosely organized and most temporary of all religious groups. Unlike sects, cults—often under the direction of a charismatic leader—call for an unusual lifestyle. Jim Jones and Father Divine, for example, believed that they were divinely chosen to lead humanity, as does the Reverend Sun Myung Moon today. In cults, the emphasis is on the individual rather than on society. Because cults operate outside the mainstream of society and are focused around one leader or prophet, their existence depends on the life and health of their leader. In some cases, they have given up their more radical teachings and have become churches, accepting more mainstream beliefs. The Seventh-Day Adventists, for example, began as a cult group that proclaimed the end of the world on a specific date; but when that date passed, it maintained many of its other beliefs. Today, it is a church with a trained clergy, a stable membership, and a formal organizational structure.

**thinking** SOCIOLOGICALLY

Select your own religion or one with which you are well familiar. Identify the following for this religion: (a) things that are considered sacred, (b) selected characteristics of the membership or its adherents, (c) selected rituals or ceremonies in which the adherents participate, (d) key beliefs of the religion, and (e) the form of social organization that exists.

# 11.3 THEORIES OF RELIGION

## 11.3a A Functionalist Approach

The universality of religion suggests to the functionalist that religion is a requirement of group life and that it serves both manifest and latent functions. Unlike most people today, who view religion as primarily a private and personal experience, Durkheim, as discussed earlier in the chapter, believed that the primary function of religion was to *preserve and solidify society*. Noting that worship, God, and society are inseparable, he paid little attention to the other functions of religion. This perspective assumes that religion is the central focus for integrating the social system. By developing the awe that members of society feel for moral norms, religion functions to hold society together. This social solidarity is developed through rituals such as church or synagogue services, baptisms, bar (or bat) mitzvahs, Christmas caroling and gift-giving, and the multitude of observances and ceremonies practiced by specific religious groups.

A second function, related to promoting social solidarity, is to *create a community of believers*. A religion provides a system of beliefs around which people may gather to belong to something greater than themselves and to have their personal beliefs reinforced by the group and its rituals. Those who share a common ideology develop a collective identity and a sense of fellowship.

A third function is to *provide social control*. Religion reinforces social norms, providing sanctions for violations of norms and reinforcing basic values, such as property rights and respect for others. Society's existence depends on its members' willingness to abide by folkways and mores and to interact with one another in a spirit of cooperation and trust.

**Cult**
Extreme form of religious organization that calls for a totally new and unique lifestyle, often under the direction of a charismatic leader

This list of *manifest functions* performed by religion could be continued. Religion serves to *provide answers to ultimate questions*. Why are we here? Is there a supreme being? What happens after death? Religions provide systems of belief based on the faith that life has a purpose and that someone or something is in control of the universe. They make the world seem comprehensible, often by attributing familiar, human motives to supernatural forces. In addition, religion also provides *rites of passage*, *ceremonies*, and *rituals* designed to give sacred meaning and a social significance to birth, the attainment of adulthood, marriage, death, and other momentous events.

Religion also helps to *reconcile people to hardship*. All societies have inequality, poverty, and oppression, and everyone experiences pain, crises, prejudice, and sorrow. By belonging to a religion, people may come to feel that they are special in some way—that they will be rewarded in the future for having suffered today. Many religions call for caring, mercy, charity, kindness, and other prosocial behaviors. They may provide moral, ethical, social, and even financial support to those in need.

Religion can also *cultivate social change*. Many religious groups criticize social injustice, existing social morality, and community or government actions. Some take action to change unfavorable conditions. The churches have been a major force in the civil rights movement, for example. Many protests against the Vietnam War were a result of religious teachings about love and peace. Religious groups opposed to social reforms have mounted other major protests, in opposition to the right to have an abortion, equal rights for homosexuals, and the women's rights movement.

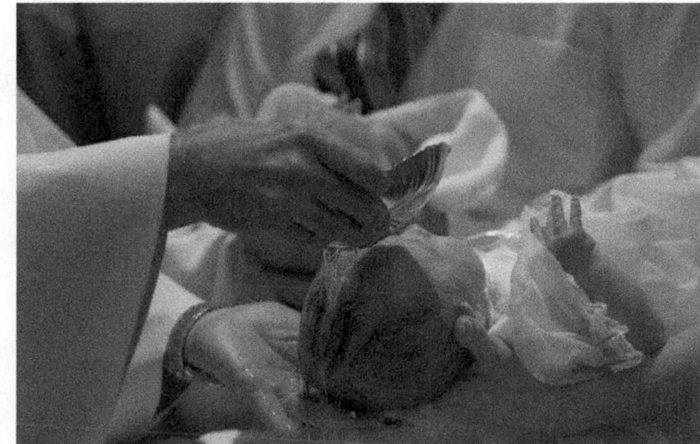

Durkheim believed religion served to preserve and solidify society through rituals such as baptisms, church services, and gift-giving. He also believed that those who share a common ideology develop a collective identity and a sense of fellowship. (iStockphoto)

Some latent functions of religion concern mate selection, experience in public speaking, and psychic rewards for donating funds or labor to worthy causes. Other groups and systems may be able to fulfill some of these manifest or latent functions, but many social scientists argue that particular functions provided by religion cannot be adequately met by other means. Other social scientists might suggest that some of the functions of religion may not be needed by society.

While religion performs many basic functions for society and individuals, it is likely to have dysfunctions as well. If it serves to preserve and solidify society, to create a community of believers, to reinforce social norms, and to reconcile people to hardship, it also can serve to divide society, create bias against the nonbeliever, exclude nonmembers of the group, and maintain the status quo. Religion can be dysfunctional in forcing people to accept inequities and in inhibiting its members from acting to change them. It can be dysfunctional in convincing its followers to reject this world for a future life in which rewards are guaranteed, and it can often inhibit the search for and acceptance of new truths, new ideas, and additional knowledge.

Examples of religion as both a source of integration and conflict are evident throughout the world. Some fundamentalist teachings of Islam have been interpreted to convince youth that it is honorable to die in wars for their country. In Northern Ireland, protests and violence abound between Catholics and Protestants. In the Middle East, the conflicts between Jews and Muslims are intense. In India and Pakistan, caste and class conflicts linked to religious traditions cause death and destruction. In many countries, Jews are persecuted. Overpopulation and wars can be justified in the name of religion. As mentioned elsewhere, to have in-groups is to have out-groups. To believe that there is only one Truth is to reject all ideas that challenge prejudices.

## APPLYING THE FUNCTIONALIST APPROACH TO RELIGION

Some useful insights provided by the functionalist approach are that religion serves a variety of essential social functions and that an understanding of religion is closely linked to an understanding of an entire culture.

For example, can we understand Israel without knowing about Judaism, Saudi Arabia without knowing about Islam, or the United States without knowing about Christianity? Judeo-Christian religions penetrate most of our lives—even though we may be unaware of it and may not subscribe to any particular religion. This is exemplified even by our legal tender, on every piece of which is the phrase, "In God We Trust." Our entire economic system is imbued with religious overtones.

The knowledge that religion serves basic social functions may be useful in a number of careers. Notably, people whose jobs lead them to deal with foreign cultures might benefit from a thorough understanding of the major religions in those countries. Consider, for example, the difficulties that politicians, diplomats, and military personnel from the United States might have in dealing with the governments in the Middle East if they do not first understand the basic religions in these countries, their influence on Middle Eastern culture, and how they contrast with the Protestant ethic, one of the mainstays of U.S. culture. In the war with Iraq in 2003, many Americans came to realize just how important it is to understand the impact of a country's religious traditions on its culture. Many American soldiers, other military personnel, medical personnel, news reporters, and others who observed the war had to adjust to what they thought were the odd attitudes that the Arab world has toward such things as gender roles, alcohol use, and the female body. Imagine what it must be like for someone from the Middle East who comes to the United States, where many religious viewpoints are tolerated.

*Using the same type of advertising in the Middle Eastern countries as is used in the United States would be a mistake because gender roles are viewed differently. (iStockphoto)*

Because religion plays such a key part in a society's values, norms, roles, and beliefs, people involved in international business may benefit by fully understanding a country's religious traditions. This could be especially true in the advertising of products. Even though most advertisements in the United States are still geared toward traditional gender roles, for example, many are beginning to cater to the changing roles of women and men in American society. Considering again the example of Islam, we see that using this type of advertising would be a serious mistake in Middle Eastern countries, where religion plays a central role in keeping marriage and homemaking the central occupations of women.

## 11.3b A Conflict Approach

As discussed in previous chapters, the conflict approach focuses on the exploitation of the poor by the elite. The classical Marxist perspective suggests that religion, like other social structures, can be understood only in the context of its role in the economic system.

In sharp contrast to the functionalist approach, conflict theorists view religion as a tool that the elite use to get the poor to obey authority and to follow the rules established by the privileged. Religion counsels the masses to be humble and to accept their condition. In the words of Karl Marx, religion "is the opiate of the masses" because it distracts them from finding practical political solutions to their problems. The powerless find an illusion of happiness through religion and look forward to future life after death, where the streets will be paved with gold and life will be joyful and everlasting. Marx urged revolution so that people could experience during life the joy and freedom that religion postpones until after death. In American society, we supplement that illusion of happiness by focusing upon individualism and meritocracy. Loosely, meritocracy advocates that "you get what you deserve and you deserve what you get." These two belief systems shore up the religious ideas that help to hold the inequality and lack of action in place.

Most theorists today would agree that religion serves interests other than those of the ruling class, but it is unquestionably true that there are strong relationships between religion and social class. Churches are highly segregated along racial and economic lines. In the United States, a number of denominations are largely or wholly black. Although the ideals of religious faith are supposed to unite people across the great chasms carved by race and ethnicity, social scientists have long noted that church attendance is perhaps the most highly segregated activity in the United States. In 2008, in a campaign interview, President Barack Obama reiterated this observation by saying, "The most segregated hour of American life occurs on Sunday morning" (National Public Radio, 2008).

Within the white population, different religious groups tend to attract people of similar educational and occupational levels. For example, few factory workers are Episcopalians, and few professional people and company executives are Baptists or members of Pentecostal groups. Some groups, such as the Roman Catholic Church, have working-class as well as wealthy members; however, the data generally show that occupation and income vary with religious affiliation.

Is religion related to class conflict? In a general way, the answer is yes. Religious affiliation is related to class, and many social controversies result from perceptions that differ according to social class. Opinions on such issues as prayer in public schools, the teaching of creationism, abortion, women as clergy, the Equal Rights Amendment, and homosexuality vary both by class and by religion. The conservative positions are generally supported both by fundamentalist and Pentecostal churches and by people who have lower incomes and less education.

## APPLYING THE CONFLICT APPROACH TO RELIGION

In pointing out how religion is related to class conflict, the conflict approach yields some other useful findings. One is that occupation and income vary with religious affiliation. This is an important fact for church leaders to consider. By knowing that the members of a particular religious congregation are likely to be from a particular social class, ministers, priests, deacons, rabbis, and others could address the relevant needs of that congregation and might formulate examples to which the people can relate.

In Latin America, a branch of religious teaching known as "liberation theology" has been gaining wide acceptance. Liberation theology directly applies church policy and intervention to the social and class conflicts that plague Latin American society. Church leaders who support this approach speak out against repressive government policies, promote land reform, and generally act as advocates for the peasant population. Although not condoned by Catholic leadership in Rome, many priests praise liberation theology as an example of the applicability of religion to social welfare.

Understanding the relationship between social class and religious affiliation could be useful for you personally. You can learn a great deal about a community, for instance, by noticing its variety of churches. If you see a fairly broad representation of Baptist, Methodist, Catholic, and Episcopalian churches and Jewish synagogues, you know that the community has a fairly wide range of income and educational levels and probably a diversity of political attitudes. However, a preponderance of one type of church or temple might be a reflection of a community with less cultural diversity and less tolerance for differences.

## thinking SOCIOLOGICALLY

1. Evaluate the major social functions of religion provided in this chapter. Can you give examples to illustrate each function? Do these functions exist for all religions?
2. From the conflict perspective, how does religion serve the elite?

# 11.4 RELIGIONS OF THE WORLD

The world population is more than 7 billion. About 16% of these people are listed as nonreligious (see Figure 11-1). Thus, whether we refer to Asia, to Russia and other countries in the Commonwealth of Independent States, to North America, or to Africa, the majority of people in the world adhere to or profess adherence to some religion.

It is difficult to obtain accurate counts of the number of adherents to the world's religions. The procedures used by different countries and groups to measure religious membership vary widely. Some assessments include only adults; others include everyone who attends services. Some people may be included in several different religious groups, such as Confucianism, Taoism, and Shintoism. Some religions forbid counts of their members. In countries where a particular religion has prevailed for many centuries (such as Christianity in Europe and Hinduism in India), the entire population may be reported as adherents. While most of us are likely to be familiar with one or two specific religions, we may be less familiar with others. We now briefly examine some major ones.

**Christianity**
One of the principal religions of the world, followers of which profess faith in the teachings of Jesus Christ

**Judaism**
The oldest religion in the Western world and the first to teach monotheism, the Jews are both an ethnic community and a religious group.

## 11.4a Christianity and Judaism

More than 2 billion people adhere to **Christianity**, and more than 14 million adhere to Judaism in the world today. Christians, who comprise about one-third of the world's population (see Table 11-2), profess faith in the teachings of Jesus Christ as found in the New Testament of the Bible, whereas adherents to **Judaism** find the source of their beliefs in the Hebrew Bible (called the "Old Testament" by Christians), especially in its first five books, which are called the "Torah." The Torah was traditionally regarded as the primary revelation of God, originally passed on orally and eventually written.

**Figure 11-1** Religions of the World and Number of Adherents

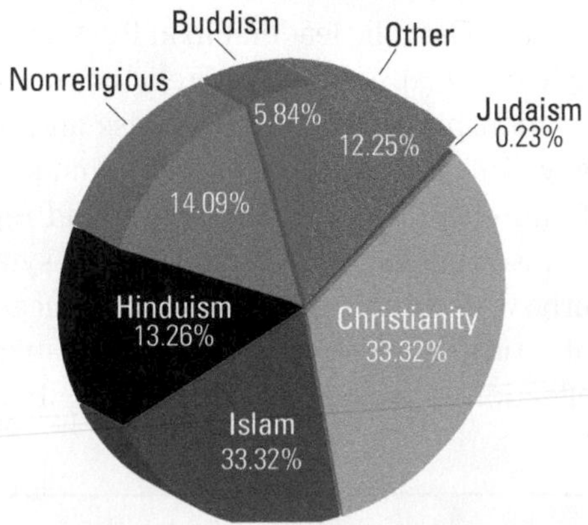


*Note.* Percentages are based on estimates of the numbers of adherents of different religions in the world population in 2007.

Adapted from CIA World Factbook 2009.

Judaism is the oldest religion in the Western world. It comprises both a religious and an ethnic community. It was the first religion to teach monotheism, which was based on the Old Testament verse "Hear O Israel, the Lord our God, the Lord is one" (Deuteronomy 6:4). Jews, the people who identify with and practice Judaism, believe that God's providence extends into a special covenant with the ancient Israelites: to bring God's message to humanity by their example. As a result, the emphasis is on conduct rather than on doctrinal correctness. Adherents to Judaism have a considerable measure of latitude in matters of belief because their beliefs have never been formulated in an official creed. This lack of an official creed also meant that Judaism did not stop developing after the Bible was completed. One result of this development was the traditional Jewish prayer book, which reflects the basic beliefs of Judaism as well as changes in emphasis in response to changing conditions.

*A Shinto ceremony in Japan (iStockphoto)*

Judaism has a system of law that regulates civil and criminal justice, family relationships, personal ethics and manners, and social responsibilities to the community, as well as worship and other religious observances. Individual practice of these laws varies greatly. Some widely observed practices concern strict adherence to kosher foods, daily prayer and study, the marital relationship, and the meaning of the yarmulke (skullcap) and tefillin (worn on the forehead and left arm during morning prayers).

The Jewish religious calendar, which is of Babylonian origin, consists of 12 lunar months, amounting to approximately 354 days. Six times over a 19-year cycle, a 13th month is added to adjust the calendar to the solar year. The Sabbath is from sunset Friday to sunset Saturday.

Male children are circumcised on the eighth day after birth as a sign of the covenant with Abraham. At age 13, Jewish boys undergo the rite of becoming a bar mitzvah to signify adult status and a responsibility for

**Table 11-2** Estimates of World Adherents to Religions

|  |  |
|---|---|
| Christianity: | 2.1 billion |
| Islam: | 1.5 billion |
| Secular/Nonreligious/Agnostic/Atheist: | 1.1 billion |
| Hinduism: | 900 million |
| Chinese traditional religion: | 394 million |
| Buddhism: | 376 million |
| Primal-indigenous: | 300 million |
| African traditional & diasporic: | 100 million |
| Sikhism: | 23 million |
| Juche: | 19 million |
| Spiritism: | 15 million |
| Judaism: | 14 million |
| Baha`i: | 7 million |
| Jainism: | 4.2 million |
| Shinto: | 4 million |
| Cao Dai: | 4 million |
| Zoroastrianism: | 2.6 million |
| Tenrikyo: | 2 million |
| Neo-Paganism: | 1 million |
| Unitarian-Universalism: | 800 thousand |
| Rastafarianism: | 600 thousand |
| Scientology: | 500 thousand |

*Note.* Sizes shown are approximate estimates, and are here mainly for the purpose of ordering the groups, not providing a definitive number. This list is sociological/statistical in perspective.

Retrieved from http://www.adherents.com/Religions_By_Adherents.html

performing the commandments. A similar ceremony for girls, the bat mitzvah, is a more recent innovation.

Christianity diverged from Judaism in ancient Israel. Christians considered Jesus to be the Jewish savior, or Messiah, and incorporated the traditional Hebrew writings of Christ's followers into the canon of their faith, the Bible. After Christ's death (and, as Christians believe, his resurrection), his teachings spread to Rome and many other centers of the Roman Empire. When the Roman Empire split in AD 1054, so did the Christian Church; it came to be called the Orthodox Church in the East and the Roman Catholic Church in the West. The Roman Catholic Church was united under popes until the sixteenth century. Today, of the estimated 2 billion plus Christians, nearly 57% are Roman Catholic. Slightly more than one-third are Protestant, and the rest are Eastern Orthodox.

Christians, like Jews, believe in one god (monotheism); but for most Christians, their God takes the form of a Holy Trinity: Father, Son, and Holy Spirit. Christians experience God as the Father, Jesus Christ as the Son of God, and the Holy Spirit as the continuing presence of God. Also, most Christians worship on Sunday instead of Saturday, which is the Jewish Sabbath. They also practice baptism by water when they become adherents or give a public testimony of their acceptance of Christ and of Christ's divinity. Christians also take the Eucharist, a sacred meal recalling the last supper that Jesus had with his disciples. The breaking of bread and the drinking of wine—symbolizing the body and blood of Christ, respectively—are sacred acts (sacraments) to most Christians. Prayer and preaching are also important Christian functions.

**BVT*Lab***

Visit www.BVTLab.com to explore the student resources available for this chapter.

## 11.4b Islam

There are nearly 1 billion Islamic adherents in the world. Followers of **Islam** follow the teachings of the Qu'ran (Koran) and of Muhammad, a prophet. Islam means "surrender, resignation," and "submission." A person who submits to the will of Allah, the one and only God, is called a Muslim (sometimes spelled Moslem). This surrender involves a total commitment to faith, obedience, and trust in this one God. The insistence that no one but God be worshiped has led many Muslims to object to the term "Muhammadanism," a designation widely used in the West but thought to suggest that Muhammad, a great prophet of Islam, is worshiped in a manner that parallels the worship of Christ by Christians.

*Followers of Islam follow the teachings of the Koran and of Muhammad, a prophet. In this photo, Muslim children read the Koran. (iStockphoto)*

It is sometimes assumed that Islam originated during the lifetime of Muhammad (AD 570–630), specifically during the years in which he received the divine revelations recorded in the Muslim sacred book, the Koran. Many Muslims, however, believe that the prophet Muhammad simply restored the original religion of Abraham.

Islam encompasses a code of ethics, a distinctive culture, a system of laws, and a set of guidelines and rules for other aspects of life. The Muslim place of worship is the mosque, and the chief gathering of the congregation takes place on Fridays. Muslims profess their faith by repeating, "There is no God but God, and Muhammad is the messenger of God." The Muslims also have a deep awareness of the importance of a fellowship of faith and a community of believers.

**Islam**
One of the world's principal religions, followers of which adhere to the teachings of the Koran and of Muhammad, a prophet

The Koran includes rules for ordering social relationships. It is especially explicit about matters pertaining to the family, marriage, divorce, and inheritance. The family is basically authoritarian, patriarchal, polygamous, patrilineal, and largely patrilocal. Women are clearly subordinate to men and receive only half the inheritance that male heirs receive. Muslim males may marry non-Muslim women but in countries where the

Muslim holy law is the law of the state, Muslim women may not marry outside their faith. A Muslim male may take up to four wives (polygyny) and traditionally can divorce a wife by simple pronouncement and dowry repayment. Children, especially sons, are perceived as desirable.





sociologyatwork

## Helping Religious Refugees Readjust

Baila Miller received a doctorate in sociology at the University of Illinois at Chicago Circle. She used her sociological training in a variety of ways. She was a member of the faculty doing applied research in gerontology in the Department of Medical Social Work at the University of Illinois at Chicago. Prior to that, she handled publications and training for SPSS, a computer software company; before that she was the assistant director of research at the Jewish Federation of Metropolitan Chicago.

It was at the Jewish Federation where Miller first used her sociological training to earn a living. When Miller was asked how she used her sociological training in her work at the Jewish Federation, she responded, "The federation raises charitable funds and allocates them to Jewish causes in Israel and overseas and to local Jewish social welfare, health, and educational institutions. The office of research and planning where I worked was a small department—just three people. We were responsible for analyzing the budgets of some of the agencies we supported, for preparing service statistics for submission to the United Way, for collecting and analyzing data needed by our volunteer committees, and for carrying out special research projects."

It was in these special research projects that Miller found the fullest application of her training. "In one project we completed a survey of the Jewish population of greater Chicago," she says—a survey that presented unique problems among population studies because the U.S. Bureau of the Census does not collect data on religious affiliations in its decennial census. "We wanted to determine many things about the Jewish community: How many people were there? Where did they live? How did they maintain their Jewish identity? Did they participate in religious observances and in Jewish education? What were their service needs and how could a Jewish agency meet [these needs]? Should we have concentrated on services for the elderly or on childcare for two-career families? Who were the Jewish poor?"

Clearly, many areas of Miller's sociological training came into play with this one study alone. In addition to needing knowledge of various types of quantitative and qualitative research techniques, she needed to know about substantive areas in sociology—such as minority groups, religious groups, population, community, families, and social psychology—which were invaluable to her research.

Another project with which Miller was involved at the Jewish Federation was a study of the adjustment of Soviet Jewish émigrés to life in various communities in the United States. Miller analyzed data about Soviet Jewish émigrés in a number of ways. First, at the individual level, she studied how these people adjusted to American life in terms of occupational achievement, language acquisition, social and cultural involvement in the Jewish community, and maintenance of Jewish identity. She looked at the effects of background characteristics—social and economic status and place of origin in the former Soviet Union—and of mediating factors, such as the type of resettlement services that were offered in various communities in this country. Second, on the community level, she looked at aggregate measures of differences in adjustment in various cities in the United States. This included an investigation of comparable studies that were done in 13 U.S. cities and a cross-cultural analysis of the similarities and differences with other large refugee or émigré groups, particularly Asians and Mexicans. Finally, she did a policy analysis of different programs offered by Jewish agencies and national refugee organizations in order to determine their effectiveness.

Although laws are changing in many Islamic countries and the education of women has increased dramatically, fewer females than males attend school; even fewer women receive a higher education. Marriage and housekeeping are considered the proper occupations of women. Therefore, it is not surprising that Islam is finding it difficult to come to terms with the scientific ideas and the technology of the Western world. Since it is difficult to accurately report the number of Muslims in the United States due to the U.S. Census not reporting religious identification, we have to estimate the members to be from 7 million to 8 million based on recent studies (Ali, 2008).

## 11.4c Hinduism

The greatest majority of the 786 million Hindus in the world are residing in India, Pakistan, and Nepal. The state religion of Nepal is Hinduism. Until 2008, the King of Nepal was considered a dependent of the Hindu god Vishnu. In India, approximately 85% of the population is Hindu. **Hinduism** has evolved over about 4,000 years and comprises an enormous variety of beliefs and practices. It hardly corresponds to most Western conceptions of religion because organization is minimal, and there is no religious hierarchy.

Hinduism is so closely intertwined with other aspects of the society that it is difficult to describe it clearly, especially in regard to castes. Hindus sometimes refer to the ideal way of life as fulfilling the duties of one's class and station, which means obeying the rules of the four great castes of India: the Brahmans, or priests; the Kshatriyas, warriors and rulers; the Vaisyas, merchants and farmers; and the Sudras, peasants and laborers. A fifth class, the Untouchables, includes those whose occupations require them to handle "unclean" objects.

*Ganesh is the Hindu god of success. Hindu belief holds that the universe is populated by a multitude of gods (polytheism) who behave much as humans do, and worship of these gods takes many forms. (iStockphoto)*

These classes encompass males only. The position of women is ambiguous. In some respects, they are treated as symbols of the divine; yet in other ways, they are considered inferior beings. Traditionally, women have been expected to serve their husbands and to have no independent interests; however, this is rapidly changing.

Although caste is a powerful influence in Hindu religious behavior, a person's village community and family are important as well. Every village has gods and goddesses who ward off epidemics and drought. Hindu belief holds that the universe is populated by a multitude of gods (polytheism) who behave much as humans do, and worship of these gods takes many forms. Some are thought to require sacrifices, others are worshiped at shrines or temples, and shrines devoted to several gods associated with a family deity are often erected in private homes.

To Hindus, the word *dharma* means the cosmos, the social order. Hindus practice rituals that uphold the great cosmic order. They believe that to be righteous, a person must strive to behave in accordance with the way things are. In a sense, the Hindu sees life as a ritual. The world is regarded as a great dance determined by one's karma, or personal destiny and the final goal of the believer is liberation from this cosmic dance. Hindus also believe in *transmigration of souls*: After an individual dies, that individual's soul is born again in another form, as either a higher or a lower being, depending on whether the person was righteous or evil in the previous life. If an individual becomes righteous enough, the soul will be liberated and will cease to be reborn into an earthly form and will exist only as spirit.

**Hinduism**
One of the world's principal polytheistic religions, with no religious hierarchy but a close involvement with society and the cosmic order, that is practiced mainly in India and Pakistan

A fundamental principle of Hinduism is that our perceptions of the external world are limitations. When we think about one thing, we are cut off from the infinite number of things that we are not thinking about but could be. If we think of nothing, we become in tune with the universe and freed of these limitations. One means of doing this is through meditation.

The actual belief systems of India are extremely confusing to Westerners because so many different tribal religions have been assimilated into Hinduism; but the basic nature of polytheism, in general, and of Hinduism, in particular, permits new gods to be admitted.

## 11.4d Buddhism

**Buddhism** has about 376 million adherents. It is impossible to precisely determine the number of Buddhists because many people accept Buddhist beliefs and engage in Buddhist rites while practicing other religions, such as Shintoism, Confucianism, Taoism, or Hinduism.

Buddhism is thought to have originated as a reaction against the Brahmanic tradition of Hinduism in the fifth century BC. At this time, a prince named Siddhartha Gautama was born in northern India to a prosperous ruling family. As he grew older, the suffering he witnessed among the people distressed him. At age 29, he left his wife and family to go on a religious quest. One day, while sitting under a giant fig tree, he passed through several stages of awareness and became the first Buddha, the enlightened one. He decided to share his experience with others and became a wandering teacher, preaching his doctrine of the "Four Noble Truths": (1) This life is suffering and pain. (2) The source of suffering is desire and craving. (3) Suffering can cease. (4) The practice of an "eightfold path" can end suffering. The eightfold path consisted of right views, right intentions, right speech, right conduct, right livelihood, right effort, right mindfulness, and right concentration. It combined ethical and disciplinary practices, training in concentration and meditation, and the development of enlightened wisdom. This doctrine was Buddha's message until age 80, when he passed into final nirvana, a state of transcendence forever free from the cycle of suffering and rebirth.

*A Buddhist monk prays. Buddhism is thought to have originated as a reaction against the Brahmanic tradition of Hinduism in the fifth century BC. (iStockphoto)*

After Buddha's death, legends of his great deeds and supernatural powers emerged. Stories were told of his heroism in past lives, and speculations arose about his true nature. Some groups viewed him as a historical figure, whereas others placed him in a succession of several Buddhas of the past and a Buddha yet to come. Differing views eventually led to a diversity of Buddhist sects in different countries. Some remained householders who set up Buddha images and established many holy sites that became centers of pilgrimage. Others became monks, living in monastic communities and depending on the laity for food and material support. Many monks became beggars, and in several Southeast Asian countries they still go on daily alms rounds. They spend their days in rituals, devotions, meditation, study, and preaching. Flowers, incense, and praise are offered to the image of the Buddha. These acts are thought to ensure that the monks will be reborn in one of the heavens or in a better place in life, from which they may be able to attain the goal of enlightenment.

**Buddhism**
One of the world's principal religions, adherents of which follow the teachings of Buddha, the enlightened one, who preached a doctrine of "Four Noble Truths"

In every society where Buddhism is widespread, people combine Buddhist thought with a native religion, supporting the monks and paying for rituals in the temples. These societies are also organized around other religions, however.

Today, the integration of Buddhism into many cultures has resulted in different interpretations of the way to Buddhahood. Yet we can supposedly reach Nirvana by seeing with complete detachment, which is seeing things as they really are without being attached to any theoretical concept or doctrine.

## 11.4e Confucianism

**Confucianism**, which has about 5.8 million adherents, is associated primarily with China, the home of nearly 180 million adherents to Chinese folk religions. Confucianism has influenced the civilizations of Korea, Japan, and Vietnam, as well as China. Confucianism is the philosophical and religious system based on the teachings of Confucius, who was born to a poor family in 551 BC, in what is today Shantung Province in China, and was orphaned at an early age. As a young man, he held several minor government positions; however, he became best known as a teacher, philosopher, and scholar. Distressed by the misery and oppression that surrounded him, he dedicated his life to attempting to relieve the suffering of the people.

By talking with younger men about his ideas to reform government so that it served the people rather than the rulers, Confucius attracted many disciples. He emphasized the total person, sincerity, ethics, and the right of individuals to make decisions for themselves. Although Confucius was not a religious leader in the usual sense of the word, he believed that there was a righteous force in the universe and yet his philosophy was founded not on supernaturalism but on humanity. He said that virtue is to love people, and wisdom is to understand them.

The basic philosophy of Confucius is found in his many sayings: "All people are brothers." "Sincerity and reciprocity should be one's guiding principles." "The truly virtuous person, desiring to be established personally, seeks to establish others; desiring success for oneself can help others to succeed." "The superior person stands in awe of three things: the ordinances of heaven, great persons, and the words of sages." The ideals of Confucius were motivated not by the desire for rewards or an afterlife but simply by the satisfaction of acting in accordance with the divine order.

Confucius had a pervasive influence on all aspects of Chinese life—so much so that every county in China built a temple to him. Everyone tried to live in accordance with the Confucian code of conduct. His values guided human relations at all levels—among individuals, communities, and nations. His thought guided conduct in work and in the family. Even today, the Chinese who profess to be Taoists, Buddhists, or Christians still generally act in accordance with Confucian ideals.

**Confucianism**

One of the world's principal religions, found mainly in China, adherents of which follow the teachings of Confucius

One of the books in the classical literature of Confucius is the *Book of Changes*, or the *I Ching*. This book is familiar to many Americans and is used to guide a person's behavior and attitude toward the future.

### thinking SOCIOLOGICALLY

Given the tremendous variability in religious beliefs and practices around the world, consider statements such as these:

1. Religious truth is only found in a literal interpretation of the Bible.
2. Religion is a social creation.
3. Whether there is no god, one god, or many gods is only relevant in terms of what people believe.

# 11.5 RELIGION IN THE UNITED STATES

Christianity predominates in the United States. The Roman Catholic Church is the largest religious group in the United States with more than 57 million adult members (25% of the adult population). When combined, more than half (around 51%) of the adult population (around 116 million) in this country are non-Catholic Christians, including around 112 million Protestants, 3 million Mormons, and 800,000 Greek Orthodox (U.S. Census Bureau, *Statistical Abstract*, Table 74, 2011). Protestants belong to such churches as the National and Southern Baptist conventions, the Assemblies of God, the United Methodist Church, and the Lutheran Church, to mention just a few. There are about 2.7 million adult members of Jewish congregations. Around 85% of the population clearly identifies with one or another religious group.

The United States, which has no state church, has more than 200 denominations and is greatly influenced by a variety of religious groups and belief systems. Williams (1980) conceptualizes American religion as interplay between two forces: the structured and the unstructured, the major religious communities and the informal groups that he calls "popular religions." These two trends developed, he says, in response to the demands of life in a new country. Faced with a diverse population, a new political system, and rapid technological change, Americans sometimes have found organized religions too limited and in response to the demands of a new nation, they have developed new religious movements.

# 11.6 THE DEVELOPMENT OF RELIGIOUS MOVEMENTS

Although guided by different practices, there is a commonality about the nature of faith and the relationship of faith to social commitments, very much guided by a sacred adherence to the American value of individualism (Madsen, 2009). Some so-called liberal religious groups have downplayed the supernatural aspects of Christianity and have emphasized the importance of ethical conduct and a remote, depersonalized God. Others worship a personal god and express their beliefs emotionally. Those who worship in this way seek signs of divine intervention in their daily lives.

The proliferation of sects accompanied the breakdown of the feudal structure and the development of industrialization. One wave of groups, known as the Pietist sects, rejected worldliness in favor of pacifism, communal living, and aspiration toward perfection. The Amish and the Hutterites are American groups descended from these sects. Another sect is the Religious Society of Friends (Quakers), who came to Pennsylvania from England. Quakers believe in an "inner light," and that people mystically partake of the nature of God. Thus, they see no need for a religious structure (e.g., clergy or churches) interceding between God and human beings.

*A group of Amish children walk along a road. The Amish are considered to be the descendants of the Pietist sect that rejected worldliness in favor of pacifism, communal living, and aspiration toward perfection.* (AP Wide World Photo)

Another theme in American religious life is **millennialism**, the belief that a dramatic transformation of the earth will occur and that Christ will rule the world for a thousand years of prosperity and happiness. One millennial movement took place among the Millerites in the 1830s. William Miller, the founder, was convinced that the Second Coming of Christ would happen in 1843. When it did not, he changed the date to 1844. Again nothing happened. Some of his followers, who believed that the Second

**Millennialism**

The belief prevalent among certain Christian sects that there will be a dramatic transformation of life on earth and that Christ will rule the world for a thousand years of prosperity and happiness

Coming had occurred invisibly and spiritually, founded the Seventh-Day Adventists. A more recent example of millennialism is Christian Exodus, a group that incorporates Evangelical Christianity and paleoconservative beliefs as a response to social crises that they believe have resulted from liberalized social values and economic uncertainty. Christian Exodus feels that these values have threatened a Christian way of life and that the way to salvation is through the electorate. The group's focus is aimed at dominating South Carolina politics as an attempt to create policies that reinforce traditional Christian values (Sweet & Lee, 2010).

Other religious movements have been based on divine revelation. One American prophet who received a divine revelation was Joseph Smith, who founded the Church of Jesus Christ of Latter-Day Saints (Mormons) in 1830. His following was recruited from the rural people of upstate New York. About thirty years later, Mary Baker Eddy began a movement in the urban middle class, known as the Christian Science movement. Ms. Eddy's revelation was that illness could be controlled by the mind. This sect developed into a denomination when people of wealth and status became adherents.

*Pentecostalism involves a practice similar to divine revelation. It is believed that the participants are able to "speak in tongues." (AP Wide World Photo)*

*Pentecostalism* involves a practice similar to divine revelation. Pentecostal Christians hold highly emotional services that resemble revivals. Participants also "speak in tongues" (*glossolalia*), in which they go into ecstatic seizures and utter a rapid flow of apparently meaningless syllables that are claimed to be a direct gift from the Holy Spirit.

An offshoot of Pentecostalism is *faith healing*, which experienced a rapid growth after World War II. In faith healing, the fundamentalist preacher asks members of the congregation who are sick or disabled to come forward. The preacher asks the disabled person and the rest of the congregation to call upon the power of the Lord to heal: "In the name of Jesus, heal." If their faith in Christ is strong enough, the blind will see, the lame can throw away their crutches, and so on. Followers of faith healers come primarily from the poor or working classes, who often do not have health insurance, adequate financial resources, or sometimes an awareness of what is available or where to go for adequate medical treatment.

A recent manifestation of the interplay between churches or denominations and fundamentalist groups of the sect type concerns the teaching of evolution in the public schools. Most educated people in the United States accept Darwin's theory of biological evolution. Many fundamentalist Christians, however, interpret the Bible literally and believe that God created heaven and earth in exactly the 6 days it specifies. The creationists are urging that creationism be given "equal time" with evolution in school science classes. The basic assumptions of scientists and religious fundamentalists are in direct conflict: Science is based on deductions drawn from empirical reality, whereas creationism is based on divine revelation and denounces empirical evidence that contradicts Biblical accounts. The issue of whether creationism should be taught in the public schools was temporarily muted in 1982 when a federal district judge in Arkansas ruled that the two-model approach of the creationists is simply a contrived dualism that has no scientific factual basis or legitimate educational purpose. The ruling contended that because creationism is not science, the conclusion is inescapable that the only real effect of teaching creation theory is the advancement of religion. What the creation law does, in effect, is to make the teaching of creationism in the public schools unconstitutional.

A ruling in the opposite direction, which illustrates the impact of fundamentalism on our judicial system, took place in 1987. A federal district judge in Alabama ruled that about 40 social studies books be removed from the public schools because they taught what creationists called "secular humanism." The judge ruled that secular humanism was a religion that gave credit to humans rather than to God.

## 11.6a Secularization

There is a trend in modern religion toward secularization. **Secularization** means to focus on this world and on worldly things such as science, reason and technology, as distinguished from the church, religious affairs, and faith. It means that problems are solved by humans through their own efforts (the essence of so-called secular humanism), as opposed to unquestioned faith in supernatural powers and a focus on the next world or an afterlife. It means a trend toward the declining influence of religion in the lives of people and in the institutions of society. Today, for example, marriages are assumed to be decided between humans, not foreordained by a god. Tragedies such as automobile accidents are explained in terms of human interactions and the laws of science, not as manifestations of divine will.

This way of thinking is extremely disturbing to fundamentalists and to right-wing evangelicals. To them, the idea that human beings are in control of their own destiny and that individuals themselves can change the condition of their lives without divine providence or intervention is unimaginable and unbelievable, if not evil and sinful. To emphasize materialism, consumption, and the here and now runs counter to giving up your "sinful ways," trusting in God, and focusing on salvation and the hereafter.

At a Catholic mass in Cameroon, Pope Benedict XVI urged Cameroon's bishops to defend against secularization. Secularization means that problems are solved by humans through their own efforts as opposed to unquestioned faith in supernatural powers. (AP Wide World Photo)

Stark and Bainbridge (1981) argue that secularization is a major trend but that it is not a new or modern development and does not presage the demise of religion. It is a process that goes on in all societies while countervailing intensification of religion goes on in other parts. The dominant religious organizations are always becoming more *secularized* (worldly) but are supplanted by more vigorous and less worldly religions. They demonstrate that secularization is one of three interrelated processes that constantly occur in all societies. Secularization itself generates two countervailing processes: revival and religious innovation. Revival is born out of secularization, as protest groups and sect movements form to meet the demand for a less worldly religion and to restore vigorous otherworldliness to a conventional faith. *Religious innovation*, also stimulated by secularization, leads to new faiths and new religious traditions. The birth of these new faiths will not be found in the directories of major church listings but will be found in lists of obscure cult movements.

Cults flourish where conventional churches are weakest. Stark and Bainbridge provide evidence that in America, there are very robust *negative* correlations between church membership rates and cult activity rates. The states and cities that have low church membership rates have the highest rates of membership in cults. Centuries ago, Christianity, Judaism, Islam, and Buddhism began as cults that rose to power because of the weaknesses in the dominant religions of their time. Stark and Bainbridge argue that the same process is happening today. Thus, in America, as in most societies, the history of religion is not only a pattern of secularization and decline but also equally one of birth and growth. While the sources of religion are shifting constantly, the amount of religion remains fairly constant.

## 11.6b Religiosity and Church Attendance

**Secularization**
The process through which beliefs concerning the supernatural and religious institutions lose social influence

Religiosity, the level of religious belief and behavior (Grant, 2008) is a qualitative factor that is difficult to assess accurately. While very difficult to measure, church attendance is one indication of the importance of religion. According to a 2010 Gallup Poll, 43.1% of Americans say they go to religious services weekly or almost weekly, up slightly from

## Table 11-3 Church Attendance in the United States

How Often Do You Attend Church, Synagogue, or Mosque?

| | % At least once a week | % Almost every week | % About once a month | % Seldom | % Never | Sample Size |
|---|---|---|---|---|---|---|
| 2010 (Jan–May) | 35 | 8 | 11 | 25 | 20 | 146,355 |
| 2009 | 35 | 8 | 12 | 25 | 20 | 353,849 |
| 2008 | 34 | 8 | 12 | 26 | 20 | 311,591 |

Adapted from "Americans' church attendance inches up in 2010: Increase accompanies rise in economic confidence," by Frank Newport, June 25, 2010, Gallup.
Retrieved from http://www.gallup.com/poll/141044/Americans-Church-Attendance-Inches-2010.aspx

42.1% in 2008 (see Table 11-3). Political affiliation, race, age, gender, marital status, education, and geographic location all seem to be related to church attendance (see Table 11-4). The highest rates of frequent church attendance are found among Conservatives (55%), blacks (55%), Republicans (55%), people over 65 years old (53%), Hispanics (52%), Southerners (51%), married people (48%) and women (47%). The lowest rates are found among Liberals (27%), Asians (31%), 18- to 29-year-olds (35%), single people (35%), Westerners (37%), Easterners (38%), Independents (38%), and men (39%).

Yet church attendance may not be an accurate measure of religiosity because people go to churches, synagogues, temples, or mosques for many reasons: to worship God, see friends, enjoy music, meet social expectations, and so on. Public opinion polls consistently indicate that a high percentage of people believe in God (more than 90%) and a life after death (about 75%), and they overwhelmingly want their children to have religious

## Table 11-4 Church Attendance in the United States

Frequent Church Attendance, January–May 2010, by Demographic Group

| Demographic Group | % | Demographic Group | % |
|---|---|---|---|
| Conservative | 55 | 50 to 64 | 43 |
| Non-Hispanic black | 55 | Some college | 41 |
| Republican | 66 | Non-Hispanic white | 41 |
| 65+ | 53 | 30 to 49 | 41 |
| Black Hispanic | 52 | Moderate | 39 |
| Southern | 51 | Democrat | 39 |
| Married | 48 | Men | 39 |
| Women | 47 | Independent | 38 |
| White Hispanic | 46 | East | 38 |
| Midwest | 44 | West | 37 |
| College graduate | 44 | Not married | 36 |
| Postgraduate | 44 | 18 to 29 | 35 |
| High school or less | 44 | Asian | 31 |
| SAMPLE AVERAGES | 43 | Liberal | 27 |

*Note.* Percentage saying they attend "at least one a week" or "almost every week."
Adapted from "Americans' church attendance inches up in 2010: Increase accompanies rise in economic confidence," by Frank Newport, June 25, 2010, Gallup.
Retrieved from http://www.gallup.com/poll/141044/Americans-Church-Attendance-Inches-2010.aspx

training. The discrepancy between church attendance figures and religious beliefs indicates that factors other than formal religious organizations influence religious thought. Until fairly recently, social scientists have not had a satisfactory way of measuring overall religiosity within societies. Sociologists have used indicators such as attendance at religious services, prayer and meditation, membership in churches and other religious organizations, religious beliefs and attitudes, and the subjective importance of religion. Rather than seeing these as individual indicators, Grant (2008) used them to arrive at an "aggregate religiosity" to measure the overall religiosity of a society. Using this measure, Grant found that there was a sharp rise in religiosity in the United States in the 1950s, a decline beginning in the 1960s, and a slower decline since the 1970s.

## 11.6c The Electronic Church

Through television, many people in the United States "attend church" without ever leaving their homes. Somc televangelists became national celebrities in the 1980s through this medium, amassing a huge financial empire through a variety of marketing techniques.

The notoriety of some of these TV evangelists increased as unusual activities were picked up by the press and sensationalized. Oral Roberts announced that God had told him that he would die unless he raised millions of dollars by a certain date. Jim and Tammy Bakker used Praise the Lord (PTL) funds for a Christian theme park, several expensive homes for their personal use, a new Corvette and houseboat, and a luxurious air-conditioned doghouse. Both Jim Bakker and Jimmy Swaggart were caught in indiscrete sexual relationships. Pat Robertson, who "speaks in tongues" and receives prophecies directly from God, ran for president of the United States. Jerry Falwell started the Moral Majority and became actively involved in supporting conservative political candidates and right wing social causes, before passing away in May 2007. Several, such as Jerry Falwell and Bob Jones, established universities that only accept "born-again" instructors and that serve as bastions of fundamentalist Christian teachings. Some, such as Robert Schuller—who had a congregation of 10,000 at his "Crystal Cathedral" in California as well as international members worldwide until he sold it in 2013—have established worldwide ministries while retaining a direct affiliation with a church or denomination (Reformed Church of America) rather than becoming sect-like.

Why does televangelism tend to be dominated be right-wing and fundamentalist ministers rather than preachers of mainstream denominations? Although no simple answers are available, some clues may lie in their message and in their organization. The message is simple, clear, precise, and based on a literal interpretation of the Bible. In a pluralistic society with social and moral ambiguities over the role of women, freedom of speech and expression, sexual norms, family planning, abortion and the like, it is comforting to believe that social as well as personal problems can be solved by a doctrinaire return to traditional gender roles and social values and a faith in God. The claim can be made that television is not friendly to intellectual discussions of ambiguous moral issues that are more commonly expressed by seminary graduates and the leadership in more established denominations.

The *organization* is often established around the charismatic quality of a single person (almost always male). These persons select their advisors and boards to back them and to establish an independent media network that is seldom accountable to other organizations or institutions. The leaders understand the value of showmanship and make appeals (often highly emotional) in the name of God to save souls, cleanse an immoral nation, and support their ministry. Unless an organization becomes established and institutionalized to provide continuity of the television program, the ministry is likely to dic with the removal or death of the charismatic leader.

In functional terms, the success of the electronic church is explained in terms of what it does for people: that is, its religious functions. Among others, it may provide answers to ultimate questions, reconcile people to hardship, and advocate the return to less complex and more traditional ways. The extent to which it facilitates social integration, creates a community of believers, and provides rituals is questionable, however. It is unlikely that many people kneel for prayer or join hands with others in front of a TV set. On the other hand, the millions of dollars sent to television preachers indicate that they are important to many Americans and fill various needs.

## 11.6d Ecumenism

One response to the current trend toward secularization has been **ecumenism**. The ecumenical movement calls for worldwide Christian unity. Interdenominational organizations such as the National Council of Churches are attempting to reconcile the beliefs and practices of different religious groups.

### thinking SOCIOLOGICALLY

1. Is religion a key factor in maintaining the status quo, a key factor in stimulating social change, both, or neither?
2. What types of variables influence the involvement of religious groups in politics? Do the variables change depending on the sociological theory you are using? Describe and explain.
3. How is secularization related to or caused by changes such as industrialization, urbanization, an increasingly educated population, political conservatism or liberalism, changing roles of women, and so forth?

## 11.6e A New Religious Consciousness

A number of new religious groups have sprung up in the United States over the past few decades. Many of them emphasize the personal religious experience rather than a rational, bureaucratic religious organization. The ideas of many of these new groups, such as the Moral Majority, Children of God, Messianic Jews, and the Christian World Liberation Front, have roots in the Christian tradition. The Reverend Sun Myung Moon's Unification Church (popularly known as "Moonies") is a combination of Protestantism and anticommunism. Others, like Synanon, Erhart Seminars Training (EST), Church of Scientology, and Silva Mind Control, grew out of the "human potential" movement of the 1960s and 1970s. Still others, such as Zen Buddhism, Yoga, and ISKCON (the organization of Hare Krishnas), are rooted in Eastern religions such as Buddhism, Hinduism, and Confucianism. Many of these religious movements demand of their members total conformity to the practices of the group and are often rigid in their teachings.

Durkheim believed that as societies become more complex and diversified, so do the forms of religious belief and practice. Some see the new religious consciousness as a search for identity and meaning. Some see these movements as a reaction against the militaristic and capitalistic values that are emphasized by contemporary American society. Others contend that the new religions have arisen in response to the climate of moral ambiguity in the United States. The decline of the established churches has undoubtedly been influential as well. In all probability, each of these factors has had an effect.

**Ecumenism**
The trend for different denominations to join together in pursuit of common interest in a spirit of worldwide Christian unity

## 11.6f Religion and Other Institutions

The relationship between the church and other institutions is a complex one. The institutions and the functions they perform are not always easy to differentiate. As was mentioned earlier, Max Weber argued shortly after the turn of the century that capitalism was enhanced by the work ethic of Protestantism. In the 1980s, the entry of television evangelists such as Jerry Falwell and Pat Robertson into the political arena reflected the linkage between religion and politics. Other institutional linkages include the influence of religion on school curricula and prayer, the impact of religious teachings on family size and use of contraceptives or abortion, and the influence of religion on the economy through the ownership or control of many businesses and the endorsement or non-endorsement by religious groups of various products. There is increasing evidence that many evangelical members of the power elite within the United States, especially within politics and business, have a strong sense of cohesion because of the salience of their religious beliefs, thus furthering the strength of the evangelical movement (Lindsay, 2008).

Emile Durkheim noted the key linkage between the sacred and the secular or profane when he stated that anything could be made sacred. Political rituals such as those that accompany the election of a president, family behaviors such as eating dinner together, economic goods such as automobiles, or educational events such as a graduation can all be considered sacred. These interrelationships and religious influences extend beyond the basic institutions. Note, for example, how religious principles have served as the foundation for opposition to war, restrictions on alcohol, or the disciplining of children. In today's world, although the church as a social institution has come under attack, religion and religious values continue to exert a major influence on societies, on all the institutions within them, and on the lives of individuals around the globe.

### thinking SOCIOLOGICALLY

1. How might you define "being religious"? Can you be religious without attending some church or synagogue or participating in some social group of like-minded persons?
2. Using theories and facts about religious groups and systems, discuss how and why religious groups become involved in political activities, both domestically and internationally. Provide specific examples of the types of policies with which religious groups would be concerned.

# CHAPTER 11 Wrapping it up

## Summary


1. A religion is a ritualized system of beliefs and practices related to things defined as sacred by an organized community of believers.
2. People have believed in supernatural powers throughout history. Some societies have believed that supernatural powers inhabit objects such as rocks and trees. This is known as animism. Others have assumed that supernatural powers reside in a shaman, who could be called upon to protect the group or to bring success. A third form of belief is totemism, in which a plant or animal is thought to be ancestrally related to a person or tribe.
3. Religions are sometimes differentiated by the number of gods that adherents worship. Monotheistic religions believe in one god, and polytheistic religions believe in a number of gods.
4. Religion may take a variety of forms. Mysticism is based on the belief in powers that are mysterious, secret, and hidden from human understanding. Churches are institutional organizations with formal bureaucratic structures; they are sometimes differentiated into ecclesia, which are official state religions, and denominations, which are independent of the state.
5. Sects are small separatist groups that follow rigid doctrines and emphasize fundamentalist teachings. Cults are loosely organized religious organizations whose members adopt a new, unique, and unusual lifestyle. Rather than attempting to change society, cults generally focus on the spiritual lives of the individual participants.
6. There are a number of theories about religion. The functionalist perspective examines what religion does for society. Religion is generally perceived as fulfilling social functions, such as preserving and solidifying society, creating a community of believers, cultivating social change, and providing a means of social control. It also fulfills personal functions such as answering ultimate questions, providing rites of passage, and reconciling people to hardship.
7. The conflict perspective views religion as a tool used by the dominant individuals and groups to justify their position and to keep the less privileged in subordinate positions.
8. More than 5 billion people are believed to be identified with or have an affiliation with one of the world's major religions. About 2 billion are Christians, who profess faith in the teachings of Jesus Christ. Another billion believe in Islam and surrender their wills to Allah, following the teachings of the prophet Muhammad.
9. Excluding the nonreligious, the third largest religious group is the followers of Hinduism, which is closely linked to the traditional caste system of India. Hindus have a vast array of religious practices and beliefs.
10. Followers of Buddhism believe that they can avoid human suffering by following an eightfold path of appropriate behavior. Confucianism, based on the life and teachings of Confucius, is both a philosophy and a religion and is closely linked to Taoism and Shintoism, as well as to Buddhism.
11. The United States has no state church, and a wide variety of religious groups exist in this country. There are two contrasting trends in contemporary religious practice. One type of group emphasizes formal religious organization, whereas the other emphasizes an informal, personalized, emotional belief system. Throughout American history, religious life has been influenced by folk religions, sects, Pentecostal groups, and groups that believe in millennialism, divine revelation, and faith healing.
12. Currently, religion is being studied in new ways as a result of developments in qualitative and quantitative research techniques and computer technology. The use of these and other techniques has revealed a trend toward secularization, which is counter intuitively believed to contribute to the emergence of cult activities.
13. U.S. church attendance has leveled off at an estimated 40%, but a large majority of the population still professes a belief in God and in life after death.

14. Televised religious programs reach millions of persons in their homes. Along with these developments have come increased ecumenicalism and a new religious consciousness. This new consciousness is professed by many new religious sects and movements, some derived from the Christian tradition, others from the human potential movement and Eastern religions.
15. Several explanations for the creation of these groups have been offered. It has been suggested that they have arisen in response to our diverse culture, search for identity, and need for precise, simplistic answers, or as a protest against secularization and materialism. The institution of religion in America and around the world is closely linked with the family, as well as with economic, political, and educational institutions. These institutions both influence religious beliefs and practices and, in turn, are influenced by religion.

## Discussion Questions

1. Discuss some ways in which religion affects our identity and our behavior.
2. How do you think life in America would be different if our culture was based on polytheism rather than monotheism?
3. How would you explain why some people are attracted to churches, others to sects, some to cults, and still others to no religious groups at all?
4. Regardless of an American's specific religious beliefs, we are all affected by the Protestant ethic. Explain how Protestantism has helped to shape our cultural beliefs and values, and how it may have affected you.
5. Compare the functionalist and conflict approaches to religion, and discuss how these views are different from or similar to views that you may have been socialized to believe about religion.
6. Discuss some ways in which religion effects the outcomes of peace, gender roles, politics, and so forth in the Middle East, Ireland, or Southern U.S. states, for example.
7. Select one of the religions discussed in the text other than your own (if you do not have a religion, then select any one). Explore how your involvement in family and in political, economic, and educational institutions might be different if you were a member of that religion.
8. Make a list of selected trends in religion. How would you explain them? How can they be changed?
9. Explain the appeal of TV preachers or evangelists. What accounts for their appeal, popularity, fund-raising success, and longevity?
10. Discuss the linkage between religion and life in other institutions, such as the family or school.

adidas

CHAPTER 12

# Educational Groups and Systems

## SYNOPSIS

Focal Point

## SCHOOL BULLYING

*Bullying in schools is widespread in the United States. (Shutterstock)*

Bullying, or peer-victimization, has become an increasing problem in schools. Bullying is a specific form of aggression among students that is persistent and results from an imbalance in power between the bully and the victim (Olweus, 1993, as cited in Bender & Losel, 2011). Bullying in schools is not a new phenomenon and can be found all throughout history (Billiterri, 2010). Hyojin Koo (2007, as cited in Billiterri, 2010), a Korean scholar who studied the history of bullying, found that what bullying includes and attitudes about it have changed over time. In the eighteenth to twentieth centuries, bullying generally included physical or verbal harassment related to a death, isolation, or extortion in school children. Koo found that during the 1950s and 60s, bullying evolved from robbing, stealing, and acting rowdy to persistent inattentiveness and underhandedness. Since the 1980s, bullying has come to include direct verbal taunting and social exclusion. This includes cyber-bullying as well as face-to-face.

Dan Olweus, creator of the Olweus Bullying Prevention Program, says, "A person is bullied when he or she is exposed, repeatedly and over time, to negative actions on the part of one or more other persons, and he or she has difficulty defending himself or herself." Olweus (Olweus Bullying Prevention Program, 2012) includes a variety of concerns:

1. Verbal bullying including derogatory comments and bad names
2. Bullying through social exclusion or isolation
3. Physical bullying such as hitting, kicking, shoving, and spitting
4. Bullying through lies and false rumors
5. Having money or other things taken or damaged by students who bully
6. Being threatened or being forced to do things by students who bully
7. Racial bullying
8. Sexual bullying
9. Cyber bullying (via cell phone or Internet)

Bullying in schools is widespread in the United States. In the past year, 50% of high school students admitted that they had bullied someone; 47% said that they had been bullied, teased, or taunted in a way that had upset them. Nearly 40% of bullied girls and 46% of bullied boys in grades 3 through 12 have been bullied for a year or longer (Billiterri, 2010). Research has found that bullying has no national borders and is found in many countries throughout the world (Borntrager, Davis, Bernstein, & Gorman, 2009).

The victims of bullying can suffer serious consequences including depression, low self-esteem, health problems, poor grades, and suicidal thoughts. Some of the more catastrophic results have been seen in the news in recent years. Hope Witsell, a 13-year-old Florida student, hanged herself in her bedroom after being taunted by classmates after someone had circulated a nude photo she had sent to her boyfriend. Phoebe Prince, a 15-year-old, hanged herself after alleged bullying occurred at her Massachusetts high school. Tyler Clementi, 18, committed suicide by jumping off the George Washington Bridge after classmates allegedly used a webcam to transmit images of him being involved in a gay relationship. While these are some of the most famous recent cases, the effects of bullying are widespread.

Bullying not only has negative consequences for its victims but for the perpetrators as well. Research has found that bullying at school is often associated with delinquency, violence, and other anti-social behavior in adulthood (Bender & Losel, 2011).

At least 43 states and the District of Columbia have laws to address bullying, including 6 states that address cyber-bullying and 30 that include electronic harassment. However, the creation of these laws is controversial because some feel that they may infringe on students' free speech rights.

The topic of bullying is important to sociology because it is an example of what sociologists would call a dysfunction (a negative latent function) of education.

When looking at educational systems, it is important to consider not only manifest (intended) functions but also the other functions, both positive and negative, that result from the ways in which the institution of education exists and develops within societies.

**Children in the United States** are required to go to school. They sometimes begin at age 2 or 3, long before the required age of 6 or 7, often staying in school long past age 16 (when they could legally drop out). Thus, education dominates the lives of children; and it also plays an important role in adult life, as adult students, parents, taxpayers, school employees, government officials, and voters participate in the school system. The high school graduation rate declined in the latter part of the twentieth century but has improved since then. The national graduation rate increased from 72% in 2001 to 75% in 2008, although there is a great deal of variation from state to state and between ethnic and racial groups (Dillon, 2010). For example, during that same period, graduation rates declined noticeably in Arizona, Nevada, and Utah, but increased substantially in New York and Tennessee with two states, Vermont and Wisconsin, reaching a graduation rate of almost 90%. In 2008, eight states had graduation rates below 70%. During that same time, the graduation rate was 81% of white students, 64% of Hispanic students, and 62% of black students (Rotherham, 2010).

At the same time, education in the United States produces high school graduates who are not prepared for college. ACT (American College Testing) has been collecting and reporting data on students' academic readiness for college since 1959 (ACT, 2010). ACT has benchmarks in English, reading, math and science to assess college readiness. In 2010, 28% of graduating high school students met none of the benchmarks, 15%

**Figure 12-1** College Readiness Benchmarks by Subject

In 2012, 67% of all ACT-tested high school graduates met the English College Readiness Benchmark, while 25% met the College Readiness Benchmarks in all four subjects. Of high school graduates, 52% met the Reading Benchmark and 46% met the Mathematics Benchmark. Just under 1 in 3 (31%) met the College Readiness Benchmark in Science.

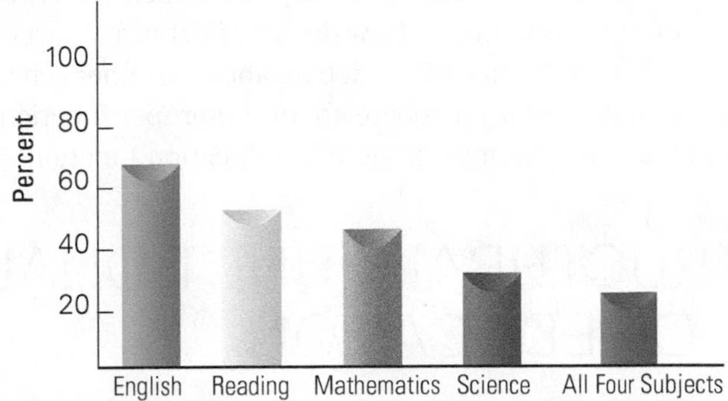


Adapted from "College Readiness Benchmarks by Subject" Copyright © by ACT, Inc. 2012. Used with permission of ACT, Inc.
Retrieved from http://www.act.org/research/policymakers/cccr12/readiness1.html.

**Figure 12-2** Number of College Readiness Benchmarks Attained

About 72% of all 2012 ACT-tested high school graduates met at least one of the four College Readiness Benchmarks in English, Reading, Mathematics, or Science. 28% of all graduates did not meet any of the College Readiness Benchmarks, while 47% met between 1 and 3 Benchmarks. Of all 2012 ACT-tested high school graduates, 25% met all four College Readiness Benchmarks, meaning that 1 in 4 were academically ready for college coursework in all four subject areas.

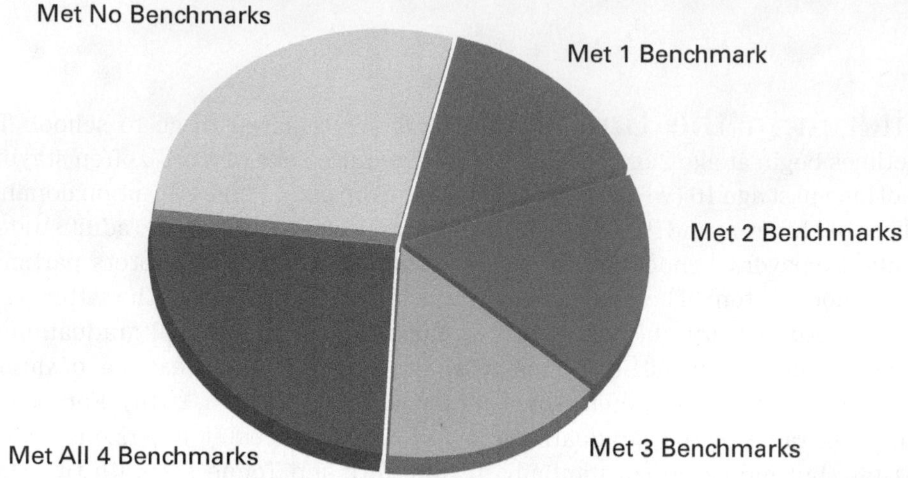


*Note.* Graph reads: In 2012, 25% of ACT-tested high school graduates met all four College Readiness Benchmarks, 15% met 3 Benchmarks, 17% met 2 Benchmarks, 15% met 1 Benchmark, and 28% met none of the Benchmarks. Percentages may not sum to 100% due to rounding.



Retrieved from http://www.act.org/research/policymakers/cccr12/readiness4.html.

met one benchmark, 17% met two benchmarks, 15% met three benchmarks, and only 24% met all four benchmarks (see Figures 12-1, 12-2 and 12-3). Less than one in four students were academically ready for college coursework in all four subject areas.

Why is education so important? We all know some of the reasons we believe in the value of education. We learn science, the arts, and skills for employment; and we learn to make informed judgments about our leisure activities, our political involvement, and our everyday lives.

Is this all that we get from education? What else does it accomplish for society? What part does our education system play in creating a literate population and in selecting people for occupations that match their talents? What part does it play in maintaining the stratification system and in justifying the unequal distribution of wealth in society? What part does education play in shaping socially acceptable behavior and curtailing inappropriate behavior, such as bullying? How does it affect other parts of our lives such as our identity and self-esteem? Much of the debate about whether schools are doing the job they are supposed to do is really a debate about the proper function of schools. The goal of this chapter is to help you understand how education functions in society today.

# 12.1 STRUCTURAL FUNCTIONAL THEORY OF EDUCATION

Structural functional theory recognizes the family as an important agency of socialization. It is in the family that the child learns the culture's values, norms, and language—how to be a social person. By the age of 5 or 6 years, the child has developed a unique social personality; in a properly functioning family, the child is socialized to adjust to the

**Figure 12-3** College Readiness Benchmarks—Attainment and Near-Attainment

About 9% to 15% of graduates were within 2 scale points of meeting an ACT College Readiness Benchmark in 2012, depending on subject area. This represents approximately 150,000 to 250,000 additional students who were close to being college ready within a subject area.

In 2012, 46% of graduates met the Mathematics Benchmark, while another 9% were within 2 scale points of doing so. The percentages of students within 2 scale points of the respective College Readiness Benchmark in the other subject areas were the same or greater, including 9% of graduates in English, 11% in Reading, and 15% in Science.

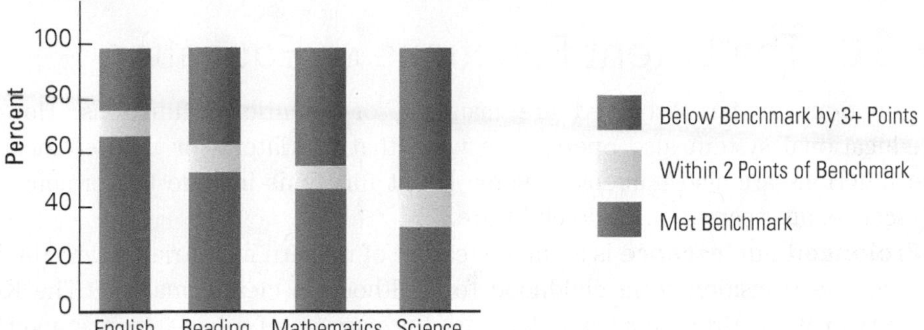


*Note:* Graph reads: In 2012, 67% of ACT-tested high school graduates met the College Readiness Benchmark in English, while 9% scored 1 or 2 points below the Benchmark, and 24% scored 3 points or more below the Benchmark. Columns may not sum to 100% due to rounding.



Retrieved from http://www.act.org/research/policymakers/cccr12/readiness3.html

routines and disciplines of the school system. How does education in the schools differ from education in the home?

## 12.1a The Manifest Functions of Education

The *manifest* or intended function of the educational system, according to structural functionalists, is to supplement family socialization. The schools use experts (teachers) to teach children the knowledge, skills, and values necessary to function in the world outside the family (Parsons, 1959).

The most obvious teaching in school is the teaching of skills. Students today are expected to learn to read, write, and do arithmetic; specially trained experts teach these skills. Schools also teach students *knowledge* about the larger world through such courses as history, geography, and science. In addition, students learn the values of the larger society, including those that pertain to large organizations. They learn to tell time and to be punctual, to cooperate with others to achieve group goals, and to obey the rules necessary for a smooth-running organization.

Another function of education is to select and develop, through evaluation and testing, those young people who have especially useful talents so that each individual will be as productive as his or her abilities permit. Schools give I.Q. tests to determine students' capabilities, and they give grades and achievement tests to find out how much students have learned. They also give psychological tests to help determine which occupations suit the students so that they can then guide them into vocational lines appropriate to their abilities. Some students are guided into vocational courses and the work force; others go to academic high schools and then into two- or four-year colleges. A few of the most talented (or privileged) go to elite colleges and graduate schools and then on to the professions.

A third function of the education system is to transmit new behaviors, skills, ideas, discoveries, and inventions resulting from research. Today, for example, schools teach

**BVT *Lab***

Flashcards are available for this chapter at www.BVTLab.com

typing and place less emphasis on penmanship. In some school systems, elementary school students are taught to use a computer terminal before they have mastered their multiplication tables.

The creation of new knowledge is another function of education. Our medical technology is one outstanding example of the knowledge developed in universities. Attempts have also been made to use the educational system to decrease poverty. Education develops the skills necessary to earn income, and special programs have been devised to help the poor to develop these skills. Some high schools and colleges, for example, offer students training in specific vocational skills, such as car repair, computer programming, or restaurant management. Early educational programs such as Head Start are designed to teach disadvantaged children the skills they need to keep up with their peers.

## 12.1b The Latent Functions of Education

The functions so far discussed are manifest, or intentional functions. However, the educational system also operates in ways that are latent, or unintentional and these functions are also influential. Some latent functions include the prolonging of adolescence, age segregation, and childcare.

**Prolonged adolescence** is a unique feature of modern industrial society. In other societies, the transition from childhood to adulthood is clearly marked. The Kpelle of Liberia in West Africa, for example, mark the passage of a boy into manhood by a circumcision ritual. After this ceremony, the young man is regarded as having the same responsibilities as the other men of his tribe. In our society, children have been relieved of work roles for increasingly long periods so that they can acquire an education. The age of mandatory school attendance was raised from 12 to 14 and then to 16 years, so students today have to remain in school for a longer time than they once did. Another factor that has increased the number of years they spend in school is that many jobs require a high school or college diploma. Students remain in school longer when unemployment rates are high and jobs are not available and parents have to continue to support and assume responsibility for their children during this extended education. As a result, in the United States the period of dependency on parental support sometimes continues for 2 decades or even longer. Approximately 13.5% of 25- to 34-year-olds were living with their parents in 2010 (up from around 10.7% in 1983), while homeownership declined from around 41% to around 39% for under 35-year-olds during that same time period (see Figure 12-4).

**Prolonged adolescence**

A latent function of education that serves to maintain dependency on parents and keep young people out of the job market

**Age segregation**

The separation of groups by age, such as occurs in our education system

**Age segregation** is the separation of some age groups from the larger population. Children in schools spend their time with children of the same age—their peers. The peer group is an important agency of socialization. Peer groups sometimes develop into distinct subcultures, whose members dress alike, listen to the same music, eat the same foods, wear similar hairstyles and makeup, and develop code words and slang—a language of their own. One such age-segregated subculture evolved in the late 1960s. During that decade, adolescents and college students were often in conflict with families, schools, and businesses. Fathers and sons stopped speaking over the length of the sons' hair, and students were expelled from schools and colleges and denied jobs because they wore long hair and blue jeans. The plethora of bare-chested young men and barefooted youths prompted signs to appear on storefronts, announcing "Shirts and shoes required." Students in the late 1960s learned values of equality and individual worth in school but found that the larger society did not reflect these values.

*Children in schools are segregated according to age so that they may socialize with their peers.* (Shutterstock)

Our education system has also developed other latent functions, such as childcare. This function has become

**Figure 12-4** Percent of 25- to 34-Year-Olds Living with Parents vs. Homeownership Rate for Those Under 35 Years Old

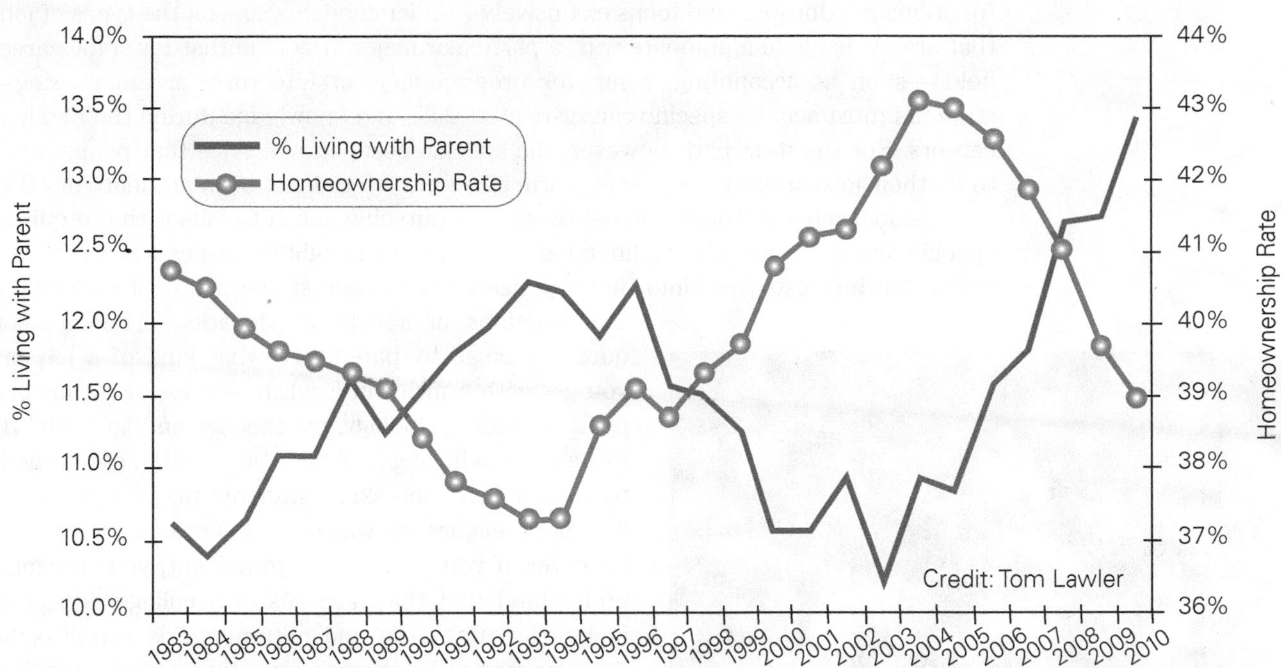


Adapted from "Under 35: Living with parents vs. homeownership rate" by Bill McBride.
Retrieved from http://www.calculatedriskblog.com /2010/12/under-35-living-with-parents-vs.html, December 10, 2010. ASEC: Conducted by Census Bureau

increasingly important in American society because in many families, both parents must work simply to make ends meet. Although the hours that children are in school—9 to 3—are often not convenient for working parents, they could not even consider working if their children were not in school. Some school systems are so attuned to their supervisory, childcare function that they offer after-school playgroups—for a nominal fee—to take care of children until a parent gets off work and can take the child home.

In sum, structural functionalists believe that the educational system fulfills both manifest and latent functions. It reinforces the socialization process that started with the family, prepares children for work in a complex industrial society, and guides them into the occupations most appropriate to their abilities and to society's needs. Some latent functions of education include the segregation of age groups, the extension of adolescence, and supervisory childcare.

## APPLYING THE FUNCTIONS OF EDUCATION

Understanding the functions of education is important for teachers, counselors, school administrators, parents, students, and employers. If teachers, for example, concentrate their efforts exclusively on providing specific academic skills to students, the schools may fail to teach values and norms such as honesty, punctuality, respect, trust, civic responsibility, competition, and cooperation. As a result, undue pressure on students by parents and counselors to succeed academically might turn some students into scholars who lack competence in social skills, and academically poor students might become alienated from the entire educational process. By no means are we suggesting that high academic achievement should not be emphasized. However, it may not be the only measure of a successful education for every student.

Understanding the many functions of education is especially important for college students. One of the most difficult decisions you and other students must make early in your college career is your choice of a major. Most often, students lose sight of the many functions of education and focus exclusively—understandably so—on the types of jobs that are available to a graduate with a particular major. It is true that for some career fields—such as accounting, computer programming, architecture, or engineering—students must acquire specific career-related skills and knowledge during their college careers. For the most part, however, the specific occupational skills that people need to do their jobs are learned in some form of on-the-job training or in graduate or other professional schools. Therefore, unless you are pursuing one of the fields that require a specific major—especially in a liberal arts college—you might do just as well to select a major that interests you. Unfortunately, many parents and students do not understand the functions of a college education. The common question asked by parents is, what kind of a job can you get with a major in English—or sociology, history, political science, biology, psychology, and so forth? By mistakenly believing that the sole function of college is to learn specific job skills, students may be pressured to select majors in which they have little interest. However, if you (and just as important, your parents) understand that the functions of a college education include learning social and cultural norms as well as the development of basic communicative, critical thinking, and interpersonal skills, you might select a major that better suits your needs and desires.

*It is important for college students to understand the many functions of education. (iStockphoto)*

College students and their parents are not the only ones who misunderstand the various functions of a college education. Personnel in college placement offices and employers who are hiring college graduates often make similar mistakes in associating careers only with particular majors. Business majors will not necessarily be better as sales representatives, sociology majors will not necessarily be better as city planners, and English majors will not necessarily be better as journalists. By not understanding the many ways a college education serves a student, college graduates may be channeled into careers for which they are not particularly suited and not considered for jobs in which they might excel.

## 12.2 CONFLICT THEORY OF EDUCATION

Conflict theorists might argue that educational systems help sustain inequalities between the haves and have-nots in a society. Thus, the school system, through a **hidden curriculum**, teaches values and norms that are necessary to maintain the stratification system in society. The educational system is also used to justify giving higher-status jobs to the children of elites and lower-status jobs to children of the poor.

### 12.2a The Hidden Curriculum

**Hidden curriculum**

The teaching and learning of things such as obedience, competition, and patriotism that are not part of the stated curriculum

Schools require students to learn, albeit subtly, how to behave appropriately for their position in society. This learning is not a part of the stated curriculum—the acknowledged subjects—such as reading, writing, or arithmetic. It is a part of a hidden curriculum, in which students learn such things as obedience, competition, and patriotism. No one ever announces that these qualities are being taught. Nevertheless, if students are to be educated for a job, they must learn to obey rules, to do whatever a superior orders them to do, to work as hard as they can—or at least harder than their coworkers—and to be loyal to superiors, the organization, and the nation in which they work. Both the values and the norms of the elite are a part of the hidden curriculum.

## 12.2b The Teaching of Values

Conflict theorists believe that schools teach children the values of the group in power. Children are taught patriotism by saying the "Pledge of Allegiance" and by studying the history and geography of the United States and of their own states and communities. They learn that the United States is a great country founded by prominent leaders who believed in freedom for all. Students learn about the democratic system of government, the fairness of representation, and the importance of the vote. They are taught to value the capitalist system, in which everyone has the right to accumulate as much private property as possible and to pass it on to their children.

*Children learn patriotism by reciting the "Pledge of Allegiance." (iStockphoto)*

The importance of teaching values can be appreciated by looking at the conflicts that sometimes arise in schools. Teachers may be fired if they teach high school students the advantages of socialism or the disadvantages of capitalism. The topics omitted from school curricula also shed light on the teaching of values. Students are seldom instructed on the family systems or sexual practices of people in other cultures. They are rarely taught about great philosophers who have criticized the United States' political or economic systems, nor are they generally made aware of the people who have suffered under these systems. Students who reach a college sociology course that attempts to analyze both strengths and weaknesses of social systems are often shocked by what they learn.

## 12.2c The Learning of Norms

According to conflict theorists, students learn to conform to the standards of behavior of those in power through the educational process. For example, students are told when to stand in line, when to take turns, when to talk, when to be quiet, when to read, when to listen, when to hang up their coats—the list goes on and on. Students are not taught when to complain, when their rights are being infringed upon, when their time is being wasted, or when to use their freedom of speech. Rules are an important part of the complex organization of a school, and acceptance of certain rules is vital to the maintenance of the social order.

Students are also expected to compete with other students in school. They are taught that they must do better than others to receive attention, good grades, and privileges. Those who do not compete—who instead pursue the activities they enjoy—may fail, be separated from their peer group, and be labeled as slow, hyperactive, disabled, or otherwise deviant. In short, they are punished.

The competition, however, is unfair because it is based on the norms of the middle class, not those of working-class ethnics or inner-city blacks. Some ethnic groups, for example, find it embarrassing to compete scholastically, to display that they know more than someone else, and the result is that they do not enter into the competition.

Most teachers come from the middle class and teach students their own values and norms. They tend to teach middle-class literature rather than the literature that might be more germane to their students. When stories about middle-class children in the suburbs with a house, a lawn, a pet dog, and a car are used to teach reading to 5-year-old inner-city children who have never had houses to live in, lawns to play on, pet dogs, or cars to ride in, the meaning of the story is as incomprehensible as if the story were written in a foreign language.

## 12.2d Credentialism

Conflict theorists argue that the credentials, diplomas, and degrees given by schools represent learning that is not essential to doing most jobs (Collins, 1979). Nevertheless, some jobs afford wealth and prestige to those who hold these credentials. Because such jobs are scarce and so many people want them and compete for them, those who control these jobs can require qualifications of their applicants that have little to do with the skills needed for the job. Instead, the qualifications can serve to place upper-class persons in higher-status or elite jobs, middle-class people in middle-class jobs, working-class people in blue-collar or lower-paying service jobs, and the poor in the lowest-status, lowest-paying jobs society has to offer.

**Credentialism** is the practice of requiring degrees for jobs whether or not the degrees actually teach skills necessary to accomplish the jobs. Everyone—from assembly-line workers to physicians—learns much more than is necessary to do his or her work. Physicians, for example, must complete 4 years of college, 4 years of medical school, and a 1-year internship to become general practitioners. Those who want to specialize need an additional 3 or more years of training. Communist societies such as China and Cuba successfully train people in a much shorter time to take care of most of the health needs of the society. The system in the United States perpetuates the prestige of physicians by demanding credentials that can be obtained only by those who have the time and money to enter this high-prestige profession. In addition, physicians come to form their own subculture of shared values and beliefs during their years of training.

Collins (1979) also argues that the jobs requiring a great deal of education do not necessarily require the skills people learn in school, but the jobs do require the cultural norms learned in school. When college-educated people enter management positions, the elite can rest assured that the managers will make decisions consistent with the cultural norms.

In sum, conflict theorists believe that the group in power, to legitimate their position, runs the educational system. They teach values and norms useful in maintaining their position, use an unfair competitive system to legitimate upper-middle-class success, and insist on certification of skills beyond those necessary to do a job. The upper-middle class has the competitive advantage, but everyone learns the values and norms that maintain the system.

Most American education is public—the schools are open to everyone. Local and federal governments fund schools, so there are strong ties between the educational system and the political system. Education is paid for through tax dollars and although it is controlled locally, it complies with all the laws of the land. Those who head federal, state, and local school bureaucracies interpret these laws. Students, parents, and teachers have little opportunity to influence decisions in the bureaucracy.

The bureaucracy of a local school system is headed by a local school board, which adopts a budget, sets policies, and directs the supervisor of schools. The superintendent develops guidelines based on the policies of the school board and directs the principals of the schools in the area. The principals make rules for the local schools, based on the guidelines of the supervisor and they direct the teachers to carry out the rules. The teacher establishes rules for the classroom in accordance with the principal's direction and teaches the students.

The people residing within the school district's boundaries usually elect local school boards, although in about 10% of the districts the mayor appoints them. Traditionally, school boards consisted primarily of white, male business or professional people, although in the past decades more women and minorities have won elections to school boards. At times, board members come into conflict with groups in their school districts.

**Credentialism**

The practice of requiring degrees for most high-paying jobs, whether or not the degrees actually signify skills necessary to accomplish the job

Disagreements have ranged from monitoring hairstyles to how to offer vocational training, from discipline to teaching the basics of reading, writing, and arithmetic. Some critics argue that school boards would better represent their communities if the board members represented a wider range of the community, including those from ethnic and other minority groups, labor, faculty, and the student body.

The Center for Public Education lists five reasons that school boards matter (http://www.nsba.org):

1. School boards look out for children, first and foremost. Education is not a line item in a school board's budget—it is the ONLY item.
2. School boards are advocates for their communities when decisions are made about children's education.
3. School boards set the standards for achievement in their communities, incorporating their community's view of what students should know and be able to do at each grade level.
4. School boards are the public link to public schools. They are accessible to the public and accountable for the performance of their schools.
5. School boards are the education watchdog for their communities, ensuring that taxpayers get the most for their tax dollars.

Public schools are opened to everyone. Education is paid for through tax dollars. (iStockphoto)

Although the United States emphasizes local control of schools, it is somewhat misleading to suggest that school boards operate independently because the federal government passes many laws that affect the educational system (e.g., the No Child Left Behind Act of 2002). Schools must respect the rights protected by the U.S. Constitution; they must allow religious freedom and offer equal opportunity. The federal government influences such issues as prayer in school, the teaching of evolution, equal opportunity for minorities, and the education of the handicapped, including provisions for children with special educational needs. School boards must comply with federal laws regarding these and other concerns.

With the exception of maintaining the constitutional rights of citizens, the federal government had only a limited role in public education from the founding of the nation until the mid-twentieth century. Early on, some laws—such as the Lands Ordinance Act of 1785, the Northwest Ordinance of 1787, and the Morrill Act during the Civil War—set aside funds from the sale of unsettled land to fund public education. After the Civil War, Congress required new states to establish systems of non-sectarian education. In 1917, Congress approved direct aid to public education. However, it was not until 1950 that the federal government became directly involved in the composition of schools when the U.S. Supreme Court ruled that racial segregation in schools was unconstitutional. With the demands of the Cold War and the impending awareness that the United States was starting to fall behind other countries educationally (as evidenced by the Soviet launch of Sputnik, the first space satellite), the federal government began to take direct steps to influence the curriculum in public schools with the passage of the National Defense Act, which provided funds to states for teaching science, math, and foreign languages. Educational concerns have been a part of every presidency since the early 1960s (Jost, 2010) (see Table 12-1).

States also have constitutions, which cannot contradict federal law. Within the restrictions of federal law and the state constitution, the states pass laws that set standards for the schools. They certify teachers, set the number of days that students must attend school, determine school holidays, and establish minimum requirements for the curriculum and for graduation.

Within the limits set by the state and federal governments, local school boards set policy to be carried out by school principals and teachers, who must teach course content and follow schedules set by higher authorities (Scimecca, 1980). The evaluation of teachers is heavily based on cooperation with the principal and local school board, rather than on creativity or teaching skills. Furthermore, teachers today are overwhelmed by the paperwork of the bureaucracy—seating charts, report cards, attendance records, schedules, and lesson plans—which takes considerable time away from teaching (Ballantine, 1983). The National Education Association (NEA) reports that teachers spend an average of 50 hours per week on instructional duties, including

**Table 12-1** Role of the Federal Government in Education

| | |
|---|---|
| **1950s to 1970s** | |
| 1954 | U.S. Supreme Court ruled racial segregation in public schools unconstitutional |
| 1958 | In response to Cold War threats, National Defense Education Act provided aid to states for teaching math, science, and foreign languages |
| 1965 | President Lyndon B. Johnson signed Elementary and Secondary Education Assistance Act, the first broad federal aid for public schools and established Title I which allocates funds to schools with a high proportion of "educationally deprived students" |
| 1979 | President Jimmy Carter signs law creating U.S. Department of Education |
| **1980s to 1990s** | |
| 1981 | President Ronald Reagan cut federal spending on education by 20% |
| 1983 | Federal government study *A Nation at Risk* depicted in U.S. education system as failing and lagging behind other countries |
| 1988 | President George H. W. Bush pledged to be the "education president" in his campaign platform |
| 1989 | President Bush hosted "education summit" with few concrete results |
| 1991 | President Bush proposed "America 2000" legislations, but the bill was killed by Congress |
| 1992 | President Bill Clinton stressed education in his campaign platform |
| 1994 | President Clinton enacted "Goals 2000" calling for states to develop education standards, and the Improving American Schools Act linked Title I funds to the adoption of standards |
| **2000 to present** | |
| 2001–2002 | President George W. Bush enacts "No Child Left Behind" (NCLB) calling for annual testing of students in reading and math and enacting penalties for schools that do not meet standards, tying federal funding to the achievement of standards |
| Mid-2000s | Negative reactions to NCLB because of an overemphasis on standardizing exams, and the perception that schools were unfairly labeled as underperforming without providing help to improve them, thus providing incentives for schools to lower standards rather than to raise them |
| 2008 | President Barack Obama stressed education in his campaign platform |
| 2009 | Congress approved a $4.3 billion stimulus for "Race to the Top" grants to states with education reform plans; 41 states participated |
| 2010 | State governors and education leaders propose common core standards in English and math and President Obama proposes "Blueprint for Reform" calling for revising NCLB |

Adapted from *CQ Researcher*, April 16, 2010, Vol. 20 No. 15, p. 347.

an average of 12 hours each week on non-compensated school-related activities such as grading papers, bus duty, and club advising. Furthermore, teachers spend an average of $443 of their own money each year to meet the needs of their students (www.nea.org), and in 2005 the IRS started allowing teachers to deduct $250.00 of those expenses from their yearly tax returns. Also, as with any bureaucracy, the school-system bureaucracy denotes a stratification system.

## 12.3 STRATIFICATION IN THE SCHOOL SYSTEM

Like other social systems, schools reflect stratification and can promote still further stratification. The school that children attend can have an enormous influence on their life chances. Those who attend first-rate elementary and high schools can go on to prestigious colleges and can obtain high-paying jobs. At the other end of the spectrum, those who receive a poor education may become so frustrated that they quit without graduating. Some critics contend that schools are biased in favor of middle- and upper-class students at all levels, from the federal education bureaucracy to the local school board.

*Socioeconomic segregation in neighborhoods seems to define how students see themselves in the social hierarchy.* (iStockphoto)

### 12.3a Students

Traditionally, schools have been segregated by socioeconomic status in the United States because children go to neighborhood schools, and neighborhoods are segregated. Students of different races often attend different schools for the same reason. Many African and Hispanic Americans live in inner-city neighborhoods and go to predominantly African and Hispanic American schools. They also have a higher high school dropout rate than whites, although the dropout rate for all groups has declined by almost 50% since 1980 (see Table 12-2).

Lower-class students do not learn to read and write as well as those from higher-class backgrounds. As a result, they may come to believe that they are not capable of accomplishing what their contemporaries at other schools can accomplish. This lowers their achievement motivation, and they may become apathetic or alienated from the system.

Bowles and Gintis (1976) theorized that the wealthy, powerful class has benefited from neighborhood school systems that segregate students. In segregated school systems, students learn their place in the stratification system. Upper-class students learn about the hierarchy and the need to follow the rules of a hierarchy. They also learn that they can someday take their rightful place among the wealthy and powerful. They are actively socialized into the social system. Lower-class students also come to believe that upper-class people have a legitimate right to rule (Oakes, 1982). Intelligence tests have been shown to perpetuate the beliefs of all classes that the wealthy have a right to rule.

### 12.3b Biased Intelligence Tests

In 1916, Lewis M. Terman designed a test to measure what was called an "intelligence quotient," or "I.Q." The test was used for assessing a person's attainment of skills used in upper-middle-class occupations that involved manipulating numbers and words. The purpose of the test was to select students who were good at such manipulations to go on

**Table 12-2** Status Dropout Rates of 16- to 24-year-olds in the Civilian, Non-Institutionalized Population, by Race/Ethnicity: Selected Years, 1990–2010

| | White | Black | Hispanic | Asian/ Pacific Islander | American Indian/ Alaska Native |
|---|---|---|---|---|---|
| 1990 | 9.0 | 13.2 | 32.4 | 4.9! | 16.4! |
| 1995 | 8.6 | 12.1 | 30.0 | 3.9 | 13.4! |
| 1998 | 7.7 | 13.8 | 29.5 | 4.1 | 11.8 |
| 1999 | 7.3 | 12.6 | 28.6 | 4.3 | ‡ |
| 2000 | 6.9 | 13.1 | 27.8 | 3.8 | 14.0 |
| 2001 | 7.3 | 10.9 | 27.0 | 3.6 | 13.1 |
| 2002 | 6.5 | 11.3 | 25.7 | 3.9 | 16.8 |
| 2003 | 6.3 | 10.9 | 23.5 | 3.9 | 15.0 |
| 2004 | 6.8 | 11.8 | 23.8 | 3.6 | 17.0 |
| 2005 | 6.0 | 10.4 | 22.4 | 2.9 | 14.0 |
| 2006 | 5.8 | 10.7 | 22.1 | 3.6 | 14.7 |
| 2007 | 5.3 | 8.4 | 21.4 | 6.1 | 19.3 |
| 2008 | 4.8 | 9.9 | 18.5 | 4.4 | 14.6 |
| 2009 | 5.2 | 9.3 | 17.6 | 3.4 | 13.2 |
| 2010 | 5.1 | 8.0 | 15.1 | 4.2 | 12.4 |

*Note.* Race categories exclude persons of Hispanic ethnicity.

!Interpret data with caution. The coefficient of variation (CV) for this estimate is 30% or greater. ‡Reporting standards not met (too few cases).

Adapted from "The Condition of Education 2012" (NCES 2012-045), Indicator 33, U.S. Department of Education, National Center for Education Statistics. (2012).

*I.Q. tests were used to segregate the upper class from the lower class. Occupations were assigned accordingly. (iStockphoto)*

to advanced training. Terman and others believed that it measured an inherited genetic trait called "intelligence." They assumed that those who scored low on the test lacked intelligence and were less capable of learning than those who did well. It was argued that those who did poorly should be assigned to lower-class jobs.

The initial critics of intelligence tests argued that I.Q. tests do not measure an inherited characteristic; rather they measure a person's knowledge of upper-middle-class culture, which is why immigrants, the working class, the poor, and blacks score low while upper-middle-class Americans score high. For example, many I.Q. tests are mostly vocabulary tests, and the words that separate the average from the high scorers are words such as "amanuensis," "moiety," and "traduce." While some of the content of intelligence tests has been revised to address these criticisms, research has found that it is not only the content of the intelligence tests that can lead to a bias against lower socioeconomic groups but also the standardized nature of the tests and testing settings. Studies show that standard testing situations have a disruptive effect on how well people from lower socioeconomic groups perform when the students are told that the test is a measure of their intellectual ability. However, the test scores of lower socioeconomic students matched the test scores of students from higher socioeconomic backgrounds when the same test was not presented as a measure of intellectual ability (Croziet & Outrevis, 2004). Studies such as these suggest that standardized intelligence tests do not measure intrinsic ability. Critics say that the test serves the stratification system by creating a myth that convinces the lower classes that their station in life is part of the natural order of things (Karier, 1986). They come to believe that they are not capable of advancing in society to the higher positions, partly because they are not capable of attending prestigious private schools.

# 12.4 AMERICAN PRIVATE SCHOOLS

As of 2007, there were 33,740 private schools in the United States. Of these private schools in 2007–2008, 68% had a religious orientation (Brougham, Swain, & Keaton, 2009). By far the most common private schools in the United States, those serving a broad segment of the population, are the **parochial schools** run by the Catholic Church (22.2% of private schools) and founded to serve Catholics who want both an academic and a religious education for their children.

A newer phenomenon in American society is the growth of private religious schools not associated with the Catholic Church. These schools (13.8% of private schools) are sometimes referred to as "Christian schools," even though most private schools in the United States already have a Christian tradition. Some of the newer schools are affiliated with Protestant churches, and some have no formal link to traditional religion. Some of these schools developed to provide an alternative to racially integrated schools, and some to provide a place to teach an alternative set of values to students from those taught in the public schools. Currently, the number of students that these schools serve is about one-third the number of parochial-school students.

Other private preparatory schools have a very long history in this country; they are more expensive and they serve a wealthier student body. Finally, private schools of higher education offer an expensive education and serve only a small segment of society. Private systems are generally recognized as providing an education that is superior to those provided by the public schools.

## 12.4a Parochial Schools

Researchers (Byrk, Lee, & Holland, 1993) have found that Catholic-school students perform better than public high school students. They also found that school performance was not as closely linked to socioeconomic background in the Catholic high schools as it was in public schools. There are many reasons for the stronger performance of students in Catholic schools, including effective discipline, more monitoring of students' work, and higher expectations of the teachers for all students. For example, students in Catholic schools are more likely to take academic courses than they are in public schools, regardless of their ability or socioeconomic background. Students in Catholic schools are more likely to be groomed for college, whether they are financially able to go or not (Lee & Smith, 1995). In public schools, on the other hand, students from lower socioeconomic backgrounds are more likely to be steered into general or vocational curricula, and they are less likely to see a future connected with academic performance; thus, quite naturally, they will not work hard at academics.

**Parochial schools**
Schools run and maintained by a religious body or organization rather than the public at large

## 12.4b Private Preparatory Schools

The wealthy in America do not usually send their children to public schools, but rather to private **preparatory** ("prep") **schools** and then to private universities. Most of the elite private preparatory schools were founded in the late 1800s, as the American public school system developed. These private schools stated that their goals were more than intellectual development. For example, Groton, founded in 1884 in Massachusetts, stated in its opening announcement the following: "Every endeavor will be made to cultivate manly, Christian character, having regard to moral and physical as well as

**Preparatory schools**
Private schools, usually of a select and elite nature, that are intended to offer an intensive education in both academic and social/cultural activities

intellectual development" (McLachlan, 1970, p. 256). These prep schools offer a very intensive education, both in academics and in sports and cultural activities. It is generally accepted that these students receive an education superior to most, if not all, public high schools. The cost of tuition at Groton, for the 2010–2011 school year, was $48,895 for boarding students and $37,020 per year for day students.

Furthermore, students learn to see themselves as a select, exclusive group. In a study of administrators and faculty of 20 prestigious prep schools, as well as freshmen and seniors at those schools, Cookson and Persell (1985) found that students believed that they belonged to an exclusive, elite group. They also believed that because family and school provided all the friends they needed, they had no interest in meeting other people.

The exclusive nature of preparatory schools bothered both outside critics and the schools themselves, and efforts have been made to admit some students who would normally not be able to finance such an education. One such program was "A Better Chance," also known as the "ABC" program (Zweigenhaft & Domhoff, 2003, 1991). ABC enabled talented, inner-city minority students to attend some of the most prestigious prep schools with children of some of the wealthiest families in the United States. The minority students flourished both academically and socially, and well over 90% continued their education at highly selective colleges and universities. In spite of these accomplishments, these minority students still tended to be limited in their careers to middle-management positions. According to the National Center for Educational Statistics, the average cost for a year at a private school ranged from $9,000 to $36,000 per student in 2006.

## 12.4c Selective Private Colleges

Admittance to selective colleges and universities is no simple task, as many college students know by the time they read this text. The most prestigious colleges do not select students on the basis of intelligence and achievement alone. Studies of how Harvard University (2011–2012 tuition plus fees, $52,650) selects its students demonstrate how selection for college works against the student from a middle-class background who has little to offer except good grades (Karen, 1990; Klitgaard, 1985). Harvard does not select only students of high scholastic aptitude. They believe that the quality of their educational program would suffer because those who entered Harvard with very high grades but who found themselves in the bottom 25% of the class at Harvard would be unhappy (Klitgaard, 1985). Harvard would rather select some students who were not outstanding academically who would be happy to be in the bottom 25% of the class. Even though Harvard does choose applicants with truly outstanding academic records on the basis of intelligence alone, it also tries to choose students based on other criteria.

Elite institutions, such as Harvard, seek to select young people on the basis of what they will be able to contribute to society. (iStockphoto)

Harvard's Admissions Committee includes a few faculty members, but it is comprised primarily of professional admissions officers who specialize in searching for students who would add a "well-rounded" dimension to the student body. They sort applications according to a variety of criteria, such as scholastic aptitude; whether the student is the child of a Harvard graduate, an athlete, or a public or private school graduate; from what area of the country the student comes; or whether the student is a foreign candidate.

The outcome of this selection process, according to Karen (1990), is that those from prep schools have an advantage over those from public schools and that those from elite prep schools have the greatest advantage.

Children of alumni and athletes have a great advantage, minority groups have an advantage if they went to elite prep schools, and Asians are at a disadvantage.

Harvard, like many elite institutions, hopes to improve the lives of young people; however, it also wants its educational program to have an impact on the society as a whole. It attempts to select young people on the basis of what they will be able to contribute to society. A young person who has been educated in one of the best private schools and whose family has important connections in business or government is more likely to hold, eventually, a key position in society. Education will probably have a greater added value in that person's career than educating a person with no such contacts. Most selective American colleges are believed to have similar procedures.

Although our prestigious colleges are respected worldwide for providing a high-quality education, most of the American educational system has come under attack in the past 2 decades.

In 2010–2011, the average total price of attendance (tuition plus room and board) for full time students at a public 2-year college was approximately $8,000 per year, approximately $16,000 per year at a public 4-year college, and approximately $33,000 per year at a private 4-year institution. Studies show a slow down in college tuition increases (National Center for Education Statistics, 2011).

## 12.5 THE FAILURE OF AMERICAN SCHOOLS

America and foreign nations, alike, have been increasingly concerned about the failure of American public schools to educate young people. Comparisons with other countries reveal that Americans do very poorly on test scores, especially in science and math. As explained in the first part of this chapter, high school graduates are woefully inadequately prepared for college work in English, reading, math, and science.

**BVT*Lab***

Visit www.BVTLab.com to explore the student resources available for this chapter.

Performance in some other areas is equally poor. The National Association of Education Progress' *The Nations Report Card, Civics 2010* found that fewer than half of American eighth graders knew the purpose of The Bill of Rights and only 1 in 10 demonstrated an acceptable knowledge of the checks and balances of the legislative, executive and judicial branches of the Federal government (Dillon, 2011). Unfortunately, 75% of high school seniors could not identify the effect of United States foreign policy on other countries, nor could they name a power of Congress granted by the Constitution.

## 12.6 WHY STUDENTS DO NOT LEARN

A variety of reasons are given to explain why American students do not learn in school. They include low socioeconomic statuses of families and pupils, poor resources in school facilities, inadequate curricula, students discouraged from striving toward success, and high dropout rates.

### 12.6a Financial Problems

Whatever the problems are in our educational system, they probably are not due simply to a lack of money. Money spent, per pupil, on public school education has risen significantly in the past half-century, as shown in Table 12-3. The increase has been more rapid than could be explained by a rising cost of living. Some of this money has been used to increase the number of teachers and staff, with the result being a steady decrease in the number of students per instructional staff member (Table 12-4).

## Table 12-3 Current Expenditures per Pupil in Fall Enrollment in Public Elementary and Secondary Schools: Selected Years, 1961–1962 through 2008–2009

| School Year | Expenditures in Unadjusted Dollars | Expenditures in Constant 2009–2010 Dollars[1] |
|---|---|---|
| 1961–1962 | 393 | 2,835 |
| 1970–1971 | 842 | 4,596 |
| 1980–1981 | 2,307 | 5,773 |
| 1986–1987 | 3,682 | 7,174 |
| 1991–1991 | 4,902 | 7,933 |
| 1995–1996 | 5,689 | 7,981 |
| 1996–1997 | 5,923 | 8,079 |
| 1997–1998 | 6,189 | 8,293 |
| 1998–1999 | 6,508 | 8,572 |
| 1999–2000 | 6,912 | 8,849 |
| 2000–2001 | 7,380 | 9,135 |
| 2001–2002 | 7,727 | 9,399 |
| 2002–2003 | 8,044 | 9,574 |
| 2003–2004 | 8,310 | 9,679 |
| 2004–2005 | 8,711 | 9,849 |
| 2005–2006 | 9,145 | 9,960 |
| 2006–2007 | 9,679 | 10,276 |
| 2007–2008[2] | 10,298 | 10,543 |
| 2008–2009 | 10,591 | 10,694 |

*Note.* Beginning in 1980–81, state administration expenditures are excluded from "current" expenditures. Current expenditures include instruction, student support services, food services and enterprise operations. Beginning in 1988–89, extensive changes were made in the data collection procedures.

[1]Constant dollars based on the Consumer Price Index, prepared by the Bureau of Labor Statistics, U.S. Department of Labor, adjusted to a school-year basis. [2]Revised from previously published figures.

Adapted from "Digest of Education Statistics, 2011" (NCES 2012-001), Table 191 and Chapter 2. U.S. Department of Education, National Center for Education Statistics (2012).

## Table 12-4 Public and Private Elementary and Secondary Pupil/Teacher Ratios: Selected Years, Fall 1955 through Fall 2015

| Year | Pupil/Teacher Ratio | | |
|---|---|---|---|
| | Total | Public | Private |
| 1955 | 27.4 | 26.9 | 31.7 |
| 1960 | 26.4 | 25.8 | 30.7 |
| 1965 | 25.1 | 24.7 | 28.3 |
| 1970 | 22.4 | 22.3 | 23.0 |
| 1975 | 20.3 | 20.4 | 19.6 |
| 1980 | 18.6 | 18.7 | 17.7 |
| 1985 | 17.6 | 17.9 | 16.2 |
| 1990 | 17.0 | 7.2 | 15.6 |
| 1995 | 17.1 | 17.3 | 15.7 |
| 2000 | 15.9 | 16.0 | 14.5 |
| 2005 | 15.4 | 15.6 | 13.5 |
| 2010 (projected) | 14.9 | 15.2 | 12.6 |
| 2015 (projected) | 14.8 | 15.1 | 12.4 |

SOURCE: "Digest of Education Statistics," National Center for Education Statistics.

## 12.6b School Facilities

James Coleman and a team of sociologists have done a series of studies (1966; 1997; 1990) to compare the facilities of schools in black and white neighborhoods. Coleman found that the schools were the same age, spent the same amount of money per pupil, and had equivalent library and laboratory facilities. Teacher qualifications and class size were also the same. He concluded that the differences in achievement were related to the students' socioeconomic backgrounds, not to differences in the school facilities. Coleman also found that black students performed better in white schools and recommended busing students to promote integration. Busing was carried out in many localities, but both black and white citizens disliked busing children to schools in other neighborhoods. Many argued that it interfered with the concept of neighborhood schools and local control.

## 12.6c Inadequate Curricula

Much of the problem in students not learning, according to the National Commission on Excellence in Education, is the deterioration of school curricula in the public schools. Today, about half of all students in high school take a general studies course, compared to only 12% in 1964. While most of the courses in a general studies program are traditional academic studies such as English, history, or science, 25% of the credits earned in general studies are in physical and health education, work experience, remedial courses, and electives such as bachelor living. Only 31% of high school students take intermediate algebra, only 6% take calculus, and total homework assignments require an average of less than 1 hour a night. It has already been noted that parochial schools have an advantage over public schools, in part because they continue to emphasize academic subjects. The National Commission urged a greater emphasis on academic subjects in the public schools, recommending 4 years of English and 3 years each of math, science, and social studies. However, most states have failed to meet these standards.

Meanwhile, the United States concerns itself with issues such as a so-called politically correct curriculum, the values that are taught, the future career potential of students, and other issues not related to academic subjects.

## 12.6d The Self-Fulfilling Prophecy

There are many ways to discourage students from achieving in the classroom. One way is to discourage students from believing that learning and achievement are possible. Rosenthal and Jacobson (1968) found that students do not learn as well when their teachers believe that the students are not very bright. If teachers have learned that lower class and minority students do not perform well on I.Q. and achievement tests, they will have lower expectations of them in class. Even if they do perform well, teachers may fail to recognize their talents, give them lower grades, and confuse and frustrate them. Thus, a **self-fulfilling prophecy** is at work.

This self-fulfilling prophecy was evident in a study of pupil-teacher interaction, where it was found that teachers asked black students simpler questions than they asked white students. If a black pupil could not answer a question, the teacher asked somebody else. If a white pupil could not answer a question, however, the teacher gave an explanation. Teachers also praised and complimented white students more than black students when they gave correct answers (Weinberg, 1977).

**Self-fulfilling prophecy**
A prediction that comes true because people believe it and act as though it were true

## 12.6e High Dropout Rate

Worse than the students who finish without adequate preparation are those who do not finish at all. Dropout rates for young people ages 16–24 have declined from 12.1% to 7.4% between 1990 and 2010. However, these rates are still considered high, and dropout rates are even higher in minority communities (see Table 12-2).

### thinking SOCIOLOGICALLY

1. Using sociological perspectives about education as the basis for your ideas, what types of changes in your college's curriculum would you recommend to the administration at your school?
2. Discuss the extent to which the curriculum in your college is guided by a traditional Western intellectual perspective or a multicultural perspective. In light of this, what are the functions of your school's curriculum?
3. If you were to become a high school teacher, what personal assumptions would you have to address? Do you hold stereotypes about particular groups? Do you believe that children learn differently because of gender? Social class? How would being an observant sociologist guide your work as a teacher?

# 12.7 IMPROVING THE SCHOOLS

A variety of changes to the public school system are being tested in order to improve the schools in the United States. Some of these changes are discussed in the following sections.

## 12.7a Magnet Schools

**Magnet schools**
Schools with special programs designed to attract exceptional students

In recent years, magnet schools have been developed in segregated school districts. **Magnet schools** are schools with special programs designed to attract exceptional students. These students voluntarily travel outside of their neighborhoods to go to the magnet schools. The hope is that white students will be attracted to schools with heavy black enrollment, and thus integration will be achieved. One fear of magnet school programs is that tax dollars and the best students in a district will be concentrated in magnet schools, and other schools will be left with mediocre programs and students. Most magnet schools are new, so it is too early to judge their success conclusively. Some early research findings suggest that magnet schools are not achieving the goal of integration. One study (Rossell, 2003) found that the more magnets that exist in a voluntary desegregation plan, the greater the "white flight" and the less interracial exposure. This may be because magnet schools are disruptive, and the more magnets, the more disruption. In areas that have mandatory desegregation plans, this is not as much the case since there is already considerable disruption without the magnets. However, in voluntary desegregation areas, the effectiveness of magnet schools on achieving integration can be increased if demand, location and structure are considered in their planning.

*Magnet schools have special programs designed to attract exceptional students, and provide one option that is being tested to improve the public school system in the United States.* (AP Wide World Photo)

## 12.7b Decentralized Bureaucracies

Another approach to improving the schools is to **decentralize** the **bureaucracy**, in other words, put more of the decision-making processes in the hands of local schools instead of giving all authority to the school boards. This approach is being attempted in the Chicago school system (Muwakkil, 1990), but with considerable debate and conflict. Chicago has a very large school system, where the relatively elite Central Board of Education has been distant from the less aristocratic local schools over which it rules. Chicago has worked very hard to recruit ethnic and racial minorities onto the school board of this mostly minority-populated school system. Now that they have succeeded in getting minority representation on the school board, critics want to decentralize and some believe the real intent is to take power away from the now-integrated school board. In other words, the intent is to reinstitute discrimination via a different mechanism.

Instead of the school board running the schools, the schools in Chicago are now to be run by parent-controlled local school councils (LSCs). The LSCs have the right to hire and fire principals, select textbooks, and develop curricula. Many have chosen to fire the principals and are under attack for discrimination and other unfair practices. Some critics argue that parents, especially in the poorest districts, are not equipped to carry out the responsibilities of the LSCs. Whether these changes actually will improve Chicago's schools remains to be seen.

## 12.7c Vouchers

A third approach to improving our educational system is to give parents a choice of schools to which to send their children. If they choose a private school, they will receive a **voucher** for state funds with which to pay the tuition. The Supreme Court of the State of Wisconsin ruled on June 10, 1998, that the Milwaukee voucher program, which will allow up to 15,000 children to attend any religious or private school, does not violate the state or federal constitution. This decision was appealed all the way to the United States Supreme Court. The high court ruled 8–1 not to hear the appeal and thus allowed the verdict in Wisconsin to stand. Government-run voucher programs are very controversial and have been heavily criticized. Those who support the idea of choosing a school believe that parents will choose the best schools for their children. Schools will have to upgrade in order to compete for students, or they will not be able to stay open. Critics of the system argue, however, that parents may not be in the best position to choose a school and may be offered a shoddy product. Furthermore, the number of good schools is limited and most students will have to remain in the Milwaukee school system, which has admittedly been doing a poor job of educating its students. Lastly, some critics claim vouchers are nothing more than unfair discounts for the rich who can already afford the full cost of expensive private schools like Groton. To be sure, according to the National Conference of State Legislators, over three-quarters of the funds for Arizona's voucher program go to students already in private schools, with less than a fifth going to students from public schools (Spartenburg County Legislative Delegation, 2005). The end result, say the critics, is that voucher systems not only weaken public education by draining money from public schools, they also fail to provide enough money for middle- and working-class parents to send their children to the same elite private schools that wealthy students attend.

*In some states, parents receive state paid vouchers to help pay for private school tuition. However, this method is very controversial and has received much criticism.*
*(AP Wide World Photo)*

**Decentralized bureaucracies**
Putting the decision making processes in the hands of the people or local units rather than in the hands of a centralized few

**Voucher**
State-backed credit that gives parents the option to send their children to private schools by using state funds to pay for the tuition

## 12.7d New Management

Chelsea, Massachusetts, has turned over the management of the city schools to Boston University (Ribadeneira, 1990), and those educators now run the local schools. This approach has also been met with criticism. Critics argue that the university is authoritarian and patronizing. Teachers complain that they are left out of the decision-making process. Hispanic leaders complain that the university has failed to consider bilingual education. This, like other experiments in reform, has met with considerable conflict from the community.

Other approaches being considered or attempted include paying teachers on the basis of merit, involving business and industry more extensively in the educational system, having children begin school at age 4, and increasing the length of the school day and the school year. A wholesale increase in schooling is a risky proposition at best, however, when we do not know why students are not performing well. If schools, however subtly, are encouraging our lower classes and minority students to fail—as would be indicated by the high dropout rate among these students—increasing the school day, the school year, and the number of requirements might also increase the apathy and discouragement felt by these students. Likewise, if school is too strongly oriented toward middle-class occupations and is therefore discouraging to people from the lower classes, and if job opportunities do not increase, might the involvement of the business community in the schools make matters worse? Simple solutions to remedy our very complex problems in education and stratification will probably not work.

**BVT *Lab***

Improve your test scores. Practice quizzes are available at **www.BVTLab.com**

## 12.7e Creating Future Goals

Although differences in achievement have been related to family background and to the quality of the schools, one variable—future opportunity—has been given little consideration. However, a program begun almost accidentally may demonstrate that future opportunity is most important when considering achievement. In 1981, multimillionaire Eugene Lang returned to his old school in East Harlem to speak to the sixth-grade graduating class, a group of minority students living in one of the poorest neighborhoods in the country ("I Have a Dream" Foundation, 2008). He told them that he would pay for the college education of anyone in the class who would stay in school. He also changed their poor environment by giving them his friendship and moral support through tutoring, career counseling, and other advantages that wealth can bring. In a school where typically only half of students graduate and where only 1 or 2 in 100 have grades high enough for college admission, 90% of Lang's group of hopeful sixth-graders stayed in school through high school; more than half had grades that would enable them to attend college. Perhaps a promising future is necessary for success in school, especially if teachers as well as students believe that success is possible. Perhaps a belief that the students can and will attend college is as necessary in public high schools as it is in parochial high schools. Perhaps the United States should look at a different system of rewards for work accomplished in school.

# 12.8 CONTEST AND SPONSORED MOBILITY

**Contest mobility**
A competitive system of education in which those who do best at each level are able to move on the next level

In the United States, students can get as much education as they are willing and able to pay for, as long as they maintain the grades necessary for acceptance at the next higher level. This system has been labeled **contest mobility** (Turner, 1960) because students can continue as long as they meet the standards of each level. The high school graduate can apply to college, the 2-year college graduate can apply to a 4-year institution, and the college graduate can apply to a graduate school. Once out of school, the contest continues as students compete with each other for jobs.

However, the contest is not based entirely on performance. As was stressed earlier, the most prestigious schools in America do choose students who have good grades, but they also choose students with lower grades who are likely to make outstanding contributions to society (Klitgaard, 1985). These students are often children of people in powerful government or business positions. Education is also limited by the ability to pay. Poor students in the United States have been able to get grants and loans to help pay college costs; yet middle-income families in the United States must pay thousands of dollars a year, on average, to attend a public or private college.

By contrast, Japan and most European countries have a system known as **sponsored mobility**. In these countries, students must pass qualifying examinations to gain admittance into different types of high schools and colleges. Once they pass the exams, however, their education is sponsored; furthermore, if they do their work, they are assured of success both in school and upon completion of their studies. They do not pay any tuition for their higher education (Johnstone, 1986). In Britain and in Sweden, students receive grants and loans for living expenses and are discouraged from working while in school. Of course, students in these countries who do not earn good grades cannot further their education.

**Sponsored mobility**
A system of education in which certain students are selected at an early age to receive advanced education and training

Within these systems, educational tracks vary. Students may receive a classical education leading to a university degree, a business education, or engineering and technical training. Once they enter a particular track, they rarely change to another type of education. A student in business school, for example, is unlikely to switch to a university.

## thinking SOCIOLOGICALLY

1. How would you change job qualifications or credentials so that students would be more eager to perform?
2. Do you think that guaranteed jobs for top performers would increase school performance?
3. How would you change the school system so that it would be less costly?

# CHAPTER 12 Wrapping it up

## Summary

1. Structural functional theory argues that education in a complex industrial society supplements what families can teach their children and that it helps children to acquire both the complex skills and the knowledge necessary to function in the world. The educational system also selects students on the basis of their talents and abilities to meet the needs of society, directing the most talented into advanced education and training for positions of leadership while directing those with less talent to the positions in which they will serve society best. Educational institutions also create new knowledge and new technology, which they teach to the next generation. They create innovation and change so that society can advance.
2. Conflict theory argues that education is a means by which powerful groups prevent change; they use the educational system to teach children their values and norms, so everyone will believe that the position of the powerful is justified. Powerful groups promote children and give diplomas and degrees on the basis of how well students know their culture. Children of the wealthy usually receive prestigious credentials from prestigious schools and move into high-paying, prestigious jobs, while those from the lower classes tend to remain in lower-class jobs.
3. The American educational system was begun by the Puritans and developed into our modern system of elementary schools, secondary schools, colleges, and universities.
4. Schools are complicated bureaucracies—directed and financed by local, state, and federal boards—which determine curricula, testing procedures, and other requirements for certification. Superintendents, principals, and teachers implement the various rules and standards; students, upon meeting the standards, receive the appropriate diplomas and degrees.
5. Stratification is pervasive in the educational system. School board members are likely to be business leaders, and teachers are likely to be from the middle or working classes. Students are segregated into rich or poor neighborhood schools. Intelligence tests are biased toward upper-middle-class culture.
6. Private schools in the United States include Catholic and other religious-based parochial schools, private preparatory schools, and private colleges. Selective private colleges have a complicated admissions system that does not select exclusively on the basis of grades, thereby allowing class-based differences to play a stronger role in selection.
7. Education in the United States has been criticized because tests show that American students perform well below those in other industrialized countries. Schools have been criticized for lacking funding, strong curricula, and good facilities.
8. School systems are trying solutions such as magnet schools, decentralized bureaucracies, vouchers, and management by universities.
9. European school systems differ from the American system, not only by providing a better education, but also by sponsoring students who academically qualify for further education. College tuition is provided by the national governments.
10. Some critics argue that too much education is required now and that this requirement is detrimental to the working class, who cannot afford it when, at the end of their courses of study, they do not experience the upward mobility in occupations that they had hoped to gain.

## Discussion Questions



1. What do you see as some specific latent and manifest functions of education in your college?
2. To what extent does your school emphasize credentialism in your selection of courses and major?
3. Discuss ways in which your own educational experience has served to maintain your socioeconomic position in society.
4. If you believed that children were naturally lethargic, how would you structure schools? If you believed that children were naturally geniuses, how would you structure schools? Given the nature of your own school experience, what assumptions about children do you suppose have been made?
5. How might your school experience have been different if you had gone to a more integrated school? A less integrated school? Be specific.
6. How might your school experience have been different if you had gone to a school with more money? A school with less money? Be specific.
7. If there were fewer opportunities to go to college in the United States, but tuition were free, would this improve or diminish your chances of finishing college? Does your answer have anything to do with your socioeconomic status?
8. If there were fewer educational credentials for jobs and more emphasis on job experiences, would this improve your chances for a good career or make your chances more difficult? Does your answer have anything to do with your socioeconomic status?
9. Discuss the positive and negative functions of contest and of sponsored mobility for individuals and for society.
10. Make up a list of issues for the board of trustees of your college to consider that would improve education where you are.

CHAPTER 13

# Political and Economic Groups and Systems

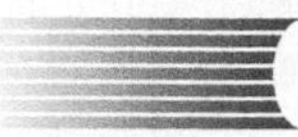

## SYNOPSIS

## Focal Point

# GOVERNMENT AND THE AMERICAN ECONOMY

The final months of 2012 were fraught with anxiety about the U.S. economy going over a fiscal cliff. The "fiscal cliff" was a popular expression used to describe the potential economic effects of tax increases, government spending cuts, and a reduction in the government budget scheduled to begin in 2013, if laws remained unchanged. It was a complex government economic situation mired in years of policies stemming from a number of presidential administrations (CBS Detroit, 2012). The fiscal cliff was one of the biggest news stories in the final weeks of 2012, with a key obstacle to reaching a solution being the ideological difference between Democrats and Republicans in Congress. Much attention was given to the significant differences between the political parties in reaching a solution, and yet this wrangle with issues concerning the economy was nothing new in U.S. politics. In 2009, the American Recovery and Reinvestment Act had underscored the deep ideological divide between Democrats and Republicans about the proper role of government in economic activity. When Congress enacted the economic stimulus package in 2009, nearly every Democrat supported the bill whereas most Republicans rejected it. The dispute centered on the question of whether the federal government should intervene in the economy by boosting government spending to stimulate economic growth. Republicans claimed the stimulus bill reflected a broader socialist agenda by the Democrats that would undercut economic performance and individual drive in the United States. The Democrats disagreed, saying the stimulus money would not only boost economic growth but also reinforce capitalism by creating thousands of jobs in the private sector.

The political divide over the American Recovery and Reinvestment Act and the debates pertaining to preventing the fiscal cliff in 2012 are important because they highlight a major subject of sociological inquiry—the differences between economic systems. The American economy today is essentially capitalist. That is, government regulation and control over the U.S. economy is limited. Moreover, any idea that the U.S. economy is somehow socialist has no merit. Socialist economies are state-run, and everyone has employment for life. Still, it is indisputable that the U.S. government plays a major role in guiding the American economy. Why then do so many Americans oppose socialism? For that matter, why do some Americans criticize capitalism? To answer these questions, it pays to examine the extremes of the two systems. Consider the following two hypothetical cases. While neither of these descriptions is an accurate depiction of the Unites States, they represent stereotypes fostered by critics of each system.

Imagine the United States is completely capitalist with no government regulation or interference in the economy. Everyone is free to accumulate as much wealth as possible. Corporate and personal income taxes are things of the past. Employees are exploited through low wages in order to maximize profits. As competition grows, so does corporate espionage. Without public schools, only the wealthy can afford primary or college educations. Meanwhile, banks raise interest rates as high as 90% on business loans, cutting deeply into company profits. Without regulation, banks can do whatever they want. Large corporations have difficulty raising capital as well. With rampant insider trading, confidence in the stock market is perpetually low. Large corporations simply cannot sell enough shares to accumulate adequate amounts of capital. Pollution increases because it is more cost-effective for large corporations not to have pollution-controls. Air and water pollution lead to rapid environmental deterioration as well as an increase in illnesses. Travel becomes prohibitively expensive. First, since everyone pays expensive tolls on all the privately owned roads, it's not cost-effective to send negotiators from place to place. Second, the cost of gasoline is enormous because of price-fixing by multinational petroleum companies.

*The U.S. economy is based on capitalism. (iStockphoto)*

Now imagine the U.S. economy is entirely socialist. All land, factories, banks, and stores are government owned. The pursuit of profit is a capital crime. Citizens can own personal items, such as clothing and bicycles, but are prohibited from owning any property that generates profit such as apartments for rent. The economy is highly regulated to meet national economic goals. However, to meet these goals, central planners regularly deprive Americans of the latest technology and fashion. Everyone has a free education, but schools are dilapidated because no tax revenue is available to pay for new buildings and equipment. The teachers, moreover, are mostly unqualified because nobody with talent goes to college willingly. Because everyone gets paid equally under socialism, there's no incentive to work hard. Government officials, therefore, resort to tactics of intimidation and tyranny to generate economic productivity. For example, the government may force students to major in certain subjects when professionals in those fields are in short supply. The government may also tell students where to live and work after graduation. It does not matter if anyone agrees with the government; citizens do what they're told. Even with its tyrannical tactics, however, the government never generates the same level of national output as capitalist countries. That's why everyone routinely waits in long lines to get basic amenities such as bread and butter. Meanwhile, citizens who are sick receive free medical care, but the quality of treatment is substandard. Most doctors are mediocre as well. It's easy to understand. When professionals earn the same amount as high-school dropouts, they're not motivated to provide superior service.

Clearly, neither of these scenarios is an accurate depiction of these economic systems. However, it also seems clear that there needs to be a balance between laissez-faire competition and government intervention in order to have a stable economy. The United States is one of the most capitalist countries on earth. However, political wrangling over the government's role in the economy is as old as the republic. In every period, however, one thing remains constant: The government plays a major role in fostering the economic power of the United States. A key goal of this chapter, then, is to provide students with the ability to analyze and evaluate different economic systems and the effects of policies like the American Recovery and Reinvestment Act on society.

As the opening vignette to this chapter suggests, there is a very close connection between government and the economy. To survive, people need food, shelter, and healthcare. Except for those who live in the tropics, people also need clothing and a source of heat. To be accepted in modern American society, however, we need a great deal more—soap, deodorant, toothpaste, shoes, and various types of clothes for different occasions. We also enjoy the luxuries our society provides—such as plates, knives, forks, furniture, cars, sporting equipment, radios, televisions, the Internet, iPods, tablets, and so on. All these things, from the most basic necessities to the most expensive luxuries, are produced by our economic system. The **economic system** is the social system that provides for the production, distribution, and consumption of goods and services.

Yet, at the same time, an economic system affects and is affected by a system of laws that regulate what people can and cannot do. Laws also regulate what and how goods can be produced, distributed and consumed. In large, complex societies, many decisions must be made about the duties and responsibilities of citizens and also about their rights and privileges. If the society is to be orderly, people must obey the rules that are made. **Politics** is the use of power to determine who gets what in society. The political institution establishes and enforces the laws and punishes those who disobey them. It can levy taxes, distribute scarce resources, sponsor education, plan the economy, encourage or ban religion, determine who can marry and who is responsible for children, and otherwise influence behavior. The study of political groups and systems, then, is the study of power.

**Economic system**
The social institution that provides for the production, distribution, and consumption of goods and services

**Politics**
The use of power to determine who gets what in society

## 13.1 TYPES OF POWER

**Power** is generally viewed as the ability to control the behavior of others, to make decisions about their rights and privileges, and to see to it that people obey the rules

**Power**
The ability to control or influence the behavior of others, even without their consent

or other expectations of the powerful. Max Weber (1946) pointed out that there are several types of power. **Physical force** is one obvious type. An individual or an army can be captured and put into handcuffs or prison by a stronger individual or army. Often, however, sheer force accomplishes little. Although people can be physically restrained, they cannot be made to perform complicated tasks by force alone.

**Latent force**, or the threat of force, is more powerful than force alone. Kidnappers can get what they want by demanding ransom in exchange for the victim's life. The kidnappers want the money and hope that the threat of murder will produce it—a dead victim does not do the kidnapper any good. Similarly, a ruler can say, "Either perform your duty or you will go to jail," hoping that the threat of jail will make the citizen perform the desired duty. Putting the citizen in jail, however, would not really help the ruler. Latent force can sometimes produce results in situations in which direct force would not.

Controlling a society through force, whether actual or latent, is expensive and inefficient. It does not bring about the cooperation necessary for society to function productively. A group that relies on force to maintain its power faces a constant threat of being overthrown by its citizens, whereas more reliable types of power do not depend on force for their effectiveness. **Legitimate power**—such as the power to make and enforce rules that benefit all—is power that is accepted by the people in a society as being necessary and beneficial.

**Authority** is power accepted as legitimate by those it affects. The people give the ruler the authority to rule, and they obey willingly without the need for force. Weber, who was a master at classifying the abstract concepts needed to understand society, identified three types of authority: (1) traditional authority, (2) charismatic authority, and (3) legal authority. In **traditional authority**, the leader of the group leads by tradition or custom. In a patriarchal society, the father is the ruler and is obeyed because this practice is accepted by those ruled. When the father dies, his eldest son becomes ruler and has authority based on the nation's customs. Rulers who have traditional authority are usually born into their positions, and their competence to rule is not usually at issue. Also, the bounds of authority for traditional rulers are fairly broad—their power can range from settling minor disagreements to dictating who can marry whom.

The second type of authority, **charismatic authority**, is based on the personal attributes of the leader. Sometimes, a person can win the confidence, support, and trust of a group of people who then give the leader the authority to make decisions and set down rules. A charismatic leader attracts followers because they judge him or her to be particularly wise or capable. Martin Luther King, Jr., was this kind of leader. King gained followers because he was a speaker who addressed people with sincerity and a sense of mission. He won their respect. With their support, he was able to lead a political fight to improve the position of blacks in the United States.

The third type of authority, **legal authority**, is based on a system of rules and regulations that determine how the society will be governed. In the United States, the U.S. Constitution sets down the bases for the government's authority, giving Congress the legal authority to enact laws and the president the legal authority to carry them out. The president also directs the military when it is needed to enforce the law and brings before courts or pardons those who break it. The courts interpret the laws and make judgments about whether the laws have been broken.

Weber was especially concerned with some of the characteristics of legal authority. The power granted by legal authority is based on the rules and regulations governing the office. The power of the individual officeholder is limited by those rules, and the individual has power only as long as he or she adheres to those rules. Legal authority rests in the organization, and the organization attempts to serve its own interests and to meet its own goals. Thus, power in the United States rests in organizations—not in the will of the individual citizens.

The federal bureaucracy in the United States, for example, has grown so much in recent years that its size has become an issue in presidential elections. Candidates

**Physical force**

A type of power backed by sheer force, such as an army or physical might

**Latent force**

A type of power in which force is threatened

**Legitimate power**

Controlling the behavior of others through having people accept authority as necessary and beneficial to all

**Authority**

Power accepted as legitimate by those it affects

**Traditional authority**

The right to rule granted to someone on the basis of tradition, as with a patriarch or king

**Charismatic authority**

Authority granted to someone on the bases of his or her personality characteristics

**Legal authority**

Authority based on a system of rules and regulations that determine how a society will be governed routinely promise to cut back on the number of federal employees. Once in office, however, they find that the bureaucracy has ways of resisting major cutbacks and that it is almost impossible to make substantial reductions—even in the president's own executive branch. Because presidents cannot afford to antagonize the people on whom they rely to implement their policies, the bureaucracy often continues from administration to administration without significant reduction in size.

## APPLYING POWER AND AUTHORITY

Power is not something that is used only by political leaders or army officers. Most of us use it from time to time in our daily personal and professional lives. If you know the various types of power and authority, you may be able to increase your effectiveness as a parent, employer, business executive, teacher, doctor, politician, police officer, and in many other roles. Although Weber probably did not have these roles in mind when he was developing his ideas regarding power and authority, we can extrapolate how these concepts might be applied to everyday roles.

There are different forms of power and authority. For example, parents can rely on a type of traditional authority to control their children rather than resorting to latent or physical force. (iStockphoto)

As a parent, for example, you have the ability, for the most part, to control (or at least try to) your children through traditional authority. Typically, you would have little need to justify your demands, and you would not have to rely on latent or physical force when you want them to clean their rooms or to be home by midnight. "Because I said so" is a sufficient explanation for parents to give for demands they make of their children. However, a teacher who uses the same type of explanation to get students to complete a reading assignment will probably suffer a loss of students' respect and diminished overall effectiveness. Often, teachers are more effective when they rely on legal authority, in which the students are firmly reminded that to learn the material and get a passing grade, they must comply with the rules. In some instances, talented teachers can inspire their students to work hard through their charismatic personalities, but charismatic authority would be unlikely to work in most classrooms. However, charismatic authority could be an extremely effective form of control and leadership for political leaders, ministers, or even managers of sports teams. Generally, then, a more effective way of leading people is to be aware of the different forms of power and authority and to be sensitive to what works best in various situations, rather than merely to rely on one method that worked well in one situation.

## 13.2 POLITICAL STRUCTURES IN MODERN SOCIETIES

As societies become wealthier and more complex, political systems grow more powerful. In very primitive and simple societies, there was no ruler and decisions were made as a group. As societies evolved from uncomplicated bands, they grew wealthier; their rulers were able to control larger areas with their armies. States developed. **States** are societies with institutional means of political regulation (government and laws), military defense, and a way to finance these activities (Hall, 1986). At first, controlled areas were small; later, cities and the surrounding areas came under the power of individual rulers. These territories were called **city-states**. Today, most of the world is organized into

**States**
Societies with institutional government and laws as a means of political regulation, military defense, and a way to finance these activities

**City-state**
A city and the surrounding area ruled independently of other areas

**nation-states**, large territories ruled by a single institution. Nation-states developed in Europe several centuries ago, but they arose in Africa only during the past century.

There are two types of legal political rule in modern societies: democracy, in which the people control the government, and *totalitarianism*, in which the state rules the people. Neither of these types is found in a pure form, and many countries have a mixed power structure. In analyzing modern societies, however, it is useful to describe power structures in terms of their ideal types.

## 13.2a The Democratic State

In its ideal form, a **democracy** is a power structure in which people govern themselves. Philosophers such as Jean Jacques Rousseau, John Locke, John Stuart Mill, and John Dewey believed that people knew what was in their own best interests and could learn how to protect these interests within the political system. They also believed that the experience of being politically involved would develop better citizens (Orum, 1978). One major problem with democracies, however, is the likelihood that **oligarchies**, or ruling elites, will develop (Michels, 1911). As a result, instead of all people sharing in their own governance, a few people have a monopoly of power and rule for everyone. Michels (1911) believed that in nation-states and other large organizations, the rise of a few to dominate power was inevitable. He called this the **iron law of oligarchy**.

An early attempt to practice democracy was made by the Greek city-state of Athens, but it was actually an oligarchy. Leadership was rotated, and all government responsibility was shared among the citizens. This system is evident in the Greek use of the term **citizen**, referring to those who were considered members of the city-state and who were entitled to the freedoms and privileges granted to members of that state. Only a small percentage of the population of Athens were citizens; because there were so few, every citizen could participate directly in the political process. However, the great majorities of the city's inhabitants—the slaves, women, and foreigners—were not considered citizens and had no political standing.

Changes in social attitudes have raised women, the lower socioeconomic classes, and other groups from the low status they occupied in ancient Greece to the status of citizens in modern Western civilization. Nonetheless, true democracy continues to be impossible because of the unwieldy size of modern political populations. As a result, modern democracies have chosen a system of representation by which the population elects officials to act as their agents. The elected officials, in turn, appoint the upper-level civil servants and justices of the court. Therefore, when we refer today to "democratic" power structures, we mean those in which people are allowed to vote for elected representatives. It is assumed that the elected representatives will be removed from office if they are not responsive to the desires of the people. Although representative governments of this sort have laws to limit the power of officials and to protect the rights of individuals—especially their rights to equality and to dissent—there is no question that the elected officials and the people they appoint have a great deal of power.

Even in modern democracies, elites may use their power to form an oligarchy. They maintain power by manipulating the electorate. They may, for example, stuff ballot boxes and miscount votes. They may use the mass media to distribute information selectively, advertising favorable information and covering up information that the electorate may not favor. When an oligarchy develops in large bureaucratic governments, the elite sets policy, the bureaucracy carries out that policy, and the citizens believe that the rule is still legitimate, as long as they are allowed to vote (Etzioni-Halevey, 1997).

**Nation-state**
A large territory ruled by a single political institution

**Democracy**
A power structure in which people govern themselves, either directly or through elected representatives

**Oligarchy**
Government by a small elite group

**Iron law of oligarchy**
In democratic societies, the inevitable rise of a few elite leaders who dominate power

**Citizen**
One who is considered a member of a state and who is entitled to the privileges and freedoms granted to members of the state

**Totalitarianism**
A power structure in which the government has total power to dictate the values, rules, ideology, and economic development of a society

## 13.2b The Totalitarian State

**Totalitarianism** is a system of rule in which the government has total control. The government dictates the society's values, ideology, and rules. It controls the educational system and plans education based on the skills and technology that the rulers believe the society needs. It also controls economic development, which is planned in advance; and production is based on the needs of the society, as determined by the leaders.

Totalitarian societies do not permit dissent. Their goal is to develop a unified population, one that is not divided by differing religious loyalties or political views. They eliminate dissenters through violence, imprisonment, or expulsion, especially when the societies are just developing.

Democratic and totalitarian societies have several characteristics in common, and they often have similar ideologies. Both types of government may believe in freedom and equality for their citizens. For example, in both types of societies, citizens may be free to vote on some issues. Another ideological similarity is that each considers its own system superior to the other. The most conspicuous similarity, however, is their bureaucratic organization. Bureaucracies of enormous complexity and power run both democratic and totalitarian systems, and political parties play an important role in shaping and unifying the organizational structures under each.

Continuing and escalating turmoil in the Arab world raises questions about whether or not Western-style democracy can occur in Arab countries. Some say "No" because Islam is not a democratic religion. In fact, there is no Arabic word for democracy. Also, due to abundant oil revenues, citizens do not pay taxes in some Arab countries and thus do not hold the government accountable; and Western democracies had reinforced many of the autocratic regimes that protestors are trying to take down. Still others consider support for democracy to be very broad in the Arab world and believe that it is not affected by degree of religiosity. Evidence of support for democracy, some contend, comes from large voter turnouts in 2005 during times of dire risks to physical safety (Flamini, 2011).

*The government has total control in a totalitarian state.* *(AP Wide World Photo)*

## 13.2c Political Parties

**Political parties** are groups of citizens formed with the express intent of gaining control of the political body of the state. They exist in both democratic and totalitarian states. Parties nominate candidates to run for office, provide personnel for bureaucratic posts, and make public policy. Their goal is not only to influence government but also to manage it.

Political party systems differ in structure, organization, and reasons for existence. Some parties form around a particular person, such as Charles de Gaulle's Gaullist Party in France, which was a strong force in French politics even after the death of its founder. Other parties exist to promote a specific issue. The Green Party of West Germany was created to support environmental and antinuclear legislation. The National Woman's Party was founded at the beginning of this century in the United States to represent the interests of a particular minority. Most powerful parties, however, are not organized around a single issue. They concern themselves with managing the entire government and the many issues that government addresses.

A party's role in government is strongly influenced by the number of parties in a particular governmental system. Totalitarian states have only one party, so there is no competition for control of the government. Nevertheless, unless the party is run by the military and order is maintained by force, the political party must react to public opinion while encouraging support for the government. The party also selects candidates for public office and then presents them to the general public. Since there are no competing candidates in one-party systems, nomination ensures election. In addition, the party defines issues and must convince the electorate to support its stand on these issues.

**Political parties**
Groups of citizens formed with the express intent of gaining control of the political body of the state

The issues not brought up by the party are not debated, but every effort is made to win support from the public for the activities that the party does undertake.

Two or more political parties are found in democratic countries. This allows competition between candidates and debate over competing issues. In a two-party system, such as in the United States, one party must gain a majority of the votes; thus each party tries to attract the voters in the moderate center. Because they have to avoid taking any stand that would alienate this central group of moderate voters, both parties have to be moderate and dare not offer creative solutions to problems. They can only support the status quo. Thus, the voter has little real choice.

In governments with more than two political parties, the parties do not have to seek moderation or win a majority of votes. Instead, they take a definite stand and offer creative solutions to problems in order to satisfy a group of people who are committed to a particular issue—a labor issue, an antiwar issue, or an environmental issue. They then nominate a candidate who will take a strong stand on the chosen one or two issues. Because it is very difficult for such a candidate to get a majority of votes, parties compromise with each other and form coalitions even when they hold opposing positions on a variety of issues. Government policies can change dramatically with each election, depending on which party or coalition of parties gains power. Nevertheless, the voters have a clear choice on a variety of issues when they cast their ballots.

## 13.3 TYPES OF ECONOMIC SYSTEMS

To produce goods and services for a society, an economic system requires land on which to produce food and to build factories. It also needs raw materials, tools, and machinery to process them; and it needs labor. Economic systems in modern societies vary according to who owns the land, the factories, the raw materials, and the equipment. These *means of production* may be *privately owned*—that is, owned by individuals—or may be *publicly owned* by the state. **Capitalism** is a system based on private ownership. **Socialism** is a system based on state ownership of the means of production. Once again, these pure economic systems are only ideal types. In practice, in capitalist societies, some property is owned by the state; in socialist societies, some property is privately owned, such as small plots of land used to grow food for the local market. No society is purely capitalist or purely socialist. *Mixed economies*, in which private and public ownership are both practiced extensively, are called **welfare capitalism** or **democratic socialism**.

Although all existing economic systems are based on capitalism, socialism, or some combination of the two, one other system deserves mention, even though it has never been developed in a major nation. **Communism** is an economic system that is the goal of communist political parties throughout the world. It is a system in which the ownership of the means of production is held in common by all citizens. A society's economic system has a powerful influence on how it produces and distributes goods.

**Capitalism**
An economic system in which all of the means of production are privately owned

**Socialism**
An economic system based on state ownership of the means of production

**Welfare capitalism/ democratic socialism**
A mixed economy in which private and public ownership are both practiced extensively and one in which the goods and services vital to the society, such as transportation systems and medical care, are run by the state

**Communism**
An economic system in which members of the society jointly own the means of production

### 13.3a Capitalism

The United States has a capitalist economic system; that is, one or more individuals own the means of production, the land and the factories. The many groups and individuals who own stock—stock being shares of the corporation—own most large corporations, whereas one person, a family, or a few individuals may own many small businesses. Individuals who own the means of production are *capitalists*. In this sense, most Americans are not capitalists because they do not derive income from owning a business. Even though Americans may own cars, clothes, and television sets, those are consumer goods. They do not provide profit to the owner. Even homes that increase in value over the years and that produce a profit when sold do not produce income when the owners use them as a personal residence. Capitalists earn income from what they own; consumers spend income for what they own.

Capitalism is a **market economy**—that is, the goods sold and the people who buy and sell them determine the prices at which they are sold. Products which no one wants to buy or sell are not traded. If everyone needs a product—fuel, for example—the product will be sold for as much money as people will pay for it. In a **free-market** system, all people are theoretically free to buy, sell, and make a profit, if they can. There are, however, prohibitions against selling some things, such as illegal drugs, and some services, such as sexual favors. The free-market system is the reason that capitalism is so strongly associated with freedom.

## 13.3b Socialism

Socialism differs from capitalism in that the means of production are owned by the state. Socialist systems are designed to ensure that all members of the society have some share of its wealth. Ownership is social rather than private. So-called communist systems, such as in Cuba, are actually socialist systems because the government owns all of the industries in the country.

Socialism also differs from capitalism in that the marketplace does not control the economy. It has a **planned economy**—the government first decides what goods the society needs, what are luxuries, and what can be done without altogether; then it controls what will be produced and consumed and sets prices for these goods. Thus, there is no free market. The Soviet Union, for example, faced with a severe housing shortage after World War II, gave high priority to building low-cost housing for its population but gave very low priority to building automobiles.

## 13.3c Welfare Capitalism

Welfare capitalism, sometimes called "democratic socialism," is found in most western European countries. In Sweden and Great Britain, some industries are privately owned, and others are state owned. Generally, the state owns the industries most vital to the country's well-being, such as the railroads and the communications industry. The government pays for the most crucial needs—such as medical care, education, and old-age benefits—with tax dollars. As a result, the taxes in welfare capitalist countries are quite high in order to pay for these benefits.

Whether a country is more or less capitalistic can sometimes be determined by comparing the taxes collected to the **gross domestic product (GDP)**, the total value of all final goods and services produced within the borders of a country per year. Often, the greater the proportion of the GDP that goes to taxes, the more social programs the country has. The GDP includes all necessities, luxuries, and military supplies produced for a price within the borders of a country. It does not include anything not produced for profit. The worth of the work of housewives, for example, is the largest item not included in the GDP. As you can see from Table 13-1, GDP in the United States is high compared to other countries.

The GDP does not indicate what the various countries produce; neither does it show for what the tax dollars are spent. The United States, which spends much of its tax money on the armed forces, includes military spending in its GDP. Many other countries, on the other hand, spend little of their tax revenue on the military and spend a great deal on health, social planning, and the reduction of poverty. Thus, while the United States has the highest GDP in the world (outside of the combined European Union), its GDP per capita (the amount spent per person) falls to 11th place (see Table 13-2). As a result, these countries—such as Japan, France, and Sweden—all have populations with longer life expectancies than are found in the United States, with the U.S. being in 51st place (see Table 13-3). These countries have combined capitalism with social programs paid for through taxation and government spending programs.

**Market economy**

An economy in which the price and production of goods are determined by what people are willing to pay in the market place

**Free market**

An economic system in which all people are theoretically free to buy, sell, and make a profit

**Planned economy**

An economy in which the production and prices of goods are planned by the government

**Gross domestic product (GDP)**

The total value of all final goods and services produced within the borders of a country per year

**Table 13-1** Top 20 Countries' GDP (in Billions, U.S. Equivalent)—2011

| Rank | Country | GDP (Purchasing Power Parity) |
|---|---|---|
| 1 | European Union | $15,480 |
| 2 | United States | $15,080 |
| 3 | China | $11,300 |
| 4 | Japan | $4,444 |
| 5 | India | $4,421 |
| 6 | Germany | $3,114 |
| 7 | Russia | $2,383 |
| 8 | Brazil | $2,294 |
| 9 | United Kingdom | $2,288 |
| 10 | France | $2,214 |
| 11 | Italy | $1,847 |
| 12 | Mexico | $1,667 |
| 13 | Korea, South | $1,554 |
| 14 | Spain | $1,406 |
| 15 | Canada | $1,395 |
| 16 | Indonesia | $1,125 |
| 17 | Turkey | $1,075 |
| 18 | Iran | $990 |
| 19 | Australia | $915 |
| 20 | Taiwan | $875 |

Adapted from Central Intelligence Agency, the World Factbook. 2012.

**Table 13-2** Top 20 Countries' GDP Per Capita—2011

| Rank | Country | GDP Per Capita (Purchasing Power Parity) (US$) |
|---|---|---|
| 1 | Qatar | $102,800 |
| 2 | Liechtenstein | $89,400 |
| 3 | Luxembourg | $80,700 |
| 4 | Macau | $74,900 |
| 5 | Bermuda | $69,900 |
| 6 | Singapore | $60,900 |
| 7 | Jersey | $57,000 |
| 8 | Falkland Islands (Islas Malvinas) | $55,400 |
| 9 | Norway | $55,300 |
| 10 | Hong Kong | $50,700 |
| 11 | Brunei | $50,500 |
| 12 | United States | $49,800 |
| 13 | United Arab Emirates | $49,000 |
| 14 | Switzerland | $45,300 |
| 15 | Guernsey | $44,600 |
| 16 | Kuwait | $43,800 |
| 17 | Cayman Islands | $43,800 |
| 18 | Gibraltar | $43,000 |
| 19 | Austria | $42,500 |
| 20 | Australia | $42,400 |

Adapted from Central Intelligence Agency, the World Factbook. 2012.

**Table 13-3** Life Expectancy at Birth, Top 60 Countries—2012

| Rank | Country | Life Expectancy at Birth | Rank | Country | Life Expectancy at Birth |
|---|---|---|---|---|---|
| 1 | Monaco | 89.68 | 32 | Saint Pierre and Miquelon | 80.00 |
| 2 | Macau | 84.43 | 33 | Austria | 79.91 |
| 3 | Japan | 83.91 | 34 | Faroe Islands | 79.85 |
| 4 | Singapore | 83.75 | 35 | Malta | 79.85 |
| 5 | San Marino | 83.07 | 36 | European Union | 79.76 |
| 6 | Andorra | 82.50 | 37 | Luxembourg | 79.75 |
| 7 | Guernsey | 82.24 | 38 | Belgium | 79.65 |
| 8 | Hong Kong | 82.12 | 39 | Virgin Islands | 79.47 |
| 9 | Australia | 81.90 | 40 | Finland | 79.41 |
| 10 | Italy | 81.86 | 41 | Korea, South | 79.30 |
| 11 | Liechtenstein | 81.50 | 42 | Turks and Caicos Islands | 79.26 |
| 12 | Canada | 81.48 | 43 | Wallis and Futuna | 79.12 |
| 13 | Jersey | 81.47 | 44 | Puerto Rico | 79.07 |
| 14 | France | 81.46 | 45 | Bosnia and Herzegovina | 78.96 |
| 15 | Spain | 81.27 | 46 | Saint Helena, Ascension, and Tristan de Cunha | 78.91 |
| 16 | Sweden | 81.18 | | | |
| 17 | Switzerland | 81.17 | 47 | Gibraltar | 78.83 |
| 18 | Israel | 81.07 | 48 | Denmark | 78.78 |
| 19 | Iceland | 81.00 | 49 | Portugal | 78.70 |
| 20 | Anguilla | 80.98 | 50 | Guam | 78.50 |
| 21 | Netherlands | 80.91 | 51 | United States | 78.49 |
| 22 | Bermuda | 80.82 | 52 | Taiwan | 78.48 |
| 23 | Cayman Islands | 80.80 | 63 | Bahrain | 78.29 |
| 24 | Isle of Man | 80.76 | 54 | Chili | 78.10 |
| 25 | New Zealand | 80.71 | 55 | Qatar | 78.09 |
| 26 | Ireland | 80.32 | 56 | Cyprus | 78.00 |
| 27 | Norway | 80.32 | 57 | Panama | 77.96 |
| 28 | Germany | 80.19 | 58 | British Virgin Islands | 77.95 |
| 29 | Jordan | 80.18 | 59 | Costa Rica | 77.89 |
| 30 | United Kingdom | 80.17 | 60 | Cuba | 77.87 |
| 31 | Greece | 80.05 | | | |

Adapted from Central Intelligence Agency, the World Factbook. 2012.

## 13.3d Communism—A Utopian Idea

Communism is an economic system that does not exist in any of the world's larger societies. The basic premise of communism is that all property should be held in common and that distribution of goods and services should be based on the principle developed by Marx (1964, p. 258), "From each according to his ability, to each according to his needs!" Thus, in the ideal communist society, workers would do their best to serve the needs of the society and would be assured of receiving whatever they needed.

Communism has been achieved in some small communities. It was especially popular in the nineteenth century in the United States when there were an estimated 100 communes with a total of more than 1,000,000 members (Etzioni-Halevey, 1997). Religious sects—such as the Shakers, Rappists, Zoarites, Amana Communists, and

Perfectionists—formed most of these communes. One notable example was the Oneida community in Oneida, New York. All members of this religious society shared the property, buildings, and industries of the community. They also shared the work, rotating in their jobs so that no one would long suffer the burden of the heaviest or the least pleasant work, and no one would become attached to a particular job. Groups did work so that fellowship was a part of cooking, cleaning, farming, and whatever else had to be done. There was no monogamous marriage, which they believed would have implied the ownership of another person. The community planned the birth of children; and when children were born, they were members of the community, not possessions of their parents. The Oneida community was very successful in carrying out its ideal of communism and providing its with fellowship and security. However, neighbors of the commune did not approve of their practices, especially their lack of marriage; and the community was forced to disband.

Communist communities have also been popular in the twentieth century—especially in Europe in the 1930s and in the United States in the 1970s. Most of the recent communes were not religious groups. They did not put a strong emphasis on work, and they failed because they could not sustain themselves.

Communism, like socialism, requires a major redistribution of wealth. Individuals would no longer own the farms, factories, and other means of production. Many capitalists, in fact, confuse socialist systems with communist systems and use these words almost interchangeably. They are, however, very different systems. In socialism, the government controls the economy. In communism, the people themselves control the economy.

# 13.4 THEORIES OF POLITICAL AND ECONOMIC DEVELOPMENT

Although political and economic systems are considered two separate social institutions, they are, as the opening vignette of this chapter suggests, closely intertwined. The relationship between who holds the power that determines the rules within a society and the types of political systems that exist are closely related to how a society meets its needs for goods and services and the types of economic systems that exist. Therefore, we will link our theoretical discussions about the development of political and economic systems.

## 13.4a Structural Functional Theory

Structural functionalists believe that a society is built on a common set of values. Accordingly, political and economic systems reflect those values. The values of U.S. society include, among other things, work, achievement, equal opportunity, the freedom to run our own lives, and the freedom of the individual to accumulate and own private property. These values are learned and perpetuated through socialization.

In a legal system of authority, a society's values shape its laws and political policies. If people value achievement, the law will protect the right to achieve. If people value freedom, the law will protect freedom, and social policy will encourage freedom. No one will be forced to practice a particular religion, for example, and marriage will be a matter of personal choice. Political institutions pass laws and develop policies that reflect the values of the population. Often, the political institution must extend itself into international affairs to protect the society's values. It may limit the import of foreign goods to protect its own workers and negotiate with other nations in order to allow trade for the benefit of its own citizens. It protects its citizens from aggressive acts and maintains armed forces to carry out its international functions.

Structural functionalists believe that the political institution holds the values of the dominant society and arbitrates conflicts when they arise. One person might act on a value of freedom by marrying more than one spouse, or members of a subculture might feel free to use illegal drugs. It is the political system that decides which values must be upheld and which must be limited to maintain social order. In the United States, where freedom is a value, constant arbitration is necessary to protect the freedoms of the individual without impinging on the other values of society.

Similarly, a society's values shape its economic system. If a society values individual freedom to accumulate wealth and property, structural functional theory contends that society will have a capitalist economic system. Capitalism evolved in the U.S. because immigrants coming to this country brought with them the desire to be free to determine their own economic welfare. Thus, capitalism reflects core values of the U.S. Conservative economists have been describing capitalism as a vast cooperative system for centuries. In *The Wealth of Nations*, written in 1776, Adam Smith pointed out the beautiful balance that is achieved through the "principle of supply and demand." This principle ensures that social needs will be met because it is profitable to meet them. When there is a demand, someone will profit from supplying it. People need food, clothing, and medical care, for example, so huge industries have developed to meet these needs. By tending to their self-interests, this theory suggests, everyone who produces a necessary product or service will profit and will, thereby, benefit both themselves and society.

In recent years, structural functionalists have been concerned about the large number of people who seem unable to find profitable means of supporting themselves. Most structural functionalists do not fault the capitalistic system, but they do recognize that some dysfunctions make it difficult for some individuals and groups to have an equal opportunity in the marketplace. A child growing up in an urban ghetto or on an impoverished Indian reservation is unlikely to get the education needed to land jobs that pay well. Even when members of minority groups do manage to get a good education, racism and stereotyping may prevent them from finding a profitable occupation. As a result, the benefits of a capitalistic system are not equally available to all. Another dysfunction concerns the development of monopolies, which limit competition and thereby narrow the range of opportunities available in the marketplace. When one corporation dominates the sale of a good or service, it disrupts the market economy and can set its own price.

**BVT** ***Lab***

Flashcards are available for this chapter at **www.BVTLab.com**

## 13.4b Conflict Theory

Conflict theory assumes that societies are drawn together by people's need for resources—food, shelter, and other necessities—rather than being based on a set of common values. Some groups get a larger share of the resources, and they use these resources to gain power. Just as they hire people to work for their financial interests in the economic sphere, they use their resources to hire people to protect their power interests in the political sphere. They use their wealth to influence political leaders to support their economic interests, and they bring about the downfall of individuals or governments that oppose their interests.

The history of Europe provides many examples of how economic groups have used legal power to protect their own interests (Pirenne, 1914). At first, European merchants in the Middle Ages sold their goods at strategic points along heavily traveled highways. Eventually, however, they built towns at those points and passed laws restricting others from trading, thus using their political power to create a monopoly of trade. These merchants dominated the cities of Europe for several centuries by passing laws to protect their interests.

In the fifteenth and sixteenth centuries, as worldwide shipping increased, nation-states became powerful and used their political power to protect their shippers. When machinery came into use and manufacturing grew, the manufacturers initially required no political support. They preferred a laissez-faire economy, a free and competitive market. Workers were plentiful, and industry could hire them for very low wages and could fire them at will. The workers, who suffered greatly under this system, eventually caused serious civil disturbances; the industrialists had to develop a legal system to protect their own interests.

In the *Communist Manifesto*, Marx described the development of both capitalism and communism as historical events. When most people produced needed goods directly from farming, there was an agricultural economic system. As industrialization developed and trading of manufactured articles increased, however, the economy came to be based on money, or capital. Marx realized that as some people increased their store of capital, they would be able to buy more and more factories and other means of production. Those who did not own any means of production would be forced to sell their only asset—their labor—to the factory owners. As the owners grew richer and more powerful, they would buy up more and more of the means of production and would force still more people to rely on their labor for subsistence. Eventually, Marx believed, the number of workers would grow so large that competition would reduce wages to a minimum, and an entire class of impoverished workers would develop. He felt that conditions among the working class would ultimately deteriorate to the point that they would revolt, overthrow the owners, and develop a system in which the means of production would be owned communally and would be operated for the benefit of all.

Max Weber (1946) agreed with Marx's fundamental view of the economic order, but he differed slightly in his assessment of the means and outcome of oppression. Weber was concerned with the growth of bureaucracy. Bureaucracies operate in accordance with rational rules and procedures rather than humanitarian principles. With the compartmentalization of responsibility, it would be possible for a company to become extremely ruthless in the pursuit of profit, even if it meant that thousands of workers and the population at large would suffer. Those who made the decisions would be far removed from those who actually carried them out and who were in a position to observe their consequences. Weber was less optimistic than Marx; Weber believed that eventually bureaucracies would grow so rich and powerful that no human effort could dislodge them. Even today, some conflict theorists contend that giant multinational corporations are too powerful to be controlled by individuals—or even nations—and that the world will come under progressively greater corporate control.

Conflict theorists believe that in every age, the wealthy have used both laws and force to protect their wealth. Why, then, do the great majority of people support the laws of the wealthy? According to conflict theorists, it is because the rich use their wealth and power to control the mass media. They teach their values to the majority of people by controlling the schools, the press, radio, television, and other means of communication. They try to legitimate their power by convincing the population that the rich have a right to their wealth and that they should have the power to restrict trade, hire and fire workers, and otherwise restrict the behavior of the majority to maintain their own position. Unlike the structural functionalists, who believe that the values of the society shape the political and economic systems, conflict theorists believe that the political and economic systems shape the values of society.

## APPLYING KNOWLEDGE OF POLITICAL SYSTEMS

Knowledge of the different types of political structures and systems in modern societies is useful in a number of ways. First, academic sociologists can learn a great deal about a culture by understanding its political systems. By knowing how close a country is to being democratic or totalitarian and knowing the nature of its political parties, sociologists can gain insight into some of the values and behaviors of a people.

Certainly, politicians and diplomats need to know about the nature of the various political systems. A U.S. diplomat could not effectively negotiate with a foreign diplomat without first thoroughly understanding that the rules, policies, and decision-making processes are likely to be very different from those of the United States.

Corporations involved in international business also need to have a thorough knowledge of foreign political structures. The policies that offer a great deal of freedom to American businesses are not found in all countries. Tax laws, tariffs, import and export laws, and other regulations greatly affect the way a business operates. Before making massive investments in an international business, then, corporate executives need to scrupulously study how the politics of a country will affect their ability to make a profit.

On the clinical side, understanding the nature of various political systems might help therapists and social workers to counsel immigrants who are having problems of adjustment. For someone who is used to being overtly controlled, the freedom offered by some democracies could be difficult to handle. New responsibilities, expectations, and rules about making personal decisions might be disorienting. For example, teachers and school counselors might also find themselves in a position where they have to help foreign students who are seeking education to adjust.

The issue of helping people adjust to new political systems is especially relevant today, considering the sweeping political changes that have been occurring in Eastern Europe. Imagine the psychological and sociological turmoil that could envelop people who have lived within very controlled political environments when their country democratizes almost overnight, as it seems to have happened in many cases. The classical sociologist Emile Durkheim said that when people are faced with sudden changes in their lives (either positive or negative), they might experience anomie—a condition in which their old goals, values, and norms lose their meaning, leaving them with unclear guidelines for their lives. Perhaps private therapists, teachers, counselors, journalists, politicians, and other public speakers could use a sociological knowledge of political groups and systems to help people adjust to new situations brought about by rapid political change.

Finally, anyone who travels abroad would benefit from understanding the political systems of foreign countries. Suppose that you decide to visit, work, or attend school in a European or Asian country. Do you know the rights you would have in, say, Greece, Italy, France, or China? If you happened to be accused of a crime, would you have the same rights as a U.S. citizen? Do you know, for example, that possession of marijuana is a more serious crime in many other countries than it is in the United States? To protect yourself and avoid unnecessary expenses or delays in time, you might carefully study the ways in which other political systems operate in such countries before you travel.

## 13.5 THE POLITICAL SYSTEM IN THE UNITED STATES

The United States has a democratic political system. Citizens are expected to rule the country by participating in the political process—debating issues, joining one of the two major political parties or remaining independent, voting for officials, and then expressing their opinions to officeholders.

The elected officials serve in a diverse, decentralized system of federal, state, and local governments. Each level of government has a system of checks and balances. The legislative branch makes the laws, the executive branch carries out the laws, and the judicial branch interprets the laws. Our system of government is representative, but how representative is it in practice? Who holds the power? Which groups influence government the most? There are two opposing perspectives on power in America. The first is that a powerful elite holds all of the power, and the second is that power is divided among many diversified groups.

## 13.5a The Power Elite

C. Wright Mills (1956) argued that a **power elite**—consisting of leaders in the upper echelons of business, the military, and the government—runs the United States. These leaders, Mills contended, are likely to come from similar backgrounds and have similar beliefs and values. There is no actual conspiracy among these leaders to promote the interests of their own high social stratum; but they nevertheless tend to support the same policies because those policies support their common interests. Recent research, especially by Domhoff (2011) supports the theory that there is a power elite who holds power in United States political affairs.

One example of the operation of a power elite is what has come to be known as the "military–industrial complex." This complex evolved during World War II when some of the checks and balances regulating the defense department were dismantled. The absence of these checks and balances meant that the American defense industry was producing for a consumer, the American taxpayer, for whom price was not negotiable. As a result, unprecedented profits were made. In this way, United States military actions in foreign countries such as Korea and Vietnam kept the defense industry employed, and the industry became a decisive force in governmental policy.

## 13.5b Political Pluralism

Many sociologists believe that numerous groups in the United States play a significant role in political decision-making. David Riesman and his colleagues (1950) described the power system of the United States as one of **political pluralism**—rule by many different groups. A variety of special interest groups try to influence legislation. They form lobbies that represent various industries, labor groups, religions, educational groups, and other special interests. These groups try to protect their own interests by pressuring politicians for favorable legislation and fighting against legislation they dislike. Thus, Riesman et al. believed, no single group had absolute power because different groups would balance one another's actions when they had competing interests.

There is little question that a variety of interest groups exist in the United States today. The issue for critics of pluralism is whether these various groups have any real power. Political pluralists believe that many groups are equally powerful and balance the power of other groups. Those who believe that a governing class or a military–industrial complex is most powerful fear that other groups are not strong enough to counteract the power of the elite, no matter how active and well organized they are.

Two types of groups are frequently in the news in American politics: *political action committees*, which contribute money to political campaigns, and *lobbies*, which attempt to influence legislation. Both types clearly have more power than individuals who do not belong to such groups. Questions remain about whether either type of group has enough power to counteract the power of elites or whether these groups actually tend to represent and extend the power of elite groups.

## 13.5c Political Action Committees (PACs)

**Political action committees (PACs)** are organizations formed to raise money for political campaigns. Candidates running for office need a great deal of money for political advertising, office overhead, transportation, and other needs. The expenses can reach tens of millions of dollars per campaign. As a rule, the people who are elected to political office have spent more money than their opponents; PACs help to pay these election expenses.

**Power elite**

A small group of people who hold all of the powerful positions and cooperate to maintain their social positions

**Political pluralism**

A political system in which many diverse groups have a share of the power

**Political action committees (PACs)**

Organizations formed to raise money for a political campaign

PACs represent many special interest groups—often groups that are at variance with one another. Business groups, labor groups, and professional groups—all sponsor PACs. Some of the largest are the National Conservative PAC, Fund for a Conservative Majority, National Congressional Club, Realtors Political Action Committee, National Rifle Association (NRA), Political Victory Fund, Republican Majority Fund, American Medical Association (AMA), and the Fund for a Democratic Majority. Many of the most powerful favor the Republican Party, but others favor the Democratic Party. Those that have business interests often split their contributions, giving money to members of both parties. Nonetheless, although PACs support both parties and a variety of candidates, they do not represent a cross-section of American voters. Only groups with moneyed connections can possibly raise the sums needed to be influential in funding candidates.

A few PACs, particularly very conservative groups, have used PAC money to try to defeat **incumbents**, the elected officials who already hold office and are trying to be reelected. Most PAC money, however, goes to incumbents and tends, therefore, to maintain the power structure as it is. Currently there exists a very high rate of reelection of incumbents to the U.S. Congress, partly because they have access to PAC money.

Each PAC is allowed to contribute up to $5,000 to each politician per election unless it is a presidential campaign, in which case up to $10,000 is allowed. PACs are not permitted to persuade politicians to take a particular stand; of course, they support only politicians who will support their cause. Oil and gas PACs, for example, support those members of Congress who vote for bills that will help the oil and gas industry; real estate PACs support only members who vote for bills that will help the real estate industry, and so on.

Although PACs are not technically allowed to persuade politicians to take political stands, thousands of associations and groups are permitted to try to influence both politicians and civil servants. These groups are commonly called "lobbies."

*Political action committees (PACs) are organizations formed to raise money for political campaigns, and they represent many special interest groups. U.S. Congress incumbents who have access to PAC money seem to have a higher reelection rate.* (AP Wide World Photo)

## 13.5d Lobbies

**Lobbies** are organizations of people who wish to influence the political process on specific issues. Unlike political parties, lobbies do not nominate candidates or hope to manage the government. Their goal, rather, is to persuade elected and appointed officials to vote for or against a particular regulation or piece of legislation. Groups of people with a common interest often form an association with the express purpose of influencing the legislative process. Thousands of such associations are based within blocks of the United States Capitol, where they monitor the legislation being considered. They maintain close contact with government officials and scrutinize the work of bureaucrats when budgets are being prepared or hearings are being held, so that they can influence the government to their own best interest. Because most national associations are federations of state and local associations, they have influence at every level of government, from the smallest town to the federal government.

Some of the largest and best-known associations are those involved in manufacturing. The list is endless, including the National Association of Manufacturers (NAM), the Chamber of Commerce of the United States, the Chemical Specialties Manufacturers Association, the National Asphalt Pavement Association, the Evaporated Milk Association, the National Association of Retail Druggists, and the National Cemetery Association. Whom these organizations hire to lobby for them is a subject of serious debate.

**Incumbent**
One holding an elected office

**Lobby**
An organization of people who want to influence the political process on a specific issue

It is estimated that as many as 1 in 10 Americans depends on defense spending for their livelihood; these individuals, the corporations for whom they work, and the military are well organized to lobby Congress for money for defense spending. The National Defense Industrial Association, founded in 1997, has 1,100 corporate members who are defense contractors and 27,000 additional members from industry, universities, and the Pentagon. The Aerospace Industries Association has 154 associate member companies and 83 member companies. There are also the Navy League, the Air Force Association, the Association of the U.S. Army, the Armed Forces Communications and Electronics Association, the Shipbuilders Council of America, the Electronic Industries Association, and the Society of Naval Architects and Marine Engineers.

There are also some lobby groups who are concerned with issues unrelated to business. They are supported by donations from the public, and they lobby for issues related to the public good. Such groups include Common Cause, the National Wildlife Federation, the ACLU, and the Center for Science in the Public Interest.

The workings of the powerful automobile lobby show how much time, energy, and money are involved in influencing the political process. During the early 1960s, Ralph Nader, a public interest lobbyist, launched an attack on the faulty design of American automobiles in his book *Unsafe at Any Speed*. After the book was published, Nader continued to work for improved auto safety. In response, Congress considered passing legislation to set safety standards for cars; the auto lobby, led by Henry Ford, moved in to stop the legislation (Dowie, 1977). Ford went to Washington and spoke to the Business Council, an organization of 100 executives of large organizations who come to Washington from time to time to advise government. He visited members of Congress, held press conferences, and recruited business support; yet he still failed to stop the passage of the Motor Vehicle Safety Act, which was signed into law in 1966. Ralph Nader ran for president of the United States in 2000.

A regulatory agency was then made responsible for setting guidelines for auto safety. The Ford Motor Company responded by sending representatives to the agency to argue that poor drivers, unsafe guardrail designs, poor visibility, and a variety of other highway and driving hazards were responsible for accidents. They contended that not only was the automobile safe but also that the regulations requiring improvements would increase the cost of cars and would save few lives.

In 1968, despite these lobbying efforts, the regulatory agency issued new safety standards designed to reduce the risk of fire in automobiles after a rear-end crash. As required by law, the agency scheduled hearings on the regulation. Ford responded with a report stating that automobile fires were not a problem. The agency then had to conduct several studies to determine whether fire was a problem. It found that 400,000 cars burned up every year and that 3,000 people burned to death. It again proposed safety standards; Ford again responded, arguing that although burning accidents do happen, rear-end collisions were not the cause. The agency researched this question and found that rear-end collisions were, in fact, the cause in most cases. Again, regulations were proposed, again Ford responded, and again research was conducted. The total delay in developing regulations was 8 years. The regulations eventually did pass; however, during those 8 years, the company managed to defeat regulations requiring other safety measures. For example, it was 20 more years before air bags were finally installed in automobiles.

*A regulatory agency found that 400,000 cars burned up every year and that 3,000 people burned to death. After 8 years of delays, new safety regulations were finally passed. (iStockphoto)*

This account of one corporation's reluctance to comply with a safety regulation shows that big business has enormous, but not absolute, power over government. It also shows how time-consuming and expensive the business of lobbying is. It can be practiced only by organizations with much wealth and power, and bureaucratic organizations have much more power than any individual citizen.

**thinking** SOCIOLOGICALLY

1. Use the knowledge of political groups and systems provided in this chapter to discuss whether the government should further limit the amount of money that PACs can contribute to political campaigns.
2. Using the information about lobbies and PACs, develop arguments to support and oppose the two views of political power groups offered in this chapter—the power elite and political pluralism.

# 13.6 THE ROLE OF THE INDIVIDUAL

Special interest groups can use their power to try to influence political decisions. However, what is the role of the individual? As stated earlier in this chapter, American citizens are expected to participate in the political process by voting, debating issues, either joining one of the two major political parties or remaining independent, and expressing their views to their elected officials. People learn these and other responsibilities through the process of political socialization.

## 13.6a Political Socialization

In most American communities, many children watch the mayor lead the Fourth of July Parade and learn that the mayor is a good and benevolent leader. Most youngsters also learn that other leaders, likewise, give time and money to make the community a better place to live. During elections, children often learn about political parties as their families discuss candidates, and frequently they identify with a political party on an emotional level long before they can understand political issues. To a child, the president of the United States is to the country what the father is to the family: a leader, provider, and protector.

Children learn at an early age that political leaders and other leaders work to make the community a better place to live. They see the president of the United States as a leader, provider, and protector. (AP Wide World Photo)

Political socialization of this sort continues when children enter school. Through formal courses in history, literature, and government, they learn to respect society's norms and political systems. Leaders are presented in history books as role models for society's norms. In an interesting study of how history books portray George Washington, Schwartz (1991) found that in the early part of the nineteenth century, when the United States believed that our leaders should be genteel, Washington was described in biographies as remote, of flawless virtue, refined, and with a dignified air. After the Civil War, Americans wanted their leaders to be more populist; thus, historians were criticized for making Washington sound cold, harsh, stern and soulless—a human iceberg. Historians described him at this point as one who loved life, children, flashy clothes, good wine, good houses, cards, and dirty jokes. After 1920, in order to fit into the growth of business, historians began to describe Washington as a good businessman, a captain of industry. Thus, whatever characteristics were considered admirable in a given period, those were the characteristics emphasized when discussing our first president.

Not all children emerge from their family and school socialization with the idea that political leaders are benevolent, caring, achieving people, of course. They may accumulate contradictory evidence along the way, perhaps having experiences with parents, teachers, or others who indicate that leaders are not to be trusted. They may also acquire a distrust of the political system by listening to parental complaints about lack of jobs or other conditions that result from political decisions and that cause family hardship. Schools teaching middle-class values may fail to convince a child living in poverty that the political system is fair and benevolent; realities in the child's environment may provide harsh evidence that not everyone can move from a log cabin to the White House. Children from Appalachia and urban ghettos have been much less apt to support the American political system than middle-class American children (Dowse & Hughes, 1972). Political socialization exists as much in the daily interactions between adults and children as it does in the more formalized school settings. This is especially true in both urban and rural lower socioeconomic areas where children become acquainted with the political realities of the gap between the rich and the poor (Lay, 2006).

## 13.6b Political Socialization in the Mass Media

By the time that children finish school, they have developed political attitudes that will shape their political behavior in adult life. However, political socialization still continues, especially through the mass media, which reinforce childhood socialization. Much mass media socialization presents political issues in emotional terms. Slogans that promise a better America without offering data about how this is to be done are seeking an emotional response from voters, a response resembling the one a child feels for the mayor leading the Fourth of July Parade. Although these emotional appeals for voter support are routinely criticized as "flag waving," emotion is believed to play a very large role in voter choice.

**BVT Lab**

Flashcards are available for this chapter at **www.BVTLab.com**

What is the price one pays to run for president? The Center for Responsive Politics calculated that the total amount spent by presidential candidates, senate and house candidates, political parties and independent interest groups trying to influence the federal election in 2012 was approximately 6 billion dollars, up from nearly 5.3 billion dollars in 2008, 4.1 billion in 2004, and 3.1 billion in 2000. In 2012, the presidential election alone accounted for around 2.6 billion dollars. Certainly the majority of this money does not come from PACs, but PACs do play an important contributory role. In the 2012 presidential election, PACs contributed more than 540 million dollars to the candidates and politically active non-profits contributed around 350 million dollars (OpenSecrets.org, 2012). This does not account for the hundreds of millions of dollars contributed "off the books." The issue of campaign funding has become a controversial issue because, clearly, the amount of money that candidates have to spend on their campaigns is a powerful component of political socialization and can have significant effects on the outcomes of elections.

## APPLYING POLITICAL SOCIALIZATION

By being aware that some politicians use emotional ploys, you can increase your ability to critically evaluate their political statements, positions, and campaign platforms. Some politicians—particularly those who have training in acting or public speaking—have mastered this ability to manipulate people's emotions. This skill provides them with a great deal of charismatic authority, which affords them considerable political clout. Often, politicians can muster overwhelming public support for policies that are devoid of any meaningful substance or that are even—at times—not in the best interests of the population. However, politicians can also use emotion to sway the population to accept meaningful and beneficial policies. As voters, you need to be particularly critical of political proposals that are directed more to your hearts than to your minds. The most effective way for the mass media to influence people is to present information in such a way that there is only one obvious conclusion (Goodin, 1980). The media often give only one side of an issue; if the so-called obvious solution is heard frequently enough, it will seem to make sense to most people. Often, for a year or two before an election, we hear a candidate mentioned as the obvious choice for the party. The candidate might even say that if people do not have jobs, they obviously do not want jobs. If people do not vote, they are obviously not interested. These statements are not obvious at all; but unless contradictory information is provided, they may seem obvious enough and will probably be accepted by the majority of the public.

In the United States, there is concern that the mass media express only the views of the large corporations that generally own them. Few newspapers, for example, are still locally owned and compete with other locally owned newspapers. Gannett Company dominates the newspaper business, owning a national newspaper, *USA Today*, plus local newspapers, radio and television stations, and even most of the nation's billboards. There are only a few major television networks, including ABC, CBS, NBC, and FOX. Thus, information about politics may be severely limited, and the information presented may represent only the viewpoint of the mass-media owners.

When only one side of an issue is heard, people will tend to believe only that side. (AP Wide World Photo)

The federal government also provides information to its citizens regarding health, agriculture, education, labor, housing, and population statistics. This information is dispensed in a variety of ways: county agricultural agents, public health centers, libraries, newspapers, radio, and television. Many of the statistics used by sociologists are collected and published by government agencies. Sociologists are well aware, however, that the government also attempts to shape public opinion; it sometimes reports information that presents a misleading description of a problem. Government unemployment figures, for example, count only those unemployed persons who are still known to be actively seeking work; they do not report the number of people who have given up the search for a job. This practice artificially lowers the statistics on unemployment in the country.

---

**thinking** SOCIOLOGICALLY

1. What features of the United States political system increase legitimate authority?
2. Given our low voter turnout, is legitimate authority decreasing?
3. Are the social values reflected in the United States political system the values of all the people or the values only of more powerful people?

## 13.6c Political Participation

The United States has one of the lowest voter turnouts in the democratic world (see Table 13-4). In 2012, only 53.6% of the voting age population chose to vote (see Table 13-5 and Table 13-6). Four years later, the statistics looked much the same; of those registered to

**Table 13-4** Ranking of Voter Turnout Percentages in Selected Democratic Nations in Recent National Elections (by Most Recent Year Available)

| Rank | Country | Year | Turnout of Voting-Age Population |
|---|---|---|---|
| 1 | Sweden | 2010 | 84.6% |
| 2 | Austria | 2008 | 81.7% |
| 3 | Italy | 2008 | 80.5% |
| 4 | Germany | 2009 | 70.8% |
| 5 | Japan | 2009 | 69.3% |
| 6 | Spain | 2011 | 68.9% |
| 7 | United Kingdom | 2010 | 65.8% |
| 8 | Israel | 2009 | 64.7% |
| 9 | Mexico | 2012 | 62.5% |
| 10 | Canada | 2011 | 61.4% |
| 11 | France | 2007 | 59.9% |
| 12 | Republic of Korea | 2012 | 54.3% |
| 13 | USA* | 2012 | 53.6% |
| 14 | Switzerland | 2011 | 49.1% |

*USA data adapted from George Mason University United States Election Project. Retrieved from http://elections.gmu.edu/Turnout_2012G.html.

Other data adapted from the Institute for Democracy and Electoral Assistance, Voter Turnout Database. Retrieved from http://www.idea.int/vt/viewdata.cfm.#

*The United States has one of the lowest voter turnouts in the democratic world.* *(AP Wide World Photo)*

vote in the 2004 presidential election, only 88.5% of registered voters and 55.3% of the voting age population cast a ballot. In 2008, 89.6% of registered voters and 56.8% of the voting-age population voted. Voter turnout hurts the Democratic Party because the blocks of people who do not vote—the young, the poor, and blacks—are statistically more apt to be Democratic. When voter turnout is low, the Republican Party is more likely to win elections, and social programs that help the poor and minority groups are more likely to be ignored.

A variety of explanations for the lack of voter participation have been proposed. One set of explanations attributes the lack of voter participation to social-psychological reasons, the attitude of the voter. Potential voters stay away from the polls for a variety of reasons. They may believe that their votes do not make a difference, or they don't feel any civic obligation to participate. Perhaps they do not like either party's candidate, or they may be equally satisfied with all candidates. Voters may lack the education to know either the importance of voting or the issues being considered; they may be too young or too poor to care—in a word, they are *apathetic*. Those who believe that social-psychological reasons are the reasons that people do not vote also tend to believe that if government is less than perfect, the voters have no one to blame but themselves. If they seek change, they should give politics more attention.

However, critics of this theory argue that people are not staying away from the polls because of apathy. In this nation, before the twentieth century, and in other nations currently, people have participated at much greater rates than they do in the United States now. In most European nations, the young, the poor, and the less educated all vote as often as the old, the rich, and the more educated. If apathy and social-psychological attitudes are to explain a lack of voter participation, such explanations

**Table 13-5** Voting in General and Presidential Elections, 1960–2012

| Year | Voting-Age Population | Voter Registration | Voter Turnout | Turnout of Voting-Age Population (Percentage) |
|---|---|---|---|---|
| **2012** | **240,926,957** | **NA** | **130,234,600** | **53.6%** |
| 2010 | 235,809,266 | NA | 90,682,968 | 37.8% |
| **2008** | **231,229,580** | **NA** | **132,618,580** | **56.8%** |
| 2006 | 220,600,000 | 135,889,600 | 80,588,000 | 37.1% |
| **2004** | **221,256,931** | **174,800,000** | **122,294,978** | **55.3%** |
| 2002 | 215,473,000 | 150,990,598 | 79,830,119 | 37.0% |
| **2000** | **205,815,000** | **156,421,311** | **105,586,274** | **51.3%** |
| 1998 | 200,929,000 | 141,850,558 | 73,117,022 | 36.4% |
| **1996** | **196,511,000** | **146,211,960** | **96,456,345** | **49.1%** |
| 1994 | 193,650,000 | 130,292,822 | 75,105,860 | 38.8% |
| **1992** | **189,529,000** | **133,821,178** | **104,405,155** | **55.1%** |
| 1990 | 185,812,000 | 121,105,630 | 67,859,189 | 36.5% |
| **1988** | **182,778,000** | **126,379,628** | **91,594,693** | **50.1%** |
| 1986 | 178,566,000 | 118,399,984 | 64,991,128 | 36.4% |
| **1984** | **174,466,000** | **124,150,614** | **92,652,680** | **53.1%** |
| 1982 | 169,938,000 | 110,671,225 | 67,615,576 | 39.8% |
| **1980** | **164,597,000** | **113,043,734** | **86,515,221** | **52.6%** |
| 1978 | 158,373,000 | 103,291,265 | 58,917,938 | 37.2% |
| **1976** | **152,309,190** | **105,037,986** | **81,555,789** | **53.6%** |
| 1974 | 146,336,000 | 96,199,020[1] | 55,943,834 | 38.2% |
| **1972** | **140,776,000** | **97,328,541** | **77,718,554** | **55.2%** |
| 1970 | 124,498,000 | 82,496,747[2] | 58,014,338 | 46.6% |
| **1968** | **120,328,186** | **81,658,180** | **73,211,875** | **60.8%** |
| 1966 | 116,132,000 | 76,288,283[3] | 56,188,046 | 48.4% |
| **1964** | **114,090,000** | **73,715,818** | **70,644,592** | **61.9%** |
| 1962 | 112,423,000 | 65,393,751[4] | 53,141,227 | 47.3% |
| **1960** | **109,159,000** | **64,833,096[5]** | **68,838,204** | **63.1%** |

NA = not available. NOTE: Presidential election years are in boldface.

[1] Registrations from Iowa not included.

[2] Registrations from Iowa and Mo. not included.

[3] Registrations from Iowa, Kans., Miss, Mo., Nebr., and Wyo. not included. D. C. did not have independent status.

[4] Registrations from Ala., Alaska, D.C., Iowa, Kans., Ky., Miss., Mo., Nebr., N.M., N.C., N.D., Okla, S.D., Wis., and Wyo. not included.

[5] Registrations from Ala., Alaska, D.C., Iowa, Kans., Ky., Miss., Mo., Nebr., N.M., N.C., N.D., Okla., S.D., Wis., and Wyo. not included

Read more at National Voter Turnout in Federal Elections: 1960–2012 http://www.infoplease.com/ipa/A0781453.html#ixzz2QjrSzTQ8.

Adapted from Federal Election Commission. Data drawn from Congressional Research Service reports, Election Data Services Inc., and State Election Offices.

ought to hold in other twentieth-century democratic, industrialized societies, as they do in the United States.

Critics of social-psychological theories argue that the reasons for a lack of voter participation are found in the social structure of voting procedures. Piven and Cloward (1989), for example, argue that voter participation in this country was high before 1880 and that many of the issues in elections were populist issues that stimulated

**Table 13-6** Who Voted in the 2008 Presidential Election?

| | Registered | Voted | Registered Who Voted |
|---|---|---|---|
| **Total, 18 years and older** | 71% | 63.6% | 89.6% |
| **Race** | | | |
| White, non-Hispanic | 73.5% | 66.1% | 90.0% |
| African-American black | 69.7% | 64.7% | 92.9% |
| Asian | 55.3% | 47.6% | 86.1% |
| Hispanic | 59.4% | 49.9% | 84.0% |
| **Age:** | | | |
| 18- to 24-Year-Olds | 58.4% | 48.5% | 83.0% |
| 25- to 34-Year-Olds | 66.4% | 57.0% | 85.8% |
| 35- to 44-Year-Olds | 69.9% | 62.8% | 89.8% |
| 45- to 54-Year-Olds | 73.5% | 67.4% | 91.6% |
| 55- to 64-Year-Olds | 76.6% | 71.5% | 93.3% |
| 65- to 74-Year-Olds | 78.1% | 72.4% | 92.7% |
| 75 and older | 76.6% | 67.8% | 88.6% |
| **Income:** | | | |
| Under $20,000 | 63.7% | 51.9% | 81.5% |
| $20,000–29,999 | 67.1% | 56.3% | 83.9% |
| $30,000–39,999 | 71.1% | 62.2% | 87.5% |
| $40,000–49,999 | 72.6% | 64.7% | 89.1% |
| $50,000–74,999 | 78.2% | 70.9% | 90.7% |
| $75,000–99,999 | 81.9% | 76.4% | 93.3% |
| $100,000 and Above | 79.6% | 91.8% | 91.8% |
| Income Not Reported | 53.4% | 49.0% | 91.7% |
| **Education:** | | | |
| No High School Diploma | 50.5% | 39.4% | 78.0% |
| High School Graduate or GED | 64.1% | 54.9% | 85.6% |
| Some College or Associate's Degree | 75.3% | 68.0% | 90.4% |
| College Graduate | 81.2% | 77.0% | 94.8% |
| Advanced Degree | 85.8% | 82.7% | 96.4% |

Adapted from U.S. Census Bureau, Current Population Survey, November, 2008.

the participation of farmers and of the working class. However, after the election of 1880, powerful business leaders formed oligarchies in both parties; and as both parties then supported business issues almost exclusively, competition between the parties collapsed. The populists were shut out of party politics.

The business leaders of both parties were concerned about the waves of immigrants flowing into this country and wanted to restrict their power to influence elections; they were concerned about the power that black people had been developing since the Civil War. In order to restrict these groups, they instituted reforms dealing with registration and voting procedures. They instituted poll taxes, official ballots, registration lists that required a worker to be away from work in order to get on the list, literacy tests, residency requirements, and other complicated voting procedures. While many of these restrictions have been declared illegal, the procedures for registering and voting are still burdensome in this country (Piven & Cloward, 1989). Registration sometimes requires traveling to the county seat or even to the state capital. In addition to the difficulties of registering to vote, there are too many elections, too many elected officials, and too many **referenda**—that is, questions on the ballot concerning everything from building roads to changing the qualifications for elected officials. In some countries, registration is automatic when the voter reaches an eligible age. In other countries, voting is mandatory, and people who do not vote are fined.

**Referenda**

Questions on a ballot to be decided by the electorate

Typically, people in the United States who do vote tend to remain very loyal to either the Republican or the Democratic parties, a loyalty based primarily on emotional ties formed during the earlier socialization process. Approximately 85% to 95% of both parties voted for their own party affiliation in the 2008 election (see Table 13-7). Most people do not choose a party on the basis of political opinions, usually because they are not well informed about political issues. The parties, typically, do not differ significantly on most issues, even though the 2012 presidential election was played out in the media as having radical differences between the parties, which may have affected the outcome of that election (see Table 13-8). People usually affiliate with a party and then are educated by the party's stand on the issues. Because they are loyal to their party, they accept

*In some countries voting is mandatory.*
*(iStockphoto)*

**Table 13-7** How People Voted in the 2008 Presidential Election

| | All Voters | | Whites | |
|---|---|---|---|---|
| | Obama % | McCain % | Obama % | McCain % |
| **Total** | **53** | **46** | **43** | **55** |
| **Age 18–29** | **66** | **31** | **54** | **44** |
| Republicans | 15 | 84 | 11 | 88 |
| Democrats | 95 | 4 | 92 | 7 |
| Independents | 66 | 27 | 62 | 32 |
| Men | 62 | 34 | 52 | 45 |
| Women | 69 | 29 | 56 | 42 |
| College Experience | 65 | 32 | 55 | 42 |
| No College | 66 | 31 | 50 | 48 |
| White | 54 | 44 | | |
| Black | 95 | 4 | | |
| Hispanic | 76 | 19 | | |
| **Age 30+** | **50** | **48** | **41** | **57** |
| Republicans | 8 | 90 | 7 | 91 |
| Democrats | 88 | 11 | 83 | 16 |
| Independents | 48 | 48 | 44 | 52 |
| Men | 47 | 51 | 39 | 59 |
| Women | 52 | 46 | 44 | 54 |
| College Experience | 49 | 49 | 42 | 56 |
| No College | 50 | 48 | 38 | 60 |
| White | 41 | 57 | | |
| Black | 98 | 4 | | |
| Hispanic | 62 | 36 | | |

Adapted from National exit poll conducted by NBC News.

**Table 13-8** Selected Characteristics of Voters in the 2012 Presidential Election

| | % of Voters | % Voted for Obama | % Voted for Romney |
|---|---|---|---|
| Male | 47% | 45% | 52% |
| Female | 53% | 55% | 44% |
| Married Women | 31% | 46% | 53% |
| Non-Married Women | 23% | 67% | 31% |
| White | 72% | 39% | 59% |
| Black | 13% | 93% | 6% |
| Hispanic | 10% | 71% | 27% |
| People Who Rated Economy as Poor | 31% | 12% | 85% |
| People Who Rated Economy as Not so Good | 45% | 55% | 42% |
| People Who Rated Economy as Excellent or Good | 23% | 90% | 9% |
| White Catholic | 18% | 40% | 59% |
| White Evangelical | 26% | 21% | 78% |
| No Religion | 12% | 70% | 26% |

Adapted from Washington Post Exit Polls 2012.
Retrieved from http://www.washingtonpost.com/wp-srv/special/politics/2012-exit-polls/national-breakdown/

the stand of the party. In an interesting study, Heritage and Greatbatch (1986) found that people interrupt political speeches with applause after emotion-laden slogans, not after informative analyses of domestic or foreign affairs.

While on most issues the voters will accept the stand taken by their party, this is not true of the so-called moral issues, such as race, sexual behavior, and religion. People usually have a strong opinion on moral issues; they will leave their party and either will not vote or else will vote for the other party if they disagree with their own party's stand. As a result, political parties generally try to avoid moral issues altogether and take a middle-of-the-road stand on other issues to attract the largest number of voters.

Some groups outside of the major political parties have attempted to bring moral issues into politics. They recognize that emotional issues often can easily influence a large minority of people, and they have used these issues to attract followers. They cannot, however, attract the majority of voters. If the majority of the voters agreed, for example, that abortions should be outlawed, the major political parties would also express that belief; thus, the issue would cease to be divisive.

Certainly, other factors in addition to allegiance to one's political party play a part in how people vote. Table 13-8 provides a breakdown of how some of characteristics of people were related to how they voted in the 2012 presidential election.

### thinking SOCIOLOGICALLY

While Tables 13-5, 13-6, 13-7, and 13-8 do not provide identical comparison, they do provide informative data about the 2008 and 2012 presidential elections and suggestions about what affected how people voted. Examine these tables and identify the characteristics of people that might have affected their vote in each of the elections. In what ways were they similar? In what ways were they different? How do you account for the similarities and differences between the elections?

# APPLYING SOCIOLOGICAL PERSPECTIVES ON ECONOMIC GROUPS AND SYSTEMS

Developing a sociological perspective about the nature of economic groups and systems is useful in a variety of ways. For example, all of us can learn a great deal about different societies by understanding their economic systems. In addition, sociological perspectives can aid individuals who have specialized interests. For example, politicians can gain important insights because an important aspect of international politics concerns the economic relationships among countries (for example, trade agreements regarding goods, such as oil, wheat, or other natural resources). International business executives need to understand the relationship between social systems and economic systems in order to make prudent business decisions. In addition, on a personal level individual investors in stocks, bonds, mutual funds, and so on can benefit from insights that may help them understand and predict trends in foreign markets. The world of business and investments is no longer limited to the country of residence or of origin. The practical need to understand the relationship between social systems and economic systems has never been greater and is likely to continue to grow.

For example, capitalism reflects our primary American value of individualism—according to the structural functional perspective—and capitalist policies assume that the individual alone is solely responsible for his or her life chances. Understanding the functions and dysfunctions of such capitalist policies—or those of any economic system, for that matter—is essential for policymakers. To create effective economic policies that benefit all people in a society, policymakers would do well to consider both the functions and dysfunctions of particular economic systems, regardless of their reflection of social values. Unfortunately, values—not rationality—form the basis of most public policy (and politicians risk losing public support and reelection when they lose sight of this). Rice (1985) suggests, for example, that it would be rational to have an economic policy in which the government regulates the cost and supply of oil to prevent the oil market from being monopolized by a few giant corporations; but the American value of individualism—as reflected in free enterprise—prohibits this.

Most of you will not be in a position to affect national economic policies, but many of you will be involved in work or business situations that may be arranged to reflect individualism. For example, suppose that you are the manager or owner of a retail-clothing store and you hope to achieve high sales by basing your employees' salaries on the number of sales each makes. Although individual competition might stimulate them to work harder initially, the store might eventually suffer from this policy. The competition for sales could lead to a lack of trust and lower morale among the sales personnel, and thus to a weakened work team. Some employees might quit because they are dissatisfied with working conditions. Time and money would then be lost to hiring and training new personnel. What seems like a good idea theoretically might turn out, in reality, to contain some serious dysfunctions that could undermine your original goals. By realizing that business and economic policies contain dysfunctions as well as functions, and by trying to anticipate what they might be, you might be able to avoid some problems before they arise.

# 13.7 THE AMERICAN ECONOMIC SYSTEM

Most American citizens are convinced that the capitalist system is good and cherish the freedom of the marketplace—the freedom to buy, sell, and earn a living in any way they can. We value these freedoms as much as we value our religious freedom; and, in fact, the two systems arise out of the same tradition.

In *The Protestant Ethic and the Spirit of Capitalism* (1905), Weber discussed the Puritans' influence on the American desire for profit. He noted that capitalism, the exchange of goods for profit, has existed at one time or another in all societies. In the United States, however, profit became a major goal, desired not simply to provide for one's daily needs but also to accumulate wealth.

The Puritans were *Protestant Calvinists*. Their doctrine stated that most people lived in sin but that a few had been predestined for everlasting life by the grace of God. No one on this earth could affect that predestination; God sealed people's fates. The chosen were on earth to build God's kingdom as God intended.

How did people know whether they were among the elect? They could not know; but it was believed that those who were involved in the work of the world, who appeared to be building God's kingdom, must be among the elect. Those who spent their lives in idleness, carousing, drinking, and card playing were obviously not doing God's work, and thus obviously not among the chosen. The Calvinists feared death and sought confirmation that they were among the chosen. They worked to produce goods, taking wealth as a sign that they were among the chosen. They did not spend time or money on comforts, play, or anything else that might indicate that they were not chosen; nor did they associate with people whom they believed to be outside the elect. They worked and they accumulated wealth, believing it to be an indication of self-worth. We now know this perspective as the **Protestant ethic**.

There is strong evidence that religious values play a role in present day economics as well. "Religion is an important factor in wealth accumulation … (it) keeps coming up in any model you run to explain wealth" (Keister, 2003). Even after considering other ways of accumulating wealth associated with particular denominations—such as inheritance, levels of education, and other factors—the effect of religion is still significant. According to the study, Keister found that families have a powerful influence on how people learn to save, and religion has a powerful impact on shaping family life. Specifically, the religious beliefs that children learn in their families translate into educational attainment, adult occupations, financial literacy, social connections, and other factors that influence adult wealth ownership. For example, conservative Protestants often emphasize prayer and trust in God to meet their needs, which may reduce their desire to invest. These same groups also look forward to the rewards of the afterlife and don't promote acquiring wealth as good for this life. Jews, on the other hand, don't have a strong orientation to the afterlife but do encourage pursuits that will lead to wealth accumulation, such as high-income careers and investing in this life.

Overall, the median net worth of Jewish people in the survey was $150,890, more than three times the median for the entire sample ($48,200). For conservative Protestants (which included Baptists, Jehovah's Witnesses, Seventh-Day Adventists and Christian Scientists, among others), the median net worth was $26,200, or about half the overall average; and median net worth of mainstream Protestants (including Episcopalians, Methodists, Presbyterians, Lutherans, Unitarians, and others) and Catholics were similar to each other, falling at about the average for the whole sample (Keister, 2003).

Keister also found that people who regularly attended religious services tended to be wealthier. Perhaps going to religious services provides another opportunity to be indoctrinated with beliefs that help build wealth. Also, attending services provides a social network of like others where one may meet contacts or learn investment tips.

**Protestant ethic**

The view associated with the Puritans that hard work is valuable for its own sake (according to Weber, the Protestant ethic is responsible for the high value placed on capitalism in the United States)

Overall, the results of Keister's study demonstrate the importance of family socialization processes in shaping wealth accumulation. Furthermore, the results underscore the importance of culture in shaping economic behavior and ultimately in creating social inequality.

## 13.7a The Growth of Large Corporations

The almost religious fervor with which we work for profit has contributed to the growth of large corporations. **Mass production** has also contributed to the growth of corporations. Building one car by hand is very expensive. Obviously, workers on an assembly line, using machinery, can assemble many identical parts and produce many cars in less time, at a lower cost per car. Robots cost even less than workers, and the cars can be sold at a much greater profit. Factories and mass production have replaced the shoemaker, the spinner, the weaver, the dressmaker, the furniture maker, the cigar maker, the glass blower, the potter, the butcher, the baker, and the candlestick maker. Factories, with the specialized division of labor and automation, make it possible to mass produce goods that can be sold at low prices and still bring profit to the manufacturer.

Bill Gates (AP Wide World Photo)

Profits have also been increased by **vertical expansion** of businesses, which is when a business owns everything from its raw materials to its retail outlets. If a business owns not only the factory that produces the goods but also the source of the raw materials purchased by the factory, the trucks that take the goods to market, and the stores that sell the products, the business can cut its costs at every step of the operation. It does not have to pay part of its profits to the owner of the raw material, the trucker, and the store owner. A business that owns all related businesses, from the raw material to the retailer, can increase its profits at every stage of its operation.

American corporations have expanded their operations to control the entire process from raw material to retail sales (Zwerdling, 1976). A large food store chain, for example, may own thousands of food stores and more than a hundred manufacturing and processing plants, including bakeries, milk plants, ice cream plants, soft drink plants, meat processors, and coffee roasting plants. It might manufacture its own soap, peanut butter, and salad oil; and it might own a fleet of thousands of trucks to ship these products to its stores. Members of the board of directors of the chain would also sit on the boards of banks and corporations involved in agriculture, food production, food processing, food packaging, gas and electric power, and fuel oil. By owning or influencing every stage of production from the land on which the food is grown to the retail sales outlets, such a chain becomes a very large corporation.

**Horizontal expansion**, another way to increase profits, refers to the practice of taking over similar businesses in order to gain a monopoly and reduce competition in the field. For example, a company that makes soup may buy all of the competing soup-making companies. Then, when a customer enters the grocery store, most of the soup available for purchase is made by the same company, which can define the quality standards, set the price of soup, and eliminate worry about losing sales to competition. That company controls the market.

Another form of expansion that assures continued profits is **diversification**—entering a variety of businesses in an attempt to ensure a stable rate of profit. Investors might buy a variety of stocks so that if one went down, another might remain stable or go up; they would then be protected from losing their entire investment. In the same way, corporations buy a variety of businesses so that those that are not highly profitable can be supported by those that are. Great Western United owns sugar companies,

**Mass production**
The production of many items of a product, which lowers the cost per item and reduces the time needed to make each one

**Vertical expansion**
Business expansion in order to own everything related to a business, from raw materials to sales outlets

**Horizontal expansion**
Corporations taking over similar businesses in order to gain a monopoly and reduce competition

**Diversification**
The corporate practice of entering business in a variety of areas in order to protect profits (a decrease in profits in one type of business might be made up by an increase in profits in another type, for example)

Shakey's Pizza, and a large number of real estate holdings. The real estate is extremely valuable, but it does not provide income. By diversifying, Great Western United can support its real estate holdings with income from other sources. United States Steel Corporation, when the demand for steel fell, diversified by buying other companies and changing its name to USX.

The legally structured size of corporations tells only half the story of their tremendous power. Corporate links may join corporations that appear to be unrelated. When IBM was developing computers in a highly competitive market, IBM officers and directors were on the boards of Bankers Trust Company of New York, the Rockefeller Foundation, First National City Bank of New York, Chemical Bank, Federal Reserve Bank of New York, Morgan Guaranty Trust Company of New York, the J. P. Morgan Bank, and the United States Trust Company (DeLamarter, 1986). According to DeLamarter, these banks made it difficult for competitors of IBM to finance the development of their own computer products, thus aiding IBM in its domination of the field. As corporations grow larger and more powerful, they do not confine their operations to their own country but expand, instead, internationally.

## 13.7b Multinational Corporations

Very large corporations own companies in one or more foreign nations, where they employ workers and produce and sell their products. These companies are known as **multinational corporations**. Ford Motor Company is a major example of a multinational corporation. In 2012, more than half of Ford's 172,000 employees were non-U.S. citizens. In 2012, more than half of Ford's 65 production plants were located outside of the United States (media.ford.com, 2012).

Americans own most multinational corporations. These companies often become involved in political arrangements made between the United States and other countries. They affect the economies of this country and those countries in which they have holdings in several ways. They can buy foreign materials even when the United States would like to reduce overseas spending and would prefer that they "buy American." They can play one country against another, offering to build a plant in whichever gives them the greatest advantages in taxes, cheap labor, and freedom from regulation. By closing plants, they can create unemployment problems. In a sense, multinational corporations are above the laws of any nation because they can use their vast wealth and power to dominate a nation's economy or evade its laws. The annual sales of either General Motors or Exxon are greater than the GNP of countries such as Austria, Denmark, Norway, Greece, Portugal, and the smaller nations of the world. Corporations can borrow vast amounts of money on the basis of their sales, and yet countries can tax only their GNP. As corporations increase in size, they gain progressively more power to dominate the economies of entire nations.

*Multinational businesses have had a great impact on developed nations as well as developing nations. Del Monte and Dole are examples of multinational businesses.* *(AP Wide World Photo)*

While the major increase in multinational business has been in the developed nations of the world, developing nations have also been powerfully influenced by multinationals. Large agricultural corporations, for example, have converted large tracts of farmland into huge plantations, cultivated by modern machinery to produce cash crops for worldwide shipment. Del Monte and Dole grow pineapples in the Philippines and Thailand, where there is an abundance of cheap labor; and they then ship the pineapples to United States and Japanese markets. The Gulf and Western Corporation controls land in the Dominican Republic, which is used to grow sugar for Gulf and Western's

**Multinational corporation**
Corporations that do business in a number of nations

sugar mill. The large corporations often do not own the land but enter into agreements with local landowners to grow what they need for their processing plants; and the local landowners and governments usually cooperate—even when the nutrition of their own local people suffers.

Multinational corporations have such a great impact on the nations in which they do business and are so influential in international relations that some observers believe that nations, as we know them today, will eventually vanish and that affairs of state will come to be run by the boards of directors of huge corporations. Whether this will happen and whether it would create a more peaceful and orderly world or more poverty for workers is still a matter of speculation, for now. In any case, as corporations change and grow, the nature of work also changes.

**thinking** SOCIOLOGICALLY

1. Evaluate the structural functional view that capitalism is efficient for a society, especially as corporations grow larger.
2. Evaluate Weber's stance that corporations are becoming so large that they could become ruthless in search of profits and have no regard for people.
3. If you were running a large organization, what would you consider the best way to manage your employees? Incorporating interactionist principles, explain why employers would benefit by creating primary and in-group feelings among their employees. If you were a lower-level employee, would you agree?

## 13.8 POLITICS AND THE DISTRIBUTION OF WEALTH

The economic system in our society produces wealth, but it has no responsibility to distribute wealth to all of the citizens. It is the political system that determines how the wealth is distributed. The government levies taxes and uses its funds to support programs for its citizens. In recent years, there has been much debate regarding the extent to which government should support the less privileged in society. Critics contend that the country must not drop programs that aid those unable to work because they are too young, too old, or too ill, or simply because no jobs are available. They believe that as long as the needs of society are met only when they provide profits to capitalists, the society will continue to have unemployment and poverty; and human needs will go unmet simply because it is not profitable to meet them. One such debate about government support of the low-income worker centers on the issue of the minimum wage.

**BVT*Lab***

Visit www.BVTLab.com to explore the student resources available for this chapter.

Those who encourage government action to help redistribute wealth argue that a more equitable redistribution of money would permit everyone to benefit from the wealth generated by society. Today, most government effort to help those who cannot manage financially takes the form of some type of welfare payment.

### 13.8a Welfare

Welfare consists of government payments to people who have an inadequate income. The United States Federal Government spends more than $400 billion per year to fund welfare programs. Welfare programs include the following:

1. One of the oldest alleviative poverty programs at the national level is Temporary Assistance for Needy Families (TANF), first enacted (under the

name Aid to Families with Dependent Children) as part of the landmark Social Security Act of 1935. TANF is jointly funded with state and federal revenues.

2. Medicaid, the medical insurance program for the poor
3. Supplemental Security Income (SSI), part of the Social Security system, which is designed to aid the poorest of the aged, blind, and disabled
4. General Assistance, a program to help poor people not covered by other programs

Piven and Cloward (1993) have shown that welfare payments, historically, increase when unemployment is high and discontent is widespread; however, they decrease when workers are scarce and unemployment is low. They argue that welfare payments are used to keep the unemployed from expressing their discontentment in hard times.

In what has become somewhat of a classic tongue-in-cheek, but accurate, discussion of poverty, Herbert Gans (1971) lists some advantages that the middle and upper classes derive by keeping people poor:

1. They are a source of cheap labor.
2. They can be sold goods of inferior quality that otherwise could not be sold at all.
3. They serve as examples of deviance, thereby motivating others to support the norms of the dominant group.
4. They make mobility easier for others because they are out of the competition.
5. They do the most unpleasant jobs.
6. They absorb the costs of change because they suffer the unemployment when technological advances are made by industry.
7. They create jobs for the middle class in social work and related fields.
8. They create distinctive cultural forms of music and art, which the middle class adopts.

Welfare payments to the poor comprise only a small part of the federal government's efforts to improve living conditions, but most programs are designed to assist classes other than the poor.

## 13.8b Welfare for the Well-Off

There are more government programs to help the middle and upper classes than to help the poor. Following is a partial list:

1. Veterans' benefits—such as life insurance, healthcare, educational support, housing loans, and burial grounds
2. Housing loans, available to higher-income groups, offering lower interest rates and reduced down payments
3. Business loans on favorable terms, available to owners of both small and large businesses
4. Farming subsidies to landowners who agree not to farm some of their lands or who grow products for which there are powerful lobbies, such as tobacco
5. Social Security, which is not available to the unemployed or to those who work in jobs the program does not cover and which is not taxed on incomes above a certain level
6. Medical care in hospitals built with government funds, staffed by doctors educated with government support and which use treatments developed with the help of government grants

7. College classrooms and dormitories built with government funds and financial assistance for college students

Even in the face of programs such as these, it is the programs for the poor that generally come under attack when the government tries to cut the domestic budget. Programs that benefit the middle class, especially veterans' and housing benefits, are considered sacred and are never reduced.

## thinking SOCIOLOGICALLY

1. Carefully go through this chapter, and list all of the topics that could provide insight into the policy debate about raising the minimum wage.
2. How are each of the topics selected in Question 1 useful in evaluating each side of the debate?

# CHAPTER 13 Wrapping it up

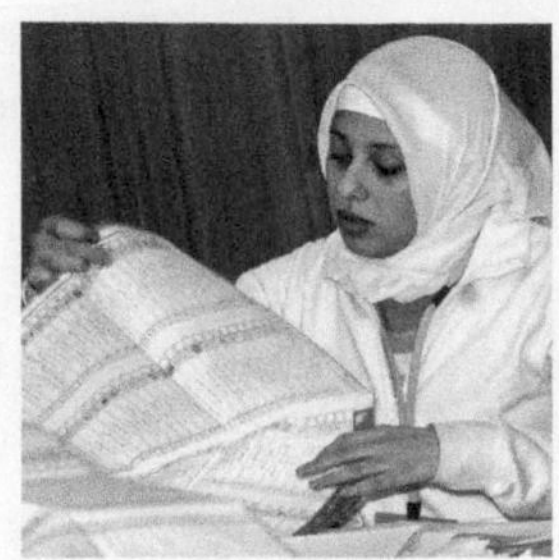

## Summary


1. A society's political institution is the structure that has the power to rule in a society. Power is the ability to control the behavior of others. Politics is the use of power to determine who gets what in society.
2. Two types of power are physical force and latent force. Physical force is an inefficient way to control a society. Latent force, making people comply by threatening them with punishment, is more effective.
3. Authority is the most effective means of power and is considered legitimate because the people believe that the ruler has a right to rule; thus, they comply voluntarily. Traditional authority is derived from accepted practices or customs. Legal authority is based on a system of legislated rules and regulations. Charismatic authority comes from the personal traits of the leader.
4. A society's economic system provides for the production and distribution of the goods and services the society uses. Sociologists study economic systems to better understand how the production of goods influences social life.
5. There are currently two basic types of economic systems: capitalism and socialism. In *capitalism*, the property needed to produce resources and goods is privately owned, and goods are sold for a profit. The United States is the most capitalistic of modern nations; however, even in this country, some property is not privately owned.
6. In *socialism*, the property needed to produce goods and resources is owned by the state, and production is planned by the state.
7. In a *welfare capitalism* system, some property is private and some is owned by the state.
8. *Communism* is a system in which the members of the society own the means of production in common. Communism has had some success in small communities, but it has not been developed on a national scale.
9. Structural functionalists believe that political and economic systems reflect societal values. If a society values freedom, monogamy, hard work, and achievement, laws will be passed to enforce these values. Members of the society will comply with the law because it reflects their own beliefs.
10. Structural functional theorists point out that capitalism reflects social values favoring private property and the freedom to determine one's own economic course. Functionalists believe that capitalism persists because it functions well, providing profit to whoever supplies any needed goods.
11. Structural functionalists also believe that the political system must try to resolve conflicts in values. The value of freedom, for example, may come into conflict with the value of hard work, and the government must arbitrate to ensure that behavior does not infringe on either value. Some subcultures teach values that conflict with those of the larger society, but the government must protect the values of the dominant society.
12. Conflict theorists believe that some groups gain power because they possess a large share of society's resources. They use these resources to acquire power and use the law and the political system to protect their own wealth. The rich teach the population through the schools and the mass media that their wealth, power, and laws are legitimate. In other words, they shape the values of the society to serve their own interests. Conflict theorists argue that capitalism both creates a monopoly of wealth and alienates workers.
13. Modern societies have two types of legal power structures: democratic systems and totalitarian systems. Democratic systems allow citizens to participate in their own governance. Totalitarian systems have powerful governments that control the society.
14. Political parties are groups of citizens formed with the express intent of gaining control of the political body of the state. They exist in both democratic and totalitarian states. Parties nominate candidates to run for office, provide personnel for bureaucratic posts, and make

public policy. Their goal is not only to influence government but also to manage it.

15. Debate about how power is distributed in the United States has continued for many years. Theorists have argued, on the one hand, that a power elite made up of business and government officials controls the power and, on the other hand, that there are a variety of diversified groups that protect their own interests.
16. In the United States, socialization legitimates legal authority, and political socialization begins early. Youngsters learn about political leaders and political parties at home and in the community. Socialization continues in school, and most children learn to respect the political system, although poor children are more likely to question government and its practices.
17. Voter participation is low in this country. Social-psychological explanations do not fully explain why voters do not vote. Instead, the structure of our political parties and our registration and voting procedures explain much of our low voter participation.
18. Most Americans remain loyal to one political party and permit it to guide them on important issues. On moral issues, however, voters tend to act more independently.
19. The American economic system reflects values held by its people. These values were strongly influenced by the Puritans, who believed that God chose those who accumulated wealth. Americans value *growth*, the individual right to accumulate wealth. In considering the influence of different denominations of religion, there appears to be a correlation between religion, family values, and the accumulation of wealth.
20. Through *vertical expansion*, American corporations have grown from large factories to giant corporate systems that control every step in the manufacturing process, from raw materials to retail sales. Some corporations have grown through *horizontal expansion* to monopolize most of the sales in a field, and others have grown through *diversification* to own a number of different types of unrelated businesses. Businesses may also be linked by being owned or controlled by the same bank or wealthy individual.
21. Many very large multinational corporations do business in many countries.

## Discussion Questions

1. Discuss how knowledge of different types of power could be useful in your everyday life. Use examples of specific social situations in which you are routinely involved.
2. Discuss the advantages of authority as a source of power.
3. Select a policy or a piece of legislation currently in the news, and examine it from the structural functional and conflict perspectives on political systems.
4. Discuss which would be a more efficient form of government—democracy or totalitarianism.
5. Discuss the role of political parties in government.
6. Discuss whether you think that power in the United States is monopolized by a few, as in the military–industrial complex, or is broadly distributed, as in a pluralistic model.
7. Discuss the advantages and disadvantages of a one-party political system, a two-party political system, and a political system with multiple parties.
8. What kinds of abuses might result from PACs and lobbies?
9. Examine your own political attitudes and how they have been developed through socialization.
10. Do you believe that a political party educates voters who have chosen the party, or do voters choose a party after educating themselves on issues? Discuss how this difference shapes the nature of authority.
11. Make a list of the socialistic programs that exist in the United States. Which of these programs should be eliminated? What programs do you think should be added to the list?
12. Discuss the traditional values of American society that spur our economy. What values are changing, and what new values are evolving that spur the economy?
13. Consider the advantages and the disadvantages of Sweden's system of having large tax bills and more social programs, compared to the United States having lower taxes and fewer programs.
14. Compare how structural functional theory and conflict theory would explain the growth of multinational corporations.
15. What are the advantages and disadvantages of very meager welfare payments? What would they be for very generous welfare payments?
16. What are some of the reasons for providing government programs to improve the standard of living of the middle class and the wealthy?

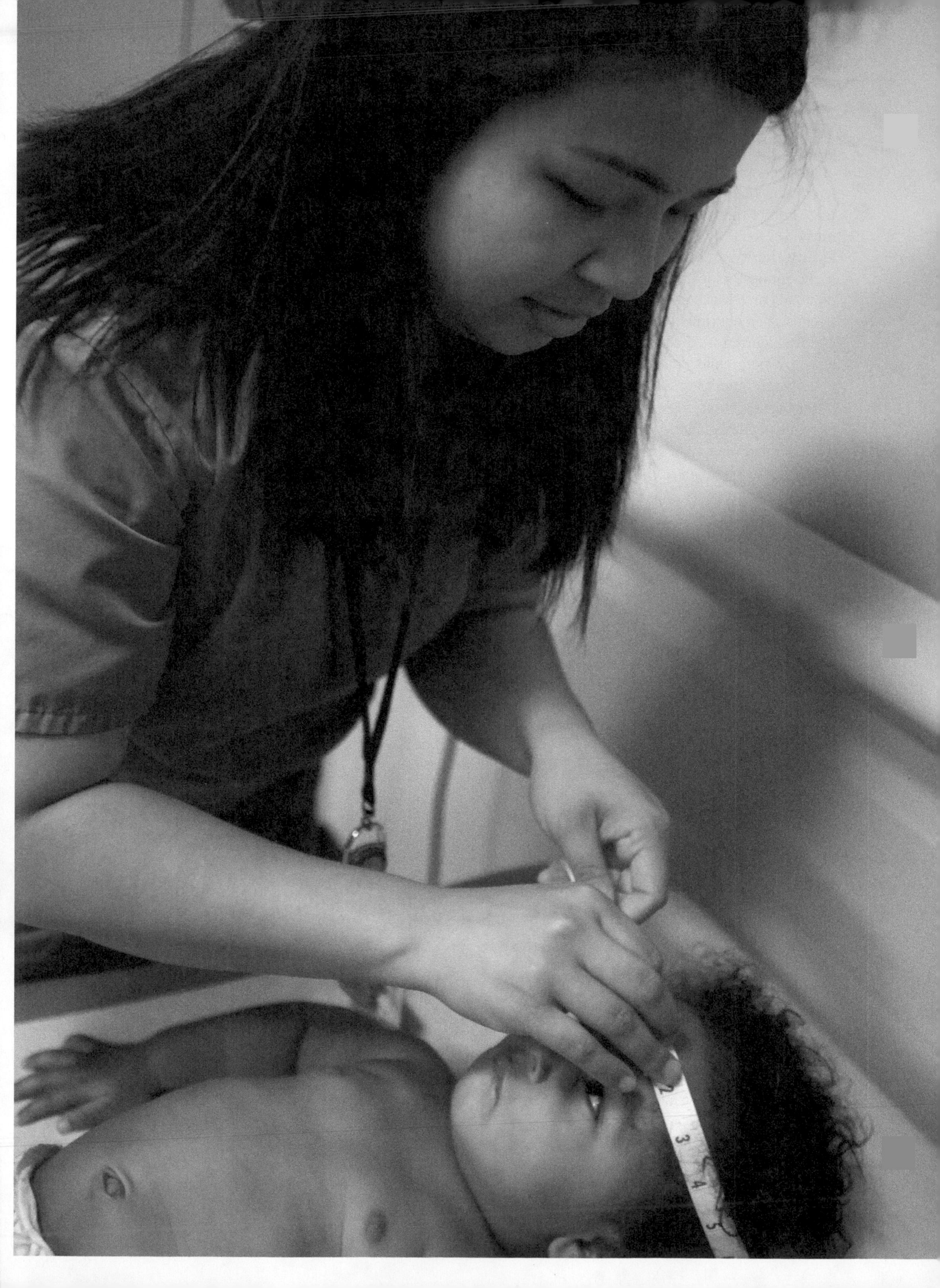

# CHAPTER 14

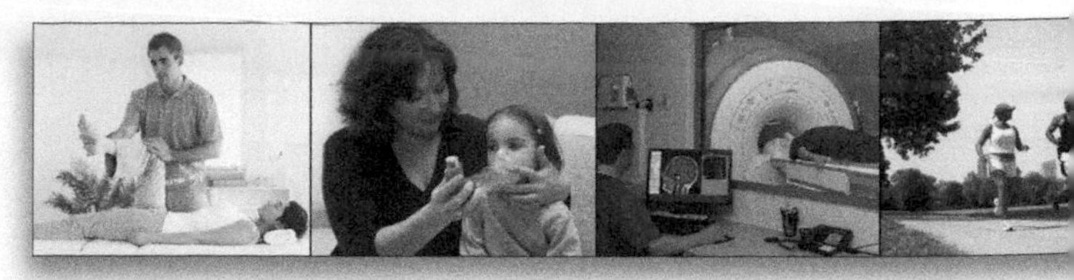

# Healthcare Groups and Systems

## SYNOPSIS

Focal Point

## HEALTH AS A SOCIAL FACT

Health, both physical and psychological, is often thought of as an individual condition of people's lives. However, when we look at statistics about health conditions, it becomes clear that health is a social fact. As you read in Chapter 1, Emile Durkheim defined social facts as "every way of acting, fixed or not, capable of exercising on the individual an external constraint." Social facts stem from collective forces rather than individual ones. They are external to individuals and resistant to individual will. While there certainly are aspects of our health that may be affected by our individual decisions (such as the decision to smoke cigarettes), when looked at collectively, the statistics regarding health suggest that health is as much a social fact as it is a biological fact. Consider the following statistics compiled by the *Centers for Disease Control and Prevention (CDC) Health Disparities and Inequalities Report, United States 2011*:

- In all states of the U.S., lower income residents report fewer average healthy days.
- Air-pollution related disparities associated with fine particulates and ozone, which often lead to health problems, are often determined by geographical location. Racial/ethnic minority groups are more likely to live in affected geographic areas and experience a disparately larger impact on their health.
- Infants born to black women are 1.5 to 3 times more likely to die than infants born to women of other races/ethnicities.
- Men of all races/ethnicities are approximately four times likely to die in motor vehicle crashes than women, and death rates are twice as high among Native Americans.
- Men of all ages and race/ethnicities are approximately four times more likely to die by suicide than females. The suicide rate among Native Americans and non-Hispanic whites is more than twice that of blacks, Asian Pacific Islanders and Hispanics.
- Rates of drug-induced deaths increased between 2003 and 2007 among men and women of all race/ethnicities, with the exception of Hispanics, and rates are highest among non-Hispanic whites. Prescription drug abuse now kills more persons than illicit drugs, a reversal of the situation 15 to 20 years ago.
- Men are much more likely to die from coronary heart disease, and black men and women are much more likely to die of heart disease and stroke than their white counterparts.
- Rates of preventable hospitalizations increase as incomes decrease. There also are large racial/ethnic disparities in preventable hospitalizations, with blacks experiencing a rate more than double that of whites.
- Racial/ethnic minorities, with the exception of Asians/Pacific Islanders, experience disproportionately higher rates of new human immunodeficiency virus diagnoses than whites, as do men who have sex with men (MSM).
- Hypertension is by far most prevalent among non-Hispanic blacks (42% vs. 28.8% among whites), while levels of control are lowest for Mexican Americans. Although men and women have roughly equivalent hypertension prevalence, women are significantly more likely to have the condition controlled. Uninsured persons are only about half as likely to have hypertension under control than those with insurance, regardless of type.
- Rates of adolescent pregnancy and childbirth have been falling or holding steady for all racial/ethnic minorities in all age groups. Disparities persist, however, as birth rates for Hispanics and non-Hispanic blacks are 3 and 2.5 times those of whites, respectively.
- More than half of alcohol consumption by adults in the United States is in the form of binge drinking. Younger people and men are more likely to binge drink and consume more alcohol than older people and women. The prevalence of binge drinking is higher in groups with higher incomes and higher educational levels, although people who binge drink and have lower incomes and lower educational attainment levels binge drink more frequently. When they do binge drink, they drink more heavily. American Indian/Native Americans report more binge drinking episodes per month and higher alcohol consumption per episode than other groups.
- Tobacco use is the leading cause of preventable illness and death in the United States. Despite overall declines in cigarette smoking, disparities in smoking rates persist among certain racial/ethnic minority groups, particularly

among American Indians/Alaska Natives. Smoking rates decline significantly with increasing income and educational attainment.

Consider that each of the above healthcare disparities pertains to social or demographic characteristics rather than individual traits. While it is true that some of the results (such as alcohol and tobacco consumption) seem to be the result of individual choices, the fact that some behaviors are disproportionate in some social groups suggests that there is something about being in those groups that leads to the disparities.

Healthcare is one of the most hotly debated and controversial political issues in the United States. The "Patient Protection and Affordable Care Act" (popularly referred to as "Obamacare") illustrates this deeply controversial issue. One controversy about the plan involves the extent to which government should play a part in insuring affordable healthcare for its citizens, as well as economic considerations that have potential effects for the economy as a whole. As with other political differences about the economy, the controversies surrounding "Obamacare" are also fraught with ideological differences that manifest themselves in practical approaches. Every society must give serious attention to the health of its population if it is to survive. Illness disrupts society inasmuch as members who are ill cannot fulfill their social roles, they use scarce resources such as medicines, and they require the time and attention of healthy persons to take care of them. In extreme instances, illness has destroyed entire societies, sometimes even killing everyone. Because of these factors, every society has developed ways of coping with illness. We often think of health and illness in strictly biological terms and believe that the diagnosis and treatment of illness are based on a scientific analysis of a biological problem. Social factors, however, play a major role in defining who is well and who is ill; they also influence how illness is treated. An understanding of these social factors is critical to developing sound healthcare policies.

# 14.1 THE SOCIAL NATURE OF HEALTH AND ILLNESS

The World Health Organization has defined health to be, in the most idealistic terms, the "complete physical, mental and social well-being and not merely the absence of disease and infirmity." It is difficult to estimate how many people would be considered totally healthy according to this perfect definition. Does anyone ever have complete physical, mental, and social well-being all at the same time? Rather than use such an all-encompassing definition, others in the health field prefer to define *health* as the body in a state of equilibrium. Our biological systems should function in a particular way, and we are healthy when they function as they should.

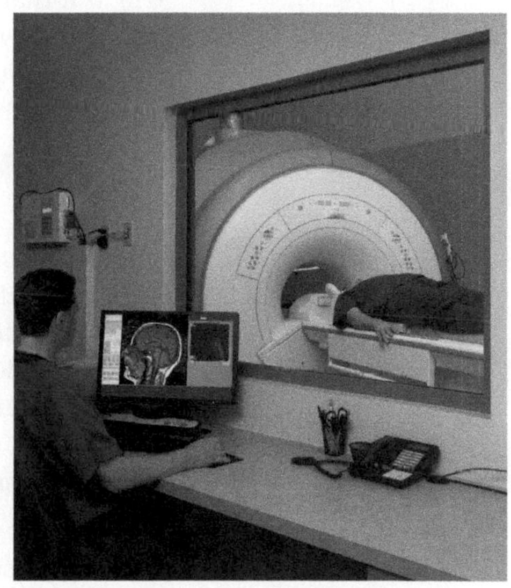

*Diagnostic tests using advanced technologies help detect illness.*
*(iStockphoto)*

Others prefer to define *health* as the absence of illness—but illness is an equally difficult term to define. **Pathological illnesses** are those in which the body is clearly diseased or malfunctioning in some way, as when viruses cause measles and chicken pox, cancer cells develop and grow, or an artery to the heart is blocked. These conditions are either obvious when examining the patient, or they are detected in laboratory tests involving X-rays, microscopes, or the more advanced technology available today. Not all biological abnormalities are considered illnesses, however. Herpes simplex, for example, was not considered an illness until venereal herpes became widespread and life-threatening to newborn infants.

**Pathological illness**
An illness in which the body is clearly diseased or malfunctioning in some way

**Statistical illness**
An illness in which one's health varies from the norm

**Statistical illnesses** are those in which a person's health varies from the norm. For example, high blood pressure is a statistical illness indicating that the person's blood pressure is considerably higher than is deemed normal. The trouble with defining statistical illnesses is in knowing whether or not the norm is actually healthy. In the case of high blood pressure, the norm in the United States (140/95) is probably too high for optimal health. A much lower blood pressure, 100/60, is probably desirable. However, that level is so abnormally low in the United States that if it were used as a standard, everyone would be classified as ill.

Depression is considered a form of mental illness. Researchers, however, are looking for biological causes of depression. (iStockphoto)

Mental illnesses are even more difficult to define than physical ones. Those with cyclothymia have more extreme mood swings than normal, but everyone has some mood swings. We are all depressed sometimes. So how depressed must a person be before being labeled as having the illness called "major depression"? Comparing an individual's behavior and verbalizations to the norm makes the diagnosis. Whether our behavior is considered healthy or ill continues to be determined by social criteria.

# 14.2 THEORETICAL PERSPECTIVES ON ILLNESS

How does society handle illness? Who decides when we are ill and when we are well? Why is it that we can sometimes miss school or work while at other times when we feel just as bad we are not excused? Should illness be decided objectively on the basis of biological criteria? Sociologists do not believe that an objective view of illness can ever be achieved because illness is social as well as biological.

## 14.2a A Functional Explanation of Illness

Talcott Parsons (1951) pointed out that people are classified as ill not on the basis of their physical condition but on the basis of how they are functioning in society. If people do not function well in their social roles, especially in family and work roles, they are considered deviant and disruptive to society. To maintain social order, such people are labeled "ill" and are placed in a **sick role**—a set of expectations, privileges, and obligations related to their illness. The expectations of the sick role vary somewhat, depending on the person and the illness, but generally involve three assumptions:

1. *Sick people are expected to reduce their performance in other roles.* Those with a serious case of the flu—who have a high temperature and other symptoms—may be excused from all other roles. Those suffering from a mild case of flu may be expected to perform work or student roles as usual, but they will be expected to reduce social and recreational roles. The sick role reflects a society's need to have members participate in the work of that society. The first roles relinquished are those that are for pleasure. The last ones relinquished are work roles.
2. *Sick people are expected to try to get better.* They should do whatever they can to improve their health and not linger in their illness.
3. *Sick people are expected to take the advice of others.* Children must take the advice of parents, and adults must listen to their doctor or to the family members who are caring for them. Sometimes, children take care of their parents. Although children would not usually tell their parents how

**Sick role**
A set of expectations, privileges, and obligations related to illness

to behave, in the event of a parent's illness, children give extensive advice. Furthermore, if the advice is not accepted, the advice-giver often becomes very hurt or angry.

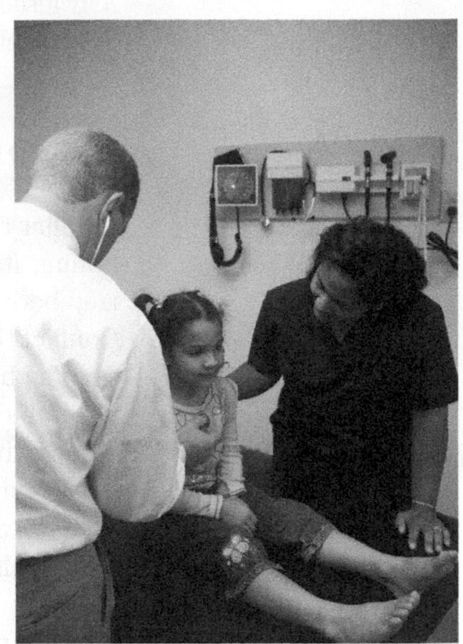

Physicians are the only individuals legally qualified to diagnose and treat illness. (Shutterstock)

Society places the power to declare who is sick in the hands of physicians. Only the physician has the legal right to diagnose and treat illness. The physician can excuse you from work or school, admit you to a hospital, or have you declared disabled or too ill to stand trial in a court of law. A person's self-diagnosis is not adequate. He or she must go to a doctor to be seriously considered ill. If the doctor does not agree with the patient's diagnosis, the individual is labeled "well."

The sick role varies, depending on a variety of social circumstances such as age, gender, and the influence of caregivers. Elderly people are expected to be ill and are easily placed in the sick role. It is also acceptable for women to be ill unless they have responsibility for young children—women are rarely excused from childcare duties. The caregiver also influences the sick role. If he or she accepts the illness, the sick person will play the role more fully; but if the caregiver is someone who works staunchly under all but the most dire circumstances, the sick person may be required to perform work roles. Some mothers are happy to bring soup and tender loving care to their children for long periods of time. Other mothers believe that their children should be up and about as soon as possible. Although the sick role expectations may vary, it does place a person in the social order with a set of both responsibilities and privileges to guide behavior, so that the social order can be kept integrated and functioning.

## APPLYING THE SICK ROLE

At one time or another, everyone will become sick or be required to care for someone who is sick. It is therefore important to acknowledge the existence and implications of the sick role. If, by being placed in a sick role, a person is expected to reduce his or her performance in other roles, is expected to try to get better, and is expected to take the advice of others, then labeling someone as "sick" becomes a useful device in their treatment and path to recovery. People often have ailments that require them to suspend their routine roles in order to return to proper health. Sometimes, though, people are unable to do this, either because they feel compelled to continue to function in their role as worker, parent, or student, or because they are unable to be excused. For example, have you ever felt sick yet continued your routine of play or work and later, when diagnosed as sick by a parent or a doctor, decided that resting was the proper thing to do? The label "sick" serves the important function of not only allowing but also requiring that the sick role become the predominant one, at least temporarily.

It is also important to understand the social consequences of such a label and how it might work to a person's disadvantage. Suppose that a person with a physical limitation is labeled as "sick." This can be negative in a few ways. First, although that person might be able to perform adequately in a job, he or she might not be given an opportunity because of the expectation that sick people reduce their performance in other roles. Similarly, some people who are "sick" may be stigmatized or feared. AIDS victims, for example, are often shunned, even though AIDS cannot be transmitted through casual contact. Second, a person with a physical limitation who is labeled "sick" may come to conform to the expectations associated with the sick role. Clearly, the sick role is a powerful social phenomenon that can be applied to the detriment or advantage of people's physical and mental health.

While various factors affect sick role performances, playing the sick role produces various consequences for the sick person. Dr. Christine Laine (1997) found that patients who are active and engaged with regard to their own healthcare fare better than patients who are less active or adopt the sick role. Although there may be perceived advantages to letting the professionals do the work, the end result is that those who adopt the sick role may lessen their chances of attaining "optimal outcomes" (Laine, 1997). As stated earlier, older, sicker, and less-educated patients are more likely to adopt the sick role.

## 14.2b The Conflict Perspective on Illness

Conflict theorists believe that the healthcare system is an elite system intent on maintaining its power. The healthcare system legitimizes its power by claiming a specialized body of knowledge and uses its power to gain wealth and maintain the status quo. Conflict theorists contend, for example, that the system of giving birth in hospitals rather than at home or in birthing centers persists because it is convenient for doctors and profitable for hospitals (Rothman, 2000). Deliveries are made by doctors rather than by midwives because it provides employment for doctors, not because it is necessary or better for women and babies. Conflict theorists also note that insurance programs such as Medicare, the federal health insurance program for the elderly, are structured such that wealthy people receive more benefits than the poor (Davis, 1975).

In the United States, from 2002 to 2011, the cost of healthcare for a typical family of four has more than doubled from $9,235 to $19,393 (see Figure 14-1). Conflict theorists argue that much of the diagnosis and treatment of diseases benefits the large medical corporations more than the patients. Although drug companies sell drugs of questionable safety and effectiveness for the common cold, they do not like to manufacture **orphan drugs**—those that are valuable in the treatment of rare diseases but not profitable to the manufacturer. Manufacturers of high-technology medical equipment may sell rarely used, expensive devices to many hospitals within a locality, when one device could be shared by several hospitals (Waitzkin, 2000). This raises hospital costs by encouraging physicians to engage in more testing and procedures that must be paid for by the patient, in order to justify the expensive device.

**Orphan drugs**
Drugs that are valuable in the treatment of rare diseases but are not profitable to manufacture

**Figure 14-1** Milliman Medical Index of Healthcare Costs in the U.S.

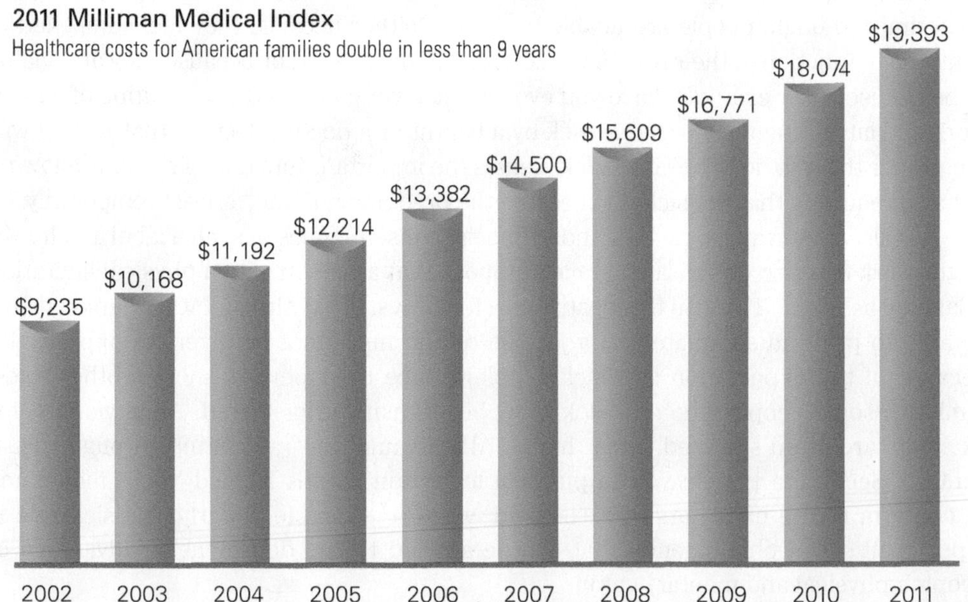


Adapted from Milliman Research Report.
Retrieved from http://publications.milliman.com/periodicals/mmi/pdfs/milliman-medical-index-2011.pdf

Physicians, who usually represent the upper middle class, may use their power to control patients and to maintain the status quo. Physicians have the power to excuse people from work or to refuse to excuse them. Availability of adequate health insurance often plays a role in patient care. For example, well-paid specialists can put well-insured business executives with back pain into a hospital for days or weeks of treatment. On the other hand, for a similar back condition, public health clinic physicians may give inadequately insured laborers painkillers and send them back to work. Physicians declare who is eligible for insurance payments for illness and disability and who must return to work. Physicians can declare criminals insane and unable to stand trial. Elite criminals are more likely to obtain the services of prestigious psychiatrists, who declare the accused to be insane, whereas lower-class criminals cannot afford such services; if these lower-class criminals receive any psychiatric attention, such services are likely to be publicly funded, which makes it probable that the criminal will stand trial and go to prison. Thus, the sick role and illness are used to perpetuate the existing social system.

## 14.2c Symbolic Interaction and Illness Behavior

Because illness is social, symbolic interaction has played a major role in the study of medical groups and systems. For example, researchers who study symbolic interaction explore the meanings that patients give to symptoms and illness. Patients are the first to recognize their own illness and to decide to visit a doctor, who then takes a medical history. How the patient describes symptoms influences the diagnosis, and patients describe their illness based on what society teaches them. They learn that nausea and dizziness are signs of illness (unless they are smoking their first cigarette, in which case they ignore it). They learn that headaches or stomach pains require a drugstore remedy, but chest pains require a visit to the doctor. They learn that if they are tired at night, they need to go to bed; but if they are tired in the morning, they must ignore it and go to class or to work, as expected. These experience-based facts and hearsay knowledge are not necessarily good diagnoses, however; pains in the head or stomach, as well as nausea, dizziness, and fatigue, are symptoms that may indicate serious as well as mild diseases.

Children learn about the causes of disease as they grow up. They learn that if they do not wear a sweater, boots, or a coat, they will catch cold. If they do not eat right or get enough sleep, they will get sick. If they go outdoors for fresh air and exercise, they will be healthier. Then, when they get sick, they wonder what they did wrong. As adults, we tend to blame sick people when they develop heart disease or cancer. Did they eat too much or drink too much? Did they live stressful lives? Surely, they must have done something wrong. We accept a great deal of guilt and blame for our health in this society, even though there is no evidence that we can prevent death, little evidence that we can even forestall death significantly, and a great deal of evidence that the environment influences our health more than our own behavior does.

We also learn medical theories of illness as we grow up. We learn that viruses, germs, or other enemies of the body attack us from outside and that we must ward off attack, if not with boots and sweaters, then with drugs, food, vitamin C, rest, exercise, prayer, or whatever else is fashionable at the time. The approach of the Native Americans was more peaceful. They believed that illness occurred when there was an imbalance with nature; treatments were designed to bring the ill person back into harmony with nature. These treatments were often successful.

During earlier ages, illnesses were classified in a religious context. Lepers and alcoholics were sinners. The ill were disfavored by the gods or possessed by a devil that had to be exorcised. Exorcists, priests, shamans, or religious leaders of other types were called upon to treat the ill person. Ceremonies were performed, gods were called upon to remove the illness, and the shaman was well paid for these talents.

Today, we have great faith in medical science and believe our current good health is the result of good medicine. History shows that, in fact, improved nutrition and sanitation played the most important role in eradicating diseases in the past and that poorer nutrition and a polluted environment are important factors causing today's illnesses.

## 14.3 THE CHANGE IN ILLNESS OVER TIME

Prior to industrialization in Europe, the major killing diseases were **infectious diseases** caused by germs and viruses. Infectious diseases such as tuberculosis, influenza, pneumonia, and the plague were the most common and they often killed children. This pattern continued until the twentieth century and then changed, according to **epidemiologists** (the people who study the social distribution of disease and illness). Today, the diseases that kill the most people are heart disease, cancer, and stroke, which are called **degenerative diseases** because they slowly disable the body as we get older. Both infectious diseases and degenerative diseases have proven to be related to environmental conditions.

### 14.3a The Age of Infectious Diseases

In the Middle Ages, diseases were widespread. Whenever crops failed, there was a food shortage. Transportation was not good enough to bring in large supplies of food, so the population became undernourished, weak, and increasingly susceptible to infection. Devastating plagues swept Europe from 1370 on. In some areas, one-third to one-half the population died. Often, when the plague hit a city, people fled to the countryside, dying on the way or carrying the plague deep into rural areas.

The causes of the plague and other diseases were not understood. In the cities, human waste was thrown into the streets. People did not concern themselves with cleanliness and did not use soap and water. It was considered immoral to concern oneself with the flesh and immodest to wash below the waist (Thompson, 1976).

When it was discovered that rats carry the plague and that germs cause infections, urban sanitation systems were developed. Supplies of water were brought to cities, and sewage systems were built. The improvement of sanitation may have added more to the average life expectancy than all modern medical advances.

Improvements in nutrition played an even more dramatic role in reducing the death rate. It is believed that nutrition improved in Europe when the potato came into widespread use, in about the middle of the eighteenth century. The potato is rich in nutrients and easy to store and ship from place to place. Until the development of potato crops, infectious diseases were rampant and the average life expectancy was probably less than 40 years.

Modern medicine may have helped to reduce the death rate from infectious diseases in two important ways. *Antibiotics*, such as penicillin, were developed to cure infections; *vaccines*, such as for measles, were developed to prevent diseases. There is no question that antibiotics save lives; but researchers McKinlay and McKinlay (1981) argue that vaccines actually affected the death rate only slightly, reducing it by 3.5% at most. The infectious diseases that were the major causes of death in 1900—influenza, pneumonia, tuberculosis, diphtheria, typhoid, scarlet fever, measles, and whooping cough—were declining steadily as causes of death long before modern vaccines were discovered. They continued to fall after the vaccines were introduced, but not appreciably. Poliomyelitis, commonly called polio, is an exception. It showed a very noticeable decline soon after the vaccine came into widespread use. Otherwise, the reduction in infectious diseases was largely a result of better nutrition, better sanitation, and better housing.

**Infectious diseases**
Diseases caused by germs and viruses that can be spread from one person to another

**Epidemiology**
The study of the spread of diseases

**Degenerative diseases**
Those diseases that slowly disable the body as one gets older, such as heart disease and cancer

### 14.3b Current Causes of Death

Poor nutrition is still widespread among the poor of most nations, and starvation and infectious diseases are persistent problems. However, the causes of death in industrial societies are dramatically different. Recently, the major causes of death in the United States and most other industrial nations have been heart disease, cancer, chronic respiratory diseases, and stroke (see Table 14-1). Although heart disease and strokes have been declining slightly, these and other more rare diseases that damage the heart and blood vessels cause more deaths in the United States than any other disease. The American diet is believed to contribute significantly to these diseases.

The American diet, along with pollution, is also blamed for the increasing cancer rate. Cancer caused nearly 568,000 deaths in 2011 (Table 14-1). Most experts in the field estimate that 80%–90% of all cancer cases are the result of environment or diet (American Cancer Society, 2010). In 2010, approximately 171,000 cancer deaths were caused by tobacco use. The American Cancer Society states that all cancers caused by tobacco use and heavy use of alcohol can be prevented completely. About one-third of all other cancer deaths are the result of being overweight, obesity, poor nutrition or lack of physical activity—and thus could also be prevented. Cancers related to infectious agents (such as hepatitis B and HIV) are also preventable, as well as cancer caused by overexposure to ultraviolet rays. The risk of *carcinogens* (cancer-causing products) in the environment has been known since 1942, when publications urged that measures be taken to minimize cancer hazards on the job (Agran, 1975); but little effective action has been taken. Those who work with rubber, steelworkers, workers who produce dyestuffs, miners, dry cleaners, painters, printers, petroleum workers, and others who are exposed to benzene, insecticides, copper, lead, and arsenic suffer from higher than normal cancer rates. Cancer rates are also higher in neighborhoods where these industries are located.

Accidents, the fifth most common cause of death, are the leading cause of death for persons under age 35. Motor vehicle accidents, which account for half of these deaths, have declined as speed limits were reduced to 55 miles per hour and the use of seat belts increased. White males between the ages of 15 and 25 have the highest death rate from automobile accidents.

**Table 14-1** Ten Leading Causes of Death in the United States, 2011

| Cause of Death | Number of Deaths |
|---|---|
| Heart disease | 599,413 |
| Cancer | 567,628 |
| Chronic lower respiratory diseases | 137,353 |
| Stroke (cerebrovascular diseases) | 128,842 |
| Accidents (unintentional injuries) | 118,021 |
| Alzheimer's disease | 79,003 |
| Diabetes | 68,705 |
| Influenza and pneumonia | 53,692 |
| Nephritis, nephrotic syndrome, and nephrosis | 48,935 |
| Intentional self-harm (suicide) | 36,909 |

Adapted from Centers for Disease Control and Prevention, "Leading Causes of Death." Retrieved from http://www.cdc.gov/nchs/faststats/lcod.html

## 14.3c Alcoholism: Moral Failure or Major Disease?

Alcoholism is a major killer of Americans and would probably appear on the list of major killers if all deaths due to alcoholism were listed on death certificates. According to the National Institute on Alcohol Abuse and Alcoholism, nearly 17.6 million adults in the U.S. have an alcohol problem (National Institute on Alcohol Abuse and Alcoholism, 2011). Among children ages 13 to 17, there are 3 million alcoholics. Untold numbers of heart attack victims are probably victims of alcoholism. Many cancer victims—especially those with cancer of the mouth, throat, larynx, esophagus, pancreas and liver—are really victims of alcoholism. While the number of alcohol related driving fatalities has decreased from 26,100 (60% of fatalities) in 1982 to 9,878 (38% of fatalities) in 2011, these deaths are still both prevalent and preventable (see Table 14-2).

It is believed that alcoholism is the underlying cause of many deaths. Alcoholism seems to be a physical disease that cannot be cured by willpower. (Shutterstock)

In 1956, the American Medical Association (AMA) declared that **alcoholism** is a disease with identifiable and progressive symptoms; that if it is untreated, it leads to mental damage, physical incapacity, and early death. The physical nature of the disease was described shortly thereafter by Jellineck (1960). It was demonstrated that alcoholism occurs in people who have inherited a body chemistry that fails to metabolize alcohol the way normal people do. Instead, the body produces toxic substances that cause widespread damage in the body and changes that cause the body to require more alcohol to function. While genetic makeup partially contributes to alcoholism, the extent to which one's social environment plays a part in the progression of the disease should not be overlooked. Thus, the victim is addicted to alcohol because once having introduced alcohol into the body, the victim must continue to drink in order to continue to function. Sooner or later, however, the body will be poisoned to the extent that the victim cannot function with or without alcohol. Because alcoholism has historically been viewed as a sin, a crime, a moral lapse, or a psychological illness, physicians prefer not to use it as a cause of death in order to protect the reputation of the family and thus it does not appear on the list of common causes of death.

**Alcoholism**

A disease related to the drinking of alcohol that has identifiable and progressive symptoms (if untreated, alcoholism can lead to mental damage, physical incapacity, and early death)

### thinking SOCIOLOGICALLY

1. Because we give personal meanings to health and illness, we do not always recognize the threat of illness objectively. Have you ever thought you were well when you were ill? Have you ever not noticed one of your own symptoms of a disease?
2. At any time, have you learned anything about alcoholism that led you to believe that alcoholics are weak-willed people rather than people who are ill?
3. What are some possible short-term consequences of assigning someone the "sick role"? Long-term consequences? The older, sicker, and less educated are more likely to take on the sick role. Sociologically, how do you explain this?

**Table 14-2** Alcohol-Related Driving Fatalities in the U.S. 1982–2011

| Year | Total Fatalities Number | Alcohol-Related Fatalities Number | Alcohol-Related Fatalities Percentage |
|---|---|---|---|
| 1982 | 43,945 | 26,173 | 60 |
| 1983 | 42,589 | 24,635 | 58 |
| 1984 | 44,257 | 24,762 | 56 |
| 1985 | 43,825 | 23,167 | 53 |
| 1986 | 46,087 | 25,017 | 54 |
| 1987 | 46,390 | 24,094 | 52 |
| 1988 | 47,087 | 23,833 | 51 |
| 1989 | 45,582 | 22,424 | 49 |
| 1990 | 44,599 | 22,587 | 51 |
| 1991 | 41,508 | 20,159 | 49 |
| 1992 | 39,250 | 18,290 | 47 |
| 1993 | 40,150 | 17,908 | 45 |
| 1994 | 40,716 | 17,308 | 43 |
| 1995 | 41,817 | 17,732 | 42 |
| 1996 | 42,065 | 17,749 | 42 |
| 1997 | 42,013 | 16,711 | 40 |
| 1998 | 41,501 | 16,673 | 40 |
| 1999 | 41,717 | 16,572 | 40 |
| 2000 | 41,945 | 17,380 | 41 |
| 2001 | 42,196 | 17,400 | 41 |
| 2002 | 43,005 | 17,524 | 41 |
| 2003 | 42,643 | 17,013 | 40 |
| 2004 | 42,518 | 16,919 | 39 |
| 2005 | 43,443 | 16,885 | 39 |
| 2006 | 42,532 | 15,829 | 37 |
| 2007 | 41,059 | 15,387 | 37 |
| 2008 | 37,261 | 13,846 | 37 |
| 2009 | 33,808 | 12,744 | 38 |
| 2010 | 32,885 | 10,228 | 31 |
| 2011 | 32,367 | 9,878 | 38 |

Retrieved from http://www.alcoholalert.com/drunk-driving-statistics.html

## 14.4 THE AMERICAN HEALTHCARE SYSTEM

The American healthcare system consists of physicians, nurses, and other healthcare workers who treat illness primarily as a biological event, to be prevented or cured on an individual basis. Illness, however, can be viewed as a social phenomenon and can often be eliminated in society before many individuals are stricken.

## 14.4a The Social Model of Illness

Historically, the greatest strides in reducing illness have been changes in lifestyle, particularly in nutrition, sanitation, and shelter. The **social model of illness** suggests that much disease is caused by social conditions and that changing those conditions can cure it. Some observers believe that taking a social approach could also reduce death rates from modern causes, such as heart disease, cancer, and automobile accidents. Food supplies, for example, could be improved by having a more varied assortment of whole grain foods on the market, as well as foods that do not contain sugar or excessive amounts of fat or salt. Vegetables and fruits could be improved by practicing farming methods that put nutrients into the soil and keep pesticides out of the fruit. More efficient water systems could reduce waste and provide purer drinking water. A modern transportation system could reduce air pollution and accidents. Early detection of AIDS and safe sex practices could reduce the spread of this disease. All of these improvements would need to be accomplished through social reorganization and social change, however.

## 14.4b The Medical Model of Illness

Currently, almost all of our research and healthcare are based on a **medical model of illness**, in which sickness is viewed as an individual problem requiring individual treatment. Cures for heart attacks and cancer are applied after the patient is sick. People are taken to shock trauma centers after the automobile accident occurs. Even when preventive measures are considered, the responsibility rests with the individual. People must seek good food to eat by searching for stores that sell sugar-free and pesticide-free foods, for example; they must treat their own water if they want pure water to drink. They must find ways to get proper exercise individually.

The American healthcare system is designed to maintain the medical model of illness, with a full complement of physicians, nurses, and other staff, plus hospitals, the pharmaceutical industry, and modern medical technology. Of every healthcare dollar, 93 cents is spent trying to cure people after they get sick. Physicians played a major role in building the healthcare system we have today.

## 14.4c The Profession of Medicine

The profession of medicine, for which an MD degree is required, is now one of the most prestigious professions in the United States—but this has not always been true. In the early years of United States history, there were very few doctors. Women took care of the ill members of the family and the community, and also delivered babies. Older women often gained considerable experience in these activities and would be consulted whenever someone was particularly ill or a baby was born. Many of the women of the community would gather for births, so younger women observed and understood the birthing process before they had their own children. A doctor was rarely needed.

There were only a few physicians in this country at the time of the American Revolution; they had been trained in Europe, where they studied Latin or Greek. There was little science taught in universities in those days, and no medical science. Most physicians learned to practice medicine by being an apprentice to a physician, taking on more and more responsibility until they were able to venture out on their own, often to the frontier to seek patients who needed their services. The medicine practiced was often **heroic medicine**, a dramatic intervention by the physician. Patients were bled, blistered, and given poisonous laxatives in an attempt to kill the disease. Often, the treatment killed the patient. Most people went to doctors only when they were desperate. Doctors were often poor and had little work to do. They sometimes had to beg in the streets to survive (Rothstein, 1970).

**Social model of illness**
The view that many diseases are caused by social conditions and that they can be cured by changing social conditions

**Medical model of illness**
A model of illness in which sickness is viewed as an individual problem requiring individual treatment

**Heroic medicine**
Dramatic medical treatments such as bleeding, blistering, or administering poisonous laxatives

By the early 1800s, many physicians were entering the profession, some of whom had been trained in Europe, some trained in apprenticeships, and some not trained at all. There was also a populist health movement at this time. Many groups formed health clubs, started to eat health foods, and learned the best healing remedies from the women in the community. Some populists even set up medical schools to train and graduate physicians in one or another favorite type of remedy. This situation concerned the physicians who had been educated in Europe; they knew that in Europe, the profession was held in high esteem and felt that it was necessary to create the same respect for medical authority here in the United States (Starr, 1982).

In about 1800, European-educated physicians were able to get state legislatures to pass laws forbidding healers without formal education from practicing medicine, but the laws were unpopular and were soon repealed. In 1847, physicians formed the AMA (American Medical Association) and adopted the Hippocratic Oath as a vow to practice good and ethical medicine. They lobbied states to ban abortion, which had been widely practiced until that time and had been an important source of income to women healers who were not physicians. By this method, the AMA effectively made it impossible for these women to earn a living in the practice of medicine.

In 1910, another major move limited the practice of medicine to wealthy males. Abraham Flexner published the "Flexner Report," which stated that most existing medical schools were inadequate. Congress responded to the Flexner Report by giving the AMA the right to determine which schools were qualified to train physicians—an important power in controlling the profession. All seven medical schools for women and most medical schools for blacks were closed, eliminating women and most blacks from the practice of medicine. Part-time schools were also closed, eliminating those who could not afford full-time study. The medical field remained open only to white males of the upper classes; a shortage of physicians developed, making medicine a very lucrative profession. Today, medical care has become a huge industry in the United States. The AMA has power and influence over hospitals, medical education, prescription drugs, the use of medical technology, and the qualifications for receiving insurance payments.

The most common type of medical practice is private practice on a **fee-for-service** basis, in which the physician is paid for each visit and each service rendered. In this type of practice, the physician is self-employed and must establish an office with expensive equipment. In the office, the physician provides **primary medical care**, which is the first general, overall care the patient requires. It may include a medical history, checkup, and treatment of minor cuts, colds, sore throats, and other ailments. The primary care physician usually has privileges at a nearby hospital (i.e., the hospital permits the physician's patients to be treated there under the physician's supervision and care). There, patients may go to have surgery, deliver babies, and receive tests or other services.

**Fee-for-service**

A medical payment system in which the physician is paid for each visit and each service rendered

**Primary medical care**

The first general, overall care the patient needs

## 14.4d Hospitals

Hospitals provide **secondary medical care**, which is more specialized than the general practitioner provides; **secondary care givers** are those who deliver the specialized care. Hospitals were once poorhouses or places where people went to die. When there was little specialized knowledge of complex treatment procedures, there was no advantage to putting people in the hospital for treatment. Babies were born at home, and tonsils were removed using the kitchen table as an operating table. As medical knowledge increased and hospitals came to be better equipped and more convenient places for doctors to treat patients, hospitals and their specialized staffs of physicians, nurses, and technicians drew large numbers of patients needing short-term specialized care.

There are now many types of hospitals. The most common is the community **voluntary hospital**, a nonprofit facility that treats patients who need short-term care. Most of these hospitals are in the suburbs, and money to build some of them was provided by the Hill-Burton Act of 1954. The only restriction made by Congress was that such hospitals should do some charity work. Otherwise, physicians had complete

**Secondary medical care**

Care that is more specialized than the care that a general practitioner provides

**Secondary care givers**

Those who provide more specialized care than that provided by a general practitioner

**Voluntary hospital**

A nonprofit hospital that treats patients who need short-term care control over the new buildings and where they were built. As a result of the Hill-Burton Act, a large number of hospitals were built; due to the surplus, however, many have now been closed.

A second type is the **municipal hospital**, which is built by a city or county. These hospitals are often the only ones available to treat the poor and often have names such as "City General" or "County General." They are noted for their busy emergency rooms, which serve as primary care centers for those urban poor who do not have personal physicians. This method of providing primary care is far more expensive than it would be if health clinics were more widely available. Unfortunately, when government budgets are strained, rather than provide more cost-effective clinic care, hospital funding may be cut, emergency rooms may be closed, and sometimes the hospitals themselves are closed, eliminating a vital source of healthcare for many, especially poor people.

A third type is the **proprietary hospital**. These are privately owned, usually by physicians or by hospital corporations. Such hospitals have been growing rapidly. They can control costs by refusing patients who cannot pay, by specializing in less expensive short-term procedures, and by not investing in the variety of equipment and services that are costly but not profitable—thus, they can treat their patients at lower costs than nonprofit hospitals.

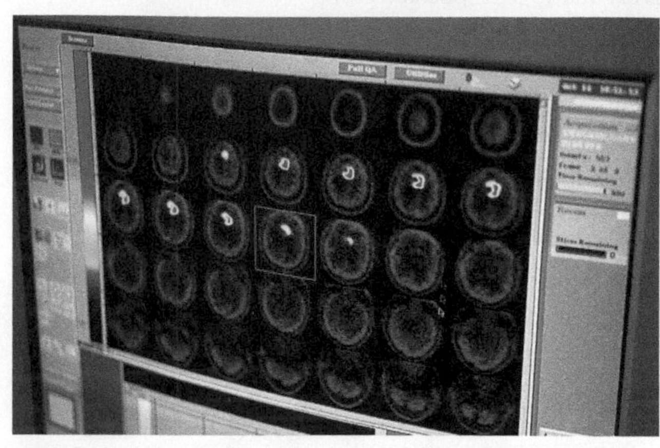

*Positron emission tomography (PET) technology is used to help diagnose illness. (AP Wide World Photo)*

A fourth type of hospital, developed with federal funds after World War II, is the **medical center**, which trains new physicians, conducts research, and gives **tertiary medical care**—long-term care requiring complex technology, usually at great expense. It uses specialized modern equipment—such as artificial kidneys, heart-lung machines, computed axial tomography (CAT) scanners, as well as 3-D computed tomography (CT) scanners, magnetic resonance imaging (MRI), positron emission tomography (PET), single photon emission computed tomography (SPECT), coronary care units, electronic fetal-monitoring machines, radioisotopes, ultrasound, and fiber optics. This equipment may or may not be safe or effective, and the federal government does not regulate much of it. It is also extremely expensive. An MRI scanner can cost 1 million to 3 million dollars to buy, and each scan costs the patient or the insurance company about $1,000 (Squires, 1990).

**Municipal hospital**
A hospital built and operated by a city or county

**Proprietary hospital**
A hospital that is privately owned usually by physicians or corporations

**Medical center**
A major hospital that trains new physicians, conducts research, and provides tertiary medical care

**Tertiary medical care**
Long-term care requiring complex technology

**Fetal monitoring**
Measuring the vital signs of the infant as it is being born

In a well-planned medical system, the very expensive technology used in tertiary care is centrally located in medical centers, to which patients are referred from their community hospitals. In a free economy such as ours, corporations are eager to sell their very expensive equipment to all hospitals and hospitals, competing to fill their beds, have sometimes purchased high technology regardless of the community need. Every hospital wants to have its own coronary care unit, CT scanner, fetal monitors, and all of the other technology. Tertiary healthcare, which theoretically should be limited to a few medical centers, is now hardly distinguishable from secondary healthcare.

This extension of the secondary healthcare system to provide tertiary services has the obvious disadvantage of being very costly. Almost 40 cents of every medical care dollar is spent in hospitals, much of it to buy and operate equipment. Having spent so much on costly equipment, hospitals and doctors feel pressured to use it. Ordinary head injuries get CT scans, and almost every baby being born is subject to **fetal monitoring**, which measures the heart rate of the infant being born and is not an exact science. Changes in the patterns measured are often treated with alarm, and the mother may be unnecessarily subjected to a cesarean section, which involves surgically opening the womb. Cesarean sections, considered major abdominal surgery, have increased from less than 5% to more than 30% of all births since the introduction of fetal monitoring. Technology, then, is expensive to buy and use, and it requires teams of medical technicians to operate the equipment. The largest staff group in the hospital, however, consists of the people who actually take care of the patients—the nurses.

## 14.4e Nurses

In the early days of medicine, nurses were considered gentle and caring people who wiped fevered brows and otherwise tenderly cared for patients. Nurses played the roles of wife to the doctor and mother to the patient. In the days before advanced scientific knowledge, nursing duties were not very different from what was done at home. As medicine has changed, the role of the nurse has changed. However, the nursing profession has had difficulty changing its image, partly because of the way in which nurses are educated. Today, there are nearly 3 million registered nurses in the United States, and they make up the largest healthcare occupation (Bureau of Labor Statistics, 2012).

To be a nurse, one must get certification as a registered nurse (RN). The educational requirements for RNs vary. Originally, they were trained in hospitals in a 3-year program with some classroom work to supplement their on-the-job training. Hospitals gained their labor for 3 years, while the nurses paid only room, board, and sometimes a modest fee for tuition. Most nurses were from the working class, and the low-cost training gave them entry to a profession that was far superior in salary and working conditions to the typical kind of factory job they might otherwise obtain.

Advances in medical technology brought changes to this educational system. As scientific knowledge accumulated in the 1950s and 1960s, nurses needed more time in the classroom. This was expensive for hospitals, however. During these same 2 decades, 2-year community colleges, 4-year colleges, and universities were expanding—and these schools wanted students to prepare for occupations. At that point, the needs of the schools matched the needs of hospitals, so the latter continued to train nurses in the hospital but turned the classroom education over to schools. The 2-year colleges awarded the RN certification after 2 years of school, and the 4-year colleges awarded the RN certification after 4 years. Two-year colleges served the working classes, and 4-year colleges served upper-middle-class women. In addition, some nurses were still trained entirely by hospitals.

As a result of this change in education, some nurses have 2 years of college training, some have 4 years, and some have no formal college training but more practical hospital training. The goals of the different groups vary. Nurses with 4 years of college training would like to change the image of nursing to an upper-class profession with more autonomy, more respect, and better salaries. The 4-year nurses have not won the support of many less-educated nurses because the new standards would require several more years of education for them. Nurses have not won the support of physicians either. Physicians now have authority over them and do not want to relinquish it.

To date, nurses work at inconvenient hours, such as evenings, nights, and weekends, and holidays. They work under the strict supervision of the physician, and even though they spend more time with patients they must follow the physician's directions at all times. They also are not paid as well as many other professionals with 4-year degrees. Hospitals, suffering under increasing budgetary pressures, resist the efforts of nurses to improve their professional standing.

Even those who specialize in a field such as nurse midwifery have difficulty in finding autonomous ways to practice their profession. Nurse midwives are trained to deliver babies, and they use methods that are, in the opinion of many, safer than the drugs and surgical procedures used by physicians. At present, nurse midwives also have difficulty obtaining hospital privileges and must practice under the supervision of a physician.

**BVT*Lab***

Visit www.BVTLab.com to explore the student resources available for this chapter.

## 14.4f Other Healthcare Workers

Although physicians, hospitals, and nurses make up the core of the American healthcare system, many other professionals are involved in healthcare. Hospital administrators are sometimes physicians; however, in recent years, they are more likely to have been trained in business administration or healthcare administration (Sager, 1986). They have a staff working with them who have a variety of special skills, such as keeping medical records, purchasing medical supplies, and performing all of the tasks necessary to keep a hospital running.

Medical research is conducted by physicians or by researchers trained in other sciences, such as biology and chemistry. Research takes place in hospitals, in centers devoted to research, or in corporations that produce pharmaceuticals (drugs) or medical equipment.

**Registered dietitians (RDs)**, important members of the hospital staff, plan regular meals and special diets for patients. Registered dietitians are licensed by their own association of dietitians. **Nutritionists** have similar concerns; however, their education, theories, and licenses are quite different from those of dietitians. Dietitians more and more refer to themselves as nutritionists; and in many states dietitians are lobbying legislatures to ban nutritionists who lack RD certification from advising people on what to eat. Neither group is allowed to diagnose or treat diseases; they can only recommend proper eating programs.

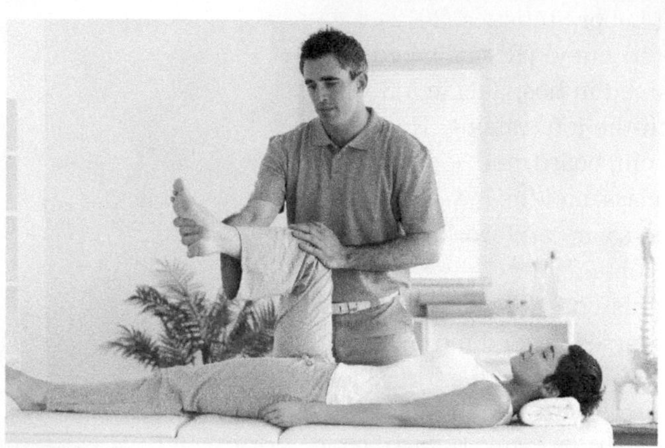

*Chiropractic healing is a form of medicine.* (Shutterstock)

**Chiropractors** have been outside of the healthcare system for the most part. *Chiropractic* healing is a Greek term for healing by manipulating the body with the hands. Today, chiropractors are primarily concerned with manipulating the spine, but they may also use X-rays and other modern technologies. In addition, they may also educate their patients about nutrition and a healthy lifestyle as preventive measures. Physicians generally do not recognize chiropractic healing as a legitimate form of medicine; during the nineteenth century, when physicians were building their profession, they lobbied legislatures to have chiropractors outlawed. Chiropractors, who had their own professional association, managed to survive; today many people recognize that their work is beneficial. A Gallup Poll commissioned by the American Chiropractic Association (ACA) estimates that around 28 million people in the United States see a chiropractor each year.

Many other health workers are even farther from the mainstream of American medicine. Acupuncture and acupressure are not now generally recognized as legitimate forms of healing in the United States, although recent research is bringing new attention to these methods. Rolfing and other forms of massage are also outside of the mainstream, as are herbal medicines, yoga, relaxation techniques, and a wide variety of other techniques used elsewhere in the world. The American healthcare system is dominated by physicians and hospitals, which favor expensive modern technologies and pharmaceuticals.

## APPLYING SOCIOLOGY TO HEALTHCARE

Although healthcare is typically thought to be the sole domain of the medical profession, social science can provide important clues to help diagnose and treat much physical and mental illness. Social scientists can help point out the interplay between social, environmental, and psychological factors in both illness and disease and in their treatment and prevention.

Using a social model of illness in connection with a medical model, healthcare workers might be encouraged to explore how the values and norms of a society might help or hinder the development of disease, or how the beliefs and attitudes about

**Registered dietitians (RDs)**

Licensed members of hospital staffs who plan regular meals and special diets for patients

**Nutritionist**

A person who specializes in proper eating programs

**Chiropractors**

Those who practice healing by manipulating the body, especially the spine a specific illness might affect a return to good health. For example, if alcoholism is still viewed as a moral failure or a lack of willpower, how might this interfere with the prevention of disease in people who are genetically at high risk? How might this hinder a person from admitting to having the disease, being willing to seek help, or gaining the support of friends and family while receiving treatment? If AIDS is seen as a disease caused by males' sexual preferences or by intravenous drug use, how might this interfere with prevention, diagnosis, or treatment of this disease in a heterosexual teenager who does not use intravenous drugs?





## 14.5 PAYING FOR MEDICAL CARE

The United States spends nearly 2 trillion dollars on healthcare expenses per year—more than any other industrialized country and more than 2.5 times the amount spent by any other member of the Organization for Economic Cooperation and Development (OECD) (Johnson, 2010). Yet, it ranks with Turkey and Mexico as the only OECD countries without universal healthcare. The healthcare reform plan signed into law under President Obama in 2010 is designed to make healthcare more affordable and more accessible. Prior to the reform plan, 45.7 million people in the U.S. did not have health insurance (Clemmit, 2009). The healthcare reform plan is designed to extend coverage to 32 million uninsured people by expanding Medicaid, providing government subsidies to help low- and middle-income families buy insurance, create regulated insurance markets where people without employer-sponsored insurance can buy subsidized coverage, and use Medicare to cut health costs for individuals (Clemmit, 2010). There are avid supporters and opponents to the plan, and it has become one of the most politically controversial and divisive laws in recent times. Supporters feel that healthcare is a right for every American and that lack of sufficient healthcare ultimately hurts U.S. productivity. In addition, supporters feel that the savings to Medicare and Medicaid (as a result of raising Medicare taxes on high income people) will reduce the federal deficit. Opponents believe that the law creates unwarranted entitlements and that the cost of healthcare reform will lead to escalating federal spending on healthcare.

### 14.5a Health Insurance

Private health insurance began during the Great Depression, when physicians had to wait months or even years to get paid for their services (Starr, 1982). Physicians developed Blue Cross, a nonprofit insurance system, to be sold to groups of workers. Employers offered to pay part of the insurance premium for workers instead of giving them raises and the program was such a success that in the 1950s, private insurance companies began to offer health insurance. The benefits of health insurance were many. Workers were insured, companies could show their concern for the workers, and there was a large flow of money into the healthcare system. The income of physicians increased dramatically; hospitals were able to afford high-technology medical equipment, which benefited the industries that produced it.

Those who did not benefit from health insurance were the retired, the unemployed, part-time workers, and workers in jobs without fringe benefits. They saw health costs rise and found physicians and hospitals less interested in charity work. To help these people, the United States began the **Medicare** program for retired workers and the **Medicaid** program for the poor. All of these insurance systems paid whatever the physician and hospital charged, and prices soared.

**Medicare**
Federally sponsored health insurance for people age 65 or older

**Medicaid**
Federally sponsored health insurance for the poor

Some people would like to have the federal government provide a national health insurance program that would cover everyone, but others fear that a further infusion of money into the healthcare system would cause further cost increases. History has shown us that as more money is available for healthcare, the costs of healthcare increase. The medical profession vigorously opposes cost control, considering it an interference with their right to practice medicine as they see fit.

Nevertheless, actions have been taken to resist the rising cost of insurance. In 1983, the federal government began to limit the amount of money it would pay through Medicare and Medicaid. The government devised **diagnostic related groups (DRGs)**, which set a maximum payment for any treatment; hospitals have had to limit the length of stay and the number of tests given to Medicare and Medicaid patients in order to treat them within the limits of the DRGs. Corporations have responded to rising insurance costs by eliminating insurance as a fringe benefit. Instead, corporations are hiring physicians to run clinics for the specific purpose of providing healthcare for workers. They find that they are able to contain costs and provide cheaper care directly, rather than through insurance. More and more workers have also responded to the high costs of health insurance by turning to prepaid healthcare.

### 14.5b Prepaid Healthcare

In the United States, the emphasis has been on fee-for-service care, in which the doctor charges a fee for each visit. However, another type of healthcare provider, the **health maintenance organization (HMO)**, is growing rapidly. HMOs are prepaid plans in which a fee is paid in advance, and most—if not all—necessary healthcare is provided at no additional cost.

HMOs have four goals: (1) to provide preventive medicine and early detection of disease; (2) to practice the best scientific medicine possible when a disease is detected; (3) to reduce hospitalization through the use of preventive medicine and early detection of disease; and (4) to reduce medical costs through better use of tests, procedures, and hospitalization.

Because their healthcare is prepaid, HMO members do not hesitate to have regular checkups and to visit their doctors when illness occurs. Since HMO physicians now practice in large groups, they can communicate with one another easily, they have access to all the necessary equipment and other services, and they have resources and schedules that allow ongoing educational programs. Medical testing can be done knowledgeably, reducing the use of unnecessary tests. Preventive medicine and good medical care reduce hospitalization and medical costs. HMOs also trim costs by using auxiliary medical personnel, such as nurses and physicians' assistants, whenever possible. Physicians are motivated to keep costs down because HMOs share cost savings with them in the form of bonuses. Some HMOs even have their own hospitals and are motivated to run these efficiently for further cost savings.

## 14.6 HEALTH MOVEMENTS

### 14.6a Health and the Second Great Awakening

The "Second Great Awakening" was a popular religious movement that swept through the northeastern part of the country in the early part of the nineteenth century. Because health was linked to religious values, people considered slovenliness, gluttony, and neglect of one's health to be sinful. It is not surprising, then, that this religious movement was accompanied by a health movement, where sweeping changes in attitudes about the care of one's body accompanied concern for one's soul. A leader in this health movement was Sylvester Graham, a Presbyterian minister who believed that foods should be simple, not concocted from complicated recipes. He recommended eating fruits and vegetables, which were unpopular at the time; although he did not know about vitamins or other scientific nutritional matters, he recommended eating the whole kernel of wheat (Root & Rochemont, 1976). Graham developed a wheat cracker and traveled through the

**Diagnostic related group (DRG)**

The group that devises the schedule of payment limits set by the federal government for Medicaid and Medicare recipients

**Health maintenance organization (HMO)**

A prepaid healthcare plan in which a fee is paid in advance for all necessary healthcare

Northeast, preaching his dietary religion and gaining many followers. Boarding houses were set up to serve the Graham crackers and other foods recommended by Graham. Oberlin College reserved part of its cafeteria for those following the Graham diet.

The health movement developed an ecumenical spirit when Seventh-Day Adventists became followers of Dr. Graham. Mother Ellen Harmon White, a Seventh-Day Adventist, founded the Western Health Reform Institute in Battle Creek, Michigan, a sanitarium to restore health to the ailing. She hired Dr. John Harvey Kellogg to manage it. Kellogg thought that chewing on dried, crispy foods would benefit the teeth, and he added them to the menu. One patient, Charles Post, was treated for ulcers at the sanitarium for 9 months. Although not cured of ulcers, he believed that the food business might be profitable and developed a drink called Postum and later a cereal, Post Toasties. Kellogg soon followed suit, and the development of packaged foods began. While Americans are still concerned about the food they eat, the more dynamic health movement today is centered on drinking habits.

## 14.6b Modern Concerns About Diet and Exercise

Recent concerns about diet and exercise are not religiously motivated and do not have the strength of movements with a religious or spiritual motivation. Modern concerns about diet began with the peace movement of the late 1960s, which also opposed pollution and rejected both chemically filled foods and food packaging that added to litter and pollution. Health food stores sprang up to serve foods without chemicals, such as dyes, hormones, antibiotics, pesticides, and other nonfood ingredients. Foods were sold in bulk and used a minimum of packaging. Food additives account for $1.5 billion in sales for American chemical companies, who assure us that they are safe; most Americans are satisfied with that assurance.

*Before automation and automobiles, people were more physically active out of necessity. This is probably the first time in history that exercise could be classified as a social movement. (iStockphoto)*

This is probably the first time in history that exercise can be classified as a social movement. In the past, people got a good deal of exercise quite naturally. Heavy labor had not been replaced by automation; everyone knows that Abraham Lincoln walked miles to school, as did our grandparents and some of our parents. Today, heavy labor has been replaced by automation, and the automobile has replaced walking. In order to get exercise, a special time of the day must be set aside for such activity, as it no longer occurs naturally in the course of the day.

Americans are showing some concern about diet and exercise in order to reduce their chances of contracting heart disease and cancer. While there may be some improvement in this area, the percentage of overweight people in the United States has not been reduced over the past 20 years. In fact, the incidence of obesity in the United States has risen dramatically over the past 20 years, and research shows the situation may be worsening. A 2009–2010 survey conducted by the Center for Disease Control's National Center for Health Statistics, the nation's principal health statistics agency, found that 36% of adults age 20 and older were obese (see Figures 14-2 and 14-3).

Furthermore, according to the same data, the numbers of children who are overweight continues to increase as well, which in turn means that these children have an increased chance of being overweight adults. Obese children account for 10% of those ages 2 to 5, 20% of 6- to 11-year-olds, and 18% of those ages 12 to 19 (see Figure 14-4).

Overall, there are a variety of factors that play a role in obesity. In general, behavior, environment, and genetic factors have a part in causing people to be overweight and obese. "Despite obesity having strong genetic determinants, the genetic composition of the population does not change rapidly. Therefore, the large increase in … [obesity]

**Figure 14-2** Prevalence of Obesity Among Adults Aged 20 and Over, by Sex and Age: United States, 2009–2010

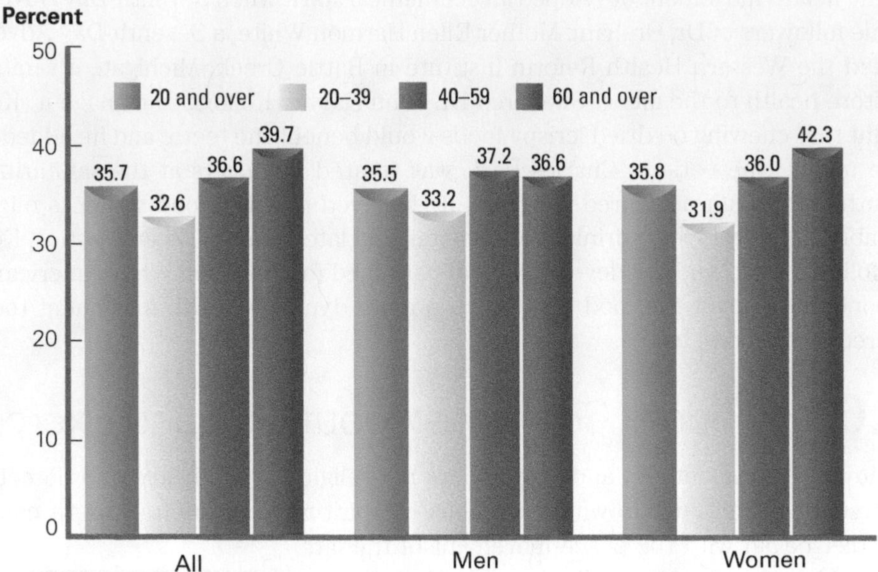


Adapted from the Center for Disease Control's National Center for Health Statistics, "NCHS Data on Obesity." Retrieved from http://www.cdc.gov/nchs/data/factsheets/fact_sheet_obesity.pdf

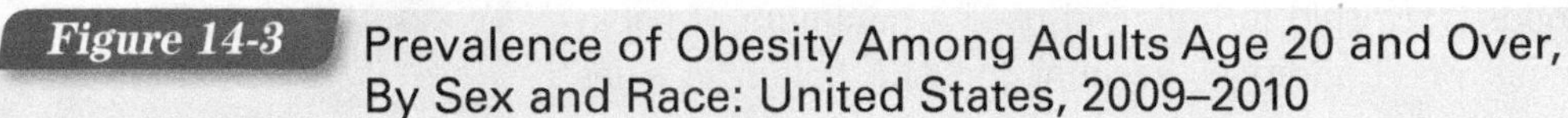

**Figure 14-3** Prevalence of Obesity Among Adults Age 20 and Over, By Sex and Race: United States, 2009–2010

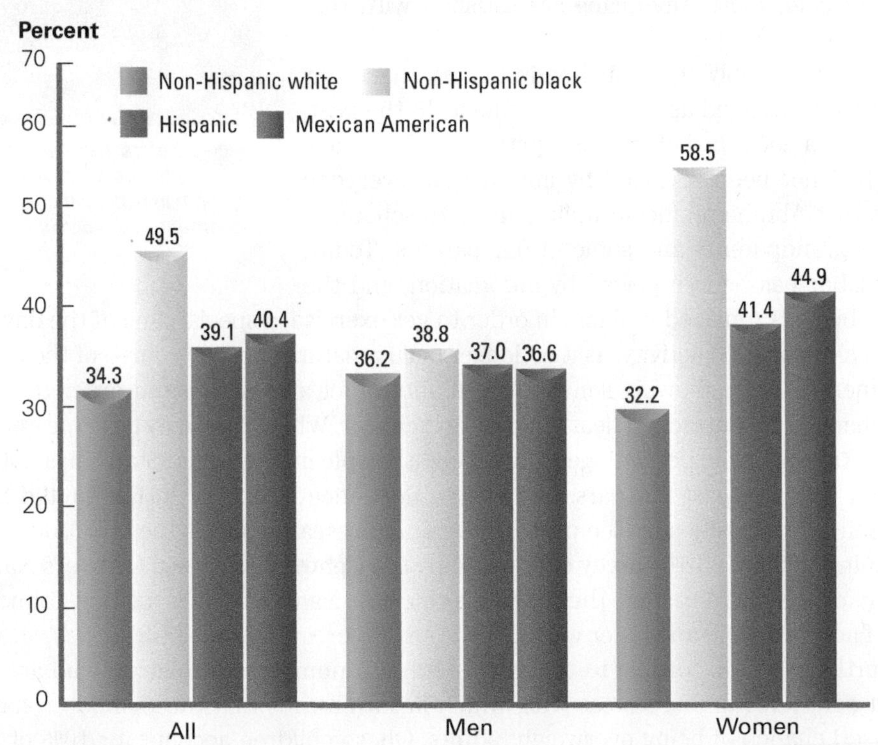


Adapted from the Center for Disease Control's National Center for Health Statistics, "NCHS Data on Obesity." Retrieved from http://www.cdc.gov/nchs/data/factsheets/fact_sheet_obesity.pdf.

**Figure 14-4** Prevalence of Obesity Among Children and Adolescents Age 2–19, by Sex and Age: United States, 2009–2010

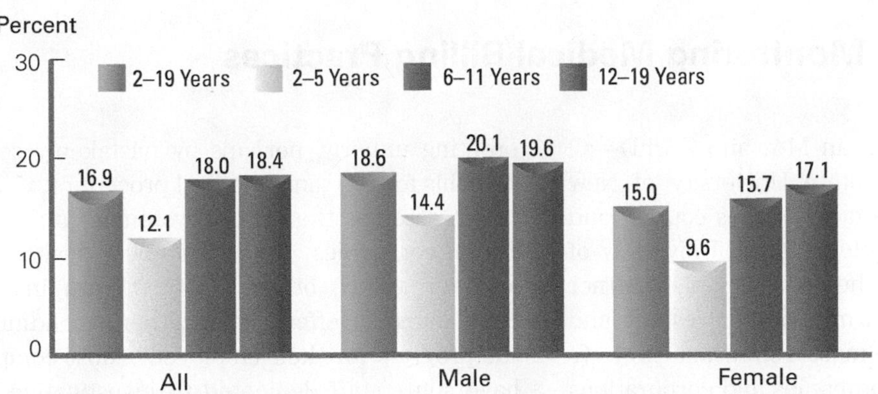


Adapted from the Center for Disease Control's National Center for Health Statistics, "NCHS Data on Obesity." Retrieved from http://www.cdc.gov/nchs/data/factsheets/fact_sheet_obesity.pdf

must reflect major changes in nongenetic factors" (Hill & Trowbridge, 1998). Behavior and environment are most readily manipulated and are the greatest areas in which prevention could occur.

While our culture has succeeded in producing fast and convenient food, more and more options, and super-size portions, we have not succeeded in getting off the sofa. Furthermore, because of technological innovations, our need to exert actual physical energy is diminished so that we increasingly are taking in more calories than we burn. According to the Behavioral Risk Factor Surveillance System, in 2000 more than 26% of adults reported no leisure time physical activity (Centers for Disease Control and Prevention, 2004).

# 14.7 HEALTHCARE IN OTHER COUNTRIES

Unlike the American healthcare system, where up to one third of the population gets less than the care they need (Basch, 1999), other countries have found ways to distribute healthcare to all. The healthcare systems of Great Britain and China illustrate other possibilities of how healthcare planning can work.

## 14.7a The British Healthcare System

At the beginning of the Industrial Revolution, Great Britain had a **laissez-faire** economy—an economy with little government planning and intervention. Healthcare depended on **noblesse oblige**, the moral obligation of the rich to give to the poor and the suffering. Unfortunately, the economy produced a great many poor and suffering people whom the rich did not take care of. The British economic system gradually progressed from laissez faire to welfare capitalism, in which the government takes a major responsibility for the welfare of its people within the capitalist system. The move to welfare capitalism was inspired, in part, by the need for an adequate healthcare system.

In the nineteenth century, Great Britain was forced to use government money to provide some medical care for its people; and since 1911, Great Britain has had national health insurance, which has covered the medical expenses of workers (Denton, 1978; Light, 2003). Their wives and children were not insured, however; they either did not go to doctors or else postponed treatment until it was too late. After World War II, the poor

**Laissez faire**
An approach to the economy in which there is no government planning or intervention

**Noblesse oblige**
The obligation of the rich to give to the poor and suffering

sociologyatwork

## Monitoring Medical Billing Practices

Henry Pontell has a BA, an MA, and a PhD—all in sociology—from the State University of New York at Stony Brook. He now teaches courses and does research in criminology at the University of California. In addition, he is a general partner in his own consulting firm, Pontell, Jesilow and Associates. One of his most significant projects was to help insurance companies and corporations prevent and detect incorrect billings by healthcare providers.

The cost effectiveness of healthcare is very much an issue today, with healthcare consuming more than 11% of the GNP. It is a major concern of the government, which administers the Medicare and Medicaid systems; of individual consumers, who must pay ever increasing insurance premiums or risk having to pay enormous medical bills out of their own pockets; and of businesses, which have traditionally offered health insurance for their employees.

"In many companies," Pontell explains, "healthcare is the fastest growing operating expense, and they're looking for ways to hold down costs. Some are making greater use of prepaid plans such as HMOs. Others are going to copayment, in which the company requires employees to pay part of the cost of insurance themselves. In effect, they're reducing employees' benefits. Another approach is simply to offer plans that provide less extensive coverage."

Pontell's company attacked the problem from a different angle—cutting down the incidence of fraud and abuse on the part of medical practitioners. Improper billing is a sizeable problem. In the Medicare and Medicaid systems, Pontell says, between 10% and 20% of all resources are lost to fraud and abuse. Fraud occurs when a healthcare practitioner knowingly exploits the system, perhaps billing an insurer for services he or she did not actually provide. Abuse is unintentionally profiting unfairly, perhaps by mistakenly sending two bills for the same medical procedure.

In essence, the Pontell system is quite simple. Some companies run their own health insurance programs; others contract with insurance companies, in effect paying them to administer the program for their employees. Most companies have some staff dedicated to investigating cases of potential fraud; however, they rarely have the resources to do comprehensive investigations of thousands, or sometimes millions, of claims. Pontell's objective was to help them use their resources more effectively. "Through my research, I've developed a program for reviewing a company's records of claims filed by different physicians." What it yields is a list of names of physicians whose billing of the company is aberrant in some way. It is then up to the company to investigate these practitioners further.

"To conduct this work successfully," Pontell says, "I drew on my training in research methods, human relations, criminological theories relating to white-collar crime, criminal deterrence, medical sociology, law, and the professions. My sociological background is also helpful in two other ways: first, in relating the value of my service to executives in many different industries, and second, in interacting with and coordinating the efforts of corporate executives, insurance investigators, computer analysts, healthcare personnel, and my research staff."

Besides doing his consulting on medical billing practices, Pontell and his associates have written a book, *Prescriptions for Profit*, which fully describes the ways in which abuses can and have occurred within the health field. Pontell is a prime example of a sociologist who has blended an academic and an applied sociological career. He not only conducts criminological research but also puts to use the knowledge he uncovers.

health of the people and the large number of elderly in the population created a serious problem, and the British developed the National Health Service (NHS), which provides healthcare for everyone and is funded by tax revenues.

The NHS has three branches, which are patterned after the healthcare system that already existed in Great Britain. General practitioners deliver primary healthcare, treating the sick in their communities. Consultants, physician specialists in hospitals, provide secondary healthcare. The third sector is the public health sector, consisting of nursing homes, home nursing services, vaccination services, health inspections, and other community health services.

Physicians lost their autonomy when the government took control. General practitioners are now paid according to the number of patients for whom they provide care. This system does not provide the independence of a fee-for-service practice, but it does allow physicians more control over their income than working for straight salaries. Physicians are also allowed to see private patients and to charge them whatever they are willing to pay. This dual setup has been criticized for creating a two-class medical system, but very few patients want private care.

The working class is especially pleased with the NHS. Any citizen can go to a general practitioner without paying a fee; if hospitalization is required, the general practitioner refers the patient to a hospital consultant, again without charge. To control the costs of such a system, patients who do not have serious problems may have to wait for weeks or months for a consultation, as those who do have serious problems are seen first. The citizens of Great Britain have been very happy with the system.



## 14.7b Healthcare in the People's Republic of China

The most dramatic development of a healthcare system occurred in China after the Communist takeover in 1949. Before that time, the huge Chinese population suffered from malnutrition, poor sanitation, and poor health. Medical care was almost totally lacking. When the Communists came into power, disease and starvation were rampant (Denton, 1978). There was a shortage of doctors, and the few doctors available were divided between Eastern and Western medical practices. Because the Communists had few resources, they had to make efficient use of what little they had.

They did not try to develop scientific medicine after the model set by Western physicians. They combined Western medicine with traditional Chinese medicine, using acupuncture and herbs along with some Western drugs and technology. The Communists also trained enormous numbers of so-called **barefoot doctors** to serve as unpaid health workers. The peasants in the communes selected commune members for training to become barefoot doctors. Trainees are not chosen on the basis of their academic or intellectual achievements but rather on the basis of their political attitudes and their attitudes toward people. They are required to support the political system, as well as the communes they serve.

To become barefoot doctors, the trainees receive 3 to 18 months of training in both Eastern and Western medical techniques. They then serve in their communes, emphasizing preventive medicine by developing sanitary systems and practices in the community, by teaching peasants proper hygiene and healthcare, and by vaccinating the population. As volunteers, they also work at ordinary jobs, side by side with the peasants for whom they provide care; they can thereby easily recognize those who have poor health habits or illnesses. They treat simple illnesses and emergencies and direct the more seriously ill to better-trained doctors and nurses.

**Barefoot doctors**

People chosen by the peasants in the communes in Communist China to provide medicine and treat simple illnesses and emergencies, who receive 3 to 18 months of training

Urban areas have *Red Guard doctors*, who are not as well trained as the barefoot doctors. In addition, there are *worker doctors*, who work in factories. These doctors receive less training because highly trained full-time physicians and nurses are available in urban areas. The Red Guard and worker doctors serve the same grass roots function as the barefoot doctors—serving without pay, stressing preventive medicine such as sanitation and inoculations, and generally looking after the health of members of their communes.

When hospitalization is necessary for an illness, individuals must pay for it. A variety of insurance plans are available to cover the costs of hospital care, but the costs are not high. Open-heart surgery, the most expensive procedure, costs about 2 weeks' wages for the average worker—far less than in the United States.

The Chinese Communists emphasize equality. Although most doctors work in urban areas, they are transferred to rural areas if the need develops. They are not free to practice where they wish. They are expected to help nurses to care for patients, and differentiating the various types of doctors and nurses along class lines is forbidden.

When the Communists began their healthcare system, the number of educated people available to administer the large bureaucracy was inadequate. Because physicians were the most educated and capable people in the society, they became the leaders of the healthcare system regardless of their political leanings. As the Communists increased their power, they became concerned about the independence of the Ministry of Public Health and its practices. They felt that this group did not place enough emphasis on treating rural populations and that this group focused on curative rather than preventive medicine (Maykovich, 1980). By 1955, the Communists had developed more political leaders to rule the Ministry of Public Health, along with physicians. Conflicts developed, and some errors were made because the politicians were not trained in medicine; however, the conflicts generally broadened the work of the ministry because the politicians insisted on emphasizing areas that do not ordinarily interest physicians. The conflict between the interests of physicians and political interests has continued. Currently, the emphasis is on what interests the physicians—developing better technology and more sophisticated procedures for treating complicated illnesses.

The ancient art of herbal medicine is currently one of the main focuses in the Chinese healthcare system. (iStockphoto)

Along with their interest in technology, the Chinese are doing more than any other country to develop the ancient art of herbal medicine, the use of plants in natural healthcare systems (Ayensu, 1981). Beijing (formerly known as Peking by Westerners) has an Institute of Medical Materials, and Guangzhou (formerly known as Canton) has the Provincial Institute of Botany for the study of herbal medicines. Thousands of medicinal plants are under cultivation for use in biological evaluations and chemical studies, and every year thousands of barefoot doctors are taught about the use of these herbs in healthcare. Medicinal plants have been used to treat venereal diseases, leukemia, high blood pressure, ulcers, poor digestion, skin cancer, and countless other diseases. They can be used as heart stimulants, diuretics, sedatives, and to induce abortion. The value of herbs is widely known throughout the world; for example, 25% of prescription drugs in the United States are based on flowering plants.

## thinking SOCIOLOGICALLY

1. How could we reduce U.S. healthcare costs?
2. How could we provide healthcare efficiently to all of those who do not have insurance and cannot afford to pay for healthcare?
3. Why doesn't the United States have a national health service similar to Great Britain?
4. How can the conflict theory of health and illness help to explain the high cost of healthcare?

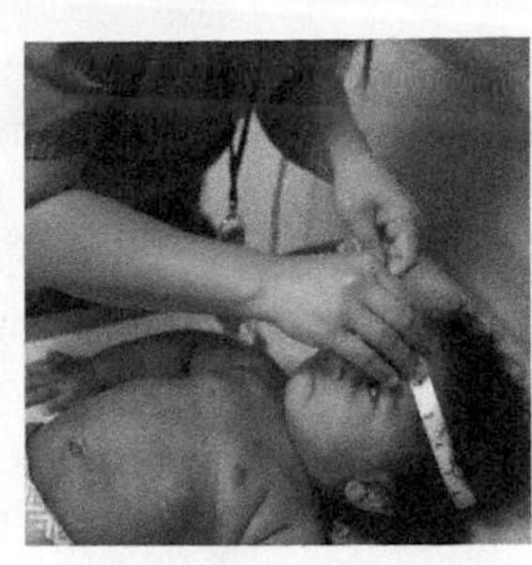

# CHAPTER 14 Wrapping it up

## Summary

1. Health and illness are of interest to sociologists because they are defined socially, as well as biologically, and because society needs a healthy population to survive.
2. *Pathological illnesses* are those in which the body is diseased or malfunctioning.
3. *Statistical illnesses* are those in which a person's health deviates from the norm.
4. Structural functionalists, who emphasize the integrative, functional characteristics of society, note that a sick role exists to integrate ill people into the social structure. This sick role involves certain expectations. For example, sick people are expected to get better and to resume their major roles, thereby ensuring the smooth functioning of society.
5. Conflict theorists contend that physicians share the viewpoint of elite classes in society and use their power over patients to maintain the social system.
6. Symbolic interactionists study the learned meanings associated with illness. In many societies, illness has been associated with sin or demons, and treatment often has had religious overtones.
7. In preindustrial days, when nutrition and sanitation were poor, infectious diseases were the greatest health hazard. The major health hazards now are heart disease, cancer, and stroke. Many of the occurrences of these diseases are caused by alcoholism.
8. AIDS, an infectious disease, could reach epidemic proportions.
9. Changing social structures often cause changes in prevailing illnesses—for example, industrialization and its accompanying pollutants are a major cause of cancer.
10. In the American healthcare system, the medical model of illness prevails. The individual is considered responsible for prevention, and the healthcare system becomes involved only when a person is already sick. The social causes of illness receive little attention.
11. Physicians developed their profession through the nineteenth and twentieth centuries to be powerful and prestigious. Most physicians provide primary healthcare.
12. Secondary care is provided by hospitals, which have specialized equipment and staff. There are several kinds of hospitals: nonprofit voluntary hospitals, tax-supported municipal hospitals, and privately owned proprietary hospitals.
13. Tertiary healthcare, the very highly specialized care developed with modern technology, is given in medical centers, which also conduct research and train physicians. Since the other types of hospitals have purchased specialized technology as well, the cost of medical care has greatly increased.
14. Most nurses work in hospitals. Nursing is still a relatively low-paying profession that reflects its origins as an occupation for working-class women.
15. A wide variety of other healthcare workers—including technicians, administrators, and dietitians—work in hospitals. Many others work outside of traditional medical settings. Dentists are well-respected healthcare workers; however, nutritionists, chiropractors, and acupuncturists still struggle to have their practices accepted.
16. Healthcare, with its emphasis on expensive technology, has become very costly. Health insurance—such as Blue Cross/Blue Shield, insurance issued by private companies, and Medicare and Medicaid issued by the federal government—were first designed to help pay costs. As more money became available, however, costs rose further.
17. A major departure in healthcare delivery from the fee-for-service system and health insurance is the HMO. By using resources more efficiently, HMOs may provide a better, less costly system.
18. Health movements have called for improved diets and have provided treatment for alcoholism and related diseases. These movements typically have a religious or spiritual motivation.

19. Medical care in other countries reflects practices in their social systems. Great Britain's healthcare system has evolved from the laissez-faire economic system with its belief in noblesse oblige to a welfare system within the capitalist framework.
20. China has developed a healthcare system using both Eastern and Western medical knowledge. It has been able to integrate the system with its political system, and it has developed a corps of barefoot doctors who provide preventive healthcare in rural areas. China has also done research on the more sophisticated use of traditional medicines.

## Discussion Questions

1. Discuss why it is important to understand the difference between pathological and statistical illness.
2. What are some positive and negative functions of the sick role for people with pathological illness and for people with statistical illness?
3. If you had the power to set social norms, when would you put people in the sick role, and when would you insist they perform their normal roles?
4. Does your definition of illness match current norms?
5. What are some advantages and disadvantages of the social model of illness and of the medical model of illness? Has the social model of illness become more valued in recent years? Explain and illustrate your answer.
6. Who benefits financially from the current healthcare system?
7. Who would lose financially if the United States were to change to a plan similar to the National Health Service in Great Britain?
8. Discuss the relative merits and disadvantages of voluntary hospitals, proprietary hospitals, and medical centers.
9. How does the medical care in various countries reflect their social systems?
10. If you had the power to set social norms, what changes would you make, based on a social model of illness, to end the AIDS epidemic?
11. Discuss your thoughts as to why successful health movements are related to religious or spiritual movements.
12. Compare the training of a physician in this country with that of the herbalist in other societies. Is there a similarity in the way each learns social roles?

*We have come to a turning point in the human habitation of the earth.*

BARRY COMMONER

# PART FIVE

# Human Ecology and Change

While sociology, as a scientific discipline, is about understanding stable patterns of social behavior from the interpersonal to the global level, much of sociology has developed as a response to and an explanation of social change. Some of the predominant social changes that have led to the emergence of sociological explanations in social institutions—such as economics, politics, family, religion, health-care, education—have been discussed in the previous section, along with issues and problems related to those changes. Social change takes place through the interplay of structural and interpersonal dynamics. Changes in characteristics of the population and the social, cultural, political, and environmental conditions have been interwoven throughout history. It is important to understand these interconnections in order to help understand the direction the world will take in the immediate and long-term future.

京B E8736
京B E4491

CHAPTER 15

# Population and Ecology

## SYNOPSIS



If you are like most people, you worry about the population a great deal, even though you may not realize it. By population, we mean the number of people in a society. The population affects your chances of finding a job and a spouse. If you do marry, it is likely to influence the age of your spouse, whether you have children, and how many you will have. It may also affect your chances of being promoted, your taxes, the age at which you will retire, and your income after retirement.

Not only does the size of the population affect our life chances and the ways in which we live, but the age of the population, also, has implications for our personal lives and for societies as a whole. All societies expect different behaviors from people of different ages. In dress, music, leisure, sex, work, and so forth, what may be expected and appropriate for the young might not be expected or appropriate for the elderly. In many countries, including the United States, people are living longer than ever before; and an aging population creates new concerns for both individuals and societies. Many

Focal Point

# ENVIRONMENT

While the major threats to the environment are now commonplace knowledge, people in the United States and many other countries have a history of taking natural resources and the environment for granted. In the prosperous decades following World War II—the 1950s and 1960s—cultural values in the United States did not include high regard for the environment or concern for energy conservation. For example, U.S. energy consumption doubled between 1950 and 1972, increasing as much during that time as it had in the entire 175 previous years of American history (Skolnick & Currie, 1997). Table 15-1 shows oil demand in the United States and the totality of countries in the Organization of Economic Cooperation and Development (OECD) from 1973 to 2011.

The early 1970s, however, marked the end of this "state of environmental unconsciousness." In 1970, President Richard Nixon created the Environmental Protection Agency (EPA), thus bringing environmental issues to the fore of national attention, where they have remained since (Melville, 1989). Although there has been some success in environmental protection since the 1970s—for example, the phasing out of leaded gasoline has curtailed *some* forms of air pollution and regulations about the dumping of toxic wastes and raw sewage have improved the water quality in some lakes and streams—the pressures of a growing population and an expanding economy have led to increased environmental pollution and, in the words of William K. Reilly (head of the EPA under former President George H. W. Bush), to "an array of environmental problems even more daunting than the pollution crises of the past generation" (Melville, 1989).

Environmental issues are difficult to address for a number of reasons (Melville, 1989). First, many of today's pressing environmental hazards are invisible and thus difficult to call to the public's attention. It is much easier to mobilize public support for problems that are readily apparent, such as polluted water, air, and land. However, it is difficult to reach consensus about problems that cannot be seen—such as acid rain, contaminated groundwater, carbon-dioxide emissions and their resultant greenhouse effect, or ozone-layer depletion.

Second, responsibility for environmental pollution is widespread. We are all partially responsible for environmental protection. For example, we drive cars, fly planes, and operate lawn mowers. We use wood stoves and electricity generated by burning fossil fuels; utilize industries, such as dry cleaners, that emit pollutants; and improperly dispose of used products, such as batteries.

Third, it is costly for industries to meet strict environmental regulations. Some argue that protecting the environment comes at some risk to the economy, and thus we live within a culture that accepts a certain amount of pollution as a by-product of industrialized society.

Fourth, environmental problems are global in scope. For example, air pollution is not only the result of fossil fuel use in the United States but also because of its use worldwide. In 2013, Beijing, China, had air pollution levels 30 to 45 times above recommended safety levels (Reuters, 2013). Because the source of the problem is global rather than local—that is, the result of the habits of 7 billion inhabitants of the planet—many people feel that it makes little difference what they do as individuals or perhaps even as a nation. However, this belief took a turn in 2006/2007 when the phrase "**Going Green**" was introduced to the public. The concept of going green—which was started in order to gain the public's interest in cutting back on the usage of oil, electricity, and those machines that require these types of energy to operate—has seen a tremendous boost over the last year. From Hollywood to Washington, D.C., the public is becoming more aware of the need for the United States to take the lead in this ecological battle. It provided the platform for many presidential candidates for the 2008 election; and in the early part of 2007, former Vice President Al Gore won an Academy Award for his documentary film on global warming. This cemented the gap between the film industry and politics, plus it created a platform to which the majority of society not only relates, but also weighs in on.

**Going green**
The phrase that defines people who are mindful of what they consume, mindful of others, and who are working towards protecting the environment both nationally and internationally

Although the environment seems to be a topic more suited to engineers, chemists, biologists, and geologists, it is important to sociologists as well because of the interrelationships that exist between population and the environment. Rapid population growth and the concomitant increased social needs have led to increased industrialization. From the structural functional perspective, the social wellbeing and high standard of living that industry functions to provide are accompanied by the latent dysfunction of environmental pollution. At first glance, this gives the impression that industry itself is to blame for environmental problems. However, as James Coleman and Donald Cressey suggested a few decades ago, "The origins of the environmental crisis are not to be found in a few polluting industries but in the basic social organization and cultural outlook of the modern world" (1990, p. 538). Thus, the key to understanding environmental pollution lies in understanding our cultural ideals and the ways in which our social life is organized. Natural scientists study and explain the physical ways in which the balance of nature is disturbed; sociologists and social scientists study and explain the intricacies of society and culture that often lead to practices that disturb the balance of nature.

individuals do not look forward to growing old because they associate attractiveness, health, and productivity with the young. For the society as a whole, an increasing aged population arouses concerns about financial support, healthcare, housing, productivity, and other issues.

An example of how an aging society presents new concerns has been cited in Sweden (Ekman & et al., 2001) where bicycling has almost doubled between 1980 and 1992–93 among persons ages 25 to 64. For the elderly (age 65 or older), the bicycle is a common means of transport, in both Sweden and a number of other countries. The risk of dying due to bicycling was about 3.7 times greater among the elderly than among children age 14 or under. The elderly also face a greater risk of being injured than do their younger counterparts. For all ages, the risk is 7.4 times higher for a bicyclist than for a car driver. The risk for the elderly is about 3 times greater than for the average bicyclist, and as much as 6 times higher for the age group 75 to 84 years. The author states, "With some few exceptions, there is no doubt that society has neglected the problem." He attributes the neglect to the fact that decision-makers have a tendency to focus on the relatively young. However, people are living longer today and the elderly are healthier, which indicates the need for greater interest and more intervention. "We have signs of an epidemic, but one that can be ameliorated or prevented" (Ekman & et al., 2001).

Sometimes, we also worry about population problems in the larger world. Poverty, disease, accident and death rates, world hunger, the problems of crowded cities, vanishing farmlands—all are population problems. To avoid sounding all too gloomy, we should point out that some of the most practical things we can do to resolve these problems

**Table 15-1** Petroleum Consumption in the United States, OECD Countries and the World 2004–2011 (1,000 Barrels/Day)

| Year | United States | Total OECD | World |
|---|---|---|---|
| 2011 | 18949.459 | 46380.293 | 88170.297 |
| 2010 | 19180.127 | 46846.813 | 87251.203 |
| 2009 | 18771.400 | 46280.363 | 84741.367 |
| 2008 | 19497.965 | 48355.262 | 85554.277 |
| 2007 | 20680.379 | 50037.309 | 85944.177 |
| 2006 | 20687.418 | 50143.840 | 85155.727 |
| 2005 | 20802.162 | 50445.219 | 84089.133 |
| 2004 | 20731.150 | 50100.129 | 82582.820 |

Adapted from EconStats, International Petroleum.
Retrieved from http://www.econstats.com/fut/xeiam11_ea74.htm

involve studying the population in hopes of influencing it. We may be able to better understand our own lives, plan sensible social policies to shape the world's future, and develop sound business, investment, and economic strategies by understanding the size, age, sex ratios, and movements of the population. The study of these various characteristics of society is called "demography."

# 15.1 DEMOGRAPHY AND THE STUDY OF POPULATION

**Demography** is the study of the size and makeup of the human population and how it changes. Demographers want to know how many babies are being born, what diseases are in the population, how long people live, how populations age, whether they stay in the same place or move about, and whether they live in remote regions or crowded urban areas.

*The population—the number of people in a society—affects a number of aspects in life, including your job, your spouse, and your children. Population problems in the larger world can include poverty, disease, and world hunger. (iStockphoto)*

## 15.1a Collecting the Data

Demographers' main concern is counting people. In fact, the word *demography* is often used to refer to the study of population statistics. Societies have always realized how important it is to know about their members and since early times have kept some form of **census**—a count of the population—usually with a record of the age and sex of its members. Written records of deaths can be found in early Greek and Egyptian accounts. The Bible says that when Jesus was born, Mary and Joseph were on their way to be counted in a Roman census.

The first census in the United States was carried out in 1790; and censuses are still carried out once every 10 years, with questionnaires mailed to all known households and interviewers going door to door for those who are not contacted or do not respond by mail.

The census is often criticized for underreporting people, especially the poor and homeless. Some people do not receive the questionnaires or do not bother to return them. Interviewers do not find some people—sometimes because the job is not organized or done properly and sometimes because people avoid being found. Because state and local governments receive federal funds based on population counts, these governments are quick to complain that their populations have been undercounted.

A smaller census is made every year and is more accurate than the 10-year census because it is based on a carefully chosen random sample (see Chapter 2 for a discussion of sampling) of the population. The smaller, yearly census also has the advantage of being done by more highly experienced interviewers; and there is less need to hire as many temporary, inexperienced people, as is required for the 10-year census. Additionally, **vital statistics**—records of all births, deaths and their causes, marriages, divorces, some diseases, and similar data—are recorded in each state and reported to the National Center for Health Statistics. Most modern nations keep records as accurate as those of the United States. Even underdeveloped nations attempt to record their populations; and although data from these countries may be relatively inaccurate, they provide enough information to assess world population trends.

Three variables can cause the size of the population in a given region to change: (1) births, (2) deaths, and (3) migrations. Demographers measure these factors in terms of their rates.

**Demography**
The statistical study of population, especially data on birth rates, death rates, marriage rates, health, and migration

**Census**
An official count of the number of people in a given area

**Vital statistics**
Records of all births, deaths and their causes, marriages, divorces, and certain diseases in a society

## 15.1b Fertility

**Fertility** is a measure of the rate at which people are born. **Mortality** is a measure of the rate at which people die. **Migration** is the movement of people into or out of a geographical area. To understand how populations change, it is necessary to understand how demographers measure these factors. Fertility data indicate the rate at which babies are born. The crude birth rate is simply the number of births per one thousand people; but if we want to predict how many babies will actually be born, more information is needed. We must know the **age-sex composition** of the society, and the number of males and females in the population, along with their ages. A population with few women will have few children. The ages of the females are especially important because children and older women do not have babies.

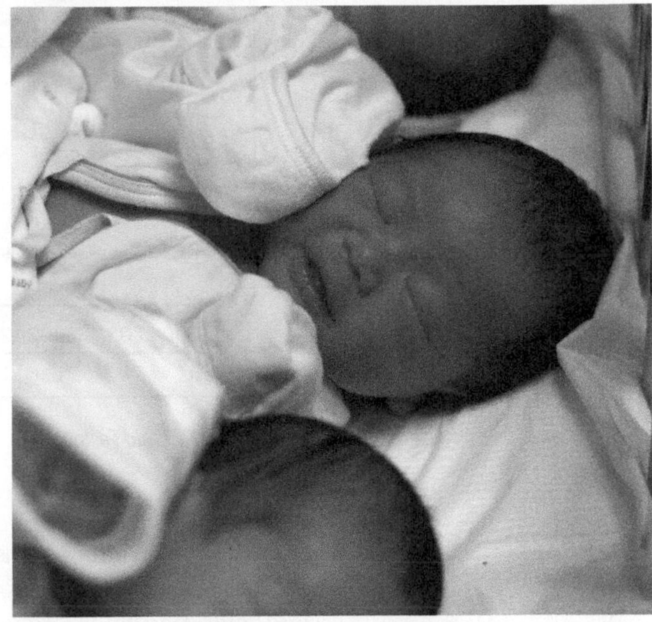

The birth rates in a society are affected by the society's age-sex composition: the number of males and females in the population and their ages. In most societies, the number of men and women is about equal, and more children are born to women in the middle of their childbearing years. (Shutterstock)

In most societies, about 105 males are born for each 100 females, but women live longer than men. Thus, there may be more men at younger ages, but there are more women in older groups. During the childbearing years, the number of men and women is usually about equal, except in societies suffering from wars in which large numbers of men are killed or in societies experiencing a great deal of migration. Areas from which men have moved have a surplus of women, whereas the areas they move into have a surplus of men; and a society with unequal numbers of men and women will have a low birth rate.

Demographers generally assume that women are fertile from age 15 to age 49. They also know that more children are born to women in the middle of their childbearing years. However, some women in their childbearing years choose not to have children, and few have as many as they potentially could. An individual woman's potential for bearing children is called her **fecundity**. Although women can potentially have 20 to 25 children, very few have this many. In recent years, worldwide fertility rates have been declining (see Figures 15-1A and 15-1B).

Fertility varies greatly among societies and among subcultures within societies. The number of children born in a society is affected by three major factors: wealth, environment, and societal norms about marriage and children. Generally, richer nations have lower birth rates than poorer nations. The same relationship between wealth and birth rates holds within nations: the upper classes usually have lower birth rates than the poor classes.

Fertility rates are also different between rural and urban areas. Women in rural areas usually have more children than those in cities. In rural areas, children are needed to help with farm labor; yet in modern urban areas, children are not productive. Rather, they are an expense to house, feed, clothe, and educate. They may also decrease a family's income when a parent must either pay for childcare or stay home to care for them. Many demographers believe that the birth rate of the world will decline, and perhaps drop sharply, as underdeveloped nations become more industrialized and urban.

A society's norms regarding the value of children and the age at which marriage is considered acceptable have a strong effect on fertility rates. In countries in which women marry young, the birth rates are higher than those in which they marry later because of differences in the number of childbearing years. Norms about the number of children a family should have and about the acceptability of birth control and abortion also affect the birth rate. Separation by war, work away from home, and conflicts between spouses also reduce the birth rate, whereas a cultural practice of abstaining

**Fertility**
A measure of the rate at which people are being born

**Mortality**
A measure of the rate at which people are dying

**Migration**
Movement of people into or out of an area

**Age-sex composition**
The number of men and women in the population, along with their ages

**Fecundity**
A woman's potential for bearing children

**Figure 15-1A** World Birth Rates (Births/1,000 Population), 2000–2012

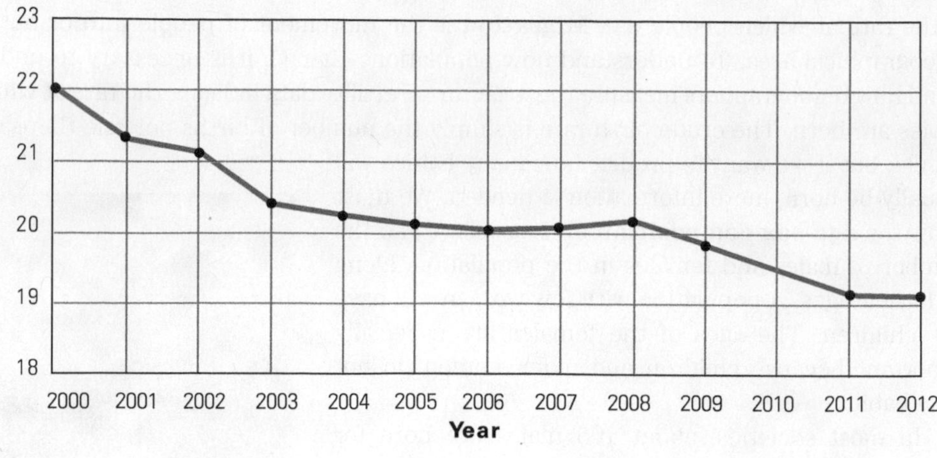


| 2000 | 2001 | 2002 | 2003 | 2004 | 2005 | 2006 | 2007 | 2008 | 2009 | 2011 | 2012 |
|---|---|---|---|---|---|---|---|---|---|---|---|
| 22 | 21.37 | 21.16 | 20.43 | 20.24 | 20.15 | 20.05 | 20.09 | 20.18 | 19.86 | 19.15 | 19.14 |

Adapted from *CIA World Factbook*

from intercourse during menstruation may make intercourse more likely during fertile periods and may result in an increased birth rate. In addition to the fertility rate, mortality and migration rates also influence the population size.

## 15.1c Mortality

*Mortality* is a measure of the rate at which people die. The crude death rate is the number of deaths in a given year per one thousand people. Like the crude birth rate, however, the crude death rate does not provide enough information to predict how

**Figure 15-1B** U.S. Birth Rate (Births/1,000 Population), 2000–2012

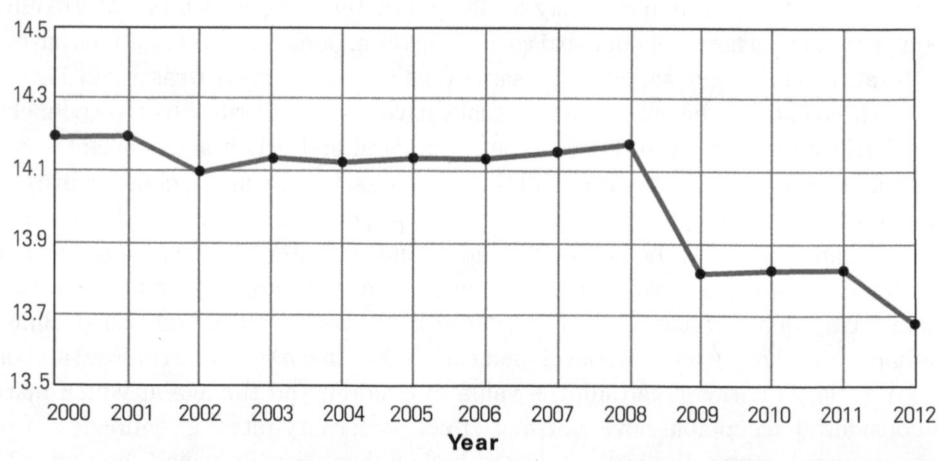


| 2000 | 2001 | 2002 | 2003 | 2004 | 2005 | 2006 | 2007 | 2008 | 2009 | 2010 | 2011 | 2012 |
|---|---|---|---|---|---|---|---|---|---|---|---|---|
| 14.2 | 14.2 | 14.1 | 14.14 | 14.13 | 14.14 | 14.14 | 14.16 | 14.18 | 13.82 | 13.83 | 13.83 | 13.68 |

Adapted from *CIA World Factbook*

many people will die or to compare death rates among populations. For a more accurate estimate of the death rate, demographers consider age and gender. A population with many old people will have a higher death rate than a comparatively young population; and because women live longer than men, a population with many women will have a lower death rate. Demographers often use an **age-adjusted death rate**, a measure of the number of deaths at each age for each sex (usually per 100,000 living at that age). Demographers can also compute life expectancy by predicting how many of each age cohort, or age group, will die at each age.

Mortality, like fertility, varies with wealth. When people, especially infants, have adequate food, shelter, and medical care, they are less likely to die of disease. The rate of *infant mortality*, death in the first year of life, was very high in the Middle Ages. Now it is lower, and the average life expectancy has been greatly increased. Infant mortality is low and life expectancy high in more developed nations, such as the United States, Canada, and European countries. When compared to the average infant mortality of all countries worldwide, the United States fares favorably well (see Figures 15-2A and 15-2B). However as of 2012, of the 30 industrialized countries in the world, the United States has the fifth highest infant mortality rates, worsening slightly from the sixth highest in 2009. If we take out the low-income countries from this list, the U.S. worsens to the third highest rate (see Table 15-2).

Researchers have uncovered what they hope to be a one-time blip in infant mortality rates in the United States. Infant mortality rates rose in 2002 for the first time in decades. Our nation's infant mortality rate edged upward from 6.69 deaths per 1,000 live births in 2001 to 6.75 deaths per 1,000 in 2002 (see Figure 15-2A). In explaining the higher infant mortality rate, researchers point to the surge in older women having babies; the popularity of fertility treatments; and paradoxically, advancements in identifying and saving fetuses in distress. Because we have the ability to identify fetuses in distress and deliver them early, they are dying at higher rates in early infancy (Stein, 2004).

An increase in infant mortality is cause for attention because the infant mortality rate usually reflects the general wellbeing of the larger society. However, life expectancy in the United States continues to rise because of our ability to prevent, detect, and treat cancer, accidents, stroke, and heart disease.

**Age-adjusted death rate**
The number of deaths occurring at each age, for each sex, per 100,000

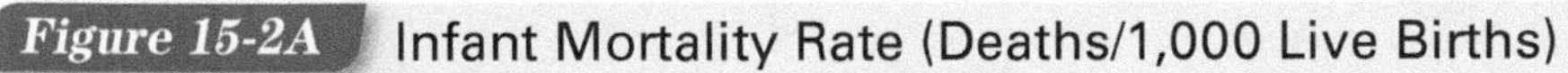
**Figure 15-2A** Infant Mortality Rate (Deaths/1,000 Live Births)

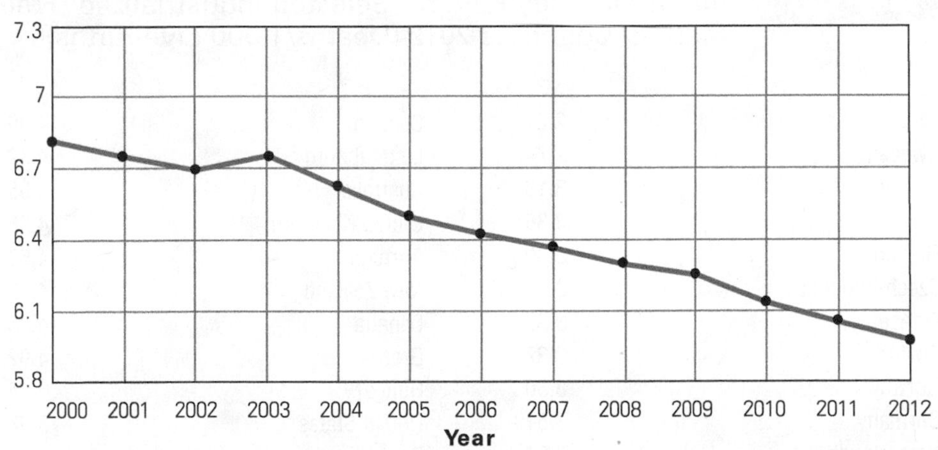


| 2000 | 2001 | 2002 | 2003 | 2004 | 2005 | 2006 | 2007 | 2008 | 2009 | 2010 | 2011 | 2012 |
|---|---|---|---|---|---|---|---|---|---|---|---|---|
| 6.82 | 6.76 | 6.69 | 6.75 | 6.63 | 6.5 | 6.43 | 6.37 | 6.3 | 6.26 | 6.14 | 6.06 | 5.98 |

Adapted from *CIA World Factbook*

**Figure 15-2B** Infant Mortality Rates in the World, 2000–2012

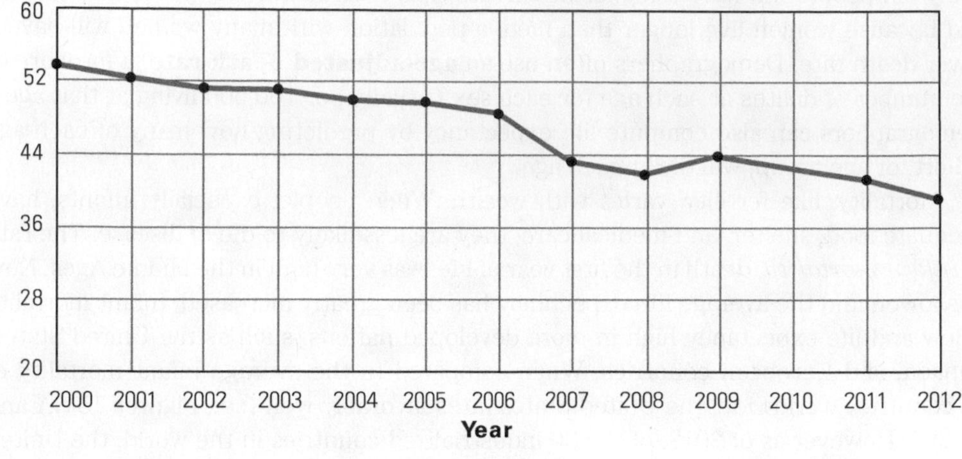


| 2000 | 2001 | 2002 | 2003 | 2004 | 2005 | 2006 | 2007 | 2008 | 2009 | 2011 | 2012 |
|---|---|---|---|---|---|---|---|---|---|---|---|
| 54 | 52.61 | 51.55 | 51.38 | 50.31 | 50.11 | 48.87 | 43.52 | 42.09 | 44.13 | 41.61 | 39.48 |

Adapted from *CIA World Factbook*

People in China (Macau), Andorra, and Japan have the longest life expectancies in the world. An infant born in these countries can expect to live, on average, more than 80 years. The death rate is higher and the life expectancy shorter in India, Africa, South America, and Southeast Asia, where poverty is widespread (CIA World Factbook, 2009).

Death rates also vary by class within nations. In the United States, for example, poor people have a higher rate of infant mortality and a shorter life expectancy than the rich; blacks have a larger proportion of poor people, higher rates of infant mortality, and shorter life expectancies than whites (Centers for Disease Control and Prevention (CDC), 2004). The more important factor in infant mortality, however, is poverty, not

**Table 15-2** Infant Mortality Rate for Selected Industrialized (Free-Market) Countries 2012 (Deaths/1,000 Live Births)

| Country | Rate | Country | Rate |
|---|---|---|---|
| Japan | 2.21 | Belgium | 4.28 |
| Sweden | 2.74 | Luxembourg | 4.39 |
| Iceland | 3.18 | Australia | 4.55 |
| Italy | 3.36 | United Kingdom | 4.56 |
| Finland | 3.40 | Portugal | 4.60 |
| Czech Republic | 3.70 | New Zealand | 4.72 |
| France | 3.37 | Canada | 4.85 |
| Spain | 3.37 | Greece | 4.92 |
| Norway | 3.50 | Hungary | 5.24 |
| Germany | 3.51 | United States | 5.98 |
| Netherlands | 3.73 | Poland | 6.42 |
| Switzerland | 4.03 | Slovakia | 6.47 |
| South Korea | 4.08 | Mexico | 16.77 |
| Denmark | 4.19 | Turkey | 23.07 |
| Austria | 4.26 | | |

Adapted from *CIA World Factbook*

race. Black infants born to parents living in predominantly white neighborhoods, indicating higher income, have lower infant mortality rates than white infants living in predominantly black neighborhoods, where poverty is greater (Yankauer, 1990).

## 15.1d Migration

Migration is the movement of people into or out of a geographical area and includes the following: **immigration**, movement into an area, and **emigration**, movement out of an area. Migration is harder to define and measure than birth or death rates. To be considered a migrant, how far must a person move, and how long should the person remain in the new place? In the United States, moving within a county is not considered migration, but moving from one county to another is. Migrant workers, who travel about the country doing farm labor, are not technically considered migrants because rather than remaining in a new location after the work season is over, they return to their original starting point and take up jobs in that area.

Why do people move? Demographers speak in terms of push factors and pull factors. **Push factors** are those that push people away from their homes: famines, wars, political oppression, loss of jobs, or bad climate. Some Eastern Europeans, for example, have migrated to the West where jobs are more plentiful. **Pull factors** are those that make a new place seem more inviting: the chance to acquire land or jobs, the discovery of riches such as gold or oil, or the chance to live in a more desirable climate. Discoveries of gold in California, for example, drew fortune seekers from all over the world.

*Migration is difficult to define. Migrant workers travel around the country doing farm labor but are not technically considered migrants because they return to their original starting point after the work season is over, rather than remaining in the new locations to which they travel. (iStockphoto)*

In prehistoric times, waves of migrants moved out of Africa and Asia into the Middle East and eastern Europe. Later, tribes moved further into Europe, spreading their culture as they moved. It is assumed that these waves of migration were caused by push factors, such as changes in climate, changes in food supply, or pressure from increasing populations in Asia, as well as pull factors, such as Europe's more favorable climate.

The population of Europe increased slowly throughout the Middle Ages. When Columbus first came to America, a new wave of migration began. It started slowly, but it is estimated that more than 60 million Europeans eventually left Europe. Many later returned, so the net migration—the actual population change—was much lower (Heer, 1975).

Between 1820 and 1970, 46 million migrants entered the United States (Thomlinson, 1976). In a single peak year, 1854, a total of 428,000 immigrants came to this country. This group consisted mainly of Irish leaving their country because of the potato famine and Germans leaving because of political turmoil in their country. A second peak was reached around the turn of the century when immigrants averaged a million per year. Most of the Europeans who entered the United States at that time were from Italy or other southern and eastern European countries.

A more long-term, great migration occurred between 1619 and 1808, when 400,000 Africans were forced to migrate to the United States as slaves. Considering all the Americas, between 10 million and 20 million Africans were brought to the Western Hemisphere (Thomlinson, 1976).

Immigration restrictions were first imposed in the United States in 1921 and again in 1924 in order to slow the rate of immigration. During this period, most immigrants were from Canada, Mexico, Germany, the United Kingdom, or Italy. After 1965, immigration quotas were relaxed; and a new wave of immigrants entered the country, changing dramatically the origins of American immigrants. About 2.4 million Asians, or about 46% of all immigrants, entered the United States during the 1980s. Another 2 million, or

**Immigration**
Movement of people into an area

**Emigration**
Movement of people out of an area

**Push factors**
Natural or social factors that cause people to move out of an area

**Pull factors**
Natural or social factors that cause people to move into an area

38% of all immigrants, came from Mexico and other parts of Latin America (Information Please Almanac, Atlas & Yearbook, 1991). As of 2008, this new pattern of immigration showed no sign of abatement. Certainly, in 2008 a record number of immigrants (1,046,539) naturalized, two-fifths of whom came from Latin America and Asia. The top countries of birth of new citizens in 2008 were Mexico, India, the Philippines, China, and Cuba. However, since 2008 the number of naturalizations from these countries has shown a consistent annual decline (see Table 15-3).

Besides legal immigration, the United States is also home to one of the largest diasporas of undocumented immigrants in the world. Most illegal immigrants in the United States come from Latin America and enter the country via the U.S.–Mexico border. The lure of the American dream drives these immigrants into the United States by the millions. Indeed, for 2008, the U.S. Department of Homeland Security conservatively estimated that the United States was home to over 11 million undocumented immigrants. As with the rate of naturalization, the flow of undocumented immigrants has declined since 2008, but only slightly (Figure 15-3). Since the terrorist attacks on September 11, 2001, the flow of undocumented immigration into the United States has been curtailed somewhat by stronger border security. However, hundreds of thousands still enter the United States illegally every year. For most Americans, it's a source of pride that so many people from around the world would risk their very lives just to live in the United States. Still, the aftershocks of the 9/11 attacks regularly remind Americans that not every immigrant has the best interests of the United States in mind. As a result, in the decades to come, the issue of undocumented immigration will continue to be a major source of political debate.

*The United States is home to one of the largest populations of illegal immigrants. Although the flow of these immigrants was curtailed somewhat after 9/11, hundreds of thousands of illegal immigrants continue to enter the country for the opportunities it offers.* *(AP Wide World Photo)*

When they arrive in the United States, immigrants may work at very low-paying jobs, such as in clothing factories or as doormen. Some are able to begin small businesses of their own. Many immigrants are better off than they were in their country of origin, but others who are more highly educated and trained for professions are unable to find work to match their qualifications; they, too, must work at the very low-paying jobs available to them. There is some research evidence that the influx of low-wage immigrant workers into the Los Angeles area has kept wages there from rising for the population as a whole (Vernez & Ronfeldt, 1991). Because of recent restrictions, however, admissions for categories such as temporary agricultural workers and holders of NAFTA visas for professionals declined to 650,000 in 2003—a continued decline from 2002 levels of 688,000 (UNFPA, 2004).

**Table 15-3** Persons Naturalized by Country of Origin: Top Five 2008–2011

| Country | 2008 | 2009 | 2010 | 2011 |
|---|---|---|---|---|
| Mexico | 231,815 | 111,630 | 67,062 | 94,783 |
| India | 65,971 | 52,889 | 61,142 | 45,985 |
| Philippines | 58,792 | 38,934 | 35,465 | 42,520 |
| China | 40,017 | 37,130 | 33,969 | 32,864 |
| Cuba | 39,871 | 24,891 | 14,050 | 21,071 |

Adapted from "Homeland Security Annual Report, U.S. Naturalizations: 2011."
Retrieved from http://www.dhs.gov/xlibrary/assets/statistics/publications/natz_fr_2011.pdf and from "Homeland Security Annual Report, U.S. Naturalizations: 2010." Retrieved from http://www.dhs.gov/xlibrary/assets/statistics/publications/natz_fr_2010.pdf

**Figure 15-3** Unauthorized Immigrant Population: 2000–2011 (in Millions)

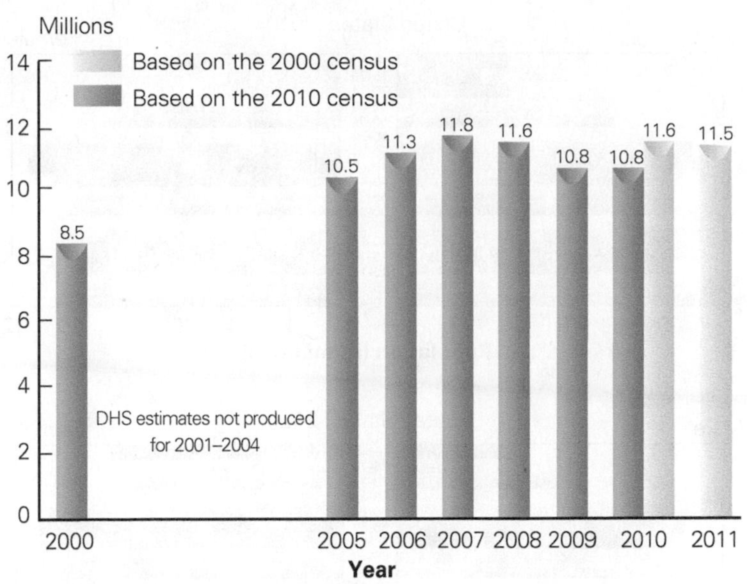


*Note.* The 2010 estimate was revised for consistency with estimates derived from the 2010 Census.
Adapted from Homeland Security, "Population Estimates. Estimates of the Unauthorized Immigrant Population Residing in the United States: January 2011."
Retrieved from http://www.dhs.gov/xlibrary/assets/statistics/publications/ois_ill_pe_2011.pdf

Migration within the United States has also been extensive. Throughout this country's history, people have moved predominantly from east to west and from rural to urban areas. After World War I, when immigration was restricted and the supply of laborers entering the country was limited, Northern cities recruited Southern blacks to fill labor jobs. Many blacks moved to Northern cities, far exceeding the number of jobs or the housing available. The migrants could not return to the South because they didn't have money to make the return trip or a home waiting for their return. Even today, we can see the pattern of inadequate jobs and housing for blacks living in Northern cities.

The rate of population change is determined by all the foregoing factors. If the birth rate is high and the mortality rate is low, the population increases. If the mortality rate is high compared with the birth rate, the population will decline. Where migration enters the picture, the population can grow or decrease very rapidly. Even relatively small changes in demographic patterns can make long-term, sweeping changes in the lives of people in the population. For example, people born when birth rates are high in the United States have many different experiences from people born when birth rates are low.

# 15.2 POPULATION TRENDS AND LIFE EXPERIENCES

Figure 15-4 is a population pyramid, a graph that shows how many males and females from each age category there are in the United States today. In the middle column, find the category containing your age group, noting that the bars extending to the left and right represent the males and females born in those years. By looking at the bottom of the graph, you can determine the number of people of your age and sex in the population. If you are between ages 15 and 19 as of 2010, the left line tells us how many females in your age group live in the United States while the right line tells us how many males of your age group reside in the United States. Notice also how the pyramid

**Figure 15-4** Age-Sex Population Pyramid, United States, for the Years 2010, 2020 (est.), and 2050 (est.)

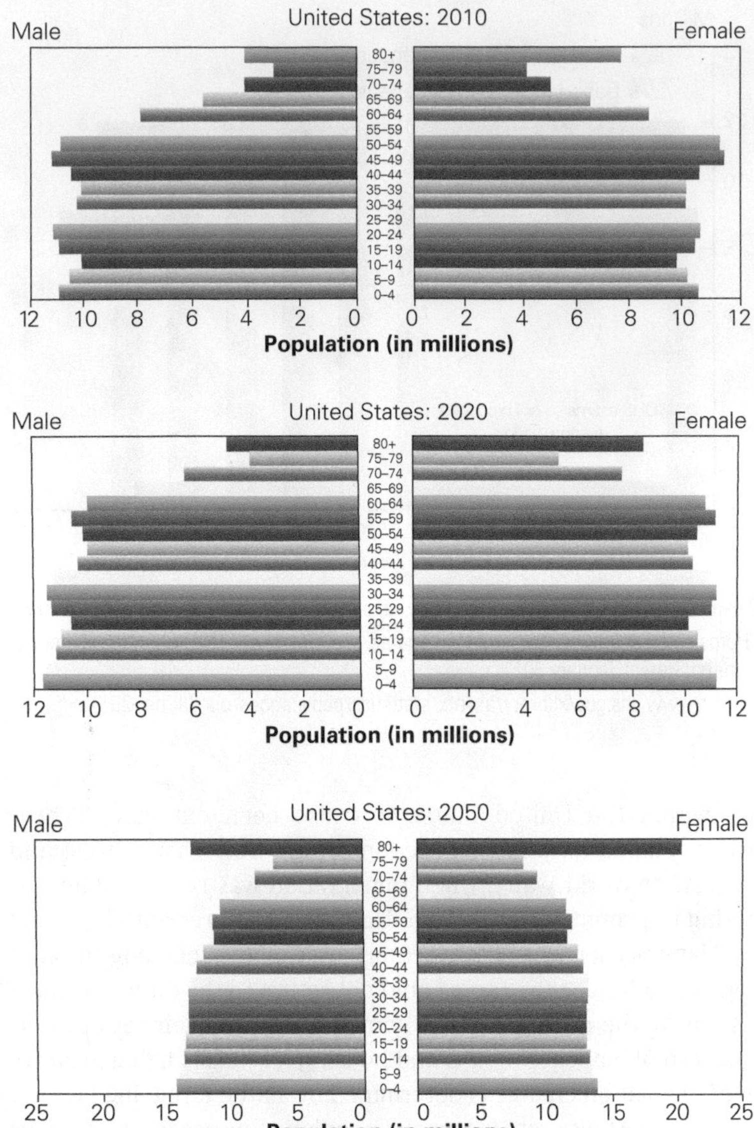


Adapted from U.S. Census Bureau, International Database.
Retrieved from http://www.nationmaster.com/country/us/Age_distribution

bulges out for the ages between 45 and 64 and between 15 and 29. The bulge for 45- to 64-year-olds represents the people born during what is called the "baby boom," and the bulge for 15- to 29-year-olds represents their children. Compare the 2010 population pyramid of the United States with those of India and Germany, which serve as examples of countries with much older and much younger populations, respectively (see Figures 15-4 and 15-5).

Why were so many people born during those baby boom years? During the depression of the 1930s and World War II in the 1940s, many people postponed having children. After the war, the country was both peaceful and affluent. Those who had postponed having children began families, and those who were just entering their 20s began having children, too. The result was a disproportionate number of babies born in the 1950s and 1960s, compared to other decades.

**Figure 15-5** Population Pyramids of a Young Population (India) and an Older Population (Germany)

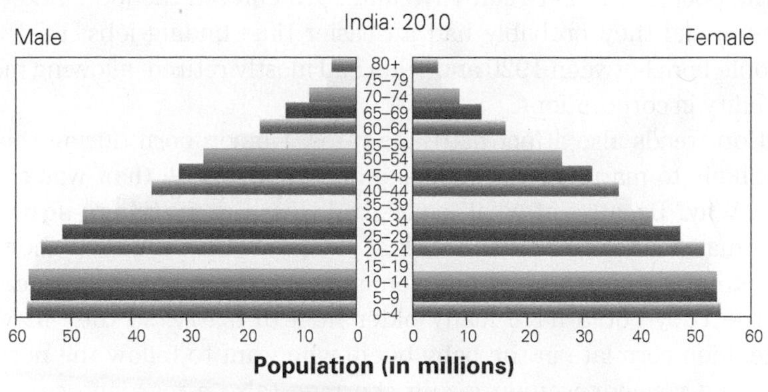


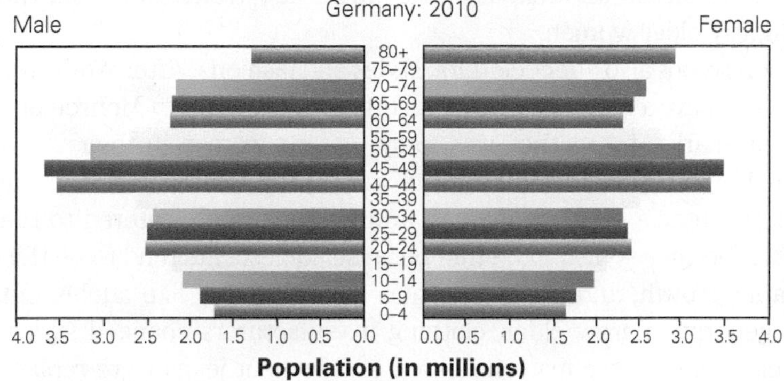


Adapted from U.S. Census Bureau, International Database.

How has the baby boom affected the lives of people born during those years? First, it may have affected their education. Children might not have gone to nursery school because the schools were full. Schools were crowded because there were not enough schools to take care of so many children, and many children attended schools in temporary classroom buildings. When students reached college age, they faced strong competition to gain entrance to colleges, which were overcrowded trying to deal with the surge in population. At the end of the baby boom, schools closed because there were fewer students to fill all the space that had been created. Some students, especially those in suburban areas, watched their elementary schools close when they left them, went to a junior high school that was closed while they were there, moved to a second junior high, and saw that one close before they had finished senior year.

Students born between 1975 and 1979 had a very different educational experience. Their experience was similar to those who were born in the 1930s and followed the baby boom of the 1920s. Harter (1987) describes the generation of the 1930s as the "good-time" cohort. When they went to school, there was plenty of space in school, plus a full complement of athletic teams, glee clubs, debating societies, and other extracurricular activities. The cohort of the 1930s could participate without facing much competition. So it was with those born between 1975 and 1979. There was plenty of room in school for them throughout their educational years, and there has not been the extreme competition for a place in college. In fact, colleges were competing for students to attend their schools and made every effort to recruit students and provide them with scholarships and loans so that they were able to attend. The lack of competition may also have reduced the amount of studying and learning that had taken place in school.

When baby boom children completed their education, unemployment rates were high. Many people were competing for jobs, and only a small part of the work force was retiring to create more job openings. About a generation later, the drop in the unemployment rate in 1984 was largely a result of a drop in the number of young people entering the job market.

When the people born between 1975 and 1979 entered the job market, there were fewer of them; and they probably had an easier time finding jobs. Furthermore, the bulge of people born between 1920 and 1929 had mostly retired, allowing more room for upward mobility in corporations.

Population trends also affect marriage rates. Women born during the baby boom were more likely to marry at an older age or to stay single than was true in earlier generations. Why? Because of what is referred to as the **marriage squeeze**. Women traditionally marry older men, and a look at the population pyramid shows that there was a shortage of older men for these women to marry (a marriage squeeze). Women born after the baby boom have many older men to marry, so they may marry at a younger age. Men born late in the baby boom who want to follow the normative practice of marrying younger women face a shortage (also a marriage squeeze), and so far they have not shown an inclination to start a new trend and avoid the squeeze by marrying slightly older women.

Population trends also affect clothing styles and fashions. After World War II, the mark of beauty was to have a more well-developed figure, like Marilyn Monroe or Betty Grable. Therefore, the market for clothes was found among women in their 20s and 30s, who had been unable to buy clothes during the war. Youngsters born during the baby boom, however, represented a big, new market; and manufacturers catered to them beginning in the 1960s. It became stylish to be thin because adolescents tend to be thin during their period of rapid growth, and a whole nation dieted to look like adolescents. When the baby boom generation grew older, clothing manufacturers changed styles to meet the market for clothes for more mature figures; and low-cut jeans were replaced by stretch blue jeans with a fuller-cut thigh and an elastic waist. Also, the health club business began to boom because this age group wanted to stay thin and look young. Ski resorts suffered a slump, however, because as members of the baby boom got older, they began staying home, having children, and watching their budgets. Thus, there were not enough younger people to replace them on the slopes. Golf, a gentler sport, began to increase in popularity.

**Marriage squeeze**

The effects of an imbalance between the number of males and females in the prime marriage ages due to rising or falling birth rates and the median age differences at marriage

Housing costs are also affected by population trends. Housing prices increased dramatically when baby boom young adults bought houses, but then dropped as demand eased. Retirement homes also saw a boom when those born in the 1920s retired, but

*Population trends affect aspects of society including marriage rates and fashion. For example, the mark of feminine beauty after World War II was to have a fuller figure like Marilyn Monroe. In contrast, today's view of beauty is to be thin to mirror the body of an adolescent.* (AP Wide World Photo)

prices fell when those born in the 1930s retired. Through studying population trends, we can see that consumer interests become very predictable.

Population trends may also determine government policies that affect you in your old age. In the year 2020, most of the baby boom will have reached age 60; many will be collecting Social Security, while others will still hold powerful positions in business and government. Moreover, because this age group will be a large voting bloc, they may be able to control decisions about continuing the support of Social Security benefits. Because the smaller population just younger than the baby boom may have a large tax burden to help support all the people in retirement, it is to be hoped that the younger population will be fully employed.

Knowledge of this population trend can help us do more than merely hope for the best, however. Because policymakers today know with certainty that there will be massive numbers of people in need of Social Security through 2025, they can take the necessary steps now to avert a future breakdown in the Social Security system. By studying population and predicting how it will affect our lives, we can tailor public policy planning to accommodate these shifts in population trends.

Population trends may affect business and investment decisions, both on the personal and corporate levels. Consider, for example, how corporations that provide services for the elderly will prosper when the baby boom reaches retirement age. Nursing homes, retirement villages, and pharmaceutical products for the aged are likely to experience explosive growth as a result of this population trend. Other services, such as automated car washes, house cleaning and yard services, and restaurants may also develop due to the increased numbers of the elderly. Think of how this knowledge can help businesses plan for those needs. New businesses in new fields may open up and may offer opportunities to those shrewd enough to anticipate the future needs of the population. Different nations have different population pyramids and must plan, therefore, for very different future needs of the population. As shown in the population pyramid in Figure 15-5, countries in which a large proportion of the population is very young, such as India, can be expected to grow rapidly as children mature and have children of their own. Here the care and education of the young will be of primary importance. In Germany, where the proportion of young people is smaller, the population cannot be expected to grow. However, they have a larger proportion of elderly and will need to plan for their care.

**BVT*Lab***

Improve your test scores. Practice quizzes are available at **www.BVTLab.com**

**thinking** SOCIOLOGICALLY

1. If the United States were a very young population, such as India, what social problems would probably be more prevalent than they are today? What social problems would probably be less prevalent?
2. If the United States were an older population, such as Germany, what social problems would probably be more prevalent than they are today? What social problems would be less prevalent?

## **15.3** DEMOGRAPHIC ASPECTS OF AGING

The aging of the population is of increasing demographic concern in most industrialized nations. Never have so many people lived so long.

One key question in investigations of an aged population concerns the age at which people are considered elderly. Most of us know of men and women over age 70 who look, think, and act young and others who seem old at age 35 or 45. Nevertheless, social policy and much of the available data in the United States define the elderly population as those 65 years of age and over. This cutoff point is somewhat arbitrary; however, it is widely used by gerontologists, and we follow it in this chapter. Yet, it is not universal; and today many gerontologists distinguish between the "young-old" (those ages 55 to 74) and the "old-old" (those 75 and over). You should recognize that numbers such as these are statistical generalizations and that wide variations exist in people's life expectancy, income, activity, and so forth.

## 15.3a Numbers of the Elderly: The Graying of America

The population age 65 and older is projected to double over the next 3 decades, from nearly 40 million to nearly 80 million. In 2030, people age 65 plus are expected to make up 20% of the population. The Census Bureau projects the 65-plus population to be almost 55 million in 2020, 72 million in 2030, over 81 million in 2040, and around 88.5 million in 2050. The U.S. will rank third in the world in population of those 65 and older.

The population age 80 and older is the fastest growing segment of the older population. In 2010, the 80-plus-year-olds made up 3.7% of the population; by 2050 the percentage of this age group is projected to grow to be 7.4% of the population. The 80-plus population will grow to more than 32.5 million in 2050. The U.S. will rank second in the world in this population (U.S. Bureau of the Census, 2010). (See Figure 15-6.)

*The population of people age 65 and older is projected to double over the next 3 decades.* (Shutterstock)

These numbers are not wild speculation. These people have already been born, and—barring any major wars or diseases—nearly three-fourths of those currently living can expect to reach old age. These numbers can, of course, be influenced by migrations of people into or out of the United States, in addition to the unexpected death factor.

This pattern of growth raises many questions relating to work, leisure, health, housing, family life, and other matters. One approach gerontologists have taken in considering how changes in these areas will affect society involves examining the relationship between the elderly and the rest of the population.

One way to examine the relationship between the old and the young is by calculating the **dependency ratio**—the ratio between the number of people in the dependent population and the number of people in the supportive or working population. The dependent population includes both the aged and children. Dependency ratios are an indicator of the potential burden on those in the working-age population. Using data provided by the U.S. Bureau of the Census, we can compute this ratio by dividing the number of people under age 20 plus the number of people age 65 and over by the number of people ages 20 to 64, and then multiply by one hundred.

A figure that excludes children is an *old-age dependency ratio*, which can be determined by dividing the number of persons over a specific age by the number of those in the supportive or working population. The total dependency ratio is projected to increase from 67 to 85 between 2010 and 2050, the result of a large increase in the old-age dependency ratio (22 to 35, as all of the baby boomers move into the age 65 and over category) (U.S. Bureau of the Census, 2010). (See Figure 15-7).

**Dependency ratio**
The ratio between the number of persons in the dependent population and the number of people in the supportive or working population

Today's lower birth rate will result in fewer workers to support each elderly, non-working person. Thus, we can expect issues such as Social Security, healthcare costs, and support services to become increasingly serious concerns. Shifts in dependency ratios will create problems of familial and societal support of the aged throughout this century; and such problems will become even more serious mid-century, at about the time most of you will be considering retirement. According to the U.S. Bureau of the

**Figure 15-6** Age and Sex Structure of the Population for the United States: 2010, 2030, and 2050

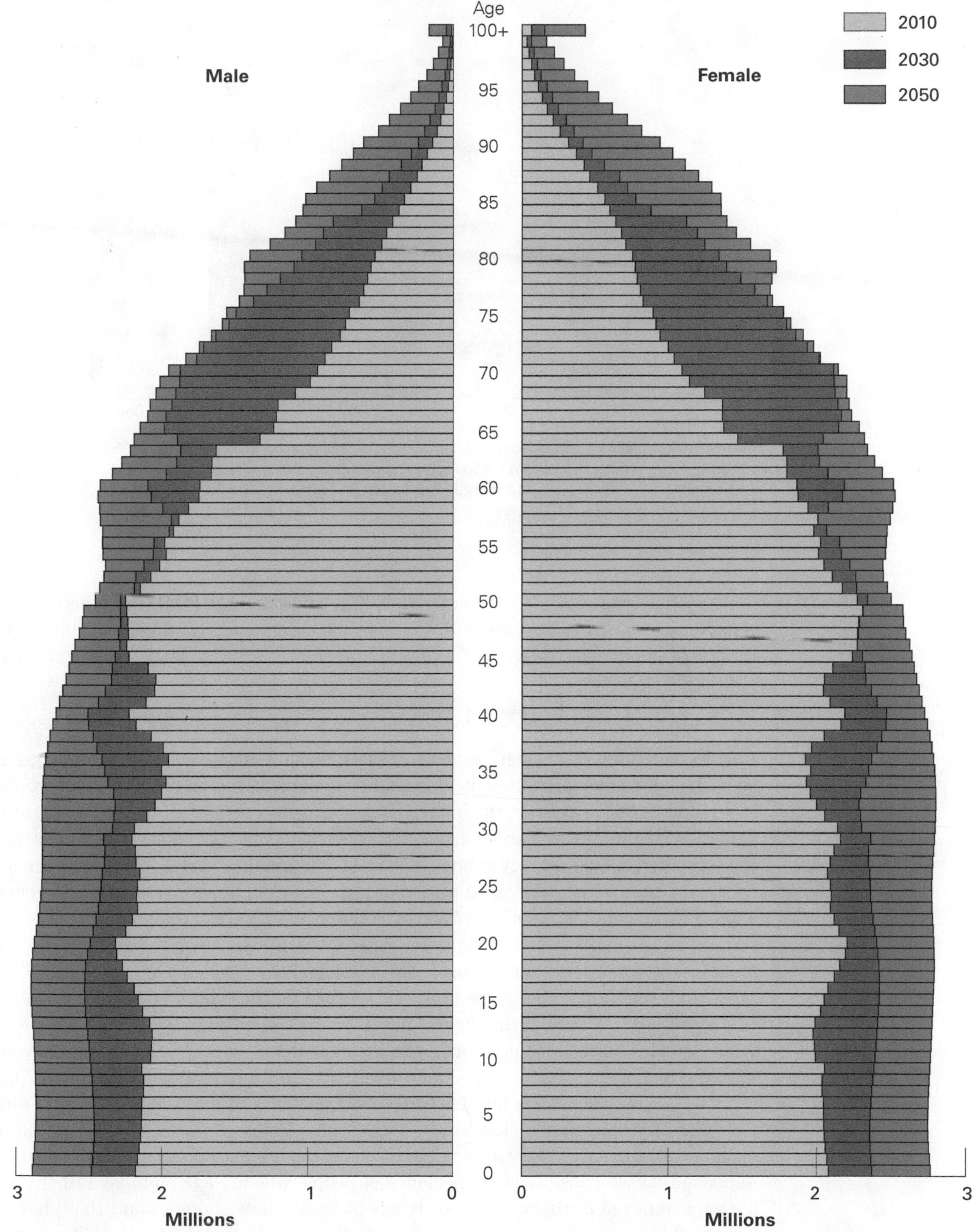


Adapted from U.S. Census Bureau, 2008.

**Figure 15-7** Dependency Ratios for the United States 2010–2050

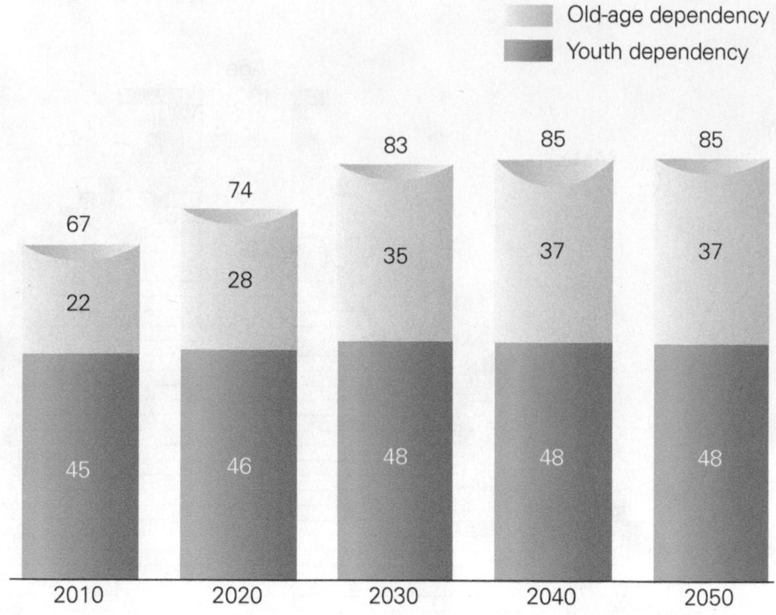


*Note.* Total dependency = ([Population under age 20 + Population aged 65 years and over] / [Population aged 20 to 64 years]) × 100. Old-age dependency = (Population aged 65 years and over / Population aged 20 to 64 years) × 100. Youth dependency = (Population under age 20 / Population age 20 to 64 years) × 100
Adapted from U.S. Census Bureau, 2008.

Census, there were 50,545 centenarians in 2000, a 35% increase from 1990. This number is expected to further increase to 324,000 by 2030 and to nearly 500,000 in 2050 (U.S. Bureau of the Census, 2008).

## 15.3b Life Expectancy

**Life expectancy** is the average years of life remaining for people who attain a given age. The most commonly cited life expectancy figure is based on birth. In other words, how many years, on average, can infants born in a given year expect to live? A glimpse at Table 15-4 shows these figures for selected countries. In many industrialized countries, the estimated life expectancy at birth as of 2011 was greater than 80 years. However, for many countries in the developing world, life expectancy at birth was less than 50 years, and for some countries less than 5 years. You may want to take a moment to consider some reasons as to why these figures vary so extensively. However, at this point, we focus on the United States and the life expectancy of older persons here.

Within the United States, the projected lifespan for those born in 2009 is 78.2 years (both genders, all races); this figure, however, varies considerably by sex and race. White females born the same year have a life expectancy of 80.9 years (white females have the highest level of life expectancy of all races and genders), compared with 76.2 years for white males; black females had a life expectancy of 77.4 years, compared with 70.9 years for black males (Kochanek, Xu, Murphy, Minino, & Kung, 2011). Instead of dealing with life expectancy at birth, what about the life expectancy of older persons? Suppose that we consider life expectancy of people who are age 65 today rather than life expectancy at birth. People who are age 65 today (those born around 1950) have a projected life span of an additional 18.8 years. That would give them a total life span of 83.8 years. However, in 1950, their projected lifespan was 68.2 years. The projected life span of someone born in 2000 was 76.8 years. Yet, people who were 10-year-olds in 2009 are projected to live another 68.8 years, giving them a life span of 78.8 years. This means

**Life expectancy**
The average years of life remaining for persons who attain a given age

**Table 15-4** Life Expectancy at Birth for Selected Countries, 2012 (Est.)

| Country | Life Expectancy | Country | Life Expectancy |
|---|---|---|---|
| Japan | 83.91 | Greenland | 71.25 |
| Singapore | 83.75 | Guatemala | 71.25 |
| Italy | 81.86 | Bangladesh | 70.06 |
| France | 81.46 | Bolivia | 67.90 |
| Sweden | 81.18 | India | 67.14 |
| United Kingdom | 80.17 | Kenya | 63.07 |
| United States | 78.49 | Liberia | 57.41 |
| Mexico | 76.66 | Uganda | 53.45 |
| China (mainland) | 74.84 | Namibia | 52.17 |
| Brazil | 72.79 | Zimbabwe | 51.82 |
| Peru | 72.73 | Afghanistan | 49.72 |
| Philippines | 71.94 | South Africa | 49.41 |

Adapted from "CIA World Factbook, 2012."
Retrieved from https://www.cia.gov/library/publications/the-world-factbook/rankorder/2102rank.html

that the older we get, the more our projected life span increases and that we cannot look only at the year of birth as the predictor of lifespan. This suggests that lifespan is not determined by biological factors alone but by a variety of social factors such as gender, race, geographic location, income, and others (see Table 15-5).

**thinking** SOCIOLOGICALLY

1. What are some implications of a changing dependency ratio in terms of (a) Social Security, (b) labor force demands, (c) healthcare, and (d) intergenerational relationships?
2. Recognizing the difference in life expectancy and life span, why has life expectancy increased in the United States and many other countries while the life span has remained virtually unchanged? What possibilities do you see for changes in either life expectancy or the life span over the next several decades?
3. Pretend you are going to take an elderly person on a tour of your university campus. What are things you would consider as you plan your tour? What does this tell you about your own beliefs concerning the elderly?

## 15.3c Social Characteristics of the Elderly

The elderly population, like the rest of the population, varies in terms of sex (male or female), marital status, living arrangements, geographical distribution, labor force participation, and other characteristics. Many characteristics are related in some way to the fact that women greatly outnumber men. Of the 37.8 million people over age 65 in the U.S. in 2009, 43% were men and 57% were women. Elderly women far outnumber elderly men. This factor has a major impact on conditions such as marital status and living arrangements.

**Table 15-5** Lifespan by Age as of 2009 and 2010 Estimates

| Age | Expectation of years to live (2009) | Expectation of years to live (2010) |
|---|---|---|
| 0 | 78.6 | 78.7 |
| 1 | 78.1 | 78.2 |
| 5 | 74.2 | 74.3 |
| 10 | 69.2 | 69.3 |
| 15 | 64.3 | 64.4 |
| 20 | 59.4 | 59.5 |
| 25 | 54.7 | 54.8 |
| 30 | 49.9 | 50.0 |
| 35 | 45.2 | 45.3 |
| 40 | 40.5 | 40.6 |
| 45 | 35.9 | 36.0 |
| 50 | 31.5 | 31.5 |
| 55 | 27.2 | 27.2 |
| 60 | 23.1 | 23.1 |
| 65 | 19.2 | 19.2 |
| 70 | 15.5 | 15.5 |
| 75 | 12.2 | 12.2 |
| 80 | 9.2 | 9.2 |
| 85 | 6.6 | 6.6 |
| 90 | 4.7 | 4.7 |
| 95 | 3.3 | 3.3 |
| 100 | 2.4 | 2.4 |

Adapted from National Vital Statistics Reports, p. 27, Table 6. (Sherry, Jiquan, & Kochanek, 2012). Retrieved from http://www.cdc.gov/nchs/data/nvsr/nvsr60/nvsr60_04.pdf.

Elderly men and women differ sharply in their marital status and living arrangements (see Table 15-6). About three-fourths of all older men are married and living with their spouse, compared with less than half of the women. The most dramatic difference in marital status between the sexes is shown under the category "widowed." In 2009, of people over age 65, nearly 13% of the men and 41% of the women were widowed. These differences are due to the fact that men tend to marry younger women and die at younger ages. Also, elderly widowed men have remarriage rates about seven times higher than those of women. As noted earlier, the notion that most old people end up in nursing homes and other long-term care institutions is a myth: Only about 5%, or 1 in 20, is institutionalized.

*Many characteristics of the elderly population are related to the fact that women greatly outnumber men.*
*(Shutterstock)*

Geographically, the elderly are heavily concentrated in metropolitan areas and in a few states. Compared with those under age 65, elderly persons are less likely to live in the suburbs. In the early 1990s, as was true a decade earlier, about two-thirds lived in metropolitan areas. Black and Hispanic elderly are especially concentrated in central cities, whereas whites are more likely to live outside the central city. In 2009, there were 10 states

**Table 15-6** Persons 65 Years Old and Over, Characteristics by Sex: 1990 to 2010

| | Total | | | | Male | | | | Female | | | |
|---|---|---|---|---|---|---|---|---|---|---|---|---|
| Characteristics | 1990 | 2000 | 2005 | 2010 | 1990 | 2000 | 2005 | 2010 | 1990 | 2000 | 2005 | 2010 |
| Total (million) | 29.6 | 32.6 | 35.2 | 38.6 | 12.3 | 13.9 | 15.1 | 16.8 | 17.2 | 18.7 | 20.0 | 21.8 |
| **Percent Distribution** | | | | | | | | | | | | |
| Marital status: | | | | | | | | | | | | |
| Never married | 4.6 | 3.9 | 4.1 | 4.3 | 4.2 | 4.2 | 4.4 | 4.1 | 4.9 | 3.6 | 3.9 | 4.5 |
| Married | 56.1 | 57.2 | 57.7 | 57.6 | 76.5 | 75.2 | 74.9 | 74.5 | 41.4 | 43.8 | 44.7 | 44.5 |
| Spouse present | 54.1 | 54.6 | 54.8 | 55.2 | 74.2 | 72.6 | 71.7 | 71.7 | 39.7 | 41.3 | 42.0 | 42.4 |
| Spouse absent[1] | 2.0 | 2.6 | 2.9 | 2.4 | 2.3 | 2.6 | 3.2 | 2.8 | 1.7 | 2.5 | 2.7 | 2.1 |
| Widowed | 34.2 | 32.1 | 30.3 | 28.1 | 14.2 | 14.4 | 13.7 | 12.7 | 48.6 | 45.3 | 42.9 | 39.9 |
| Divorced | 5.0 | 6.7 | 7.9 | 10.0 | 5.0 | 6.1 | 7.0 | 8.7 | 5.1 | 7.2 | 8.5 | 11.1 |
| **Educational Attainment** | | | | | | | | | | | | |
| Less than 9th grade | 28.5 | 16.7 | 13.4 | 10.2 | 30.0 | 17.8 | 13.2 | 10.2 | 27.5 | 15.9 | 13.5 | 10.1 |
| Completed 9th to 12th grade, but not high school diploma | [2] 16.1 | 13.8 | 12.7 | 10.3 | [2] 15.7 | 12.7 | 11.9 | 9.7 | [2] 16.4 | 14.7 | 13.3 | 10.8 |
| High school graduate | [3] 32.9 | 35.9 | 36.3 | 36.4 | [3] 29.0 | 30.4 | 31.6 | 32.0 | [3] 35.6 | 39.9 | 39.9 | 39.8 |
| Some college or associate's degree | [4] 10.9 | 18.0 | 18.7 | 20.6 | [4] 10.8 | 17.8 | 18.4 | 19.7 | [4] 11.0 | 18.2 | 19.0 | 21.2 |
| Bachelor's or advanced degree | [5] 11.6 | 15.6 | 18.9 | 22.5 | [5] 14.5 | 21.4 | 24.9 | 28.4 | [5] 9.5 | 11.4 | 14.3 | 18.0 |
| **Labor Force Participation:[6]** | | | | | | | | | | | | |
| Employed | 11.5 | 12.4 | 14.5 | 16.2 | 15.9 | 16.9 | 19.1 | 20.5 | 8.4 | 9.1 | 11.1 | 12.9 |
| Unemployed | 0.4 | 0.4 | 0.5 | 1.2 | 0.5 | 0.6 | 0.7 | 1.6 | 0.3 | 0.3 | 0.4 | 0.9 |
| Not in labor force | 88.1 | 87.2 | 84.9 | 82.6 | 83.6 | 82.5 | 80.2 | 77.9 | 91.3 | 90.6 | 88.5 | 86.2 |
| Percent below poverty level[7] | 11.4 | 9.7 | 9.8 | (NA) | 7.8 | 6.9 | 7.0 | (NA) | 13.9 | 11.8 | 11.9 | (NA) |

(NA) = Not available.

[1]Includes separated. [2]Represents those who completed 1 to 3 years of high school. [3]Represents those who completed 4 years of high school. [4]Represents those who completed 1 to 3 years of college. [5]Represents those who completed 4 years of college or more. [6]Annual averages of monthly figures.

Except as noted, adapted from U.S. Census Bureau, Current Population Reports, "The Older Population in the United States: March 2002," P20-546, 2003, and earlier reports; "Educational Attainment," <http://www.census.gov/population/www/socdemo/educ-attn.html>; "Families and Living Arrangements," <http://www.census.gov/population/www/socdemo/hh-fam.html>; and "Detailed Poverty Tabulations from the CPS," <http://www.census.gov/hhes/www/cpstables/032010/pov/toc.htm>.

Adapted from U.S. Bureau of Labor Statistics, Employment and Earnings, January issues. See footnote 2, Table 586. [7]Poverty status based on income in preceding year.

with more than 1 million people age 65 and over: California (4 million), Florida (3 million), New York (2.7 million), Pennsylvania (1.9 million), Texas (2.5 million), Illinois (1.7 million), Ohio (1.6 million), Michigan (1.3 million), North Carolina (1.2 million), and New Jersey (1.2 million). More than half of the total elderly population of the United States is found in these 10 states (U.S. Census Bureau 2010). Alaska has the smallest number of elderly persons—only 53,000 or 7.6% of its population. Florida is the state with the highest proportion of persons over age 65—18.9%. During the past decade, the largest increases in the elderly population were in the Southern and western states.

## Applying Demographic Aspects of Aging

The demographic aspects of aging are useful in a number of ways. Politicians and other policymakers are discovering that they need to understand the demographics of this growing constituency, such as knowing how many people will be over age 65 and identifying their social characteristics.

This understanding is important in determining the nature and form of policies and laws regarding mandatory retirement, pension plans, Social Security, Medicaid, Medicare, disability provisions, and so forth. Effective politicians realize that millions of older persons are active in special interest groups that can wield strong political pressure and support, such as the Gray Panthers, the National Retired Teachers Association, the National Council of Senior Citizens, and the American Association of Retired Persons (AARP). The AARP alone has a stunning 40 million members and more than 4,000 local chapters. Organizations such as these often apply their efforts toward improving the lives of older Americans by offering travel possibilities and insurance plans, as well as through selective lobbying efforts at the state and local level. To be politically effective, politicians cannot ignore the needs of this substantial and increasingly powerful group of Americans.

Business leaders and advertisers also need to be aware of the various demographic characteristics of the elderly. How will the needs of consumers change, as the population grows older? What kinds of products should research-and-development (R&D) departments of corporations be concerned with when planning for future corporate growth? Advertisers particularly must be concerned with elderly demographics. No longer can advertising campaigns focus exclusively on the young; as the median age of the population climbs, so does the age of consumers who have a large disposable income. In fact, if you pay close attention to television commercials and magazine ads, you will notice that more and more middle-aged and elderly models, actors, and actresses are being used.

Considering that the percentage of the population over age 65 is steadily increasing, community planners need to consider this age group in many aspects of their plans for the near future. For example, are there enough municipal parks? Are they conveniently located? Do they contain the facilities that will be needed by the elderly? If the number of elderly people in the population is increasing, it might make more sense to include park facilities that the aged are more likely to use (such as picnic areas, walking paths, botanical areas, and so forth) rather than increasing the number of basketball courts or bicycle paths. Planners also need to ensure that there will be adequate nursing home facilities and retirement villages, increased availability of low-cost housing and apartments, and adequate medical facilities that specialize in the healthcare of the elderly.

Awareness of the demographics of aging can also be useful for you personally. As you formulate your career plans, you may want to consider what types of services will be needed by the growing population of elderly. Will some careers or occupations be more highly rewarded because of increased demand? How will the increased population of elderly people affect your family planning, finances, and investments? There may be investment opportunities that you can take advantage of by knowing that the population of the United States is getting older. Knowing that there will be increased competition—and thus, rising costs—for retirement homes, cemetery plots, and so forth, may affect the way you plan for your future.

---

## 15.4 THE WORLD POPULATION EXPLOSION AND THE DEMOGRAPHIC TRANSITION



Until about 200 years ago, both birth and death rates were very high. As a result, the size of the world population remained stable. For every person who was born, someone died. Then a dramatic change took place. First, in industrial nations in the early part of the nineteenth century, the death rate dropped because of improvements in nutrition and sanitation. For several generations, however, the birth rate remained high. (This is the period when what we now refer to as the "population explosion" began.) Then, in about

sociologyatwork

## Monitoring Population Trends

Mathew Greenwald received his PhD in sociology from Rutgers University. Prior to opening up his own consulting firm—Mathew Greenwald and Associates, Inc.—he was the director of the social research services department of the American Council of Life Insurance (ACLI). While with the ACLI, he supervised a 10-person staff, designated to monitor past social changes and to predict future social change. Insurance companies use the results of this type of work to construct policies and to prepare for the future.

Greenwald explains that, because whole-life insurance policies can run for 50 or 60 years, insurance companies have an interest in the long view. "Of course, some aspects of the social world are so volatile that it's difficult to say what will be happening 15 years from now," Greenwald says. However, it is still possible to make predictions. "For example, we know that Social Security will be in trouble in 2011. That's when the first year of the baby-boom generation, those born in 1946, will be retiring. We also expect important medical breakthroughs in such areas as cancer research. Certain trends in computerization and global economics will probably also continue. Thus, while there's a lot we can't know, some trends can be accurately predicted; and the more we know, the easier it is to make decisions."

Here is where his sociological training came in. "The sociological perspective is of crucial importance," Greenwald says. "It's really a certain type of logic, a guide for analysis. It provides a structure for assessing situations. I might approach a family-related problem by looking at it in terms of statuses and roles, for example. More concretely, my training is useful in developing questionnaires and doing survey research. Besides my coursework in methods and statistics being useful, my work in theory, health, population, and the family also has been very valuable."

Greenwald provides an example of how sociological knowledge is useful in making predictions for insurance companies. "The primary purpose of life insurance is to replace income if a family breadwinner dies or is disabled, so the insurance business is bound up with many basic social institutions. We use survey research to keep track of a number of trends on an ongoing basis, including attitudes toward death, retirement, and family responsibility. We also use demographic data about factors such as health, birth rates, death rates, divorce rates, and the number of women working." As you might expect, major social developments influence the sales of life-insurance policies. "Now that families are more dependent on wives' income, women are buying much more insurance than they did previously. We're also finding that sales among Afro-Americans and Hispanics are increasing as these groups become more affluent."

In addition to following demographic trends, Greenwald and his department often undertook special projects. For example, one study concerned the public's sense of control over key aspects of their lives. Their findings: "Sadly, we found that people feel they have less control than they did a few decades ago, especially over the long term." This is probably the result of a number of factors, such as a volatile economic system, political turmoil at home and abroad, terrorism, and wars. "It's unfortunate," he says. "People who don't feel that they have much control are less likely to take a stand and try to change the situation—they don't take advantage of the control they do have. As [that] concerns the insurance business, there's evidence that feelings of lack of control are associated with ill health."

Although Greenwald is no longer with ACLI, he still maintains his ties to the life-insurance industry; his own company mostly does surveys that focus on market research for life-insurance companies. These surveys are used to develop new products, assess the effectiveness of advertising, enhance client relationships, and anticipate how to respond to changes in the social environment.

1850, the birth rate began to decrease, and the rate of population increase slowed. This change from high birth and death rates to low birth and death rates with a period of rapid population growth in between is known as the **demographic transition**. It occurs as a society evolves from a traditional pre-modern stage to a modern industrial stage; most European nations and other industrial countries have already passed through it. Other countries, particularly those in the developing world, still have very high birth rates in rural areas because children are highly valued for the tasks they do and for the security they provide when their parents reach old age. It is in these countries that population growth continues at very high rates. It took the human race from the beginning of history until 1850 to reach a population of 1 billion people; it took only an additional 100 years to reach 2 billion, and only 35 more years to reach 4.8 billion. Currently, the world is populated with more than 7 billion people, only a dozen years after it reached 6 billion. In *The World Population Prospects: The 2011 Revision*, the United Nations predicted that the world's population would reach 10.1 billion by the end of the twenty-first century (United Nations, Department of Economic and Social Affairs, 2012). While growth in industrialized countries is slowing down, growth in Africa may triple by the end of the century because fertility is not declining as rapidly as expected in some poor countries. Further, the population of the United States is growing faster than in other developed countries because of high immigration and higher fertility among Hispanic immigrants. The population of the United States, currently around 315 million, is expected to rise to 478 million by 2100. Still, this pales to the projected increase in some countries in Africa—such as Nigeria, currently at around 165 million and expected to reach 730 million by century's end (Gillis & Dugger, 2011) (see Figures 15-8A and 15-8B).

**Demographic transition**
The change from high birth and death rates to low birth and death rates with a period of rapid population growth in between (this transition occurs as a society evolves from a traditional pre-modern stage to a modern industrial stage)

**Figure 15-8A** World Population Growth

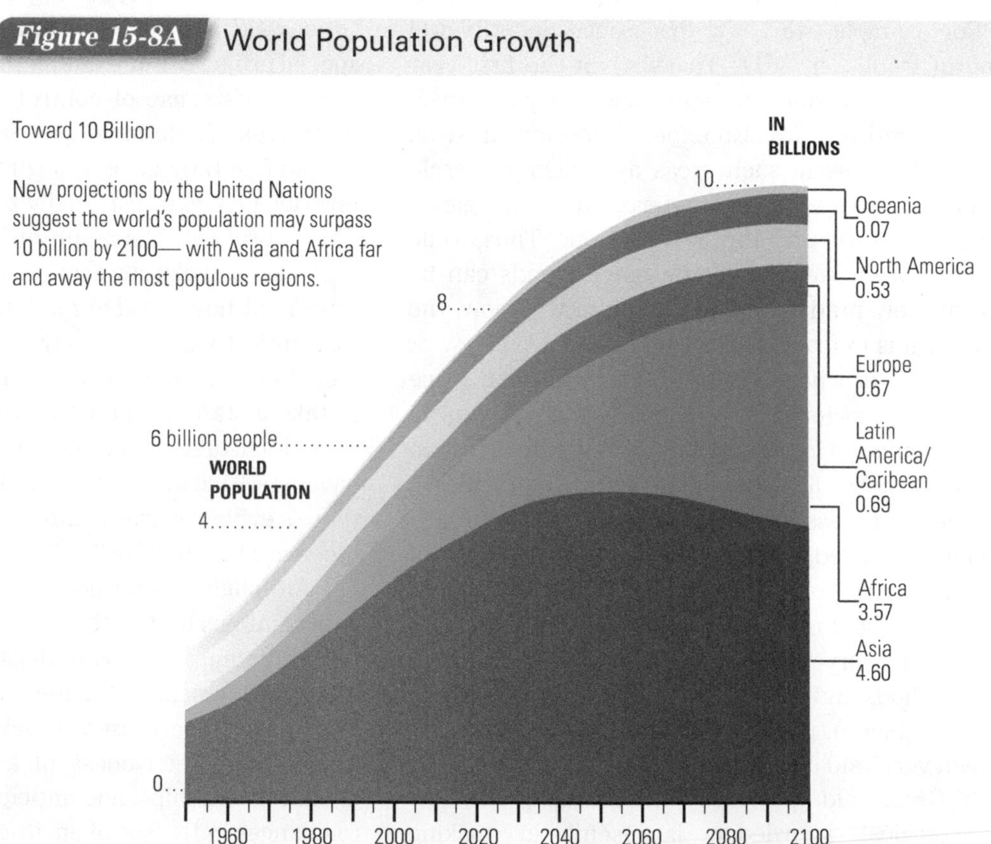


SOURCE: United Nations. Excerpted from NY Times "U.N. Forecasts 10.1 Billion People by Century's End." May 3, 2011.

**Figure 15-8B** World Population Growth by Selected Countries

Population forecasts for selected countries

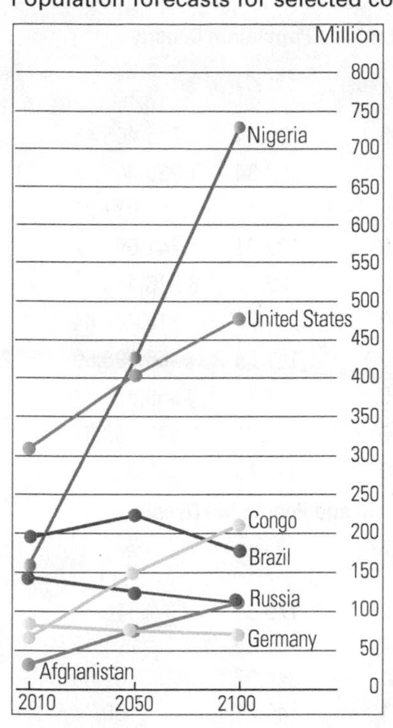


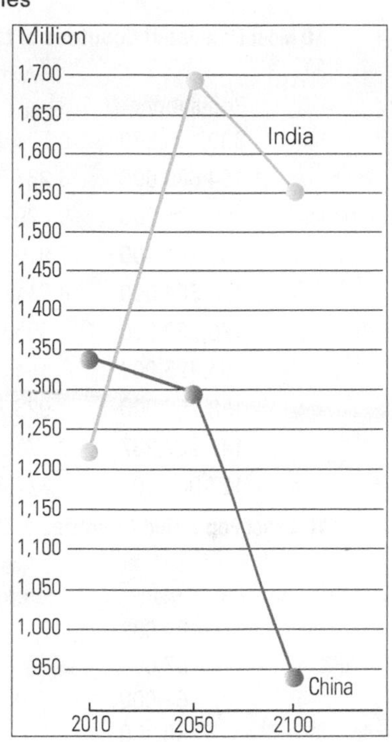


SOURCE: U.N. Population Prospects, 2010 Revision.

## 15.4a Population Density

The population explosion has dramatically increased the number of people in the world, but migrations have not distributed people evenly over the face of the earth. Whereas the population is sparse in many areas of the world, in some regions it is extremely dense. Such areas cannot provide the natural resources needed to maintain their population.

*Although the world's population has dramatically increased over the last 200 years, people are not distributed evenly over the face of the earth. For example, in China, where there are more than 1 billion people, the population density is only 361 people per square mile due to the country's large size; in many smaller countries, on the other hand, the population density is so great that the land cannot support the people. (iStockphoto)*

Population density is measured as the number of people per unit area, such as square kilometer or square mile (Rosenberg, 2011). The measure can sometimes be confusing, as it is not necessarily related to the size of the population (see Table 15-7). The United States, although it has absorbed millions of immigrants, has a relatively low population density. In some remote areas, the density is only 5 people per square mile. In major cities during the business day, on the other hand, the population density is as high as 100,000 people per square mile. For the entire United States, the density is 83.38 people per square mile (Worldatlas, 2012).

The other highly industrialized nations of the world have a higher population density than the United States. In Europe, it is very high. The developing nations are less densely populated than European countries, but they are not highly industrialized and therefore have less wealth to support them. China, the largest nation in the world, now has a population of more than 1 billion people, but its area is so great that its population density is only 361 people per square mile. There

**Table 15-7** The 10 Most and 10 Least Populated Countries of the World and Their Population Density, 2010

**10 Most Populated Countries of the World and Population Density**

| Country | Population | Area (sq. km.) | Persons per sq. km. | Area (sq. mi.) | Persons per sq. mi. |
|---|---|---|---|---|---|
| China | 1,339,190,000 | 9,596,960.00 | 139.54 | 3,705,405.45 | 361.42 |
| India | 1,184,639,000 | 3,287,590.00 | 360.34 | 1,269,345.07 | 933.27 |
| United States of America | 309,975,000 | 9,629,091.00 | 32.19 | 3,717,811.29 | 83.38 |
| Indonesia | 234,181,400 | 1,919,440.00 | 122.01 | 741,099.62 | 315.99 |
| Brazil | 193,364,000 | 8,511,965.00 | 22.72 | 3,286,486.71 | 58.84 |
| Pakistan | 170,260,000 | 803,940.00 | 211.78 | 310,402.84 | 548.51 |
| Bangladesh | 164,425,000 | 144,000.00 | 1,141.84 | 55,598.69 | 2,957.35 |
| Nigeria | 158,259,000 | 923,768.00 | 171.32 | 356,668.67 | 443.71 |
| Russia | 141,927,297 | 17,075,200.00 | 8.31 | 6,592,768.87 | 21.53 |
| Japan | 127,380,000 | 377,835.00 | 337.13 | 145,882.85 | 873.17 |

**10 Least Populated Countries of the World and Population Density**

| Country | Population | Area (sq. km.) | Person per sq. km. | Area (sq. mi.) | Persons per sq. mi. |
|---|---|---|---|---|---|
| Andorra | 84,082 | 468 | 179.66 | 180.7 | 465.32 |
| Dominica | 67,000 | 754 | 88.86 | 291.12 | 230.14 |
| Marshall Islands | 63,000 | 181 | 348.07 | 69.88 | 901.49 |
| Saint Kitts & Nevis | 38,960 | 261 | 149.27 | 100.77 | 386.61 |
| Liechtenstein | 35,904 | 160 | 224.4 | 61.78 | 581.19 |
| Monaco | 33,000 | 2 | 16,500.00 | 0.77 | 42,734.82 |
| San Marino | 32,386 | 61 | 530.92 | 23.55 | 1,375.07 |
| Palau | 20,000 | 458 | 43.67 | 176.83 | 113.1 |
| Tuvalu | 10,000 | 26 | 384.62 | 10.04 | 996.15 |
| Nauru | 10,000 | 21 | 476.19 | 8.11 | 1,233.33 |
| Vatican City | 800 | 1 | 800 | 0.39 | 2,071.99 |

Adapted from World Atlas. Retrieved from www.worldatlas.com

are places in the developing world where the population density is so very high that the land cannot begin to support the human life in the area, and the poverty is devastating.

## 15.4b Population and Ecology

How large a population can survive on the earth's resources? The study of the interrelationships between living organisms and the environment is called **ecology**. In the case of human beings, the concern is that the environment will not be able to support human life with the necessary food, water, and other basic necessities if the population should get too large.

Interestingly, theories about the relationship between population and the environment were initially developed during a period when it was feared that there were too few people to produce what society needed. Between 1450 and 1750, European traders were exporting Europe's products in exchange for gold and silver. In some areas, however, one-third to one-half of the population had been killed by the plague. Many writers argued that if the population were larger, there would be a better ecological balance. More products could be produced and exported, which would bring more gold and silver to the merchants. If the population were large enough, labor would be cheap, wages could be kept low, the people would have little to spend, and increases in imports would not be needed. Thus, all increased production could be traded for gold, silver, or merchandise valuable to the traders.

**Ecology**
The study of the interrelationships between living organisms and the environment

The political activity of this period was designed to encourage a high birth rate. The birth rate did increase, and by 1750, writers had begun to worry about overpopulation. The most famous of this second group of writers was Thomas Malthus.

## 15.4c Malthus's Theory of Population

Thomas Robert Malthus (1766–1834) argued in his *Essay on the Principle of Population* that because of the strong attraction between the two sexes, the population could increase by multiples, doubling every 25 years. According to **Malthusian theory**, the population would increase much more rapidly than the food supply. That is, the population would increase in a geometric progression (i.e., 2, 4, 8, 16, 32, and so on), while the food supply would increase in an arithmetical progression (i.e., 1, 2, 3, 4, 5, and so on). The predicted result was a runaway population growth with insufficient food to feed the exploding numbers of people. Malthus believed that the more intensively land was farmed, the less the land would produce, and that even by expanding farmlands, food production would not keep up with population growth. Malthus contended that the population would eventually grow so large that food production would be insufficient, and famine and crowding would cause widespread suffering and would increase the death rate—acting as nature's check on overpopulation. Malthus suggested, as an alternative, that the birth rate be decreased, especially through postponing marriage until a later age.



Malthusian theory created much debate. Writers such as John Stuart Mill and the economist John Maynard Keynes supported his theory. Others have argued against it. Karl Marx, for example, contended that starvation was caused by the unequal distribution of the wealth and its accumulation by capitalists.

During the depression of the 1930s, the debate changed because the birth rate fell sharply in industrial nations. Some predicted that the human species would die out—first the Caucasians, then other races. Schemes were proposed to encourage families to have more children by giving them allowances for each child born. Many economists, however, believed that even in societies with smaller populations, people could prosper and industry could grow if the provided wealth were redistributed to poor families to increase consumption. Government spending on programs for the poor and unemployed could be increased; low interest rates could be used to encourage spending on houses, cars, and other consumer goods.

The birth rate rose sharply after World War II, especially in the underdeveloped nations; people starved in Bangladesh, Africa, and India. Birth control programs were instituted, and it was argued that the only way to eliminate starvation was to reduce the birth rate. Malthusian theory became popular once again. Malthus's contention that food production could not increase rapidly was much debated when new technology began to give farmers much greater yields. Malthus's contentions were revised. The **neo-Malthusian theory** developed, revising his theory to include more information—such as taking into account the effects of technology—but still predicting the fact that population cannot grow indefinitely without dire consequences.

The debate continues, nevertheless; and some social thinkers continue to believe that population explosion is not necessarily a threat. The French sociologist Dupreel (1977) argued that an increasing population would spur rapid innovation and development to solve problems, whereas a stable population would be complacent and less likely to progress.

**Malthusian theory**

The theory proposed by Thomas Malthus stating that population expands much faster than the food supply, resulting in starvation for much of the population when it grows too large

## 15.4d World Food Distribution Today

Before World War II, Africa, India, and Asia exported grain to other nations, primarily to the industrial nations of Europe (George, 1977). Why, then, are people in these underdeveloped nations starving today?

Some analysts argue that the land in overpopulated areas has been farmed too intensively to provide food for large populations and thus has been ruined. Even the

**Neo-Malthusian theory**

Revision of Malthusian theory about food production and population growth that includes more information, such as taking into account the effects of technology

United States, with its comparatively low population density, has lost 10%–15% of its farmland through soil erosion since the time of the European immigration (Humphrey & Buttel, 1982). In parts of Asia, Latin America, and Africa, the problem is much worse because overuse of the land is causing it to deteriorate very rapidly. In Africa, the size of the Sahara Desert is estimated to be increasing by 30 miles a year because the land cannot sustain the population using it.

Other observers of the world food situation have criticized American corporations for creating the world food shortage. They contend that because we had a surplus of grain, we encouraged underdeveloped nations to grow nonfood cash crops, such as cotton and rubber, or nonnutritious foods, such as coffee, tea, and sugar. The United States would lend money and supply fertilizer and farm equipment only to nations that agreed to grow products needed in the United States. In Brazil, for example, the United States encouraged soybean production, while American corporations own all the soybean-processing plants and receive most of the profit from soybean production.

*Overuse of land in areas, including the U.S., Africa, India, and Asia, has led to deterioration and starving populations. The Sahara Desert in northern Africa is estimated to be increasing by 30 miles each year because the land cannot sustain the population using it. (iStockphoto)*

In the past few decades, many underdeveloped nations have become increasingly dependent on American grain imports because they use their own land for nonfood products. In the 1970s, the price of grains rose dramatically; and critics argue that the United States, having acquired a monopoly of the food supply, increased prices to make enormous profits. Today, the cash crops grown by other nations cannot be sold at prices high enough to buy all the grain needed from the United States. Thus, poor people everywhere starve because they do not have land on which to grow food or the money to buy food, even when enough food is produced in the world to feed its entire population.

## 15.4e Population and Other Natural Resources

Food production and distribution is only one of the problems that occur as the world population increases. As was noted in the introduction to this chapter, environmental problems are serious in nature and global in scope. Humans need water just as we need food, and the earth's large human population is rapidly polluting the available water. Waste from modern life, including the many chemicals that are now produced each year, find their way into small streams and large seas, making the water unfit for human consumption. It also makes water unfit for fish, thereby reducing the hope of turning to the sea as a source of additional food.

The increased population also affects the air we breathe. As the population increases, more and more rural areas become densely settled; and atmospheric pollution is exacerbated by the toxic elements emanating from cars, planes, industrial smoke, and other sources. Almost every human activity generates dust; when these particles become airborne, they seed the clouds and increase the rainfall. On the east coast, especially in Canada and New England in recent years, pollution from Midwestern industries has caused acid rain to fall, killing fish and changing the composition of the land on which it falls. Another pollution-related problem is that as the cloud cover increases with airborne pollutants, it has a *greenhouse effect*, holding warmth from the sun close to the earth rather than letting it escape into the upper atmosphere. As a result, some scientists suggest that the warming climate is responsible for the both the reconfiguration of icebergs and the creation of new ones, which could raise the sea level and flood coastal areas. In 2012, a 46-square-mile chunk of ice broke off of Greenland's Peterman Glacier. This created an iceberg twice the size of Manhattan. These types of changes in the composition of Arctic regions, such as Greenland, can have significant consequences like increases in sea levels, changes in atmospheric conditions, changes in animal and plant life, and other far reaching environmental outcomes (Huffington Post, 2012).

Our forests are also being rapidly depleted. Trees are cut down to make room for people, to provide fuel, and to provide wood for houses, furniture, and other products. The loss of forests not only means the loss of these wood products but also affects the ecological balance between the earth and the atmosphere. In particular, plants consume an excess of carbon dioxide and give off an excess of oxygen; this crucially affects the ratio of oxygen to carbon dioxide in the air we breathe.

As these natural resources are lost—and the loss will be rapid if we do not use resources wisely—conflict will occur. People who lack the necessary resources to survive will fight those who do have resources. Although conflict in the world is usually expressed in political terms, these conflicts are not based on political ideology. They are conflicts over scarce resources. The United States involvement in the Middle East is motivated largely by our desire to safeguard our supplies of oil. Latin American countries such as El Salvador and Nicaragua cannot provide for the peasants who have been driven off their land by the larger agriculturalists—a dilemma that induces revolution. As suggested by conflict theory, if revolutions and inequalities are to be eliminated, increasing population must be accompanied by an end to the unregulated freedom to pursue wealth and a more equitable rationing of the world's scarce resources.

*The increase in the world population is affecting natural resources such as forests, which are rapidly being cut down to provide fuel, houses, furniture, and other products, as well as to make room for people. Such loss of natural resources negatively affects the ecological balance between the earth and the atmosphere, which in turn will cause conflict as people fight to survive the negative effects.* (iStockphoto)

**thinking** SOCIOLOGICALLY

Suppose that you were hired by an environmental protection group to help lobby for stricter environmental regulation. How could you use knowledge of demography and population to help in gathering public support for environmental protection?

## 15.4f Political Policies Regarding Population

Although a more even distribution of resources would solve some of the world's hunger problems, and careful planning would help us to preserve what resources we still have, ultimately, our population must be controlled. The current policies of most governments are now aimed at reducing the birth rate to improve the standard of living. After World War II, Japan initiated a program legalizing abortion and encouraging contraception. Soon afterward, India and most other Asian nations began such programs. In spite of programs to discourage births, however, many nations still experienced a population explosion. China toughened its policies most severely, limiting Chinese families to having only one child.

In the 1960s, the United States began to offer millions of dollars worth of contraceptive aids, especially intrauterine devices and birth control pills, to underdeveloped countries that requested help in controlling their populations. The federal government also provided funds to states to open family-planning clinics and disseminate information about contraceptives in this country. These programs have succeeded in reducing birth rates in many nations; however, they have also been severely criticized, for several reasons.

First, some of the contraceptive methods used in underdeveloped nations are those considered unsafe and banned in the United States. Users in other countries, not warned of the dangers, unknowingly risk infection, heart attacks, strokes, and death when they use these contraceptives. Second, lowering the birth rate in underdeveloped nations deprives parents of children, who are an asset in rural areas. They can help carry water and grow food on family plots and care for their parents in illness and old age. Thus, the policies implemented to reduce poverty in industrial nations could well increase poverty for families living in some rural areas. When planning policy, it is crucial to consider all the factors at work in the countries that will be affected.

## 15.4g Zero Population Growth

The goal of current world population policy is **zero population growth**, which is achieved when parents have only two children, just enough to replace themselves. If this practice were followed, the population would remain the same generation after generation. In reality, of course, some people do not have children, and some children die before reaching adulthood; thus, zero population growth could be attained if couples averaged slightly more than two children each. Given current rates of infant mortality and the number of women who actually have children, the population would remain stable if couples averaged 2.1 children. In the United States, the rate has been steady at 1.9, below the zero growth rate. Many underdeveloped nations have much higher birth rates, however, so the world population explosion is continuing. Increasing population and associated ecological problems will continue to be crucial issues in the future. A more equal and careful distribution of resources is essential to preventing starvation and pollution. This relationship between population and ecology illustrates the need for a sociological understanding of the interrelationships between population size and social institutions.

**Zero population growth**

A population policy that encourages parents to have no more than two children to limit the growth of the population

### thinking SOCIOLOGICALLY

1. Predict what the future would be like, both the good and the bad, if all birth control and abortion were eliminated from the world.
2. Predict what the future would be like, both the good and the bad, if the entire world achieved zero population growth.

# CHAPTER 15 Wrapping it up

## Summary

1. All societies differentiate behavior by age. Age, an ascribed status, includes social expectations about appropriate behaviors for persons who have lived a certain number of years. *Aging*, the process of growing older, is accompanied by biological, psychological, and social changes as people move through the life course.
2. The systematic study of the aging process is known as *gerontology*. *Social gerontology*, a subfield of gerontology, focuses on the social and cultural aspects of age and of the aging process.
3. Expectations about the behavior considered appropriate for people of a given age are age norms. Many such norms reflect inaccurate stereotypes and may lead to ageism, which is prejudice and discrimination based on age.
4. The elderly are considered to be those age 65 and over. Some gerontologists differentiate between the *young-old* (55–74) and the *old-old* (75 and over). Demographically, the percentage of elderly people in the total population is increasing, as is life expectancy, although there are considerable variations due to sex and race. Interestingly, the life expectancy of those who reach old age has increased very little, and the life span is basically unchanged. The proportion of older people who do not work is increasing in comparison to the younger working population; this proportion is known as the *old-age dependency ratio*.
5. The social characteristics of the elderly vary widely according to sex, marital status, living arrangements, geographical distribution, labor force participation, and other factors. Women greatly outnumber men, and many women are widows. Most of the elderly live in their own homes or with their families. Geographically, they tend to live in metropolitan areas, and they are heavily concentrated in some states. The proportion of the elderly in the labor force has dropped considerably over the past several decades.
6. The lifestyles of the elderly vary greatly, depending on their social class and income. Women and blacks are the groups most likely to live in poverty. The most common source of income for the aged is Social Security. A minimal income is available to those not on Social Security through the Supplemental Security Income (SSI) program.
7. Demography is the study of population statistics. Demographers study census data on the number of people in the population and records of births and deaths to compute the birth and death rates.
8. The crude birth and death rates are computed by determining the number of births and deaths per one thousand people. Neither of these measures takes age or sex into account, even though these factors also influence the number of births and deaths.
9. Populations remain stable when people are born at the same rate at which they die. Population increases when the birth rate exceeds the death rate and decreases when the death rate exceeds the birth rate.
10. Populations may also change through migration. Push factors are conditions that encourage people to move out of an area; pull factors encourage people to move into an area.
11. The size of the population affects each of us quite personally. Whether we are born into a growing or a shrinking population has a bearing on our education, the age at which we marry, our ability to get a job, the taxes we pay, and many other aspects of our lives.
12. The population explosion of the past 200 years occurred because of improvements in nutrition and sanitation, which lowered the death rate. In industrial nations, the birth rate has also dropped, but rapid population growth continues in many Third World countries.
13. Population densities vary greatly in different parts of the world. Generally, the most densely populated countries are industrialized nations of Europe and Japan.
14. *Ecology* is the interrelationship between organisms and their environment.

15. Malthusian theory states that because the population grows faster than the food supply, starvation is inevitable if population growth is not controlled. Although his arguments have received much support through the years, critics contend that the world produces enough food to feed everyone and the problem arises because food is distributed unequally.
16. Some underdeveloped nations raise cash crops that neither feed the people nor bring in enough money to buy food. Some observers believe that the United States, which is the world's largest food exporter, encouraged other countries to grow nonfood cash crops and then, having cornered the grain market, raised prices to increase profits.
17. Other problems affecting food production, vis-à-vis population, stem from pollution of the air and water and the destruction of forests.
18. Most nations are now attempting to reduce their birth rates, and contraceptives have been distributed throughout the world for this purpose.
19. The goal of world population policy is zero population growth, calculated to be an average of 2.1 children per family.

## Discussion Questions

1. List a number of age norms that exist for teenagers or those in their early 20s. How would you explain their existence and differentiation from those existing for younger or older persons?
2. Discuss some ways in which shifts in the dependency ratio might affect family life. How have changes in the dependency ratio affected life in your family over the past two or three generations?
3. What types of social changes, social problems, and social benefits might occur from the increase in life expectancy?
4. Discuss changes in marital status and living arrangements by age. What types of factors other than widowhood affect marital status and living arrangements?
5. It was stated that the elderly are heavily concentrated in a few states. Why? What are some social implications (recreation, transportation, consumer spending, healthcare, etc.) of this geographical distribution?
6. Discuss how the age and sex of a population can affect its fertility and mortality rates.
7. Based on the conflict perspective, discuss how migration can maintain the position of elites in a society.
8. Based on a functionalist viewpoint, describe when a high fertility rate would be functional and when it would not be.
9. What are some factors that could lead to rapid changes in the rate of population change? Using this information, what kinds of changes do you predict in the rate of population change in your lifetime?
10. Assume that because of increasing rates of cancer and AIDS, the life expectancy of the United States declines dramatically. How would that change society when you reach age 60?
11. If the world were purely capitalist, what would happen to the rates of starvation in the world? Why? What if it were purely socialist?
12. Discuss all of the ways in which your life has been shaped by the year of your birth and the number of people your age.
13. Discuss how the relationship between population and ecology is evident today.

I NEED THIS OVERPRICED SOFTWARE FOR COLLEGE
BUT THEY TOOK AWAY MY TORRENTS <3 :(
SO YOU THOUGHT YOU COULD TAKE OVER THE INTERNET.
TELL ME ALL ABOUT HOW YOU FAILED.
@GlobalProtestRS

CHAPTER 16

# Social Change and Social Movements

## SYNOPSIS

Focal Point

## CENSORSHIP

After having read much of this book, you probably realize that one of the central themes of sociology—and some would argue, one of the central themes of a liberal arts education—is the notion that many aspects of social reality are not defined absolutely. For example, political and religious beliefs, standards of morality, and the cultural value of specific works of art and literature are often open to interpretation. Simply stated, people often disagree about what is true, false, good, or bad. When this is the case, competing groups often attempt—through censorship—to manipulate public opinion to accept their respective interpretations. Understanding how public opinion is shaped is an important topic in the study of collective behavior.

One of the most famous cases of censorship in the late twentieth century, and one which brought censorship to international attention, resulted in a death warrant—issued by the Iranian leader at the time, Ayatollah Khomeini—against author Salman Rushdie for his book, *The Satanic Verses.* Khomeini and his followers regarded the book as blasphemy against the Muslim religion, the belief system that lies at the heart of Iranian social and political life. Censorship—the prohibition of some types of information—is deeply rooted and openly espoused in many cultures of the Middle East and Asia, and in countries with repressive governments. Within the past few years, censorship in China has become a very contentious issue as the Chinese government has tried, largely unsuccessfully, to limit the freedom of discussion about sensitive issues that could diminish the power of the government. However, censorship also occurs in free countries, including the United States.

*Censorship is a way to prohibit some types of information in order to manipulate public opinion. (iStockphoto)*

Censorship has long been a controversial issue in the United States, even though the First Amendment to the U.S. Constitution decrees that, "Congress should make no law ... abridging the freedom of speech, or of the press." For example in 1798, second President of the United States John Adams signed into law the Alien and Sedition Acts, which made it a crime to speak, write, or publish materials "with intent to defame ... or bring into contempt or disrepute" members of the government. Under this law, some newspapers were shut down and their editors imprisoned. (It is interesting to note that in 1991, the leaders of the reform movement for democracy in the Soviet Union temporarily shut down *Pravda*, a major newspaper in the Soviet Union, because of its overtly communistic orientation.) The Alien and Sedition Acts expired in 1801 under President Thomas Jefferson. Jefferson argued that people should have free access to all information because they would be able to recognize falsehood from the truth (Orr, 1990). Jefferson felt that Americans should be free to voice any opinion or to express themselves in any way, as long as it does not directly cause harm to any individual or to society. The rationale for this position is that censorship would be a greater harm to America's ideals than the expression itself.

In spite of the dysfunctions of censorship, censorship is still a major issue in the United States. In 1990, many members of the U.S. Congress demanded that the National Endowment of the Arts (NEA) cease its funding of offensive art after Robert Mapplethorpe—a recipient of NEA funding—displayed photographs depicting acts of homosexuality and other sexual behavior.

More recently, the issue of censorship has been in the news surrounding songs written in protest to the Iraqi invasion. Many country stations throughout much of the United States pulled the recording artists Dixie Chicks from their play lists after Natalie Maines, the lead singer, expressed embarrassment and shame that the president of the United States was from Texas, the state that is also home to the country trio.

With the global spread of electronic communication through such social networking vehicles as Facebook, Twitter, Instagram and the like, censorship has become an important issue in developing countries and countries undergoing rapid changes. In 2012, for example, the Chinese government issued regulations requiring Internet users to provide their real names to providers and assigned Internet providers responsibility for deleting "forbidden postings and reporting them to authorities" (Bradsher, 2012). This ruling was part of stepped-up censorship regulations during a period when the revelation of sexual and financial scandals led to the resignation of numerous Chinese officials. Cyber-censorship became a worldwide concern after the reporting of events surrounding "Arab Spring"—social movements pertaining to the democratization of a number of Middle Eastern countries—were severely curtailed by Arab governments. According to the press freedom group Reporters Without Borders, "Never have so many countries been affected by some form of online censorship, whether arrests or harassment of netizens, online surveillance, website blocking or the adoption of repressive Internet laws" (Marshall, 2012).

Perhaps now more than ever, with the widespread use of social networking via the Internet, the issue of censorship raises a number of important sociological questions. How are definitions of social reality created and maintained? Who benefits from censorship—society, or the groups that are attempting to prohibit the dissemination of some information? What part does censorship play in accelerating or inhibiting social movements? Should opinions that differ from our own and that could be hurtful to some groups be protected? Is freedom of speech being taken away? Does complete freedom of speech for everyone limit the freedoms of some? How far is too far when speaking over the public airwaves? Who has the power to determine what is censored? This chapter addresses these and other questions about collective behavior and social movements.

The towns and cities of the United States and the rest of the world have been changing rapidly for many years. The communities in which many of you were brought up have probably undergone dramatic changes during your lifetime, or even since you entered college. Some of these changes are readily apparent: one of your favorite old buildings may have been razed to make way for a new office complex, or perhaps a new park has been created near your home. Other changes, although less tangible, are equally important. The streets on which you played on as a child may now be considered unsafe after dark. You may have trouble finding a summer job because several large businesses have left your city.

Likewise, whole societies have undergone change, some quicker than others. The reasons for changes such as these are many. We touched on a number of them in earlier chapters. Form of government, the family, changing gender roles, bureaucracies, and ethnicity—the list of factors that influence change is vast. Social change from the community level to the societal level and the forces that underlie them are the subject of this chapter.

# 16.1 THE ORIGIN AND DEVELOPMENT OF COMMUNITIES

A **community** is a collection of people within a geographic area who share some degree of mutual identification, interdependence, or organized activity. Sociologists apply this term to a variety of social groups, including small North American Indian tribes, towns, communes, and large urban centers. As this chapter shows, urban communities have become larger and more diverse throughout the course of human history.

## 16.1a Early Community and Urban Development

**Community**
A collection of people within a geographic area who share some degree of mutual identification, interdependence, or organization of activities

The first communities, which originated more than 35,000 years ago, were small bands that hunted and foraged for food. Their means of subsistence dictated the size and activity of the group; they were nomadic, moving frequently to new areas as food ran out. There were few status distinctions among members of these communities, although males and older persons had somewhat higher status and more power than others. Apparently, there were few conflicts among hunting-and-gathering bands, and there was little evidence of war-making tools or group attacks.

Roughly 10,000 years ago, humans learned to produce and store their food. This Neolithic revolution, as it is called, ushered in the era of horticultural communities. **Horticultural communities** were essentially small-scale farming communities that relied on tools such as the hoe to till the soil. Though horticulture is tedious, back-breaking work, it doubled the number of people that the land could support—from one to nearly two persons per square mile (David, 1973). Stable communities developed around fertile agricultural regions; and in the more fertile areas, a surplus of food was produced, which freed some members of the community from agricultural activities. As agricultural techniques improved, horticultural communities became larger and more diverse. Artisans who produced the tools and implements necessary for survival were the first specialists in history (Childe, 1951). It was during this era that the first urban communities emerged. Urban communities grew slowly for the next several thousand years because of the inefficiency of horticultural techniques—it took about 50 horticulturists to produce enough surplus to support one urban resident—and also because of the primitive political and social organization (Davis K., 1973)

*Nomadic communities frequently move to new places as food runs out. (AP Wide World Photo)*

## 16.1b Pre-Industrial Urban Communities

The introduction of metals, the invention of the plow, the use of animals for transportation and farming, and the refinement of irrigation techniques helped usher in a new era in human history around 3000 BC—the Agrarian Age (Lenski, 1966). The development of writing and counting and the evolution of political and social organizations were also essential to the spread of agrarian society. These technological advances increased surpluses so that still more people were freed from agriculture. Cities grew larger and their activities became more diverse. Around 1600 BC, Thebes, the capital of Egypt, had a population of over 200,000. Athens had a population of 150,000 or so during the same period (Childe, 1951). By AD 100, Rome had an estimated population of over 500,000.

This trend of urban growth ended when Rome fell in the fifth century AD and subsequent wars and plagues reduced the size of cities. The rate of agricultural innovation was slow because human energies were redirected toward the technology of war. The social system became more rigid; status and occupations were determined on the basis of heredity rather than achievement or ability.

In the eleventh century, cities, especially those along natural routes and junctures, began to flourish after feudal wars subsided. As the food surplus increased, the population in the cities became more specialized. In fourteenth-century Paris, for example, tax rolls listed 157 different trades (Russell, 1972). In addition to artisans, cities also had specialists in other areas, such as government, military service, education, and religion. Each major urban activity led to the development of an institution devoted to its performance and churches, shops, marketplaces, city halls, and palaces became the prominent features of medieval cities.

**Horticultural communities**
Small-scale farming that relies on tools such as the hoe to till the soil

## 16.1c Community Development in the Industrial Era

It was not until the end of the eighteenth century that cities began to grow rapidly, due largely to the effects of the Industrial Revolution. The social and economic forces that converged at this time eventually changed Western Europe and later the United States from rural to urban societies. The growth of the number of people who live in urban rather than rural areas and the subsequent development of different values and lifestyles is referred to as **urbanization**. Agricultural innovations—crop rotation, soil fertilization, and the selective breeding of animals—brought larger and larger surpluses.

At the same time, the development of manufacturing in the cities attracted many people. As the nineteenth century progressed, cities became much larger and grew into centers of commerce and production. At the same time, however, they were also the locus of poverty and disease. As migration from rural areas increased, the city population became more heterogeneous. The variety of occupations, ethnic backgrounds, dialects, and lifestyles in these urban areas stood in sharp contrast to the relatively homogeneous populations of small towns and rural communities.

Population diversity, poverty, cramped living quarters, inadequate garbage disposal and sewage facilities, and other social and economic problems placed a tremendous strain on the urban political order. Cities became centers of unrest. Riots and revolutions, strikes by workers, and numerous clashes among members of different social groups were a significant part of nineteenth-century urban history. Many of the problems that arose in European cities during this era persist, to some degree, in all Western nations and in Developing World nations, in a different way.

Most major cities in developing countries—such as Calcutta, India—have "squatter" settlements. *(AP Wide World Photo)*

## 16.1d Developing World Urbanization

Prior to 1900, urbanization outside of Western Europe and North America was limited in both scale and extent to colonial expansion. Throughout this century, however, the situation has been changing dramatically. During the past 50 years, while the urban population increased in the more developed regions of the world, the increase was most dramatic in Developing World countries, the least industrialized countries. In Latin America and Africa, for example, the urban population increased eightfold.

By the end of World War II, the colonial powers had relinquished control to the local governments of the colonies they had created. In each developing nation, one city became the focus of change and progress. Because these focus cities had improved health conditions and facilities, more jobs, and better education, they drew masses of people. The newly created governments, usually controlled by military juntas or other totalitarian regimes, were unable to keep pace with this rapid growth, however; and those who had moved from the country found that they had exchanged lives of rural poverty for lives of urban poverty.

Much of this Developing World urban growth became concentrated in what are called "squatter" settlements, where people would settle temporarily—squat—along railways, highways, the banks of streams, or on vacant government land. Most major cities in developing countries have squatter areas: Manila in the Philippines; Calcutta, India; Lima, Peru; and Saigon, Vietnam. These areas (a) lacked all the basic amenities, (b) were physically decrepit and highly disorganized, and (c) became centers of squalor, illiteracy, sickness, and human depravity. However, they played an important role in solving the housing shortage and the other complex problems associated with migration from rural to urban centers. On closer examination, they

**Urbanization**
The growth of the number of people who live in urban rather than rural areas and the process of taking on organizational patterns and lifestyles characteristics of urban areas

were found to provide access to the jobs and services of the central city. Many squatter areas developed highly organized self-help efforts over a period of a few years. The residents gave shelter, security, and assistance to one another; and many of these settlements provided opportunities to continue rural values and ways of living, thereby easing the transition to the density and fast pace of the city.

To Western observers, the solution to these problem areas was to relocate the inhabitants and provide housing, usually outside the central city limits. However, these solutions rarely solved the problems of most squatters because they involved heavy costs for investment (and interest), maintenance, and transportation and did not originate in the self-help efforts of the squatters themselves. Often funded by developed nations, these efforts tended to follow patterns established in the Western world, ignoring the values and priorities of the Developing World residents themselves. They also tended to overlook the importance of urban community services and failed to follow through on a long-term basis with a commitment to the residents themselves. These problems, which have existed in most Developing World countries throughout modern history, are more severe today than ever before because of rapid urban population growth.

**BVT *Lab***

Flashcards are available for this chapter at **www.BVTLab.com**

This rapid urban population growth in the Developing World and elsewhere shows no sign of abatement, either. Over 250 cities in the world have populations of a million or more. Five of the largest metropolises have over 20 million inhabitants each. In addition, we can see from Table 16-1 that most of the world's mega-cities are located in the Developing World. Given the extreme levels of poverty found in many of these large and densely populated areas, one may question whether solutions are available to deal with the enormous problems and whether living conditions can be made humane and livable. Topics related to this issue are addressed later in this chapter.

# 16.2 URBANIZATION IN THE UNITED STATES

## 16.2a Population Trends

The major population shift from rural to urban areas in the US did not begin until the Civil War. An *urban area*, according to the United States Bureau of the Census, is a city or town that has at least 2,500 inhabitants. In 1800, 6% of the population of the United States lived in urban areas; this increased to 20% by 1860. The period of greatest urban development took place during the 60-year period between 1860 and 1920; by 1920, slightly more than half the population lived in urban areas. This figure has continued to increase. America's urban population increased by 12.1% from 2000 to 2010, compared to the national overall population growth rate of 9.7%. Urban areas currently account for 80.7% of the U.S. population, compared to 79.0% in 2000 (Proximity, 2013). Table 16-2 shows the size of the 10 largest cities in the United States in 2010 as compared to 1990.

*The large, densely populated cities of the early 1900s have given way to the growth of metropolitan areas.* (iStockphoto)

The shift of the population from rural to urban areas has paralleled the growth of jobs and opportunities in the industrial and service sectors of the economy. Because of their early industrial and commercial development, northeastern states such as New York and Pennsylvania were among the first to urbanize. A few years later, Midwestern cities such as Chicago and Detroit became large urban centers. The Western states experienced strong urban growth only after World War II, as a result of the growth of the defense industries.

**Table 16-1** World's Largest Metropolitan Areas, 2012

Numbers shown include population within the recognized metro area of the city, and they include people living in the immediate surrounding area outside of the established border of the city.

| World Rank | City | Country | Metro Population |
|---|---|---|---|
| 1 | Tokyo | Japan | 32,450,000 |
| 2 | Seóul | South Korea | 20,550,000 |
| 3 | Mexico City | Mexico | 20,450,000 |
| 4 | New York City | United States of America | 19,750,000 |
| 5 | Mumbai | India | 19,200,000 |
| 6 | Jakarta | Indonesia | 18,900,000 |
| 7 | Sáo Paulo | Brazil | 18,850,000 |
| 8 | Delhi | India | 18,680,000 |
| 9 | Õsaka/Kobe | Japan | 17,350,000 |
| 10 | Shanghai | China | 16,650,000 |
| 11 | Manila | Philippines | 16,300,000 |
| 12 | Los Angeles | United States of America | 15,250,000 |
| 13 | Calcutta | India | 15,100,000 |
| 14 | Moscow | Russian Fed. | 15,000,000 |
| 15 | Cairo | Egypt | 14,450,000 |
| 16 | Lagos | Nigeria | 13,488,000 |
| 17 | Buenos Aries | Argentina | 13,170,000 |
| 18 | London | United Kingdom | 12,875,000 |
| 19 | Beijing | China | 12,500,000 |
| 20 | Karachi | Pakistan | 11,800,000 |
| 21 | Dhaka | Bangladesh | 10,979,000 |
| 22 | Rio de Janeiro | Brazil | 10,556,000 |
| 23 | Tianjin | China | 10,239,000 |
| 24 | Paris | France | 9,638,000 |
| 25 | Istanbul | Turkey | 9,413,000 |
| 26 | Lima | Peru | 7,443,000 |
| 27 | Tehrãn | Iran | 7,380,000 |
| 28 | Bangkok | Thailand | 7,221,000 |
| 29 | Chicago | United States of America | 6,945,000 |
| 30 | Bogotá | Columbia | 6,834,000 |

Adapted from U.S. Census Bureau and *Times Atlas of the World*

## 16.2b The Metropolitan Community

The large, densely populated cities of the early 1900s have given way to the growth of metropolitan areas. The U.S. Bureau of the Census describes a **metropolitan statistical area (MSA)** as a large population nucleus, together with adjacent communities that have a high degree of social and economic integration with that nucleus. The metropolitan community is the organization of people and institutions that perform the routine functions necessary to sustain the existence of both the city and the area around it.

**Metropolitan statistical area (MSA)**
A county or group of counties with a central city and a population of at least 50,000, a density of at least 1,000 persons per square mile, and outlying areas that are socially and economically integrated with the central city

The growth of metropolitan areas has been rapid and dramatic. Because of new developments in technology, in transportation, and in social structures, the concentration of large numbers of people has become possible. These same developments have

**Table 16-2** 25 Largest Cities in the Unites States, 2010 with Comparisons to 1990

| | 4/1/2010 Census Population | 4/1/1990 Census Population | Size Rank 2010 | Size Rank 1990 |
|---|---|---|---|---|
| New York, NY | 8,175,133 | 7,322,564 | 1 | 1 |
| Los Angeles, CA | 3,792,621 | 3,485,398 | 2 | 2 |
| Chicago, IL | 2,695,598 | 2,783,726 | 3 | 3 |
| Houston, TX | 2,099,451 | 1,630,553 | 4 | 4 |
| Philadelphia, PA | 1,526,006 | 1,585,577 | 5 | 5 |
| Phoenix, AZ | 1,445,632 | 983,403 | 6 | 10 |
| San Antonio, TX | 1,327,407 | 935,933 | 7 | 9 |
| San Diego, CA | 1,307,402 | 1,110,549 | 8 | 6 |
| Dallas, TX | 1,197,816 | 1,006,877 | 9 | 8 |
| San Jose, CA | 945,942 | 782,248 | 10 | 11 |
| Jacksonville, FL | 821,784 | 635,230 | 11 | 15 |
| Indianapolis, IN | 820,445 | 741,952 | 12 | 13 |
| San Francisco, CA | 805,235 | 723,959 | 13 | 14 |
| Austin, TX | 790,390 | 465,622 | 14 | 25 |
| Columbus, OH | 787,033 | 632,910 | 15 | 16 |
| Fort Worth, TX | 741,206 | 447,619 | 16 | 29 |
| Charlotte, NC | 731,424 | 395,934 | 17 | 33 |
| Detroit, MI | 713,777 | 1,027,974 | 18 | 7 |
| El Paso, TX | 649,121 | 515,342 | 19 | 22 |
| Memphis, TN | 646,889 | 610,337 | 20 | 18 |
| Baltimore, MD | 620,961 | 736,014 | 21 | 12 |
| Boston, MA | 617,594 | 574,283 | 22 | 20 |
| Seattle, WA | 608,660 | 516,259 | 23 | 21 |
| Washington, DC | 601,723 | 606,900 | 24 | 19 |
| Nashville-Davidson, TN | 601,222 | 510,784 | 25 | 26 |

Adapted from "Top Fifty Cities in the U.S. by Population and Rank,"
Retrieved from Infoplease.com http://www.infoplease.com/ipa/A0763098.html#ixzz2IcWT5k2Z

also enabled a population dispersed over a wide area to become part of a larger, integrated community.

Metropolitan growth was caused, initially, by a shortage of space for industrial development, new housing, and new highways. Businesses were forced to design their facilities to fit the space that was available. Because streets were narrow and heavily congested, the transportation of goods was tedious and costly. Room for storage and loading was scarce. The land adjacent to the cities was ideal. It was inexpensive, property taxes were low, and businesses could design their facilities to suit their needs. The development of the steam engine and later the electric trolley facilitated the transportation of goods and employees over a wider area. After the 1920s, the increase in motor vehicles and the accompanying growth of highway systems stimulated unprecedented metropolitan development. Trucking became an important method of moving goods and supplies. Manufacturing and industry moved to the suburbs, which drew people and a variety of small businesses and stores to follow. After World War II, hundreds of suburbs developed, each of which had its own government, school system, and public services.

The suburban growth paralleled a slower growth and a recent decline in the population of central cities.

A metropolitan area that extends beyond the city and the MSA is the **megalopolis**, which is a continuous strip of urban and suburban development that may stretch for hundreds of miles. One example exists between Boston and Washington, DC, on the East Coast. This megalopolis covers 10 states, includes hundreds of local governments, and has a population of nearly 50 million. Other megalopolis areas are forming between San Francisco and San Diego on the West Coast and between Chicago and Pittsburgh in the Midwest. Sometime in the next 50 years, half of the United States population may live in one of these three enormous population conglomerations.

**Megalopolis**
A continuous strip of urban and suburban development that may stretch for hundreds of miles

## 16.3 URBAN ECOLOGY

In recent years, *ecology* has come to be associated with the biological and natural world of plants and animals and how they are affected by pollution and other environmental influences. However, the term is also concerned with populations and communities. In this context, it is the study of the interrelationships of people and the environment in which they live. **Urban ecology** is concerned not only with urban spatial arrangements but also with the processes that create and reinforce these arrangements.

**Urban ecology**
The study of the interrelationships between people in urban settings and the social and physical environment in which they live

**Table 16-3** Fastest-Growing Metropolitan Areas in the United States, 2010–2011, by Percentage and by Numeric Increase

| The 10 Fastest Growing Metro Areas from April 1, 2010, to July 1, 2011 | | |
|---|---|---|
| Rank | Area / County | Increased |
| 1 | Kennewick–Pasco–Richland, WA | 4.3% |
| 2 | Austin–Round Rock–San Marcos, TX | 3.9% |
| 3 | Hinesville–Fort Stewart, GA | 3.4% |
| 4 | McAllen–Edinburg–Mission, TX | 3.0% |
| 5 | Raleigh–Cary, NC | 2.9% |
| 6 | Warner Robins, GA | 2.9% |
| 7 | Provo–Orem, UT | 2.7% |
| 8 | Charleston–North Charleston–Summerville, SC | 2.6% |
| 9 | Myrtle Beach–North Myrtle Beach–Conway, SC | 2.6% |
| 10 | Yuma, AZ | 2.6% |
| **The 10 Metro Areas with the Largest Numeric Increase from April 1, 2010, to July 1, 2011** | | |
| 1 | Dallas–Fort Worth–Arlington, TX | 154,774 |
| 2 | Houston–Sugar Land–Baytown, TX | 139,699 |
| 3 | Washington–Arlington–Alexandria, DC, VA, MD, WV | 121,911 |
| 4 | New York–Northern New Jersey–Long Island, NY, NJ, PA | 118,791 |
| 5 | Los Angeles–Long Beach–Santa Ana, CA | 115,964 |
| 6 | Miami–Fort Lauderdale–Pompano Beach, FL | 105,490 |
| 7 | Atlanta–Sandy Springs–Marietta, GA | 90,345 |
| 8 | Riverside–San Bernardino–Ontario, CA | 80,146 |
| 9 | Phoenix–Mesa–Glendale, AZ | 70,349 |
| 10 | Austin–Round Rock–San Marcos, TX | 67,230 |

Adapted from U.S. Census.
Retrieved from http://www.census.gov/newsroom/releases/archives/population/cb12-55.html

## 16.3a Urban Processes

Urban areas are not static; they change continually. The urban environment is formed and transformed by three processes: (1) concentration and deconcentration, (2) ecological specialization, and (3) invasion and succession.

The term **concentration** refers to increasing density of population, services, and institutions in a region. As people migrate to the city to find jobs, living quarters become scarce and the institutions that serve the people become strained. This starts an outward trend, called **deconcentration**, as land values and property taxes increase, and the services and public facilities decline. As a result, the core of the city—the central business district—eventually comes to consist of businesses that use space intensively and can afford to pay the economic costs. These consist of prestigious department and retail stores, financial institutions, high-rise luxury apartments, and other highly profitable ventures.

People, institutions, and services are not randomly distributed in the city. Different groups and activities tend to be concentrated in different areas. This phenomenon is called **ecological specialization**. Commercial and retail trade concerns are generally found in a different part of the city than are manufacturing and production. Similarly, public housing and low-rent tenements are seldom located near suburban residences. The basic principle at work here is that people and institutions usually sort themselves into spatially homogeneous groups. As we have indicated, this homogeneity may result from economic factors: people gravitate toward places they can afford. Personal preference is also influential, as is evident from the existence of ethnic communities and areas that attract people with a particular lifestyle, such as Greenwich Village and Chicago's Gold Coast.

Changes in community membership or land use result from **invasion** by other social groups or land users, which leads to **succession**, as the old occupants and institutions are replaced by the new. One example of invasion and succession is evident when a major industry buys a sizable tract of urban land, destroys the single-family dwellings, and converts the land to commercial or industrial use. In metropolitan Detroit, for example, a huge automobile assembly complex displaced the residents of an ethnic community called "Poletown."

Perhaps the most notable case of invasion and succession is reflected in the changing racial composition of central cities. The "white flight" of the 1960s, 1970s, and 1980s changed the racial composition of large cities—such as Detroit, Atlanta, and Washington, DC—from predominantly white to predominantly black. A related development is the "ghettoization" of inner cities, which occurs as minorities become trapped in central cities that have diminishing tax bases, deteriorating housing, and inefficient public services.

Deteriorating housing and inefficient public services are the result of diminishing tax bases brought on by processes called invasion and succession.

**Concentration**

An urban ecological process in which population, services, and institutions come to be gathered most densely in the areas in which conditions are advantageous

**Deconcentration**

Movement outward from the city because of increases in land values and taxes and declines in services and public facilities

**Ecological specialization**

The concentration of homogeneous groups and activities into different sections or urban areas

**Invasion**

An ecological process in which new types of people, organizations, or activities move into an area occupied by a different type

**Succession**

An urban process of replacing old occupants and institutions with new ones

## 16.3b Urban Structure

The three ecological processes just described are the basis for several different models of urban structure. One of the most influential models during the early development of ecological theory was the **concentric zone model**, developed by Ernest W. Burgess (Burgess, 1925) in the 1920s (see Figure 16-1). According to this theory, a city spreads out equally in all directions from its original center to produce uniform circles of growth. Each zone has its own characteristic land use, population, activities, and institutions. At the center of the city is the business district, which consists of retail stores, civil activity centers, banks, hotels, and institutional administrative offices. Zone 2, the transitional zone, contains older factories, wholesale and light manufacturing businesses, and low-rent tenements. It is in this zone that immigrants or migrants are likely to live when they first arrive in the city. At the turn of the century, first-generation European immigrants made their home in this zone; however, today it is populated by minorities—African Americans, Hispanic Americans, and other ethnic groups. Zone 3 marks the edge of the residential areas and consists of progressively more expensive houses and apartments, ending finally with the commuter zone.

**Concentric zone model**
A model of urban structure, showing that cities grow out equally in all directions from their original centers, producing uniform circles of growth that have their own distinctive land use, population, activities, and institutions

Burgess's zone theory has been criticized since many cities do not fit the concentric zone pattern, which is more characteristic of commercial-industrial cities than of administrative cities. *Commercial-industrial cities* are those built around industry, such as Detroit, Cleveland, and Pittsburgh. These cities have a high proportion of blue-collar

**Figure 16-1** Ecological Models of Urban Structure

Three generalizations of the internal structure of cities:

**Districts:**

1. Central business district
2. Wholesale light manufacturing
3. Low-class residential
4. Middle-class residential
5. High-class residential
6. Heavy manufacturing
7. Outlying business district
8. Residential suburb
9. Industrial suburb
10. Commuter zone

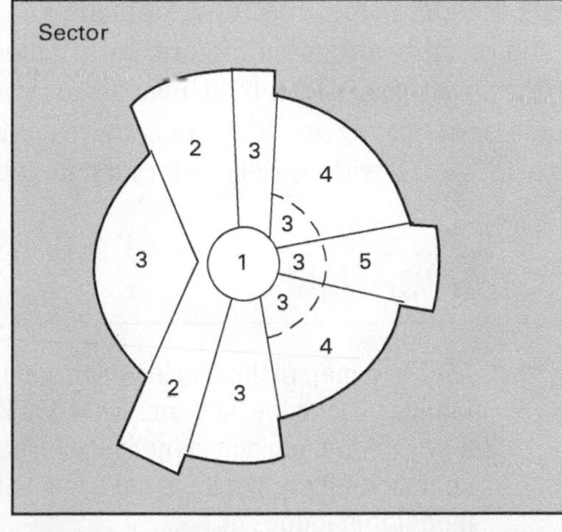


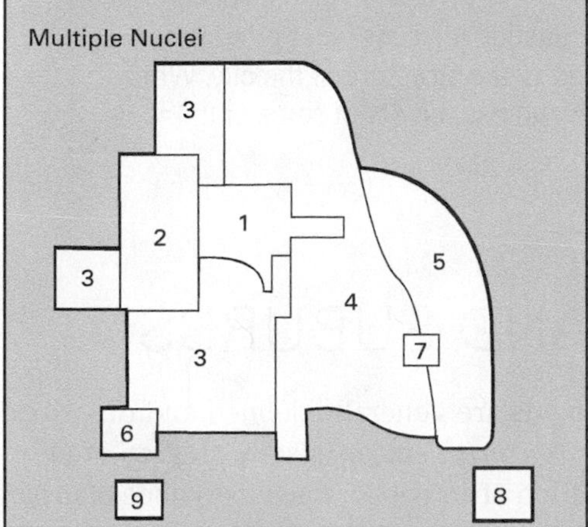


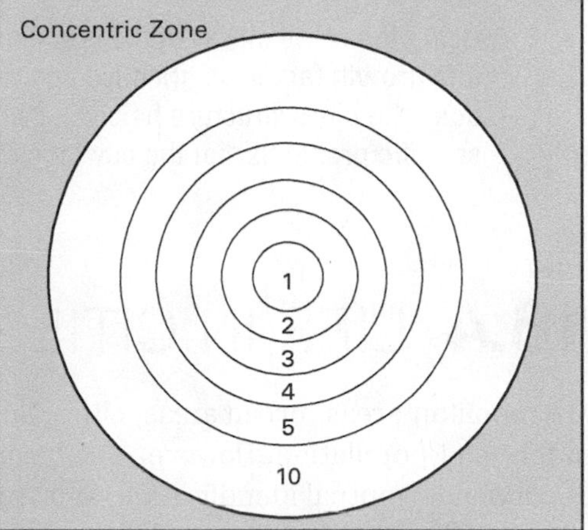


Reprinted from "The Nature of Cities" by Chauncy D. Harris and Edward L. Ullman in Vol. 242 of *The Annals of the American Academy of Political and Social Science*, November 1945.

workers. *Administrative cities*—such as Washington, DC and New York City—rely heavily on government, education, and nonindustrial businesses. Also, it seems to more accurately describe cities such as Chicago that developed at the turn of the century than cities such as Houston, Phoenix, and San Diego that are developing today.

There are two major alternatives to Burgess's theory. One is the **sector model**, formulated by Homer Hoyt (Hoyt, 1939). According to Hoyt, the city is organized into pie-shaped wedges radiating from the central business district. Patterns of land use—industrial, high-income residential, and low-income tenements—tend to extend outward from the city core in internally consistent sectors or wedges. An industrial zone might radiate from the core in one wedge and spread into the suburbs, whereas high-income housing might push outward from the core in another wedge. Hoyt noticed this pattern in several large cities, notably Minneapolis and San Francisco.

*Hoyt noticed patterns of land use in several large cities such as San Francisco. (Shutterstock)*

The third theory of spatial growth rejects the idea of a single urban core or center, maintaining instead that areas of different land use have different centers. This is the **multiple-nuclei model** formulated by Harris and Ullman (1945). In their view, each area expands from its center, and the form of expansion may fit either the concentric or the sector zone models. In many ways, the multiple-nuclei model describes the growth of metropolitan areas better than the growth of central cities.

These three models do not reflect every possible variety or pattern of growth. Urban expansion is influenced by a variety of factors, including rate of migration into the city, cultural and historical precedents for urban development, and the physical characteristics of the land. As a result of these and other factors, Latin American cities, for example, do not fit American growth patterns; cities built near major waterways grow differently from other cities. Sociologists today are developing more complex models of urban development that take into account a wide variety of factors, including social, economic, and cultural variables.

### thinking SOCIOLOGICALLY

1. Locate a map of the city in which you live or a nearby city with which you are familiar. Using the map and what you know about the city, determine which, if any, of the ecological models of urban structure discussed in this chapter it seems to follow. If it does not seem to fit any of these models, try to develop a model that it does fit.
2. Using the same city as in the preceding question, discuss what processes and growth factors might have contributed to the structure of the city. What does the city's structure help you discern and explain about some of the specific problems that the city faces?

**Sector model**
An explanation of the ecology of cities as a series of pie-shaped wedges radiating from the central business district, each with its own characteristics and uses

**Multiple-nuclei model**
The model of urban development showing that cities have areas of different types of land use, each of which has its own center or nucleus

## 16.4 LIFE IN CITIES AND SUBURBS

Metropolitan areas, urban areas, cities, and towns are generally defined and described in terms of population. However, the term *community* suggests some degree of interdependence, mutual identification, or organization of activities. The emergence of urban communities has altered human lifestyles and values. The size, complexity, and density of urban communities have given rise to new forms of social organization, new behaviors, and new attitudes. One of the major questions with which sociologists have grappled is why urban communities are different from rural areas in so many ways, besides just the fact that they are larger and more densely populated. Sociologists have long recognized that there are qualitative differences between urban and rural life; Ferdinand Tönnies (1887), a German sociologist, made a distinction in this regard over a century ago. He called the small, rural villages of his boyhood gemeinschaft (communities) and the centers of activity *gesellschaft* (associations).

A **gemeinschaft** community is characterized by a sense of solidarity and a common identity. It is a primary community rooted in tradition. Relationships among neighbors are intimate and personal, and there is a strong emphasis on shared values and sentiments—a "we" feeling. People frequently interact with one another and tend to establish deep, long-term relationships. Many small towns and communes have these characteristics.

A **gesellschaft** community, in contrast, is based on diverse economic, political, and social interrelationships. It is characterized by individualism, mobility, impersonality, the pursuit of self-interest, and an emphasis on progress rather than tradition. Shared values and total personal involvement become secondary. People live and work together because it is necessary or convenient, and people are viewed more in terms of their roles than as unique individuals. In a large city, for example, one is likely to interact with a police officer as a public servant or authority figure that has stereotyped characteristics and obligations. In a small town, on the other hand, residents would be likely to know a police officer personally. Rather than viewing the officer as a manifestation of a certain form of authority, one would know the officer as an individual with unique character traits. Historically, there has been a shift from gemeinschaft to gesellschaft relationships as a result of role specialization, and more generally, of bureaucratization. In the nineteenth century, Weber labeled this as a change from a "traditional" to a "rational" society. In the twentieth century, American sociologists have used these ideas as a springboard for their own theories. In the next two sections, we examine some of these theories about the quality of life in cities and suburbs.

An Amish family is an example of gemeinschaft community. (AP Wide World Photo)

## 16.4a City Life

Robert Redfield (1941), an American sociologist, developed a typology similar to those formulated by nineteenth-century scholars. He distinguished a **folk society** (which is small, isolated, homogeneous, and kin-oriented) from an urban society (which is large, impersonal, heterogeneous, and fast-paced). Around the same time, Louis Wirth, a colleague of Redfield's at the University of Chicago, described the effects of large numbers, density, and heterogeneity on urban life. In "Urbanism as a Way of Life" (1938), Wirth argued that as the population in an area becomes denser, lifestyles diversify, new opportunities arise, and institutions develop. At the same time, density increases the number of short-term, impersonal, and utilitarian social relationships that a person is likely to have.

According to Wirth, these three factors—large numbers, density, and heterogeneity—create a distinctive way of life, called "urbanism." Urbanism consists of distinctive characteristics: an extensive and complex division of labor; an emphasis on success, achievement, and social mobility, along with a behavioral orientation that includes

**Gemeinschaft**
A traditional community characterized by a sense of solidarity and common identity and emphasizing intimate and personal relationships

**Gesellschaft**
A modern community characterized by individualism, mobility, and impersonality, with an emphasis on progress rather than tradition

**Folk society**
A community described by Redfield as small, isolated, homogenous, and kin-oriented

rationality and utilitarianism; a decline of the family and kinship bonds and a concurrent rise of specialized agencies that assume roles previously taken by kin; a breakdown of primary relationships and the substitution of secondary group-control mechanisms; the replacement of deep, long-term relationships with superficial, short-term relationships; a decline of shared values and homogeneity and an increase in diversity; and finally, segregation on the basis of achieved and ascribed status characteristics.

Stanley Milgram (1970) has focused on the effects of urbanism. In midtown Manhattan, for example, someone can meet 220,000 people within a 10-minute walking radius of his or her office and not recognize a single person. Such experiences, says Milgram, may cause "psychic overload" and result in the detached, "don't get involved" attitude that is frequently cited as a part of big-city life. There have been a number of recorded incidents, for instance, in which people have been mugged, raped, or beaten in plain view of pedestrians who refused to help the victim.

These views of urban life give the impression that it is cold, violent, and alienating. Scholars have viewed city living conditions as the cause of crime, mental illness, aggression, and other serious problems. However, recent studies by sociologists have questioned the validity of this assessment. Certainly, these negative aspects of city life do exist; the real question is how typical or widespread they are. Several studies have found that there is considerable cohesion and solidarity in the city, particularly in neighborhoods where the residents are relatively homogeneous in terms of social or demographic characteristics. The findings of early sociologists may have accurately described the central core of American cities such as Chicago during periods of rapid growth, but contemporary research illustrates that a variety of lifestyles and adaptations can be found in cities.

Several decades ago, Herbert Gans (1962) presented research showing the diversity of urban lifestyles that is likely to remain true today. He argued that there are at least five types of residents in the city: cosmopolites, singles, ethnic villagers, the deprived, and the trapped.

*Cosmopolites* usually choose to remain in the city because of its convenience and cultural benefits. This group includes artists, intellectuals, and professionals who are drawn by the opportunities and activities generally found only in large urban centers. They are typically young, married, and involved in upper-middle-class occupations.

*Singles* like to live in the city because it is close to their jobs and permits a suitable lifestyle. The central city, with its nightclubs and singles-only apartments, offers a basis for social interaction. It gives singles opportunities to make friends, develop a social identity, and eventually find a mate. Many of these people are not permanent urban residents; they live in the city only until they marry or have children, at which time they move to the suburbs.

*Ethnic communities consist of working-class individuals who chose a specific area in which to settle. Because of their shared cultural heritage, the area in which they settled developed under the influence of their culture, creating areas such as Chinatowns.* (Shutterstock)

The third group identified by Gans, *ethnic villagers*, generally consists of working-class people who have chosen to reside in specific areas of the city. Their neighborhoods often develop a distinctive ethnic color as shops, restaurants, and organizations spring up. The Chinatowns of New York and San Francisco, the Hispanic areas of San Antonio and San Diego, and the Polish communities of Chicago and Detroit are neighborhoods of this type. Because of their strong ethnic ties, they usually do not identify as strongly with the city, nor do they engage in many of the cultural, social, or political activities that take place beyond their ethnic community. Their identity and allegiance are tied to the ethnic group and local community to a far greater extent than to the city. A strong emphasis is placed on kinship and primary group relationships, and members of other groups are often perceived as intruders or outsiders.

The fourth group, the *deprived*, is composed of the poor, the handicapped, and racial minorities who have fallen victim to class inequality, prejudice, or personal misfortune. They live in the city because it offers inexpensive housing and holds the promise of future job opportunities that will enable them to move to a better environment.

Finally, the *trapped* are those who cannot afford to move to a newer community and must remain in their deteriorating neighborhoods. The elderly who live on pensions make up much of this group; because many have lived in the city all their lives, they tend to identify strongly with their neighborhoods. The deprived and the trapped are the most frequent victims of the problems of the city. They are more likely to be the targets of assault, mugging, extortion, and other crimes than other city residents. In high-crime areas, many of these people live isolated lives and are terrified by the ongoing violence in their neighborhoods.

## 16.4b Suburban Life

The dominance of **suburbs**, communities surrounding and dependent on urban areas, is a recent phenomenon although the population movement to the suburbs began at the end of the nineteenth century. Suburbs grew as a result of both push and pull factors. The problems of the city drove residents to the suburbs; and the positive aspects of suburban life—cleaner air, lower property taxes, larger lots, and a chance to own a home—also attracted people. Because the move involved a substantial capital investment, this transition was made primarily by the more affluent.

**BVT *Lab***

Visit www.BVTLab.com to explore the student resources available for this chapter.

The growth of the suburbs was also influenced by technological developments, especially those in transportation. Before the 1920s, trains and electric trolleys were the major means of mass transportation to and from the central city. Accordingly, the first pattern of suburban growth was star-shaped, as communities sprang up along the railway and trolley corridors radiating from the center of the city. The automobile gave the suburban movement a significant boost by permitting the development of land not located near a railway or trolley corridor.

After World War II, the suburbs took on a different appearance. The increased affluence of American workers and the mass production of relatively inexpensive housing enabled many lower-middle-class and blue-collar families to become suburbanites (i.e., residents of the suburbs). The type of housing that emerged in the post–World War II suburbs, called "tract housing," was based on mass-production techniques. Neighborhoods and sometimes whole communities of similar houses were constructed. As the population began to shift to the suburbs, so did the retail trade and small businesses. The result was an unprecedented growth of suburban shopping centers.

The rapid growth of suburbs in the 1950s and early 1960s caused a great deal of concern among many social commentators. Suburban life was characterized as a "rat race" dominated by a preoccupation with "keeping up with the Joneses." Suburbanites were seen as anxious, child-oriented, status-seeking people who led empty, frustrating lives (Bell, 1958; Gordon, Gordon, & Gunther, 1961; Mills, 1951). The typical suburbanites were viewed as more concerned with household gadgets, status symbols, and getting into what they consider to be the right organizations than with understanding the world around them or achieving individuality. These views generated what sociologists call the "myth of suburbia." Recent research has given us reason to doubt that the patterns of behavior found in the suburbs are due to suburban residence and even that there is a distinctively suburban way of life.

The suburbs and the people who live there are actually quite diverse. Most of you can differentiate suburbs by the types of housing and land areas that accompany it. Most cities have one or two identifiable suburban communities of the affluent, which are occupied by white, upper-middle-class executives and professionals. Other identifiable communities consist of white-collar and upper-working-class residents with their three-bedroom, two-and-one-half-bathroom homes with an attached two-car garage. A third type of suburban community is that of the blue-collar, less educated and less affluent

**Suburbs**

The communities that surround a central city and are dependent on it resident. These homes, without garages, are small and are the least expensive type of suburban housing. In all categories, a primary reason cited for moving to the suburbs is the desire to own a home. A second important reason is to find a suitable environment in which to raise children. Other factors common to most suburbanites are a desire for open spaces and for a less hectic pace.

**thinking** SOCIOLOGICALLY

1. Would you say that the town in which you live could be characterized as a gemeinschaft or a gesellschaft? Why? Discuss some features and qualities of the town that lead you to characterize it in this way.
2. Discuss the accuracy of the statement, "People who live in cities are different from people who live in suburban or rural areas."
3. How accurate do you find Gan's classification and description of the five types of urban residents? As you reflect, can you identify these types from your own experiences?

## 16.4c Urban Problems

The most severe problems in urban areas are found in the central cities: poverty, unemployment, crime, noise and air pollution, waste disposal, water purity, transportation, housing, population congestion, and so on. Although the suburbs are by no means immune to these problems, they generally do not experience them to the same degree as central cities. The central cities are beset by a number of crises, some of which are becoming worse. In this section, three problems are discussed: poverty and unemployment, crime, and schooling.

Among the most serious issues facing cities today are the related problems of poverty and unemployment. The economic vitality of central cities has diminished over the years, as industry, affluent taxpayers, and jobs have moved out. The result has been a steady deterioration of housing and public services and the loss of high-paying jobs. The least fortunate of city residents are forced to live in slums and ghettos.

**Slums** are overcrowded streets or sections of a city marked by poverty and poor living conditions—resulting from the dirt, disease, rodents, and other health hazards that accompany concentrations of housing with poor plumbing, garbage disposal, and sanitation facilities. Slum residents—such as racial minorities, the elderly, women who head large families, and addicts—are often victims of social injustice and personal misfortune. Over the years, research has shown that slum living has a number of detrimental effects on health: residents of slums are more likely than others to contract diseases and to become seriously ill; they have poorer overall health and shorter life spans; and they are more apt to have poorer self-images and experience psychological problems such as depression and alienation.

The most serious poverty and its accompanying social problems occur in ghettos. A **ghetto** is an area, usually a deteriorating one, in which members of a racial or ethnic minority are forcibly segregated. Urban areas that are no longer of interest to the more affluent majority tend to become ghettos. A ghetto is a social and economic trap that keeps members of the minority group within a controllable geographic area. Crane (1991) describes ghettos as neighborhoods that have experienced epidemics of social problems: epidemics of crack, gang violence, teenage childbearing, and so forth. His assumption is that social problems are contagious and are spread through peer influence within ghetto neighborhoods. He found that the neighborhood effect on the pattern of dropping out of school and of childbearing—the two variables he studied among teenagers—was precisely the one implied by an epidemic hypothesis. Urban ghettos, the worst areas of large cities, produced sharp, epidemic jumps in both dimensions.

**Slums**
Slums are overcrowded streets or sections of a city marked by poverty and poor living conditions

**Ghetto**
An area in a city in which members of a racial or ethnic minority are forcibly segregated

**Figure 16-2** Perceptions of Trend in Crime Nationally, 1989–2011

Is there more crime in the U.S. than there was a year ago, or less?

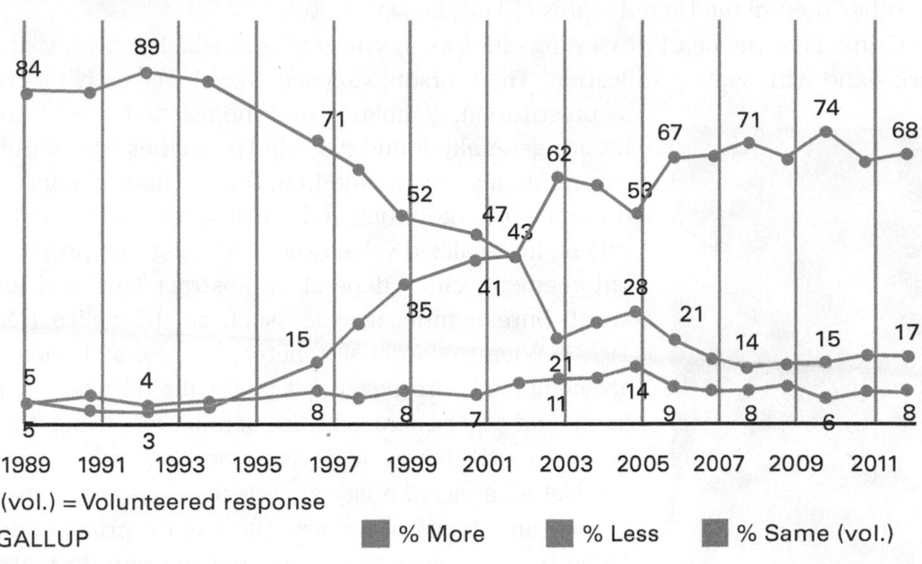


Adapted from Gallup Wellbeing.
Retrieved from http://www.gallup.com/poll/150464/americans-believe-crime -worsening.aspx

The jobs for which the less affluent central-city residents are qualified are usually low paying and scarce, and the unemployment rate is twice as high as the rate in the suburbs. The departure of industry and manufacturing jobs has left inner-city residents with jobs characterized by high turnover, low wages, and few opportunities for advancement. It is not unusual to find a person who heads a family and works full-time barely earning enough

**Figure 16-3** Perceptions of Trend in Crime Locally, 1989–2011

Is there more crime in your area than there was a year ago, or less?

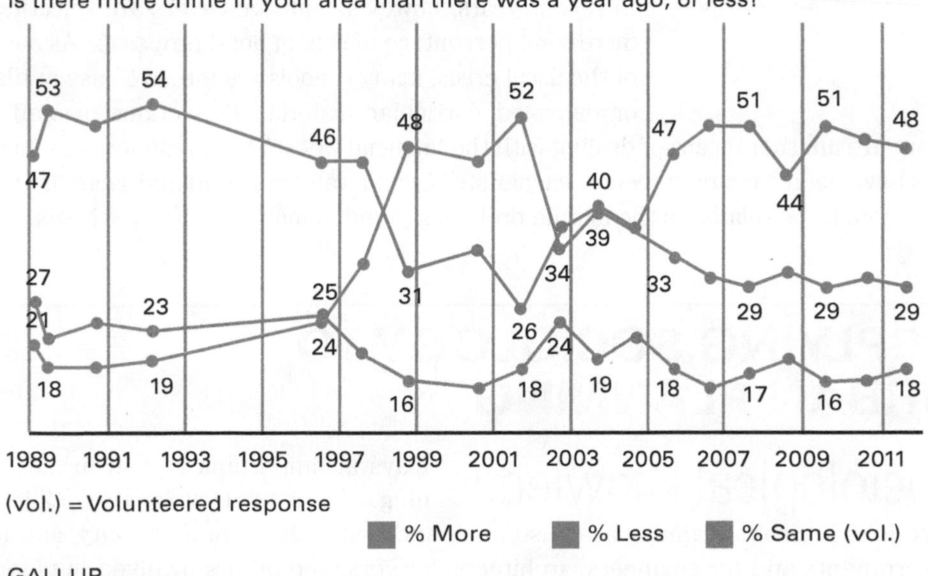


Adapted from Gallup Wellbeing.
Retrieved from http://www.gallup.com/poll/150464/americans-believe-crime-worsening.aspx

to stay above the poverty line. With recent cuts in federal aid to job-training programs, it is unlikely that the situation of these city residents will improve in the near future.

Crime is another serious urban problem. Urban households have historically been, and continue to be, the most vulnerable to property crime, burglary, motor vehicle theft, and other theft in the United States (Klaus, 2004).

Crime is at the heart of viewing cities as unsafe places in which to live, visit, and work—and with some justification. Theft, arson, violence, illegal vice activities (such as prostitution, gambling), and the use and sale of narcotics are generally found more in large cities where there is greater anonymity. In addition, the methods of control are different in large cities and small towns. Whereas towns rely on internalized values and primary-group pressure for enforcement, cities depend on abstract laws and impersonal, bureaucratic agencies such as the police (Dinitz, 1973). When high density, heterogeneity, and anonymity are combined with poverty, a physically decayed environment, and other characteristics of inner city living, there is great potential for social deviance and violence.

*Inadequate financing and violence are just two of the major problems that schools face today.*
*(AP Wide World Photo)*

Not all areas of a city experience the same crime rate or the same types of crimes. The highest crime rates are found in the inner city sectors, and the rate decreases as one moves toward the fringes of the urban area. Zonal differences in crime tend to persist, however, even when the physical characteristics and the occupants of a zone change.

Another urban problem area is schooling. Today, city schools are faced with a variety of major problems, two of which are inadequate financing and social disorder, including violence. Many cities have a very difficult time keeping pace with the accelerating costs. This difficulty is accentuated by inequalities in school funding: Urban schools generally have a much lower per-student expenditure allowance than schools in the suburbs. City schools have reacted to this funding problem in several ways. In some areas, school bond increases have been used to retain financial solvency. In recent years, however, irate taxpayers are rejecting an increasing percentage of school bond proposals. As a result of the fiscal crisis, many schools are forced to use outdated or damaged curricular material. Reductions in staff and salary are another means of dealing with the financial woes. These responses to funding cuts have been a factor in recent teacher strikes and walkouts. Staff and salary cutbacks also seem to be related to the morale problems found in many inner-city schools.

## APPLYING SOCIOLOGY TO URBAN PLANNING

Sociological knowledge plays an important part in urban planning. Some professional sociologists have jobs in urban planning as consultants and researchers for state, city, and local governments and for engineers, architects, lawyers, and others involved in planning cities and communities. Before engineers design a new road going through a neighborhood, for example, they might want to know how the increased traffic flow will influence the social organization of the community. Municipal governments might need to know how a neighborhood renewal project might influence the social organization of a particular community before they begin the project. Will the residents' networks of cooperation and exchange be disrupted? How will leisure time and work roles be affected? Will the project impose middle-class values on a lower-class culture?

Andrew Collver (1983), in an article on housing and environmental planning, suggests six ways in which sociology can contribute to urban planning:

*Regional Data Collection and Analysis* To plan a workable community or neighborhood, the planners—policymakers, engineers, architects, lawyers, and others—should understand the developmental trends of the larger region in which it is located and how its location both serves and is served by the larger metropolitan system. Is the population of the region growing? How much migration in and out of the area is there? How are the age patterns of the population changing? What are the various types of income, religious, and ethnic groups within the community, and how well integrated are they? Answers to questions such as these require some knowledge of social stratification, minority groups, and demography, as well as knowledge of sociological research methods.

*Neighborhood Life-Cycle Analysis* This entails examining the history of the neighborhood and its trend of growth or decline, rather than just examining the neighborhood at a single point in time. Is the average income level of the residents rising or declining? Are new businesses opening, or are old businesses closing, or both? Is the middle class moving in or out? As Collver (1983) points out, "to try to attract middle-class homeowners back to an inner-city neighborhood that lacks such essential elements as architectural charm, good schools, and convenient access to work and recreation would be an exercise in frustration." A sociological analysis of a community can help to create plans that are more in line with the natural tendencies of the community.

*Preparation of Long-Range Community Plans* Long-range plans are not always effectively carried out, but they are a useful way for urban planners to reach common understandings and assumptions about what should be done. This increases the level of communication among the planners and helps to make them of one mind. Sociological knowledge can be a helpful way to create workable plans from the stated goals of community leaders. Suppose, for example, that one of the stated goals of the community government is to create an ethnically and racially diverse neighborhood of middle-income people. Knowledge of prejudice, minority groups, values, norms, roles, culture, and so forth would be useful in devising a means to achieve the community's goals.

*Critical Review and Evaluation of Alternative Courses of Action* What kind of impact will the proposed urban plan have? What are some possible alternatives to the plan? If they are inferior to the plan chosen, why are they inferior? How can architectural and environmental impact be assessed and managed? Knowledge of people's lifestyles and the effects of spatial arrangement, density, crowding, heterogeneity, and other factors offer insight into the impact of a plan. Field experiments are a means of testing policies before they are actually implemented. Similarly, field experiments can be conducted to assess the impact of various alternative-planning measures before selecting one. Collver notes also that impact analysis is required by federal and state regulations.

*Project Evaluation* Once a project has been completed, planners must determine whether it met its goals. Outcome evaluation would be one way of assessing the results of an urban planning project. Knowledge of the methodology of outcome evaluation research could be used to help fine-tune the plan being evaluated. There are four steps in evaluation research: specification (defining or identifying the goals of the project), measurement (the information needed to evaluate the goal), analysis (the use of the information to draw conclusions), and recommendation (the advice given regarding what should be done, based on the analysis).

*Creation of Social Inventions or Alternative Structures* How can the necessary functions of a community be met in new and better ways? Developing such inventions might require changes in basic ideologies and institutions. Could a neighborhood or community, for example, share the use and maintenance of common property rather than having individual property owners? This would require a restructuring of our basic ideology of private ownership, and yet this seemingly revolutionary idea is what lies behind the movement toward condominiums and cooperative apartments. A sociological analysis of our basic ideologies and institutions may help free us from some confinements that are not practical or beneficial in every situation.

# 16.5 COLLECTIVE BEHAVIOR

Most facets of social life follow patterns of rules and norms. People generally have a daily routine and conform to the roles expected of them. In the same way, such organizations as schools, churches, factories, and governments are highly structured institutions that tend to be stable and relatively static. In these organizations, decisions are made through some semblance of logical, rational discussion. There is, however, another dimension of social life in which the activities are relatively spontaneous, unstructured, and unstable. This category includes such group activities as panics, demonstrations, riots, fads and fashions, disasters, and social movements. These actions, which may also follow certain patterns and established norms and rules, are instances of what sociologists call "collective behavior."

## 16.5a What Is Collective Behavior?

**Collective behavior**

The spontaneous, unstructured, and transitory behavior of a group of people in reaction to a specific event

**Institutionalized behavior**

Recurrent behavior that follows an orderly pattern with a relatively stable set of goals, expectations, and values

Sociologists use the term **collective behavior** to refer to spontaneous, unstructured, and transitory behavior of a group of people in response to a specific event. Some types of collective behavior that sociologists study include panics, riots, crowds, fads, and fashions.

Collective behavior can be contrasted with **institutionalized behavior**, which is recurrent and follows an orderly pattern with a relatively stable set of goals, expectations, and values. Examples of routine, predictable behavior would be going to class, commuting on a train, and going to church. If some unusual event takes place—an earthquake, train wreck, or fire, for example—collective behavior takes over. When people are confronted with an unfamiliar event for which no norms or rules have been established, they may behave in ways that differ radically from their normal conduct. People generally leave a theater in a calm, orderly fashion without pushing or shouting. However, if a fire breaks out, their conventional behavior would change to screams, shoving, and a rush for the exits. The ordinary norms break down and are replaced by new ones. Such actions occur infrequently, however, and only under special conditions.

*The term collective behavior refers to spontaneous, unstructured, and transitory behavior of a group of people in response to a specific event. For example an audience at a concert will sometimes wave their hands to show the band their appreciation. (Shutterstock)*

Sociological theories and perspectives on collective behavior are useful to those whose occupations lead them to deal with large numbers of people. By understanding, for example, the preconditions of collective behavior, police, religious leaders, politicians, organizers of sports events, concert organizers, architects, designers, and city planners and others might be able to create more effective ways to channel large numbers of people. Concert halls, sports arenas, convention halls, apartment complexes, subways, airports, and other places that hold large numbers of people could be designed in ways that impede the formation of destructive collective behavior.

## 16.5b Preconditions of Collective Behavior

An example of institutionalized behavior is commuting on a train. (iStockphoto)

Some specific social conditions tend to increase the likelihood of collective behavior. Rapid social change creates tensions and conflicts that sometimes lead to collective actions and violence. Social diversity and the associated inequalities in the distribution of wealth and of opportunities have produced many social movements—the women's movement, the Gray Panthers, the civil rights movement, and the labor movement. The mass media also play an important role in the dissemination of information of all types, from the trends in fashion and trends in music to student protests, prison riots, and more.

Neil Smelser, in his *Theory of Collective Behavior* (1962), identified the following six factors that, when they exist simultaneously, will produce collective behavior:

1. **Structural conduciveness**, the most general precondition, is the extent to which a society's organization makes collective behavior possible. A society that has no stock market cannot have a stock market crash. A country that has only one race or religion will not have race or religious riots. Note that structural conduciveness does not cause collective behavior. Rather, it is a measure of the existence of conditions in which it can occur. The fact that some aspect of a society is structurally conducive does not mean that collective behavior will happen; it means that, given certain other conditions, it could.
2. A **structural strain** is any kind of conflict or ambiguity that causes frustration and stress. Structural strains may be caused by conflicts between real and ideal norms, by conflicts between goals and the available means to reach them (anomie), or by the gap between social ideals (full employment, wealth, equality) and social realities (unemployment, poverty, and discrimination by age, race, and gender). Widespread unemployment among teenage blacks is an example of a structural strain.
3. People develop **generalized beliefs** about the conditions causing the strain. The women's movement, for example, began to grow only after the belief became widespread that women were discriminated against in employment, education, and other areas. Mobs form and riots take place only when people share a perception of some injustice or unfair treatment. Generalized beliefs may be based on known facts, shared attitudes, or a common ideology. The truth or accuracy of the beliefs is unimportant—the important thing is that they are shared.
4. A **precipitating factor** must trigger a collective response. The precipitating event itself is sometimes fairly insignificant. An unwarranted search may start a collective protest in an overcrowded prison. Commodity trading may proceed quietly until a rumor arises that frost has severely damaged the expected orange harvest. The precipitating event can also be a more serious incident, of course. News that a police officer has shot a black youth can inflame a tense racial situation. As was true of generalized beliefs, a precipitating event need not be true or accurately communicated to exert an

**Structural conduciveness**
The extent to which a society's organization has the conditions that make a particular form of collective behavior possible

**Structural strain**
Any conflict or ambiguity in a society's organization that causes frustration and stress; often seen as a precondition for collective behavior

**Generalized belief**
A stage in the development of collective behavior in which people share a common identification and interpretation of a problem

**Precipitating factors**
Events that trigger a collective response

influence. Even an unfounded rumor can lend focus and support to a belief and can increase the likelihood of a collective response.

5. **Mobilization for action** occurs once a precipitating event has taken place; people have to be persuaded to join the movement. Sometimes, an event mobilizes a group spontaneously, as when the crowd boos the umpire for making a bad call or when a crowd panics if someone yells "Fire!" Sometimes leaders emerge from within the group to encourage participation, which is what occurred during the formation of the Solidarity labor movement in Poland in 1980, when Lech Walesa, an unemployed electrician, quickly became the leader and spokesperson for the group. In other cases, outside leadership steps in to organize the people and push them into action, which is what often happened during the era when labor unions were being formed in this country. Collective behavior begins when mobilization for action takes place.
6. The **operation of social control** consists of the actions of the mass media, government, and other groups when they try to suppress or influence collective behavior. In the case of a potential strike, management might agree to listen to grievances, make a few changes, or raise wages slightly. If the strike takes place, it might fire striking workers and hire new ones. If social control cannot prevent collective action before it starts or halt it once it has begun, the collective behavior continues.

**Mobilization for action**

A stage in the development of collective behavior during which people are persuaded to join the movement

**Operation of social control**

A stage in the development of collective behavior in which the mass media, government, and other groups try to suppress or influence collective behavior

Smelser's model should be applicable to a wide variety of collective behaviors. As an example, we use the 1991 police assault of a black motorist, Rodney King, in Los Angeles. The incident, shown many times on national television and reported in most newspapers in the country, involved four white, baton-wielding police officers striking Rodney King more than 50 times after he was pulled over in his car for speeding. What caused this event to make national headlines and led thousands of citizens to demand the resignation of Los Angeles Police Chief Daryl Gates?

First, the circumstances were structurally conducive to a hostile outburst. It involved issues of race differences (black versus white) and power differences (police officers versus a motorist). Second, structural strains in the United States between blacks and whites, as well as between criminals and victims, are common. Note for example, how politicians often exploit fears over racial quotas, affirmative action, the early release of prisoners, and so forth to win elections. Concerns over the rights of the criminal exceeding the rights of the victim are widespread. These and many other structural strains were present in the Los Angeles police incident. Third, a shared generalized belief existed about inequalities, injustices, and unfair treatment of blacks by whites, as well as of officers toward selected violators of the law. It is likely that most people are aware of instances of racism and brutality in police departments. Nonetheless, the existence of these three conditions, all quite common, seldom leads to collective action. What was different about this event?

*Officers are seen here kicking and beating a man with nightsticks. The witnessing of these events, and existing structural strains within the society, triggered a collective response: rioting. (AP Wide World Photo)*

A key factor differentiating this event from others was the videotaping of the brutal beating of an unarmed single black man by a group of white police officers. This videotape, frequently aired over national television, was a precipitating factor (our fourth precondition) that triggered a collective response. Denial was no longer a possible police or community response. The fifth determinant of collective behavior was the mobilization of people to take action. The action suggested was not merely toward the police officers but also toward the person in charge of them: police chief Daryl Gates. Social control, the sixth determinant, came with a commission report recommending that the chief step down, the involvement of Los Angeles Mayor Bradley in demanding police reform, and other measures to convince the public that corrective actions would follow.





**thinking** SOCIOLOGICALLY

1. Select an example of collective behavior that took place in your state or community. Can you identify preconditions that encouraged it?
2. Can you cite an example during your lifetime in which collective behavior has produced positive social change?

# 16.6 CROWDS

## 16.6a Characteristics of Crowds

A **crowd** is a temporary group of people in face-to-face contact who share a common interest or focus of attention. This common interest may be unexpected and unusual, but it is not necessarily so. Although people in a crowd interact a good deal, the crowd as a whole is organized poorly, if at all. According to Turner and Killian (1993), crowds have four features that make them a unique area for study: anonymity, suggestibility, contagion, and emotional arousability.

1. *Anonymity*. People who do not know those around them may behave in ways that they would consider unacceptable if they were alone or with their family or neighbors. During a riot, the anonymity of crowd members makes it easier for people to loot and steal. In a lynch mob, brutal acts can be committed without feelings of shame or responsibility. Whatever the type of crowd, the anonymity of the individuals involved shifts the responsibility to the crowd as a whole.
2. *Suggestibility*. People who are seeking direction in an uncertain situation are highly responsive to the suggestions of others and become very willing to do what a leader or group of individuals suggests, especially given the crowd's anonymity.
3. *Contagion*. As people interact, the crowd's response to the common event or situation increases in intensity. If they are clapping or screaming, their behavior is likely to move others to clap or scream; and contagion increases when people are packed close together. An alert evangelist, comedian, or rock singer will try to get the audience to move close to one another to increase the likelihood of contagion and to encourage the listeners to get caught up in the mood, spirit, and activity of the crowd.
4. *Arousability*. Anonymity, suggestibility, and contagion tend to arouse emotions. Inhibitions are forgotten; people become emotionally charged to act, sometimes in uncharacteristic ways. During the Beatles concerts of the early 1960s, for example, teenage girls who were presumably quite conventional most of the time tried to rush on stage and had to be carried away by police.

**Crowd**
A temporary group of people in face-to-face contact who share a common interest or focus of attention

Although these four aspects of crowd behavior may be seen in almost any crowd, their intensity varies. Some crowds permit greater anonymity than others, and some have higher levels of suggestibility and contagion; one or more of these characteristics may not appear at all. The presence or absence of certain crowd features can be used to organize crowds into different categories.

## 16.6b Types of Crowds

**Casual crowd**

A crowd that is high in anonymity but low in suggestibility, contagion, emotional arousal, and unity

**Conventional crowd**

A crowd, such as the spectators at a baseball game, whose members are anonymous but share a common focus and follow established social norms and rules

**Acting crowd**

A crowd that acts on the basis of aroused impulse and thus one that may be volatile, aggressive, and dangerous

**Mobs**

Emotionally aroused groups ready to engage in violent behavior

**Riot**

A form of collective behavior involving mass violence and mob action

Every crowd shares a common focus. However, some crowds are very low in emotional arousal and are highly unstructured, whereas others are quite emotional, aggressive, and even dangerous to one's safety. Herbert Blumer (1939) identified and differentiated **casual crowds** (non-emotional, unstructured crowds such as people gathering to watch a street musician) from **conventional crowds** (more highly structured crows such as spectators at a sporting event or airline passengers). Both of these types of crowds have common purposes and are guided by norms.

The type of crowds that attract the most public attention are called **acting crowds**, the behavior of which is centered around and typifies aroused impulses. The two most dramatic forms of acting crowds are mobs and riots.

**Mobs** are groups that are emotionally aroused and ready to engage in violent behavior. They are generally short-lived and highly unstable. Their violent actions often stem from strong dissatisfaction with existing government policies or social circumstances; extreme discontentment with prevailing conditions is used to justify immediate and direct action. Disdainful of regular institutional channels and legal approaches, mobs take matters into their own hands.

Mob violence has erupted in many different circumstances. During the French Revolution of the 1780s and 1790s, angry mobs stormed through Paris, breaking into the Bastille prison for arms and calling for the execution of Louis XVI. In nineteenth-century England, enraged workers burned the factories in which they worked. Lynchings of blacks in the United States for real or imagined offenses continued into the twentieth century, often with little or no opposition from the formal agencies of control—police, courts, and public officials. Although lynch mobs are uncommon today, occasional instances of mob behavior take place over civil rights issues such as busing or housing, during political conventions and rallies, and among student or labor groups angry about perceived injustices.

Howard Rheingold proposed that cyberspace and the coming generation of fast wireless devices and their experienced users could change the way mobs are created. Rheingold states that "the coming generation of fast wireless devices will make ad hoc 'swarming' a potent force for cultural transformation" (Andrews, 2002). Social protesters have managed to use technology effectively, in part because it is still largely unregulated. However, with national security changes taking place, it remains to be seen whether or not technology will change the way action is mobilized.

*Riots are collective actions involving mass violence and mob action. Most riots result from an intense hatred of a particular group with no specific person or property in mind.*
*(AP Wide World Photo)*

**Riots** are collective actions involving mass violence and mob actions. The targets of their hostility and violence are less specific than those of mobs, and the groups involved are more diffuse. Most riots result from an intense hatred of a particular group with no specific person or property in mind. Destruction, burning, or looting may be indiscriminate; unfocused anger can lead to violent acts against any object or person who happens to be in the wrong area at the wrong time. Like mobs, rioters take actions into their own hands when they feel that institutional reactions to their concerns about war, poverty, racial injustices, or other problems are inadequate.

The race riots of the 1960s in Watts in Los Angeles, Harlem in New York, and other areas in many cities are the most commonly cited examples of rioting. These riots, which generally occurred in black ghettos, involved widespread destruction of property followed by extensive looting. The National Advisory Commission on Civil Disorders (Kerner Report, 1968) found that riots are associated with a number of factors, including discrimination, prejudice, disadvantaged living conditions, and frustration over the inability to bring about change.

# 16.7 THEORIES OF ACTING-CROWD BEHAVIOR

## 16.7a The Classical Perspective

The **classical perspective** of acting-crowd behavior suggests that people in a crowd lose their conscious personalities and act impulsively on the basis of their instincts rather than reason. This perspective was articulated in what is probably the most influential single book ever written on collective behavior, *The Crowd: A Study of the Popular Mind* (1895), by the French sociologist Gustave Le Bon (1841–1931). He mentions two key concepts in the classical view of crowds: collective mind and mental unity. He believed that crowds cause people to regress. According to this view, crowds are guided by instinct, not by rational decisions. Under the influence of crowds, even conventional, law-abiding citizens may act impulsively and be guided by unconscious influences. Crowds do not reason; they respond instantly to the immediate situation. Why? First, the anonymity of the collective gives each person in a crowd a feeling of power. Then, contagion sweeps through the crowd like a virus passing from one person to another. Finally, the participants become as suggestible as if they had been hypnotized. The result is the unquestioned acceptance of and obedience to the leaders.

**Classical perspective**
A view of acting crowd behavior that suggests that people in a crowd lose their conscious personalities and act impulsively on the basis of their instincts rather than reason

## 16.7b The Interactionist Perspective

The **interactionist perspective** assumes that people in crowds reinforce and heighten one another's reactions. Often referred to as the contagion model, it was developed by Herbert Blumer (1939), who—like Le Bon—believed that crowd behavior is often irrational and emotional. Blumer, however, rejected the idea that it stems from a group or collective mind. He believed that crowd behavior results from what he called "circular reactions" operating in a situation of social unrest. In a situation of social unrest, interactions reinforce and heighten the unrest. If one group, for example, shouts, "Let's get him," others model this behavior and usually adopt the same feelings and ways of expressing them. The reactions of these others increase the fervor of the original group, which in turn excites the rest of the crowd even further. In the absence of widespread unrest, such a reaction would never begin. Three types of circular reactions are milling, collective excitement, and social contagion.

**Interactionist perspective**
A view of crowd behavior that emphasizes how people in crowds reinforce and heighten one another's reactions

In a milling crowd, people move about aimlessly. **Milling** tends to make people preoccupied with one another and less responsive to the usual sources of stimulation. Like hypnotic subjects who become increasingly preoccupied with the hypnotist, milling individuals grow more preoccupied with others in the crowd and become increasingly inclined to respond quickly, directly, and without thinking.

**Milling**
The stage in the development of crowd behavior during which people move about aimlessly, grow increasingly preoccupied with others, and become increasingly inclined to respond without thinking

**Collective excitement** takes place when milling reaches a high level of agitation. People in the grip of collective excitement are emotionally aroused. They respond on the basis of their impulses; they are likely to feel little personal responsibility for their actions; and under the influence of collective excitement, they may behave in an uncharacteristic manner (Blumer, 1939).

**Social contagion** comes about wherever milling and collective excitement are intense and widespread. What is fascinating about social contagion is that it can attract people who were initially just indifferent spectators. They get caught up in the excitement and grow more inclined to become involved. Unlike Le Bon's theory, this theory does not suggest the existence of a group mind. Rather, people's interactions tend to heighten in intensity until the group is capable of spontaneous behavior.

## 16.7c The Emergent-Norm Perspective

The **emergent-norm perspective**, first proposed by Turner and Killian (1993), emphasizes how norms influence crowd behavior and how new norms emerge and are maintained. Whereas Le Bon and Blumer stress similarities in the behavior of crowd members, the emergent-norm perspective focuses on differences in crowd members' behavior.

According to this view, crowds do not behave as a homogeneous unit. Observers may think they act as a unit, but divergent views and behaviors may go unrecognized or be dismissed as unimportant. When attention is focused on the acting crowd, people frequently overlook those who remain silently on the sidelines, those who passively lend their support, and those who express little excitement. People behave differently because they act in accordance with different norms. Norms influence all social conduct, and new norms arise during novel situations such as mob actions or riots. Some may accept norms that make violence and looting acceptable. Others may define the situation differently and choose to leave or remain uninvolved.

As an example and a test of the emergent-norm explanation of collective behavior, Aguirre, et al. (2011) analyzed the crowd responses to a fire at The Station nightclub in Rhode Island in 2003, which killed 100 persons and left 200 injured. The fire was ignited by the pyrotechnics at a Great White rock concert. It was the fourth deadliest fire in U.S. history. Aguirre and his colleagues discovered that while the fire had all the requisites for panic, panic-like behaviors were not prevalent. While it is true that many of the victims who died competed with each other for escape from the building, Aguirre et al. concluded that they were helping each other until the very end. They also found that for the survivors, cooperation and care for each other in their groups was a key factor in their survival. Rather than an expected panic, norms of helping had emerged through interpretation and interaction with one another.

The process by which norms emerge occurs daily in any context of human social interaction and communication. All of us are dependent on those around us to define and determine what a given event means. When others in the group shout, run, or express fear, we are likely to feel tremendous pressure to conform to their behavior. An untrained observer may note the one dominant behavior and describe the group members as unanimous in their definition, mood, and behavior. More careful observation, as emergent-norm theory suggests, would reveal that unanimity is an illusion and that differential expression does take place.

## 16.7d The Game Perspective

The **game perspective** on crowd behavior suggests that crowd members think about their actions and consciously try to act in ways that will produce rewards (Berk, 1974). Unlike other theories, which assume that crowds behave irrationally, game theory stresses the importance of rational decisions. People weigh the rewards and costs of various actions and choose the course that is most likely to lead to a desired end.

**Collective excitement**
In the interactionist perspective on crowd behavior, the stage during which milling reaches a high level of agitation

**Social contagion**
A stage in the development of crowd behavior during which the crowd's response to a common event increases in intensity and the crowd's behavior moves others to behave in the same way

**Emergent-norm perspective**
A view of collective behavior that emphasizes how new norms emerge and influence the behavior of crowds

**Game perspective**
A view of crowd behavior that suggests that members think about their actions and consciously try to act in ways that will produce rewards

Looting, for example, may yield a reward such as a television set. If few people are looting, the chances of arrest may be fairly great—and a potential looter may choose not to take the risk. If, on the other hand, there are thousands of people looting stores, the chances of arrest are quite low—and the person may decide to join in. Milling about before engaging in violent action may be used as a time for assessing various courses of action and for evaluating the strength of support. According to this perspective, violence is not necessarily irrational. It may be the result of a conscious decision that it will be useful in acquiring a desired end: civil rights, jobs, housing, new leaders, or something else. When many people desire the same goal, collective action can increase their chances of achieving it.

*When thousands of people are looting, others may join in because they feel that there is less of a chance that they will be arrested.* (AP Wide World Photo)

### thinking SOCIOLOGICALLY

1. How might the emergent-norm and game perspectives be applied to explain the acting-crowd behavior of the Brazilian nightclub event?
2. The rock group the Grateful Dead, which came into existence in the late 1960s, is still popular, especially among its faithful fans known as "Dead Heads." The band has ceased touring since the death of Jerry Garcia. Even though they attracted large crowds, the Grateful Dead concerts were notably peaceful and orderly. This is ironic because the group seemed to represent very free, liberal, nontraditional, antiestablishment values. Use the knowledge of collective behavior found in this chapter to examine why Grateful Dead concerts were usually orderly and devoid of dangerous outbreaks of collective behavior.
3. Use knowledge contained within this chapter, including insights that you have gained from the preceding example of Grateful Dead concerts, to develop a strategy that concert and sporting-event organizers could use to try to protect against potentially dangerous outbreaks of collective behavior

## 16.8 SOCIAL MOVEMENTS

While crowds are temporary collectives of people in close proximity to one another, social movements tend to be more geographically diffuse and longer lasting. A **social movement** is a collective effort to bring about social change and to establish a new order of social thought and action. Movements involve more than a single event or community; they begin during periods of unrest and dissatisfaction with some aspect of society, and they are motivated by the hope that the society can be changed.

**Social movement**
Collective non-institutionalized efforts to bring about social change and establish a new order of social thought and action

Initially, social movements tend to be poorly organized, lack an identity, and are spontaneous. As they develop, however, they acquire an established leadership, a body of customs and traditions, divisions of labor, social rules and values, and new ways of thinking. This process of institutionalization leads to the development of formal organizations, and ultimately to new social systems.

## 16.8a Types of Social Movements

In the United States, a number of social movements have had a significant effect on changing public attitudes and the development of policies and laws, such as the civil rights movement, the feminist movement, the environmental movement, the peace movement, and the gay rights movement. The emergence of the Tea Party in the United States is an example of a contemporary social movement that is having widespread effects. Perhaps some of the most notable social movements today are the prodemocracy movements occurring in the Middle East, such as the youth-led movement in Egypt that led to the resignation of President Hosni Mubarak. Each of these movements has involved a collective effort to bring about social change and to establish a new social order. Various authorities have used different schemes to classify such movements.

Within the past few decades, beginning in the final years of the twentieth century, some social movements have expanded beyond the borders of any one country and have become international in scope. One such movement is the global social justice movement. The global social justice movement emerged both as a critique of negative social and political environments and the desire to make globalization more socially sustainable and democratic. Some of its manifestations have occurred in the form of protests at top international summits such as the World Trade Organization (WTO), the G8 (representatives of the governments of eight major economies), and the International Monetary Fund (IMF). One of the distinguishing features of the global social justice movement is that it has been organized across national borders and has challenged traditional nation-state based forms of politics (Wennerhag, 2010).



Turner and Killian (1993) organize social movements in terms of their orientation. *Value-oriented movements* advocate social changes concerning various groups, which result in broader adherence to the central values of the larger society. The civil rights, gay liberation, and women's movements, for example, are efforts to fulfill the American values of equality, freedom, and justice. *Power-oriented movements* aim to achieve power, recognition, or status. The Nazi movement in Germany and the Bolshevik Revolution in Russia are extreme examples of this type of movement. *Participant-oriented movements* focus on personal rewards and fulfillment for their participants. Back-to-nature and evangelical movements are of this type.

Actually, there are as many different kinds of movements as there are goals. *Reactionary movements* advocate the restoration of the values and behaviors of previous times. *Conservative movements* attempt to protect the status quo and resist change. *Resistance movements* are aimed at preventing or reversing changes that have already occurred. *Reformist movements* try to modify some aspect of society without destroying or changing the entire system. *Revolutionary movements* believe in the overthrow of the existing social order as a means of creating a new one. *Nationalistic movements* hope to instill national pride and a sense of identity with one's country. The goal of *utopian movements* is to create the perfect community. *Religious movements* want to convert or modify the existing belief system in accordance with a religious principle. *Expressive movements* would like to change people's emotional reactions to help them cope with prevailing social conditions. Some movements have several purposes or combine the features of several types of movements. Regardless of the way they are categorized, they all involve collective efforts to initiate (or sometimes resist) a new order of social thought and action.

## 16.8b The Development and Life Cycle of Social Movements

Social movements develop most frequently in complex, non-totalitarian societies. They evolve through a series of stages that closely parallel those suggested by Smelser as preconditions of the development of any type of collective behavior. Blumer (1939) divided the development of movements into four steps, as follows:

1. The stage of **social unrest** parallels Smelser's stages of conduciveness and structural strain. This stage is characterized by unfocused restlessness and increasing disorder. Often, people are unaware that others share the same feelings and concerns. Rumors abound, and persons become increasingly susceptible to the appeals of agitators. These agitators do not advocate any particular ideology or course of action; rather, they make people more aware of their discontentment and raise issues and questions to get people thinking.
2. Social unrest is followed by the stage of **popular excitement**. During this period, unrest is brought into the open. People with similar concerns begin to establish a rapport with one another, and they openly express their anger and restlessness. Then the group begins to acquire a collective identity, and more definite ideas emerge about the causes of the group's condition and how the situation can be changed. Leaders help define and justify feelings, clarify the issues, provide direction, stir up excitement, identify the opposition, and point out obstacles that must be overcome. They also offer a vision of what things could be like after the movement succeeds. In the past, social reformers such as Martin Luther King, Jr., charismatic leaders such as Gandhi, and prophets such as Christ have led movements such as these.
3. In the **formalization** stage, a formal structure is developed; rules, policies, and tactics are laid out. The movement becomes a disciplined organization capable of securing member commitment to stable goals and strategies. At this stage, movements make concerted efforts to influence centers of power (Turner & Killian, 1993). The stable organization of the movement and the establishment of various programs and committees serve to keep members involved after the initial urgency has died down. The leadership shifts from agitators, reformers, or prophets to statespersons or intellectual leaders and administrators. The intellectual leaders develop the ideology, symbols, and slogans that keep the movement alive. The administrators work on procedures, tactics, and organization. It is at this stage that movements often split into factions or break down completely due to differences of opinion over such questions as how the movement should proceed, how radical its tactics should be, and what types of concessions should be granted.

   In the formalization stage, it becomes clear that the success of social movements requires more than just successful leadership. A group of committed followers is also needed. It has traditionally been assumed that followers are drawn from the ranks of the discontented, the deprived, the frustrated, and the angry. A more recent perspective, **resource mobilization theory**, suggests that the success of a social movement depends not only on those who benefit from it directly but also on their ability to mobilize other individuals and groups to contribute time, money, and influence to the cause—even though they may not directly benefit.
4. Social movements reach the final stage in the life cycle of social movements through **institutionalization**. During this stage, the movement becomes integrated into society. It may have a permanent office and personnel hired to continue its efforts. At this point, it may also have accomplished its primary purpose and may disappear into the network of institutions that already exists. In other instances, the success of a movement leads to the development of new social movements. Some movements never reach this stage—they are suppressed by formal or informal powers and disappear or go underground. At the institutional stage, the unrest, discontent, and popular excitement have largely ceased and are replaced by formal offices, organized groups, and structured activities.

**Social unrest**
The stage in the development of a social movement that is characterized by unfocused restlessness and increasing disorder

**Popular excitement**
The stage in the development of a social movement during which social unrest is brought into the open and people with similar concerns begin to organize

**Formalization**
The stage in the development of a social movement in which a formal structure is developed, and rules, policies, and tactics are laid out

**Resource mobilization theory**
The theory that the success of a social movement depends not only on those who benefit from it directly but also on its ability to mobilize other individuals and groups to contribute time, money, and influence

**Institutionalization**
The process by which orderly, stable, structured, and increasingly predictable forms of behavior or interaction are developed

Social movements are important and powerful vehicles of social change, but they are not the only reason that social change occurs. We turn now to a discussion of theories of social change.

**thinking** SOCIOLOGICALLY

1. Using Blumer's and Smelser's ideas concerning social movements, what role might the Internet play in developing and shaping future social movements? What sort of role, if any, do you currently see the Internet playing in the development of social movements?
2. The spring of 2011 marked the beginning of a new modern wave of collective behavior and social movements in the Middle East by people, mostly of the current generation, seeking the advancement of democratic conditions. Most notably, these have occurred in Egypt, Libya, Tunisia, Bairhan, and Syria; certainly, however, they are not confined to these countries. As a way of reviewing the material in this chapter, find a few news articles on any of the events stemming from "Arab spring." Discuss them in terms of the theories and ideas of collective behavior and social movements found in this chapter.

# 16.9 THEORIES OF SOCIAL CHANGE

## 16.9a Evolutionary Theory of Change

During more optimistic periods of our history, social change was regarded as progress. When society changed, it was assumed to be getting better. Evolutionary theory suggests that societies evolved from the simple and primitive to the more complex and advanced, just as animal life progressed from the simplest one-celled organisms to the most complex animal, the human being. Herbert Spencer, a classic evolutionary theorist, believed that as a society grows, the functions of its members become more specialized and better coordinated into the larger system; and thus, there is progress. Spencer was very influential for many years, especially in the United States, where growth was equated with progress.

Evolutionary theory is less popular today. Change may create social problems rather than social progress, and Spencer's optimistic theory is regarded with some skepticism. Conflict theorists are among those who do not believe that continuous evolution is progress.

## 16.9b Conflict Theory of Social Change

Conflict theorists are in many ways as optimistic as evolutionary theorists, but they do not assume that societies smoothly evolve to higher levels. Instead, change comes about as oppressed groups struggle to improve their lot. Thus, change is a result of conflict and struggle; however, the result still is, generally, an improvement in society. Each stage of conflict leads to a higher order. As oppressed groups are able to work their way out of oppression, society is able to provide more justice and equality for all. This is a positive view and very optimistic, especially compared with the views of some cyclical theorists.

## 16.9c Cyclical Theories of Change

**Cyclical change theory**
The view that societies go through a cycle of birth, maturation, decline, and death

The most pessimistic cyclical theorists think that decay is inevitable. One such theorist was the historian Oswald Spengler (1918), whose **cyclical change theory** suggests that every society is born, matures, decays, and eventually dies. The Roman Empire rose to power and then gradually collapsed, just as the British Empire grew strong and then deteriorated. Spengler contended that social change might take the form of progress or of decay but that no society lives forever.

Most sociologists believe that this view is too rigid and that although societies may have cycles of change, the cycles are not preordained. Pitirim Sorokin (1889–1968), a Russian social theorist who lived through the Russian Revolution of 1917, did not equate change with progress; neither did he believe that all societies are inevitably destined to decay. He noted, rather, that societies go through various stages. At different stages, he suggested, they emphasize religious beliefs, scientific beliefs, or the pleasures of art, music, and the beauty of nature. They shift from one cycle to another, moving first in one direction and then in another, as the needs of the society demand. Sorokin is still respected for these ideas and has greatly influenced the attempts of structural functionalists to explain social change.

*The cyclical change theory is the belief that a society is born, matures, decays, and dies. The Roman Empire is one such example.* (Shutterstock)

## 16.9d Structural Functionalism and Social Change

Structural functionalists—who believe that society is a balanced system of institutions, each of which serves a function in maintaining society—suggest that when events outside or inside the society disrupt the equilibrium, social institutions make adjustments to restore stability. An influx of immigrants can bring new ideas into a community that then spread throughout the society. A natural disaster, a famine, or a war may disrupt the social order and force the social institutions to make adjustments. Like Sorokin, the structural functionalists do not necessarily consider social change, per se, to be good or bad—rather, it is the process through which societies lose and regain their equilibrium.

The term *cultural lag* is often used to describe the state of disequilibrium. When an event such as an increase in population or a depletion of natural resources causes a strain in a society, it takes some time for the society to understand the strain and to alter its values and institutions to adapt to the change. Just as the human body must adjust its functioning to adapt to changes, societies adjust to maintain and restore themselves.

# 16.10 SOCIAL CHANGE THEORIES AND UNDERDEVELOPED NATIONS

Sociologists have developed theories to explain why social change has occurred differently and at different rates in industrialized and underdeveloped nations. Although Europe (and later the United States) industrialized, other nations did not. Attempts to explain this lack of development have evolved around two different theoretical points of view: modernization, which has its roots in evolutionary theory, and dependency theory, which is also known as world systems theory.

## 16.10a Modernization in Underdeveloped Nations

Evolutionary theorists tend to assume that today's underdeveloped nations in Africa, South America, and other areas that do not have modern industry—such as is found in Europe and North America—will pass through the same stages that industrialized nations passed through in their quest for modernization. **Modernization** is the process whereby preindustrial countries emerge as urban societies with lower birth

**Modernization**

The process whereby pre-industrial countries emerge as urban societies with lower birth rates, more goods and services, and better nutrition and healthcare rates, more goods and services, better nutrition and healthcare, improved housing, and some luxuries.

A closer comparison, however, suggests that contemporary nations may not be able to take the same course as those that are already industrialized. The United States developed into an industrial society due to its work ethic, its lack of competition from other countries, and its vast supply of natural resources, including its excellent land for agriculture and its minerals, such as iron and coal. The United States can also attract the labor it requires through immigration and can stop immigration when no more workers are needed.

Many underdeveloped nations simply lack the same abundance of natural resources. Tropical forests and arid deserts cannot easily be developed to produce grain. Oil, coal, iron, and lumber are unavailable in many countries. Many of these items must be purchased from other countries to meet the needs of the ever-growing native population. To purchase these necessities, Developing World countries have borrowed enormous sums and now have huge debts to the International Monetary Fund (a specialized agency of the United Nations run by 186 member countries), the World Bank (an international organization owned by 184 countries for the purposes of aiding in the reconstruction and development of countries) and various private lenders. Whereas in recent years much attention has been given in the news to the debt crises in industrialized countries of the world, in 2010 international capital flows to developing countries totaled more than a trillion dollars, an increase of 68% from 2009 (The World Bank, 2012).

To pay these debts, Developing World countries have tried to develop cash crops that can be exported to pay for the goods that the country must buy. These agricultural products are usually not foods, but such products as coffee, cotton, and flowers. Unfortunately, because the land has been taken over for cash crops, the native population no longer has land on which to grow food. They do not have jobs in agriculture, either, because most of the work is done with farm machinery. Part of the rural population has moved into the already crowded cities hoping to find work; but work is scarce, and pay is poor. Often the poor live on the streets or in makeshift homes that provide little shelter. Dysentery and pneumonia are common, especially among children. The need for medical care puts further strain on the resources of the population.

*Products such as coffee are used as cash crops to pay for goods that the Developing World countries need to buy.*
*(iStockphoto)*

Inasmuch as undeveloped nations cannot compete with the large multinational industries, they sometimes invite those industries to come into their countries to do business, hoping that these industries will provide employment for the natives and income for the country. This is rarely successful. Employment opportunities are usually too few and limited to the lowest-paying jobs. When the goods are exported, the profits go to the multinational corporation and not to the host country.

Thus, while the United States developed its industry with control over its population, abundant natural resources, and no competition from other world industries, developing nations have tried to modernize with too large a population, too few natural resources, and too much competition from worldwide industries. Not surprisingly, they have been unable to support their people. In trying to do so, they have gone into debt to such an extent that the world banking system is threatened by bankruptcy as a result of the unpaid debts of these nations.

Dependency theorists agree that underdeveloped nations are suffering. However, their understanding of the cause of the problems is very different.

## 16.10b Dependency or World Systems Theory

**Dependency theory**
Conflict theory stating that underdeveloped nations cannot industrialize because they are dependent on the nations already industrialized

**Dependency theory** was inspired by Marx and has been developed by conflict theorists, who believe that underdeveloped nations cannot industrialize as the Western world did because they have been made dependent on the Western world. One must look at the entire world system, and not just at individual regions, if one is to understand social change. **World systems theory** states that **core nations** (those that are already industrialized) dominate the economies of **peripheral nations** (underdeveloped nations), taking wealth from the peripheral nations to further their own development.

Wallerstein (2000) argues that the northwestern European core nations first exploited the eastern and southern European nations; and when exploration opened trade in the sixteenth century, they went on to exploit North and South America, Africa, and India. The Europeans took raw materials from the rest of the world, used them to produce manufactured goods, and then sold manufactured goods to the peripheral nations at high cost, driving these nations into poverty.

This exploitation is still common. Del Monte and Dole, multinational corporations, grow pineapples in the Philippines and Thailand and ship them to the United States, now a core nation. The Gulf and Western Corporation grows sugar in Central America for sale in the United States. Coffee and bananas are other major products taken exploitatively from Latin American nations. The pharmaceutical industry also takes raw materials from peripheral countries, manufactures medicines, and sells those medicines back to these countries at high prices (Gereffi, 1983). The profits from these diverse ventures go to the core nations' stockholders, not to the peripheral nations that provided the raw materials.

*Coffee and bananas are other major products taken exploitatively from Latin American nations. (iStockphoto)*

Gereffi (1983) suggests that these exploited countries could begin to remedy this situation by putting a ban on the purchase of all but the most essential manufactured products until they develop their own industries; they could nationalize the industries of foreign corporations in their own countries. However, this would require a revolutionary change in ideology in many cases. As long as the elites in peripheral nations cooperate with business from the core nations, such changes are not possible.

Wallerstein (2000) believes that there are worldwide forces uniting to change this ideology and to oppose such extreme inequality. He believes that these movements are growing in strength and will bring an end to capitalistic exploitation and the powerful national systems—as we know them today—over the next 2 centuries.

The totalitarian nations of Eastern Europe saw dramatic social changes in the past decade. Clearly, these are conflicts over extreme inequality. Many of the people involved in these changes see capitalism as a means to greater equality, but others may not be willing to give up the personal security of socialism in exchange for the economic insecurity of capitalism. It will be interesting to watch what solutions the countries of Eastern Europe find to solve their problems and how the rest of the world responds to the needs of these countries. World systems theory has done a great deal to alter our perception of the world, and it has generated a great deal of scholarly research by viewing the world as one large, complex system. It will be interesting to see whether world systems theory will influence ongoing political actions of nations.

**World systems theory**
Conflict theory stating that core nations dominate the economies of peripheral nations

**Core nations**
Industrial nations that exploit underdeveloped, peripheral nations

**Peripheral nations**
Underdeveloped nations who are exploited by core nations

## 16.10c Social Change Theory: A Synthesis

Few theorists today are so optimistic that they believe societies inevitably improve; few are so pessimistic that they believe that societies inevitably decay. Most integrate the ideas of Sorokin, the structural functionalists, and the conflict theorists. Societies do change, but the changes are not necessarily good or bad. Societies attempt to remain stable; although a stable society is usually better than a chaotic one, stability sometimes causes harsh conditions, injustice, and oppression. When this happens, conflicts arise; society is forced to change perhaps for the better, but not necessarily so.

Change and stability, then, are processes that can take place simultaneously in any society. At any given time, one or the other will dominate, depending on the society's needs. Change is inevitable, and it is often beneficial.

### thinking SOCIOLOGICALLY

1. Which theory or combination of theories do you think best describes how society changes?
2. How have social changes in the past decade shaped your personal development? Take into consideration institutional and technological changes.
3. Examine Figures 16-4 and 16-5. How do you think the variation in Internet usage around the world both accounts for and reflects social movements and social change? How do you think these tables reflect the various theories of social change?

**Figure 16-4** Internet Users in the World, Distribution by World Regions 2012 Q2

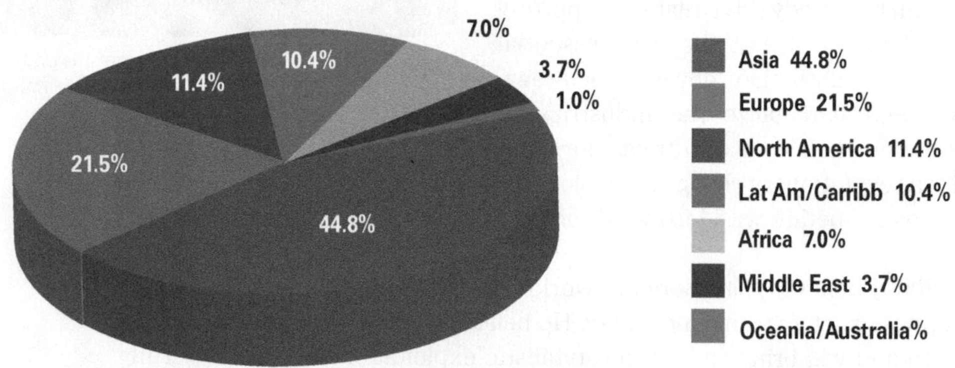


Basis: 2,405,518,376 Internet users on June 30,2012 copyright © 2012, Miniwatts Marketing Group

**World Internet Usage and Population Statistics—June 30, 2012**

| World Regions | Population (2012 est.) | Internet Users Dec. 31, 2000 | Internet Users Latest Data | Penetration (% of Population) | Growth 2000–2012 | Users (% of Total) |
|---|---|---|---|---|---|---|
| Africa | 1,073,380,925 | 4,514,400 | 167,335,676 | 15.6% | 3,606.7% | 7.0% |
| Asia | 3,922,066,987 | 114,304,000 | 1,076,681,059 | 27.5% | 841.9% | 44.8% |
| Europe | 820,918,446 | 105,096,093 | 518,512,109 | 63.2% | 393.4% | 21.5% |
| Middle East | 223,608,203 | 3,284,800 | 90,000,455 | 40.2% | 2,639.9% | 3.7% |
| North America | 348,280,154 | 108,096,800 | 273,785,413 | 78.6% | 153.3% | 11.4% |
| Latin America/Caribbean | 593,688,638 | 18,068,919 | 254,915,745 | 42.9% | 1,310.8% | 10.6% |
| Oceania/Australia | 35,903,569 | 7,620,480 | 24,287,919 | 67.6% | 218.7% | 1.0% |
| World Total | 7,017,846,922 | 360,985,492 | 2,405,518,376 | 34.3% | 566.4% | 100.0% |

Figure and Table adapted from Internet World Stats.
Retrieved from http://www.internetworldstats.com/stats.htm.

**Figure 16-5** Facebook Users in the World by Region, 2012

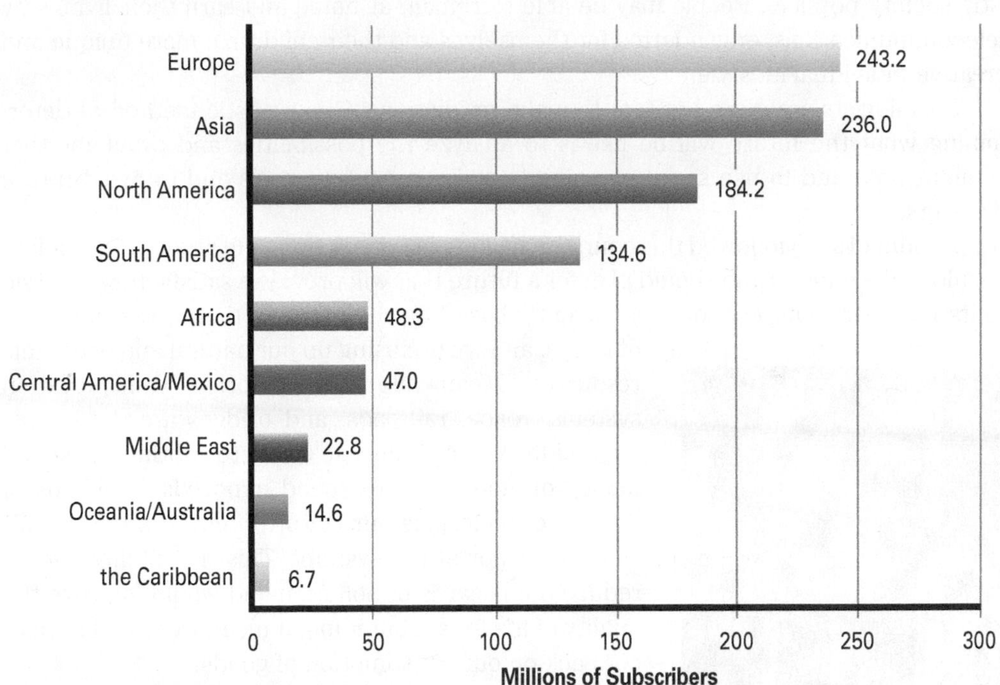


The total number of Facebook subscribers in the world was estimated to be 937,407,180 on September 30, 2012. Copyright © 2012, Miniwatts Marketing Group

**Facebook Users for 2011 and 2012**

| Geographic Regions (in order by size) | Facebook Users March 31, 2011 | Facebook Users March 31, 2012 |
|---|---|---|
| Europe | 200,260,360 | 232,835,740 |
| Asia | 131,556,800 | 195,034,380 |
| North America | 173,640,240 | 173,284,940 |
| South America | 69,594,760 | 112,531,100 |
| Central America | 28,090,240 | 41,332,940 |
| Africa | 27,414,240 | 40,205,580 |
| Middle East | 15,779,440 | 20,247,900 |
| Oceania/Australia | 12,333,780 | 13,597,380 |
| Caribbean | 5,362,600 | 6,355,320 |
| World Total | 664,032,4640 | 835,525,280 |

Adapted from Internet World Stats, "Usage and Population Statistics." Retrieved from http://www.internetworldstats.com/facebook.htm

## APPLYING SOCIOLOGY TO THE FUTURE

Futurists, people who attempt to describe what the future will be like, range from the most pessimistic doomsayers to the greatest optimists. The doomsayers predict an economic depression far worse than the depression of the 1930s. The wisest investment, they say, is to buy a piece of land in a very remote part of the country, build a substantial shelter that will be well hidden from the hordes of the poor and starving who will be roaming the countryside when the economy collapses, and bury near the shelter a supply of dehydrated food, guns, and other basic equipment needed to survive alone in the wilderness.

The optimists predict an end to poverty and drudgery and believe that human innovation will solve our problems. For example, computers may make a more individualistic society possible. People may be able to remain at home and earn their livings by telecommunications, engendering for themselves and their children a more unique and creative individual lifestyle.

Sociologists are more hesitant to make predictions. One realistic method of determining what the future will be like is to analyze the possibilities and problems that it might hold and to use social planning to strive for future goals and to avoid future disasters.

Etzioni (1980) followed this course in making his predictions. He argues that society should make choices and should plan for a future that will provide a satisfactory lifestyle to its members. Our economy is currently based on the consumption of vast amounts of goods, and we are using up our natural and economic resources. Meanwhile, our factories, transportation systems, roads, railroads, and bridges are deteriorating rapidly. We must choose either to continue to spend money on goods—or to spend hundreds of billions of dollars to modernize our factories and to build an efficient transportation system. This rebuilding would reduce the hazards of pollution and would improve the quality of life for all, but it might mean we would have to cut back on our consumption of goods.

*The choices of a society affect the future of it. The infrastructure of our country—such as factories, railroads, and bridges—is deteriorating.* (Shutterstock)

Etzioni used the typical approach of sociologists in his study of social change, which is to try to understand the social system. Our social system is based on a profit-oriented economy, and we manufacture products that can be sold for a profit. Our system functions to support a cycle of production and consumption; it does not, however, support modernization of factories or an efficient use of resources, unless such actions provide a profit. By understanding that our system now functions only when profits are made, it is possible to predict what will happen if we continue to function as we have in the past. We will use up all our resources.

Nonetheless, innovations can be made, institutions can be changed, and values and goals can be altered. A society can change its course and move in a new direction. We cannot, today, optimistically assume that progress will be inevitable and that we do not have to plan to reach our goals. Neither is there reason to be so pessimistic that we resign ourselves to becoming victims of a social system in decline. Furthermore, we cannot blithely assume that society will run its course from good times to bad and then bounce back to good times again because we could, in the meantime, destroy all life on earth. By understanding how societies function, we can make choices, alter our social institutions, and develop lifestyles that will reduce conflict, avoid ecological devastation, and support human life in the ever-increasing numbers that seem inevitable. We can plan to use our resources wisely.

Sociologists who study society from a historical perspective, observing the relationship between social changes and social problems—for example, increased automobile use and today's energy problems—are likely to be frustrated by the practice of solving problems as they arise rather than trying to find long-range solutions. These solutions might require better technology to control auto emissions or clean up oil spills, for example. In any case, more effective solutions can be developed if we understand the social basis of the problems.

Our problems are caused, in part, by a cultural lag in our awareness of future needs. Social planning could help us to change our social systems and to improve the situation. Those who have a vested interest in our current system might resist change, which would create a certain amount of conflict; yet such conflict might be beneficial to society. Sociology, by helping us to understand social change, can help us to direct it. For example, academic sociologists will continue to study how changes affect our social institutions and will help us to predict future trends. Professional sociologists in the workplace may use knowledge of sociology to help policymakers and social planners design long-range solutions to social and technological problems, and nonprofessional sociologists in the workplace may use knowledge of social change to help them foresee and plan for business trends and consumer needs. Indeed, you may use knowledge of social change and other sociological theories to plan for your family's future.

Sociology originally grew out of an attempt to understand and do something about the social problems related to changes brought about by modernization. Thus, as Shostak notes, "It was conceived as a way of managing social change and helping humankind stay in charge of events" (1985, p. 172). Although it may be impossible to predict with certainty the impact of technological or institutional changes on the whole social system, sociology does alert us to the important fact that a change in one part of the system will continue to reverberate throughout the system long into the future. Armed with this knowledge and with the knowledge of the other theories, perspectives, and concepts sociology offers, humankind may be better equipped to shape its social institutions, and you may be better equipped to shape your own life. The authors hope that this introduction to the study of sociology has sparked your own sociological imagination so that you can think about the good life for you in terms of social as well as individual accomplishments.

# CHAPTER 16 Wrapping it up

## Summary

1. Urban communities can exist only when there is a group of people to grow and process food for the urbanites. A degree of social organization is also necessary to transform a crowded group of people into a social group that behaves in an orderly and predictable manner.
2. The first urban communities developed approximately 10,000 years ago during the horticultural era. This development was possible because of increased food production and the creation of regular surpluses. Several thousand years later, technological advances—such as the plow, metallurgy, use of animals, counting, and writing—and the increasing complexity of social and political organization enabled cities to grow to unprecedented sizes.
3. The fall of Rome in the fifth century AD marked the beginning of a precipitous decline in city size and complexity that lasted for nearly 600 years. Urban communities did not begin to grow substantially again until the late eighteenth century with the dawn of the industrial age. Urban populations then increased dramatically; and within a few decades, more people lived in cities than in rural areas.
4. The most dramatic increase in urban population is in Developing World countries, the least developed countries. Some of this urban growth became concentrated in squatter settlements. Today, there are about 250 cities in the world with increasing populations of more than 1 million people, and there is little hope of this trend abating.
5. In the United States today, three-fourths of our population live in urban areas, which have increased in size as well as in number. The rapid industrial and population growth in large cities during the early part of the twentieth century caused people and industries to move from central cities to the sparsely populated areas outside of them. This process resulted in the modern metropolis.
6. A *metropolitan statistical area (MSA)* is a large population nucleus combined with adjacent communities that have a high degree of social and economic integration with that nucleus. A megalopolis results from the overlap of two or more metropolitan areas.
7. Urban ecology is the study of the interrelationships of people and the environment in which they live. It includes urban processes: (a) concentration and deconcentration as people move into and out of geographical areas, (b) ecological specialization, and (c) invasion of and succession by new and different social groups in land areas.
8. Various models of urban structure and spatial growth include the *concentric zone model of cities*, spreading out equally in all directions producing uniform circles of growth; the *sector model of cities*, as organized into pie-shaped wedges radiating from the central business district; and the *multiple nuclei zone model of cities*, which has various centers as well as duplicate areas of business, industrial, shopping, and residential locations.
9. Cities and suburbs, while often described in terms of population, also involve a sense of community. Gemeinschaft communities are characterized by a sense of intimacy, common identity, and tradition, in contrast to gesellschaft communities, which are characterized by impersonality, self-interest, and an emphasis on progress.
10. In contrast to popular stereotypes, cities and suburbs have quite diverse populations. Early sociologists believed that city living was unhealthy and encouraged family breakdown, violence, and depersonalization. Recent research, however, shows that a variety of people and lifestyles are found in the city. A number of people prefer the city because of its social and economic advantages.
11. Suburban life is also quite diverse, and suburbanites do not differ in lifestyle or values

from city residents with similar demographic and social characteristics.

12. Our cities face a number of problems today—notably poverty and unemployment, crime, and inadequate schools. Slum areas and ghetto areas experience the most serious social problems.
13. The downtown areas of many cities are being revitalized, and a number of residential neighborhoods are being given a new appearance as a result of urban renewal and urban homesteading projects. Some urban neighborhoods are being rejuvenated by gentrification efforts.
14. Collective behavior is spontaneous, loosely structured, and transitory. Institutionalized behavior, by contrast, is more orderly and has stable goals, expectations, and values.
15. Certain conditions increase the likelihood of collective behavior. Smelser described six of them: (1) *structural conduciveness*, the existence of conditions or situations in which collective behavior is possible; (2) *structural strain*—some type of frustration, stress, conflict, or dissatisfaction in society; (3) *generalized belief*, a shared understanding of the reasons for the strain and stress; (4) *precipitating factors*, events that trigger a collective response; (5) *mobilization for action*, in which individuals or groups encourage participation in collective behavior; and (6) the *initiation of social controls*, in order to counter the conditions just listed.
16. The most common type of spatially proximate collective behavior is the *crowd*. The characteristics of crowds are anonymity, suggestibility, contagion, and emotional arousability.
17. Crowds vary in type, ranging from very unemotional and highly unstructured crowds to very emotional, active crowds, such as mobs or rioting crowds.
18. There are four major theories of acting-crowd behavior. The classical theory of Le Bon posited the existence of a collective or group mind that has a regressive influence on behavior, which tends to be irrational, irritable, and impulsive.
19. Bulmer's interactionist theory focused on social interactions and a circular reaction process that generates milling, collective excitement, and social contagion.
20. The emergent-norm theory of Turner and Killian emphasized how norms influence crowd behavior and how the emergence of new norms causes a divergence of crowd views and behaviors.
21. Bark's game theory stressed the rational decision-making process involved in crowd behavior and suggested that people consciously weigh the rewards and costs associated with various kinds of collective activity.
22. Social movements are organized collective efforts to bring about social change and establish a new order of social thought and action. Turner and Killian classify movements in terms of their orientation, whereas other authorities use different classification schemes.
23. As social movements develop, they generally go through four distinct stages: social unrest, popular excitement, formalization, and institutionalization. Although all social movements grow through roughly the same process, the goals of different movements can vary considerably. Their success depends heavily on their ability to effectively mobilize resources.
24. Society is changing so rapidly that sociology has become, in many respects, the study of social change.
25. Evolutionary theory proposes the optimistic view that change is progress, in which growth is always good, and that stagnation leads to decay.
26. Conflict theorists are also optimistic about social change, but they believe that conflict will occasionally arise to correct adverse social developments. The outcome of such conflict, they say, will be better social systems.
27. Cyclical theorists can be very pessimistic. They assume that societies grow, reach a peak, and then inevitably decay. Some cyclical theorists, however, do not assume that change is always for the better or the worse. Societies move back and forth, they contend, emphasizing first one value, then another, as the needs of the society change.
28. Structural functionalists have been concerned primarily with stability, but they recognize that society changes occasionally. Often, a change that affects one social institution will be followed by cultural lag, a disruption in the functioning of society until other institutions adjust to the change.
29. Most sociologists agree that society is orderly and that social institutions function to maintain order. They also agree that conflicts may arise when the existing social order causes hardship for the members of a society but that such conflicts can be beneficial.
30. Modernization theorists believe that underdeveloped nations have different natural resources, different values, and a different work ethic—all of which have caused their patterns of

growth to differ from those of the developed, or core nations.

31. Dependency or world systems theorists believe that less developed nations are exploited by the nations that developed first.
32. In the future, it is hoped that we will be able to plan innovations that will improve our ecology and our ways of relating to one another.

## Discussion Questions

1. Discuss the types of factors that historically led to the location and growth of urban areas.
2. What are some of the problems associated with Developing World urbanization?
3. What are some factors that have led to urbanization in different areas of the United States?
4. Compare the reasons for the growth of metropolitan statistical areas and of nonmetropolitan areas.
5. Discuss how the urban processes of concentration and deconcentration, ecological specialization, and invasion and succession form the basis of different models of urban structure.
6. Does your city, or one with which you are familiar, fit any one of the three models of urban structure described in this chapter? Why or why not?
7. Why is it argued that relationships and communities shift from gemeinschaft to gesellschaft characteristics with increasing urbanization?
8. Describe conditions that characterize a slum and a ghetto. Why does either exist?
9. Identify two urban problems of the city in which you live or a nearby city and discuss them, using a sociological perspective.
10. What is meant by urban renewal? Discuss the impact on families of tearing down houses in blighted areas to build new apartments or housing units.
11. Examine the pros and cons of such activities as downtown revitalization, homesteading, and gentrification.
12. How does collective behavior differ from institutionalized behavior? Give examples of each type of behavior.
13. Select an incident of collective behavior that has occurred recently, and discuss the preconditions that might have led to it.
14. Explore the different types of crowds and crowd behavior that tend to exist or have existed in your college campus, community, or the city where you live.
15. How do mobs and riots differ? Are either or both less likely when and where people know one another?
16. Select examples not provided in the text that illustrate each of the theories of acting-crowd behavior. Discuss how the theories can be used to explain each of the respective examples you have selected.
17. Examine the development and life cycle of a contemporary social movement or any other social movement in which you might be interested.
18. Discuss how the geography of the United States led to its development as a modern industrial nation.
19. Discuss how closely linked American ideology is to what Weber called "rationalism," as opposed to an ideology linked to traditionalism.
20. Discuss how the American political system developed as a result of geography and of rationalism.
21. Why does the United States have a less developed railroad system than Europe and Japan?
22. Discuss ways in which the United States could change its transportation system and the advantages and disadvantages to such changes.
23. Discuss the reasons why Developing World nations cannot develop industries the way the United States did.
24. Predict the future. Are you an optimist or a pessimist?

## A

**Account** .................................. 116
An effort at maintaining the self by explaining the reasons for or facts surrounding the behavior

**Achieved status** ........................ 85
A status that you choose voluntarily or attain through effort or ability

**Acquaintance rape** .................. 236
Rape by someone who is known to the person being raped (such as in date rape)

**Acting crowd** ........................... 450
A crowd that acts on the basis of aroused impulse and thus one that may be volatile, aggressive, and dangerous

**Advanced horticultural societies** 162
Societies with irrigation systems and other advanced farming practices

**Affective neutrality versus affectivity** ............................ 89
A pattern variable that pertains to expectations about the extent to which emotions are part of role relationships

**Age-adjusted death rate** ........... 399
The number of deaths occurring at each age, for each sex, per 100,000

**Age segregation** ..................... 308
The separation of groups by age, such as occurs in our education system

**Age-sex composition** ............... 397
The number of men and women in the population, along with their ages

**Aggregate** ............................ 91
Any collection of people together in one place that interact briefly and sporadically

**Agrarian societies** .................... 162
Complex societies with farming, armies, merchants, and a concentration of wealth in the hands of a few people

**Alcoholism** .............................. 374
A disease related to the drinking of alcohol that has identifiable and progressive symptoms (if untreated, alcoholism can lead to mental damage, physical incapacity, and early death)

**Altruistic suicide** .................... 17
Suicide that results from being overly integrated into groups and the group meaning taking on more importance than the individual

**Amalgamation** ........................ 197
The process by which different racial or ethnic groups form a new group through interbreeding or intermarriage

**Anglo conformity** .................... 196
A form of assimilation in which the minority loses its identity completely and adopts the norms and practices of the dominant WASP culture

**Animism** ................................ 278
The religious belief that spirits inhabit virtually everything in nature and control all aspects of life and destiny

**Anomic suicide** ....................... 17
Suicide that results from sudden changes in society or in one's life, leading to a disruption in the patterns that guide one's life

**Anomie** ................................. 142
When deviance arises from the incongruence between a society's emphasis on attaining certain goals and the availability of legitimate, institutionalized means of reaching those goals

**Anthropology** .......................... 10
The study of the physical, biological, social, and cultural development of humans, often on a comparative basis

**Artifacts** ................................ 73
Physical products or objects created through human actions

**Ascribed status** ....................... 85
A status obtained involuntarily or without effort on the part of the individual

**Ascription versus achievement** ... 90
A pattern variable that pertains to whether interactions within a role should be guided by the ascribed or the achieved status of those who are interacting in a particular relationship

**Assimilation** ........................... 196
The process through which individuals and groups forsake their own cultural tradition to become part of a different group and tradition

**Associational (or organizational) group** ................................... 91
A group of people who join together to pursue a common interest in a organized, formally structured way

**Authoritarian personality theory** ... 192
The view that people with an authoritarian type of personality are more likely to be prejudiced than those who have other personality types

**Authority** ........................... 228, 332
Power accepted as legitimate by those it affects

**Autonomy** .............................. 228
The ability to decide how work will be done

## B

**Barefoot doctors** ..................... 387
People chosen by the peasants in the communes in Communist China to provide medicine and treat simple illnesses and emergencies, who receive 3 to 18 months of training

**Beguines** ............................... 224
Communes existing during the Middle Ages that consisted of peasant women who chose not to marry and who took vows of celibacy

**Beliefs** ................................. 70
Views that people share about what is true or what really exists

**Bilateral lineage** ..................... 250
A descent system in which influence, wealth, and power are assigned to both sides of the family

**Blaming the victim** .................. 139
A type of reasoning that implies that social problems are caused by the people facing them

**Blended families** ..................... 253
Families composed of at least one formerly married spouse, the children of the previous marriage or marriages, and new offspring

**Bourgeoisie** .......................... 14

The class of people who own the means of production

**Buddhism** ............................. 291

One of the world's principal religions, adherents of which follow the teachings of Buddha, the enlightened one, who preached a doctrine of "Four Noble Truths"

**Bureaucracy** .......................... 100

A hierarchical, formally organized structural arrangement of an organization based on the division of labor and authority

## C

**Capitalism** ............................. 336

An economic system in which all of the means of production are privately owned

**Caste system** .......................... 164

A system of stratification in which one's social position is ascribed at birth, one's value is assessed in terms of religious or traditional beliefs, and in which upward social mobility is impossible

**Casual crowd** .......................... 450

A crowd that is high in anonymity but low in suggestibility, contagion, emotional arousal, and unity

**Categorical group** .................... 91

A group of people who share a common characteristic but do not interact or have any social organization

**Census** ................................ 396

An official count of the number of people in a given area

**Charismatic authority** ............... 332

Authority granted to someone on the bases of his or her personality characteristics

**Chiropractors** .......................... 380

Those who practice healing by manipulating the body, especially the spine

**Christianity** ............................ 286

One of the principal religions of the world, followers of which profess faith in the teachings of Jesus Christ

**Church** ................................ 281

An institutionalized organization of people who share common religious beliefs

**Citizen** .................................. 334

One who is considered a member of a state and who is entitled to the privileges and freedoms granted to members of the state

**City-state** ............................. 333

A city and the surrounding area ruled independently of other areas

**Class-consciousness** ......... 16, 182

Awareness among members of a society that the society is stratified

**Class system** .......................... 163

A system of stratification found in industrial societies in which one's class is determined by one's wealth and in which vertical social mobility is possible

**Classical perspective** ............... 451

A view of acting crowd behavior that suggests that people in a crowd lose their conscious personalities and act impulsively on the basis of their instincts rather than reason

**Closed system** ........................ 164

A system of stratification in which there is no movement from one rank to another

**Collective behavior** ................. 446

The spontaneous, unstructured, and transitory behavior of a group of people in reaction to a specific event

**Collective conscience** ............... 16

A collective psyche that results from the blending of many individual mentalities, but exists above any one individual

**Collective excitement** ............... 452

In the interactionist perspective on crowd behavior, the stage during which milling reaches a high level of agitation

**Communism** .......................... 336

An economic system in which members of the society jointly own the means of production

**Community** ............................ 429

A collection of people within a geographic area who share some degree of mutual identification, interdependence, or organization of activities

**Comparable worth** .................... 228

Evaluating and rewarding different occupations equally if the work in each occupation requires the same level of skill and is of equal value to the employer

**Complementary needs** ............... 256

A theory of mate selection based on the idea that people marry those who provide the maximum need gratification when needs tend to be complementary rather than similar

**Concentration** ........................ 436

An urban ecological process in which population, services, and institutions come to be gathered most densely in the areas in which conditions are advantageous

**Concentric zone model** ............... 437

A model of urban structure, showing that cities grow out equally in all directions from their original centers, producing uniform circles of growth that have their own distinctive land use, population, activities, and institutions

**Concept** ................................ 36

An abstract system of meaning that enables us to perceive a phenomenon in a certain way

**Conflict theory** .................. 23, 144

A social theory that views conflict as inevitable and natural and as a significant cause of social change

**Confucianism** .......................... 292

One of the world's principal religions, found mainly in China, adherents of which follow the teachings of Confucius

**Conjugal families** ..................... 245

Families consisting of a husband and wife, with or without children

**Content analysis** ..................... 44

The procedure of systematically extracting thematic data from a wide range of communications

**Contest mobility** ........................ 324

A competitive system of education in which those who do best at each level are able to move on the next level

**Control group** .......................... 41

In an experiment, the group not exposed to the independent variable that is introduced to the experimental group

**Conventional crowd** ................. 450

A crowd, such as the spectators at a baseball game, whose members are anonymous but share a common focus and follow established social norms and rules

**Core nations** .......................... 459

Industrial nations that exploit underdeveloped, peripheral nations

**Counterculture** .......................... 77

A subculture that adheres to a set of norms and values that sharply contradict the dominant norms and values of the society of which that group is a part

**Credentialism**.......................... 312

The practice of requiring degrees for most high-paying jobs, whether or not the degrees actually signify skills necessary to accomplish the job

**Crime** .................................. 149

A violation of a criminal statutory law accompanied by a specific punishment applied by some governmental authority

**Crowd** .................................. 449

A temporary group of people in face-to-face contact who share a common interest or focus of attention

**Cult** ..................................... 282

Extreme form of religious organization that calls for a totally new and unique lifestyle, often under the direction of a charismatic leader

**Cultural lag**............................ 73

The tendency for non-material culture to lag behind material culture

**Cultural pluralism** .................... 197

The situation in which the various ethnic groups in a society maintain their distinctive cultural patterns, subsystems, and institutions

**Cultural relativism**.................... 64

The belief that cultures must be judged on their own terms rather than by the standards of another culture

**Cultural transmission theory** ...... 145

The theory that a community's deviance may be transmitted to newcomers through learning and socialization

**Cultural universals** .................. 78

Aspects of culture that are shared by all people, such as symbols, shelter, food, and a belief system

**Culture** ................................ 61

A system of ideas, values, beliefs, knowledge, norms, customs, and technology shared by almost everyone in a particular society

**Cyclical change theory**............... 456

The view that societies go through a cycle of birth, maturation, decline, and death

## D

**De facto segregation**................. 198

School assignment based on residence boundaries in which blacks and whites live in separate neighborhoods

**De jure segregation** ................. 198

The legal assignment of children to schools solely because of race

**Decentralized bureaucracies** ...... 323

Putting the decision making processes in the hands of the people or local units rather than in the hands of a centralized few

**Deconcentration** ..................... 436

Movement outward from the city because of increases in land values and taxes and declines in services and public facilities

**Degenerative diseases** .............. 372

Those diseases that slowly disable the body as one gets older, such as heart disease and cancer

**Democracy**............................ 334

A power structure in which people govern themselves, either directly or through elected representatives

**Demographic transition** ........... 416

The change from high birth and death rates to low birth and death rates with a period of rapid population growth in between (this transition occurs as a society evolves from a traditional pre-modern stage to a modern industrial stage)

**Demography** .......................... 396

The statistical study of population, especially data on birth rates, death rates, marriage rates, health, and migration

**Denominations** ....................... 281

Well-established and highly institutionalized churches

**Dependency ratio** .................... 408

The ratio between the number of persons in the dependent population and the number of people in the supportive or working population

**Dependency theory** ................. 458

Conflict theory stating that underdeveloped nations cannot industrialize because they are dependent on the nations already industrialized

**Dependent variable** ................. 39

A variable that is changed or influenced by another variable

**Descriptive research**.................. 45

Research that describes social reality or provides facts about the social world

**Deviance** .............................. 131

Variation from a set of norms or shared social expectations

**Diagnostic related group (DRG)** ... 382

The group that devises the schedule of payment limits set by the federal government for Medicaid and Medicare recipients

**Differential association theory** ... 145

The theory that deviance results when individuals have more contact with groups that define deviance favorably than with groups that define it unfavorably

**Differential reinforcement** ........ 146

The view that the acquisition and persistence of either deviant or conforming behavior is a function of what behaviors have been rewarded or punished

**Direct relationship** .................. 39

A relationship between two variables in which an increase in one variable is accompanied by an increase in the other; compare with inverse relationship

**Disclaimers** ........................... 116

An aspect of maintaining our presentation of self in which we deny behavior that contradicts how we wish to be viewed

**Discrimination** ....................... 193

Overt unequal and unfair treatment of people on the basis of their membership in a particular group

**Displacement**.......................... 201

A process occurring in split labor markets in which higher paid workers are replaced with cheaper labor

**Diversification** ....................... 357

The corporate practice of entering business in a variety of areas in order to protect profits (a decrease in profits in one type of business might be made up by an increase in profits in another type, for example)

**Division of labor** .................... 162

The assignment of inter-related specialized tasks within a social system in order to accomplish a goal

**Downward mobility** ................. 180

A move to a position of lower rank in the stratification system

**Dramaturgical approach** ........... 115

An approach to the study of interaction in which interaction is compared to a drama on stage; the importance of setting and presentation of self are emphasized

**Dysfunctions** .......................... 21

In structural functional theory, factors that lead to the disruption or breakdown of the social system

## E

**Ecclesia** ................................ 281

An official state religion that includes all or most members of society

**Ecological specialization** ........... 436

The concentration of homogeneous groups and activities into different sections or urban areas

**Ecology** ................................ 418

The study of the interrelationships between living organisms and the environment

**Economic determinism** .............. 14

The idea that economic factors are responsible for most social change and for the nature of social conditions, activities, and institutions

**Economic system** .................... 331

The social institution that provides for the production, distribution, and consumption of goods and services

**Economics** ............................ 10

The study of how goods, services, and wealth are produced, consumed, and distributed

**Ecumenism** ............................ 298

The trend for different denominations to join together in pursuit of common interest in a spirit of worldwide Christian unity

**Egalitarian** ............................ 251

The norm of authority in the family in which decisions are equally divided between husband and wife

**Egoistic suicide** ....................... 17

Suicide that results from lack of social integration into meaningful groups, leaving the individual with a sense of being isolated

**Emergent-norm perspective** ........ 452

A view of collective behavior that emphasizes how new norms emerge and influence the behavior of crowds

**Emigration** ............................ 401

Movement of people out of an area

**Endogamy** ............................ 251

A marriage norm requiring a person to marry someone from his or her own group

**Epidemiology** .......................... 372

The study of the spread of diseases

**Equal Right Amendment (ERA)** ...... 232

A proposed amendment to the Constitution of the United States, which was not ratified, that gave equal rights to women

**Estate system** .......................... 164

A system of stratification in which one's social position is ascribed by law or through inheritance

**Ethnic antagonism** .................... 200

Mutual opposition, conflict, or hostility among different ethnic groups

**Ethnic group** .......................... 188

Group of people characterized by cultural traits that reflect national origin, religion, and language

**Ethnocentrism** ........................ 63

The view that one's own culture is superior to others and should be used as the standard against which other cultures are judged

**Ethnographic research** .............. 40

A form of descriptive research focusing on the sociology of meaning through close observation of sociocultural phenomena

**Evaluative research** ................. 47

Research that measures how well a program or project works in relation to its goals

**Evolutionary theory** ................. 30

A theory of social development that suggests that societies, like biological organisms, progress through stages of increasing complexity

**Exchange theory** .................... 28

A theory of interaction that attempts to explain social behavior in terms of reciprocity of costs and rewards

**Exclusion** ............................ 201

Attempts to keep cheaper labor from taking jobs from groups that receive higher pay

**Exogamy** ............................... 251

A marriage norm requiring a person to marry someone from outside his or her own group

**Experimental design** ................. 41

A scientific procedure in which at least two matched groups, differing only in the variable being studied, are used to collect and compare data

**Experimental group** ................. 41

In an experiment, the group to which an independent variable is introduced, with that variable not being introduced in the control group

**Explanatory research** .............. 46

Research that attempts to explain why things do or do not happen by examining the relationship between social variables

**Exploratory research**................. 45

Research that attempts to answer the question "what" by explaining a new social phenomenon

**Expressive role** ....................... 120

A role that emphasizes warmth and understanding rather than action or leadership—and is traditionally associated more with women than with men

**Extended family** ....................... 246

A family that goes beyond the nuclear family to include other nuclear families and relatives such as grandparents, aunts, uncles, and cousins

**External means of control**........... 133

Pressures or sanctions that are applied to members of society by others

## F

**False consciousness**.................. 182

Lack of awareness of class differences and acceptance of upper-class rule

**Family** .................................. 245

A group of kin united by blood, marriage, or adoption who share a common residence for some part of their lives and assume reciprocal rights and obligations with regard to one another

**Family of orientation** ................ 246

The nuclear family into which one was born and in which one was reared

**Family of procreation** .............. 246

The nuclear family formed by marriage

**Fatalistic suicide** .................... 17
Suicide that results from oppressive social conditions that lead one to a fatal sense of hopelessness

**Fecundity** .............................. 397
A woman's potential for bearing children

**Fee-for-service** ........................ 377
A medical payment system in which the physician is paid for each visit and each service rendered

**Feminization of poverty** .............. 232
An increase in the proportion of women below the poverty line, particularly female heads of households

**Fertility** .............................. 397
A measure of the rate at which people are being born

**Fetal monitoring** ........................ 378
Measuring the vital signs of the infant as it is being born

**Folk culture** .......................... 77
The culture of the working class or ethnic groups

**Folk society** .......................... 439
A community described by Redfield as small, isolated, homogenous, and kin-oriented

**Folkways** ............................. 71
Norms of conduct of everyday life that bring only mild censure or punishment if they are violated

**Formal external controls** ........... 135
Generally occur in a public setting such as a courtroom

**Formal organization** ................. 98
Large social group deliberately organized to achieve certain specific, clearly stated goals

**Formalization** ........................... 455
The stage in the development of a social movement in which a formal structure is developed, and rules, policies, and tactics are laid out

**Fraternal polyandry** ................. 250
A form of polyandry where brothers are co-husbands

**Free market** .......................... 337
An economic system in which all people are theoretically free to buy, sell, and make a profit

**Frustration-aggression theory** ...... 191
The theory that prejudice results when personal frustrations are displaced to a socially approved racial or ethnic target

**Functional alternatives** .............. 22
Meeting functions of the system in ways other than initially intended

**Fundamentalism** ..................... 281
The belief that the Bible is the divine word of God and that all statements in it are to be taken literally, word for word

## G

**Game perspective** .................... 452
A view of crowd behavior that suggests that members think about their actions and consciously try to act in ways that will produce rewards

**Gemeinschaft** .......................... 439
A traditional community characterized by a sense of solidarity and common identity and emphasizing intimate and personal relationships

**Gender** ................................ 219
A social status that refers to differences between the sexes, specifically to differences in masculinity and femininity

**Gender identity** ....................... 124
The social construction of boys and girls, men and women, as opposed to their biological characteristics

**Gender roles** .......................... 219
The expectations for behavior deriving from culturally created definitions of masculinity and femininity

**Generalized belief** .................... 447
A stage in the development of collective behavior in which people share a common identification and interpretation of a problem

**Generalized others** ................. 112
The assumption that other people have similar attitudes, values, beliefs, and expectations, and therefore that it is unnecessary to know a specific individual in order to know how to behave toward that individual

**Genocide** ............................. 199
The deliberate destruction of an entire racial or ethnic group

**Geography** ............................. 11
The study of the physical environment and the distribution of plants and animals, including humans

**Gesellschaft** .......................... 439
A modern community characterized by individualism, mobility, and impersonality, with an emphasis on progress rather than tradition

**Ghetto** .................................. 442
An area in a city in which members of a racial or ethnic minority are forcibly segregated

**Going green** .......................... 394
The phrase that defines people who are mindful of what they consume, mindful of others, and who are working towards protecting the environment both nationally and internationally

**Gross domestic product (GDP)** ...... 337
The total value of all final goods and services produced within the borders of a country per year

**Group marriage** ....................... 249
A form of marriage in which several or many men are married to several or many women

## H

**Health maintenance organization (HMO)** ................. 382
A prepaid healthcare plan in which a fee is paid in advance for all necessary healthcare

**Heroic medicine** ..................... 376
Dramatic medical treatments such as bleeding, blistering, or administering poisonous laxatives

**Hidden curriculum** ..................... 310
The teaching and learning of things such as obedience, competition, and patriotism that are not part of the stated curriculum

**High culture** .......................... 77
The materials and ideas of wealthy, affluent, or upper classes (in contrast to popular culture)

**Hinduism** ............................. 290
One of the world's principal polytheistic religions, with no religious hierarchy but a close involvement with society and the cosmic order, that is practiced mainly in India and Pakistan

**History** ................................. 11
The study of the past; social history is concerned with past human social events.

**Horizontal expansion** ............... 357
Corporations taking over similar businesses in order to gain a monopoly and reduce competition

**Horticultural communities** ......... 430
Small-scale farming that relies on tools such as the hoe to till the soil

**Hunting-and-gathering societies** ... 162
Small, often nomadic societies that have no agriculture and live on food that is found

**Hypothesis** ............................. 39
A statement about the relationship between variables that can be put to an empirical test.

## I

**I** ......................................... 112
The acting, unselfconscious person

**Ideal culture** .......................... 78
The norms and values that people profess to follow

**Ideal type** .............................. 100
A model of the hypothetical, pure form of an existing entity

**Ideology** ................................ 182
A set of ideas about what society is like, how it functions, whether it is good or bad, and how it should be changed

**Idioculture** ............................ 79
The system of knowledge, beliefs, behaviors, and customs that is unique to a given group

**Immigration** ........................... 401
Movement of people into an area

**In-group** ............................... 93
A social group to which people feel they belong and with which they share a consciousness of kind

**Incest** .................................. 251
Socially forbidden sexual relationships or marriages with certain close relatives

**Incumbent** ............................. 345
One holding an elected office

**Independent variable** .............. 39
A variable that causes a change or variation in a dependent variable

**Industrial societies** .................. 163
Societies with great division of labor, highly specialized work, and a great concentration of wealth

**Inequality** .............................. 161
Differences between groups in regard to wealth, status, or power

**Infectious diseases** .................. 372
Diseases caused by germs and viruses that can be spread from one person to another

**Informal external controls** ......... 135
Positive and negative controls—such as smiling, frowning, and high-fives—used to influence behavior

**Instincts** ................................ 109
Biological or hereditary impulses, drives, or behaviors that require no learning or reasoning

**Institutional discrimination** ......... 194
The continuing exclusion or oppression of a group as a result of criteria established by an institution

**Institutional racism** .................. 195
Racism that is embodied in the folkways, mores, or legal structures of a social institution

**Institutional Review Boards (IRBs)** 49
Committees on college/university campuses and in research organizations that provide oversight of research that is conducted on human subjects

**Institutionalization** .................. 455
The process by which orderly, stable, structured, and increasingly predictable forms of behavior or interaction are developed

**Institutionalized behavior** ........... 446
Recurrent behavior that follows an orderly pattern with a relatively stable set of goals, expectations, and values

**Institutions** ............................ 74
A stable cluster of values, norms, statuses, and roles that develops around a basic social goal

**Instrumental role** ..................... 120
A role that emphasizes accomplishment of tasks—such as earning a living to provide food and shelter—and is traditionally associated more with men than with women

**Integration** ............................ 196
The situation that exists when ethnicity becomes insignificant and everyone can freely and fully participates in the social, economic, and political mainstream

**Interactionist perspective** ......... 451
A view of crowd behavior that emphasizes how people in crowds reinforce and heighten one another's reactions

**Intergenerational mobility** ......... 180
A change of social position or rank, up or down, from one generation to the next, such as when children have a higher status than their parents

**Internal means of control** ........... 133
Learned patterns of control that exist in the minds of individuals and make them want to conform to social norms

**Intragenerational mobility** ......... 180
A change of social position or rank, up or down, within one's own lifetime

**Invasion** ................................ 436
An ecological process in which new types of people, organizations, or activities move into an area occupied by a different type

**Inverse relationship** .................. 39
A relationship between two variables such that an increase in one variable is accompanied by a decrease in the other; compare with direct relationship

**Iron law of oligarchy** ........... 101, 334
In democratic societies, the inevitable rise of a few elite leaders who dominate power; the perspective that a formal organization would be dominated by a small self-serving group of people who achieve power and promote their own interests

**Islam** ................................... 288
One of the world's principal religions, followers of which adhere to the teachings of the Koran and of Muhammad, a prophet

## J

**Judaism** ................................ 286
The oldest religion in the Western world and the first to teach monotheism, the Jews are both an ethnic community and a religious group.

## K

**Kinship** ................................ 248
The web of relationships among people linked by common ancestry, adoption, or marriage

## L

**Labeling theory** ........................146
A theory that emphasizes how certain behaviors are labeled "deviant" and how being given such a label influences a person's behavior

**Laissez faire** ...........................385
An approach to the economy in which there is no government planning or intervention

**Language** .............................. 66
The systematized use of speech and hearing to communicate feelings and ideas

**Latent force** ...........................332
A type of power in which force is threatened

**Latent functions** ........................ 21
The unintended consequences of a social system

**Law of human progress** .............. 12
Comte's notion that society has gone through three stages: the theological, the metaphysical, and the scientific

**Laws** .................................. 72
Formal, standardized expression of norms enacted by legislative bodies to regulate certain types of behavior

**Legal authority** ........................332
Authority based on a system of rules and regulations that determine how a society will be governed

**Legitimate** .............................181
To make the power of the dominant group acceptable to the masses so they let the dominant group rule without question

**Legitimate power** .....................332
Controlling the behavior of others through having people accept authority as necessary and beneficial to all

**Life chances** ..........................164
The opportunities a person has to improve his or her income and lifestyle

**Life expectancy** .......................410
The average years of life remaining for persons who attain a given age

**Lobby** ..................................345
An organization of people who want to influence the political process on a specific issue

**Looking-glass self** .....................113
A process occurring in social interaction and having three components

## M

**Macrosociology**..........................6
A level of sociological analysis concerned with large-scale structures and processes, such as war and unemployment

**Magnet schools** ........................322
Schools with special programs designed to attract exceptional students

**Malthusian theory** .....................419
The theory proposed by Thomas Malthus stating that population expands much faster than the food supply, resulting in starvation for much of the population when it grows too large

**Manifest functions** ................. 21
The intended consequences of a social system

**Market economy** .....................337
An economy in which the price and production of goods are determined by what people are willing to pay in the market place

**Marriage squeeze** .....................406
The effects of an imbalance between the number of males and females in the prime marriage ages due to rising or falling birth rates and the median age differences at marriage

**Mass expulsion** ........................199
Expelling racial or ethnic groups from their homeland

**Mass media** ...........................119
Forms of communication—such as television, popular magazines, and radio—intended for a large audience

**Mass production** .....................357
The production of many items of a product, which lowers the cost per item and reduces the time needed to make each one

**Master status** .......................... 85
A particular status in one's status set that takes priority over the others

**Matriarchal** ...........................251
A family structure in which the wife dominates the husband

**Matrilineal** .............................250
A family structure in which descent and inheritance are traced through the mother's line

**Matrilocal** .............................250
A family norm that newly married couples should live with the wife's family

**Me** ......................................112
The part of the self that sees self as object, evaluates self, and is aware of society's expectations of self

**Mean** .................................. 43
A measure of central tendency computed by adding the figures and dividing by the number of figures, also known as the average

**Mechanical solidarity** ...............163
The idea of Durkheim in which people do similar work but are not very dependent on one another (in contrast to organic solidarity, in which people are very dependent on others)

**Median** ................................ 43
A measure of central tendency, in which half the figures fall above and half the figures fall below; also known as the midpoint

**Medicaid** .............................381
Federally sponsored health insurance for the poor

**Medical center** ........................378
A major hospital that trains new physicians, conducts research, and provides tertiary medical care

**Medical model of illness** ...........376
A model of illness in which sickness is viewed as an individual problem requiring individual treatment

**Medicare** .............................381
Federally sponsored health insurance for people age 65 or older

**Megalopolis** ..........................435
A continuous strip of urban and suburban development that may stretch for hundreds of miles

**Melting pot**.............................196
A form of assimilation in which each group contributes aspects of its own culture and absorbs aspects of other cultures, such that the whole is a combination of all the groups

**Methodology** .......................... 39
The rules and guidelines outlined and followed in social research

**Metropolitan statistical area (MSA)** .............................. 433
A county or group of counties with a central city and a population of at least 50,000, a density of at least 1,000 persons per square mile, and outlying areas that are socially and economically integrated with the central city

**Microsociology** ........................... 6
The level of sociological analysis concerned with small-scale units such as individuals in small group or social interactions

**Middle-range theory** ................. 20
A set of propositions designed to link abstract theory with empirical testing

**Migration** ............................. 397
Movement of people into or out of an area

**Millennialism** .......................... 293
The belief prevalent among certain Christian sects that there will be a dramatic transformation of life on earth and that Christ will rule the world for a thousand years of prosperity and happiness

**Milling** ................................ 451
The stage in the development of crowd behavior during which people move about aimlessly, grow increasingly preoccupied with others, and become increasingly inclined to respond without thinking

**Mind** ................................... 112
The process of using a language and thinking

**Minority group** ....................... 189
A group that is subordinate to the dominant group in terms of the distribution of social power, defined by some physical or cultural characteristics, and is usually—but not always—smaller in number than the dominant group

**Mobilization for action** .............. 448
A stage in the development of collective behavior during which people are persuaded to join the movement

**Mobs** ................................... 450
Emotionally aroused groups ready to engage in violent behavior

**Mode** ................................... 43
The most frequent response in a body of data

**Modernization** ....................... 457
The process whereby pre-industrial countries emerge as urban societies with lower birth rates, more goods and services, and better nutrition and healthcare

**Modified-extended family structure** ................................ 247
The family structure in which individual nuclear families retain considerable autonomy yet maintain connections with other nuclear families in the extended family structure

**Monogamy** ............................. 249
The marriage of one man to one woman

**Monotheism** .......................... 279
The belief in one god

**Mores** .................................. 72
Norms of conduct associated with strong feelings of right or wrong, violations of which bring intense reaction and some type of punishment

**Mortality** ................................ 397
A measure of the rate at which people are dying

**Mortification of self** ................. 126
Stripping the self of all the characteristics of a past identity, including clothing, personal possessions, friends, roles and routines, and so on

**Mos** ...................................... 72
Singular form of *mores* (from the Latin)

**Multinational corporation** ......... 358
Corporations that do business in a number of nations

**Multiple-nuclei model** .............. 438
The model of urban development showing that cities have areas of different types of land use, each of which has its own center or nucleus

**Municipal hospital** ................. 378
A hospital built and operated by a city or county

**Mysticism** ............................. 280
The belief that spiritual or divine truths come to us through intuition and meditation, not through the use of reason or via the ordinary range of human experience and senses

## N

**Nation-state** .......................... 334
A large territory ruled by a single political institution

**Nature-nurture debate** ............... 109
A longstanding debate over whether behavior results from predetermined biological characteristics or from socialization

**Negative sanctions** ................. 133
Actions that discourage individuals from a particular behavior

**Neo-Malthusian theory** ............... 419
Revision of Malthusian theory about food production and population growth that includes more information, such as taking into account the effects of technology

**Neolocal** ................................ 250
A family norm that newly married couples should establish residences separate from those of both sets of parents

**Noblesse oblige** ....................... 385
The obligation of the rich to give to the poor and suffering

**Nonmarital cohabitation** ............ 267
An intimate arrangement in which two unmarried and unrelated adults share a common household or dwelling

**Norms** .................................. 65
Formal and informal rules of conduct and social expectations for behavior

**Nuclear families** ..................... 246
Families in which two or more persons are related by blood, marriage or adoption and who share a common residence

**Nutritionist** ............................ 380
A person who specializes in proper eating programs

## O

**Observational research** ............ 39
Research in which the researcher watches what is happening and makes no attempt to control or modify the activity being observed

**Oligarchy** ............................. 334
Government by a small elite group

**Open system** .......................... 163
A system of stratification in which it is possible to move to a higher or lower position

**Operation of social control** ......... 448

A stage in the development of collective behavior in which the mass media, government, and other groups try to suppress or influence collective behavior

**Operational definition** ............... 38

A definition of a concept or variable such that it can be measured

**Organic solidarity** ..................... 163

Durkheim's term for the integration of society that results from the division of labor

**Organizational deviance** ...............5

Occurs when events are created by or exist within organizations that do not conform to the organization's goals or expectations and that produce unanticipated and harmful outcomes

**Organized crime** ..................... 149

Groups expressly organized to carry out illegal activities

**Orphan drugs** .......................... 370

Drugs that are valuable in the treatment of rare diseases but are not profitable to manufacture

**Out-group** ............................ 93

A group to which people feel they do not belong, with which they do not share consciousness of kind, and with which they feel little identity

## P

**Parochial schools** ..................... 317

Schools run and maintained by a religious body or organization rather than the public at large

**Pathological illness** .................. 367

An illness in which the body is clearly diseased or malfunctioning in some way

**Pathology of normalcy** .............. 72

The concept that cultural norms are not always beneficial for a society, group, or individual

**Patriarchal** ............................. 251

A society in which men have the power and authority and are dominant.

**Patrilineal** ............................ 250

A family system in which descent and inheritance are traced through the father's line

**Patrilocal** ............................ 250

A family norm that newly married couples should live with the husband's family

**Pattern variables** ...................... 89

Sets of contrasting role expectations regarding judgement, emotions, depth of the relationship, self or collective focus and the extent to which ascribed or achieved statuses guide the relationship

**Peer group** ....................... 94, 119

An informal primary group of people who interact in a personal, direct, and intimate way; an informal primary group of people who share a similar or equal status and who are usually of roughly the same age

**Peripheral nations** ..................... 459

Underdeveloped nations who are exploited by core nations

**Physical force** ........................ 332

A type of power backed by sheer force, such as an army or physical might

**Planned economy** ..................... 337

An economy in which the production and prices of goods are planned by the government

**Play** ..................................... 111

According to Mead, a way of practicing role-taking

**Political action committees (PACs)** ................. 344

Organizations formed to raise money for a political campaign

**Political parties** ....................... 335

Groups of citizens formed with the express intent of gaining control of the political body of the state

**Political pluralism** .................... 344

A political system in which many diverse groups have a share of the power

**Political science** ..................... 10

The study of power, government, and political processes

**Politics** ................................ 331

The use of power to determine who gets what in society

**Polyandry** ............................. 249

The marriage of one woman to more than one husband at the same time

**Polygamy** ............................. 249

The marriage of one man or woman to more than one person of the opposite sex at the same time

**Polygyny** ................................ 249

The marriage of one man to more than one wife at the same time

**Polytheism** .............................. 279

The belief in and worship of more than one god

**Popular culture** ........................ 77

Trends, social activities, and shared experiences of everyday people (in contrast to elite culture)

**Popular excitement** .................. 455

The stage in the development of a social movement during which social unrest is brought into the open and people with similar concerns begin to organize

**Positive sanctions** ..................... 133

Actions that encourage individuals to continue a behavior

**Poverty** ................................ 169

Having fewer resources than are required to meet the basic necessities of life, according to rates based, usually, on a government index of income relative to size of family and farm/nonfarm residence

**Power** ............................. 161, 331

The ability to control or influence the behavior of others, even without their consent

**Power elite** ............................. 344

A small group of people who hold all of the powerful positions and cooperate to maintain their social positions

**Precipitating factors** ................. 447

Events that trigger a collective response

**Prejudice** ............................. 191

A preconceived attitude or judgment, either good or bad, about another group that usually involves negative stereotypes

**Preparatory schools** ................. 317

Private schools, usually of a select and elite nature, that are intended to offer an intensive education in both academic and social/cultural activities

**Presentation of self** ................. 115

The way we present ourselves to others and how our presentation influences others

**Priests** .................................. 280

Religious leaders who owe their authority to the power of their office

**Primary group** ........................ 92
A small, informal group of people who interact in a personal, direct, and intimate way

**Primary labor market** ............... 226
The labor market reserved for people who will advance to high-level positions

**Primary medical care** ............... 377
The first general, overall care the patient needs

**Principle of legitimacy** ............... 253
Malinowski's idea that every society has a rule that every child should have a legitimate father to act as the child's protector, guardian, and representative in society

**Profane** ................................ 277
That which belongs to the realm of the everyday world; anything considered mundane and unspiritual

**Projection** ............................. 191
A psychological explanation of prejudice that suggests that people transfer responsibility for their own failures to a vulnerable group, usually a racial or ethnic group

**Proletariat** ............................ 14
The group in capitalist societies that does not own the means of production and has only labor to sell

**Prolonged adolescence** ........... 308
A latent function of education that serves to maintain dependency on parents and keep young people out of the job market

**Prophets** ................................ 280
Religious leaders who have authority on the basis of their charismatic qualities

**Proposition** ............................ 39
A statement of the relationship between two or more concepts or variables

**Proprietary hospital** ................. 378
A hospital that is privately owned usually by physicians or corporations

**Protestant ethic** ....................... 356
The view associated with the Puritans that hard work is valuable for its own sake (according to Weber, the Protestant ethic is responsible for the high value placed on capitalism in the United States)

**Psychology** ............................ 10
The study of human mental processes and individual human behavior

**Pull factors** ............................. 401
Natural or social factors that cause people to move into an area

**Push factors** .......................... 401
Natural or social factors that cause people to move out of an area

## Q

**Qualitative methods** ................. 39
The gathering and reporting of non-numerical data used to determine the essential characteristics, properties, or processes of something or someone

**Quantitative methods** .............. 39
The gathering of numerical data that is usually used to test a hypothesis or examine the relationship between variables

## R

**Racial group** ........................... 187
A socially constructed category that distinguishes by selected inherited physical characteristics

**Racism** ................................. 194
The belief that one racial group is superior to others, typically manifested through prejudice and discrimination

**Radicalism** ............................. 202
Labor groups joining together in a coalition against the capitalist class

**Random sample** ........................ 42
A sample selected in such a way that every member of a population has an equal chance of being chosen

**Real culture** .......................... 78
The norms and values that people actually follow and practice, which may or may not be the same as the ideal culture

**Reference group** ..................... 94
A group with which people identify psychologically and to which they refer in evaluating themselves and their behavior

**Referenda** ............................. 353
Questions on a ballot to be decided by the electorate

**Registered dietitians (RDs)** ......... 380
Licensed members of hospital staffs who plan regular meals and special diets for patients

**Relative deprivation** ................. 95
A feeling of being deprived, not because of objective conditions, but because of comparison to a reference group

**Relativistic view** ..................... 135
The view that deviance can be interpreted only in the sociocultural context in which it occurs

**Reliability** ............................. 42
The extent to which repeated observations of the same phenomena yield similar results

**Religion** ................................ 278
An organized community of believers who hold certain things sacred and follow a set of beliefs, ceremonies, or special behaviors

**Resocialization** ........................ 126
Socialization to a new role or position in life that requires a dramatic shift in the attitudes, values, behaviors, and expectations learned in the past

**Resource mobilization theory** ...... 455
The theory that the success of a social movement depends not only on those who benefit from it directly but also on its ability to mobilize other individuals and groups to contribute time, money, and influence

**Riot** ..................................... 450
A form of collective behavior involving mass violence and mob action

**Role** ..................................... 85
The social expectations or behaviors associated with a particular status

**Role ambiguity** ........................ 86
A situation in which the expectations associated with a particular social status are unclear

**Role conflict** .......................... 87
A situation that exists when differing expectations are associated with the same role or when two or more of an individual's roles have differing expectations

**Role set** ............................... 86
Multiple roles that are attached to individual statuses

**Role strain** ............................ 86
A situation that occurs when differing and incompatible roles are associated with the same status

**Role-taking** .............................111
Assuming the roles of others and seeing the world from their perspective

## S

**Sacred** .................................277
Objects and ideas that are treated with reverence and awe

**Sample** ................................. 42
A number of individuals or cases drawn from a larger population

**Sanctions** .............................133
Rewards and punishments that are used to encourage proper behavior

**Sapir-Whorf hypothesis** ........... 67
The hypothesis that societies with different languages perceive the world differently because their members interpret the world through the grammatical forms, labels, and categories their language provides

**Scapegoating**..........................191
A psychological explanation of prejudice that involves blaming another person or group for one's own problems

**Secondary analysis** .................. 41
The use of existing information that was gathered or exists independently of one's own research

**Secondary care givers** ...............377
Those who provide more specialized care than that provided by a general practitioner

**Secondary group** ..................... 92
A group in which the members interact impersonally, have few emotional ties, and come together for a specific, practical purpose

**Secondary labor market** ............226
The labor market in which jobs pay poorly, there is little job security, and there are few promotions or salary increases

**Secondary medical care** ............377
Care that is more specialized than the care that a general practitioner provides

**Sector model** ..........................438
An explanation of the ecology of cities as a series of pie-shaped wedges radiating from the central business district, each with its own characteristics and uses

**Sects** ...................................281
Religious groups that have broken away from a parent church, follow rigid doctrines and fundamentalist teachings, and emphasize "otherworldly" rewards, rejecting or deemphasizing contemporary society

**Secularization** ........................295
The process through which beliefs concerning the supernatural and religious institutions lose social influence

**Segregation** ...........................198
The separation of a group from the main body usually involving separating a minority group from the dominant group

**Self** ......................................110
The sense of one's own identity as a person

**Self-fulfilling prophecy** ......... 114, 321
A prediction that comes true because people believe it and act as though it were true

**Self-orientation versus collective-orientation** .............. 89
A pattern variable pertaining to whether or not we should be focused on our own self-interests or the interests of the group within role relationships

**Serial or sequential monogamy** ...249
Marriage to a number of different spouses in succession, but only one at any given time

**Sex** ......................................219
The biological and anatomical characteristics that differentiate males and females

**Sexual harassment** .................235
Sexual advances made by coworkers or superiors at work

**Shamanism**.............................278
The religious belief that certain persons (shamans) have special charm, skill, or knowledge in influencing spirits

**Sick role** ...............................368
A set of expectations, privileges, and obligations related to illness

**Significant others** .....................111
Important people in the lives of children, especially with regard to socialization

**Simple horticultural societies** ...... 162
Societies that grow food using very simple tools, such as digging sticks

**Slave system** ...........................164
A system of stratification in which there exists a basic belief in the ownership of humans as labor

**Slums** ...................................442
Slums are overcrowded streets or sections of a city marked by poverty and poor living conditions

**Social class** ...........................164
A category of people who have approximately the same amount of power and wealth and the same life chances to acquire wealth

**Social conflict** ........................ 14
A view of Karl Marx that social conflict—class struggle due to economic inequality—is at the core of society and is the key source of social change

**Social contagion** .....................452
A stage in the development of crowd behavior during which the crowd's response to a common event increases in intensity and the crowd's behavior moves others to behave in the same way

**Social differentiation** ...............161
The difference or variation of people based on selected social characteristics such as class, gender, race, or age

**Social dynamics** ..................... 12
Comte's term for social processes and forms of change

**Social facts** .......................... 16
Reliable and valid pieces of information about society

**Social group** .......................... 91
A group in which people physically or socially interact

**Social learning theory** ...............146
The view that deviant and conforming behaviors are strongly influenced by the consequences that follow them

**Social model of illness** .............. 376
The view that many diseases are caused by social conditions and that they can be cured by changing social conditions

**Social movement** .................... 453
Collective non-institutionalized efforts to bring about social change and establish a new order of social thought and action

**Social network** ....................... 97
The linkage or ties in a set of relationships

**Social psychology** .................... 10
The study of how individuals interact with other individuals or groups and how groups influence the individual

**Social science** ....................... 10
A science that has human behavior, social organizations, and society as its subject matter

**Social statics** .......................... 12
Comte's term for the stable structure of a society

**Social status** .......................... 166
The amount of honor and prestige a person receives from others in the community; also, the position one occupies in the stratification system

**Social stratification** ................. 161
The ranking of people according to their wealth, prestige, or party position

**Social system** .......................... 21
A set of interrelated social structures and the expectations that accompany them

**Social unrest** .......................... 455
The stage in the development of a social movement that is characterized by unfocused restlessness and increasing disorder

**Socialism** ............................. 336
An economic system based on state ownership of the means of production

**Socialization** .......................... 108
The process of learning how to interact in society by learning the rules and expectations of society

**Society** ............................... 61
A group of interacting people who live in a specific geographical area, who are organized in a cooperative manner, and who share a common culture

**Sociobiology** .......................... 109
The study of the biological and genetic determinants of social behavior

**Sociocultural learning theories** ... 146
Theories that deal with the processes through which deviant acts are learned and the conditions under which learning takes place

**Socioeconomic status (SES)** ...... 167
An assessment of status that takes into account a person's income, education, and occupation

**Sociological imagination** .............. 5
The ability to see how history and biography—together—influence our lives

**Sociological perspective** .............. 5
A way of looking at society and social behavior that involves questioning the obvious, seeking patterns, and looking beyond the individual in an attempt to discern social processes

**Sociology** ................................. 3
The study of human society and social life and the social causes and consequences of human behavior

**Specificity versus diffuseness** ...... 89
A pattern variable that pertains to expectations about the scope or breadth of role relationships

**Split labor market** ..................... 180
A labor market in which some jobs afford upward mobility and others do not

**Sponsored mobility** ................. 325
A system of education in which certain students are selected at an early age to receive advanced education and training

**States** .................................. 333
Societies with institutional government and laws as a means of political regulation, military defense, and a way to finance these activities

**Statistical group** .................... 91
A group formed by sociologists or statisticians in which members are unaware of belonging and have no social interaction or social organization

**Statistical illness** .................... 367
An illness in which one's health varies from the norm

**Status** .................................. 85
The socially defined position an individual occupies

**Status set** ............................. 85
The combination of all the statuses any individual holds at a given time

**Stereotypes** .......................... 190
Widely held and oversimplified beliefs about the character and behavior of all members of a group that seldom correspond to the facts

**Strain theories** ....................... 142
Theories of deviance suggesting that the experience of socially induced strain, such as anomie, forces people to engage in deviant activities

**Stratification** .......................... 200
The structured ranking of entire groups of people that perpetuates unequal rewards and power in a society

**Stratified sampling** .................. 43
Sampling in which a population is divided into groups and then subjects are chosen at random from within those groups

**Structural assimilation** ............... 196
One aspect of assimilation in which patterns of intimate contact between the guest and host groups are developed in the clubs, organizations, and institutions of the host society

**Structural conduciveness** ........... 447
The extent to which a society's organization has the conditions that make a particular form of collective behavior possible

**Structural functionalism** ........... 21
The theory that societies contain certain interdependent structures, each of which performs certain functions for the maintenance of society

**Structural strain** ........................ 447
Any conflict or ambiguity in a society's organization that causes frustration and stress; often seen as a precondition for collective behavior

**Subcultures** .......................... 76
Group of people who share in the main culture of a society but also have their own distinctive values, norms, and lifestyles

**Suburbs** ................................ 441
The communities that surround a central city and are dependent on it

**Succession** .............................. 436
An urban process of replacing old occupants and institutions with new ones

**Survey research** ........................ 40
A quantitative research technique that involves asking people questions about the subject being studied

**Symbol** ................................ 65
Something that is used to represent something else, such as a word, gesture, or object used to represent some aspect of the world

**Symbolic interaction theory** ......... 25
The social theory stressing interactions between people and the social processes that occur within the individual that are made possible by language and internalized meaning

**Symbolic interaction theory** ......... 111
The social theory stressing interactions between people and the social processes that occur within the individual that are made possible by language and internalized meanings

**Systematic sampling** .................. 43
Obtaining a sample from a population by following a specific pattern of selection, such as choosing every 10th person

## T

**Taboos** ................................ 72
Mores that prohibit something

**Technology** ............................ 73
The application of nonmaterial and material knowledge by a society to maintain its standard of living and lifestyle

**Tertiary medical care** ............... 378
Long-term care requiring complex technology

**Theory** ................................. 20
A set of logically and systematically interrelated propositions that explain a particular process or phenomenon

**Totalitarianism** ...................... 334
A power structure in which the government has total power to dictate the values, rules, ideology, and economic development of a society

**Totemism** ............................ 279
The worship of plants, animals, and other natural objects as gods and ancestors

**Traditional authority** ................ 332
The right to rule granted to someone on the basis of tradition, as with a patriarch or king

**Traditional indigenous** .............. 10
Refers to ethnic groups who are native to a land or region

**Trained incapacity** .................... 101
The situation that exists when the demands of discipline, conformity, and adherence to rules render people unable to perceive the end for which the rules were developed

## U

**Universalism versus particularism** .......................... 89
A pattern variable that pertains to expectations about how we should judge or evaluate each other in role relationships

**Upward mobility** .................... 180
Movement in the stratification system to a position of greater wealth, status, and power

**Urban ecology** ....................... 435
The study of the interrelationships between people in urban settings and the social and physical environment in which they live

**Urbanization** .......................... 431
The growth of the number of people who live in urban rather than rural areas and the process of taking on organizational patterns and lifestyles characteristics of urban areas

## V

**Validity** ............................... 42
The extent to which observations actually measure what they are supposed to measure

**Values** ................................. 67
Ideas and beliefs shared by the people in a society about what is important and worthwhile

**Variable** ............................... 37
A characteristic such as age, class, or income that can vary from person to person; a concept that can have two or more values

**Verstehen** ............................. 19
Understanding human action by examining the subjective meanings that people attach to their own behavior and the behavior of others

**Vertical expansion** ................. 357
Business expansion in order to own everything related to a business, from raw materials to sales outlets

**Vital statistics** ........................ 396
Records of all births, deaths and their causes, marriages, divorces, and certain diseases in a society

**Voluntary associations** ............... 102
An organization people join because they share the organization's goals and values and voluntarily choose to support them

**Voluntary hospital** .................... 377
A nonprofit hospital that treats patients who need short-term care

**Voucher** ................................ 323
State-backed credit that gives parents the option to send their children to private schools by using state funds to pay for the tuition

## W

**Welfare capitalism/democratic socialism** .............................. 336
A mixed economy in which private and public ownership are both practiced extensively and one in which the goods and services vital to the society, such as transportation systems and medical care, are run by the state

**Women's movement** .................. 230
The social movements led by women to gain political and economic equality

**World systems theory** ............... 459
Conflict theory stating that core nations dominate the economies of peripheral nations

## Z

**Zero population growth** ........... 422
A population policy that encourages parents to have no more than two children to limit the growth of the population

# REFERENCES


## A

ACT. (2010). The condition of college and career readiness. Retrieved from www.act.org

Ade-Ridder, L. (1990). Sexuality and marital quality among older married couples. In T. H. Brubaker (Ed.), *Family relationships in later life* (2nd ed.). Newbury Park, CA: Sage Publications.

Adorno, T. W., Frenkel-Brunswik, E., Levinson, D. J., & Sanford, N. R. (1950). *The authoritarian personality.* New York, NY: Wiley.

Agnew, R. (1985, September). A revised strain theory of delinquency. *Social Forces, 64*, 151–167.

Agran, L. (1975, April 12). Getting cancer on the job. *The Nation*, 433–437.

Aguirre, B. E., Quarantelli, E. L., & Mendoza, J. L. (1988, August). The collective behavior of fads: The characteristics, effects, and career of streaking. *American Sociological Review, 53*, 569–584.

Aguirre, B., Torres, M. R., Gill, K. B., & Hotchkiss, L. H. (2011, March). Normative collective behavior in the Station Building Fire. *Social Science Quarterly, 92*(1), 100–118.

Akers, R. L. (1977). *Deviant behavior: A social learning approach* (2nd ed.). Belmont, CA: Wadsworth.

Akers, R. L., et al. (1979, August). Social learning and deviant behavior: A specific test of a general theory. *American Sociological Review, 44*, 636–655.

Albrecht, S. L., Thomas, D. L., & Chadwick, B. A. (1980). *Social psychology.* Englewood Cliffs, NJ: Prentice Hall.

Ali, L. (2008, November). *Islam & Obama.* Retrieved April 14, 2009, from The best daily beast: http://www.newsweek.com/id/168062

Allport, G. (1954). *The nature of prejudice.* Boston, MA: Beacon Press.

Alzheimer's Association. (2010). Alzheimer's disease facts and figures. *Alzheimer's and Dementia, 6.*

American Anthropological Association. (1998, May 17). *Statement on "race".* Retrieved April 17, 2013, from http://www.aaanet.org/stmts/racepp.htm

American Association of Suicidology. (2012). *Fact sheets.* Retrieved November 28, 2012, from Reliable information about suicide: http://www.suicidology.org/resources/suicide-fact-sheets

American Cancer Society. (2010). *Cancer facts and figures.* Retrieved from Atlanta: American Cancer Society: http://www.cancer.org/research/cancerfactsfigures/cancerfactsfigures/cancer-facts-and-figures-2010

American Management Association. (2004). *AMA 2004 workplace testing survey: Medical testing.* New York, NY: American Management Association.

American Sociological Association. (2009). *21st century careers with an undergraduate degree in sociology.* Washington, DC: American Sociological Association.

AmeriStat. (2003, March). Diversity, poverty characterize female-headed households. *Tabulations from the Census Bureau's Current Population Survey.*

Andrews, P. (2002, November 18). Mob behavior being altered by technology. *The Seattle Times.*

Annie E. Casey Foundation, The. (2004). *City and rural kids' count data book.* Baltimore, MD: Anna E. Casey Foundation. Retrieved from http://www.aecf.org/upload/publicationfiles/da3622h401.pdf

Annual Demographic Survey. (2002, March). *2002 Annual Demographic File (technical documentation revised on C4-C06-ALLF-06-US1).* Retrieved from United States Census Bureau: http://www.census.gov/mp/www/cat/people_and_households/current_population_survey.html

Anooshian, L. J. (2003, September). Social isolation and rejection of homeless children. *Journal of Children in Poverty, 9*(2), 115–134.

Aoki, M. (1988). *Information, incentives and bargaining in the Japanese economy.* Cambridge, England: Cambridge University Press.

Arber, S., Nigel, G. G., & Dale, A. (1985, November). Paid employment and women's health: A benefit or a source of role strain? *Sociology of Health and Illness, 7*, 375–400.

Arcaro, T., & Kilgariff, C. (2002). Humanistic sociology and Darwin: An argument for a sociobiological approach. *Association for Humanist Sociology Annual Conference.* Madison.

Argetsinger, A., & Roberts, R. (2006, December 6). Mary Cheney and partner are about to be moms. *The Washington Post.*

Atchley, R. (1976). *The sociology of retirement.* New York, NY: John Wiley.

Atchley, R. (1991). *Social forces and aging: An introduction to social gerontology* (6th ed.). Belmont, CA: Wadsworth.

Atchley, R. C. (1982). The process of retirement: Comparing men and women. In M. Szinovaxz (Ed.), *Women's retirement: Policy implications of recent research* (pp. 153–168). Beverly Hills, CA: Sage Publications.

Austin, S. (1976, January 4). Crisis in New York City. *New York Times*, 40.

Ayensu, E. S. (1981, November). A worldwide role for the healing powers of plants. *Smithsonian, 12*, 86–97.

## B

Babbie, E. (1977, 1980). *Society by agreement.* Belmont, CA: Wadsworth Publishing Co.

Badgett, M. L., & Folbre, N. (2003). Job gendering: Occupational choice and the marriage market. *Industrial Relations, 42*(2).

Bales, R. F. (1953). The equilibrium problem in small groups. In T. Parsons, R. F. Bales, & E. A. Shils, *Working papers in the theory of action.* Glencoe, IL: Free Press.

Ballantine, J. H. (1983). *The sociology of education.* Englewood Cliffs, NJ: Prentice-Hall.

Bandura, A., & Walters, R. H. (1959). *Adolescent aggression.* New York, NY: Ronald.

Barber, M. (2007). An assimilation theory of ethnicity and race. *American Sociological Association Conference.*

Basch, P. F. (1999). *Textbook on international health.* New York, NY: Oxford University Press.

Basile, K. C., Chens, J., Black, M. C., & Saltzman, L. (2007). Prevalence and characteristics of sexual violence victimization among U.S. adults, 2001–2003. *Violence and Victimization, 22*(4), 437–448.

Basirico, L. A. (1983). *Glass consciousness: Social organizations and social interaction in the stained glass world.* Ann Arbor, MI: University Microfilms International.

Basirico, L. A. (1986). The art and craft fair: A new institution in an old art world. *Qualitative Sociology, 9*, 339–353.

Basirico, L. A., & Bolin, A. (2010). The joy of culture. In T. Arcaro, & R. Haskell, *Understanding the global experience: Becoming a responsible world citizen* (pp. 26–48). Allyn and Bacon.

BBC News. (2002, March 15). *Saudi police 'stopped' fire rescue.* Retrieved June 4, 2009, from BBC News: http://news.bbc.co.uk/2/hi/middle_east/1874471.stm

BBC News. (2004, March 1). Home care call for terminally ill. *BBC News UK.*

BBC News. (2006, December 7). *Cheney lesbian daughter pregnant.* Retrieved May 22, 2009, from BBC News: http://news.bbc.co.uk/1/hi/world/americas/6217056.stm

Bean, F. D. (1983, Summer). The baby boom and its explanations. *Sociological Quarterly, 24*, 353–365.

Becker, H. S. (1974). The labeling theory reconsidered. In P. Rock, & M. McIntosh, *Deviance and social control.* London: Tavistock.

Bell, W. (1958). Social choice, life styles, and suburban residences. In W. Dobriner, *The suburban community.* New York, NY: Putnam.

Belsky, J. (1990, July/August). Infant day care child development, and family policy. *Society, 27*, 10–12.

Bem, S., & Bem D. (1976). Training the woman to know her place: The power of a nonconscious ideology. In S. Cox (Ed.), *Female psychology: The emerging self* (pp. 180–191). Chicago, IL: SRA.

Benac, N., & Cass, C. (2012, November 10). Face of U.S. changing; Elections to look different. *Associated Press.*

Bender, D., & Losel, F. (2011). Bullying at school as a predictor of delinquency, violence and other anti-social behavior in adulthood. *Criminal Behavior and Mental Health, 21*, 99–106.

Berg, I. (2003). *Education and jobs: The great training robbery.* Clinton Corner, New York, NY: Perchero Press/Eliot Werner Publications.

Berger, B. (1960). *Working class suburbs.* Berkeley, CA: University of California Press.

Berger, P. (1963). *Invitation to sociology.* New York, NY: Doubleday.

Berk, R. (1974). *Collective behavior.* Dubuque, IA: Brown.

Berk, S. F. (1985). *The gender factory: The apportionment of work in American households.* New York, NY: Plenum Press.

Bernard, J. (1981). *The female world.* New York, NY: Free Press.

Bernstein, R. (1990, October 14). In U.S. Schools: A war of words. *New York Times Magazine*, 34.

Bertakis, K. D., & Azari, R. (2010). Patient gender differences in the predictors of medical expenditure. *Journal of Women's Health, 10*, 1925–1932.

Bilge, B., & Kaufman, G. (1983, January). Children of divorce and one-parent families: Cross-cultural perspectives. *Family Relations, 32*, 59–71.

Billiterri, T. J. (2010, December 10). Preventing bullying. *CQ Researcher, 20*(43), 1013–1036.

Bird, C. (1999). Gender, household labor, and psychological distress: The Impact of the amount and division of housework. *Journal of Health and Social Behavior, 40*, 32–35.

Blake, J. (1981). Family size and the quality of children. *Demography, 18*, 421–442.

Blake, J. (1981b, March). The only child in America: Prejudice versus performance. *Population and Development Review, 7*, 43–54.

Blake, J. (1989). *Family size and achievement.* Berkeley, CA: University of California Press.

Blakemore, J. E., & Hill, C. A. (2008). The child gender socialization scale: A measure to compare traditional and feminist parents. *Sex Roles, 58*, 192–207.

Blanchard, C. M. (2008). *The Islamic traditions of Wahhabism and Salafiyya.* CRS Report, Order Number RS21695.

Blau, P. (1964). *Exchange and power in social life.* New York, NY: Wiley.

Blau, P. M., & Duncan, O. D. (1967). *The American occupational structure.* New York, NY: Wiley.

Blumer, H. (1939). Collective behavior. In A. McClung, *Principles of sociology.* New York, NY: Barnes and Noble.

Bonacich, E. (1972, October). A theory of ethnic antagonism: The split labor market. *American Sociological Review, 37*, 547–559.

Bonacich, E. (1975, November). Abolition, the extension of slavery, and the position of free blacks: A study of split labor markets in the United States, 1830–1863. *American Journal of Sociology, 81*, 601–628.

Borntrager, C., Davis, J. I., Bernstein, A., & Gorman, H. (2009). A cross-national perspective on bullying. *Child Youth Care Forum, 38*, 121–134.

Bose, C. E., & Rossi, P. H. (1983, June). Prestige standings of occupations as affected by gender. *American Sociological Review, 48*, 316–330.

Boserup, E. (1981). *Population and technological change.* Chicago, IL: University of Chicago Press.

Bowles, S., & Gintis, H. (1976). *Schooling in capitalist America.* New York, NY: Basic Books.

Boyer, E. (1986, November 6). College: The undergraduate experience in America. *Chronicle of Higher Education, 33*(10), 16.

Broder, J. M. (2010, October 28). Panel says firms knew of cement flaws before spill. *New York Times*. Retrieved from www.nytimes.com

Bromley, D. G. (2000). *Religious movements homepage at the University of Virginia*. Retrieved April 29, 2013, from The World Religions & Spirituality Project VCU: http://religiousmovements.lib.virginia.edu

Brougham, S. P., Swain, N. L., & Keaton, P. W. (2009). Characteristics of private schools in the U.S.: Results from the 2007–2008 private school universe survey, 2009–2013. *National Center for Education Statistics, Institute of Education Sciences*.

Bureau of Labor Statistics. (2012, March 29). *Bureau of labor statistics, registered nurses.* (U. S. Labor, Producer) Retrieved April 30, 2013, from Occupational Outlook Handbook: http://www.bls.gov/ooh/healthcare/registered-nurses.htm

Burgess, E. W. (1925). The growth of the city. In R. E. Park, & E. W. Burgess, *The city* (pp. 47–62). Chicago, IL: University of Chicago Press.

Burgess, E., & Park, R. E. (1921). *Introduction to the science of sociology.* Chicago, IL: The University of Chicago Press.

Burke, R. J., & Weir, T. (1976, May). Relationship of wives' employment status to husband, wife and pair satisfaction and performance. *Journal of Marriage and the Family, 38*, 279–287.

Burton, N. (2011, March 23). *Black Populations Decline in Major Cities.* Retrieved April 17, 2013, from The Root: http://www.theroot.com/buzz/black-populations-decline-major-cities

Byrk, A. S., Lee, V. E., & Holland, P. B. (1993). *Catholic schools and the common good.* Cambridge, MA: Harvard University Press.


## C


California Environmental Protection Agency. (2002, January 31). *Study links air pollution and asthma.* Retrieved from California Environmental Protection Agency News Release: http://www.arb.ca.gov/newsrel/nr013102.htm

Caplow, T., Bahr, H. M., Chadwick, B. A., Hill, R., & Williamson, M. H. (1982). *Middletown families: Fifty years of change and continuity.* Minneapolis, MN: University of Minnesota Press.

Carpenter, C. (2007, April). Workspace drug testing and drug use. *Health Services Research, 42*(2), 795–810.

Carroll, J. (2006, June 19). *Public continues to support right-to-die for terminally ill patients.* Retrieved November 26, 2012, from Gallup: http://www.gallup.com/poll/23356/public-continues-support-righttodie-terminally-ill-patients.aspx

Cashion, B. G. (1982, April). Female-headed families: Effects on children and clinical implications. *Journal of Marital and Family Therapy*, 77–85.

Cassano, M., & Perry-Parrish, C. (2007). Influence of gender on parental socialization of children's sadness regulation. *Social Development, 16*(2), 210–231.

Catalyst. (2011). *Catalyst*. Retrieved April 25, 2013, from www.catalyst.org

Catalyst. (2012, November). *Women CEOs of the Fortune 1000*. Retrieved November 17, 2012, from Catalyst: http://www.catalyst.org/publication/271/women-ceos-of-the-fortune-1000

CBS Detroit. (2012, December 31). *What is the fiscal cliff.* Retrieved January 13, 2013, from CBS Detroit: http://detroit.cbslocal.com/2012/12/31/what-is-the-fiscal-cliff/

CBS News/New York Times. (2006, January 27). The New York Times/CBS News Poll. *The New York Times*.

CBSNews. (2013, May 31). *War on drugs unsuccessful, drug Czar says*. Retrieved April 17, 2013, from CBS News: http://www.cbsnews.com/2100-250_162-6480889.html

Centers for Disease Control. (2010, May 24). *Asthma control: Improving quality of life, and reducing deaths and costs.* Retrieved January 13, 2013, from Centers for Disease Control and Prevention: http://www.cdc.gov/asthma/aag/2010/overview.html

Centers for Disease Control. (2012). *Understanding intimate partner violence.* Retrieved November 20, 2012, from CDC Factbook Page: http://www.cdc.gov/violenceprevention/pdf/ipv_factsheet-a.pdf

Centers for Disease Control and Prevention (CDC). (2004). Births: Preliminary data for 2003. *NVSR, 53*(9), 18.

Centers for Disease Control and Prevention. (2013, February 19). *National marriage and divorce rate trends*. Retrieved March 26, 2013, from Centers for Disease Control and Prevention: http://www.cdc.gov/nchs/nvss/marriage_divorce_tables.htm

Chan, J. (2011, January). Racial profiling and police subcultures. *Canadian Journal of Criminology and Criminal Justice, 53*(1), 75–78.

Chang, J. (2011, May 25). Culture clash complicates China's Brazil push. *Associated Press*.

Chappell, N. L. (2008). Aging and mental health. *Social Work in Mental Health, 7*(1–3), 122–138.

Chasin, B. H. (1997). *Inequality and violence in the United States*. Atlantic Highlands, NJ: Humanities Press.

Cheal, D. (1988). *The gift economy*. Boston, MA: Routledge & Kegan Paul.

Cheal, D. J. (1983, November). Intergenerational family transfers. *Journal of Marriage and the Family, 45*, 805–813.

Childe, V. G. (1951, April). The urban revolution. *Town Planning Review, 21*, 3–17.

Chirot, D. (1994). *How societies change*. Thousand Oaks, CA: Pine Forge Press.

Chun, J. J. (2008). The limits of labor exclusion: Redefining the politics of split labor markets under globalization. *Critical Sociology, 34*(3), 433–452.

CIA World Factbook. (2009). *Field listing-life expectancy at birth*. Retrieved April 11, 2009, from https://www.cia.gov/library/publications/the-world-factbook/fields/2102.html

Clark, K. B., & Clark, M. P. (1947). Racial identification and preference among negro children. In L. Hartley (Ed.), *Readings in Social Psychology*. New York, NY: Holt, Reihnart, and Winston.

Clark, R. E., & Clark, J. (1989). *The encyclopedia of child abuse*. New York, NY: Facts on File.

Clarke-Stewart, A. K. (1989, February). Infant day care: Maligned or malignant? *American Psychologist, 44*, 266–273.

Cleage, P. (1993). *Deals with the devil: And other reasons to riot*. New York, NY: Balantine.

Clemens, A. W., & Axelsen, L. J. (1989). The not-so-empty nest: The return of the fledgling adult. In A. Schnaiberg, & S. Goldenberg, *From empty nest to crowded nest: The dynamics of incompletely launched young adults* (Vol. 34). Family Relations.

Clemmit, M. (2009, August 8). Health care reform: Is universal coverage too expensive? *CQ Researcher, 19*(9), 693–715.

Clemmit, M. (2009, October 19). Medication abuse. *CQ Researcher, 19*(35), 837–860.

Clemmit, M. (2010, June 11). Health care reform: Is the landmark new plan a good idea? *CQ Researcher, 20*(22), 505–528.

Cohen, A. K., & Hodges, H. M. (1963, Winter). Characteristics of lower blue-collar class. *Social Problems, 10*, 307–321.

Cohen, H. S. (1985). Sociology and you: Good living. In R. A. Strauss, *Using sociology: An introduction from the clinical perspective*. New York, NY: General Hall.

Coleman, J. S. (1990). *Equality and achievement in education*. Boulder, CO: Westview Press.

Coleman, J. S., et al. (1997). *Redesigning American education*. Boulder, CO: Westview.

Coleman, J. S., et al. (1974). *Youth: Transition to adulthood. Report of the panel on youth of the President's Science Advisory Committee*. Chicago, IL: University of Chicago Press.

Coleman, J. S., et al. (1966). *Equality of educational opportunity*. Washington, DC: U.S. Department of Health, Education and Welfare.

Coleman, J. W., & Cressey, D. R. (1990). *Social problems* (4th ed.). New York, NY: Harper Collins Publishers.

Collins, R. (1979). *The credential society: A historical sociology of education and stratification*. New York, NY: Academic Press.

Collver, A. (1983). Housing and environmental planning. In H. Freeman, R. R. Dynes, P. H. Rossi, & W. F. Whyte, *Applied sociology* (pp. 275–286). San Francisco, CA: Jossey-Bass.

Coltrane, S., & Collins, R. (2001). *Sociology of marriage and the family: Gender, love and property* (5th ed.). Belmont, CA: Wadsworth.

Columbia University. (2003). *National survey of American attitudes on substance abuse VIII: Teens and parents*. Columbia University. New York, NY: National Center on Addiction and Substance Abuse at Columbia University.

Compa, L. (1986, November 16). To cure labor's ills: Bigger unions, fewer of them. *Washington Post*, H1.

Conner, K. A. (1992). *Aging America: Issues facing an aging society*. Englewood Cliffs, NJ: Prentice Hall.

Cookson, P. W., & Persell, C. H. (1985). *Preparing for power: America's elite boarding schools*. New York, NY: Perseus Book Group.

Cooley, C. H. (1909). *Social organization*. New York, NY: Scribner's.

Coon, H. M., & Kemmelmeier, M. (2001, May). Cultural orientations in the United States: (Re)Examining differences among ethnic groups. *Journal of Cross-Cultural Psychology, 32*, 348–364.

Corea, G. (1985). How the new reproductive technologies could be used to apply the Brothel model of social control over women. *Women's Studies International Forum, 8*, 299–305.

Cornfield, D. B. (1986, March). Declining union membership in the Post-World War II Era: The united furniture workers of America, 1939–1982. *American Journal of Sociology, 91*, 1112–1153.

Coser, L. (1977). *Masters of sociological thought*. New York, NY: Harcourt Brace Jovanovich.

Council of Economic Advisers. (1998, September). *Changing America: Indicators of social and economic well-being by race and hispanic origin*. Council of Economic Advisers. Retrieved from The Council of Economic Advisers for the President's Initiative on Race: http://www.gpo.gov/fdsys/pkg/GPO-EOP-CHANGINGAMERICA/pdf/GPO-EOP-CHANGINGAMERICA.pdf

Council of the Great City Schools. (2006, June). Urban school superintendents. *Urban Indicator, 8*(1). Retrieved April 14, 2009, from http://www.cgcs.org/images/Publications?indicator_06.pdf

Cowgill, D. (1974). Aging and modernization: A revision of the theory. In J. Gubrium (Ed.), *Late life communities and environmental policy*. Springfield, IL: Charles C. Thomas.

Cowgill, D., & Holmes, L. (1972). *Aging and modernization*. New York, NY: Appleton-Century-Crofts.

CQ Researcher. (2009, October 9). Medication abuse: Is tighter regulation of prescription drugs needed. *CQ Researcher, 19*(35), 837–860.

Cracy, D. (1999, November 12). Bible belt leads U.S. in divorces. *Associated Press*.

Cragun, R. T., & Nielsen, M. E. (2009). Fighting over 'Mormon': Media coverage of the FLDS and LDS churches. *Dialogue: A Journal of Mormon Thought, 42*(1), 65–1004.

Crane, J. (1991, March). The epidemic theory of ghettos and neighborhood effects on dropping out and teenage childbearing. *American Journal of Sociology, 96*, 1226–1259.

Crawford, J. (2009, December 11). Is bilingual education best for English language learners? *CQ Research, 19*(43), 1045.

Criss, M. M., et al. (2009, August). Family, neighborhood and peer characteristics as predictors of child adjustment: A longitudinal analysis of additive and mediation models. *Social Development, 18*(3), 511–535.

Croziet, J.-C., & Outrevis, M. (2004). Socioeconomic status and intelligence: Why test scores do not equal merit. *Journal of Poverty, 8*(13), 91–107.

Cumming, E., & Henry, W. (1961). *Growing old: The process of disengagement*. New York, NY: Basic Books.

Current Population Reports. (2001). *see U.S. Bureau of the Census, Current Population Report)*.

Currie, E., & Skolnick, J. H. (1988). *America's problems: Social issues and public policy*. Glenview, IL: Scott, Forestman/Little, Brown.

Curtis, S. (1977). *A psycholinguistic study of a modern day wild child*. New York, NY: Academic Press.

## D

Dahrendorf, R. (1951). *Class and class conflict in industrial society*. Palo Alto, CA: Stanford University Press.

Darling, S., Brocchetto, M., & Ford, D. (2013, January 28). *Fire rips through crowded Brazil nightclub, killing 233*. Retrieved from CNN: http://www.cnn.com/2013/01/27/world/americas/brazil-nightclub-fire/index.html

David, K. (1973). The first cities: How and why did they arise? In K. Davis, *Cities: Their origin, growth, and human impact.* San Francisco, CA: W. H. Freeman.

Davis, K. (1975). Equal treatment and unequal benefits: The medicare program. *Milbank Memorial Fund Quarterly, 53*(4), 449–458.

Davis, K., & Moore, W. E. (1945, April). Some principles of stratification. *American Sociological Review, 10*, 242–249.

Davis, W. H. (1970, January 10). Overpopulated America. *New Republic*, 13–15.

DeLamarter, R. T. (1986). *Big blue: IBM's use and abuse of power.* New York, NY: Dodd.

Demarco, G. (2009, May 22). *Mother gives birth to twins with different dads*. Retrieved from NBCNews.com Today Parenting: http://today.msnbc.msn.com/id/30864533/?GT1=43001

DeNavas-Walt, C., Proctor, B. D., & Smith, J. C. (2012). *Income, poverty, and health insurance coverage in the United States: 2011.* U.S. Department of Commerce, Economics and Statistics Administration, U.S. Census Bureau. Washington, DC: The United States Census Bureau.

Denton, J. A. (1978). *Medical sociology.* Boston, NY: Houghton Mifflin.

DePaulo, B. M., & Kashy, D. A. (1998, January). Everyday lies in close and casual relationships. *Journal of Personality and Social Psychology, 74*(1), 63–79.

Deutscher, G. (2010, August 26). Does your language shape how you think? *New York Times Magazine*.

Dillon, S. (2010, November 30). U.S. graduation rate is rising. *New York Times*. Retrieved from www.nytimes.com

Dillon, S. (2011, May 4). Failing grades on civics exam called a 'crisis'. *The New York Times*.

Dinitz, S. (1973, May). Progress, crime, and the folk ethic. *Criminology, 11*, 3–21.

DiSalvo, D. (2010, September 13). Forget the myths about sex and aging: Libidos rage at any age. *Psychology Today*.

Dixon, M., et al. (2008). More than just letting them play: Parental influence on women's lifetime sport involvement. *Sociology of Sport Journal, 25*, 538–559.

Dollard, J., Miller, N. E., Doob, L. W., Mower, O. H., & Sears, R. R. (1939). *Frustration and aggression.* New Haven, CT: Yale University Press.

Domhoff, G. W. (2011). *Wealth, income, and power*. Retrieved April 30, 2013, from Who rules America: http://www2.ucsc.edu/whorulesamerica/power/wealth.html

Domhoff, G. W. (2013, February). *Wealth, income, and power*. Retrieved April 2013, from Who Rules America: http://whorulesamerica.net/power/wealth.html

Domhoff, W. G. (2005). *Who rules America: Power, politics and social change.* New York, NY: McGraw Hill.

Dowd, J. (1975, September). Aging as exchange: A preface to theory. *Journal of Gerontology, 30*, 584–594.

Dowd, J. (1980). *Stratification among the aged.* Monterey, CA: Brooks/Cole.

Dowie, M. (1977, September-October). Pinto madness. *Mother Jones, 2*(8), 43–47.

Dowse, R. E., & Hughes, J. A. (1972). *Political sociology.* New York, NY: Wiley.

Duberman, L. (1976). *Social inequality: Class and caste in America.* Philadelphia, PA: Lippincott.

Duke, A. (2009). *'Octomom' seeks to trademark for tv, diaper line*. Retrieved April 29, 2013, from CNN.Com/US: http://www.cnn.com/2009/US/04/15/octuplet.mom/index.html?iref=allsearch

Dupreel, E. G. (1977). Demographic change and progress. In J. Overbeek, *The evolution of population theory* (pp. 80–85). Westport, CT: Greenwood Press.

Durkheim, E. (1893). *The division of labor in society.* New York, NY: Free Press.

Durkheim, E. (1915). *The elementary forms of the religious life.* New York, NY: Free Press.

Durkheim, E. (1951). *Suicide: A study in sociology.* Glencoe, IL: Free Press.


## E


Ehrenreich, B. (2001). *Nickel and dimed: On (not) getting by in America.* New York, NY: Metropolitan Books.

Ehrenreich, B., & English, D. (1979). *For her own good: 150 years of experts' advice to women.* Garden City, NY: Anchor Books.

Eitzen, S., & Zinn, M. B. (2007). *In conflict and order: Understanding society* (11th ed.). Boston, MA: Allyn and Bacon.

Ekman, R., et al. (2001, January). Bicycle-related injuries among the elderly; A new epidemic? *Public Health, 115*(1), 38–43.

Elder, G. (1974). *Children of the great depression.* Chicago, IL: University of Chicago Press.

Elkin, F., & Handel, G. (1989). *The child and society: The process of socialization* (5th ed.). New York, NY: Random House.

Ellis, W., & Zarbatany, L. (2007, July/August). Peer group status as a moderator of group influence on children's deviant, aggressive, and prosocial behavior. *Child Development, 78*(4), 1240–1254.

Epstein, R. (2000). The dangerous claims of the animal rights movement. *The Responsive Community, 10*(2), 28–37.

Eshleman, J. R., & Bulcroft, R. A. (2006). *The Family* (11th ed.). Boston, MA: Allyn and Bacon.

Etzioni, A. (1980). *A sociological reader on complex organizations* (3rd ed.). New York, NY: Holt, Rinehart and Winston.

Etzioni-Halevey, E. (1997). *Classes and elites in democracy and democratization: A collection of readings.* New York, NY: Routledge.


## F


Fairchild, E., & Dammer, H. R. (2005). *Comparative criminal justice systems.* Belmont, CA: Wadsworth.

Farley, L. (1978). *Sexual shakedown.* New York, NY: Warner Books.

Farrington, D. P., & Ttofi, M. M. (2009). How to reduce school bullying. *Victims and Offenders, 4*, 321–326.

FBI. (2011). *Federal Bureau of Investigation 2009 financial crimes report.* Federal Bureau of Investigation. Washington, DC: Federal Bureau of Investigation.

Feagin, J. R., & Feagin, C. B. (2002). *Race and ethnic relations.* Upper Saddle River, NJ: Prentice Hall.

Feagin, J. R., & Parke, R. (1990). *Building American cities: The urban real estate game* (2nd ed.). Englewood Cliff, NJ: Prentice Hall.

Federal Interagency on Aging-Related Statistics. (2012). *Older Americans 2012: Key indicators of well-being.* Washington, DC: U. S. Government Printing Office.

Fein, D. J. (2004). Married and poor: Basic characteristics of economically disadvantaged couples in the U.S. *ABT Associates*. Retrieved from www.mdrc.org/publications/393/workpaper.html

Fine, G. A. (1979). Small groups and culture creation: The idioculture of little league baseball teams. *American Sociological Review, 44*, 733–745.

Finsterbush, K., & Mars, A. B. (1980). *Social research for policy decisions.* Belmont, CA: Wadsworth.

Fisher, B. S., Cullen, F. T., & Turner, M. G. (2000). *The sexual victimization of college women.* Washington, DC: Department of Justice (U.S.), National Institute of Justice, Publication NCJ182369.

Flamini, R. (2011, May 3). Turmoil in the Arab world. *CQ Global Researcher, 5*(9), 209–236.

Florida, R., & Kenney, M. (1991, June). Transplanted organizations: The transfer of Japanese industrial organization to the U.S. *American Sociological Review, 56*, 381–398.

Foster, G. M. (1952). Relationships between theoretical and applied anthropology: A public health program analysis. *Human Organization, 11*, 33–37.

Fox News. (2005, October 13). *Opinion dynamics poll.* Retrieved from FoxNews: http://www.foxnews.com/search-results/search?q=Opinion+Dynamics+Poll+2005&submit=Search

Fox, C., & Harding, D. J. (2005, January). School shootings as organizational deviance. *Sociology of Education, 78*, 69–97.

Fox, K. D., & Nichols, S. Y. (1983, March). The time crunch: Wife's employment and family work. *Journal of Family Issues, 4*, 61–82.

Frankel, M. T., & Rollins, H. A. (1983). Does mother know best? Mothers and fathers interacting with preschool sons and daughters. *Developmental Psychology, 19*, 694–702.

Freeman, H. (1979). *Toward socialism in America.* Cambridge, MA: Schenkman.

Friedrich, E. (1902). *The origin of the family, private property and the state.* Chicago, IL: Charles H. Ken.

Fromm, E. (1965). *The sane society.* New York, NY: Holt, Rinehart and Winston.

Fuchs, S. (2006). What makes sciences 'scientific'? In J. H. Turner, *Handbook of sociological theory.* New York, NY: Springer Sciences and Business Media.

## G

Gallup. (1991, January). The Gallup Poll Monthly June,1990. *36*, p. 52.

Gallup Wellbeing. (2011, October 31). *Gallup Wellbeing.* Retrieved January 22, 2103, from Most Americans Believe Crime is Worsening: http://www.gallup.com/poll/150464/americans-believe-crime-worsening.aspx

Gamble, W. C., & Yu, J. J. (2008). Adolescent siblings' looking glass self-orientations: Patterns of liabilities and associations of parenting. *Journal of Youth adolescence, 37*, 860–874.

Gamson, W. A. (1975). *The strategy of social protest.* Homewood, IL: Dorsey Press.

Gans, H. (1974). *Popular culture and high culture: An analysis and evaluation of taste.* New York, NY: Basic Books.

Gans, H. J. (1962). *The urban villagers.* New York, NY: Free Press.

Gans, H. J. (1967). *The Levittowners: Ways of life and politics in a new suburb.* New York, NY: Random House.

Gans, H. J. (1971, July/August). The uses of poverty: The poor pay all. *Social Policy*, 20–24.

Gans, H., & Gans, H. J. (1971, July/August). The uses of poverty: The poor pay all. *Social Policy*, 20–24.

Gelles, R. J. (1995). *Contemporary families: A sociological view.* Thousand Oaks, CA: Sage.

George, S. (1977). *How the other half dies: The real reasons for world hunger.* Montclair, NJ: Allanheld, Osmun.

Gereffi, G. (1983). *The pharmaceutical industry and dependency in the third world.* Princeton, NJ: Princeton University Press.

Gillis, J., & Dugger, C. (2011, May 3). UN forecasts 10.1 billion people by century's end. *NY Times.*

Gladwell, M. (2000). *The tipping point: How little things can make a big difference.* New York, NY: Little Brown and Co.

Glass, J., & Fujimoto, T. (1994, June). Housework, paid work, and depression among husbands and wives. *Journal of Health and Social Behavior, 35*(2), 179–191.

Glass, T. (1992). *The 1992 study of the American school superintendency: America's education leaders in a time of reform.* Arlington, VA: American Association of School Administrators.

Glassner, B., & Berg, B. (1980, August 647–664). How Jews avoid alcohol problems. *American Sociological Review, 45.*

Glaze, L. E. (2011, December). *Correctional populations in the United States, 2010.* Retrieved October 25, 2012, from Bureau of Justice Statistics: http://bjs.ojp.usdoj.gov/index.cfm?ty=pbdetail&iid=2237

Glazer, N., & Moynihan, D. P. (1970). *Beyond the melting pot* (2nd ed.). Cambridge, MA: Massachusetts Institute of Technology Press.

Glazer, S. (1989, December 15). Getting a grip on influence peddling. *Congressional Quarterly's Editorial Research Reports, 22*, 697–711.

Godard, J. (2009, October). The exceptional decline of the American labor movement. *Industrial and Labor Relations Review, 63*(1), 82–108.

Goffman, E. (1959). *The presentation of self in everyday life.* Garden City, NY: Doubleday/Anchor.

Goffman, E. (1961). *Encounters.* Indianapolis, IN: Bobbs-Merrill.

Goffman, E. (1967). *Interaction ritual: Essays on face-to-face behavior.* Garden City, NY: Doubleday/Anchor.

Gold, D., Crombie, G., & Noble, S. (1987). Relations between teachers' judgments of girls' and boys' compliance and intellectual competence. *Sex Roles, 16*, 351–358.

Goldberg, S., & Lewis, M. (1969). Play behavior in the year-old infant: Early sex differences. *Child Development, 40*, 21–30.

Goldman, K. L. (1984). Stress management: The importance of organizational context. *Clinical Sociology Review, 2*(133–136), 133–136.

Goodin, R. E. (1980). *Manipulatory politics.* New Haven, CT: Yale University Press.

Gordon, M. (1964). *Assimilation in American life.* New York, NY: Oxford University Press.

Gordon, M. M. (1978). *Human nature, class and ethnicity.* New York, NY: Oxford University Press.

Gordon, R., Gordon, K., & Gunther, M. (1961). *The split level trap.* New York, NY: Bernard Geis Associates.

Gotham, F. (2001, January). A city without slums: Urban renewal, public housing, and downtown revitalization in Kansas City, Missouri. *American Journal of Economics and Sociology, 60*(1), 285–316.

Goudreau, J. (2012, July 16). *Top 20 best paying jobs for women in 2012.* Retrieved November 17, 2012, from Forbes: http://www.forbes.com/sites/jennagoudreau/2012/07/16/the-20-best-paying-jobs-for-women-in-2012/

Gouldner, A. W. (1954). *Patterns of industrial bureaucracy.* New York, NY: Free Press.

Gove, W. R., & Geerken, M. R. (1977, February). The effect of children and employment on the mental health of married men and women. *Social Forces, 56*, 66–76.

Granovetter, M. (1974). *Getting a job: A study of contacts and careers.* Cambridge, MA: Harvard University Press.

Grant, J. T. (2008). Measuring aggregate religiosity in the United States: 1952–2005. *Sociological Spectrum, 28*, pp. 460–476.

Greely, A. (1989). *Religious change in America.* Cambridge, MA: Harvard University Press.

Greenstein, T. N. (2000, May). Economic dependence, gender, and the Division of Labor in the home: A replication and extension. *Journal of Marriage and the Family, 62*, 322–335.

Greenwald, R., Hedges, L. V., & Laine, R. D. (1996). The effect of school resources on student achievement. *Review of Educational Research, 66*, 361–396.

Greven, P. (1991). *Spare the child: The religious roots of punishment and the psychological impact of child abuse.* New York, NY: Knopf.

Griffin, L. J., Wallace, M. E., & Rubin, B. A. (1986, April). Capitalist resistance to the organization of labor before the New Deal: Why? How? Success? *American Sociological Review, 51*, 147–167.

Grinc, R. M. (1994, July). Angels in marble: Problems in stimulating community involvement in community policing. *Crime and Delinquency, 40*, 437–468.

Grodsky, E., Warren, J. R., & Felts, E. (2008). Testing and social stratification in American education. *Annual Review of Sociology, 34*, 385–404.

Growette-Bostaph, L. (2008). Predicting officer performance in motor vehicle stops: An example of the repeat phenomenon. *Policing: An International Journal of Police Strategies & Management, 31*(1), 19–35.

Grusky, D., & Ryo, E. (2006). Did Katrina recalibrate attitudes toward poverty of inequality? A test of the 'dirty little secret' hypothesis. *DuBois Review, 3*(1), 59–82.

Gumbel, A. (2004, July 21). America sings a new song of celebrity censorship. *The Independent.*

## H

Hakuta, K. (1986). *Mirror of language: The debate on bilingualism.* New York, NY: Basic Books.

Hall, T. D. (1986, June). Incorporation in the world system: Toward a critique. *American Sociological Review, 51*, 390–402.

Hamlin, J. (2001). *List of rape myths.* Retrieved November 20, 2012, from Sociology of rape, University of Minnesota Duluth: http://www.d.umn.edu/cla/faculty/jhamlin/3925/myths.html

Hampton, D. R., Summer, C. E., & Webber, R. A. (1982). *Organizational behavior and the practice of management* (4th ed.). Glenview, IL: Scott, Foresman.

Harris, C., & Ullman, E. L. (1945, November). The nature of cities. *Annals of the American Academy of Political and Social Science, 242*, 7–17.

Harris, D. K., & Cole, W. E. (1980). *Sociology of aging.* Boston, MA: Houghton Mifflin.

Harter, C. L. (1987). The 'good times' cohort of the 1930s: Sometimes less means more (and more means less). In S. W. Menard, & E. W. Moen, *Perspectives on population: An introduction to concepts and issues* (pp. 372–376). New York, NY: Oxford University Press.

Haugen, E. (1987). *Blessings of Babel: Bilingualism and language planning.* Berlin: Mounton de Gruyter.

Hayes, C. (1951). *The ape in our house.* New York, NY: Harper and Row.

Healy, J. M. (1990). *Endangered minds: Why our children don't think.* New York, NY: Simon and Schuster.

Heer, D. M. (1975). *Society and population.* Englewood Cliffs, NJ: Prentice-Hall.

Henricks, T. S. (2012). *Selves, societies and emotions: Understanding the pathways of experience.* Boulder, Co: Paradigm Publishers.

Henslin, J. M. (1990). *Social problems* (2nd ed.). Englewood Cliffs, NJ: Prentice Hall.

Heritage, J., & Greatbatch, D. (1986, July). Generating applause: A study of rhetoric and response at party political conferences. *American Journal of Sociology, 92*, 110–157.

Herminda, A. (2002, July 31). *Saudis block 2,000 websites.* Retrieved June 4, 2009, from BBC News World Edition: http://news.bbc.co.uk/2/hi/technology/2153312.stm

Hernanel, S. (2010, May 12). *Obama shifts strategy away from war on drugs, will now focus on prevention and treatment.* Retrieved April 17, 2013, from Boston.com: www.Boston.com

Herr, N. (2007). *Internet resources to accompany the source book for teaching science.* Retrieved October 10, 2012, from Television & Health: http://www.csun.edu/science/health/docs/tv&health.html

Herrnstein, R. J., & Murray, C. (1996). *The bell curve: Intelligence and class structure in American life.* New York, NY: Simon and Schuster.

Heward, W. L. (2000). *Exceptional children: An introduction to special education.* Upper Saddle River, NJ: Prentice Hall.

Hewlett, S. A. (1986). *A lesser life: The myth of women's liberation in America.* New York, NY: William Morrow.

Higins, G. E., et al. (2010). Primary socialization theory: An exploratory study of delinquent trajectories. *Criminal Justice Studies, 23*(2), 133–146.

Hill, J. O., & Trowbridge, F. L. (1998). Childhood obesity: Future directions and research priorities. *Pediatrics*, 571.

Hilton, J. M., Angela-Cole, L., & Wakita, J. (2010). A cross cultural comparison of factors associated with school bullying in Japan and the United States. *The Family Journal: Counseling and Therapy for Couples and Families, 18*(4), 413–422.

Hobbs, D. F. (1965). Parenthood as crisis: A third study. *Journal of Marriage and the Family, 27*, 367–372.

Hochshild, A. R. (2003). *The commercialization of intimate life: Notes from home and work.* San Francisco & Los Angeles, CA: University of California Press.

Hoffman, L. W. (1985, Spring). The changing genetics/socialization balance. *Journal of Social Issues, 41*, 127–148.

Homas, G. C. (1974). *Social behavior: Its elementary forms* (2nd ed.). New York, NY: Harcourt Brace Jovanovich.

Horgan, J. (1990b, April 2). Your analysis is faulty. *The New Republic*, 22–24.

Hostin, S. (2008, May 23). *Commentary: Appellate court wrong on FLDS.* Retrieved April 29, 2013, from CNN.com/crime: http://www.cnn.com/2008/CRIME/05/23/flds.appeals/index.html?iref=allsearch

Howard, E. (1902). *Garden cities of tomorrow.* London: Faber and Faber.

Hoyt, H. (1939). *The structure of residential neighborhoods in American cities.* Washington, DC: Federal Housing Administration.

*Huffington Post.* (2012, July 19). Global warming fears: Giant iceberg breaks off from Greenland's Petermann Glacier.

Humphrey, C. R., & Buttel, F. R. (1982). *Environment, energy and society.* Belmont, CA: Wadsworth.

Humphreys, L. (1975). *Tearoom trade: Impersonal sex in public places.* New York, NY: Aldine.

## I

"I Have a Dream" Foundation. (2008). *About us: History.* Retrieved January 2, 2013, from "I Have a Dream" Foundation: http://www.ihaveadreamfoundation.org/html/history.htm

Immigration Policy Report. (2001). *Immigrant children exceed expectation. Studies show that immigrant children are assimilating.* Retrieved from Immigration Policy Report: www.ailf.org/ipc/policy_reports_2001_childre.asp

Information Please Almanac, Atlas & Yearbook. (1991). Information please almanac atlas & yearbook. *44th ed.* Boston, MA: Houghton Mifflin.

Irwin, N. (2012, October 31). Why hurricane Katrina should make us optimistic about economic impact of Sandy. *The Washington Post.*

## J

Jackman, M. R., & Jackman, R. W. (1983). *Class awareness in the United States.* Berkeley, CA: University of California Press.

Jaffee, D. (1989, June 375–388). Gender inequality in workplace autonomy and authority. *Social Science Quarterly, 70*(2).

Janus, S., & Janus, C. (1993). *The Janus Report on sexual behavior.* New York, NY: John Wiley & Sons.

Jellinek, E. M. (1960). *The disease concept of alcoholism.* New Haven, CT: Yale University Press.

Jencks, C. (1979). *Who gets ahead? The determinant of economic success in America.* New York, NY: Basic Books.

Jencks, C. (1987, February 12). Genes and crimes. *The New York Review*, 33–41.

Jensen, L. (2006). At the razor's edge: Building hope for America's rural poor. *Rural Realities, 1*(1), 1–8.

Jeste, D. V., Alexopoulos, G. S., Bartels, S. J., Cummings, J. L., Gallo, J. J., & Gottlieb, G. L. (1999). Consensus statement on the upcoming crisis in geriatric mental health: Research agenda for the next 2 decades. *Archives of General Psychiatry, 56*, 848–853.

Johnson, D. P. (1986). Using sociology to analyze human and organizational problems: A humanistic perspective to link theory and practice. *Clinical Sociology Review, 4*, 57–71.

Johnson, H. (2011, April). Immigrants and education. *Public Policy Institute of California, Just the Facts.* Retrieved from www.ppic.org

Johnson, J. A., Collins, H. W., Dupuis, V. L., & Johansen, J. H. (1985). *Introduction to the foundations of American education* (6th ed.). Boston, MA: Allyn and Bacon.

Johnson, T. (2010, March 23). Health care costs and U.S. competitiveness. *Council on Foreign Relations.* Retrieved from www.cfr.org

Johnstone, D. B. (1986). *Sharing the costs of higher education.* New York, NY: College Board Publications.

Jones, L. Y. (1980). *Great expectations: America and the Baby Boom Generation.* New York, NY: Coward, McCann & Geohegan.

Jost, K. (2009, December 11). Bilingual education vs. English immersion. *CQ Research, 19*(43), 1029–1052.

Jost, K. (2010, April 16). Revising no child left behind. *CQ Researcher, 20*(15), 336–360.

## K

Kaira, S. (2004, December 31). *Japan today - Executive impact - Unstoppable canon.* Retrieved January 9, 2013, from Bushido and other musings of a Japanophile: http://bushido-nihon.blogspot.com/2004_12_01_archive.html

Kaiser Family Foundation. (2010, January 10). Daily media use among children and teens up dramatically from five years ago. Retrieved from www.kff.org

Kalil, A., & Ryan, R. (2010, Fall). Mother's economic conditions and sources of support in fragile families. *Future of Children, 20*(2), 39–61.

Kanter, R. M. (1983). *The change masters.* New York, NY: Simon and Schuster.

Karen, D. (1990, October). Toward a political-organizational model of gatekeeping: The case of elite colleges. *Sociology of Education, 63*, 227–239.

Karier, C. (1986). *The individual, society, and education: A history of American educational ideas.* Chicago, IL: University of Illinois Press.

Kart, G. S., & Kinney, J. M. (2001). *The realities of aging: An introduction to gerontology* (6th ed.). Needham Heights, MA: Allyn & Bacon.

Katel, P. (2006, June 2). War on drugs: Should nonviolent drug users be subject to arrest? *CQ Researcher, 16*(21), 481–504.

Katel, P. (2009, December 18). Housing the homeless. *CQ Researcher, 19*(44), 1053–1076.

Keister, L. A. (2003, September). Religion and wealth: The role of religious affiliation and participation in early adult asset accumulation. *Social Forces, 82*(1), 175–207.

Kelley, B. T., Thornberry, T. B., & Smith, C. A. (1997). *In the wake of childhood maltreatment.* U.S. Department of Justice, Office of Justice Programs. Washington, DC: U.S. Department of Justice.

Kellogg, W. N., & Kellogg, L. A. (1933). *The ape and the child.* New York, NY: McGraw-Hill.

Kelly, D. H. (1979). *Deviant behavior: Readings in the sociology of deviance.* New York, NY: St. Martin's Press.

Kenney, M., & Florida, R. (1988). Beyond mass production: Production and the labor process in Japan. *Politics and Society, 16*, 121–158.

Kerner Report. (1968). *National advisory commission on civil disorders.* New York, NY: Bantam Books.

Kester, K. (2001). Ethnic identification and ethnic identity of immigrant Chinese families. *M.A. Thesis*. The University of Guelph.

Kiefer, C. W. (1990). The elderly in modern Japan: Elite, victims or plural players? In J. Sokolovsky, *The cultural context of aging: Worldwide perspective.* New York, NY: Greenwood.

Kilpatrick, D., Edwards, C., & Seymour, A. K. (1992). *Rape in America: A report to the nation.* Arlington, VA: National Victim Center and Medical University of South Carolina.

Kingsley, D. (1940). Extreme social isolation of a child. *American Journal of a Sociology, 45*, 554–565.

Kingsley, D. (1947). Final note on a case of extreme isolation. *American Journal of Sociology, 50*, 432–437.

Kitano, H. H. (1991). *Race relations* (4th ed.). Englewood Cliffs, NJ: Prentice-Hall.

Kitsuse, J. I. (1962, Winter). Social reaction to deviant behavior: Problems of theory and method. *Social Problems, 9*, 247–256.

Klaus, P. A. (2004). *Crime and the nation's households.* US Department of Justice, Bureau of Justice Statistics Bulletin.

Klitgaard, R. (1985). *Choosing elites: Selecting the "best and brightest" at top universities and elsewhere.* New York, NY: Basic Books.

Kochanek, K. D., Xu, J., Murphy, S. L., Minino, A. M., & Kung, H.-C. (2011, March 16). National Vital Statistics Report. *59*(6). Retrieved from http://www.cdc.gov/nchs/nvss.htm

Koo, H. (2007). A timeline of the evolution of school bullying in different social contexts. *Asia Pacific Educational Review, 8*(1).

Kreader, J. L., Ferguson, D., & Lawrence, S. (2005). Infant and toddler child care arrangements. *Child Care & Early Education, Research Connections: Research-To-Policy Connections, 1*, 2–5.

Krugman, P. (2012, November 4). Sandy vs. Katrina. *The New York Times.*

## L

Laine, C. (1997). Should physicians discourage patients from playing the sick role? *CMAJ, 157*, 393–394.

Lak, D. (2009, Jan 21). *Polygamy in Canada: Can it be banned. B.C. supreme court upholds polygamy laws.* Retrieved April 29, 2013, from CBC News Canada: www.cbc.ca/news/background/polygamy/

Lake, F. (2011, July 12). *Utah to legalize polygamy*. Retrieved December 12, 2012, from Weekly World News: http://weeklyworldnews.com/headlines/22693/utah-to-legalize-polygamy/

Lamanna, M. A., & Riedmann, A. (2009). *Marriages and families: Making choices and facing changes* (10th ed.). Belmont, CA: Thompson Wadsworth.

Lamb, M. E., Frodi, A. M., Hwang, C. P., Frodi, M., & Steinberg, J. (1982). Mother- and father-infant interaction involving play and holding in traditional and non-traditional Swedish families. *Developmental Psychology, 18*, 215–221.

Lambert, W. E., & Taylor, D. M. (1990). *Coping with cultural and racial diversity in urban America.* New York, NY: Praeger.

Lansing, M. (1986). The gender gap in American Politics. *Women in the World, 1975–1985*.

Lauer, R. H., & Handel, W. H. (1983). *Social psychology: The theory and application of symbolic interactionism* (2nd ed.). Englewood Cliffs, NJ: Prentice-Hall.

Lay, J. C. (2006, May). Learning about politics in low-income communities. *American Politics Research, 34*(3), 319–340.

Le Bon, G. (1895). *The crowd: A study of the popular mind.* London: Ernest Benn.

Lean, N. (2012, August 26). Norway's sane killer. *Los Angeles Times*, p. 17.

Leavitt, R. R. (1971). Women of other cultures. In V. Gornick, B. K. Moran, & eds., *Women in sexist society: Studies in power and powerlessness.* New York, NY: New American Library.

Lederer, L. (1980). *Take back the night: Women on pornography.* New York, NY: Morrow.

Lee, G. R. (1978, February). Marriage and morale in later life. *Journal of Marriage and the Family, 40*, 131–139.

Lee, S. (2012, June 20). *By the numbers: The U.S.'s growing for-profit detention industry.* Retrieved October 25, 2012, from Pro Publica: http://www.propublica.org/article/by-the-numbers-the-u.s.s-growing-for-profit-detention-industry

Lee, S. P. (2010). The moral distinctiveness of genocide. *The Journal of Political Philosophy, 18*(3), 335–356.

Lee, V. E., & Smith, J. B. (1995). Effects of high school restructuring and size on gains in achievement and engagement for early secondary school students. *Sociology of Education, 68*, 241–279.

Lee, Y. S., & Waite, L. (2010, June). How appreciated do wives feel for the housework they do? *Social Science Quarterly, 91*(2), 466–492.

Leggerman, P. M. (1979). The founding of the American sociological review: The anatomy of a rebellion. *American Sociological Review, 44*, 185–198.

LeMasters, E. E. (1957, November). Parenthood as crisis. *Marriage and Family Living, 19*, 352–355.

Lemert, E. (1951). *Social pathology.* New York, NY: McGraw-Hill.

Lemkin, R. (1946, April). Genocide. *American Scholar, 5*(2), 227–230.

Lemon, B. L., Bengtson, V. L., & Peterson, J. A. (1977). An exploration of activity theory of aging: Activity types and life satisfaction among in-movers to a retirement community. *Journal of Gerontology, 27*, 511–523.

Lenski, G. (1966). *Power and privilege.* New York, NY: McGraw Hill.

Lieberson, S., & Silverman, A. R. (1965, December). The precipitants and underlying conditions of race riots. *American Sociological Review, 30*, 887–898.

Lieberson, S., & Waters, M. C. (1988). *From many strands: Ethnic and racial groups in contemporary America.* New York, NY: Russell Sage Foundation.

Light, D. W. (2003, January). Universal health care: Lessons from the British experience. *American Journal of Public Health, 93*(1), 25–30.

Lindau, S., Schumm, L., Laumann, E., Levinson, W., & O'Muircheartaigh. (2007, August). A study of sexuality and health among older adults in the United States. *New England Journal of Medicine, 357*(8), 762–774.

Lindsay, D. M. (2008, February). Evangelicals in the power elite: Elite cohesion advancing a movement. *American Sociological Review, 73*, 60–82.

Ling, P. (1992). *America and the automobile: Technology, reform, and social change, 1893–1923.* New York, NY: Manchester University Press.

Link, T. C. (2008). Youthful intoxication: A cross-cultural study of drinking among German and American adolescents. *Journal of Studies on Alcohol and Drugs, 69*, 362–370.

Lipset, S., & Bendix, R. (1967). *Social mobility in industrial society.* Berkeley, CA: University of California Press.

Lipton, E., Savage, C., & Shane, S. (2011, January 8). Arizona suspect's recent acts offer hints of alienation. *New York Times*.

Little, P. M. (2007). *The quality of school-age child care in after-school settings.* New York, NY: Child Care and Early Education Research Connections.

Lofquist, D., Lugaila, T., O'Connell, M., & Feliz, S. (2012). *Households and Families: 2010.* U.S. Census, Department of Commerce. Washington, DC: U.S. Census Bureau.

Logan, J. (2008, September 29). China's space program: Options for U.S. China cooperation. *CRS Report for Congress*.

Lopata, H. Z. (1976). *Polish Americans: Status competition in an ethnic community.* Englewood Cliffs, NJ: Prentice-Hall.

Lorber, J. (2003). The social construction of gender. In T. E. Orr (Ed.), *The social construction of difference and inequality: Race, class, gender, and sexuality* (2nd ed., pp. 99–106). New York, NY: McGraw-Hill.

Lu, L. (2009). 'I' or 'We': Family socialization values in a national probability sample in Taiwan. *Asian Journal of Social Psychology,12*, 145–150.

Lum, T., Morrison, W. M., & Vaughn, B. (2008, January 4). *China's 'soft power' in Southeast Asia.* CRS Report for Congress.

Lupart, J., & Cannon, E. (2002, May–August). Computers and career choices: Gender differences in grades 7 and 10 students. *Gender, Technology and Development*, 233–248.

Lynd, R. S., & Lynd, H. M. (1929). *Middletown.* New York, NY: Harcourt, Brace and World.

Lynd, R. S., & Lynd, H. M. (1937). *Middletown in transition.* New York, NY: Harcourt, Brace and World.


## M


Maccoby, E. E. (1988). Gender as a social category. *Developmental Psychology, 24*, 755–765.

Maccoby, M. (1977). The changing corporate character. In G. J. DiRenzo, *We, the people: American character and social change.* Westport, CT: Greenwood Press.

Macionis, J. (2004). *Social problems.* OR, USA: Prentice Hall.

Macionis, J. (2004). *Social problems.* Des Moines, IA, USA: Prentice Hall.

Macionis, J. J. (2012). *Sociology* (14th ed.). Saddle River, NJ: Pearson.

MacLeod, J. (1995). *Ain't no makin' it: Aspirations and attainment in a low income neighborhood.* Boulder, CO: Westview Press.

MacLeod, S. (2007, July 26). *Vice squad.* Retrieved June 4, 2009, from Time Magazine: www.time.com/time/magazine/article/0,9171,1647239,00.html

Macoby, E. E. (1998). *The two sexes: Growing up apart, coming together.* Cambridge, MA: Belknap Press.

Madsen, R. (2009, March). The Archipelago of faith: Religious individualism and faith community in America today. *American Journal of Sociology, 114*(5), 1263–1301.

Malinowski, B. (1930). Parenthood: The basis of social structure. In V. Calverton, & S. D. Schmalhausen, *The new generation.* New York, NY: Macaulay.

Mann, S. A., Grimes, M. D., Kemp, A. A., & Jenkins, P. J. (1997, May). Paradigm shifts in family sociology? Evidence from three decades of family textbooks. *Journal of Family Issues*, 315–349.

Marcus, W. S. (2002, July). Tracing the bitter roots of personal violation and social displacement: A comparative phenomenological study of life histories of homeless mothers and their dependent children. *Dissertation Abstracts International, A: The Humanities and Social Sciences, 63*(1), 137A–138A.

Marger, M. M. (2003). *Race and ethnic relations: American and global perspectives* (7th ed.). Belmont, CA: Thompson/Wadsworth.

Markle, G. E., & Troyer, R. J. (1979, June). Smoke gets in your eyes: Cigarette smoking as deviant behavior. *Social Problems, 26*, 611–625.

Marklein, M. B. (1991, February 20). Learning despite language differences. *USA Today*, p. 9D.

Marsden, P. V. (1987, February). Core discussion networks of Americans. *American Sociology Review, 52*, 122–131.

Marshall, R., & Paulin, B. (1985, July–August). The wages of women's work. *Society, 22*, 28–38.

Marshall, V. W., & Levy, J. (1990). Aging and dying. In R. H. Binstock, & L. K. George (Eds.), *Handbook of aging and the social sciences* (3rd ed.). New York, NY.

Martin, L. G. (1989, July). The graying of Japan. *Population Bulletin, 44*.

Marx, K. (1964). *Selected writings in sociology and social philosophy.* New York, NY: McGraw-Hill.

Marx, K., & Engels, F. (1969 Originally published in 1847). *Communist manifesto.* Baltimore, MD: Penguin Books.

Masters, W. H., & Johnson, V. E. (1970). *Human sexual inadequacy* (1st ed.). Boston, MA: Little, Brown & Co.

Maykovich, M. K. (1980). *Medical sociology.* Palo Alto, CA: Mayfield Publishing.

McGeary, J. (2004, May 24). Pointing Fingers. *Time*, pp. 43–47, 50.

McKay, H. (2009). *Porn plot: Vivid's sordid plans for Nadya 'Octomom' Suleman*. Retrieved May 22, 2009, from FoxNews.com: www.foxnews.com/story/0,2933,500688,00.html

McKinlay, J. B., & McKinlay, S. M. (1981). Medical measures and the decline of mortality. In P. Conrad, & R. Kern, *The sociology of health and illness: Critical perspectives* (pp. 12–30). New York: St. Martin's Press.

McLachlan, J. (1970). *American boarding schools: A historical study.* New York, NY: Charles Scribner's Sons.

Mead, G. H. (1934). *Mind, self and society from the standpoint of a social behaviorist.* (C. Morris, Ed.) Chicago, IL: University of Chicago Press.

media.ford.com. (2012, December). *Ford cars, utilities and trucks all post U.S. sales gains in 2012; Company posts best December sales since 2006*. Retrieved January 8, 2013, from media.ford.com: http://media.ford.com/article_display.cfm?article_id=37527

Medvedev, Z. A. (1974). Caucasus and Altay longevity: A biological or social problem? *Gerontologist, 14*, 381–387.

Medvedev, Z. A. (1975). Aging and longevity: New approaches and new perspectives. *Gerontologist, 15*, 196–201.

Meier, B. (2012, October 17). A new painkiller crackdown targets drug distributors. *New York Times*.

Mellor, D., Fuller-Tyskiewicz, M., McCabe, M. P., & Ricciardelli, L. (2010). Body image and self esteem across age and gender: A short-term longitudinal study. *Sex Roles, 63*, 672–681.

Melville, K. (1989). *The environment at risk: Responding to growing dangers (National Issues Forum Series).* Dayton, OH: The Kettering Foundation and the Kendall/Hunt Publishing Company.

Merton, R. K. (1968). *Social theory and social structure.* New York, NY: Free Press.

Michels, R. (1911). *Political parties.* New York, NY: Free Press.

Milgram, S. (1970, March 13). The experience of living in cities. *Science, 167*, 1461–1468.

Miller, C. F., Lurye, L. E., Zosuls, K. M., & Ruble, D. (2009). Accessibility of gender stereotypes domains: Developmental and gender differences in children. *Sex Roles, 60*, 870–881.

Miller, S. M. (2007, Winter). Immoral hazards: New Orleans style. *Dissent, 54*(1), 89–90.

Millican, J. (2006, November 20). *Gender stereotypes and discussions of Armani suits dominate media's coverage of speaker-elect Pelosi*. Retrieved October 15, 2012, from Media Matters for America: http://lb0.rsc.mematt.org/research/2006/11/20/gender-stereotypes-and-discussions-of-armani-su/137366

Mills, C. W. (1951). *White collar: American middle classes.* New York, NY: Oxford University Press.

Mills, C. W. (1956). *The power elite.* New York, NY: Oxford University Press.

Money, J. (1980). *Love and love sickness: The science of sex, sender difference, and pair-bonding.* Baltimore, NY: Johns Hopkins University Press.

Money, J., & Tucker, P. (1975). *Sexual signatures: On being a man or a woman.* New York, NY: Little Brown and Co.

Moore, J. (1989). Drug testing and corporate responsibility: The 'ought implies can' argument. *Journal of Business Ethics, 8*, 270–287.

Morawski, J. G., & St. Martin, J. (2011). The evolving vocabulary of the social sciences: The case of socialization. *The Evolving Vocabulary of the Social Sciences, 14*(1), 1–25.

Morin, R. (2008, July 29). *America's four middle classes.* Retrieved October 31, 2012, from Pew Research Center Publications: http://pewresearch.org/pubs/911/americas-four-middle-classes

Morning, A. (2009). Toward a racial conceptualization for the 21st century. *Social Forces, 87*(3), 1167–1192.

Morrison, W. M., & Labonte, M. (2009, January 13). China's holdings of U.S. securities: Implications for the U.S. economy. CRS Report for Congress.

Moss, H. (1967). Sex, age, and state as determinants of mother-infant interaction. *Merrill-Palmer Quarterly, 13*, 19–36.

Mumford, L. (1962). *The transformation of man.* New York, NY: Collier.

Munroe, R. L., Hulefeld, R., Rodgers, J. M., Tomeo, D. L., & Yamazaki, S. K. (2000, February). Aggression among children in four cultures. *Cross Cultural Research, 34*(1), 3–25.

Murdock, G. P. (1949). *Social structure.* New York, NY: Macmillan.

Murdock, G. P. (1957, August). World ethnographic sample. *American Anthropologist, 59*, 664–687.

Muwakkil, S. (1990, August 5). Schools in transition. *The Washington Post Education Review.*

Myrdal, G. (1944). *An American dilemma: The negro problem and modern democracy.* USA: Harper and Row Publishers.

## N

National Center for Education Statistics. (2011). *National center for education statistics fast facts.* (Institute of Education Sciences, Producer) Retrieved December 28, 2012, from National Center for Education Statistics: http://nces.ed.gov/fastfacts/display.asp?id=61

National Coalition for the Homeless. (2009, July). *Who is homeless?* Retrieved November 1, 2012, from National Coalition for the Homeless: http://www.nationalhomeless.org/factsheets/who.html

National Council on the Aging. (2002). *American perceptions of aging in the 21st century: The NCOA's continuing study of myths and realities of aging.* National Council on the Aging. Washington, DC: AARP Andrus Foundation.

National Institute on Alcohol Abuse and Alcoholism. (2011). *Alcoholism.* Retrieved from Medline Plus: http://www.nlm.nih.gov/medlineplus/alcoholism.html

National Public Radio. (2008, March 18). *Interview with then-Illinois Senator Barack Obama.* Retrieved April 14, 2009, from NPR: http://www.npr.org/templates/story/story.php?storyId=88478467

Navasky, V. (1990). Body invaders. *The Nation, 250*, 39–40.

NBC News. (2009, May 21). *Mother has twins with two fathers.* Retrieved May 22, 2009, from NBCNews.com: www.msnbc.msn.com/id/21134540/vp/30863181#30863181

Newman, O. (1972). *Defensible space.* New York, NY: Macmillan.

Newman, W. M. (1973). *American pluralism: A study of social groups and social theory.* New York, NY: Harper and Row.

Nielsen, M. E. (2009). Opinions regarding polygamy among LDS church members: Demographic predictors. *Archive for the Psychology of Religion, 31*, 261–270.

Nir, S. M. (2012, November 4). In sight of Manhattan Skyline, living forlorn and in the dark. *The New York Times.*

Noel, D. L. (1975). A theory of the origin of ethnic stratification. In R. Norman, C. Yetman, & S. Hoy (Eds.), *Major and minority: The dynamics of racial and ethnic relations.* Boston, MA: Allyn and Bacon.

Norton, M., & Ariely, D. (2011, January). Building a better America one wealth quintile at a time. *Perspectives on Psychological Science, 6*(1), 9–12.

Novak, M. (1972). *The rise of the unmeltable ethnics.* New York, NY: Macmillan.

Novak, M. (1975). White ethnic. In N. R. Yetman, & C. H. Steele, *Majority and minority: The dynamics of racial and ethnic relations.* Boston, MA: Allyn and Bacon.

Nuehring, E., & Markle, G. E. (1974, April). Nicotine and norms: The reemergence of a deviant behavior. *Social Problems, 21*, 513–526.

## O

Oakes, J. (1982, October). Classroom social relationships: Exploring the Bowles and Gintis hypothesis. *Sociology of Education, 55*, 197–212.

Oberschall, A. (1973). *Social conflict and social movements.* Englewood Cliffs, NJ: Prentice-Hall.

O'Donnell, C. (1984, June). Major theories of the labor market and women's place within it. *Journal of Industrial Relations, 26*, 147–165.

Ogburn, W. F. (1922). *Social change with respect to culture and original nature.* New York, NY: B.W. Huebsch, Inc.

Olson, D. H., & McCubbin, H. I. (1983). *Families: What makes them work.* Beverly Hills, CA: Sage Publications.

Olweus Bullying Prevention Program. (2012). *Recognizing bullying.* Retrieved December 28, 2012, from Hazelden: http://www.violencepreventionworks.org/public/recognizing_bullying.page

Olweus, D. (1993). *Bullying at school: What we know and what we can do.* Blackwell.

OpenSecrets.org. (2012, October 31). *2012 election spending will reach $6 billion, center for responsive politics predicts.* (Center for Responsive Politics) Retrieved January 3, 2013, from OpenSecrets.org: http://www.opensecrets.org/news/2012/10/2012-election-spending-will-reach-6.html

Oral Cancer Foundation. (2011, June 27). *The problem death and disease.* Retrieved April 17, 2013, from Oral Cancer Foundation: www.oralcancerfoundation.org/tobacco/problem_tobacco.htm

Ornstein, P. (1994). *School girls: Young women, self-esteem, and the confidence gap.* New York, NY: Doubleday.

Orr, L. (1990). *Censorship: Opposing viewpoints.* San Diego, CA: Greenhaven Press.

Ortiz, F. I. (1982). *Career patterns in education: Women, men and minorities in public school administration.* New York, NY: Praeger.

Orum, A. M. (1978). *Introduction to political sociology: The social anatomy of the body politic.* Englewood Cliffs, NJ: Prentice-Hall.

## P

Parson, T., & Shils, E. A. (1951). *Toward a general theory of action.* New York, NY: Harper and Row.

Parsons, T. (1951). *The social system.* Glencoe, IL: Free Press.

Parsons, T. (1951). *Toward a general theory of action.* Cambridge, MA: Harvard University Press.

Parsons, T. (1959). The school class as social system: Some of its functions in American society. *Harvard Educational Review, 29*(4), 267–318.

Parsons, T. (1960, August). Pattern variables revisited: A response to Robert Dubin. *American Sociological Review, 25*(4), 467–483.

Parsons, T., & Bales, R. F. (1955). *Family, socialization and interaction process.* New York, NY: Free Press.

Peters, J. F. (1985, Winter). Adolescents as socialization agents to parents. *Adolescence, 20*, 921–933.

Peters, T. J., & Waterman, R. H. (1982). *In search of excellence.* New York, NY: Harper and Row.

Pettigrew, T. F. (1964). *A profile of the Negro American.* Princeton, NJ: Van Nostrand.

Pew Internet and American Life Project. (2011, July). *Pewinternet.org.* Retrieved September 2012, from Pew Internet and American Life Project: http://pewinternet.org/Static-Pages/Trend-Data-(Teens)/Whos-Online.aspx

Pew Internet and American Life Project. (2012, September). *Pewinternet.org.* Retrieved September 2012, from Pew Internet and American Life Project: http://pewinternet.org/Commentary/2012/March/Pew-Internet-Social-Networking-full-detail.aspx

Pew Research Center. (2006). *Strong public support for right to die more Americans discussing—and planning -end-of-life treatment.* Washington, DC: Pew Research Center.

Pew Research Center. (2012, August 22). *The lost decade of the middle class fewer, poorer, gloomier.* Retrieved October 31, 2012, from Pew Social and Demographic Trends: http://www.pewsocialtrends.org/2012/08/22/the-lost-decade-of-the-middle-class/

Pham-Kanter, G. (2009). Social comparisons and health: Can having richer friends and neighbors make you sick. *Social Science and Medicine, 69*, 335–344.

Phillips, D., McCartney, K., & Scarr, S. (1987). Childcare quality and children's social development. *Developmental Psychology, 23*, 537–543.

Pillemer, K. (1985, December). The dangers of dependency: New findings on domestic violence against the elderly. *Social Problems, 33*, 146–158.

Pinkus, S., Richardson, J., & Armet, E. (2000, April 2). Poll analysis: Aging in America. *Los Angeles Times.*

Pirenne, H. (1914, July). Stages in the social history of capitalism. *American Historical Review, 19*, 494–515.

Piven, F. F., & Cloward, R. (1993). *Regulating the poor: The functions of public welfare.* New York, NY: Vintage.

Piven, F. F., & Cloward, R. A. (1989). *Why Americans don't vote.* New York, NY: Pantheon Books.

Planty, M., & Truman, J. L. (2012, October 17). *Criminal victimization 2011.* Retrieved October 25, 2012, from Bureau of Justice Statistics: http://bjs.ojp.usdoj.gov/index.cfm?ty=pbdetail&iid=4494

Pontell, H., & Geiss, G. (2010). How to effectively get crooks like Bernie Madoff in Dutch. *Criminology and Public Policy, 9*(3), 475–481.

Poteat, P. (2007, November). Peer group socialization of homophobic attitudes and behavior during adolescence. *Child Development, 78*(6), 1830–1842.

Pridham, K., Becker, P., & Brown, R. (2000). Effects of infant and caregiving conditions on an infant's focused exploration of toys. *Journal of Advanced Nursing, 31*(6), 1439–1448.

Procon.org. (2011, August 17). *Euthanasia.* Retrieved November 26, 2012, from Procon.org: http://euthanasia.procon.org/view.resource.php?resourceID=000134

Proximity. (2013). *America's urban population: Patterns & characteristics.* Retrieved January 21, 2013, from Proximity: http://www.proximityone.com/urbanpopulation.htm

## Q

Quinney, R. (1979). *Criminology.* Boston, MA: Little, Brown.

## R

Radke, M. J., & Trager, H. G. (1950). Children's perceptions of the social roles of negroes and whites. *Journal of Psychology, 29*, 3–33.

Ravitz, J. (2009). *Out-of-wedlock births hit record high.* Retrieved from CNN.com/Living: www.cnn.com/2009/LIVING/wayoflife/04/08/out.of.wedlock.births/index.html?iref=newssearch

Redfield, R. (1941). *The folk culture of Yucatan.* Chicago, IL: University of Chicago Press.

Reinberg, S. (2011, July 22). C-section rate in U.S. climbs to all-time high. *USA Today.*

Reiss, I. L. (1965, November). The universality of the family: A conceptual analysis. *Journal of Marriage and the Family, 27*, 443–453.

Reitzes, D. C., & Mutran, E. J. (2004). The transition to retirement: Stages and facts that influence retirement adjustment. *Aging and Human Development, 59*(1), 63–84.

Reuters. (2013, January 22). Beijing's air pollution steps get poor reception among some in China's capital. *Huff Post Green.*

Ribadeneira, D. (1990, August 5). Schools in transition. *Washington Post Education Review.*

Rice, T. (1985). American public policy formation and implementation. In R. A. Strauss (Ed.), *Using sociology: An introduction from the clinical perspective.* Bayside, NY: General Hall.

Richards, T., & Olshan, J. (2009, February 11). *Egg on his face: Fertility doc ripped by Octomom's dad.* Retrieved May 22, 2009, from New York Post: www.nypost.com/seven/02112009/news/nationalnews/egg_on_his_face_154516.htm

Riesman, D., Glazer, N., & Denney, R. (1950). *The lonely crowd: A study of the changing American character.* New Haven, CT: Yale University Press.

Ritzer, G. (1999). *Classical sociological theory.* New York, NY: McGraw-Hill.

Rivas-Drake, D., et al. (2009). A preliminary analysis of associations among ethnic-racial socialization, ethnic discrimination and ethnic identity among urban sixth graders. *Journal of Research on Adolescence, 19*(3), 558–584.

Roethlisberger, F. J., & Dickson, W. J. (1939). *Management and the worker.* Cambridge, MA: Harvard University Press.

Rogers, E. M. (1983). *Diffusion of innovations.* New York, NY: Free Press.

Rogers, S., & Amato, P. (2000). Have changes of gender relations affected marital quality? *Social Forces, 79*, 731–753.

Romaine, S. (1989). *Bilingualism.* Oxford: England: Basil and Blackwell.

Root, W., & Romemont, R. (1976). *Eating in America: A history.* New York, NY: Ecco Press.

Rose, D. (2004, September 15). Group Animated Over 'Anti-italian' Slurs. *The New York Daily News.* Retrieved from NYDailyNews.com: http://articles.nydailynews.com/2004-09-15/news/18280405_1_don-lino-columbus-day-parade-dreamworks

Rosenberg, M. (2011, March 2). *Population density.* Retrieved from about.com: www.geography.about.com/od/populationgeography/a/popdensity.htm

Rosenthal, R. (1968). *Pygmalion in the classroom: Teacher expectations and pupil's intellectual development.* New York, NY: Holt, Rinehart and Winston.

Ross, C. E., Mirowsky, J., & Ulbrich, P. (1983b, November). Comparison of Mexicans and Anglos. *American Journal of Sociology, 89*, 670–682.

Rossell, C. (2003). The desegregation efficiency of magnet schools. *Urban Affairs Review, 38*(5), 697–725.

Rossi, P. H., & Whyte, W. F. (1983). The applied side of sociology. In H. E. Freeman, R. R. Dynes, P. H. Rossi, & W. F. Whyte, *Applied sociology.* San Francisco, CA: Josey-Bass.

Rotherham, A. (2010, November 30). Dropout rates dropping, but don't celebrate yet. *Time.* Retrieved from www.time.com

Rothman, B. K. (1986a). Midwives in transition: The structure of a clinical revolution. *The Sociology of Health and Illness: Critical Perspectives.*

Rothman, K. B. (2000). *Recreating motherhood.* New Brunswick, NJ: Rutgers University Press.

Rothman, R. A. (1978). *Inequality and stratification in the United States.* Englewood Cliffs, NJ: Prentice-Hall.

Rothman, R. A. (2005). *Inequality and stratification: Race, class, and gender* (5th ed.). Englewood Cliffs, NJ: Pearson Prentice Hall.

Rothstein, W. (1970). *American physicians in the nineteenth century: From sects to science.* Baltimore, MD: Johns Hopkins Press.

Rowe, D. C., & Osgood, D. W. (1984, August). Heredity and sociological theories of delinquency: A reconsideration. *American Sociological Review, 49*, 526–540.

Rowland, R. (1985). A child at any price? An overview of issues in the use of the new reproductive technologies, and the threat to women. *Women's Studies International Forum, 8*, 539–546.

Rubin, L. (1983). *Intimate strangers.* New York, NY: Harper and Row.

Rubin, Z. (1973). *Liking and loving.* New York, NY: Holt, Rinehart and Winston.

Ruppanner, L. (2008). Fairness and housework: A cross-national perspective. *Journal of Comparative Family Studies, 39*(4), 509–526.

Russell, J. (1972). *British medieval population.* Albuquerque, NM: University of New Mexico Press.

# S


Sadker, D. (2000, April). Gender equity: Still knocking at the classroom door. *Educational Leadership, 56*(1).

Sadker, D., & Sadker, M. (1994). *Failing at fairness: How our schools cheat girls.* Toronto, Ontario: Simon and Schuster.

Sadker, M., & Sadker, D. (1985, March). Sexism in the school room of the '80s. *Psychology Today*, 54–57.

Sadker, M., & Sadker, D. (1986, March). Sexism in the classroom: From grade school to graduate school. *Phi Delta Kappan*, 512–515.

Sager, A. (1986, July/August). Opiate of the managers. *Society, 23*, 65–71.

Salary.com. (2012). *What is a stay-at-home mom worth.* Retrieved November 17, 2012, from Salary.com: http://www.salary.com/stay-at-home-mom-infographic/

Salinger, L. M., Jesilow, P., Ponterll, H. N., & Geiss, G. (1985). Assaults against airline flight attendants: A victimization study. *Transportation Journal, 25*, 66–71.

Sanderson, S. (2001). *The evolution of human sociality: A darwinian conflict perspective.* Lanham, MD: Rowan and Littlefield.

Saraceno, C. (2011). Childcare needs and childcare politics: A multi-dimensional issue. *Current Sociology, 59*(1), 78–96.

Saul, M. (2009, April 5). *Sarah Palin's feud with Bristol Palin's ex-boyfriend Levi Johnston hits new level.* Retrieved May 22, 2009, from Daily News: http://www.nydailynews.com/news/politics/sarah-palin-feud-bristol-palin-ex-boyfriend-levi-johnston-hits-new-level-article-1.360289

Saulny, S. (2011, June 29). Race remixed: Black? White? Asian?: More young Americans choose all of the above. *New York Times*, p. U.S. Section.

Sayre, E. (2010). Relative deprivation and palestinian suicide bombings. *Asian Journal of Social Science, 38*(3), 442–461.

Schabas, W. (2000). *Genocide in international law: The crime of crimes.* Cambridge, MA: Cambridge University Press.

Schaefer, R. (2003). *Sociology* (8th ed.). New York, NY: McGraw Hill Higher Education.

Schaefer, R. T. (2005). *Race and Ethnicity in the United States* (3rd ed.). Englewood Cliffs, NJ: Pearson Prentice Hall.

Schilling, O. (2006). Development of life satisfaction in old age: Another view on the "paradox." *Social Indicators Research, 75*, 241–271.

Schmallager, F., & Pittaro, M. (2008). *Crimes of the Internet.* Upper Saddle River, NJ: Prentice Hall.

Schnabel, K. U., Alfeld, C., Eccles, J. S., K¨oller, O., & Baumert, J. (2002, April). Parental influence on student's educational choices in the United States and Germany: Different ramifications-same effect? *Journal of Vocational Behavior, 60*(2), 178–198.

Schnaiberg, A., & Goldenberg, S. (1989, June). From empty nest to crowded nest: The dynamics of incompletely launched young adults. *Social Problems, 36*, 251–267.

Schrank, T. (1979, Spring). Schmoozing with Robert Schrank: An interview with a common sense sociologist. *Successful Business.*

Schur, E. M. (1984). *Labeling women deviant: Gender, stigma, and social control.* New York, NY: Random House.

Schutt, R. K. (1990, August). The quantity and quality of homelessness: Research results and policy implications. *Sociological Practice Review, 1*(2), 77–87.

Schwartz, B. (1991, April). Social change and collective memory: The democratization of George Washington. *American Sociological Review, 56*, 221–236.

Scimecca, J. A. (1980). *Education and society.* New York, NY: Holt, Rinehart and Winston.

Scott, M., & Lyman, S. (1968, December). Accounts. *American Sociological Review, 33*, 46–62.

See, P., & Strauss, R. (1985). The sociology of the individual. In R. A. Strauss, *Using sociology: An introduction from the clinical perspective.* Bayside, NY: General Hall.

Seely, G. M. (1970). *Education and opportunity: For what and for whom?* Englewood Cliffs, NJ: Prentice-Hall.

Serbin, L., & O'Leary, K. (1975, December). How nursery schools teach girls to shut up. *Psychology Today*, 56–58.

Sermons, M. W., & White, P. (2011). State of homelessness in America January 2011: A research report. *National Alliance to End Homelessness.*

Sewell, W. H., & Hauser, R. M. (1975). *Occupation and earnings: Achievement in the early career.* New York, NY: Academic Press.

Sharp, J. M. (2004). *Saudi Arabia: Reform and U.S. policy.* CRS Report, Order Code RS21913. Retrieved October 13, 2004

Shattuck, R. (1980). *The forbidden experiment: The story of the wild boy of Aveyron.* New York, NY: Farrar, Straus and Giroux.

Shaw, C. R., & McKay, H. D. (1929). *Delinquency Areas.* Chicago, IL: University of Chicago Press.

Shepard, E. M., & Clifton, T. J. (1998). *Drug testing and labor productivity: Estimates applying a production function model.* Institute of Industrial Relations, research paper No. 18. Syracuse: LeMoyne University.

Sherry, L. M., Jiquan, X., & Kochanek, K. D. (2012, January 11). Deaths: Preliminary data for 2010. *National Vital Statistics Reports, 60*(4).

Shirey, O. C. (1946). *Americans: The story of the 442nd combat team.* Washington, DC: Infantry Journal Press.

Shostak, A. (1985). How can we all survive? Managing social change. In R. A. Strauss, *Using sociology: An introduction from the clinical perspective* (pp. 172–182). Bayside, NY: General Hall.

Siegel, C. N. (1990). The brave new world of children. *New Perspectives Quarterly, 7*, 34–45.

Silverman, K. (1991). Cruel and usual punishment. In P. Greven, *Spare the child: The religious roots of punishment and the psychological impact of physical abuse* (pp. 5–6). New York, NY: The New York Times Book Review.

Simmons, R. G., Brown, L., Bush, D. M., & Blyth, D. A. (1978, October). Self-esteem and achievement of Black and White adolescents. *Social Problems, 26*, 86-96.

Simon, G., & Manstead, A. (1983). *The accountability of conduct: A social psychological analysis.* New York, NY: Academic Press.

Simpson, G. E., & Yinger, J. M. (1972). *Racial and cultural minorities: An analysis of prejudice and discrimination.* New York, NY: Harper and Row.

Skolnick, A. (1991). *Embattled paradise.* New York, NY: Basic Books.

Skolnick, A. (1992). *The intimate environment: Exploring marriage and the family* (5th ed.). New York, NY: Harper Collins.

Skolnick, J. H., & Currie, E. (1997). *Crisis in American institutions.* New York, NY: Longman Publishing Group.

Smelser, N. J. (1962). *Theory of collective behavior.* New York, NY: Free Press.

Smith, D. (1993, March). The standard North American family. *Journal of Family Issues, 14*, 50–65.

Smithers Institute. (1992). *Report on workplace substance abuse policy.* Smithers Institute, Cornell University. Ithaca: Smithers Institute, Cornell University.

Smith-Nonini, S. (2003). Back to the jungle: Processing migrants in North Carolina's meatpacking plants. *Anthropology of Work Review, 24*(3–4 Fall and Winter).

Snell, B. (1976). American ground transport. In J. H. Skolnick, & E. Currie, *Crisis in American institutions* (3rd ed., pp. 304–326). Boston, MA: Little, Brown.

Society for Human Resource Management. (2011, September 7). *Society for human resource management.* Retrieved February 22, 2013, from Drug Testing Efficacy SHRM Poll: http://www.shrm.org/Research/SurveyFindings/Articles/Pages/lDrugTestingEfficacy.aspx

Southern Poverty Law Center. (2012). *Hate and Extremism.* Retrieved November 1, 2012, from SPLC-Southern poverty law center: http://splcenter.org/what-we-do/hate-and-extremism

Spaeth, J. (1985). Job power and earnings. *American Sociological Review, 50*, 603–617.

Spartenburg County Legislative Delegation. (2005, February 7). *Minutes.* Retrieved April 14, 2009, from http://www.co.spartanburg.sc.us/govt/depts/legdel/docs/Delegation/Minutes/February72005minutes.pdf

Spengler, O. (1918). *The decline of the West.* New York, NY: Knopf.

Spitz, R. A. (1945). Hospitalism: An inquiry into the genesis of psychiatric conditions in early childhood. *The Psychoanalytic Study of the Child, 1*, 53–72.

Spitzer, S. (1975, June). Toward a Marxist theory of deviance. *Social Problems, 22*, 638–651.

Squires, S. (1990, November 6). Million dollar images. *Washington Post Health*, pp. 12–13.

Staples, B. (2003, February 20). Editorial observer: The trouble with corporate radio: The day the protest music died. *The New York Times*.

Stark, O. (1990). A relative deprivation approach to performance incentives in career games and other contests. *Kyklos, 43*, 211–227.

Stark, R., & Bainbridge, W. S. (1981, December). Secularization and cult formation in the jazz age. *Journal for the Scientific Study of Religion, 20*, 360–373.

Starr, P. (1982). *The social transformation of American medicine: The rise of a sovereign profession and the making of a vast industry.* New York, NY: Basic Books.

Statistical Abstract. (2000). *(See U.S. Bureau of the Census, Statistical Abstract of the United States).*

Stearns, E., Buchmann, C., & Bonneau, K. (2009). Interracial friendships in the transition to college: Do birds of a feather flock together once they leave the nest? *Sociology of Education, 82*(2), pp. 173–195.

Stearns, P. R. (2008). Texas and Virginia: A bloodied window into changes in American public life. *Journal of Social History*, 229–318.

Stein, R. (2004, February 12). U.S. infant mortality rates rises 3%: First increase since '58 surprises officials as other health indicators keep improving. *Washington Post.*

Stewart, A. J., & Healy, Jr., J. M. (1989, January). Linking individual development and social changes. *American Psychologists, 44*, 30–42.

Stokes, N. M. (1986). *The castrated woman: What your doctor won't tell you about hysterectomy.* New York, NY: Franklin Watts.

Stoller, P. (1976). The language planning activities of the U.S. Office of Bilingual Education. *International Journal of the Sociology of Language, 11*, 45–60.

Strauss, V. (2011). Why 'no excuses' makes no sense: Revisiting the Coleman report. *The Washington Post*. Retrieved from http://www.washingtonpost.com/blogs/answer-sheet/post/why-no-excuses-make-no-sense-revisiting-the-coleman-report/2011/07/23/gIQAo7W7UI_blog.html

Suchar, C. S. (1978). *Social deviance: Perspectives and prospects.* New York, NY: Holt, Rinehart and Winston.

Sumner, W. G. (1980). *Folkways.* New York, NY: New American Library.

Sutherland, E. H. (1939). *Principles of criminology.* Philadelphia, PA: Lippincott.

Sutherland, E., & Cressey, D. R. (1970). *Criminology.* Philadelphia, PA: Lippincott.

Sweet, J., & Lee, M. F. (2010). Christian exodus: A modern American millenarian movement. *Journal for the Study of Radicalism, 4*(1), 1–24.

## T

Tatara, T., & Kuzmeskus, L. B. (1997). *Summaries of the statistical data on elder abuse in domestic settings.* National Center on Elder Abuse. Washington, DC: National Center on Elder Abuse.

Taylor, F. W. (1911). *Scientific management.* New York, NY: Harper and Row.

Teachman, J. D. (1983, March). Early marriage, premarital fertility, and marital dissolution. *Journal of Family Issues, 4*, 105–126.

Telegraph, The. (2002, April 4). *Wolf boy is welcomed home by mother after years in the wild.* Retrieved October 10, 2012, from The Telegraph: http://www.telegraph.co.uk/news/worldnews/europe/romania/1390871/Wolf-boy-is-welcomed-home-by-mother-after-years-in-the-wild.html

The Gallup Poll Monthly. (1990, 1991, June). The Gallup Poll Monthly. *The Gallup Poll Monthly*, pp. 36–52.

The Global Poverty Project. (2012). *Global Poverty Info Bank.* Retrieved November 17, 2012, from The Global Poverty Project: http://www.globalpovertyproject.com/infobank/women

The Harris Poll. (2005, April 27). *Majorities of U.S. adults favor euthanasia and physician-assisted suicide by more than two-to-one.* Retrieved November 26, 2012, from Harris Interactive: http://www.scribd.com/doc/37307438/2005-Harris-Poll-on-national-Death-With-Dignity-support

"Supreme Court Bolsters Gay Marriage With Two Major Rulings." Adam Liptak. June 26, 2013. The New York Times

The New York Times. (2012, December 7). Supreme court to hear two cases on same-sex marriage. *The New York Times*.

The Radicati Group. (2013). *Welcome to the radicati group site*. Retrieved April 30, 2013, from About.com: http://email.about.com/gi/o.htm?zi=1/XJ&zTi=1&sdn=email&cdn=compute&tm=3&f=00&su=p284.13.342.ip_&tt=12&bt=0&bts=0&zu=http%3A//www.radicati.com/

The World Bank. (2012). *Global development finance, external debt of developing countries.* The World Bank. Washington, DC: International Bank for Reconstruction and Development/International Development Association or The World Bank.

Therkildsen, G., & Bass, G. D. (2011, April 27). *Reducing influence peddling in government contracting*. Retrieved May 8, 2011, from Truthout: http://www.truth-out.org/opinion/item/779:reducing-influence-peddling-in-government-contracting

Thio, A. (1988). *Deviant behavior* (3rd ed.). Boston, MA: Houghton Mifflin, Harper Row.

Thomlinson, R. (1976). *Population dynamics: Causes and consequences of world demographic change.* New York, NY: Random House.

Thompson, M. S. (1985). *The "Spider Web": Congress and lobbying in the age of grant.* New York, NY: Cornell University Press.

Thu, N. A., & Zang, K. (2008, February 6). *For Vietnamese, the Year of the Rat starts with lunch; Rodent-eating takes off, in response to bird flu; Cats, snakes on menu, too*. Retrieved September 28, 2012, from The Wall Street Journal: http://online.wsj.com/article/SB120222488938344263.html?mod=relevancy

Tönnies, F. (1887). *Community and society.* (C. P. Loomis, Trans.) New York, NY: Harper and Row.

Tracik, J. (2006, March). *China's submarine challenge*. Retrieved June 15, 2009, from The Heritage Foundation: www.heritage.org/research/asiaandthepacific/wm1001.cfm

Trafford, A. (1991, July 30). Gender bias in health care is no myth. *Washington Post Health, 4*.

Troeltsch, E. (1931). *The social teachings of the Christian churches.* New York, NY: Macmillan.

Tumin, M. (1963, February). On social inequality. *American Sociological Review, 28*, 19–26.

Turk, H. (1970, February). Interorganizational networks in urban society: Initial perspectives and comparative research. *American Sociological Review, 35*, 1–19.

Turner, J. H. (2006). *Handbook of sociological theory.* New York, NY: Springer Sciences and Business Media.

Turner, R. (1960, December). Sponsored and contest mobility and the school system. *American Sociological Review, 25*, 855–867.

Turner, R. H., & Killian, L. M. (1993). *Collective behavior* (4th ed.). Englewood Cliffs, NJ: Prentice-Hall.

Turner, S. P., & Turner, J. H. (1990). *The impossible science: An institutional analysis of American sociology.* Newbury Park, CA: Sage Publications.

Tyson, W. (2007). Residence hall segregation and roommate assignment as determinants of interracial friendship among first year college students. *American Sociological Association Annual Meeting.*

## U

U.S. Bureau of the Census. (2011). *Self-described religious identification of adult population: 1990–2008*. Retrieved from Statistical Abstract of the United States Table 75: www.census.gov/hhes/www/poverty/data/threshld/thresh81.html

U.S. Bureau of the Census. (2008). *Population projections*. Retrieved November 27, 2012, from U.S. Bureau of the Census: http://www.census.gov/population/projections/data/national/2008/summarytables.html

U.S. Bureau of the Census Population Survey. (2005–2009). *U.S. bureau of the census statistical abstract of the United States*. Retrieved from Current Population Survey, 2010 Annual Social and Economic Supplement, Table FG10: www.census.gov/hhes/www/poverty/data/threshld/thresh81.html

U.S. Census. (2011). *Historical income tables: People, table P-38.* Retrieved November 17, 2012, from U.S. Census Bureau: Incomes: http://www.census.gov/hhes/www/income/data/historical/people/

U.S. Census. (2012). *International statistics: Vital statistics, health, education. Table 1336. Marriage and divorce rates by country: 1980 to 2008.* Department of Commerce. Washington, DC: US Census.

U.S. Census Bureau. (2012). *Table 3: Poverty status of people by age, race and hispanic origin: 1959–2011.* Retrieved November 26, 2012, from census.gov: www.census.gov

U.S. Census Bureau. (2012, September 28). *U.S. Census Bureau Publications-Genealogy.* Retrieved September 28, 2012, from U.S. Census Bureau Publications-Genealogy: https://www.census.gov/history/www/reference/publications/publications_-_genealogy_1.html

U.S. Census Bureau, Housing and Household Economic Statistics Division, Fertility & Family Statistics Branch. (2010). *Families and living arrangements.* Retrieved from http://www.census.gov/population/www/socdemo/hh-fam/cps2010.html

U.S. Department of Health and Human Services. (2012). *Poverty guidelines, research, and measurement.* Retrieved November 1, 2012, from U.S. Department of Health and Human Services, ASPE.hhs.gov: http://www.aspe.hhs.gov/poverty/

U.S. Department of Labor. (2010, March). Record unemployment among older workers does not keep them out of the job market. *Issues in Labor Statistics, 10–04*.

U.S. Misery Index. (2010). *How miserable do you feel?* Retrieved April 16, 2013, from United States Misery Index: http://www.miseryindex.us

U.S. State Department. (2008). "Saudi Arabia" international religious freedom report. *Bureau of democracy, human rights and labor*. Bureau of Democracy, Human Rights and Labor.

UNFPA. (2004). *State of world population.* USA: UNFPA. Retrieved from http://www.unfpa.org/public/cache/offonce/home/publications/pid/2104;jsessionid=49EDD7A25ED7AA6EAEFEECD58F8F5862

United Nations, Department of Economic and Social Affairs. (2012, April 26). *World urbanization prospects, the 2011 revision*. Retrieved January 18, 2013, from United Nations, Department of Economic and Social Affairs, Population Division, Population Estimates and Projections Section: http://esa.un.org/unpd/wup/index.htm

United State Census Bureau. (2012, September 12). *Poverty*. Retrieved April 17, 2013, from U.S. Bureau of the Census: www.census.gov/hhes/www/poverty/data/threshld/thresh81.html


## V


Van Ausdale, D., & Feagin, J. R. (1996, October). Using racial and ethnic concepts: The critical case of very young children. *American Sociological Review, 61*(5), 779–793.

Van den Berghe, P. L. (1979). *Human family systems: An evolutionary view.* New York, NY: Elsevier.

Vaughan, D. (1999). The dark side of organizations: Mistake, misconduct and disaster. *Annual Review of Sociology, 25*, 271–305.

Veevers, J. E. (1975, October). The moral careers of voluntary childless wives: Notes on the defense of a variant world view. *The Family Coordinator, 24*, 473–487.

Vernez, G., & Ronfeldt, D. (1991, March 8). The current situation in Mexican immigration. *Science, 51*, 1189–1193.

Vockell, E. L. (1991, March/April). Corporal punishment: The pros and cons. *Clearing House*, 278–283.

Vold, G. B. (1958). *Theoretical criminology.* New York, NY: Oxford University Press.


## W


Wagner, M. E., Schubert, H. J., & Schubert, D. S. (1985, March). Family size effects: A review. *Journal of Genetic Psychology, 146*, 65–78.

Waite, L. J., Bachrach, L., Hindin, M., Thomson, E., & Thornton, A. (2000). *Ties that bind: Perspectives on marriage and cohabitation.* Hawthorne, New York, NY: Aldine de Gruyter.

Waitzkin, H. (2000). *The second sickness: Contradictions of capitalist health care.* Lantham, MD: Rowman and Littlefield.

Wallace, T., & Kaleem, J. (2012, December 4). Hurricane Sandy vs. Katrina infographic examines destruction from both storms. *Huffington Post*.

Waller, W. (1938). *The family: A dynamic interpretation.* New York, NY: Cordon.

Waller, W., & Hill, R. (1951). *The family.* New York, NY: Dryden Press.

Wallertstein, I. (2000). *The essential Wallerstein.* New York, NY: Free Press.

Walmsley, R. (2009). *World prison population list.* London: United Kingdom Home Office Research, Development and Statistics Directorate.

Ware, H. (1979, February). Polygyny: Women's views in a traditional society, Nigeria, 1975. *Journal of Marriage and the Family, 41*, 185–195.

Weber, M. (1930; originally published in 1905). *The protestant ethic and the spirit of capitalism.* New York, NY: Scribner's.

Weber, M. (1946). *From Max Weber: Essays in sociology.* (H. Gerth, & W. C. Mills, Trans.) Oxford University Press.

Weber, M. (1958). *The city.* New York, NY: Free Press.

Weinberg, M. (1977). *Minority students: A research appraisal.* Washington, DC: U.S. Government Printing Office.

Weitzman, L. J. (1985). *The divorce revolution: The unexpected social and economic consequences for women and children in America.* New York, NY: Free Press.

Wennerhag, M. (2010). Another modernity is possible? The global justice movement and the transformation of politics. *Distinktion: Scandanavian Journal of Social Theory, 21*, 25–49.

Westheimer, R. K., & Lopater, S. (2005). *Human sexuality: A psychosocial perspective* (2nd ed.). Philadelphia, PA: Lippincott, Williams, and Wilkins.

Weyant, J. M. (1986). *Applied social psychology.* New York, NY: Oxford University Press.

Whorf, B. L. (1941). The relation of habitual thought and behavior to language. In L. A. Spier, I. Hallowell, & S. S. Newman, *Language, culture and personality: Essay in memory of Edward Sapir.* Menasha, MI: Sapir Memorial Publication.

Whyte, W. F. (1949). *Human relations in the restaurant industry.* New York, NY: McGraw-Hill.

Williams, P. (1980). *Popular religion in America: Symbolic change and the modernization process in historical perspective.* Englewood Cliffs, NJ: Prentice-Hall.

Williams, R. M. (1970). *American society: A sociological interpretation* (3rd ed.). New York, NY: Knopf.

Williams, W. E. (2011, July 27). *Job destruction makes us richer*. Retrieved January 8, 2013, from OwnHall.Com: ownhall.com/columnists/walterewilliams/2011/07/27/job_destruction_makes_us_richer/page/fu

Wilson, E. (1975). *Sociobiology.* Cambridge, MA: Harvard University Press.

Wilson, W. J. (1987). *The truly disadvantaged: The inner city, the underclass, and public policy.* Chicago, IL: University of Chicago Press.

Wilson, W. J. (1997). *When work disappears: The world of the new urban poor.* New York, NY: Vintage Books.

Winch, R. F. (1958). *Mate selection.* New York, NY: Harper.

Winch, R. F., Ktsanes, T., & Ktsanes, V. (1954, June). The theory of complementary needs in mate selection: An analytic and descriptive study. *American Sociological Review, 19*, 241–249.

Wirth, L. (1938, July). Urbanism as a way of life. *American Journal of Sociology, 44*, 3–24.

Wolff, E. N. (2010). Recent trends in household wealth in the U.S. rising debt and the middle class squeeze. *Working Paper*, 589.

Wood, F. W. (1990). *An American profile-opinions and behavior, 1972–1989.* Detroit, MI: Gale Research.

Woodhead, L. (2008). Gendering secularization theory. *Social Compass, 55*(2), 187–193.

World Health Organization. (2011). *Mental health.* Retrieved March 6, 2013, from World Health Organization: http://www.who.int/mental_health/prevention/suicide_rates/en/index.html

World Religions and Spirituality Project, VCU. (2010, June). *World religions and spirituality project.* Retrieved April 29, 2013, from World Religions and Spirituality Project, VCU: http://www.has.vcu.edu/wrs/resources.htm

Worldatlas. (2012). *Countries of the world.* Retrieved January 18, 2013, from Worldatlas: http://www.worldatlas.com/aatlas/populations/ctypopls.htm

Wright, J. D. (1989, September/October). Address unknown: Homelessness in contemporary America. *Society, 26*(6), 45–53.

Wyner, N. A. (2010, March). Salient egalitarian norms moderate activation of out-group approach and avoidance. *Group Processes and Intergroup Relations, 13*(2), 151–165.

## Y

Yankauer, A. (1990, June). What infant mortality tells us. *American Journal of Public Health, 80*, 653–654.

## Z

Zafirovsky, M. (2003). The rational choice approach to human studies: A reexamination. *Human Studies, 26*(1), 41–66.

Zeisel, J. (1973). *Sociology and architectural design.* New York, NY: Russell Sage Foundation.

Zeitzen, M. (2008). *Polygamy: A cross-cultural analysis.* New York, NY: Berg Publishers.

Zelditch, M. (1955). Role differentiation in the nuclear family. In T. Parsons, R. F. Bales, J. Olds, M. Zelditch, & P. E. Slater, *Family, socialization and interaction process.* Glencoe, IL: Free Press.

Zinn, M. B., & Eitzen, S. D. (2005). *Diversity in families* (7th ed.). New York, NY: Allyn and Bacon.

Zirkel, P. A. (1971). Self-concept and the disadvantage of ethnic group membership and mixture. *Review of Educational Research, 41*, 211–225.

Zolotor, A. J., & Puzia, M. E. (2010). Bans against corporal punishment: A systematic review of the laws, changes in attitudes and behaviors. *Child Abuse Review, 19*, pp. 229–247.

Zweigenhaft, R. L., & Domhoff, G. W. (2003). *Blacks in the white elite: Will the progress continue?* New York, NY: Rowman & Littlefield Publishers, Inc.

Zweigenhaft, R. L., & Domhoff, W. G. (1991). *Black and whites in the establishment: A study of race and class in America.* New Haven, CT: Yale University Press.

Zwerdling, D. (1976). The food monopolies. In J. H. Skolnick, & E. Currie, *Crisis in American institutions* (3rd ed., pp. 43–51). Boston, MA: Little, Brown.

# NAME INDEX

# SUBJECT INDEX

## D



## E



## F

## G



## H



## I

## S